Naming Names
Stories of Pseudonyms
and Name Changes
with a Who's Who

by
Adrian Room

Routlege & Kegan Paul
London and Henley

First published in 1981
by Routledge & Kegan Paul Ltd
39 Store Street,
London WC1E 7DD and
Broadway House,
Newton Road,
Henley-on-Thames,
Oxon RG9 1EN

Manufactured in the United States of America

ISBN 0-7100-0920-8

*Published by arrangement with McFarland & Company, Inc.,
Publishers, Jefferson, North Carolina USA*

Contents

Introduction

This book takes a look at the names we create for ourselves. Not so much the names we are born with, although these will also be considered, but the new names we adopt and the pseudonyms we assume.

The book is designed to work on several levels.

The first level (the six chapters that open the book) is a consideration of names in general and pseudonyms and changed names in particular. What are these names? Who adopts them? Why do they adopt them? *How* do they adopt them?

At the second level the book contains a fairly generous selection of name stories. This is really the jam of the sandwich. Here are the tales behind the well-known names, often told in the words of the personalities themselves. Why did Vladimir Ulyanov call himself Lenin? How did Greta Garbo come by her name? Who was Little Tich? They're all here.

The third level is the other half of the bread and butter that forms the sandwich. It comprises lists of names arranged by categories, and is designed both for reference and for browsing. Here are found embarrassing names, anagrammatic names, humorous names, papal names, and many more.

That, if you like, is the first half of the meal.

The other half is a Who's Who, not only of the names considered throughout the book, but of hundreds of well known or important pseudonyms and adopted names. Here you can find out the real names of the personalities that interest you, as well as their dates of birth and death. At the same time, the Who's Who is an index, giving the page numbers where some of the names are dealt with specially in the first six chapters of the book. It also indicates which of the names feature in the Names Stories. (The symbol for a name that comes in the Name Stories is a degree sign, as °George Eliot. This is used right throughout the book.) The Who's Who is thus reasonably comprehensive, ranging from A.A. (George Anthony Armstrong Willis, English humorist) to Z.Z. Zangwill, English novelist).

The book concludes with five Appendices — dessert, perhaps — listing some special names (and, in case you are bemused by all these false names, some *real* ones), and, finally, with a Bibliography.

Each section of the book except the first opens with a brief explanatory introduction outlining its aims and objectives.

That, then, is what will be found in the book. But, since it will be all things to all men, there is no need to begin at page one and work your way through. Have a look through: dip into the Name Stories (page 69), flip through the Who's Who (page 227), see what books were used as material for this book (Bibliography, page 346). Or begin at page 1 after all for an account of how we get names and how we give them...

Acknowledgments

A number of people helped in the making of this book, in a formal or informal capacity, and I should like to say how grateful I am to them for their assistance.

In particular I should like to thank:

His Honour Judge Hywel ap Robert for information about Welsh bardic names; Mr. Andrew Brown, publications manager of the Voltaire Foundation, for helpful advice and material relating to the many pseudonyms of Voltaire; Mrs. Mary Buck, librarian of the Catholic Central Library, London, for much useful information on papal names and religious names in general; Mr. J.W. Carter, director of Oldham Central Library, Lancashire, England, for background information on Ab-o'-th-Yate; Jonathan Crowther ("Azed" of *The Observer*) for lending me his personal copy of the original Who's Who of *Listener* crossword puzzle makers (or "setters") and for advice on the names of crossword setters and solvers generally, and Michael Rich ("Ploutos" of *The Listener*) for kindly presenting me with a copy of a later edition of this same Who's Who.

When it comes to the nitty-gritty, the basic research and fact-finding that a book such as this inevitably involves, I owe much to Margaret Dickson, who hunted out many necessary names and dates and facts in a variety of reference works in London libraries, and to Linda Dalling, who made available the reference resources of the BBC in order to check and re-check the dates in the Who's Who. My sincere thanks to both for their efficiency and enthusiasm.

Virtually the whole of the typescript was the work of three ladies, Jan Chatfield, Kim Reseigh, and Michelle Smith, of Ace Secretarial Services, Petersfield, Hampshire, England. Their willingness and cheerfulness when confronted with page after page of weird and wonderful names, many of them foreign, was matched only by their fine professionalism and excellent timekeeping, enabling me to meet the publisher's deadline with confidence.

Of all private correspondents who helped with suggestions and offers of names from their own collection I must specially thank Leslie Dunkling, president of the Names Society, Miss P. King, formerly on the staff of the Royal Marsden Hospital, London, and Jay Ames, a tireless and knowledgeable name buff if ever there was one, of Toronto, Canada.

For permission to quote from specific books and published articles, I am indebted to the following for the extracts as indicated:

W.H. Allen Ltd. — George Carpozi, Jr., *The Gary Cooper Story* (1971), Diana Dors, *Behind Closed Dors* (1979), David Gillard, *Beryl Gray: A Biography* (1977), Frankie Howerd, *On the Way I Lost It* (1976), Veronica Lake with Donald Bain, *Veronica* (1969), Vera Lynn, *Vocal Refrain: An Autobiography* (1975), Robert Payne, *The Great Garbo* (1976), Alan Randall and Ray Seaton, *George Formby* (1974), Edward G. Robinson with Leonard Spigelgass, *All My Yesterdays: An Autobiography* (1974), Omar Sharif with Marie Therese Guinchard, *The Eternal Male* (1977), Tennessee Williams, *Memoirs* (1976), Donald Zec, *Sophia: An Intimate Biography* (1975), Maurice Zolotow, *John Wayne: Shooting Star* (1974);

Cassell Ltd. — Sir William Connor, *Cassandra: Reflections in a Mirror* (1969);

William Collins Sons & Co. Ltd. — Peggy Makins, *The Evelyn Home Story* (1975);

Faber and Faber Ltd. — Suzanne Campbell-Jones, *In Habit...* (1979);

The Foley Agency, New York — Albert Govoni, *Cary Grant: An Unauthorized Biography* (1973);

Leslie Frewin Books Ltd. — Michael Bateman, *Funny Way to Earn a Living* (1966); Des Hickey & Gus Smith, *The Prince: Being the Public and Private Life of Larushka Mischa Skikne, a Jewish Lithuanian Vagabond Player Otherwise Known as Laurence Harvey* (1975);

Harper & Row, Publishers, Inc. — Melvin Shestack, *The Country Music Encyclopaedia* (1977);

Hodder & Stoughton Ltd. — David Winter, *New Singer, New Song* (1967);

Frederick Muller Ltd. — Joan Crawford and Jane Kastner Ardmore, *A Portrait of Joan* (1963);

John Murray (Publishers) Ltd. — Richard Buckle, ed., *Dancing for Diaghilev* (1960);

New English Library Ltd. — Adam Faith, *Poor Me* (1961);

Scholastic Book Services — Larry Bortstein, *Ali* (1976);

Times Newspapers Ltd. — articles in *The Sunday Times Colour Magazine* (March 7, 1972, September 19, 1977) and *The Times* (October 12, 1974, September 24, 1977, September 11, 1978);

TV Times — article in issue no. 8, February 15, 1979;

A.P. Watt Ltd. — Roger Lancelyn Green, ed., *The Diaries of Lewis Carroll* (1953).

I am also personally indebted to the following for permission to quote extracts as shown: Leonard R.N. Ashley, from his invaluable article "Flicks, Flacks, and Flux: Tides of Taste in the Onomasticon of the

Moving Picture Industry," in *Names*, vol. 23, no. 4 (December 1975) [on Virginia Mayo], V.G. Dmitriev, from his important book *Skryvshiye Svoyo Imya* (Moscow: Nauka Publishing House, 1977) [on Demyan Bedny, V.I. Lenin, N. Saltykov-Shchedrin, Yevgeniya Tur], and John Letts, director of the Folio Society, from his letter to the editor of *The Times* (October 8, 1977) [on Ingahild Grathmer].

I have made every effort to trace the copyright holders of material used in this book, and it is my belief that the necessary permissions have been obtained. Should there be any omissions in this respect, however, I apologize in advance and shall be pleased to make the appropriate acknowledgments in future editions.

Adrian Room
Petersfield, Hampshire, England
January 1981

As for your name, I offer you the whole firmament to choose from. (Opening words of "On Choosing a Name" by Alpha of the Plough. The sentence was spoken by the editor of the *Star* as an invitation to the English essayist to write for that paper under a pseudonym.)

With a name like yours, you might be any shape,
almost (Lewis Carroll, "Through the Looking-Glass")

1 The Nature of a Name

"What's in a name?" agonized lovelorn Juliet, for she was a Capulet, and he, her roaming romantic Romeo, was a Montague, and the two families were deadly enemies.

Shakespeare himself well knew what was in a name. One need only mention his Aguecheek and Ariel, his Benvolio and Malvolio, his Pistol and Doll Tearsheet and of course his Romeo — was there ever a more evocative name? — to see and sense the charm of well chosen names.

We shall be examining in due course and in some detail "what's in a name," but first we should touch on a more basic question: what *is* a name?

We all of us have a name. Conventionally, at any rate in the Western world, we have, as an accepted and acceptable minimum, a forename, or Christian name, and a surname, or family name. We are John Smith, or Mary Brown, or Clark Gable, or Betty Grable, or even, like the famous social leader from Houston, Texas, Ima Hogg. The names are different, and serve different purposes — a forename is essentially private property, and a surname public — but in their respective and differing ways both names carry equal weight, both actually and legally, as a means of identification.

By custom and tradition, our first name is given to us soon after we are born, at a christening or baptismal or naming ceremony, while our last name is already there, and we simply become one more member of the family to share it. In most cases, we get our names from our parents, since our forename is chosen for us by our parents and we inherit our parents' surname. Our first name is our own special individual property — although there may be hundreds of other people who also bear it — and it lasts as long as our life lasts. Our surname may well have existed for centuries and generations before us, in one form or another, and will probably continue to be borne by our own children long after our own life has ended.

Assuming that our ancestors did not deliberately change the surname that we now bear, how far back can we trace this name? Theoretically, at least, must there not have been a time, going back as far as we can, when we come to the first of our forebears to be so named? How did

1

he get his name? In other words, more generally, where did the very first names of all come from?

It is worth taking a look at this original process of name creation, since this is the process that we are chiefly concerned with in this book.

Many English, but perhaps not quite so many Americans, can trace their surnames back in written form to the Domesday Book of the late 11th century. If your name is Gridley, for example, there is a chance, admittedly an extremely slim one, that Albert Greslet was one of your ancestors. His name was recorded by the Domesday Book in Cheshire in 1086. Or if you are a Tallboy, perhaps Ralph Tailgebosc of Hertfordshire, who likewise lived nearly a millennium ago, was one of the greatest of your great-grandfathers. Both Albert and Ralph have names that to our modern eyes are recognizably personal names, in the familiar forename-surname form. A number of names cited and recorded in the Domesday Book, however, are single names, or are for example names that belong to a person who is said to be the "filius" or son of someone else. The name that today is Jarrold or Gerald, for instance, occurs in the Domesday Book as Robertus filius Geraldi — "Robert Geraldson," as it were — while people today named Bishop will find, at any rate in Northamptonshire in 1066, that their Domesday ancestor was simply called Biscop.

The Domesday Book thus also records the early stages of our present binomial (forename-plus-surname) system. Originally, therefore, people had only one name. One person with one name; quite enough. But we want to go back even further. Where did these names come from in turn? Did they have a meaning? For example, was the original Tallboy (actually Tailgebosc, as we have seen) a tall boy, and was the early Bishop a bishop? What does Gridley (or Greslet) mean, and where did Gerald come from?

The answer is both simple and complex. Simple, in that all these original names did indeed have a meaning. Complex, in that many of these early names do not mean what they seem to mean. Ralph Tailgebosc was not a tall boy but was himself the descendant of someone who was a woodcutter, from the Old French *tailler* "to cut," and *bosc*, "wood." Over the centuries his surname became smoothed and assimilated to something that had an *English* meaning and pronunciation. The original Bishop, too, although his name has not changed anything like as radically as Ralph's, was almost certainly not a bishop but a man who looked like one or, more likely, had the manners or deportment of one — an episcopal posture, if you like. His name was thus more what we today would call a nickname. Albert Greslet's surname was really a nickname, too: it means "pockmarked," literally "marked by hail," also from Old French, while Gerald, these days more common as a Christian name, meant "spear-ruler."

Woodcutter, Bishop-like person, Pockmarked person and One Who Ruled with His Spear. An impressive foursome! But we can go further back than that. We are limited by written or pictographic records, of course, but we have evidence that as long ago as 3050 B.C. there was a man named N'armer, who was the first Egyptian Pharoah. And further back still, some two thousand years before him, in about 5000 B.C., there lived a Sumerian queen named Ninziddamkiag, which is believed to mean "the queen [who] loves the faithful husband"...

Romeo was not the only one to have had an evocative name...

Our names thus have their origin where language itself has its cradle — with this Egyptian Pharoah and that Sumerian queen. More specifically, they originated where the English language did: with the Greeks, the Romans, the Celts, the Germanic peoples such as the Anglo-Saxons and the Vikings, and the Normans. All these races in fact had a naming system that was in many ways similar, since although it developed into the binomial system as we know today, or, earlier, the famous trinomial system of the Romans (praenomen, nomen and cognomen), it originally involved the conferring of a single name that had a meaning.

This single meaningful name was in many cases what we might today think of as a nickname, as we have seen, or as a descriptive title. As such, it related directly or indirectly to the person named. If directly, it perhaps described his appearance, manner, gait or general image — either what he was or what he might become. The name might consist of a single element, as the Celtic word *ruadh*, "red," for someone who was of ruddy complexion (today the name is Roy), or a double element, as the Gerald mentioned, whose name derives from the Germanic *ger*, "spear," and *vald*, "rule." (This latter name was not so much an actual description but a desirable description: the child Gerald was so named in the hope that he would grow up to be a fearless ruler-by-the-spear. Might not his name help him to do this? Even today the power or suggestiveness of a name is strong. Kirk is probably more likely to be a modern "spear-ruler" than, say, Kevin.) If a name related indirectly to a person, it would usually derive from his or her family, home area, or occupation. If the first of these, it would often derive from the name of the father or grandfather. The Greeks, for example, named the eldest son after his paternal grandfather and later children after other relatives. Sometimes, however, a Greek boy bore the same name as his father. This was the case with Demosthenes, the orator, whose name, like the Germanic Gerald, was a two-element one and meant "people-strength." (Like Gerald, too, it is a desirable image name.)* Examples of names deriving respectively from a person's place of residence and his occupation are the Anglo-Saxon Grene (modern Green), for someone who lived near the village green, and Cupere (Cooper), for a man who made or repaired wooden casks.

Women's names were formed similarly but with a feminine ending. An unmarried Greek woman would derive her name from her father, a married woman from her husband, a widow from her son.

These four categories—nickname (or descriptive), familial, residential and occupational—form the basis for most modern European and transatlantic surnames.

An interesting study, which regrettably would take up too much space to be made in this present book, would be to trace the fortunes and popularity of the original names as they evolved down the centuries, and to consider why many such names became fixed as surnames only (in the modern sense), while others remain in common use as Christian names or forenames. Of the few names we have already mentioned, for example, Bishop, Green and Cooper are more familiar today as surnames, while Gerald and Roy, although also occurring as surnames, are probably more frequent as forenames. Generally speaking, it can be said that *any* surname is capable of being put into use as a forename—Dudley and Sidney were English surnames that made this transition in the 16th century, just as later in America Chauncey and Washington were adopted as Christian names—but that many surnames, in particular familial, residential and occupational ones, just never made it.

As to why surnames exist at all, the answer is much more straightforward. Surnames were found necessary to distinguish one particular person from others, perhaps many others, who had the same single name. And the simplest way to find another name—as we shall also see when we come to look specifically at pseudonyms—is to use your own father's name, as well as your own. This, after all, is what a surname is—a name that is "super" to, or added to, your own. (The word *surname* is not related to *sir*. As the 16th-century English historian and antiquary William Camden concisely but carefully put it, in his *Remains Concerning Britain*, "The French and we termed them *Surnames*, not because they are the names of the *Sire*, or the father, but because they are *super*-added to Christian names.") And to make it clear that you are using your father's name in your capacity as a son, many surnames came to incorporate an element that actually means "son." One we have already seen, since the Latin *filius* in the Domesday Book's Robertus filius Geraldi survives, in assimilated French form, as the Fitz- that begins many surnames, while a number of recognizable Christian names have become surnames by the simple process of having the actual word "son" tacked on to them. Thus both a Fitzwilliam and a Williamson had, originally, a father named William. Parallels to this I-am-the-son-of-my-father label exist in many other languages besides English. The Jewish equivalent, and a far more ancient one, is the *bar* or *ben*, meaning "son," in such names as the biblical Simon-bar-Jonas and the Talmudic Joshua ben Hananiah (*bar* is the Aramaic form, and *ben* the Hebrew), while although not a surname in the modern sense, the Russian patronymic—the middle of three names that all Russians have, as Lev *Nikolayevich* Tolstoy or Maya *Mikhailovna* Plissetskaya—is still obligatory.

Subsequently, once a surname had been acquired, it became a

family name proper and passed on, ordinarily, from father to son and daughter in the manner we have long become accustomed to. Perhaps it is a pity that in English we call this name, at times misleadingly, as we have seen, a "surname." The French, with their *nom de famille*, and the Germans, who know it as a *Familienname*, are much nearer to the real nature of the thing.

We have referred, too, to one of the four categories of surname as *nicknames*. This also is perhaps not quite the right word here, since properly, a nickname is an additional name or an extra name, and how can one refer to a single name as an extra name when it is the only one there is? (Even the word *nickname* has become distorted. By rights it should be not "a nickname" but "an ickname," since it derives from the now rare word *eke* meaning "also.") On the other hand to call such names *descriptive* names is to be almost too wide-ranging, since in a sense the other three categories are also descriptive. A reasonable alternative might be to call such direct names, which relate to the person him or herself, *characterizing names.*

But we have so far mentioned only once the type of name that this book is really about, the *pseudonym*. And since we shall be using the word continually we must define it here, before going any further.

Literally, of course, a pseudonym is a "false name," as the two Greek elements that make up the word indicate. The term is a relatively new one. The *Oxford English Dictionary* records its earliest appearance only as late as 1846, although the adjective "pseudonymous" dates back to 1706. The most recent (sixth, 1976) edition of the *Concise Oxford Dictionary* defines a pseudonym as a "fictitious name, especially one assumed by an author." Not a false name, a "fictitious" one. The same dictionary defines *fictitious* as "assumed," when applied to a name. And this, basically, is the sense in which we shall be using "pseudonym" in the present book: as a name that, whether it subsequently becomes a person's "proper" or permanent name or not, is one that has been consciously assumed or taken on instead of, or in addition to, the person's real name. In fact, it would be better to play down the "fictitious" side to such a name and emphasize the "assumed" aspect, since we shall be considering name changes of all kinds, even legal ones undertaken by such means as a deed poll. Is there in fact any point in saying that an assumed name is a false one? Name is a name is a name, as Gertrude Stein so nearly said. (Well, she was talking about Rose, and everyone knows what would smell as sweet.)

2 Why Another Name?

Who are the people who choose to adopt a pseudonym or to change their name, and why do they do it?

Broadly speaking, people assume a new or additional name because they have to, because they are expected to, or simply because they want to. The name that they assume is then made known to the public at large, to a particular group of people, or just to one other person. An actor, for example, wants his whole public to know his new name, while a spy or secret agent operates under a cover name that is known only to a select few. An individual, on the other hand, can communicate a message to a friend or loved one in a press announcement, for example, by using a disguised name that is known to his or her correspondent alone.

Let us see who exactly the main groups of people are.

One of the most common and striking situations in which people will change their original names for new ones is the act, to a greater or lesser degree traumatic, of emigration and subsequent naturalization. A person leaves his or her native country for some reason — often driven out by war, persecution or destitution — and, arriving in another, where very likely a new language is spoken, officially or tacitly starts a new life, assumes a new identity, and takes on a new name to go with it. One of the greatest migrations in history was the mass emigration to America by around 35 million people from all parts of Europe between 1820 and 1930. In their flight from poverty, famine and persecution, inhabitants of Great Britain and Ireland, Germany and Scandinavia, Italy and the Balkans, Russia and the Austro-Hungarian Empire, many of them Jews, poured into America in the hope of setting up a new life in a country that seemed to offer refuge and opportunities. And when they eventually reached the immigrant depot at Ellis Island — "Heartbreak Island" many of them called it, for fear of being denied entry — they were faced with a number of questions, of which the first was always, "What is your name?"

Immigrant names were a constant source of difficulty. Many of the newly arrived were barely literate and could not even spell their names, with the result that officials frequently simplified or anglicized them haphazardly. This meant that a number of immigrants left Ellis Island with a new name, perhaps not even realizing this, although many, especially the more literate, acquired a new name only in due course.

6

There are two well known stories about "on-the-spot" name changes of this kind.

The first concerns a German Jew named Isaac. Confused by all the questioning, he replied, when asked his name, "Ich vergessen" ("I forget" in Yiddish). The immigrant officer recorded his name as Fergusson.

The second incident is an occurrence in °Elia Kazan's film *America, America* (1963). A Greek shoeshine boy, Stavros Topouzoglou, frightened that he may not be allowed into the country, answers to the name of a dead friend, Hohannes Gardashian. The officer tells him that if he wants to be an American, he must change his name for something shorter. "Hohannes—that's *all* you need here!" And he writes the name "Joe Arness," adding, "Well, boy, you're reborn, you're baptised again. And without benefit of clergy. Next ..."

Whimsical though such tales are, they illustrate some important realities about the process of changing one's name. First, a name change can be quite an arbitrary thing. Indeed, although many of the changes recorded in this book were undertaken consciously and deliberately, thousands of American immigrants came to have their names changed by random and gradual processes—a letter dropped here, a respelling adopted there—and changed most of all, perhaps, by what Howard F. Barker, one of America's greatest authorities on surnames, called "the abrasion of common speech." Second, the immigrant officer's comment, "You're reborn," states a basic philosophy that underlies virtually all name changes. For a human being, after all, a name is far more than a mere identification tag. It is not like a place name, for example, where *London* denotes "the capital of Great Britain" and *Fort Knox* signifies "military reservation and air base in Kentucky, where most of the U.S. gold reserves are stored." Our names not only identify us, they *are* us: they announce us, advertise us and embody us. Stavros the shoeshine boy, like many other immigrants, had his name changed for him, but many people choose a new name simply because they feel that the name itself can bestow a new image and a new persona. "In assuming a new name," the French literary critic Jean Starbinski wrote of °Stendhal, who assumed over a hundred pseudonyms, "he not only grants himself a new face, but a new destiny, a new social rank, new nationalities." On a rather different plane, but approached by the same path, the pop singer °Elton John commented, on adopting his new stage name, "I'm still the same guy, but a new name gave me a new outlook on life, and a new drive to do things."

Short of an actual physical reincarnation, a change of name is one of the most popular and efficacious ways, many believe, of becoming a new or a different person.

For the many Jews in this great immigration, the adoption of a new name was nothing new in itself. A hundred years previously, for example, Jews in many European countries had been ordered to assume fixed family names as the result of a radical change in the political and cultural climate. It was at this time, in fact, that many Germanic Jewish names arose, such as Weiss, Schwartz, Gross and Klein. These particular four names (White, Black, Large, Little) were in turn often random names, given or acquired with no relevance to the person who came to be so named. In many communities in Hungary, for instance, Jews were divided into four arbitrary groups and each of these names was assigned to every person in one of the groups.

Now, a century later, many immigrant Jews were obliged to change their name again, to an English-style surname. So widespread was the change, and so diffuse, that today it is virtually impossible to recognize a Jew by surname alone: there are thousands of Smiths, Browns and Joneses who were originally, perhaps, Kovacs, Brand or (with utter dissimilarity) Edelstein. On the other hand, it is clear that today such name changes, foreign or Jewish to English, for example, are not taking place on anything like the scale that they did in the 19th century. In 1977 the director of the U.S. Immigration and Naturalization Service stated that each year about 142,000 people assume American nationality and of these only 7,000, or 15 percent, change their name, mainly by shortening it so that it is easier to pronounce in English. As the Russian U.S. émigré newspaper *Novoye Russkoye Slovo* commented: "In recent years the number of immigrants changing their name has fallen considerably. Many newcomers to the States prefer to maintain their ties with their homeland by keeping their real name and continuing to speak their native language" (September 1, 1977).

The practical advantages of changing a foreign name to an English-sounding one are obvious, and have already been mentioned. It is self-evident that if a person wishes to assimilate fully and successfully into a community, a name that blends with the others' will be of considerable assistance. Of course, equally, there is an obverse side to this: a person who does not change his or her name will be conspicuous as a foreigner, and this may be at least a hindrance, at most a positive and highly un-desirable branding, especially in time of war. This was noticeably so in the First World War, when many Anglophones with Germanic names keenly regretted their "alien" name or were prompted to change it. The English poet, ultimately of Dutch origin, John Betjeman relates in his verse autobiography *Summoned by Bells* how he was taunted at school about his name ("Betjeman's a German spy/ Shoot him down and let him die"), and in the British royal family King George V changed the family name from Wettin to Windsor by proclamation on July 17, 1917, while Queen Mary's family changed their name from Teck to "of Cambridge" and the Battenbergs became the Mountbattens.

Would people ever change their English names to foreign ones, or to ones not native to them? The immigrants, of course, changed their native names to nonnative ones, but occasions when an English name has been changed to a foreign one, except for frivolous or satirical reasons, are not common, although cases have been recorded of Jews changing *back* to their original name from the English one that they adopted on immigration.

There are perhaps two exceptions to this tendency not to change to a foreign name. The first is for groups such as ballet dancers, who may find it helpful to assume a foreign-sounding name, especially a Russian one. Thus the dancer Hilda Boot assumed the surname Butsova, while Patrick Healey-Kay became the well known ballet star °Anton Dolin. In some instances it comes as a surprise to find that a ballerina did not originally have the Russian name by which she became famous. Tamara Karsavina was born Tamara Karsavina, but °Lydia Sokolova began her dancing career as plain Hilda Munnings.

Then, apart from special instances such as that of disguise, when the national of one country aimed to pass himself off as the citizen of another, there have been occasions when some writers have assumed a foreign name with the aim of describing their impressions of their own country apparently through the eyes of an alien observer. Oliver Goldsmith did this for his *Chinese Letters*, which originally appeared as purportedly written by a Chinese philosopher named Lien Chi Altangi. This was in the mid-18th century. On similar lines, but at the beginning of the last century, Robert Southey's *Letters of Espriella* claimed to be a collection of letters written from England by a young Spaniard, giving a picture of the times. There have been other examples of "foreigners' letters," most of which were inspired by the *Lettres Persanes* (Persian Letters) of the French writer Montesquieu. These letters comprised the supposed correspondence of two Persians, Rica and Usbek, making observations about life and *moeurs* in Paris at the end of the reign of Louis XIV.

All name changes, of course, are in the last resort voluntary affairs, although political or social pressure may be very great to make the change. Possibly the only category of person who is virtually compelled to make a name change is someone who has undergone a sex change. To undergo such a radical physical and emotional transformation and retain one's old opposite sex name would seem most undesirable. In recent times one such change (of sex and name) that became widely publicized, simply because the person concerned was, and is, a distinguished writer in his — now her — own right, was that of the distinguished English author and former editor Jan Morris, formerly James Morris. Jan Morris describes the whole experience and its consequences, including the reasoning behind the change from James to Jan, in her book *Conundrum* (1964).

A category where a name change is normally mandatory is that of persons entering a religious order, the motivation behind the change being the spiritual rebirth undergone by the entrant. We shall examine the various types of religious names adopted in Chapter 4; suffice it to say here that as a result of the second Vatican Council of 1962-1965 many Roman Catholic religious orders have dropped the giving of a name in religion altogether. In the Roman Catholic church, too, it is the usual practice, although not obligatory, for a person to take an additional name at Confirmation. The acquisition of a religious name of any kind is regarded as so significant that the bearer of the name, which is often that of a saint, will celebrate his "name-day" annually as a type of birthday — perhaps one should say "rebirth" day — on the feast day of the particular saint. In the Eastern Orthodox church the baptismal name is marked in this way, since the bearer will very likely have been named after the saint on whose feast day he or she was born.

The motivation that lies behind the assuming of a religious name — both a rebirth and a rejection of one's former worldly identification — seems to have influenced a category of name change that has been regularly observed since the 11th century. This is the change of name undertaken by a pope upon his election. It is not in fact obligatory for a pope to assume a new name, but an old custom. Although two popes, in fact, did not change their name — Adrian VI (pope in 1522-1523) and Marcellus II (in 1555) — in practice every pope has changed his name since Peter, bishop of Pavia, assumed the name John in 983. It is believed that he made this change out of reverence for St. Peter, the first pope, since in his *Epitaph* he says that he took on a new name "quia Petrus antea extiterat" ("because Peter existed before"). Most popes have come to assume the name of a predecessor — the present pope, John Paul II, took the names of *two* predecessors — but there is one name that no pope will adopt. This name is Peter, and a tradition exists, or a superstition, if one dare mention such a thing with regard to the head of the Roman Catholic church, that if a pope named "Peter II" is elected he will be the last of all popes.

The very early popes changed their names simply because their original names were pagan: John II (pope in 533-535) was formerly Mercurius, and John XII (955-64) was Octavianus. On similar lines, and encouraged by the example of John XIV, the former Peter, the first transalpine pontiffs, Bruno of Carinthia and Gerbert of Aurillac, changed their barbarous names to genuine Roman ones, respectively Gregory V (966) and Sylvester II (999). In more recent times the motives for a papal name change have become a good deal more complex, and have included such factors as veneration for a particular predecessor of the same name, a "specialization" in the works of a predecessor, or simply a coincidence of election date or of place or region of origin. Papal names form a sufficiently distinctive and interesting category for us to treat them separately, as special names, in Chapter 6.

Turning from saints to sinners, we have a noted category of name adopters in criminals of all kinds. Here, perhaps, the desire for a new name is motivated not so much by the wish to start life afresh — no spiritual rebirth here! — but to dissociate oneself with one's former, "real" self. In this, at least, renegades and members of religious orders share a common reasoning. In the case of a criminal, of course, one important objective is to avoid detection or identification, and so an actual physical disguise is often accompanied by a change of name. The name itself may be unimportant: what *is* important is that the criminal should have a name of some kind, since truly and permanently anonymous human beings do not exist. Ideally, to have no name at all would be an excellent idea, since then the murderer would stand a good chance of escaping undetected, and no one would know whodunit. But if you start life with a name, as we all do, you cannot simply abandon it without replacing it somehow. Even the Man in the Iron Mask had a name, although what it was has still not been established with any degree of certainty.

A special type of name assumed by a criminal, or even a suspect, is, of course, an alias. The word is Latin in origin, meaning "otherwise," a sense that is indicated more obviously in the alternative term for an alias — "a.k.a.," or "also known as," an abbreviation rather more common in the United States than in Britain.

Like misfortunes, aliases rarely come singly, especially when a criminal or suspect is on the run, and they are changed as often as the bearer's route and disguise. The ideal alias is one that is contained in a stolen or forged passport, which is essential if the criminal is escaping to another country. Cases of criminals with forged or illegal passports are legion. One that hit the headlines in 1977, largely because of its lurid details and bizarre nature — it actually combined sex and religion — was that of the "Mormon kidnap." A young Mormon missionary, one Kirk Anderson, claimed to have been "kidnapped and held handcuffed and manacled for three days on the orders of a wealthy lovesick woman" (*Sunday Times*, September 18, 1977). The rich and randy lady in question was Joyce, or Joy, McKinney. Among aliases used by McKinney in forged passports on her subsequent flight from the police were Mrs. Bosler, Kathie Vaughn Bare, Cathy Van Deusen, Heidi Krasler, and Mrs. Palmquist. Traveling with her as her supposed husband was Keith Joseph May, a.k.a. Bob Bosler, alias Paul Van Deusen. Miss McKinney was something of an old hand at assuming a different name, it seemed. She had previously appeared as a model in a girlie magazine as Lexi Martin, and had advertised herself ("Gorgeous Former 'Miss USA' Contestant Desires Work!") in the *Los Angeles Free Press* as Joey.

The range of uses to which a name change can be put illegally or criminally is very wide. At one end there is the murderer and his alias. At the other is the child at school who answers "Here!" at rollcall to cover up for a friend who is playing hookey. This is a trivial but genuine case of impersonation. A number of cases are known of one person temporarily or even permanently succeeding in passing himself off as another. Among the more unusual, since they involve an impersonation of the opposite sex, are the histories of the 17th-century Spanish nun Catalina de Eranso, who served with the Spanish army in Chile and Peru as Alonso Díaz Ramírez de Gúzman, and of Barbara Ann Malpass, who spent four months in Jefferson County jail in 1959 claiming to be Charles Richard Williams. In the latter case the impersonation was made for the simple, practical reason that the prisoner reckoned she could more easily pass as a male runaway than a female.

It is certainly a fact that many pseudonyms are adopted for nefarious purposes, or at least for disguise. The code names and cover names taken by spies and undercover agents are well known, from the famous, although fictional, 007 (James Bond), to the infamous Cicero, who supplied top secret documents to the Germans in the Second World War — for a sizeable consideration — and who turned out to be, or so he claimed in a book published in London in 1953, one E. Bazna. Espionage is a world of forged papers, fake identities and secret passwords, a dark world of aliases, incognitos and assumed names. Experts in the art — or science — of espionage distinguish between a cover name and an operational name. A cover name is the name adopted by an agent when he embarks on his actual operation. In doing this, he assumes the identity of either a real person or a fictional one. If the former, he will also be impersonating that person. Thus the cover name of the Russian spy K.T. Molody was Gordon Lonsdale. An operational name, by contrast, is the name by which an agent is known to his chiefs, so that he can be identified without reference being made to his real name or his cover name. Thus the British-Russian agent whose real name was Allan Nunn May had the operational name Alek.

In considering the various categories of people who assume another name, we have briefly mentioned ballerinas and, in a very limited application, a few writers. These are members of a creative profession whose names — stage names and pen names — are probably the most familiar to the world since they are in a most popular sector of society. Actors and authors, when it comes to name adoption, are prolific, and to do them justice we must devote a whole chapter to the many and varied motives that prompt them to adopt another name.

Who hath not own'd, with rapture-smitten frame,
The power of grace, the magic of a name?
(Thomas Campbell, "Pleasures of Hope")

3 Names for a Living

"Words, words, words" — and rather more — are the medium by which most full-time actors and writers earn their living, and in both of these creative categories the adoption of a pseudonym is a long-standing tradition.

Let us consider each group in turn, taking those of the stage first. And here it must be said that the term actor (and actress) should be taken in its widest sense, to embrace all men and women who perform or entertain or dance or sing or play on the stage or screen, or over radio or television — all who practice the performing arts, in fact.

Many stage names are very familiar to the public, who may indeed not realize that they *are* stage names. Actors, after all, become stars and achieve fame and win awards, and their names take on a particularly exalted or important significance.

Why do actors adopt a different name?

Many would perhaps reply, "Because it's the tradition." Some might add, "It's automatic." But if we look at the motives more closely, we can see more specific reasons.

First, in their line of work, actors assume other identities in any case. They change their true selves and become someone else, if only for one evening. This is particularly true of professional stage and film actors and actresses. In playing a part, whether it is major or a minor role, an actor will also assume not only the identity and character of another person, but also the name of that person. A name change is thus part of the job. Therefore a new name is assumed as if to emphasize that such "dual personality" is anyway part and parcel of the actor's real life. An actor is thus versatile and gifted, and in changing his own name adapts his own persona to the bread-winning business of becoming someone else, night after night. A stage name is, then, very important: not for nothing is an actor's name usually referred to as his or her "professional" name.

And apart from the psychological motive, there is also a historical one. For some years in the past, acting, especially in "higher" circles of society, was regarded as an inferior, degrading or even decadent way of life. Actors would thus change their names to avoid this undesirable

13

stigma, and to dissociate their true name — and the good name of their family — from their vocation.

Again, actors are, even today, superstitious people, believing in good fortune and fame only when it happens, and a change of name may help to avoid a possible failure on the stage. After all, if you are a flop, it is not the real you that has failed, but your alter ego. A different name may perhaps actually help to bring good luck in your performance, as well as ward against failure. We recall the reasoning behind the name change made by °Elton John in Chapter 2. For him at any rate, the transformation seemed to work!

There are also, of course, sound practical reasons for making an actor's name change desirable. We have already mentioned some of these and should now enumerate them more specifically.

(1) An actor's real name may be a very ordinary or common one. He or she therefore wishes to change it to something rather more glamorous and memorable. Thus Peggy Middleton became Yvonne de Carlo, Merle Johnson turned into Troy Donahue, and Norma Jean Baker was metamorphosed as °Marilyn Monroe. Even a change of one name is enough, so that Thomas Connery became Sean Connery, and a simple tiny addition or alteration of one letter can make all the difference: Coral Brown lost her common touch when she became Coral Browne, and Frankie Howard made people look again when he restyled his name as °Frankie Howerd.

(2) A real name may be awkward or ugly or even have undesirable connotations. Change it — to something euphonious and mellifluous! Thus did Virginia McSweeney become Virginia Valli, Nadine Judd turn into °Nadia Nerina, and Jean Shufflebottom change for the better to Jeannie Carson. Actresses, in particular, are anxious to avoid a name smacking of impropriety, which prompted Dora Broadbent to change to °Dora Bryan, Diana Fluck to be reborn as °Diana Dors, and Joanne La Cock to make her name as °Joanne Dru.

(3) Very much from the practical point of view, a stage name may simply be too long for billing. A shorter rather than a longer name is always more memorable, too. So it was not surprising that Frances Anderson-Anderson halved herself to become Judith Anderson (which even so is still not noticeably short), Michael Dumble-Smith turned into Michael Crawford, Deborah Kerr-Trimmer became trimmer as Deborah Kerr, and Roger Ollerearnshaw, the TV announcer, became Roger Shaw. A shortened name can often be an improved one, too. The late lamented °Gracie Fields had a name much more melodious and pleasantly evocative than her real name of Grace Stansfield.

(4) As applies to all names, a foreign name is often best changed by an actor to an English one. So Bernard Schwartz, Dino Crocetti and Daniel Kaminsky must have thought, to change their respectively German, Italian and Polish-sounding names to Tony Curtis, °Dean Martin, and Danny Kaye. Many stage name changes are of this type.

(5) It may happen that an actor's name is similar, or even identical, to the name of another actor. In this case he is well advised to change it, simply in order to avoid confusion. In fact the British actors' trade union, Equity, makes it a condition that no actor may perform with the same name as another. So James Stewart, the British film actor, changed his name to °Stewart Granger so as not to be confused with James Stewart, the American actor, and Melvin Kaminsky, the film comedy writer and producer changed to °Mel Brooks so as not to be muddled with Max Kaminsky, the trumpet player.

When it comes to writers, the use of a pseudonym is much more flexible, and less stereotyped, than with an actor. A written, recorded name, after all, can be much more subtly manipulated than the stage name that an actor bears in the manner of a true name. Unlike an actor's name, it can be used for a single piece of writing or genre of writing, for example, it can be permanent or temporary, meaningful or arbitrary, resemble a real name or be quite unlike a conventional name. A writer, too, can have more than one pseudonym — even as many as a hundred — and can jettison at will one pseudonym to adopt another, for whatever reason, as easily as setting pen to paper. Indeed, by the very term "pseudonym" most people understand a writer's assumed name rather than an actor's (many dictionaries will define the word in terms of a writing name), and although a stage name will undoubtedly, because of the charisma of its bearer, often acquire a "star" quality, it is the name adopted by a writer that will almost always be the more telling.

We have already touched on one or two reasons that prompt a writer to adopt another name (for disguise, or to gain prestige). We should now have a closer look at the motives for adopting a pen name — some of which, in fact, are virtually the same as the motives that lead to a stage name.

Unlike an actor, a writer may well keep two professional lives on the go at once: his "bread-and-butter" one, which exercises his conventional abilities and qualifications, and which provides him with a regular paycheck and a good degree of security — his "job," in fact — and his dedicated work as a writer, which, at any rate to begin with, may not give him the same degree of security or reward him with the same regular income, but which does give him a considerable creative satisfaction. In such cases, when a man or woman is both these, professional person and vocational writer, he or she may find it convenient or desirable to adopt a pen name for the writing activities, if only to differentiate the two sides to a single person's life. When this happens, it is the pen name that will be the better known, of course, since this is the writer's more public face. We all know James Bridie, the playwright, much better than we know the Scottish doctor Osborne Henry Mavor; we are more likely to be familiar with the detective stories of °Michael Innes than the English critical studies by J.I.M. Stewart. On the other hand, both sides of a person's creative activity may be equally well known, so that Cecil Day Lewis, the poet, has a status almost equalled by °Nicholas Blake, the detective fiction writer. To distinguish, thus, the work of A.B. the breadwinner from Y.Z. the literary creator, is one of the prime functions of a pen name. Often, of course, a person's writing may be so successful that he is able to abandon his traditional career. In such a case his literary name usually "takes over" and becomes the whole individual. This happened, for example, to Richard Gordon, who gave up his professional work as a doctor in 1952 and devoted himself entirely to writing, and to °John Le Carré, who as a result of the success of his third novel of espionage, *The Spy Who Came in from the Cold*, was able to leave the foreign service in 1964 and concentrate on full-time writing.

A writer may also assume a different name not in order to distinguish between the writing self and the professional self, but to differentiate between one aspect of his or her writing and another. A travel writer, for example, may turn his hand to mystery fiction, and will take on a second pseudonym (or a first, if he writes under his real name) to be reserved for this type of book. Or a literary critic may publish some verse under a different name. The New Zealand writer whose real name was Ruth France, for example, assumed the name Paul Henderson for her poetry. (She also adopted a male name. We shall be considering such "cross-sexing" shortly). Again, it may be convenient to use a different name for books or work written over a particular period, or even for a single publication. Christopher Caudwell, the British Marxist writer of studies of poetry and prose literature, reversed the usual process in this way, using his *real* name (Christopher St. John Sprigg) for seven detective novels written between 1933 and 1939. The Welsh-born novelist Cecil Blanche Woodham-Smith adopted the name Janet Gordon for just three novels—*April Sky* (1938), *Tennis Star* (1940), and *Just Off Bond Street* (1940)—and Leslie Seldon Truss, the British thriller writer, used the name George Selmark for a single novel, *Murder in Silence* (1939).

For a different type of distinction, a writer may choose to take on another name for contributions to a particular magazine, or when submitting work to a different publisher. The Scottish poet William Aytoun used the somewhat unconventional name Augustus Dun-shunner for his contributions to *Blackwood's Magazine*, and George Darley, the Irish writer, contributed to the *London Magazine* as John Lacy.

The reasons that motivate a writer to choose another name on practical grounds do not end there. Jean-Raymond De Kremer, the bilingual Belgian writer, called himself Jean Ray when writing in French, and John Flanders (!) for his books in Flemish, and Andrey Sinyavsky, the controversial Russian writer, used the name Abram Tertz for his allegedly subversive writings published in the West.

A different genre, a different period, a different approach, a different publisher, a different language, a different self—a writer can identify the difference by simply adopting a new name.

If the situation requires it, there is of course no reason why a writer should not assume more than one pen name. There may be a good practical value in this. From the sheer commercial side, for example, a single writer can submit articles to different journals under different names, and writers who are particularly prolific may indeed prefer to "parcel out" their writings in this way. Science fiction and fantasy writers frequently employ a whole range of names, as do crime novelists, and many publishers have stocks of ready-made pen names, so called "house names," that they allocate to their authors. And when descending to a more undemanding level of writing (and reading), as light romantic fiction and "pulp" magazines (although some such work has turned out to be above average), the adoption of a battery of pen names has for some years been standard practice.

As to the number of pen names that a writer can adopt, there are few limits. John Creasey, the crime novelist, wrote his 560 books under 28 pseudonyms; °Stendhal, the French novelist, had over a hundred pen names, with "Stendhal" itself the best known, and °Voltaire, also a pseudonym — and one of the most famous in world literature — totalled at least 173, which would seem to be something of a record (see Appendix I, page 332). For the majority of writers, however, a handful of pseudonyms suffices for most practical purposes.

It goes without saying that many of the reasons that encourage an actor to change his name (an unsuitable real name, for dissociation, for ease of distinction from a similar name, for memorability) also apply to writers, although not perhaps to quite the same extent. An actor's name is very much part of his or her image and stage personality, and it is billed and promoted in a much more blatant and "public" way than the name of a writer. An actor's name, therefore, really matters. With a writer, on the other hand, although the name is indeed of considerable significance, it is *what* is written that counts. It obviously helps to have a memorable and easily pronounceable and attractive name, but for a writer a name is much more a means of pure identification than it is for an actor. Anthony Trollope's novels achieved their classic status without their author's feeling it necessary to adopt another name, nor was Oscar Wilde ever tempted in this respect. But how far would mellifluously named °Marilyn Monroe have got as Norma Jean Baker? It is interesting to speculate. (Not that there is anything wrong or repugnant or detractive in the name — it proved no hindrance to Josephine Baker, Carroll Baker or Hylda Baker — it is just that Marilyn Monroe sounds and looks more like the name of a glamorous actress, that it has more "favorable free associations," as the ad writers say.)

There are, however, particular motivations for a writer's name change that will hardly ever apply to an actor.

The chief of these is the so called "literary mask," the need or desirability for writers to conceal their true identity (which actors will hardly wish to do). The motivation here is not so much to find a name as to escape from one. In other words, the name is regarded as a "cover-up" name, much as we saw it was for a spy or criminal in the last chapter.

Why should a writer wish to hide his or her identity?

One reason may be that he wishes to avoid censorship. When a writer has something important to say, whether as fact or fiction, and when it may be difficult to say it under his real name, either because of his own standing or because it is controversial or even unlawful or hostile to authority, the adoption of a pseudonym may be the only solution. In the past many anticlerical or generally antiestablishment writers have sought refuge in an assumed name. °Voltaire, imprisoned in the Bastille for writing a scurrilous lampoon on the French regent (the notorious libertine Philippe II, Duke of Orleans), assumed his pseudonym on his release (1718) with the aim of pursuing his powerful philosophical and sceptical writings. A century before him, a fellow Frenchman, Agrippa d' Aubigné, an ardent Protestant, attacked the evils of the establishment, in particular French monarchs such as Catherine de Médicis and her sons Charles IX and Henri III, in his classic poem *Les Tragiques* (1616). For this he assumed the initials L.B.D.D. Only some 300 years later were these letters deciphered as standing for "Le Bouc du Désert" ("The Scape-goat"). This was known to have been a nickname used for d'Aubigné — moreover at one time he lived in a small village in Brittany actually called Le Désert. D'Aubigné's poem was both antiroyalist and anticlerical. Specifically anticlerical was the work of yet another outstanding French writer, Blaise Pascal. For a bitter yet objective attack on the Jesuits he en-titled his famous eighteen letters *Lettres de Louis de Montalte à un Provincial de Ses Amis et aux RR. PP. Jésuites sur la Morale et la Politique de Ces Pères* (1656) ("Letters from Louis de Montalte to a Provincial Friend and to Their Reverend Fathers the Jesuits Concerning the Morality and the Policy of Those Fathers"). The work dealt the Jesuits a blow from which they never recovered. (It was subsequently placed on the Index and ordered to be burned by the Royal Council in 1660.)

In these three literary masks we incidentally see good examples of a permanent "take-over" pseudonym (°Voltaire) and of names used for specific single works (L.B.D.D. and Louis de Montalte). It is merely a coincidence that all three may well have derived from place-names.

Thus critics and satirists of all ages have adopted a disguised name, from d'Aubigné in the 17th century to the wry American humorist Mr. Dooley (real name Finley Peter Dunne) in the 20th. It is understandable, too, that not just critics and humanists but political activists and revolutionaries will wish to adopt a "cover" name, since the publishing of their ideology in printed form will be one of the most effective ways of disseminating their message. Escaping the watchful eye of the censor here is all-important. It was largely in order to publicize — and publish, even if only in the "underground" press — his views and theories on society and the economy that led Vladimir Ilich Ulyanov to adopt a whole number of pseudonyms, of which one, °Lenin, was to make him internationally known as a professional revolutionary. (His views and activities had in fact caused the censor and the police to keep an eye on him even at the early age of 17. For him to have published anything under his real name would have been out of the question.) °Lenin first used this particular name some time before the Revolution, in 1901. Many other Russians, both before and since the Revolution, have been obliged to adopt a pseudonym for fear of censorship or reprisals.

Another category of writers who undergo a name change are the plagiarists — those who "steal" the writing of someone else and put their own name to it. (The word derives from the Latin for "kidnapper.") In this case, of course, there is not the normal change *to* another name but *from* another name to one's own. The filching or pirating of other people's works was common among Elizabethan playwrights, when hacks would openly steal the plays of others and present them as their own. Today, of course, the stringent laws of copyright make such thieving very difficult, if not impossible.

In some instances, however, the "plagiary" may be by mutual agreement between the "thief" and his victim. At the beginning of his career, for example, Bernard Shaw found it difficult to get his writing published. He was aided by his friend, the musical conductor George Lee. Shaw would write the musical reviews and Lee would have them printed over his own name. A similar situation in which a helping hand was given arose when °Jack London aided his friend George Sterling. Sterling simply could not get his story "The First Poet" accepted. London included it in his collection of short stories entitled *Turtles of Tasman* (1916). Only some time later did Sterling reveal that he, not London, was the author of that particular story.

Very many writers, of course, are influenced by the writings of others and may unwittingly borrow from them. But this is not deliberate conscious wholesale stealing, simply unconscious (or possibly subconscious) borrowing or adaptation, and as such is not really plagiary. Milton, for example, was greatly influenced by Spenser who in turn owed a good deal to Chaucer, and Keats was influenced by all three. This does not mean that any of the four can be accused of plagiary — even if Chaucer, in turn, had borrowed from French and Italian writers!

Another type of writing involving the adoption of a different name is parody. One famous case of parody was the work entitled *Les Déliquescences d'Adoré Floupette*, a collection of *poèmes décadents* that appeared in Paris in 1885. These were taken seriously by the critics — at first, at any rate. Yet who was the deliciously named Adoré Floupette? It turned out that there was no such person, but the poems themselves were clever, if rather malicious, parodies of poems by the early French Symbolist poets — Verlaine, Mallarmé, Rimbaud, Moréas and others. The

Déliquescences (meaning approximately "Meltings" or "Liquefactions") were actually the work of two young poets, Gabriel Vicaire and Henri Beauclair.

Many examples of parody, however, do not involve a name change at all. When Stella Gibbons wrote *Cold Comfort Farm* (1932) as a caricature of a novel by Mary Webb, she did not claim to *be* Mary Webb or indeed to be anyone apart from her real self.

Cases of plagiary and parody may often be quite intriguing, even if one might think twice about reading the actual works involved. Even more interesting, and a further motive for adopting another name, are literary hoaxes. These occur when a writer claims to be someone other than who he really is — the converse of a plagiarist, in fact, and closer to a parodist. Literary hoaxes involve the donning of a real literary mask.

There are some classic examples of such hoaxes.

Washington Irving, the "Father of American Literature," began his career with a double hoax. Having already used the pseudonym Jonathan Oldstyle, Gent., for a series of satirical letters published in the *Morning Chronicle* (1802-1803), he got together with his brother William and the writer James K. Paulding to publish a series of satirical essays and poems entitled *Salmagundi; or, the Whim-Whams and Opinions of Launcelot Langstaff, Esq., and Others*. These were first published as pamphlets and subsequently (1808) in book form. But Irving was not content to stop here. The following year a number of American newspapers carried announcements signed by one Handiside, manager of the New York Columbia Hotel, to the effect that a hotel resident named Diedrich Knickerbocker had checked out of the hotel leaving a manuscript behind. The announcements described Knickerbocker's appearance and character and requested anyone who knew of his whereabouts to contact Mr. Handiside who at the same time declared that if Mr. Knickerbocker did not return to the hotel he, Handiside, would publish the manuscript to recover his losses, since the aforesaid Mr. Knickerbocker had not settled his account. All this was in fact the work of Irving, intended as a build-up for his famous burlesque whose full title was *A History of New York, from the Beginning of the World to the End of the Dutch Dynasty, by Diedrich Knickerbocker* (1809). Neither Knickerbocker nor Handiside existed, of course. Thanks to this unusual publicity the work enjoyed immense success, and a few months after publication Irving revealed himself as the true author and thus "blew" his hoax. After this he published under his real name.

Irving set something of a fashion for literary hoaxes with humorous names of this kind, especially among American writers. In the March 21, 1861, issue of the *Findlay (Ohio) Jefferson*, for example, there appeared a letter from one "Petroleum Vesuvius Nasby, late pastor uv the Church uv the New Dispensation, Chaplain to his excellency the President, and p.m. at Confederate x roads, kentucky." This illiterate and seemingly dissolute country preacher from the South appeared to be extolling slavery and supporting those who approved of it. Attentive readers could see, however, that in fact his arguments were absurd and that his apparent support for the South was given ironically. The author of this letter — it was to be the first of a series — was in fact the editor of the *Jefferson* whose real name was David Ross Locke.

Locke in turn was followed by C.F. Browne, who as Artemus Ward feigned an illiterate style not simply to entertain but in order to satirize insincerities and sentimentality. Like Shakespeare's Touchstone, he "uses his folly like a stalking horse, and under the presentation of that he shoots his wit."

Two more literary hoaxes deserve mention here. The French writer Prosper Mérimée published in 1825, at the start of his career, a selection of plays about Spanish life in the manner of Lope de Vega. Wary of possible criticism by supporters of the classical school, he ascribed the plays to a nonexistent Spanish actress, one Clara Gazul. He did more than this. A foreword to the plays, written by someone named Joseph Létrange (significantly, "Joseph the Strange") gave an account of Clara's life to date — how she had been brought up, how she had escaped from a nunnery to join a roving band of actors, and the like — and backed up this verbal background to the supposed authoress by an actual portrait of Clara, as a frontispiece to the plays. This portrait was executed by the painter Delescluze — and was in fact of the 22-year-old Mérimée wearing a mantilla and a necklace! Thus as Clara Gazul and Joseph Létrange, Mérimée not only donned a literary mask (a double one, in fact) but extended his hoax to a visual impersonation.

Pierre Louÿs (originally Louis), also a Frenchman, concocted another type of mystification. He claimed, in 1894, to have discovered and translated the songs of the unknown Greek poetess Bilitis, who had, it seemed, lived in the 6th century B.C. According to Louÿs, one Dr. Heim, an archaeologist, had discovered the tomb of the Greek woman lyricist, and as if to support the claim for her existence, subsequent editions of the *Chansons de Bilitis* even contained "her" portrait, as Mérimée's plays had done. But all of it was devised by Louÿs: there was no Bilitis, no Dr. Heim, and the portrait was simply a copy of a statue in the Louvre. The poems themselves were written by Louÿs in the style of Sappho.

Such pranks must have been highly satisfying to their perpetrators.

The ultimate in literary masks, however, is to take no name at all — to write anonymously. Many writers began their career in this way, believing that if what they wrote was worth reading, the public would buy it for its own sake, irrespective of whoever the author might be. Censor-dodgers, too, will obviously favor the anonymous approach. The trouble with such a system is — if your work has no name to it, how can the public obtain more if they want it? All that can be done is to resort to a cumbersome phrase such as "The Author of 'Confessions of a Convict'" or whatever is was called. Unless the author chooses to reveal his true identity immediately, he too will have to employ a similar awkward designation in order to be recognized as the writer of the original work.

A classic case of this kind is well illustrated by Sir Walter Scott. After a writing career that had already been under way for some twenty years—so he was not the typical anonymous beginner in this respect—Scott decided to change from verse romances, in which he was anyway largely overshadowed by Byron, to novels. There duly appeared, anonymously, in 1814, his now famous historical novel *Waverley*. Would it be a success? Scott was apprehensive: he was known as a poet, not a novelist. The book was indeed a success, but Scott was still cautious, with the result that all his following novels, up to 1827, were published as "by the Author of 'Waverley'." After this, confident that his reputation as a writer of historical fiction was assured, Scott wrote under his real name.

Among other works that were first published anonymously are Tennyson's *Poems by Two Brothers* (1927), Robert Browning's first poem "Pauline" (1833), James Fenimore Cooper's first novel *Precaution* (1820), Thomas Hardy's two novels *Desperate Remedies* (1871) and, surprisingly, *Far from the Madding Crowd* (1874), and Arthur Conan Doyle's first short stories in the *Cornhill Magazine* (1879).

Thus caution, apprehension and evasion are among the motives that prompt a writer to mask his true identity.

But why should a writer wish to disguise his or her sex?

To be more precise: why should a female writer—since in this respect the women easily outnumber the men—choose to adopt a masculine name?

However successful modern feminism may or may not be, there have certainly been times, many quite recent, when a woman writer has been obliged to assume a male name in order that her book should be widely read, or even that it should be published at all. In the Victorian era, for example, when a woman's role was basically regarded as that of wife and mother, for a feminine pen to turn out anything more powerful or unconventional than a little light romantic verse or a cosy daily diary would have been virtually unthinkable. And that a woman should produce a stark, passionate *roman d'amour* or a radical, serious work exposing the evils of racialism would have been as unlikely as for a woman to have become an M.P. or even a Prime Minister of Britain. Yet as we now know, barely a hundred years later, such things are not only possible but fully acceptable.

It was simply that "serious" and innovative writing of any kind, especially where it went against commonly held moral, religious and social beliefs, was expected to come, if it came at all, from a male author, not a female. The woman's place was not only in the home, it was as a dilettante, and if a lady took to the pen at all it was more often for the execution of elegant artwork than for the creation of a great literary masterpiece.

The year before Charlotte Brontë wrote *her* masterpiece *Jane Eyre* — in 1847, when good queen Victoria had been on the throne only ten years — she and her two sisters Emily and Anne had felt it prudent or even essential to adopt, if not actually male names, at any rate ones that were not so obviously feminine as their own. Charlotte's own account of their motive and her explanation of their precise choice of pen name is revealing, and a good guide to the attitudes of the time: "Averse to publicity, we veiled our own names under those of Currer, Ellis, and Acton Bell; the ambiguous choice being dictated by a sort of conscientious scruple of assuming Christian names positively masculine, while we did not declare ourselves women, because — without at the time suspecting that our mode of writing and thinking was not what is called 'feminine,' — we had a vague impression that authoresses are liable to be looked on with prejudice" (Elizabeth Gaskell, *Life of Charlotte Brontë*, 1847).

These "ambiguous" names were in fact short lived. The following year (1848) Charlotte admitted to being the author of *Jane Eyre*, while Emily revealed herself as the writer of *Wuthering Heights* and Anne as that of *The Tenant of Wildfell Hall* — but for a while the three sisters had been so successful in masking their sex that many reviewers believed the three authors to be three brothers.

It was not only the early Victorian authoresses who assumed a name of the opposite sex. Nearly forty years after Acton, Currer and Ellis Bell, another woman writer was to take a name that was positively masculine. This was Olive Schreiner, who in 1883 published *The Story of an African Farm* under the name of Ralph Iron. The book was a novel, but no light romance: it was an expressly feminist and anti-Christian work, which because of its fine descriptive style and originality achieved instant success. It was a controversial book, however, and when the sex of the author was revealed the controversy became a storm — which proves that the South African author was fully justified in her decision to adopt a cross-sex pseudonym.

Some two centuries before any of these andronymous authors, a number of French women writers had taken to adopting male pen names. Madeleine de Scudéry, known to her friends as "Sapho," wrote more than one novel under the name of her brother George. Her very long pseudo-historical romances *Clélie* (1654-60) and *Artamane, ou le Grand Cyprus* (1649-53), each ten volumes in length, depicted distinguished persons of her day under disguised names. But Mlle de Scudéry made no secret of the fact that she was the author of these works: her pseudonym was more an incognito, which she had not assumed with any great degree of seriousness.

Among other well known French authoresses who wrote under a masculine pen name were Amandine Dudevant (as °George Sand), Marie de Flavigny, comtesse d'Agoult (as Daniel Stern), and Delphine de Girardine (as Charles de Launay).

The practical advantages of adopting a male name, especially when it came to having your writing accepted for publication, were commented on by the French revolutionary writer Louise Michel: "I more than once had occasion to notice that when I submitted articles to a newspaper under the name Louise Michel I could wager a hundred to one that they would not be printed; but if I signed myself Louis Michel the chances of being published were much greater!" (*Mémoires*, Paris 1886).

A more straightforward way out of the difficulty that attended a woman writer was for her to sign herself simply "A Lady." Only ten authoresses so called appear in this present book, but there were very many who took the name. Indeed, in 1880 the bibliophile and pseudonymist Ralph Thomas — otherwise "Olphar Hamst" of the work listed in the Bibliography — published a fascinating volume entitled *Aggravating Ladies: being a list of works published under the pseudonym of "A Lady."* This contains over 50 identifiable "ladies" who put their pens to paper thus. Actually, the pseudonym is more satisfactory than it appears: it enables a woman writer to retain her anonymity while remaining loyal to her sex, and at the same time it has an air of respectability and appears aristocratic.

Except trivially or humorously, it has been a much rarer thing for a man to assume a female pseudonym. Whereas a female writer, to enter a male literary world, may frequently have found that the most effective passport is the adoption of a man's name, a male author is already in his man's world, and the same motives will not operate. In fact the only reason for a man to take on a female name as a writer is simply the reason that prompts him to adopt another name anyway — for any of the practical or aesthetic motives we have already mentioned.

Male writers who have thus adopted a female name are few and far between and mostly little known or of small consequence.

One exception, however, was that of the Scottish author °Fiona Macleod, whose real name was William Sharp. This was primarily a "distinction" name, used consistently for his mystical and quasi-Celtic romances and plays from 1893 until his death in 1905 — he had earlier written some poetry and biography under his real name — but perhaps there was also a genuine femininity in the writing or the personality of the man himself that motivated this particular choice of name. His pen name was so successful that the true identity of the author of the books by °Fiona Macleod was not known until after Sharp's death. It was moreover a pseudonym that he declined to acknowledge in his lifetime and under which he even appeared in *Who's Who!* Fiona, incidentally, was a "Celtic" name invented by Sharp for his pseudonym, and its subsequent popularity as a girl's name, especially in Scotland, is due entirely to him. (Sharp also used, on similar lines, the name Deidre for one of his romantic tales. This, too, has become something of a vogue name for girls. It was not invented by Sharp, however.)

In referring to women authors who chose to write as "A Lady" we were really dealing with a type of aristocratic name. Many writers of both sexes have chosen to devise a pseudonym that in one way or another suggests an aristocratic origin, even a royal one. This is of course a rather obvious way to enhance one's literary status, but it has been a steadily popular one over the centuries. The mechanics consist largely in assuming a name that includes an aristocratic particle or "honorific" such as the French *de* or German *von*. (For other ways of upgrading your name, see the next chapter.) The reasoning here is fairly straightforward, the argument being: aristocrats are more important than other people and receive greater attention; if I adopt an aristocratic name or title the public will pay more attention to my writing and will rate it highly (since the author is apparently an aristocrat) even before they have read it. But such "self-promotion," in the literal sense, became over popular as a pseudonymous device, and consequently lost its initial impact. Ralph Thomas's "aggravating ladies" were not tiresome because it was difficult attempting to track them down—there were simply too many of them. And half the "mystique" of being an aristocrat, even if a spurious one, is of course the fact that you belong to the select few, not the repetitive many.

Rather more interesting is the adoption by a genuine aristocrat of an ordinary or "common" name. This can occur either when the writer's high status makes it difficult for him or her to have a work published under his or her name—this applies in particular to royalty— or when the nature of the work, and its subject matter, makes it desirable for the high-ranking author to adopt a more lowly stance.

Such a "flight from fame" has been resorted to on more than one occasion by a king or queen, who even for private corrrespondence may well choose to become Mr. or Mrs. Thus Sarah Churchill, Duchess of Marlborough (1660-1744) corresponded with Queen Anne of England as Mrs. Freeman—a doubly symbolic name—while Queen Anne in turn wrote to the Duchess as Mrs. Morley.

One of the most prolific royal writers of the 19th century was Queen Elizabeth of Romania, who published several books of verse and prose as °Carmen Sylva—a name perhaps more lyrical than lowly— while Elizabeth itself was the pen name chosen by Countess von Arnim, later Countess Russell, for her novels, beginning with *Elizabeth and Her German Garden* (1898). (Elizabeth was her mother's first name.)

The motives that thus urge an actor or writer to assume another name are many and varied, with several factors bearing on the actual choice of name.

And now that we have considered *why* the adoption of a pseudonym may be desirable or necessary, we must see *how* such a new name is devised.

A self-made man may prefer a self-made name
(Judge Learned Hand, as Samuel Goldfish
changed his name to Samuel Goldwyn)

4 How Do You Make a Name for Yourself?

Whatever the motivation for changing your name, temporarily or permanently, the big practical question is — how do I change my name? Where do I get my new name from?

Taking all pseudonyms and changed names on the broadest possible basis, it may be said that the new name is either ready-made to a greater or lesser degree, that is, it is based on an already existing name, or else it is an invented name, derived from random or meaningful letters, syllables or words. In this chapter we shall be considering the larger of these two categories — and the one that is the more interesting, since the names mainly look like real personal names — "ready-made" names. In Chapter 5 we shall then have a look at the invented ones.

The obvious place to start is with your own name. Your own real name, that is. Many people, especially those who are changing their name more for convenience than for special effect, will prefer to choose a name that in some way echoes or suggests their original name.

If your original name is foreign-sounding to English-speaking people, the easiest thing to do is to "anglicize" it. This can usually be arranged by modifying a section of the name to resemble an English name. In some instances, especially with Germanic names, such a modification can simultaneously be a translation, as English *-son* for German *-sohn*. In other cases it will suffice simply to switch to an English name that only vaguely resembles the original. Examples are Hardy Albrecht to Hardie Albright, Vladimir Dukelsky to Vernon Duke, Gertrude Konstam to Gertrude Kingston, and George Wenzlaff to George Winslow.

In many cases such an "anglicization" is also accompanied by a shortening, so that the surnames Reizenstein, Liebermann, Kirkegaard and Breitenberger become Rice, Mann, Kirk, and Byrnes. Two classic examples of this type are Spiro Anagnostopoulos, who anglicized and abbreviated his name to Spiro Agnew — Greek surnames are notable for their length — and Josef Korzeniowski, better known as the novelist Joseph Conrad. It is noticeable that transformations like this often pay little regard to the actual literal meaning of the original name, that is, there is frequently no attempt to translate the name into English, even when this would preserve the similarity. Elsy Steinberg changed her name to Elaine Stewart, not Elaine Stone, and Nathan Weinstein, the American novelist, became Nathaniel West, not Nathaniel Vine or Nathaniel Stone. (But then he claims that Horace Greeley, the American journalist who founded the *New Yorker*, told him to "Go West, young man" — and he did!)

English-style modifications form a sizeable group, but bearers of foreign names who change to an English name quite unlike their own easily outnumber them. Thus Max Showalter became Casey Adams, Eugene Klass became Gene Barry, Louise Dantzler was reborn as Mary Brian, and Nathalie Belaieff turned into the nicely alliterative Nathalie Nattier. And even though such names are not based on the person's true name, at least they are an actual genuine or genuine-sounding English name, so in that respect are "ready-made." In practice, too, many people who favor this type of change already have an English-sounding forename which they retain (Leon Ames was Leon Waycoff, Geraldine Brooks was Geraldine Stroock, Kitty Carlisle was Catherine Holzman, and Cecil Parker was at least Cecil Schwabe).

But returning to "own-name-based" names, we find that many pseudonyms are not anglicized versions of a foreign name but merely simplified or abbreviated variants. This is the least concession that can be made to an English-speaking environment: at least they will be easier to read, remember and say, even if they do not actually look like an English name. But here again, it could be that a change of this type is intentionally made — the bearer of the name thus retains something of his or her native provenance, and so the resulting name is a convenient compromise, neither conspicuously foreign nor wholly English but somewhere between the two. In fact, such a name will still be sufficiently unusual to make it more memorable than an ordinary English name such as Jones or Adams. Examples of such names are Lionel Bart, who was Lionel Begleiter, Howard Da Silva, formerly Harold Silverblatt, Milton Berle, previously Mendel Berlinger, and Peter Tork, once Peter Torkelson. Even in non-English environments the same method can be used, with Jacques Tatischeff becoming °Jacques Tati in France, and Franz von Strehlenau assuming the simplified but not specifically German name Nikolaus Lenau in Austria.

In fact a change of this kind may often result, as we have noted, from Howard F. Barker's "abrasion of common speech." A foreign-sounding name may become smoothed down and even abbreviated by the attempts of an English-speaking tongue to pronounce it. Several actual (legal) name changes have thus come about, so that such famous American names as those of General Custer, General Pershing, General Longstreet, and Herbert C. Hoover were, several generations back, respectively Köster, Pfoersching, Langestraet and Huber (Mencken, pp. 578-9).

How else may one vary one's real name? The answer is: in any number of ways, often combining two or more devices. Among the more popular are the following:

(1) Omit your surname. Often a person's second or middle name may actually look like a surname anyway — it is often a family name, such as one's mother's maiden name — and the advantage of such a modification is that it is both simplicity itself and that it enables a person to retain his or her original name unchanged. In such a fashion, changing your name means no change at all, since your new name is your old, and your "pseudonym" is not even "pseudo"! Not surprisingly, this is a very common procedure. Thus, Edward Ashley Cooper became Edward Ashley, William Bolitho Ryall became William Bolitho, Ernest Bramah Smith, author of the *Kai Lung* novels, dropped his prosaic Smith to assume (i.e., retain) his orientally exotic middle name as a surname, and Elizabeth Allen Gillease preferred to be known as just Elizabeth Allen. (To have a middle name that is at once a Christian name and a surname is indeed a stroke of good fortune.)

Of course, variants of this procedure are possible. While dropping your surname, you can simultaneously change your second name in some way, as can be done to a surname proper. George Augustus Andrews dropped his surname and altered his middle name to become George Arliss, for example. Or you can alter your *first* name while dropping your surname, often assuming instead a pet form of it or a nickname. Thus James Barry Jackson became Michael Barry, and William Berkeley Enos became Busby Berkeley. Then if you are blessed with two middle names, you can drop both you first name and your surname and use these two as first name and surname (!). This is what the humorist George Anthony Armstrong Willis did, to become Anthony Armstrong. Sherwood Bonner did likewise: originally she was Katherine Sherwood Bonner Macdowell. Again, you can omit your surname and reverse the order of your two first names, even omitting a forename in the process. This was what George Barrington Rutland Fleet did, to become Rutland Barrington. Similarly, by process of omission and reversal, Edward Thomas Andoulewicz became Thomas Andrew.

The dropping of one half of a double-barreled surname is also an expedient device, whatever else you may do with the rest of your name. Angela Baddeley was born Madeleine Angela Clinton-Baddeley, and Sir Felix Aylmer was originally Felix Edward Aylmer-Jones.

The permutations and combinations that apply in this category can also, of course, be employed in other methods.

(2) More straightforwardly, you can simply use a forename on its own. This is a method favored by cartoonists, who like a short name for signing purposes, by artists of all kinds — both painters and "artistes" — who like a single, stylish name, and is standard practice for several types of religious names, from saints to members of religious orders. (We shall

be considering religious names as a separate category later in this chapter.) Such a name is usually a person's first name, or an abbreviated or pet form of this, but can be any forename. Examples are Fabian Forte Bonaparte, who became simply Fabian, Sabu Dastagir, known better as just Sabu ("the Elephant Boy"), and the pianist Solomon Cuttner, known professionally as Solomon. Beryl Botterill Antonia Yeoman decided that the best name for signing her cartoons was Anton, and the political cartoonist Vicky was born Victor Weisz. Cherilyn Sarkasia Lalier teamed with Sonny to become popular as simply Cher, and the film actress Ann-Margret has a double-barreled first name that she finds quite sufficient to enable her to drop her surname Olson. One of the most sensible things the Belgian wife of emperor Maximilian of Mexico did was to assume the single name Carlota. Originally, in all her grandeur, she was Marie-Charlotte-Amélie-Augustine-Victoire-Clémentine-Léopoldine. (Royalty are renowned for their lavish endowment of Christian names.) A variation of this is to use your forename as a full-length pseudonym (forename plus surname) by splitting it into two. Maybritt Wilkens did this to become May Britt, and Isaiah Edwin Leopold to be Ed Wynn. The use of a forename alone preceded by "Madame" or "Mademoiselle" or "Miss" is also popular with a number of lady artistes, from fortune-tellers to stage actresses. Mlle Augusta, the French ballerina, was born Caroline Augusta Josephine. Thérèse Fuchs, and Mlle Clairon, the famous tragic actress of the Comédie Française, started life as Claire-Josephe Hippolyte Leris de la Tude.

(3) As a kind of converse of this, you can simply use your surname alone. This is perhaps least of all a pseudonym, since the use of surname alone is established, in certain situations and for certain conventions, in a number of countries. For this reason, only a few examples are included in this book. However, Liberace is here, if only to prove that it is indeed the real surname of Wladziu Liberace, and the cartoonists Giles and Low are here for similar reasons: these are the real surnames, not concocted names, of Carl Giles and David Low. Even less of a pseudonym is a real surname preceded by "Mr." or "Mrs." Yet if we take it that a full, true name consists of a forename and a surname, this must be at least partly a pseudonym since there is an element of disguise. How many people, for example, know the Christian name of Mrs. Beeton, even less her maiden name? The famous cookbook writer was born Isabella Mary Mayson. Topol, incidentally, is the true surname of the actor Chaim Topol.

(4) A common disguise for one's real name, and one popular with writers of all kinds, is to use one's initials. Such a device is so frequently resorted to, both by established writers and private individuals alike — can you honestly say that you have never signed your name by your initials? — that, again, it hardly figures in our present collection of pseudonyms. Even so, the Russian journalist O.K., née Olga Kireyeva, is included —

she lived many years in England and aimed to promote friendship between the two countries in the latter half of the 19th century — and so of course is Q, otherwise Sir Arthur Quiller-Couch. (Initials that stand for something other than one's real name are another matter, and they are duly represented as genuine pseudonyms.)

(5) Much more enterprisingly and ingeniously, a favorite method of forming a pseudonym is to "juggle" with one's real name in some way. This can be done by reversing the order of names, for example, by making an anagram out of it or by reading it back to front (as a reversal), or simply by "recasting" the original name in a mixture of ways, adding or subtracting letters where convenient. The thriller writer John Dickson Carr, for instance, selected as two of his pseudonyms the names Carr Dickson and Carter Dickson. Edith Caroline Rivett, the writer of detective novels, took the initials of all three of her names plus the chief element of her middle name reversed to become E.C.R. Lorac (at one time she wrote also as Carol Carnac), and Patrick Reardon Connor dropped one name and altered one vowel in each of the other two to become Rearden Conner. For examples of full-blooded anagrammatic and reversal pseudonyms we need to quote the French poet and short-story writer Théophile Dondey who used an Irish-style transformation to become Philothée O'Neddy, and the English comedian Tommy Trinder who back-pedaled his surname to form the early stage name Red Nirt. A glance in the Bibliography at the end of this book will show that even one of the source authors, himself an expert on pseudonyms, appears under his pseudonymous name! This is Olphar Hamst, who was in reality the English 19th-century bibliophile Ralph Thomas. The classic example of an anagrammatic name is, of course, that of °Voltaire, formed from his real surname of Arouet (with u equating with v) plus the initials "L.J." ("j" becoming "i"), said to stand for "Le Jeune." For other varied examples of name-juggling see Name List number 18 (page 189).

(6) An extension of a pseudonym consisting solely of initials, as already mentioned, is a name that is a marked contraction of the real name. These, like the "forename only" pseudonym, are especially popular with cartoonists for a short, snappy name that can be quickly and compactly signed. Among such names are Batt (Oswald Barrett), Jak (Raymond Jackson), Jon (W.P. John Jones), and Gus (George W. Smith). This last name is formed from his initials, and thus offers another possibility for a brief name. °Erté, the French costume designer, devised his name from the two initials, as the sound in French, of his full name Romain de Tirtoff, and the French cartoonist François Lejeune did similarly to produce his pen name Jean Effel. The clown °Coco has a name that comes from the two -ko- syllables of his full name Nikolai Poliakoff, and the author of *The Book of Artemas: Concerning men, and the things that men did do at the time when there was a war* (1917), and subsequent "Artemas" books, took his name from the first syllables of his

complete name Arthur Telford Mason. Here, once again, all kinds of variations are possible. Julia L.M. Woodruff, author of now unread 19th-century novels (*Holden with Cords* and *Shiloh*), took her initials, reversed them, turned the fourth into a surname, and wrote as W.M.L. Jay! The crosswordist Afrit had a name that was not only directly derived from his real name (Alistair Ferguson Ritchie) but one that additionally means a powerful devil in Islamic mythology, one that "inspires great dread," as every dedicated crossword compiler hopes he does in his solvers. (For a look at this fearsome class of pseudonymous devisers, see Chapter 6.)

Any name actually devised from an initial comes in this group, whether forming part of a conventional pseudonym, as Danny Kaye, who began life as Daniel Kaminsky, or used on its own, as above. Obviously, some letters of the alphabet are more suitable than others for forming a traditional English-type name — if that is what is wanted. Among them are B (Bee), D (Dee), G (Gee), J (Jay), and the popular K (Kay or Kaye).

How else can a pseudonym be evolved from your real name?

You can translate it!

Of course, you can only do this if your real name in any way resembles an ordinary translatable word or words. But to translate your name is a method of creating a pseudonym that has a well established and highly respectable antecedence. Such a method was established in the Renaissance period, mainly by German scholars of the 16th and 17th centuries. These men were the "new aristocracy," and felt it appropriate to translate or in some way render their often very ordinary or even laughably earthy names into an elevated Latin or Greek form. As Paul Tabori remarked, "Schurtzfleisch (Apronflesh) or Lämmerschwanz (Sheep'stail) were scarcely the right names under which to climb Mount Olympus" (*The Natural Science of Stupidity*, 1959).

A brief list will illustrate the principle:

German original	English meaning	Classical rendering
Schneider	tailor	Agricola (Latin)
Bauer	peasant	Agricola (Latin)
Huysman (Dutch)	caretaker	Agricola (Latin)
Ackermann	ploughman	Agricola (Latin)
Kuhhorn	cow horn	Bucer (Latin)
Schwarzerd	black earth	Melanchthon (Greek)
Kremer	merchant, tradesman	Mercator (Latin)
Schultheiss	village mayor (approx.)	Praetorius (Latin)
Hausschein	house shine	Oecolampadius (Greek)
Goldschmied	goldsmith	Fabricius (Latin)
Schütz	archer	Sagittarius (Latin)
Kopernik (Polish)	small onion?	Copernicus (Latin)
Hosemann	trouser man?	Osiander (Latin)
Harmensen (Dutch)	?	Arminius (Latin)

Today, thinking little of it, we have come to accept the classical version of the name as the "real" one, so that we learn at school of Mercator's geographical projection and at university, possibly, of the Arminian doctrine rejecting predestination. We might even add a far more famous "classical" name to this list – that of Christopher Columbus, whose original Italian name was Cristoforo Colombo.

Some such names seemed particularly popular. Four Agricolas (or Agricolae) are cited here, but there were a number more. The translation itself, too, was not always entirely a faithful one. Kremer the mathematician took the opportunity of not only translating himself but promoting himself from a "tradesman" to a "wholesale merchant," *Mercator*. And where a name could not be easily translated – and even sometimes when it could – a favorite device was simply to "latinize" the name by adding "-us," as with Copernicus and Arminius, above. (The French theologian born Chauvin did this, calling himself Calvinus. Today, though, English-speakers know him as Calvin.)

In more recent times, as we have already seen (in Chapter 1), foreign immigrants to Anglophone countries have taken to translating their names – especially, like the scholars two and three centuries before them, those with German names. Schneider then becomes Taylor, Schönkind becomes Fairchild, and Weiss becomes White. Most such transformations are of Jewish names.

It is of course possible to translate or "render" from any one language to any other, as circumstances require, with the new name being a permanent acquisition or simply a temporary, even frivolous, pen name. The Laotian nationalist and author of resistance pamphlets thus adopted the name William Rabbit for one of his works, this being a translation (in part) of his real name Katay Don Sasorith, while the composer born in Italy as Giovanni Battista Lulli frenchified his name when he came to settle in France as Jean-Baptiste Lully. Some translations are almost unrecognizable, at least to an English speaker. The film star Judy Holliday started life as Judith Tuvim, her surname being Hebrew for "holiday." And how about Xanrof? This was the name adopted by Leon Fourneau, the French songwriter who wrote for the diseuse Yvette Guilbert at the turn of the century. He took his surname, translated it into Latin (*fornax*, "furnace"), then reversed it!

While considering translations and renderings, we should not overlook a type of converse procedure when a standard English name is turned into a foreign version. We quoted in Chapter 2 the need felt by a number of ballet dancers, for example, to russify their name. Hilda Boot and Patrick Healey-Kay we instanced, but there were also Romayne Austin, who was transformed into Romayne Grigorova (not in fact a direct rendering), Ethel Liggins, who turned into Ethel Leginska, and of course Lilian Marks, famous as Alicia Markova. Richard Adama, the American ballet dancer who became director of the Bremen State Opera

Ballet in Germany, was born Richard Adams, and — in the world of opera this time rather than ballet — the American singer Lillian Norton preferred to modify her name to the more distinguished Lillian Nordica. A variation on the theme was performed by the Scottish music hall dancer Elizabeth McLauchlan. Teaming with her husband Raoul (né Hugh Duff McLauchlan) she gallicized and prettified her first name to become just Babette.

Babette is a diminutive of Elizabeth, of course, and different enough almost to be regarded as a pet name or nickname. In this, it offers another possibility for evolving a pseudonym: adopt your own pet name or nickname.

There can be few people who have not had an affectionate or teasing name given them at some stage in their lives, even if only in their school days, and this could make an ideal "ready-made" pseudonym.

Many well known names, from classical times to the present, originated as nicknames. The Roman emperor Caligula has a name that arose from his upbringing among soldiers: as a boy running around camp he wore small size *caligae*, the Latin word used for the stout iron-nailed shoes worn by soldiers. His name thus literally means "Little Boots." (And how much nicer that is than Gaius Julius Caesar, his real name.) In complete contrast, the film actor Zero Mostel, really Samuel Mostel, got "zero" for his subjects at school. In spite of the uncomplimentary nickname, he chose to adopt it as his screen name. School nicknames are notorious, in fact, and have been turned to advantage by a number of personalities for use as an adopted name. Ginger Rogers was called Ginger at school, Jack Oakie (Lewis Offield) was called "Oakie" at school as he came from Oklahoma, and °Dana, the singer, has a school nickname that is Irish for "mischievous" or "naughty." (It is also a Christian name — and coincidentally a surname — in its own right, which makes it an even better name.) Other nicknames also originate in childhood, whether at school or not, and these too can be adopted. °Bing Crosby's first name is a childhood nickname, and °Cyd Charisse derived her first name from her baby brother's attempt to say "sister." °Bebe Daniels made her first film when she was only seven — a "babby" — and the disc jockey °Kid Jensen (really David Allen Jensen) was Radio Luxembourg's youngest DJ when he was still a mere kid of 18.

In a somewhat unexpected quarter, and of much more venerable vintage, it is interesting to see that many of the names of famous classical painters originated as nicknames. Botticelli — a name that itself is sometimes used as a humorous word or name today for a person's posterior — was really Alessandro Filipepi, all those five hundred years ago. His name means "little barrel," and was the nickname used by his elder brother Giovanni. Similarly Canaletto means "little Canale" (Canale was his father's real name), Masaccio means "huge great Tom" (it has the Italian augmentative ending), and °Tintoretto means "little dyer"—his father was a dyer. One of Masaccio's pupils was Masolino, whose name means "little Tom"—not only in reference to his master but as a diminutive of his own name Tommaso. It is difficult to see why the 16th-century Italian painter Giovanni Antonio Bazzi should have chosen to adopt his hardly flattering nickname of Il Sodoma, "the sodomite," but, whether flaunting it or vaunting it, °Sodoma he became.

Many nicknames actually look like real names, even °Red Buttons—Aaron Schwatt was a red-haired bellboy in his teens—but some are obviously an everyday word used as a name, such as °Twiggy (Lesley Hornby), and these "word-into-name" pseudonyms we shall be considering in Chapter 5, not here.

Very many possibilities are thus open for a pseudonym to be derived from your own name—whether your real name, or part of it, or your pet name or nickname. But supposing you want to find your ready-made name some other way?

The ridiculously obvious answer is, of course, that you can get your name from someone else. The only question is—who? Who is to be the person whose name you are to adopt? What is special about him or her, or his or her name? Where do you start?

Many pseudonyms, like charity, begin at home. That is, within the family. And one of the commonest methods of all is to adopt your mother's maiden name.

This is an eminently satisfactory method, since it is not only a genuine surname that you are acquiring but one that is in every sense of the word a real family name. From the practical point of view, too, it enables you to extend the life of a name that might otherwise have disappeared from the family. Indeed, many people already bear their mother's maiden name as one of their own middle names, in which case to adopt such a name as a pseudonym is all too easy. You simply drop your surname.

Examples of "mmn" ("mother's maiden name") adoptions, as we can conveniently call them, are easy to find. Here are a dozen people who all made this particular adoption: Constance Cummings, Ann Dvorak, Dulcie Gray, Helen Hayes, Viola Keats, Jeremy Kemp, Elsa Lanchester, °Mario Lana, Yvonne Mitchell, Anna Neagle, Romy Schneider, Simone Signoret (thus making a satisfying alliterative match) ... The list can be extended considerably.

And if not your "mmn," you can always take a name from some other member of the family, whether a near and dear one or a more remote relative.

°Julie Andrews adopted her stepfather's name, as did Truman Capote. °Diana Dors took that of her maternal grandmother, and Garry Marsh chose his father's middle name. °Vivien Leigh took her husband's middle name, rather unusually, and George Scrope, the 19th-century English geologist and MP, even more unconventionally, took his wife's maiden name. (He did this on marrying, thus reversing the usual role — a fine tribute to his 24-year-old bride, who was the daughter of William Scrope, the last of the old earls of Wiltshire.)

Some people choose to take a really historic family name. Josephine Tey, the novelist, adopted that of her great-great-grandmother, and Owen Meredith, the British statesman and poet, went way back in time to take his first name from Owen Gwynnedd ap Griffith, king of North Wales, and Meredith ap Tudor, the great-grandfather of Henry VII. Edward Robert Bulwer Lytton, as Meredith is better known (his pseudonym was for his writing), was a lineal descendant of both of these royal forebears.

It is almost axiomatic that an adoptee should acquire the name of his stepparents, usually his stepfather. But he may well have had a real name of his own to begin with, which he will relinquish. This happened to Leslie Lynch King, better known as °Gerald R. Ford, and to the famous author, °Jack London, whose actual father's name was Chaney.

The usual variations can be arranged. Paul Hamlyn, the publisher, adopted and also adapted his "mmn" of Hamburg, and Maria Karnilova, the American ballet dancer, changed her "mmn" from Karnilovich to supersede her real surname of Dovgolenko. °Jacques Offenbach, the composer, took his father's nickname, "Der Offenbacher" (he was born in Offenbach-am-Main) and Kay Hammond assumed her mother's stage name. (Kay's maiden name was Standing, and her married name Clements.) Working down-family instead of up, °Mike Todd, whose original first name was Avrom, took the first name of his son, Michael, and Mme Champseix, the 19th-century French writer, composed her pen name, André Léo, from the Christian names of both her sons.

If not from a relation, then you can always borrow someone else's name. The scope here is almost infinite, since the person whose name you choose may be known to you or not. He or she may be a public or private hero, an admired figure, a friend, a colleague — even an enemy! The act of adopting the particular person's name may be intended as a mark of homage or respect, or virtually a near-random affair. You may simply be attracted by the name itself: when pop singer Gerry Dorsey turned himself into °Engelbert Humperdinck it was not simply because of his admiration for the German classical composer's works. The adopted name may in turn already be a pseudonym. This was the case with the American comic film actress °Eve Arden, born Eunice Quedens. She based her name on that of °Elizabeth Arden (Florence Graham), the Canadian cosmetician, who herself had taken her first name from that of Elizabeth, author of *Elizabeth and Her German Garden* (1898) — who was actually Mary Annette von Arnim!

Something of the wealth of possibilities can be seen by running through the names in Name List number 23, but among the borrowings will be found the names of a leading lady (Busby Berkeley), a school-teacher friend (°Richard Burton), an admired pop singer (°Elvis Costello), an admired poet (°Bob Dylan), a bishop (°Lorenzo da Ponte), some benefactors (Carlo Farinelli), a prison guard (°O. Henry), a dead man his own age (°Joseph Arthur Markham), a noted golfer (°Ted Ray), and a general of the American Revolution (°John Wayne). For Lorenzo da Ponte to adopt the name of the bishop who christened him it was not so much a personal tribute but a standing convention, since this was customary by many converts to Catholicism — much as in London, in the 13th and 14th centuries, it was quite normal for an apprentice to assume the name of his master, and even earlier, for Roman slaves to take the names, as mentioned in Chapter 1, of *their* masters.

In Chapter 6 we shall be having a special look at the name assumed by crossword compilers, but suffice it to say here that many of them gleefully (and gloatingly) adopted the names of Spanish Grand Inquisitors, a custom initiated by one of the doyen crosswordists, Torquemada.

Another special category of creative person is the Welsh bardic poet, for whom it is traditional to adopt the name of an ancient versifier: Robert Ellis, a 19th-century minister and poet, thus took as his bardic name that of the most important Welsh poet of the 12th century, Cynddelw, which itself is also sometimes chosen as a suitable forename for a Welsh baby boy.

A much larger and more important category of name adoption is that followed by members of religious orders, and many congregations of nuns, sisters, and brothers, as well as several religious orders and congregations of men, still retain the practice of assuming the name of a saint or venerated member of the church on their admission to the community (which in the Christian church is usually at the ceremony of clothing). Until recently, too, this meant that members of many orders, such as the Catholic Friars Minor, Carmelites and Capuchins, abandoned their surname altogether on taking their new religious name — although Capuchins added to their religious name the name of their place of origin, as for example Father Pius of Chester. The adoption of a saint's name is not dependent on the sex of the novice — nuns have often received the name of a male saint.

Today, since the Second Vatican Council (as mentioned in Chapter 2), many orders have dropped the giving of a name in religion. However, the custom is by no means moribund, and the realities of the process of choosing a name are described by Suzanne Campbell-Jones in her account of the clothing of novice Franciscan sisters: "The girl put up her own choice of names, and usually two or three devolved on a favourite saint or even a favourite sister, teacher or friend. One nun took the name of Ita, not because it meant in chains, but because she knew a very nice nun by that name. Sisters still used their baptismal names for legal documents or transactions outside the convent life" (*In Habit...*, Faber & Faber, 1979).

Not surprisingly, the names of members of the Holy Family are regarded with special favor among Christian postulants. Nuns choose Mary (the mother of Christ) and Elizabeth (Mary's cousin, and mother of John the Baptist); male novices choose Joseph (Mary's husband) and John (Elizabeth's son, the Baptist). Other popular choices are names of the apostles and disciples and outstanding New Testament figures, among them Andrew, Barnabas, Bartholomew, James, John (the Baptist or the Apostle), Luke, Mark, Martha, Mary (Magdalene, if not the Virgin), Matthew, Paul, Peter, Philip, Simon (also the name of Christ's brother), Stephen, and Timothy. For nuns, too, a desirable name to acquire is Teresa, who was the founder of the reformed (discalced, i.e., "unshod") Carmelite order. The Albanian-born Mother Teresa of Calcutta, who was originally Agnes Bojaxhiu, took the name of this 16th-century Spanish Mother Teresa.

Many of the later saints have come to be known by their own Christian names, so that the mystical theologian and poet St. John of the Cross was actually baptized as John (more precisely, Juan), and St. Bernadette was christened Marie-Bernarde, with her name simply a standard French feminine diminutive (so spelled, minus the second "r") of Bernard.

Names of popes, some of which are those of saints (John, Paul) and some not (Pius, Innocent) — although these may be the names of earlier popes who were themselves saints — are especially interesting, and will be dealt with separately in Chapter 6.

Religious names are thus almost always, indeed exclusively, adopted as a mark of veneration and affection.

But if in your search for a pseudonym all else fails in your hunt for a human being with a ready-made name that you can adopt, there is another recourse. This is to adopt a fictional name — meaning not so much a fictitious name (in a sense, all pseudonyms are fictitious) but a name from fiction.

There are probably characters in fiction whom we admire as much as we would if they were real flesh and blood — possibly more, since many fictional characters are idealized — and an effective way of expressing our private liking for one of them is to adopt his or her name as our own.

Here, too, the range is very wide, although naturally not as unlimited as when choosing a real person's name. And as for who, exactly, is to be the chosen character — the selection is very much a matter of personal taste and inclination. An actor or actress may choose the name of a character in a play, whether they have actually taken the part or not; a novelist or short story writer may prefer the name of some greater or lesser hero or heroine in a similar work — or even in his or her *own* work. The actress Elizabeth Ashley, when still Elizabeth Cole, took her new surname from the first name of Ashley Wilkes, as acted by Leslie Howard (originally Leslie Stainer) in *Gone with the Wind*, and Tom Jones, who began life as Thomas Woodward, reputedly derived his name from the hero of the film (of the book) *Tom Jones*. On the other hand the two famous fictional detectives Ellery Queen and Paul Temple gave their names respectively to two two-man teams of crime novelists: the Americans Frederic Dannay and Manfred B. Lee, and the British writers Francis Durbridge and James McConnell (who used °Paul Temple as their joint pen name for mystery novels *not* about the eponymous detective!).

To adopt the name of a character that you have yourself created is not merely a way of going on a literary ego trip, but more a reward for the sweat, toil and tears—and doubtless satisfaction—that you have experienced in creating that character. You have put something of your own world into him, now let him be identified with you, his creator.

The usual variety abounds, with names deriving from a girl in a song (°Nelly Bly), the heroine of one of the writer's own novels (Margaret Howth), the hero of an opera (°Mario Lanza), a biblical hunter (°Nimrod), a Shakespearean comic character (Peter Quince), and a character in Proust (°Françoise Sagan). Dame °Rebecca West took her name from an Ibsen play, and °Dinah Shore from the song "Dinah." And what could be finer than Edward Bradwardine Waverley, the name chosen by John Croker from *two* characters in Sir Walter Scott's novel *Waverley* to reply to one Malachi Malagrowther—who was Scott himself in the guise of one of his own characters in *The Fortunes of Nigel*!

Fiction, of course, covers several genres and generations, from classical times to the present, and we have already mentioned the Renaissance fashion for classical names. Classical names—those of ancient mythological characters or even real Latin and Greek authors—have always found steady favor as a rather chic pseudonym, often, one suspects, almost as much for the impressive appearance of the name as for any actual association with the original bearer of the name.

Janus, for example, is a good example of a symbolic classical name, being that of the "two-faced" Roman god of beginnings and endings (hence January). His name has been adopted by a number of writers, including the two German theologians Johann von Döllinger and Dr. Johannes Friedrich, and the French journalist and novelist Robert le Bonnières. We have seen how the name of °Cassandra was used by William Connor; it was also adopted, perhaps less symbolically, by the Russian-born French graphic artist and stage designer (in the form Cassandre) Adolphe Mouron. The name of Alcibiades, the Athenian general and politician, was assumed by two noblemen—Albert, Margrave of Brandenberg, and George Villiers, Duke of Buckingham. It was also used by Alfred, Lord Tennyson, for an article in *Punch* published in March, 1846. The 18th- and 19th-century reformer and politician John Thelwell took the name Sylvanus Theophrastus. "Sylvanus" was a name used for one of the wood gods that followed Pan; Theophrastus was a Greek philosopher and scientist, a disciple of Aristotle. (It was also one of the real names of °Paracelsus; literally it means "god-guided.") The American 19th-century novelist Emma Embury adopted the name Ianthe for her contributions to periodicals. In Greek mythology Ianthe was a Cretan girl who fell in love with another girl called Iphis—who subsequently (or consequently?) changed into a boy and married Ianthe.

With such classical borrowings, it is often difficult to tell whether the name derives from the original character or from a later character of the same name, for example, in a play by Shakespeare or Racine. The English poet laureate Alfred Austin, for instance, in using the name Lamia for editing *The Poet's Diary*, may have taken this name direct from classical sources—Lamia lured strangers so that she could devour them—or from Keats's *Lamia* (1820). Again, there were often more than one classical personage of the same name, and without more precise indication it is impossible to tell whether Lady Mary Montagu, the 18th-century English writer of letters and poems, had in mind the Queen of Halicarnassus or the sister of Mausolus when she took the name Artemisia. And if she actually bases the name on that of Artemis—who was also, as goddess of the moon, called Diana, Cynthia, Delia, Hecate, Luna, Phoebe and Selene—we are even more in the dark, since this name has also been alluded to scores of times by Shakespeare and several poets.

Today, the vogue for classical pseudonyms is less in evidence, although columnists and journalists frequently favor a name of this type. (One of the most popular is Atticus, who still writes regularly in the *Sunday Times*. Atticus was an elegant Roman scholar and master of Greek, and a publisher and patron of the arts. His real name was Titus Pomponius. The pseudonym itself literally means "coming from Attica," i.e., from Athens, and was an epithet given by Romans to distinguished scholars and writers.)

If classical names do not appeal, the pseudonym searcher can always derive a name in a random fashion, by taking any name in existence and adopting it. That is to say, you can take any standard "ready-made" name and use it, without reference to a particular person of this name. Such names can be styled as arbitrary, since although real enough as names they have no specific origin.

At one of its lower levels of application "Mr. and Mrs. Smith" is an arbitrary name when used by an (unmarried) couple to check in at a hotel. They have not taken the name from a particular Mr. and Mrs. Smith, but have simply chosen the commonest surname in the English language as a transparent disguise.

Even so, there are degrees of arbitrariness, since the actual name adopted may be specifically that of a particular person, even though the adopter knows absolutely nothing about the person. In other words, the name is taken on simply as a name, nothing more. When David Cornwell became °John Le Carré he took the name from a shopfront in London which he had seen while sitting on top of a bus. °Adam Faith, on the other hand, found his name in a "What to name the baby" book. No doubt somewhere in the English-speaking world there is a real Adam Faith, perhaps several Adam Faiths, but Terence Nelhams had none of them specifically in mind when he chose his name.

Lists of arbitrary names are, or were, frequently held by agents and managers when engaging a new performer, much as many firms today hold lists of arbitrary trade names, evolved by computer, for possible use for a new product. °Cary Grant came by his name from such a list. And of course an excellent source of ready-made names suitable for adoption in this way is a telephone directory!Walden Cassotto is said to have found his name Bobby Darin in a phone book, as did Martha Raye, the American radio and TV comedienne who was born Margaret Reed.

An arbitrary name can, of course, be an invented one, such as °Cantinflas or °Pele, in which case it does not belong in this chapter but the next.

Some pseudonyms result from a mistake such as a misprint. They do belong here since they are certainly "ready-made," even if inadvertently.

Names of this type can be instanced by those of F. Anstey, the novelist, and °Irving Berlin, the great songwriter. They were the results of printer's errors of their real names, respectively, T. Anstey Guthrie and Israel Baline. A "mistake" name may also be a misprint of an already chosen pseudonym, not a true name. The American essayist Donald Grant Mitchell had adopted the name J.K. Marvel for his contributions to the *Morning Courier and New York Enquirer* in 1846. A typo gave him his permanent pen name of °Ik Marvel. Such misprints more readily occur when the native of one country is billed in another, in a foreign tongue. This happened to the English music hall entertainer Percy Henry Thompson, who took his stage name, Percy Honri, from the way the French printer had announced his appearance at the Folies Bergères. (There must have been many such instances. I am reminded of a friend who, on holiday in Spain, saw a movie poster announcing a film starring "Dirt Bogarde.")

When considering the evolution of personal names in Chapter 1, we saw that one source of surnames was place-names. In their more evolved form, place-names can also serve as a suitable pseudonym, especially when they indicate a place with which the name adopter has a special connection, for example as a birthplace. (Strictly speaking, the classical name Atticus, mentioned above, is a pseudonym of place-name origin, although in translated and adjectival form.)

In this category we must interpret "place-name" in its widest form, to include not just standard geographical names but names of houses, estates, streets, and fields, for example — that is, anywhere that is a place with a name. Since many place-names frequently resemble a personal name — indeed, many of them actually are a personal name (as Alberta, Washington, and, after all, America) — it is often relatively easy to convert them or adapt them as a pseudonym.

To illustrate the scope place-names in the wide sense of the word offer, we need only consider °Rock Hudson (from the Rock of Gibraltar and the Hudson River), °Conway Twitty (Conway, Arkansas, and Twitty, Texas), °George Orwell (river Orwell), °Clemence Dane (church of St. Clement Danes, London), °Arthur Lucan (Lucan Dairy, Dublin), °Cyril Hare, the British crime novelist (Cyril Mansions, Battersea, London), °Gordon Craig (the Scottish island Ailsa Craig), and Cardinal °Mindszenty (native Hungarian village of Szehimindszenty). Sometimes the pseudonym refers to the place name less obviously, more allusively, as with °Nellie Melba (Melbourne, Australia), the British novelist George Woden (Wednesbury, West Midlands, itself named after Woden, the Scandinavian god of war and wisdom), and °Stainless Stephen, the English music hall comedian (born in Sheffield, of stainless steel fame).

Some centuries back it was in fact almost standard practice for certain sectors of society to assume the name of their native town or village. This was noticeably the case with Italian painters of the Renaissance school: Caravaggio, Perugino, and Veronese, for example, whose real names were respectively Merisi, Vanucci and Cogliari, took the names of their birthplaces Caravaggio, Perugia and Verona. But in many cases of this kind, the native place name would have often been a conventional addition to the real name to start with, so that Caravaggio was properly Michelangelo Merisi da [from] Caravaggio. Another Renaissance painter, although a German one, not an Italian, was Lucas Cranach, born Lucas Müller. He also adopted the name of his birthtown, then spelled Cranach (now Kronach). (This was Lucas Cranach the Elder; his son, Lucas Cranach the Younger, kept the name.) A later painter, the Frenchman Claude Gellee, became known as Claude Lorrain, from his birthplace in the historic province of Lorraine. (It is incorrect to spell his adopted name Claude Lorraine: his surname has no "e" as it is the French adjective meaning "from Lorraine," "Lotharingian," not the name of the province itself.)

An enjoyable game is hunting for places that are named after pseudonymous persons: there are rather more than one might imagine, from all the places in Soviet Russia named for °Lenin (many of them previously for °Stalin), to London Peak, Oregon, named for °Jack London.

Place-names, when used as personal names, can be regarded just as properly "ready-made" as any name of a human being. The name, after all, is already there, in existence. It does not have to be invented. Moreover, as we have seen, it frequently *looks* like a personal name. To convert an ordinary word or phrase into a pseudonym, however, is to invent a name, since by definition a word (in this sense) is not already a name.

These, then, are the chief sources of ready-made pseudonyms — people and places. Who actually provides the name or produces it is another matter: people can adopt a name themselves or they can be suggested or noted for them. We have mentioned more than one instance of an actor or performer's being given a name by an agent or manager. Then again, in Chapter 2, it was noted that many foreign immigrants to the United States were presented with a new name on an *ad hoc* basis by the immigration officer almost as soon as they had set foot on land!

Name List number 32 details a selection of pseudonyms given by some other person to the adopter (interestingly, the vast majority of them are ready-made names, not invented ones), but here we can instance the names of Cilla Black (inadvertently given by the writer of an article about her who had forgotten her real name, White), °Adrienne Corri (given by Gordon Harbord, who also renamed °Laurence Harvey and tried to rename °Diana Dors), °Larry Grayson (by agent Evelyn Taylor), Rita Hayworth (by husband, Edward Judson), °Betty Hutton (by bandleader Vincent Lopez), °George Orwell (by publisher Victor Gollancz), and °Natalie Wood (by production executives William Goetz and Leo Spitz).

We now pass to the much more obviously "false" class of invented names.

Francis Matthews is a lousy name for the theatre.
Perhaps I should have called myself Clint Thrust.
(Francis Matthews, interviewed in "TV Times," May 25, 1978.)

5 Invented Names

Most of the names that we have so far been considering have actually looked like real names, many of them comprising a "forename" and a "surname" element. Such names resemble the real names that we know in our daily lives.

One feature that distinguishes all invented names from "ready-made" ones is their artificiality: they for the most part look nothing like a conventional name.

In general, invented names can be divided into three types: those that are ordinary words, singly or grouped, those that are an artificial concoction of letters or syllables (a rare category, as will be seen), and those that are represented not by letters at all but by some other means, as signs or symbols. There are also, of course, names that are a combination of one or more of these types, as well as names that are a combination of "real" and invented.

In the first category — pseudonyms that are clearly unlike ordinary personal names — come many names that are descriptive titles. One of Oliver Goldsmith's names, for example, was "The Citizen of the World," the novelist Chiang Yee wrote as °"The Silent Traveller," Hector McNeile wrote his Bulldog Drummond stories as °Sapper (he had been an officer in the Royal Engineers), and one of °Daniel Defoe's many pseudonyms (see Appendix II) was "An English Gentleman." We have also referred to the numerous women writers who identified themselves simply as "A Lady."

Descriptive names of this type, especially one-word ones, are frequently adopted by journalists and columnists, when they may belong either to a single regular contributor or to a variety of writers. Names such as Spectator, Onlooker, Linesman, and Diplomat turn up freely in many a newspaper and magazine. Glance through the pages of your local paper: it will be most unusual if you do not come across at least one pen name of this type. (Even legal advice given by "A Barrister" and a car test report by "Our Motoring Correspondent" produce perfectly genuine pseudonyms.)

Such descriptive names can be in any language. Until comparatively recently, there has been a taste among some writers — whether

Victorian moralists or self-important scientists — to adopt Latin names. An early name used by the poet, artist and mystic William Blake was Pictor Ignotus ("unknown painter"), William Courthope, the English critic and man of letters, briefly (from 1895 to 1901) the ceremonial Professor of Poetry at Oxford University, called himself Homo Novus ("a new man"), Colonel Parker Gillmore, a now largely forgotten writer of travel books, wrote as Ubique ("everywhere"), and in the 20th century, the English writer on sound recording and engineering Donald Aldous adopted the agreeable title Discobolus (literally "discus-thrower," although Mr. Aldous is more familiar with discs of another sort).

The writer of a first book that sold well, especially in the 19th century, was often prompted to call himself or herself simply "The Author of...." In his *Handbook of Fictitious Names*, Olphar Hamst identifies over 160 such authors, from "The Author of *Abbeychurch*" (Charlotte M. Young, who frequently adopted this formula) to "The Author of *Zohrab*" (James Morier, "a great Oriental traveller, and writer of tales"). These particular pseudonyms were used respectively by Miss Young and Mr. Morier for *Scenes and Characters; or, Eighteen Months at Beechcroft* (1847) and *Ayesha, the Maid of Kars* (1834). As we have seen, Sir Walter Scott first ventured into prose as "The Author of *Waverley*." Many other "Authors of ..." are now ill-remembered, but more durable names who hid behind this disguise were R.S. Surtees ("The Author of *Handley Cross*"), Elizabeth Gaskell ("of *Mary Barton*"), Captain Marryat ("*Peter Simple*"), Thomas Hughes ("*Tom Brown's School Days*"), Harriet Beecher Stowe ("*Uncle Tom's Cabin*"), and Benjamin Disraeli ("*Vivian Grey*").

Among other typical 19th-century descriptive pen names listed by Hamst (but not featured elsewhere in this book) are "A Citizen of the United States" (A.H. Everett), "A Clergyman's Daughter" (Eliza Smith), "A Layman" (over 20 names out of the hundreds that must have existed), "An Old Sailor" (M.H. Barker), and "A Reader Therein" (Andrea Crestadoro, for *The Art of Making Catalogues of Libraries; or, A Method to Obtain in Short Time a Most Perfect, Complete, and Satisfactory Printed Catalogue of the British Museum Library* By...).

Descriptive names such as these are purely factual, serving to identify the author of a particular book or to state a writer's role or speciality.

More interesting are the allusively descriptive names, such as Sealion (Geoffrey Bennet, English novelist and naval writer), Beachcomber (D.B. Wyndham Lewis, humorous columnist in the *Daily Express*, and J.B. Morton, his successor), and the ruggedly evocative Giant Haystacks (Luke McMasters, British professional wrestler and film and TV actor).

In its structure, the name Giant Haystacks somewhat resembles a traditional "forename-plus-surname" name, and there are a number of "words-into-name" pseudonyms that even more closely approximate to a genuine personal name. These may be descriptive in some way or entirely random.

One of the most famous names of this type — "words-into-name" — is of course °Mark Twain, if only because Mark is a standard forename anyway. (The origin of the name in the call of pilots on the Mississippi River is well known, but recounted more fully, together with many other similarly devised names, in the Name Stories, page 000). In cases such as this, it is often something of a nice distinction whether a name should be regarded as "invented" or "ready-made." Mark Twain, since it originates from two ordinary words (*"mark, twain!"* — i.e., "measure two fathoms"), should therefore be treated as an invented name. However, there was a Mark Twain in existence before Samuel Clemens, and if indeed he derived his own pen name from this other writer, his pseudonym must be classified as a "ready-made" name.

Other names devised from ordinary words are °Marti Caine ("tomato cane"), °Upton Close ("up close"), °Nosmo King ("no smoking"), Holm Lee ("homely"), and (obviously) Muddy Waters. As such, in spite of their similarity to standard personal names, they must be classified as invented names, with the similarity an agreeable, and usually intentional, coincidence.

A number of humorous pseudonyms are devised from ordinary words, among them R. Andom, °Stepin Fetchit, Lemmie B. Good, Will B. Good, °Orpheus C. Kerr ("office-seeker"), and Luke Sharp, artificially invented names all.

Again, foreign words can be exploited to invent a pseudonym. Examples are °Caran d'Ache (from Russian *karandash*, "pencil"), Felix Carmen (Latin, "happy song"), °Mata Hari (Malay, "eye of the day"), Dita Parlo (mock-Italian, "I said, I speak"), and Talis Qualis (Latin, "of such a kind as").

Very frequently, a standard personal name is combined with an ordinary word to form a pseudonym. One does not have to look far for examples, but among the many are Jimmy Driftwood, Dion Fortune, °Gary Glitter, °Maxim Gorky (Russian *gorky*, "bitter"), °Danny La Rue (French, "the street"), Peter Porcupine, and Vera Vague. Some of these, Dion Fortune, for example, closely resemble real names. Another of this type — first name "real," second "invented" — is °Veronica Lake. It is also even possible to have a name where *both* parts derive from ordinary words and where the name closely resembles a standard name, as with Patience Strong. There must surely be several genuine Patience Strongs, yet because of this particular name's provenance — the ordinary words "patience" and "strong" — it must be classified nevertheless as an invented name, just as °Mark Twain must be.

°Veronica Lake is an instance of a popular combination to form a pseudonym, real forename plus "word-into-name" surname. In names of this type the "word-into-name" element is usually to some extent descriptive. Veronica Lake was so named for her calm, cool, blue "lakelike" eyes, for example, and °Gary Glitter has a surname that is intended to indicate his "glittering" image — performance, costume and all.

An alternative method of combination is to precede a standard real name by a qualifier of some kind, normally an adjective or a noun. Examples are Haywire Mac, Aunt Lucy, Little Richard, Uncle Mac, and °Smokey Joe. Common qualifiers, as this small sample suggests, are the adjectives "Little" and "Big" and nouns indicating a relationship. Here, as always, the descriptive element may not be readily discernible. Woody Allen has a first name that probably derives from his fondness for the clarinet, a woodwind instrument, for instance. Names like this frequently have a "surname" that is actually the person's real forename, so that Little Eva is really Eva Boyd, Little Milton Milton Campbell, Aunt Lucy Lucy Bather, and °Smokey Joe Joseph Sewell. Similarly Woody Allen was originally Allen Konigsberg. Combination names of these types must of course be classified as half "ready-made," half "invented."

The category of "concocted" names — pseudonyms that are not derived from any complete word or words — is not nearly so extensive as might be supposed. A number of apparently meaningless names turn out either to be based on an already existing name or are real words after all — even if not English ones. The name Krik, for example, is not a nonsense name, but derives from the bearer's real name of Henry Crickmore, and Poy is a name consisting of three letters extracted from the full name of *Percy* Hutton Fear*o*n. These are thus abbreviated "ready-made" names. Again, °Theda Bara, seemingly a random name, is actually an anagram of "Arab death," and so an invented name, albeit a modified one.

Even such bizarre names as °Boz, Medium Tem Plum, °Mistinguett and Woon have a word- or name-based origin: respectively the childish pronunciation of "Moses" (Charles Dickens), Latin for "middle temple" (Mostyn Piggot), "Miss Tinguett" (Jeanne-Marie Bourgeois) and Ralph W*o*therspo*o*n — that is, a pet name, two Latin words, a name based on that of a character in a musical, and the bearer's real name.

An example of a "concocted" name might be °Grock (Adrien Wettach), based neither on an existing name nor a standard word but invented to go well with Brick yet be different from Brock. Even here it is possible to argue that the pseudonym is "ready-made" since it is in effect a modification of the existing pseudonym Brock. Again, the pseudonym Squibob, although apparently nonsensical, at least partly suggest "squib" and as such was a suitable humorous pen name for the American satirist George Horatio Derby.

In short, "concocted" names — pseudonyms that are meaningless in themselves — will be found to exist almost entirely in initials, but these too, must have originally had *some* significance in the mind of their creator, even if their meaning is now unknown to us. It is not known for sure, for example, why °Lewis Carroll first called himself "B.B." What do these letters indicate? We can only guess. It must surely be reasonable to assume that to Charles Lutwidge Dodgson, at least — especially to a writer who was something of a wizard with words and names — they must have meant something.

The dearth of genuinely random pseudonyms thus distinguishes this class of name from other classes such as trade names where random names (e.g., computer-devised ones) are common, and is an indication that virtually all bearers or users of pseudonyms intend that their name shall have at least some significance. Even the pseudonym X means something: that the writer wishes to remain anonymous or unidentified.

To say that a pseudonym of such-and-such a person has no meaning, simply because one has not discovered that meaning, is therefore very rash!

Closest of all to the really random pseudonym is the name that is devised not from a word or even from letters, but from a sign or symbol. The standard symbol for anonymity is the asterisk (*) or dash ($-$). Asterisks, denoting sheer anonymity, can be somewhat more meaningful if they at least indicate the number of letters in the bearer's real name. Thus, Olphar Hamst had identified one **** ******, who wrote the *Letter to* *, *&c., on the Rev. W.L. Bowles's strictures on the Life and writings of Pope*, purportedly by "The Right Hon. Lord Byron" (1821), to be actually John Murray (1778-1843), son of John Murray, founder (1768) of the famous London publishing firm of this name. (John Murray *fils* was also a publisher, and moved the firm to 50 Albemarle Street, its present address.)

Not surprisingly, Hamst, as many others before and since, found that the deciphering of asterisms is no easy task, since one has only the number of asterisks to go on apart from the actual name of the work. Such a number may be quite arbitrary. No doubt it was so in the name of **********, who wrote *Letters of Advice from a Lady of Distinction to her Niece, the Duchess of* *, *&c., shortly after her Marriage* (1819). Hamst couldn't crack this one. Knowing what we do of pseudonyms, too, we would be very unwise to suppose necessarily that these letters were indeed written by a real lady of distinction to her actual niece! Nor, it seems, did Hamst know who ☉ was, the author of "The Book of God" (1866).

Other than this brief mention, asterisms and other pseudonyms consisting of signs and symbols do not feature in this book. This is not to belittle them, however, since * is just as valid a pseudonym as °George Orwell or °Mark Twain.

We must now move to Chapter 6, where we shall be having a look at some special types of pseudonyms.

6 Names with a Difference

This chapter is dedicated to names that are special: carefully
chosen names, significant names, ambiguous names, popular names,
outrageous names, baffling names, vocational names and traditional
names. We shall be considering names so evocative and meaningful that
they almost eclipse their bearer, and names so trivial that they are mostly
long forgotten. We shall also take a necessarily speculative view of certain
"open-ended" names — ones whose story is still incomplete or unexplained.
And finally, in the light of our examination of the many aspects of
pseudonyms and name-changes, we shall pose once again, but this time
perhaps more subjectively and philosophically, the question put at the
beginning of the first chapter, "What *is* a name?"

Let us at once proceed to the specific. What did the bearers of
these names have in common? Linus, Anacletus, Evaristus, Telesphorus,
Hyginus, Anicetus, Soter, Eleutherius, Zephyrinus, Urban, Pontian,
Auterus, Fabian, Cornelius...

Roman emperors? Greek gods? Classical authors? Esoteric underground "cover" names?

Here are some more, whose owners still have the same common
identity: Paul, John, Pius, Benedict, Leo, Gregory, Clement, Innocent...

You probably guessed correctly: all the names are those of popes,
with the "classical" names above being the (real) names of very early
popes, and the more familiar names that follow being those that were
assumed by a pope — indeed, by more than one pope.

We considered papal names as a special category of pseudonym in
Chapter 2, where we saw that the motives for choosing a particular name
can be clearly stated on the one hand or obscure on the other. Here we
should take a closer look at some of the more popular names that popes
have used, and try to see why they have enjoyed such favor. Why, for
example, have several popes been named John, yet none chose Matthew,
Mark or Luke? (True, there was one pope called Mark, but this was his
real name. He pontificated for nine months in 336, many years before the
first assumed name.)

It is in fact the name John that is easily "top of the popes." No less

48

than 23 popes have assumed the name in its "neat" form — the last of these being Angelo Roncalli, who became John XXIII in 1958 — with the name used in combined form by two recent popes, John Paul I (Albino Luciani, elected 1978, and in office for only 33 days), and John Paul II, his successor (Karol Wojtyla, elected that same year, and the first non-Italian pope since 1522).

John has long been a popular Christian name at all levels, in many countries, largely thanks to the two important New Testament characters, John the Baptist and St. John the Evangelist, "the two men who were closest to Christ the Lord" — as Angelo Roncalli designated them when explaining his own reasons for choosing the name. Roncalli's account of his motives for assuming the name John, in fact, gives us as clear a picture as any regarding the popularity of the name, as well as an insight into one individual pope's choice. Apart from the biblical pedigree, the name was dear to him, he said, since it was his father's name, it was the dedication of the village church in Lombardy where he was baptized, as well as that of many cathedrals throughout the world, including the Lateran basilica of San Giovanni in Rome, and of course it was the name of 22 of his predecessors. For the future John XXIII, therefore, the name was selected on a careful combination of historical, religious, and personal grounds. Significantly, the name was in turn adopted, with specific reference to John XXIII's reforming spirit, by his two successors John Paul I and John Paul II, with the latter combining homage to both John XXIII and John Paul I, whose policies he intended to pursue.

John was thus not only the first papal name to be assumed (in 983, see Chapter 2), but flourishes as a still popular papal choice a thousand years later. What name could have a better pedigree than that!

The next most common papal name is Gregory, which has been adopted 16 times — the most recently by Bartolommeo Alberto Cappellarri, pope for 15 years from 1831. Just as John owes its popularity to two saints, so there seems little doubt that Gregory owes much of its charisma to the first pope of the name, St. Gregory the Great, of *non Angli sed angeli* fame (with reference to the English slave boys he saw in Roman marketplaces). It is almost certain that St. Gregory himself was so named after the two fathers of the Eastern church Gregory of Nazianzen and Gregory of Nyssa ("The Wonderworker"). It is a characteristically "papal" name, which may explain why its general use in Western Europe and the New World has not been particularly favored. In English-speaking countries, indeed, it is today more likely to be associated with a surname rather than a Christian name.

Following Gregory in frequency comes another typically papal name, Benedict. In English-speaking countries this is even more unpopular, except among Roman Catholics, than Gregory, although it still flourishes in Latin countries. (Its meaning, "blessed," derives direct from Latin, whereas Gregory, "watchman," comes from Greek, and John, "the

Lord is gracious," originated in Hebrew.) Who was the original Benedict who prompted 15 popes to assume the name, from Niccolò Boccasini in the 14th century to Giacomo della Chiesa ("James Church"!) in the 20th? As with John and Gregory and most common papal names, there were more than one saint of this name, the best known probably being the founder of the Benedictine order. It seems likely, however, that apart from personal references (an identification with this saint or previous pope Benedict), many popes chose the name because of its highly favorable meaning. If a pope is not "blessed," who is?

Following Benedict in frequency comes an equally meaningful name, Clement. Fourteen popes took the name, from the 11th-century Suidger to Giovanni Ganganelli in the 18th century. Can we ascribe their name to a Saint Clement? If we can, it must be to the first pope of this name, who died at the end of the first century and who has by some been identified with one of the fellow laborers of St. Paul mentioned in Paul's epistle to the Philippians (4, 3). This St. Clement was famous for the letter he sent from the church of Rome to the church of Corinth, which represented the first known example of a bishop of Rome intervening in the affairs of another church. Mild (the literal meaning of Clement) the first pope of the name may have been, but clearly not meek, and subsequent popes Clement may have had him in mind when choosing the name for their pontifical position. Again, possibly the literal interpretation of the name may have been regarded as an auspicious one.

Clement has not been a particularly popular name for English speakers, and even less popular — in fact, almost nonexistent — has been the next most common papal name, Innocent. This patently obvious name was first borne by St. Innocent in the 5th century (it was his real name), and the most recently by Michelangiolo Conti, elected as Innocent XIII in 1721. St. Innocent was hardly a distinguished man, however, either as saint or pope, and the adoption of the name by later popes would appear to be either a personal tribute to an earlier allonymous pontiff or, again, the acquisition of a favorably descriptive name. Another possibility would be a link that one of the popes of the name had with the feast day of St. Innocent (June 22) or of the Holy Innocents (December 28), or perhaps with a church dedicated to the saint or the Holy Innocents.

Seen through 20th-century eyes, the name Innocent seems a curiously bland and watery one for a pope — emphatically meek *and* mild. Just the opposite is Leo, "lion," a name adopted by exactly the same number of popes as those who chose Innocent — 13. The choice of this particular name by a pope is much more likely to be an act of homage to a previous Leo than an intention to suggest a lion-like character! Indeed, we know that Leo IX, himself a saint, chose the name as a tribute to Leo the Great (Leo I), since he aimed to put the papacy, in the 11th century, on the same sound foundations as those laid by his namesake over half a century before. Again. Leo XIII, adopting the name on his election in

1878, was paying tribute to Leo XII, whom he had always admired for his interest in education, understanding attitude towards temporal governments, and desire to make active links with lapsed Catholics. The reasonable popularity of the Christian name Leo among present-day Catholics derives largely in turn from Leo XIII himself, since this pope, the last of the name, was the first world authority to codify the duties and rights of workers and their employers (1890). We thus find, coincidentally, that the papal bearers of this name that hints at strength and power have indeed been strong-natured and of powerful spiritual stature.

The only other name that has attracted over ten popes is Pius, which once more has a transparent meaning and an apt one (if rather obviously so). Twelve popes assumed this name, over half of them comparatively recently (seven since 1775). As with Innocent, we must assume either a personal compliment or simply a desirable, and traditional, epithet behind the adoption of the name. The first pope so called (it was his actual name) was the second-century ex-slave saint who combatted Gnosticisim. Not until over a thousand years later, in 1458, did another pope come to adopt the name, with the most recent bearer being Pius XII (died 1958). Pius IX (also known euphoniously as "Pio Nono") had the longest of all pontificates (1846-1878), and we know that he took his name in deference to the memory of Pius VII, who had been his friend and who also, like himself, had been bishop of Imola. Earlier and later Piuses appear to have adopted the name on more or less conventional grounds. As a Christian name, Pius is effectively a nonstarter.

Of other names favored by popes, many are unremarkable Christian names, as Stephen (selected nine or ten times, depending on the reckoning), Alexander (eight), Paul and Adrian (six each), Nicholas (five), and Victor (three). Among the typically "papal" names have been Boniface (nine popes so called), Urban (eight), and Sixtus (five). The latter three have meanings that are all of Latin origin, respectively "doing good," "townsman" and, oddly, "sixth." (It is thought that the first pope Sixtus was so named as he was the sixth pope in line after St. Peter. It was Sixtus IV who gave his name to the fine Sistine Chapel, the pope's private chapel next to St. Peter's in Rome, famous for Michelangelo's ceiling fresco.) Most of these were adopted for reasons we have seen, with an implied or specific personal, historical or abstract reference.

In the 20th century there has been a trend away from "adjectival" names of the Benedict, Innocent and Pius type, with a reversion to genuine Christian names. The four popes since the last Pius have thus been (apparently unoriginally but with particular personal reference) John, Paul, John Paul and John Paul. Interestingly, and almost prophetically, the first John Paul was instantly allotted the ordinal number "the First" by the media in many countries, thus prompting one letter writer to appear in *The Times* asking, "How long are we to wait for Pope John Paul II?" (J.C. Davis, September 1, 1978). On the last day of the month in which this letter was printed, the same newspaper was to publish John Paul I's obituary.

Among the names, true and assumed, of the 265 popes elected to date (1981), some curiosities may be noted:

▶ Of the six popes named Adrian, the fourth was the only English one (Nicholas Breakspear) and the sixth the only Dutch (Adrian Dedel). The latter was the last pope to retain his own baptismal name and was also the last non-Italian pope before the election of the Polish cardinal Karol Wojtyla as John Paul II in 1978.

▶ Paul VI was baptized as John the Baptist (Giovanni Battista).

▶ All the popes named Stephen with an ordinal number higher than II could also be one number higher, i.e., Stephen III could be Stephen IV, Stephen IV is sometimes known as Stephen V, and so on. This is because there are two popes Stephen II, the first of whom was not consecrated (he died a few days after his election) and so was not listed in the official book of popes (*Liber Pontificalis*). This means that his successor was a "real" Stephen II or actually a Stephen III.

▶ The first pope named Boniface — otherwise St. Boniface, the "Apostle of Germany" — was originally named Wynfrid, a Germanic name meaning "friend-peace." He was renamed Boniface by Pope Gregory II.

▶ Martin V, born Oddone Colonna, was elected pope in 1417. He was only the third pope so named, however, not the fifth, since the two popes "Martin II" and "Martin III" never existed. A 13-century scribe misread the names of the two popes Marinus (as Martinus) — hence the error.

▶ Sixtus IV is not the only pope whose name has passed, specifically or generally, into the English language (see above). Gregory XIII gave his name to the Gregorian calendar, introduced by him in 1582 (and still in force), while Gregorian chant, or plainsong, is named after the first pope so named, St. Gregory the Great. The once popular card game called Pope Joan was *not* derived from a pope named John or even from the mythical female pope of this name (who was supposed to have been elected pope as John VIII in about 855 and who was allegedly born in England), but apparently comes from the French term for the game, *nain jaune* ("yellow dwarf").

Passing from popes to lesser mortals, we must now turn our attention to another special category of names, one that in fact often nicely combines a distortion of a religious name and a play on words. This category comprises the ingenious names chosen by crossword compilers.

Where papal names are historically and spiritually significant, crossword compilers' names, as is to be expected, are linguistically so. Some of them, indeed, are as satisfying to "crack" as a neat clue is to solve.

As far as the English language crossword is concerned, the way was led by compilers whose classic names (in more senses than one) have gone down in cruciverbal history, in particular names derived from Spanish Inquisitors, as Torquemada (Edward Mathers), pioneer of the cryptic clue, his successor °Ximenes (D.S. Macnutt), and *his* successor °Azed (Jonathan Crowther). (See Name Stories for detailed accounts of the latter two names.) Some names of crosswordists pay homage, directly or indirectly, to this tortuous — and torturous — trio, such as °Apex (Eric Chalkley), who aimed to "ape X," or imitate °Ximenes, and Machiavelli (Mrs. Joyce Cansfield, a rare woman compiler). Most names, however, are neat and apt versions of the compilers' true names, or have a similarly punning and/or erudite origin.

Some of the finest British crossword compilers have become known to solvers through the medium of the BBC journal *The Listener*, which publishes their work regularly. For private circulation, two "Who's Whos" of *Listener* crossword setters were compiled in 1965 and 1978, giving many of the origins of setters' pseudonyms. Let us see, therefore, how British crosswordists devise their names. (None of these names appears in the "Who's Who and Index" of the present work.) Readers of this book will by now be familiar with standard methods of pseudonym creation, so only the obscurer ones are "cracked."

Ad : Alfred Adams (1906-)

Alexis : William Geoffrey Arnott (1930-) — from subject of doctorate at Cambridge University, fragments of plays of Greek classical writer Alexis

Algol : F. Fereday (1910-   ) — formerly chief mathematician at research establishment

Babs : Stanley Beale (1907-)

Badger : James Arthur St. Hill Brock (1913- ?)

Bart : John Bartholomew Widdowson (1922-)

Buff : Colin Clarke (1943-) — from pub, Buffalo's Head, Durham, where spent much time as a student

Chabon : the Rev. H. Bacon (1917-)

Cheops : A.M. Robertson (1902-) — first puzzle was pyramidal in shape

Dogop : Donald George Putnam (1930-)

Duck : Donald Frank Manley (1945-)

Egma : David Parry Martin Michael (1910-) — Shakespearean word (see text below)

Eli : Ivor Neame Ellis (1935-)

ffancy : Robert Caffyn (1920-)

Fudge : F.J. Berry (1939-)

Jac : John Adelmare Caesar (1917-)

Jago : James C. Coulson (1951-) — in Spanish tradition

Jeffec : John F. Coldwell (1931-)

Klick : Robert William Killick (1914-)

Lascia : Leslie Barclay (1950-)

Leon : Noel Anthony Longmore (1931-)

Log : G.O. Lace (1909-)

Loki : Eve McLaughlin (1928-) — both from real name and as name of god of strife and spirit of evil in Norse mythology (and see *Thor* below)

Merlin : Richard Palmer (1947-) — apart from obvious wizardry, lives at Marlin Ridge, Pucklechurch

Mog : J.E. Morgan (1944-)

Nizam : Norman James Maclean (1939-)

Odysseus : Edward Collis (1907-) — "bestowed by editor of now defunct publication"

Peto : Peter B.G. Williams (1915-); and Helen D. Williams (1917-), his wife

Philipontes : Philip Bridges (1909-)

pH7 : Francis Fraser Ross (1917-) — "absolutely neutral" (chemical term for measure of acidity/alkalinity of a liquid)

Pipeg : E.G. Phillips (-)

Ploutos : Michael C.C. Rich (1940-) — bear in mind that he had a classical education, and was actually taught classics at school by °Ximenes

Ram : Reginald A. Mostyn (1920-)

Ramal : S. John Branch (1929-) — once again, the Spanish connection (translating his surname)

Rhombus : Robert Holmes (1907-) — professionally a mathematician, as well as partially anagrammatic

Sabre : Andrew Bremner (1951-) — initial "S" may be simply for convenience

Salamanca : Michael B. Freeman (1948-) — Spain again!

Sam : Albert John Hughes (1913-) — nickname given at school by science master

Slavko : Vatroslav Lopašić (1911-) — Croatian diminutive of Christian name

Smada : Arthur Adams (1923-)

Smokey : David A. Crossland (1948-) — "name of a recently departed dog"

Thor : Terence Patrick McLaughlin (1928-) — husband of *Loki* (and of course a famous Norse god)

Topher : John R. Cheadle (1913-) — from name of son, Christopher

Twudge : Tom W. Johnson (1947-)

Tyke : J. Conrad Frost (1912-) — "has Yorkshire affinities"

UtdtU : Reginald L. Trapp (1905- ?) — "encoding of surname" (try your hand!)

Crossword compilers' names can thus be seen to be entirely monoverbal, mostly brief and snappy, and with a distinct veering towards the classical and the classy. A few, such as Loki, Merlin and Rhombus, are both direct and allusive, and in the "lit. & fig." manner beloved of the composers of cryptic clues. Perhaps the gem of the selection quoted here is the name Egma, where the origin lies in the Shakespearean word "egma"— Costard's attempt at "enigma" in *Love's Labour's Lost*, a play whose title epitomizes the predicament of many a puzzler!

Pseudonyms among crossword solvers seem to be rarely used, presumably since they seek publicity, not obscurity. However an instance is known of two setters-turned-solvers who assumed false names to enter °Ximenes competitions. These were the cocompilers Dorothy Taylor and Alec Robins (Zander), who assumed the respective names of Mrs. B. Lewis (a next-door neighbor of Miss Taylor, with no interest in crosswords) and L.F. Leason (Mr. Robins is Jewish: "L.F." indicates the Hebrew letter aleph—or "a"—for his first name, and his mother's name was Leah, with Robins himself thus being "Leah's son" or Leason). In recent years the couple have been banned from Azed crosswords in *The Observer* for such deviousness!

Crossword setters may well have the occasional mental tussle before they can come up with a satisfactory word to fill an awkward "light," or a good clue for a word once they have entered it in their grid.

Tusslers of another sort, physical not mental, are wrestlers, and many of those who do battle in the ring will select a suitable pseudonym for themselves.

Some ring names are fairly conventional, and could apply to almost any person who has adopted a pseudonymous name. You cannot tell that Bobby Becker, Don Eagle, Paul Jones and Dusty Rhodes, for example, are wrestlers simply by their ring names. But many wrestlers specialize in some kind of act, costume, or gimmick, or fall into a particular physical or ethnic group, and as such choose a name that reflects their special quality. Let us look at some of these categories.

► "The toffs": Some wrestlers like to pose as members of the nobility, and so have names like Lord Duncum, Lord Charles Montague, Sir Norman Charles, Lord Patrick Lansdowne, and Lord Bertie Topham. One "blue blood" wrestler in Los Angeles, James Blears, changed his name legally to Lord Blears.

► "The hillbillies": Where the "lords" enter the ring wearing cloaks and monocles, the "hillbillies" appear in blue denim and rope belts. They have names like Hillbilly Spunky, Logger Larsen, Klondike Bill, Farmer Jack, Elviry Snodgrass, and Country Boy Humphrey.

► "The Indians": If you have cowboys in the ring, then you must also have Red Indians. Many wrestlers in this category are called "Chief," as Chief White Owl, Chief Kit Fox, Chief Little Wolf, Chief Big Heart, Chief Thunderbird, Chief Sunni War Cloud, and Chief Indio Cherokee. Women wrestlers of this kind are usually "Princess," as Princess Tona Tomah, Princess Rose White Cloud, and Princess War Star. Many of these really are Indians, although not Chiefs or Princesses. Others have names such as Billy Two Rivers, Johnny War Eagle, Danny Little Bear, and Tiny Roebuck.

► "The terrible Turks": A good guise for a wrestler, with bald head and fearsome moustache. Among them have been Ali Bey the Turkish Terror, Youssouf the Terrible Turk, and Humid Kala Pasha (so called because of his "excessive humidity" when wrestling). There has also, of course, been an Ali Baba.

► "The fatties": Their names speak for themselves: Haystack Calhoun, Giant Haystacks, Man Mountain Dean, and The Blimp. A woman wrestler in this generous group is Heather Feather. She weighs in and wades in at just under 390 pounds and trains on sausage pizzas.

► "The angels": Handsome wrestlers? Far from it! These are the big men with uneven eyes, hideous hooters, misshapen mouths, and fiddle-case feet. Their names are often variations on their category: The Golden Angel, The Swedish Angel, The Super Swedish Angel (billed as "the world's ugliest wrestler"), The Czech Angel, and The Polish Angel. There was even a bald woman wrestler named The Lady Angel.

For a selection of ring names of all kinds, see Appendix IV, "Ring names," page 338.

After such a show of power — an amateur tackles a *Listener* cross-word or a professional wrestler at his peril — we should perhaps come down to more homely and familiar names.

Peter Anthony, for example, and Judith M. Berrisford. These are such ordinary names that one might not even suspect they are pseudonyms. Yet they are, and moreover — to justify their mention in this chapter — are somewhat out of the ordinary run of pen names. They are in fact the names of not two individuals, but two couples — respectively Peter Shaffer and his brother Anthony, and Clifford Lewis and his wife Mary. Where two people work together like this, whether as family relatives or not, it is only natural that if they assume a pseudonym, they should take a single name.

For a couple to adopt a single pen name is fairly common, and in forming their pseudonym the usual devices are resorted to — with perhaps a wider scope for "own name" creation, since there are twice as many real names to work on. The Shaffer brothers, for example, simply used their first names as a forename and surname, while the Lewises based their joint name on the maiden name of Mary Lewis's mother (Berrisford). (What is rather unusual is that the husband-and-wife team decided in favor of a feminine pen name; normally such double pen names are masculine.)

As with all pseudonyms, variations in formation and application are possible here. °A Citizen of New York, for example, was not a single citizen, nor even two, but turns out to be three distinguished writers — Alexander Hamilton, "King of the Feds," and James Madison, fourth U.S. President, and John Jay, jurist and statesman. The pseudonym Patrick Quentin conceals the identity of no less than four writers (Richard Webb, Hugh Wheeler, Martha Kelly, and Mary Aswell), and the clearly concocted name °Smectymnuus was the joint name of five English Presbyterian ministers.

Very occasionally an inversion of this type of name occurs, when a pseudonym consisting of two names turns out to be a single individual. This is the case with "William and Robert Whistlecraft," who were not a father-and-son or fraternal team but just one man — John Hookham Frere, the early 19th-century English diplomat and author. He used the name for his humorous poem *The Monks and the Giants* (1817-1818), a mock-romantic Arthurian work — to be precise, the first four cantos of it — which came to provide a model for the much better known poem *Don Juan* by Byron, begun a year later (1819).

In all pseudonym creations there is often present a latent whimsicality. If you are "making a name for yourself," why not devise something witty and clever, and enjoy yourself in the process? An amusing or punning name will often be remembered much more vividly and effectively than a prosaic and commonplace one. One suspects, for example, that if Patsy Sloots, the film actress, had retained her real name instead of changing it to the mildly attractive but rather ordinary Susan Shaw, she would have made a greater impact on her public. (Why, her real name almost *looks* like a stage name! Could she really be Posy Slatts?)

It is not surprising, therefore, that some pseudonym bearers have turned to the creation of a comical name, or several comical names, with considerable relish. The novelist William Makepeace Thackeray must have enjoyed inventing George Savage Fitzboodle, Jeames de la Pluche, Major Gahagan, Ikey Solomons, °Michael Angelo Titmarsh, Charles James Yellowplush and their kind, much as Charles Dickens and P.G. Wodehouse, in their respective fictional works, had a genius for devising names for their characters that are often witty, occasionally outrageous, and usually entirely fitting. (The study of names of fictional characters is an important and enlightening subject, as yet mostly left untreated except by a few dedicated literary or linguistic experts. We hinted at the aptness of many Shakespearean names at the beginning of Chapter 1, for example: there is a virgin field that would richly pay the pioneer cultivator.)

And lest it be thought that the prerogative of humorous pseudonym creation belongs exclusively to writers, especially the classic American humorists (Josh Billings and °Diedrich Knickerbocker among

them), let us here cite some of the most enjoyable pseudonyms ever concocted. These are the names used by °W.C. Fields, whose offbeat
imagination gave us, among others: Mahatma Kane Jeeves, Otis
Criblecolis, Egbert Souse, Cuthbert J. Twillie, Professor Eustace McGarde,
Elmer Prettywillie, Samuel Bisbee, Elmer Finch, Gabby Gilfoil,
Professor Quail, Augustus Winterbottom, T. Frothingwell Bellows, Larson E. Whipsnade, and Woolchester Cowperthwaite. Ridiculous names,
of course — yet somehow many of them not quite beyond the bounds of
possibility as actual names. (A glance into Jack Train's *Remarkable
Names of Real People* will confirm the truth, in the matter of names, can
often be stranger than fiction. Consider Fields's fictional names above,
then compare them with such as A.A.A. D'Artagnan Umslopagaas
Dynamite Macaulay, Sir Cloudsley Shovel, Firmin A. Gryp, and Iris
Faircloth Blitch, all real flesh-and-blood human beings.)

Some of Fields's pseudonyms suggest the Dickensian, and indeed
the great comic film actor was an admirer of the works of this author,
who gave the world Edwin Drood (*Edwin Drood*), Uriah Heep (*David
Copperfield*), Ebenezer Scrooge (*A Christmas Carol*), Hon. Elijah
Pogram (*Martin Chuzzlewit*), and Peg Sliderskew (*Nicholas Nickleby*).
(Lovers of modern classical music may like to be reminded that in *The
Battle of Life* there is even a Benjamin Britain.)

Fields fans are clearly more than just a few. The dedication of
Frank Atkinson's *Dictionary of Pseudonyms and Pen-Names* is "In
memory of Otis Criblecolis." When he published a second edition of the
book (as a *Dictionary of Literary Pseudonyms*) two years later, the
dedication had become "In memory of Mahatma Kane Jeeves."

The names used by Fields were not limited to those quoted above,
and in giving only some of them we should note that multiple pseudonym
creation is a fairly widespread phenomenon, whether for practical purposes (to distinguish in some way) or simply more or less for entertainment.

There have been some record breakers, and we should perhaps
stand back a little and see them at full stretch — some of them, that is.

Frank Atkinson, in his second edition, lists the 50 names used by
Donald Sydney Rowland, a writer of apparent prolixity but unstated
provenance. He has met his readers as: Annette Adams, Jack Bassett,
Hazel Baxter, Karla Benton, Helen Berry, Lewis Brant, Alison Bray,
William Brayce, Fenton Brockley, Oliver Bronson, Chuck Buchanan,
Rod Caley, Roger Carlton, Janita Cleve, Sharon Court, Vera Craig,
Wesley Craile, John Dryden, Freda Fenton, Charles Field, Burt Kroll,
Helen Langley, Henry Lansing, Harvey Lant, Irene Lynn, Stuart
McHugh, Hank Madison, Chuck Mason, Edna Murray, Lorna Page,
Olive Patterson, Alvin Porter, Alex Random, W.J. Rimmer, Donna Rix,
Matt Rockwell, Charles Roscoe, Norford Scott, Valerie Scott, Bart
Segundo, Frank Shaul, Clinton Spurr, Roland Stan, J.D. Stevens, Mark

Suttling, Kay Talbot, Will Travers, Elaine Vinson, Rick Walters, and Neil Webb.

All quite plausible, with 18 of the 50 women's names, one a well-known literary name (John Dryden), and another (Fenton Brockley) reminiscent, perhaps coincidentally, of the name of a famous British politician (Fenner Brockway).

This is not the largest number of pseudonyms held by one person that Mr. Atkinson gives. For Lauran Bosworth Paine (1916-), the British author and biographer, for example, he lists 65 pen names, most of them very unremarkable. We know, however, that even his impressive number pales into relative insignificance beside the "centenarian" pseudonymous writers, who used over 100 names.

In his great four-volume *Dictionary of Pseudonyms*, we find Masanov, thus, listing the 106 names used by V.M. Doroshevich (1864-1922), the Russian journalist and satirical writer (including Ivanov Son of Influenza, and Wandering Minstrel, Professor of Striped and Spotted Dark Green Magic — who says the Russians are a humorless race?), and the 107 pseudonyms assumed by the writer, actor and journalist A.M. Gerson (1851-1888), from the obvious "A.G." to the unexplained "S.S." The palm, however, must go to the Russian humorist Konstantin Arsenyevich Mikhaylov (1868-), who boasted no less than 325 pen names, from "Ab." to "Z." Most of them are in fact abbreviations and variants of a particular pseudonym (such as G., G-ver, Gl., Glv., Gllivr, and the like, which all seem to indicate "Gulliver"), while others are rather pedestrian descriptive names such as Passenger, Pedagogue, and Reformer. For a humorist, indeed, the majority are not even specially amusing. Still, the record stands, and must therefore be duly noted!

Far more interesting than these are the full 173 pseudonyms adopted by °Voltaire. Since, as far as I am aware, these have never appeared before in their entirety in an English-language publication, whether in the original French or in translation, I am allocating Appendix I to them (page 332) in the hopes that they will satisfy the reader's curiosity and also be a useful passage of reference for all who need them. Appendix II, which may serve as a comparison, lists the 198 names used by Daniel Foe, otherwise °Daniel Defoe, author of *Robinson Crusoe*.

With the two enjoyable names of Doroshevich, quoted above, we are reminded of the playful nature that many pseudonyms assume. Indeed, the humor and wit — and sheer outrageousness — of many pen names is one of their most popular attributes. Everyone likes a funny name, simply because everyone enjoys a joke or relishes a pun. At the same time, the actual *use* of a humorous pseudonym may be a dead serious one. A frivolous name may mask a biting satire or cruel travesty. Thus Thomas Nash, the 16th-century English satirical pamphleteer and dramatist, chose the apparently lighthearted name Adam Fouleweather for his *Wonderful, strange, and miraculous Astrologicall Prognostication* (1591) that was an acrid reply to the savage denunciation of him by the astrologer Richard Harvey, and two hundred years later William Cobbett, the British author and politician, chose the amusing name Peter Porcupine for his perfectly serious pro-British pamphlets published in America in the 1790s.

It is the lengthy descriptive names, however, that make the most entertaining reading, whatever their purpose, and for their own sakes we must introduce a few more.

Lord John Russell, the 19th-century English statesman, entitled himself "A Gentleman who has left his Lodgings" for his *Essays and Sketches of Life and Character* (1820). This originally had a preface signed "Joseph Skillet," allegedly the lodging-house keeper who published the essays to pay the rent that the "Gentleman" had neglected to pay. In the same style, but a few years earlier, Charles Snart, an attorney of Newark, Nottinghamshire, had published a book on fishing called *Practical Observations on Angling in the River Trent* (1812). For this purpose the author described himself as "A Gentleman Resident in the Neighbourhood, who has made the Amusement his Study for upwards of Twenty Years." In both cases, as with similar diverting titles, the name of the book would precede the pen name of the author, so that Lord Russell's essays and sketches were "By a Gentleman who..." and Charles Snart's discourse on angling was written "By a Gentleman...." Such names as "One who..." are also of this type, as *A Peep at the Wiltshires Assizes, a Serio-Ludicrous Poem* (1820) by "One who is but an Attorney" (George Butt, a Salisbury, Wiltshire, solicitor), and *English History for Children, from four to ten years of Age* (1832-1833), by "One who loves the Souls of the Lambs of Christ's Flock" (the Rev. Richard Marks, a Buckinghamshire vicar). (Hamst, quoting this last multipartite name, says, "We dare not allow ourselves to comment upon a person who uses such a pseudonym as this.")

Infinitely more entertaining than these long-winded names, though, are those that combine description with fantasy, as the two Doroshevich names. Russian 19th-century writers, in fact, seem to have made such names something of a speciality. Dmitriev quotes two fine specimens.

The first was devised by V.A. Zhukovsky, a minor poet, for a frivolous "Greek ballad rendered in the Russian style" entitled *Yelena Ivanovna Protasova, or Friendship, Impatience, and Cabbage* (1811). For this, Zhukovsky assumed the name "Maremyan Danilovich Zhukovyatnikov, President of the Commission on the Construction of the Muratov House, Author of the Crowded Stables, Fire-breathing Expresident of the Old Kitchen Garden, Knight of the Three Livers, and Commander of the Gallimaufry." Zhukovsky wrote this curiosity while staying with his friends, the Protasov family, at their estate at Muratovo, just outside Moscow.

A friend of Zhukovsky, one Alexander Pleshcheyev, wrote some "critical comments" on this same ballad under what must be one of the lengthiest and weirdest pseudonyms ever devised by any writer: "Aleksandr Pleshchepupovich Chernobrysov, Active Mameluke and Bogdohan, Choirmaster of the Cowpox, Privileged Galvanist of the Canine Comedy, Publisher of a Topographical Description of Wigs, and Delicate Arranger of Divers Musical Tummy-Rumblings, Including the Fully Scored Howlings Herewith Appended." The preposterous personal name that heads the pseudonym, although based on Pleshcheyev's real name, has a meaning that works out something like "Alexander Splashnavelovich Shooblackcatoff." (The Mameluke and Bogdohan in the name are mellifluous titles of, respectively, classes of Egyptian rulers and Chinese emperors.)

Turning from the "one-off" to the common-or-garden and down-to-earth, it is interesting to see that some pseudonyms, in particular some surnames, occur fairly frequently. A survey of the 4000-plus pseudonyms in the Who's Who and Index of the present work reveals the following:

Names occurring at least five times but not more than 10: Adams, Alexander, Allan (Allen), Anthony, Barrie (Barry), Bell, Blair, Brook(e)s, Brown(e), Carter, Cooper, Davi(e)s, Dean(e), Dee, Drake, For(r)est(er), Gilbert, Graeme (Graham(e)), Grant, Hall, Hamilton, Holm (Home), Hope, Howard (Howerd), James, King, Lane, Lynn(e), Martin, Millar (Miller), Moore, Morgan, Murray, Owen(s), Parker, Ray(e), Richard(s) (Richardson), Roberts(on), Robinson, Ross, Russell, Scott, Shaw, Smith, Stevens, Stewart (Stuart), Taylor, White, Wilson.

Names occurring at least 10 times, but not more than 15: Carol (Carrol(l)), Douglas(s), Field(s), Ford(e), Hay(e)(s) (names starting Hay-), John(s) (Jones), Pa(i)ge, William(s)(on).

Of these surnames, and bearing in mind the fact that they are borne mainly by English-speakers of the late 19th or 20th century, the one striking feature is that many of them double up as first names (Allan, Carol, Douglas, Howard, John and the like). The remaining names are mostly common surnames, with a high proportion — simply coincidentally? — indicating a trade or profession (Carter, Cooper, Forester, Miller, Parker, i.e. one working in a park, Smith, Taylor). Almost exactly half the basic forms given, too, are monosyllabic (28 out of 57), which is well above the average for surnames as a whole.

It is true, of course, that the adoption of one of these particular names may simply have been a chance occurrence, such as the assuming of a family name, but the picture presented is an interesting one, indicating that first, "dual purpose" names (either forename or surname) are popular, and second, that occupational surnames are regarded favorably. Of the remaining popular names, surnames indicating a color seem to be liked (Brown, White), as do "nature" names (Brook, Dean, Field, Ford, Hay, Lane) and "good image" names (Bell, Home, Hope, King, Ray).

Both Lynn and Carol are unusual in being girls' names popular as male assumed surnames. (They exist, of course, as real surnames, but not as widely as many of the other names listed here.) It is tempting to ascribe the popularity of Carol to that most popular of pseudonymous writers, °Lewis Carroll, but there is no evidence for this. Nor, however, is there any evidence against it, since of the 11 Carrolls (or variant spellings) listed, ten were born later than the author of *Alice in Wonderland* and could indeed have been inspired to adopt this name, consciously or subconsciously. Of the other names, a few may simply have occurred here as the result of random selection — that is, it may be sheer chance that six Drakes are listed in the Who's Who and seven Shaws.

The great popularity of Page or Paige would not seem to be randomly indicated, though. Why should this name be desirable? Again, apart from being a short and simple name, it may be that one or more of the bearers suggested the name to the others — perhaps °Patti Page or °Janis Paige.

However, there are two names that are even more popular than these, at least as represented in our selection in this book. These are Gray or Grey, which occurs 16 times as a pseudonymous surname, and Lee, which comes most frequently of all, 17 times.

These two names doubtless have more to them than simply being monosyllabic color and nature names. Lee, for instance, is also a fairly popular given name, especially in the United States. Gray is not a forename, but seems to be popular simply because it is a pleasant name, a reasonably euphonious one, and a name with "gentle" associations (although as a common adjective it has a number of undesirable meanings, such as "dull," "pale," "old"). Add to Gray names such as Grayson and Greyson (four of one and one of the other), and we have the most frequently occurring pseudonymous surname in the book.

Both names have a high frequency in other collections of pseudonyms also. Of his total 3400 names, for example, Clarke has 11 Greys and 13 Lees, and Atkinson, in his "over 8000" English and American literary pseudonyms, has 17 Greys and 13 Lees. (For the record, Clarke also lists 11 Allens, 11 Carols or Carrolls, 11 Fords or Fordes, and 10 Joneses. Atkinson has 13 Allans or Allens, 13 Blakes, 11 Craigs, 19 Graemes or Grahams, 12 Hamiltons, 10 Hills, 11 Jameses, 12 Johnses or Joneses, 18 Kings, 20 Martins, 10 Millers, 14 Peterses, 12 Robertses or Robertsons, 15 Scotts, 13 Smiths, 26 Stewarts or Stuarts [nine Stewarts, 17 Stuarts], 14 Thomases, 11 Wests, 13 Williamses [and one Williamson], and 10 Wilsons. Neither author has any name more common than these. Clarke's number one name is thus Lee, as ours is, while Atkinson's is Stuart or Stewart. The majority of their top-scoring names are, as ours also are, "dual-purpose" forename-surnames.) It may even be that the popularity of such pseudonymous surnames may encourage the use of such names as real given names.

Looked at less statistically, can it be said that the pseudonyms adopted by men differ in any way from those chosen by women? On the whole, there is little difference, especially among more conventional names. Take all those Lees, for example. In virtually every case the first name, whether male or female, is quite unremarkable: Andrew, Bruce, Canada, Dickey, Steve, William for the men, and Anna, Brenda, Dorothy, Gypsy Rose, Holm, Lila, Michele, Patty, Peggy, Vanessa, Vernon (a sex disguise name) for the women. A more random dip in the Who's Who will show that most men adopt rather routine, traditional masculine names (John Abbot, Richard Amberley, John Oldcastle, Drew Pearson), and that women do likewise with their feminine names (June Allyson, °Doris Day, °Sheilah Graham, Lana Turner).

It is certainly noticeable, however, that men who care about their specifically masculine image — film actors playing tough roles, for example — do tend to choose "rugged," rather aggressive-sounding names, as °Rock Hudson, Tab Hunter, and °Paul Temple. (Note the verbal associations: rocks, hunters, temples.) Some women, too, who wish to project an exclusively feminine image — as "cuties" and "sweeties" of song or the cinema, or as sex symbols of one sort or another — likewise choose a name that is intended to have associations of romance or glamour (Renée Adorée, °Eve Arden, °Veronica Lake, Penny Singleton).

A more detailed analysis of such names is given respectively in the Name Lists numbers 33 and 34. Let us just say here that the actual letters incorporated in a name are often important, with men often choosing "forceful" letters, such as "k" and "x," and women opting for soft, seductive letters, as "l" and "s." Gutturals can be gutsy, and sibilants sexy!

A large number of pseudonyms also turn out to have a common syllabic pattern. That most frequently favored is bisyllabic forename plus bisyllabic surname, as Casey Adams, Stella Martin, Henry Oscar, with the first syllable of each name accented. But this is also a fairly common phenomenon among ordinary names, and even a brief look at the *real* names of pseudonymous writers will show that there are several of this type, as David Bingley, Douglas Christie, Mary Douglas, Walter Gibson, Eric Hiscock. Perhaps an unusually high proportion of pseudonyms, however, are alliterative, with the forenames and surname both beginning with the same letter. One has only to think of the names of some well-known movie stars to see this: Anouk Aimée, °Brigitte Bardot (if hers is indeed a pseudonym), Claudette Colbert, °Diana Dors, °Greta Garbo, °Marilyn Monroe and Simone Signoret are good examples. Nearly 200 such names are given in Name List number 40.

But among all these facts and figures, all these personal particulars and calculated analyses, are there not any pseudonyms, it will be asked, whose real identity we cannot crack? Are there not still some disguised figures whose masks have not yet been removed? The answer is yes, of course. And here we are thinking not so much of the criminal or secret agent whose false name or cover name has not yet been revealed, but of the individual whose pseudonym has successfully concealed his true identity in spite of serious and scholarly attempts to unveil it.

In some cases, of course, a person's true identity may not be disclosed until his death — this happened, for example, with the writer °Fiona Macleod and the broadcaster A.J. Alan — but there are one or two names whose real bearers are still unknown or at most conjectured.

Probably the most famous of all "uncracked" pseudonyms is that of Junius, the 18th-century author whose letters, 70 in number, in the London *Public Advertiser* between January 21, 1769, and January 21, 1772, revealed many intimate scandals of the day and were generally "agin the government" and antiroyalist (one of the letters was an impudent one addressed to King George III in person). Even today, over two hundred years later, and after much ingenious detective work and extremely thorough searching of contemporary documents, the identity of the infamous writer remains in doubt. Almost always using the name Junius, but occasionally switching to Lucius, Brutus and possibly Nemesis, the author clearly had the objective of ruining the ministry of the Duke of Grafton, Britain's incapable and ineffective prime minister for the three years 1767 to 1770 and lord privy seal from 1771 to 1775.

Who was he? After a consideration of his style — he had an original and fine command of language — his classical name (but to which Junius, actual or fictional, was the allusion, if there indeed was an allusion?), and all the other many historical and political facets of the time, some 50 names were proposed as the real author. The most likely of these is popularly held to be Sir Philip Francis (1740-1818), an Irish-born politician, who was known to have written a number of letters to the papers under pseudonyms. But this is only a conjecture. Other names suggested as the true author have been Edward Gibbon, Edmund Burke, John Wilkes, Lord Chesterfield, Thomas Paine, Lord Chatham (whom Junius loyally and actively supported), Lord Shelburne, Horace Walpole, Isaac Barré, George Grenville, Lord Temple, Henry Grattan, Alexander Wedderburn, Lord George Sackville, and Horne Tooke.

"The mystery of Junius increases his importance," wrote the author himself, and this proved to be so, if only in the form of several imitators, with pseudonyms such as Junius Ridivivus, Junius Secundus, Philo-Junius, and Junius itself. "I am the sole depository of my own secret, and it shall perish with me," also wrote the sharp-tongued satirist, whom even 20th-century technology has failed to unmask.

The *Letters of Junius* in fact made a significant contribution to journalistic history in that they established the fashion for the anonymity of leading articles in the press today.

Somewhat earlier than this, another literary name had attracted wide attention. This was one George Psalmanazar. As with Junius, his real name is unknown to this day, but unlike Junius he was an outrageous, if cunning, impostor. George Psalmanazar claimed to be a native from Formosa, which at the time of his arrival in London in 1703 was virtually an unknown island. The following year Psalmanazar published an account of Formosa with a grammar of the language spoken there. This "language" was, however, a fabrication from start to finish—he had simply concocted it. At the time literary London was taken in, but his imposture was soon exposed by Roman Catholic missionaries who had been to Formosa and who proved that the language set forth in Psalmanazar's grammar was nothing like the actual native tongue. Realizing that he had been revealed for the fraud he was, the bogus scholar publicly confessed his hoax and applied himself to more orthodox works, in particular the study of Hebrew. He died in 1763 having become a man of some repute and even the friend of Dr. Johnson.

Psalmanazar may possibly have actually been a Frenchman, or perhaps a Swiss. His year of birth is uncertain, although the year 1679 has been conjectured. He seems to have taken his name from Shalmaneser, an Assyrian prince mentioned in the Bible (2 Kings 17, 3), although it is not known what particular significance this name had for him, if any. (The name Shalmaneser itself means nothing more than "Shalman be propitious." However the Assyrian king "took" Samaria and "carried away" Israel just as the impostor "took" London and "carried away" much of the cultural world of the capital.)

A man with a false name disseminating false scholarship in a country that was not even his own and claiming to be from a country where he had never set foot takes some beating for sheer impudence!

Most of the pseudonyms assumed by false claimants to the throne and bogus pretenders have in due time come to be exposed: you cannot go about calling yourself Prince Louis or Lady Maria for long without some kind of reaction and disclosure. There is one royal pretender, however, who still remains unidentified. She was an almost exact contemporary of Junius, and although less well known than he, has a story that intrigues considerably.

This was the so-called Princess Elizaveta Tarakanova, a Russian girl born probably in 1745 who claimed to be the daughter of the Empress Elizabeth and Count Razumovsky and who in 1772, when in Paris, declared herself to be the pretender to the Russian throne under the name of Princess Vladimirskaya. Her precise origin and true name have still not been revealed. All that is certainly known is her fate—a typically "Russian" one, both romantic and tragic. In February 1775 she was arrested in Italy by Count Orlov, who 13 years before had been instrumental in putting Catherine the Great on the throne by forcing Peter III to abdicate. Orlov brought her back to Russia where the self-styled princess was imprisoned in the notorious Petropavlovsk Fortress, in St. Petersburg, where she died of tuberculosis on December 4, 1775. (A popular Russian painting by Flavitsky shows Tarakanova trapped in her cell by a rising flood: the waters of the River Neva rush through the prison bars while the wretched princess vainly seeks refuge by standing on her bed. This is melodramatic fiction, however, since the great St. Petersburg flood occurred not that year but two years later, in 1777. No doubt Flavitsky, painting his picture nearly a century later, in 1864, felt that enough mystery already shrouded the subject of his portrait to enable him to depict a more poignant fate than death by TB.)

One or two other pseudonyms of the hapless princess are known, as Miss Frank, and Mrs. (or Madame) Tremouille, but her true identity remains a secret. (Her main name of Tarakanova exists as a genuine Russian surname, meaning—somewhat unromantically, although in the end appropriately, perhaps—"cockroach.")

In the event it was Paul I who succeeded his mother Catherine to the throne in 1796.

In more recent times there has been considerable speculation about the true identity of the horror and fantasy fiction writer M.Y. Halidom. (The name itself clearly originates in the oath "by my halidom," with *halidom* meaning a holy place or thing.) The name no doubt hid the identity of more than one writer, and superseded the previously used name Dryasdust, which was that given for the author of the trilogy *Tales of the Wonder Club* (1899, 1900). This trilogy was reissued under the "Halidom" name in three separate parts a year or two later: Volume I in 1903, II in 1904, and III in 1905. The "Dryasdust" name had first appeared in 1890 for *The Wizard's Mantle*, a story about a cloak of invisibility during the Spanish Inquisition. This was reprinted, under the name Halidom, in 1903. The last story to appear by this still unidentified writer or group of writers was "The Poison Ring" (1912).

Even today there are writers active whose true identity is a closely guarded secret. Kremlinologists, for example, pay special attention to the articles that appear in the Soviet newspaper *Pravda* written by one "I. Alexandrov." No one knows for sure who he really is, but the name is believed to be that of a party official whose words carry high-level Kremlin approval. In similar fashion the English publishing trade journal *The Bookseller* carries a regular column by Quentin Oates. His role is a special and influential one, for he reviews not books but the actual reviews written by literary critics. Literary editors therefore pay special heed to his words. Acerbic Quentin Oates is widely known to be, but his identity is publishing's best-kept secret.

The professional activity of Messrs. Alexandrov and Oates is of course more narrowly directed than those of Junius, and arguably less damaging. So far, however, their masks remain firmly fixed in place, even if one day they will eventually drop and the three writers will stand revealed as their true selves.

We must mention one more name that hides an as yet unestablished true identity. This was the poet and satirist Pietro Aretino, who lived and wrote some time before any of our other "mystery men," more than two hundred years even before Junius.

Aretino, we know, was the son of a shoemaker in Arezzo, north central Italy. Pietro was born in Arezzo, we also know, on April 20, 1492. Later, he pretended to be the bastard son of a nobleman, deriving his "adopted" name from that of his native town — Aretino means "belonging to Arezzo." Over the 60 years of his life (he died in Venice on October 21, 1556) the cobbler's son gained fame (or notoriety) as a writer of vicious satires and lewd sonnets and as a leader of dissolute society in the grand style. It was his writings, especially his five comedies, that really established his reputation as a literary figure of considerable standing, above all his lively and amusing *La Cortigiana* ("Life at Court") (1534), which is an enjoyable account of lowerclass life in contemporary Rome.

We thus have a good deal of information about Aretino the man and his work. We even know what he looked like, for Titian painted his portrait (currently in the Frick Collection, New York). But we still do not know the one thing that interests us here in this book — his real name!

Yet if we are honest, we will probably admit that the mystery behind the pseudonym of the seven masked figures mentioned here — there are of course many more — actually adds to their status. The concealed or undisclosed identity of Junius makes him more powerful, just as it makes Psalmanazar more outrageous, Princess Tarakanova more tragic, M.Y. Halidom (and Dryasdust) more ghoulish, I. Alexandrov more authoritative, Quentin Oates more influential, and Aretino more colorful. The image that they hold, with the names by which they are known, is quite complete as it is, and we do not wish our concept of them to be disturbed. It is simply *because* we know that their name is not their true name that their standing in our eyes is enhanced.

The world will be a duller place when the true identity of the Man in the Iron Mask is revealed.

So let us return to the question we asked at the start of this chapter and also at the very beginning of the book: what *is* a name?

For a person, his name is very much more than a "designation by which he may be identified." The name of the thing on which I am sitting as I write this is "chair," but it is not unique, and there are hundreds and thousands of more or less similar objects in the world. "Chair" means "something to sit on" — no more. It merely identifies it as the familiar household object.

The name of my neighbor is Aubrey Plowman. But, in spite of the fact that there may well be several other Aubrey Plowmans (Plowmen?) in the English-speaking world, his name serves not only to identify him — he is Aubrey Plowman, not Joe Bloggs or °Cuthbert Bede — but virtually to embody him. He belongs to the distinct and unique Plowman family, whose characteristics and identity he himself has inherited and he himself visibly portrays and publicizes, and in that family he is the individual member, different from all others, who is Aubrey. Aubrey Plowman is Aubrey Plowman — the person who is both Aubrey-ish and Plowman-like — and there is no other person like him. (The fact that there may be others of this name is purely coincidental. All John Smiths are unique.)

Furthermore, the name of a person has an "aura," an associativeness, that mere names of objects lack. All that "chair" conjures up is — "chair." That is because it simply *means* "chair." But as a word Aubrey does not mean anything, except, in a manner dissimilar to the meaning given by ordinary words, the identity and persona of the person called Aubrey. In addition, it suggests an affinity with others who bear the name — even as a surname, perhaps — and actually as a name itself is mentally pigeonholed or classified as "rather superior," "fairly refined," "on the artistic side" or whatever. It may even, perhaps by association with Audrey or Oberon, seem rather an effeminate name. But in the final analysis, once we actually know the person so called, it basically *is* the man. To me he is my neighbor, with the traditional friendliness and helpfulness that go with this role; to his workmates he is another — yet of course basically the same — Aubrey. To his wife he is her husband Aubrey, and for her the name will have greater impact than for anyone else.

Except, of course, for Aubrey himself. He has only to catch the name on someone else's lips and he is all ears. It matters: is it him they are talking about? Quick, find out! What are they saying? What has he done or said? It is almost as if, in uttering his name, the speaker has trespassed on his property, even violated his identity and character. What a difference between, say, "a photo of Aubrey..." and "a photo of a chair..."!

Try an experiment. Say out loud the name of a casual acquaintance — a colleague at work, a shopkeeper, your bank manager, a member of that organization you belong to. Then say out loud the name of a loved one. Then finally, say your own name. Consider which has the greatest impact, the greatest significance. But also consider, how else could you adequately sum up the person you named other than by actually naming him or her?

Since a person's name is to be his or her individual ambassador in life, it is thus clearly most important that it should be suitable. And this is where the person who adopts a pseudonym has a supreme advantage over the "ordinary" person, for he has consciously adopted his name, even chosen it himself, whereas most mere mortals are stuck with the name that they were given when they were born.

In this book I have aimed to show how a number of people have adopted a new name in this way, and have examined some of the main motives that prompted them to do so.

The remainder of the book is devoted to the names themselves. Although these can, of course, be examined and enjoyed independently, it is suggested that they will be more meaningful when considered in conjunction with the six chapters that conclude here.

Wherefore art thou Romeo?
(Romeo and Juliet, II, ii)

Name Stories

This is the kernel of the book: a detailed treatment of some of the best known pseudonyms and an account of their origins, often in the words of the personalities themselves. Much of the material is based on biographies or autobiographies of the subjects, or features or articles about them, and in such cases the sources are given in square brackets.

Sources indicated by author's name only, followed by page number, refer to a title listed in the Bibliography (which begins on page 346).

Dates of birth and death are rarely given in these stories; they can of course be found in the Who's Who (which begins on page 227).

The criteria for including a name story here were that (a) the person should be reasonably well known, (b) the name itself should have an interesting or unusual origin, and (c) enough material was available to give the story. Many well known names are missing from the stories that follow: these are very likely ones whose origin I was not able to trace. There are, of course, one or two names whose origin *nobody* has yet been able to track down satisfactorily, such as that of °Molière. In the circumstances, I felt it better to include as many of these as I could if only to give such information as is known, even if it is still only an informed guess.

Ab-o'-th'-Yate : Benjamin Brierley was an English weaver by trade who came to enjoy success as a writer of stories and verse in Lancashire dialect. His early stories were narrated by a character caled "Owd Ab" (Old Abe) who in turn became the subject of later sketches. "Yate" is a Lancashire form of "gate" — meaning not "gate" but "street" and still existing in some Northern place names in this sense, as Carter Gate in Nottingham ("street of the carters"). Ben Brierley was thus "Abe from the Street," or a typical old world townee character.

Æ : George William Russell, the Irish poet and satirist, had signed an article with the pseudonym Æon. The compositor had queried the spelling of the name, so Russell opted for the diphthong alone (now often written AE or A.E.). Æon itself is a pseudoclassical pen name — Greek, "eternity" — denoting a power emanating from the supreme deity.

Affable Hawk : The Indian-style name was chosen by Sir

69

Desmond MacCarthy, the literary critic, for his articles in the *New Statesman* when he succeeded Solomon Eagle in 1913.

Anna Akhmatova : When Anna Gorenko was 17 and aspiring to be a poet, her father objected to her writings ("a decadent poetess") and told her not to bring shame on the family name. Retorting "I don't need that name," Anna chose a Tatar name—that of her great-grandmother. The Tatars of the south had always seemed mysterious and fascinating to the girl who came to be one of Russia's greatest modern poets [Amanda Haight, *Anna Akhmatova: A Poetic Pilgrimage*, 1976].

Eddie Albert : The American actor Eddie Albert Heimberger grew more than tired of announcers referring to him as "Eddie Hamburger." This was the way out.

Shalom Aleichem : Solomon J. Rabinowitz was a Russian-born Jewish novelist who settled (1905) in the U.S. after several years in Italy. He explained his name as meaning "Peace upon you"—also "You are a man and a brother, Welcome!" His pen name is regarded as a gem of Jewish lore [*The Times*, May 15, 1976].

O Aleijadinho : The name is Portuguese for "the little cripple." The Brasilian sculptor and architect António da Costa, of Portuguese and black African ancestry, was born deformed, eventually lost the use of his hands, and finally became blind. In spite of such daunting handicaps, he worked hard right to the end of his long life, using tools strapped to his wrists.

Jean Le Rond d'Alembert : The famed 18th-century French mathematician was the illegitimate son of hostess Mme de Tencin and one of her lovers, the chevalier Destouches. As a baby he was abandoned on the steps of the Paris church of Saint-Jean-le-Rond. On starting school he enrolled as Jean-Baptiste Daremberg, later changing this (presumably for euphony) to d'Alembert.

Muhammad Ali : Cassius Marcellus Clay adopted this name in 1964 when joining the Black Muslim movement after becoming the new heavyweight champion of the world (against Sonny Liston, on February 25 that year). It was given him by °Elijah Muhammad, leader of the Black Muslims in the U.S. Ali made this announcement to reporters in Miami Beach two days after gaining his title: "From now on my name is Muhammad Ali. Don't call me by my slave name. Cassius Clay was a slave name. It was given to my family by white masters. I'm a Black Muslim now. That's my religion, the religion of Elijah Muhammad. And my name is Muhammad Ali. I want you to call me that from now on." The name itself is said to denote "one who is worthy of praise" [1. Muhammad Ali with Richard Durham, *The Greatest: My Own Story*, 1977; 2. Larry Bortstein, *Ali*, 1976].

George Allan : Mite or Marie Kremnitz, née Marie von Bardeleben, was coauthor with Queen Elizabeth of Romania (°Carmen Sylva) of a number of translations and novels and stories. As °Dito und

Idem, macaronic (Italian, German, Latin) for "the same and the same," they jointly wrote (1886) the play *Anna Boleyn*.

Paula Allardyce : Many references state that the real name of this thriller writer is Charity Blackstock. This appears to be another pseudonym, however. Her real name would seem to be Ursula Torday. As Paula Allardyce she wrote *Witches Sabbath* (1961), *Adam's Rib* (1963), *Miss Jonas's Boy* (1972), and other books. She also used the name Charlotte Keppel.

Dave Allen : When David Tynan O'Mahoney, the Irish TV entertainer, was starting his career and eager for engagements he hit on one way of ensuring that his name would come high on the list of any agent's index of available comedians — he changed it to Allen, which begins with A! [*The Times*, January 12, 1977].

Fred Allen : John F. Sullivan, the radio comedian and film actor, was first a juggler, Fred St. James, soon dropping the "St." to be Fred James. Later (1921) he grew tired of telling people he wasn't a member of the Jesse James Gang and changed his name to Fred Allen "as a tribute to Ethan Allen who had stopped using the name after the revolution" (Ethan Allen was a soldier and frontiersman who, as leader of the Green Mountain Boys, captured Fort Ticonderoga in the Revolutionary War).

Don Ameche : The name is an approximation of the correct pronunciation of the American film actor's real name, Dominic Amici. But might not most people find "Amici" easier to say correctly, in spite of its Italian origin, than the rather strange looking "Ameche"?

An Craoibhín Aoibhinn : Douglas Hyde, the Irish writer and statesman, and first president of Eire, was the founder of the Gaelic League and a campaigner for the rights of the Gaelic language. His Gaelic name means "the fair maiden" and comes from the title of a traditional Gaelic song, "An craoibhín aoibhinn álainn óg" — "The fair excellent young maid."

Julie Andrews : The popular English film actress was born Julia Elizabeth Wells in 1935. She assumed the name of her stepfather, Ted Andrews, a Canadian singer. In 1969 she married Blake Edwards and used a combination of her name and his, Julie Andrews Edwards, for her book *Mandy* (1972).

Fra Angelico : The great Renaissance painter's real name was Guido di Pietro, and his religious name, as a Dominican monk, Fra (Brother) Giovanni da Fiesole. The name by which he is best known was the result of a nickname, originally "Beato Angelico" — literally "blessed angelic" — because of the angelic beauty of his character. The name became established after his death rather than during his lifetime.

Anodos : Mary Elizabeth Coleridge was the granddaughter of the elder brother of the poet and critic Samuel Taylor Coleridge. She wrote poetry from childhood, and used the name, Greek for "healthy," for her early books of verse, such as *Fancy's Following* (1896). Her wishful pen name did not, alas, grant her a long life: she died a month short of her 46th birthday.

Another Lady : Marie Dobbs used this name for her enterprising completion (in 1975) of Jane Austen's unfinished novel *Sanditon* — so that the complete work is thus by Jane Austen and Another Lady. Marie Dobbs also writes as Anne Telscombe.

Ape : Carlo Pellegrini was an Italian who came to England in 1864 and turned his hand to drawing cartoons. His first effort, drawn over the name Singe (French for "monkey"), appeared in the fashionable gossip magazine *Vanity Fair* in 1869. Two cartoons later he had changed his name to the briefer English *Ape*. The name was certainly chosen both to reflect his mischievous approach to his work and also to indicate the essential nature of a cartoon or caricature, which "apes" its subjects. Another great contributor to *Vanity Fair* was °Spy.

Apex : The crosswordist Eric Chalkley chose a doubly apt name: not only one suggesting a "top" compiler but denoting his ambition, to "ape X" — that is, to imitate °Ximenes.

Johnny Appleseed : John Chapman planted fruit trees for the frontier settlers in Pennsylvania, Ohio, Indiana, and Illinois, and as a result was nicknamed by the name that he subsequently adopted. He lives on in a number of fictional works, ranging from Vachel Lindsay to Walt Disney.

Elizabeth Arden : The famous Canadian cosmetician, Florence Graham, daughter of a Scottish father and an English mother, took her name from the novel *Elizabeth and Her German Garden* (1898) by Elizabeth, and Tennyson's poem *Enoch Arden* (1864). Her own pseudonym, of impeccable literary origin, in turn served as the inspiration for...

Eve Arden : The name chosen by the American comic film actress born Eunice Quedens. It came from a coldcream jar, the contents of which were trade named "Evening in Paris." This gave her first name. Her new surname was that of the cosmetician who was responsible for the product, and whose name was also on the jar, °Elizabeth Arden. Eve's name is thus of impeccable commercial origin!

Henry Armstrong : Not content with mere "son of Jack," the American boxer Henry Jackson assumed a more meaningful and apposite name — "strong of arm!"

Fred Astaire : The name change was not made by Frederick Austerlitz himself, but was effected by his parents, Frederic and Ann Gelius Austerlitz, when the future popular dancer and actor was only two years old (1901).

Mustafa Kemal Atutürk : The Turkish soldier and statesman Mustafa Kemal adopted his surname, meaning "father of the Turks," in 1934 when as president of the Turkish Republic he introduced compulsory registration of surnames, as one of a number of reforms (his given name

Kemal means "perfection," and was bestowed on him for his excellence in mathematics when at college in Constantinople) [Irfan & Margarete Orga, *Atatürk*, 1962].

Azed : Another leading crossword compiler, Jonathan Crowther, and another doubly significant name. His clues not only lead to answers covering all the letters of the alphabet but can at times be devious and tortuous — as was the Spanish grand inquisitor whose name he reversed, Don Diega de Deza. Crowther succeeded °Ximenes on the *Observer*, and earlier had compiled for *Varsity* and *The Listener* as "Gong," his early childhood pronunciation of his Christian name.

Azorín : The Spanish author and critic José Martínez Ruíz took his pen name from that of the eponymous hero of his autobiographical novel *António Azorín* (1903) — although he first wrote the book as Candido. Azorín itself derives from the Spanish for "hawk-like" (compare the Azores, so named by 15th-century Portuguese explorers who upon first setting foot on these islands were amazed by the large number of such birds).

Lauren Bacall : The film actress's mother left Romania for America when she (the mother) was only one or two years old, together with *her* mother and father. On arriving at the immigration office on Ellis Island, the family gave their name — Weinstein-Bacal, meaning "wineglass" in German and Russian. The officer must have written just the first half of the name, so they were Max and Sophie Weinstein (Lauren's grandparents) with their daughters Renee and Nathalie (her mother) and their son Albert. Nathalie married William Perske, but soon divorced him, upon which she decided to take the *second* half of her original name for herself and for her daughter. Thus when Lauren (although not yet Lauren!) was eight years old, her mother became Nathalie Bacal and she became Betty Bacal. By the time she was 18, Betty had added another "l" to her name, since "there was too much irregularity of pronunciation": some people rhymed it with "cackle," and others pronounced it "Bacahl." She felt that the second "l" would ensure that the last syllable of the name would be pronounced correctly, as "call." When she began her film career, director Howard Hawks wanted to find a good first name to go with her surname, and asked if there was a suitable name within her family, perhaps? Betty's grandmother's name (Sophie) did not seem to be what he wanted. Hawks said he would think of something. At lunch one day with Betty, he said he had thought of a name — Lauren — and that he was going to tell everyone that it was an old family name of Betty's, even that it had been her great-grandmother's. "What invention!" commented Lauren, who is in fact alleged to dislike the name. [Lauren Bacall, *By Myself*, 1979].

Honoré de Balzac : Balzac's "de" was self-styled. His grandfather's surname was Balssa, which was changed to Balzac by his father because of its peasant connotations. The famous French novelist used a

number of other pseudonyms ranging from Henri B. to Lord R'hoone—
the latter an anagram of his Christian name.

Anne Bancroft : Anna Maria Italiano was the daughter of Italian
immigrants to the U.S. (although herself born in New York). Even her
"real" name came as the result of a misunderstanding. Her father, on
arriving at Ellis Island, thought he was being asked his nationality and
said "Italiano, Italiano." This was recorded as his name, which is what he
was actually being asked for. Anna Maria first acted as Ann Marno, but
subsequently selected the name Anne Bancroft from a list submitted her by
Darryl F. Zanuck when she made her first film, *Don't Bother to Knock*
(1952).

Monty Banks : The Italian film actor and director Mario Bianchi moderated his name to suggest "mountebank," an English term for a
clown or charlatan that itself derives from the Italian *montambanco*: in
medieval Italy such itinerant quacks mounted on a bench to appeal to the
audience. For a while Monty Banks was married to °Gracie Fields.

Theda Bara : Theodosia Goodman was not only a stage and
screen actress but also the first "vamp." For publicity she claimed to be
the daughter of an Eastern potentate, so that her pseudonym is an
anagram of "Arab death!" At least Theda is something like Theodosia.

W.N.P. Barbellion : The English essayist and naturalist Bruce
Cummings adopted this name when he published entries from his diary in
book form, as *The Journal of a Disappointed Man* (1919). The initials, he
said, stand for Wilhelm Nero Pilate—all men of bravado. His adopted
surname seems to be based on the barbel, the name of a large freshwater
fish.

Wilkie Bard : William Augustus Smith, the English music hall
artiste, had a high, domed forehead like that of Shakespeare: hence his
nickname and subsequent stage name.

Brigitte Bardot : Most books and features on the world famous
"sex kitten" give no hint that this was anything but the French film actress's real name. Willi Frischauer's biography, for example, gives her
parents' names as Louis and Anne-Marie Bardot, and her mmn as Muscel.
Yet through all his editions Halliwell maintains that BB's real name was,
and so presumably is, Camille Javal. ("BB" was in fact a genuine
pseudonym—her initials, of course—used for her appearance as a cover
girl on "Elle" in 1948). [Willi Frischauer, *Bardot: An Intimate Biography*,
1978].

Maurice Barrymore : Herbert Blythe, the English actor, adopted his name from an old playbill hanging in the Haymarket Theatre,
London. His new surname passed to his acting children, Lionel, Ethel,
and John Barrymore.

BB : In 1937 appeared *The Sportsman's Bedside Book*. Its author
was Denys Watkins-Pitchford, who chose this pen name for it and for subsequent writings on sport (in the English huntin', shootin', fishin' sense)

and the countryside. The initials came not from the title of the book but from the size of lead shot he used — BB measuring 0.18 inches in diameter — for shooting wild geese.

Orson Bean : Dallas F. Burroughs became best known as a stage actor and comedian. He started his career (1948), however, as a magician, and this was the randomly incongruous name he selected for his conjury.

Warren Beatty : Both brother and sister made a minor adjustment to their real name when adopting their stage names. Warren Beaty added a single letter, and his sister Shirley Maclean Beaty, dropping her surname, slightly respelled her middle name — in fact her mmn — to become Shirley Maclaine.

Cuthbert Bede : The Rev. Edward Bradley, English humorist and author of *The Adventures of Mr. Verdant Green* (1835), was educated at Durham University. His pseudonym comprises the names of the two patron saints of the city of Durham, St. Cuthbert and the Venerable Bede.

Demyan Bedny : The pen name of the Russian poet Yefim Pridvorov basically derives from Russian *bedny,* "poor," reflecting the condition of the peasants and working classes before the Revolution (compare °Maxim Gorky). It was originally a nickname. He had brought a poem entitled *Demyan Bedny, the Harmful Peasant* to his editors, and on his next visit they exclaimed "It's Demyan Bedny!" In fact his uncle, himself a peasant, was called Demyan. Pridvorov — whose real name derives from a word meaning "courtier," a connotation he may well have wished to avoid — also wrote one poem (1917) as Ivan Zavodskoy ("Ivan the Factory-worker") and for a while assumed the quasi-Romanian name *Demyanesk Bednesku* [Dmitriev, p. 137].

Francis Beeding : Two thriller writers with a single pen name — John Leslie Palmer and Hilary Aidan St. George Sanders. Palmer had always liked the name Francis; Sanders had once owned a house in the Sussex village of Beeding. The pair also wrote as David Pilgrim, and Palmer alone as Christopher Haddon.

Currer Bell : In adopting the surname Bell, as did her sisters, Charlotte Brontë was not assuming the name of her husband, the Rev. Arthur Bell Nicholls, as is sometimes stated. She first used the name for her volume of poems, written jointly with her sisters, *Poems by Currer, Ellis and Acton Bell,* in 1846. It was only in 1854 that she married Arthur Nicholls, dying the following year in pregnancy.

Neil Bell : Many sources give the novelist and short story writer's name as Stephen Southwold. But this smacks of a pseudonym, since he was born at Southwold in Suffolk. Recent evidence suggests that his true name was in fact Stephen H. Critten. Stephen Southwold was the name he used for children's books. He also wrote as Paul Martens and Miles.

Bellecour : The 18th-century French playwright and comic actor who was really Jean-Claude-Gilles Colson married Beauménard, otherwise Rose-Perrine le Roy de la Corbinaye, a noted actress. After his death (1778) she remarried but still called herself Mlle Bellecour.

Belleville : Another classical French actor, but of the 17th century. Henry Legrand assumed this stage name for his tragic acting. For comedies, which were basically coarse farces, he called himself Turlupin, which subsequently became a word in the French language meaning "clown." Legrand worked closely with La Fleur and °Fléchelles to form a trio.

N. Beltov : Georgy Plekhanov, the Russian Socialist, adopted the name of the hero of °Herzen's novel *Whose Fault?* (1841-1846). Other pseudonyms adopted by Plekhanov were A. Volgin (see °Lenin) and °Simplicissimus.

Bendigo : William Thompson was a British boxer and prize fighter who subsequently became a preacher. His name is a corruption of the biblical character Abednego—one of the three "certain Jews" (Shadrach, Meshach, and Abednego) who were ordered to be cast into King Nebuchadnezzar's burning, fiery furnace for not serving his gods or worshipping his golden image. (Daniel 3 tells the story of their deliverance from this fearful fate). The British boxer, in turn, is said to have given his adopted name to the Australian mining town of Bendigo, which was developed in the gold rush (1851) by an admirer of his who took his name to boost his own reputation as a boxer!

Jack Benny : Benjamin Kubelsky, the talented radio and TV comedian, started his career (1918) as Ben Benny, but changed this since it was similar to the name of the bandleader and comedian Ben Bernie. For a while in 1926 he was Benny K. Benny [Irving A. Fein, *Jack Benny: An Intimate Biography*, 1976].

Irving Berlin : When Israel Baline, the son of a penniless itinerant synagogue cantor, published his first sheet music on May 7, 1907, his surname was misprinted thus—and he kept it that way, at the same time "anglicizing" his forename to Irving. Oddly, this famous songwriter has never learned how to read or write music or to play it on anything other than the black notes of a piano (so at least, reported a feature in *The Times*, May 13, 1978)!

Mary Berwick : Adelaide Anne Procter, the English poet, was a contributor of verses to Dickens's periodicals and author of *Legends and Lyrics* (1858) which included the famous "Lost Chord" ("Seated one day at the organ..."). She was also something of a hymnwriter. Her father was Bryan Waller Procter, better known as Barry Cornwall. It may be no coincidence that the names of father and daughter are based on places that are respectively in the extreme southwest of England and the extreme northeast. In fact Barry Cornwall's name is a near-anagram of his real name.

Isaac Bickerstaff : One of the best known, and most intriguing, of literary pseudonyms. It was assumed by three famous writers: Jonathan Swift, the British (although Irish-born) satirist and critic of *Gulliver's Travels* fame, Sir Richard Steele, the Irish-born essayist and dramatist, founder of *The Tatler*, and Benjamin West, the American mathematician. Swift used the name in a pamphlet (1708) against the almanac-maker John Partridge, Steele used it for launching *The Tatler* the following year, and West assumed the name for a series of almanacs published (1768) in Boston. Where did the unusual but somehow genuine-seeming name come from? Confusingly, there had been a contemporary Irish playwright whose real name was in fact Isaac Bickerstaffe (with the extra "e"). He had been a page to Lord Chesterfield when he was Lord Lieutenant of Ireland. But it is believed the existence of a real bearer of the name, although a contemporary, was simply a coincidence. Swift is said to have taken the name Bickerstaff from a smith's sign, adding the unusual Christian name Isaac. For his correspondence with the Duchess of Shrewsbury, Swift took the name Presto, originally her nickname for him ("Speedy!"). She herself assumed the name Stella.

Bim : Bim was always accompanied by Bom, and Bom always went with Bim. The team of *Bim-Bom*, in fact, was a single interdependent entity. It comprised a pair of Russian clowns, who first performed under the name in 1891. (The name is a meaningless one, but perhaps suggests something like "bang-bang" or "boom-boom"). There was always a single *Bim* in the person of Ivan Radunsky, a Pole by origin, but there were no less than four *Boms*: a Russianized Italian named Cortesi, a fellow Pole called Stanevsky, a Czech by the name of Viltzak, and finally an actual Russian named Kamsky. The duo began as an eccentric but versatile couple, both amusing and acrobatic, lively yet highly literate (they spoke "good" Russian, as distinct from the broken Russian affected by a number of clowns). After the tragic death by drowning of Cortesi in 1897, the second Bom presented a somewhat different image, dressing not as a conventional clown but as a gay "man about town," wearing evening dress, complete with top hat and a chrysanthemum in his buttonhole. The pair now played down the acrobatics in favor of greater verbal satire. In 1901-1904 the two toured Europe. After the Revolution, Stanevsky emigrated to his native Poland, and Bim followed suit. He returned in 1925, however, and in his partnership with Viltzak now concentrated more on the musical aspect of his turns. (The third Bom was an accomplished if unorthodox musician. One of his specialities was playing on two concertinas at once). Bim finally teamed up with Kamsky in the war years (1941-6). The first half of the 1920s produced a number of Bim-Bom imitators, such as Bib-Bob (Rashkovsky and Vorontsov), Viys-Vays (Sidelnikov and Solomenko), Din-Don, Rim-Rom, Fis-Dis and the like [Shneyer, p. 67].

Nicholas Blake : The Irish-born writer is equally famous as the poet Cecil Day Lewis (his real name) and the detective novelist Nicholas

Blake. His pseudonym derives from family names: Nicholas is the name of his younger son, Blake one of his mother's family names (she was Kathleen Blake Squires).

Fabian Bland : This was the joint pseudonym of British authors Hubert Bland and his wife Edith, née Nesbit, for *The Prophet's Mantle* (1888). Hubert Bland was a prominent member of the Fabian Society — hence the name. Before her marriage, Mrs. Bland wrote horror stories as well as children's books, masking her sex with the name E. Nesbit. (The stories were also frequently narrated by a man).

Nelly Bly : Elizabeth Seaman was a newspaper writer whose round-the-world race (1889) against a theoretical record established her name as a star reporter. (Her time was 72 days, 11 minutes, and 14 seconds — the journey itself made on or in all conceivable forms of transport). Her name was suggested by the managing editor of *The Pittsburgh Dispatch*, for which she began writing when she was 18. It comes from a character in a song by Stephen Foster, who also begot Jeanie ("with the light brown hair") and Susanna ("Don't you cry for me"). (See also °Susanna Foster.)

Marc Bolan : The British pop star was born Mark Feld. In 1965, when he was 18, the Decca record company put out his debut disc under the name Mark Bowland. Later that year he changed this to Mark Bolan.

Isabel Bolton : Mary Britton Miller, the American poet and novelist, wrote at first under her real name. Having little success, she changed her style and her name — and achieved greater recognition. But what does Isabel Bolton have that Mary Miller has not?

Bon Gaultier : The name was chosen as the joint psuedonym of Scottish poets William Aytoun and Theodore Martin for their *Bon Gaultier Ballads* (1845), in which they parodied the verse of the day. (In fact Martin had used the name earlier for some humorous pieces in *Tait's* and *Fraser's* magazines, and these attracted Aytoun's attention). The name comes from Rabelais, who in the Prologue to *Gargantua* uses the words in the sense "good fellow," "good companion," Gaultier being a generalized proper name.

Boniface : The early English missionary and martyr Wynfrith, or Winfrid, the "Apostle of Germany," was renamed by Pope Gregory II in 719 for the third-century saint Boniface who was martyred at Tarsus.

William Boot : The Czech-born English dramatist °Tom Stoppard used this name for early pieces as a drama critic when writing for the magazine *Scene* (1962). He took it from the hero of Evelyn Waugh's *Scoop*, a nature columnist. Stoppard used the name Boot for a number of characters in his plays, often complemented by another character called Moon. In 1964 he wrote a TV play called *This Way Out with Samuel Boot* which actually featured a *pair* of Boots, who represent contrary attitudes towards material possessions [*Sunday Times*, January 15, 1978].

Ludwig Börne : Löb Baruch was a German political writer of Jewish descent. Converting to Christianity (in 1818), he took a new name.

Bos : Thomas Peckett Prest and others, writers of stories for boys, and creator of the infamous character Sweeney Todd (whose name in turn was to become Cockney rhyming slang for the Scotland Yard Flying Squad), originally intended to ascribe their near-piracies of Dickens (who used the name °Boz) to "Boaz," but this was ruled out as being closer to °Boz than Bos. It was also thought to be too biblical [E.S. Turner, *Boys Will Be Boys*, 1976].

David Bowie : David Hayward-Jones, the British rock star, changed his name (in 1967) to avoid confusion with David Jones of the "Monkees." The name is apparently arbitrary, but could have been suggested by the Bowie knife. Bowie's name is also, of course, virtually synonymous with that of Ziggy Stardust, the bisexual astronaut who is the hero of Bowie's important album *The Rise and Fall of Ziggy Stardust and the Spiders from Mars* (1972). Bowie's son is named Zowie.

Boz : Charles Dickens used this name both in reports of debates in the House of Commons in *The Morning Chronicle* (1835) and in his collection of articles entitled *Sketches by Boz* (1836-1837). He explained the name as being "the nickname of a pet child, a younger brother, whom I had dubbed Moses (after Moses Primrose in Goldsmith's *The Vicar of Wakefield*) ... which being pronounced Boses, got shortened to Boz." (The name is said to have been originally pronounced "Boze.")

Willy Brandt : Herbert Ernst Karl Frahm was to become Chancellor of West Germany (1969-1974). In 1933, at the age of 20, he fled to Norway as a political refugee from Nazi Germany, when Willy Brandt was his party (Social Democrat) name. He had never known his father, so his real name was that of his mother, a salesgirl in a cooperative store [Klaus Harpprecht, *Willy Brandt: Portrait and Self-Portrait*, 1972].

Brassaï : The Hungarian-born French photographer was born Gyula Halész. He adopted his name from his native city of Brassó, Hungary — now Braşov, Romania.

Fanny Brice : Fannie Borach, the American singer and actress, grew tired of having her surname mispronounced as "Bore-ache" and "Bore-act," so changed it to something simpler. °Lauren Bacall had similar problems.

Charles Bronson : The film actor Charles Buchinsky, of Russo-Lithuanian extraction, changed his Russian-sounding name at the time of the McCarthy trials for fear of being branded as a "red." His new name was inspired by Bronson Street, off Hollywood Boulevard in Beverly Hills [Steven Whitney, *Charles Bronson: Superstar*, 1978].

Mel Brooks : Melvin Kaminsky, the American film comedy writer and producer, changed his name (in 1941) to avoid being confused with Max Kaminsky, the trumpet player. He derived it by contracting his mmn, Brookman.

Lenny Bruce : A fairly conventional "anglicization of his name by the somewhat unconventional comedian born Leonard Alfred Schneider. He married (1951) Harriet Lloyd, née Jollis, who earlier had been calling herself Honey Harlowe and, later Honey Michelle [Albert Goldman, *Ladies and Gentlemen, Lenny Bruce!*, 1975].

Dora Bryan : Dora May Lawton, the comic actress, was born with the surname Broadbent — "not a name for the stage," as Noël Coward judiciously pointed out. In selecting an alternative, she originally chose Bryant, from the match manufacturers, Bryant & May, but when the program arrived from the printers the last letter of the name was missing — and she settled for the t-less version.

Yul Brynner : The American film actor of obscure origin (Swiss-Russian? Manchurian?) claims to be really Taidje Khan, Jr., but no one has apparently been able to find out who he really is — not even his wives.

Martin Bucer : The 16th-century German Protestant reformer Martin Kuhhorn, who was professor of theology at Cambridge University from 1549 until his death, translated his name in the manner of his time. His true surname literally means "cow horn," which he latinized/graecized. He must not be confused with the 20th-century Jewish philosopher Martin Buber, or even less with Martin Luther, the 16th-century (and therefore contemporaneous) German religious reformer. Bucer wrote a work on the Psalms (1529) under the name Aretius Felinus.

Buffalo Bill : William Frederick Cody, the famed American scout and showman who ran Buffalo Bill's Wild West Show (from 1883) was so named by °Ned Buntline, as Cody had provided buffalo meat for the train construction crews. Cody's real surname was of German origin, evolving from an earlier form Kothe or Köthe.

Lawsona Bukowski : Ruth Davies, known for her portrayal of the teacher's pet Penny Lewis in the BBC-TV series about life in a comprehensive school, *Grange Hill* (1978), adopted a name that has a connection with hair. Ruth had dyed her hair with henna, the botanical name for which is *Lawsonia inermis*. This gave her first name. The second, Bukowski, is that of an actor she had admired in the film version of the musical *Hair*. She first used the name when she was about 12. Ruth Davies is the daughter of the English novelist Beryl Bainbridge, who had formerly been married to Austin Davies.

Ned Buntline : Edward Zane Carroll Judson was an American adventurer, trapper and soldier of the Far West, as well as the author of several "dime" novels. He it was who met William Cody in 1869 and nicknamed him °Buffalo Bill. Judson's own assumed surname is more mischievous than meaningful. A buntline is "one of the ropes attached to the foot of a square sail to haul the sail up to the yard for furling," says Webster.

Billie Burke : As Leonard Ashley has pointed out, Billie was a popular name amongst chorus girls. It was chosen not only by Mary William (sic!) Ethelbert Appleton Burke, who married the impresario Florenz Ziegfeld, of the Ziegfeld Follies, but also, for example, by the actress who became Billie Dove.

Richard Burton : When at school in Port Talbot, South Wales, Richard Walter Jenkins showed distinct signs of promise as an actor. As such, he became the protégé of the English teacher and school play producer Philip H. Burton, who made the 18-year-old schoolboy his legal ward and gave him his name. At the time Burton in fact saw Richard as a future politician, not an actor [*Radio Times*, November 17-23, 1979].

Alexander Bustamente : The man who became prime minister of Jamaica, himself the son of an Irish father and Jamaican mother and named William Alexander Clarke, had worked in Cuba for a while as a police inspector. The name he assumed was that of the Cuban lawyer and diplomat Sánchez de Bustamente y Sirvén (1865-1951).

Red Buttons : Aaron Schwatt derived his stage name by way of a nickname. When he was 17 (1935) and working as a bellboy at Dinty Moore's tavern in the Bronx, he wore a uniform with 48 buttons. Any bellboy or pageboy is likely to be called "Buttons" from the distinctive row of buttons on his jacket, but this particular bellboy was also red-haired — so Red Buttons he was, and Red Buttons he has stayed.

Max Bygraves : The English comedian was born Walter William Bygraves. On his first night in the RAF, aged 17 (he had lied about his age to enlist), he impersonated his idol, °Max Miller, and thereafter assumed his first name.

Cadenus : This was the name assumed by Jonathan Swift for his poem addressed to Esther Vanhomrigh, *Cadenus and Vanessa* (1713) — thereby incidentally creating the now quite popular girl's name Vanessa (formed from the first three letters of Esther Vanhomrigh's surname with "Essa," a pet form of Esther, added). Swift, more famous for his authorship of *Gulliver's Travels* (1726), had become Dean of St. Patrick's Cathedral, Dublin, in 1699, hence his nickname of "Dean" Swift. Cadenus is an anagram of the Latin for "dean," *decanus*. For another lady correspondent of Swift named Esther, see °Isaac Bickerstaff.

Marti Caine : The English entertainer and singer born Lynda Crapper adopted her name (1968) in a somewhat random manner: by opening a gardening book at the entry "Tomato cane!" [ITV program, "This Is Your Life," March 22, 1978].

Michael Caine : Maurice Joseph Micklewhite assumed his first name from his own nickname, Mike, and his surname from the film *The Caine Mutiny* (1954).

Louis Calhern : Carl Henry Vogt adopted his pseudonym under pressure from his uncle, who regarded having an actor in the family as a disgrace. The actor's stage and screen name derives from a combination of his first two names and the city of St. Louis (although he was born in New York).

Maria Callas : A classic example of a lengthy Greek name shortened to a more acceptable and manageable form. The abbreviating was not done by Cecilia Sophia Anna Maria Kalogeropoulos (married name Meneghini) but by her father, shortly after his arrival in the U.S. (1923) with his family — in the year that Maria was born.

Phyllis Calvert : Phyllis Bickle was requested to change her name by the film producer and director Herbert Wilcox. The actress chose Calvert as she felt "it had a sort of ring to it." Phyllis, it seems, she felt did not need to be changed [*TV Times*, September 22, 1977].

Cañadas : The only Englishman to have qualified as a matador in the Spanish bullring was born Henry Higgins. In the bullfighter tradition he assumed a simple Spanish name, in his case meaning "glens," "narrow valleys." Such small canyons are a feature of the countryside around Bogotá, Colombia, where Higgins was born. Having survived and triumphed over the rigors of the bullring (he qualified as a fully-fledged *matador de toros* in 1970) "El Inglés," as the Spanish called him, died tragically in a hang-gliding accident on March 15, 1978, when he was only 34.

Cantinflas : There has been speculation concerning the meaning of the name assumed by the Mexican clown and comedian born Mario Moreno Reyes. It is apparently meaningless, and was given him by one of his fans.

Robert Capa : Andrei Friedmann, the Hungarian-born American photojournalist, was famous for his war pictures. Early in his career, in order to get good prices for his work, he sold his shots as the product of "Robert Capa," an imaginary American photographer who was alleged to be so rich that he refused to sell his photos at normal prices.

Caran d'Ache : The French caricaturist born in Moscow as Emmanuel Poiré took his pseudonym from a mock French version of the Russian word for "pencil," *karandash*. (The name is also in use as the trade name for a brand of painting chalks). See also °Karandash.

Joyce Carey : The British film actress was born Joyce Lawrence. She must not of course be confused with the Irish-born novelist Joyce Cary. As a playwright Joyce Lawrence adopted the name Jay Mallory.

Carmen Sylva : The young princess Pauline Elisabeth Ottilie Luise grew up to become Queen of Romania. As a keen writer and correspondent she used a number of pen names, including Astra (1886) and Aus zwei Welten (1882). "From two worlds," the latter means — and somehow symbolizes the dual life of the royal writer, as head of state and professional authoress. With Mme Mite Kremnitz she used the joint name °Dito und Idem. Her best known pen name Carmen Sylva has a classical ring of songs and sylphs.

Joan Carroll : The American child screen actress Joan Felt acted under her own name until she was eight years old (1940), then changed to Carroll because it "sounded musical."

Lewis Carroll : One of the most famous and best-loved names in 19th-century English literature, whom most people know as the author of *Alice in Wonderland* and *Through the Looking-Glass,* was really Charles Lutwidge Dodgson, a mathematical lecturer at Oxford University. His pseudonym is a transposition and translation (or rendering) of his first two names, of course — Lutwidge to Lewis and Charles to Carroll. (Compare German Ludwig and Latin Carolus). He was requested to produce a pen name by Edmund Yates, editor of the humorous paper *The Train,* to which Dodgson was contributing (1856, six years before he told, and began to write, the story of *Alice*). He first offered Yates the name Dares, after his birthplace Daresbury, but Yates thought this "too much like a newspaper signature." So Dodgson tried again, and on February 11, 1856, wrote in his diary: "Wrote to Mr. Yates sending him a choice of names: 1. *Edgar Cuthwellis* (made by transposition out of "Charles Lutwidge"). 2. *Edgar U.S. Westhill* (ditto). 3. *Louis Carroll* (derived from Lutwidge ... Ludovic ... Louis, and Charles). 4. *Lewis Carroll* (ditto)."

Yates made his choice, saving all Alice lovers from Edgar Cuthwellis, and on March 1 Dodgson duly recorded in his diary "Lewis Carroll was chosen." This was not in fact his first pseudonym, since his early contributions to *The Train* were signed as "B.B." (it was this that prompted his editor to ask for a proper *nom de plume*). The precise origin of B.B. is not clear, although Dodgson had shown a fondness for writing over mysterious initials as self-appointed editor of the Dodgson family journal, *The Rectory Magazine.* In this, as a 15-year-old schoolboy, he contributed pieces as VX, FLW, JV, FX, QG — and BB. In her biography of Carroll, Anne Clark suggests that *B.B.* — which would appear to be one of the few initialized pseudonyms Dodgson retained for use in adult life — might perhaps stand for "Bobby Burns," since a number of the pieces contributed by the schoolboy author to *The Rectory Magazine* were mournful ballads in the style of Robert Burns.

On the other hand in *Poverty Bay: A Nondescript Novel* (1905), by Harry Furniss, the illustrator chosen by Dodgson for *Sylvie and Bruno,* the line is found: "He was known at Eton as "B.B.," short for Beau Brummell, the exquisite, whom he was supposed, by the boys at school, to emulate." Furniss was here perhaps consciously or unconsciously using Dodgson's own nickname, which had been confided to him some years before and which he now remembered. This seems quite a likely explanation for the strange double-letter name. Additionally, Francis King, reviewing Anne Clark's book in the *Sunday Telegraph* (September 9, 1979), points out that many of the names in Carroll's *The Hunting of the Snark* begin with B, including all the crew members (Bellman, Barrister, Broker, Billiardmarker, Beaver, etc.) and the Snark itself, which ultimately turns out to be a Boojum! For a pseudonym based on Carroll's own pen name, see °Caroline Lewis [1. Anne Clark, *Lewis Carroll: A Biography*, 1979; 2. John Pudney, *Lewis Carroll and His World*, 1976].

Jasper Carrott : Robert Davies, the British comedian and "cult humorist of the seventies" gave his own explanation of his name: "Jasper is a nickname I picked up when I was nine, I don't know why. There is no reason for it. I added Carrott when I was 17. I was on a golf course with a friend, when he met somebody, and said: 'Oh, this is Jasper.' And for the first time in my life, this guy said: 'Jasper who?' Carrott was the first name that came into my head. No one since school days has ever called me, or even known me, by my original name, Bob Davies" [*TV Times*, February 15, 1979]. Jasper is in fact a general nickname for any person, used either casually or contemptuously.

Nick Carter : The name was adopted by the author or authors of a series of detective novels (from about 1870) in the U.S. The character Nick Carter, from which the name came, was said to have been invented by John R. Coryell (1848-1924), the American writer of popular fiction, and passed on by him to Thomas Chalmers Harbaugh (1849-1924) and Frederick Van Rensselaer Dey (1861?-1922). These authors are also said to have written some of the romantic novels appearing under the name Bertha M. Clay.

Justin Case : If you're wondering whether anyone chose to adopt this delightfully corny name, then Hugh Barnett Cave is your man. The English-born American writer of horror fiction also wrote as Allen Beck and Geoffrey Vace.

Cassandra : Sir William Connor, columnist of the *Daily Mirror* (from 1935), was noted for his often gloomy and prophetic articles. Such prophecy is reflected in his pen name, derived from the mythological Cassandra, daughter of Priam, king of Troy, who received the gift of prophecy from Apollo. It was not his choice of name, but was chosen for him, probably by Harry Bartholomew, one of the newspaper's directors. Connor wrote (1965): "I was a bit surprised to discover that I had changed my sex; was the daughter of the King of Troy; that I could foretell in the stars when the news was going to be bad; ... that nobody believed me when I spoke the unpleasant truth" [Robert Connor, *Cassandra: Reflections in a Mirror*, 1969].

Butch Cassidy : The infamous bank robber born Robert Le Roy Parker worked as a butcher for a while when on the run from the law. "Butch" was thus a nickname. His companion in crime was Harry Longbaugh, nicknamed "The Sundance Kid" from the bank raid he had made in the town of Sundance, Nevada. The film of the fate of the two robbers (1969) helped to popularize their notoriety.

Cato : Two noted adopters of the name, which was that of Marcus Portius Cato — "Cato the Younger" (95-46BC), who sought to preserve the Roman republic against the power seekers, especially Caesar — were:

(1) William Smith, the Scottish educator and minister, who came to the U.S. (in 1751) to be provost of the College of Philadelphia. He used the name for his weekly letters to the *Pennsylvania Gazette* attacking Thomas Paine's *Common Sense* (1776), which urged the declaration of independence.

(2) (Jointly) Michael Foot, the British MP, Frank Owen, author and broadcaster, and Peter Howard, author, for their book *Guilty Men* (1938) attacking the "Men of Munich" (Neville Chamberlain, Halifax, Margesson, Simon and Hoare) for their collaboration with Hitler.

Cerberus : Sir John Colville, the English diplomat and author, chose this pseudonym for his (unpublished) book "Guiltier Men" (1977), attacking Michael Foot, Tony Benn, Jack Jones, Denis Healey, Harold Wilson, et al. by way of reversing the charges made in the book *Guilty Men* by °Cato (2). Sir John saw the name as symbolic: it was that of the many-headed hound which guarded the entrance to Hades in Greek mythology [*Sunday Times*, August 8, 1978].

Cyd Charisse : A number of sources give the film actress's "real" name as Tula Finklea. She was indeed born this. But Charisse is also her "real" name since she married (1939) the ballet teacher Nico Charisse before she started work in films. However she soon divorced him and married the actor and singer Tony Martin. Her assumed surname is thus that of an early and short-lived husband. Cyd was a product of her childhood: her baby brother called her Sid (which she respelled Cyd) when trying to say "sister." She first danced (1939) as Felia Sidorova, a name based on Finklea and the same "Sid."

John Charlton : A family-based name was chosen by the English writer Martin Woodhouse for *The Remington Set* (1975), a "rather violent detective story." This was full of cops and robbers and four-letter words, and he wrote it under a different name to avoid shocking his regular readers [*The Times*, May 20, 1978].

Chubby Checker : The name originated as a nickname for Ernest Evans, the American Negro popular musician and innovator (1961) of the twist, since he resembled a young Fats Domino. ("Chubby" is fat-faced; checkers — known as draughts in Britain — is a popular indoor table game.) The nickname is said to have been bestowed by the wife of Dick Clark, the American pop promoter.

Chiang Ch'ing : The wife of Chairman Mao was born Li Yun-ho. As a young actress she changed her name to Lan P'in, meaning "Blue Duckweed." Later she married Mao and he chose the name Chiang Ch'ing for her, meaning "Green River." She used this name, too, for her acting [*Sunday Times*, November 14, 1976].

Chung Ling Soo : William Ellsworth Campbell was an American conjuror who modeled himself on a real Chinese conjuror, Ching Ling Foo, who had made a successful tour in the U.S. Ching accused him (1914) of being an impostor, and Campbell admitted it, but the public admired him all the more for his impersonation, which he had first evolved in England. Campbell, who had used the name William E. Robinson when first arrived in the U.S., was accidentally shot to death while enacting a bullet-catching trick.

Cimabue : Bencivieni di Pepo is now known by this name as a fine 13th-century painter and mosaicist. But his name is something of a mistake! It was a family nickname, meaning literally "top dunce."

A Citizen of New York : A single pseudonym for a trio: Alexander Hamilton (who took the name Pacificus individually), American statesman and "King of the Feds," plus James Madison (individually Helvidius), fourth United States President, plus John Jay, American jurist and statesman. They adopted the name jointly for their essays in the *Federalist* in favor of the new U.S. Constitution (1787-1788). Later they assumed the joint name Publius.

Clarinda : This was the private name adopted by Agnes Maclehose, née Craig for the verses she sent Robert Burns (until 1794). He was Sylvander.

The Rev. T. Clark : In real life the Scottish novelist John Galt. He used the name for his *The Wandering Jew* (1820), one of his lesser known writings, and cunningly revealed his real name, for sharp-eyed readers, in the first letters of the last four sentences of the book: "Greatness...," "All...," "Literally...," "To...."

Jedediah Cleishbotham : One of the many humorous names adopted by Sir Walter Scott (compare Chrystal Croftangry and Captain Cuthbert Clutterbuck). He used it for the name of the imaginary editor of the four series of his *Tales of My Landlord* (1816), a supposed schoolmaster and parish clerk. The pen name is composed of a typical Puritan Christian name and a surname consisting of the Scottish dialect *cleish*, meaning "to whip," and "bottom."

Anacharsis Cloots : The name chosen by the self-styled "Orator of the Human Race," Jean-Baptiste du Val-de-Grâce, seems to be something of a pun, for Greek *anacharis* means "graceless!" In 1780 he published *La Certitude des Preuves du Mahométisme* ("The Certainty of the Proofs of Mohammedanism") under the name Ali Gier-Ber.

Upton Close : When the American journalist Josef Washington Hall was holding a government post in Shantung (1916-1919), he learned of the Japanese invasion and put "up close" on his messages to indicate that he was near the front. From this notation came his pen name.

Charles Coburn : The Scottish-born music hall comedian began life as Colin Whitton McCallum. He took his name from the Coburn Road, Bow, London. He must not be confused with Charles Coburn (1877-1961), the American actor.

Coco : The well-known name of the much-loved clown Nikolai Poliakov, English (and a champion road safety propagandist) but of Russian origin. Coco, or Koko, could in fact be an affectionate form of

Nikolai. It actually comes from the two syllables of his full name Ni*k*olai Polia*k*ov and was devised for him by the Italian circus owner Rudolfo Truzzi, to whom he was apprenticed (in Russia) [*The Times*, September 26, 1974]. There was another Russian clown Coco (properly "Koko") working in Truzzi's circus, whose real name was Alfons Frantsevich Luts (1885-1945). Although he was 15 years older than Coco, the link between the two identical names and the fact that both clowns were in the same circus would seem to be rather more than just coincidental.

Colette : Not a Christian name but the surname, used alone, of Sidonie-Gabrielle Colette, the French novelist. Her first books were written under the name Willy (her husband's pseudonym). Her own name first appeared, as Colette-Willy, in *Dialogues de Bêtes* (1904). She divorced Willy in 1906 but continued to write as Colette-Willy until 1916, after which she used Colette alone.

Carlo Collodi : The author of the famous puppet story *Le Avventure di Pinocchio* (1883), whose real name was Carlo Lorenzini, adopted his pseudonym from the birthplace of his mother (he himself was born in Florence).

Confucius : The great Chinese philosopher's name is our westernized version of his true name K'ung Fu-tzu or King-fu-tze, meaning "Kung the master." This of course will suggest the name of the Chinese sport resembling karate, kung fu — which actually means "boxing principles."

Ralph Connor : Charles William Gordon, the Canadian born writer of novels with a religious theme — he was professionally a Presbyterian minister — had a name that was the result of a mistake. He meant to use "Cannor," from the letter heading "Brit. Can. Nor. West Mission," but his editor changed this to Connor and added Ralph.

Alice Cooper : Vince Furnier, the American pop performer, chose this (female) name (in 1969) to illustrate his theory that "people are both male and female biologically" and to draw attention to his group, the Nazz (originally Earwigs, then the Spiders). He claimed it suggested a blonde folk singer — which he certainly wasn't [*Daily Mirror*, June 30, 1975].

Gary Cooper : How did it come about that "Coop" changed from Frank Cooper to Gary Cooper? The metamorphosis was the work of his Hollywood agent, Nan Collins. She came from Gary, Indiana... "'My home town was named after Elbert H. Gary. I think Gary has a nice poetic sound to it. I'd like to see you take Elbert Gary's last name for your first.' 'You mean,' he interrupted, 'Gary Cooper?' 'Yes — Gary Cooper. Say it again. Gary Cooper. Very nice. I like it. Don't you?' Gary Cooper. He ran the name around in his mind a few times. He spoke it again. 'Gary Cooper.' Then he smiled. 'I like it.' 'You see,' Miss Collins said. 'I knew you would. And you'll have to agree, Gary Cooper doesn't sound as tall and lanky as Frank Cooper'" [George Carpozi, Jr., *The Gary Cooper*

Story, 1971]. By assuming the name the actor gave a considerable boost to Gary as one of the most popular Christian names of the mid-20th-century.

Le Corbusier : The exact significance of the name chosen by the French architect Charles Édouard Jeanneret is not clear. It seems, however, that Le Corbusier was a family name and that Jeanneret detected in a cousin so named the resemblance to a crow (French *corbeau*). In 1920 Jeanneret chose Le Corbusier while Ozenfant selected *Saugnier*, his grandmother's name. (As a standard French surname, Le Corbusier appears to mean "basket-seller," from French *corbeille*, "basket.")

Mara Corday : Exactly why Marilyn Watts chose this name for her film career is not certain. Leonard Ashely suggests that she may have been influenced in her choice of name by that of the Swiss actress Paule Corday, who was also known as Rita Corday and Paula Corday, rather than by the name of Charlotte Corday, the French revolutionary who assassinated Marat in his bath (1793).

El Cordobés : This was the name assumed by the Spanish bullfighter Manuel Benítez Pérez, meaning "the man of Cordoba." He was not born in Cordoba but Palma del Rio. The name came, it is said, from a monument in Cordoba to the great matador Manuel Rodriguez (Manolete), from which he derived his inspiration to excel in the bullring.

Marie Corelli : The novelist Mary (or Minnie) Mackay was of illegitimate birth, and knowing this created the myth that her father, actually Charles Mackay, a songwriter, was Italian. In a letter to *Blackwood's Magazine* she thus claimed to be "a Venetian, and a direct descendant (through a long line of ancestry) of the great Michael Angelo Corelli, the famous composer." Mary chose the name initially for a possible musical career, with a second choice of name being Rose Trevor. Earlier she had written as Vivian Earle Clifford. Arcangelo Corelli (rather than Michael Angelo) was a real enough person, and an Italian violin virtuoso and composer of the 17th and early 18th century [Brian Masters, *Now Barabbas was a Rotter: The Extraordinary Life of Marie Corelli*, 1978].

Corno di Bassetto : When George Bernard Shaw was a music critic for *The Star* (1888-1890) he chose this name, which is the traditional Italian indication in orchestral scores for the instrument known in English as the basset horn.

Adrienne Corri : Adrienne Riccoboni, the English film actress of Italian descent, was renamed by Gordon Harbord — who also renamed °Laurence Harvey and tried to rename °Diana Dors (that is, when she was still Diana Fluck).

Baron Corvo : Here indeed is a name to conjure with! The real name of the extraordinary British writer was Frederick William Serafino Austin Lewis Mary [sic] Rolfe. He claimed to have received the title of Baron Corvo from the Duchess Sforza-Cesarini when living in Italy in the

1880s—a claim that has been neither confirmed nor disproved. The enigmatic writer himself gave three versions of the origin of his pseudonym: that it was a style offered and accepted for use as a *tekhnikym* or trade name when he denied sacred orders and sought a secular livelihood, that it came from a village near Rome and was assumed when he was made a baron by the Bishop of Emmaus, who was on a visit to Rome, and that it was bestowed by the aforementioned duchess. Rolfe had other pseudonyms, as Frederick Austin, King Clement and Fr. Rolfe. He wrote autobiographically as Nicholas Crabbe in *Nicholas Crabbe* and *The Desire and Pursuit of the Whole*, and as George Arthur Rose in (and as) *Hadrian the Seventh*. *Corvo* is Italian for "raven," moreover, and he had already adopted the raven as a heraldic device. (Perhaps Crabbe has a similar symbolic significance.) George Arthur Rose is said to derive from St. George "of the Roses" and Duke Arthur (of Brittany) murdered by King John in 1203. In C.S. Lewis's *That Hideous Strength* there is a jackdaw called Baron Corvo [1. A.J.A. Symons, *The Quest for Corvo*, 1940; 2. Donald Weeks, *Corvo*, 1971].

Elvis Costello : Declan McManus, the British rock singer, was named by Stiff Records' recording agent Jake Riviera—in a West London pub. Elvis was a tribute to Elvis Presley; Costello was the name Declan's father, Ross McManus, sometimes took as a singer. Elvis Costello was promoted with the slogan "Elvis is King" [*Sunday Times Magazine*, October 15, 1978].

Charles Egbert Craddock : Mary Noailles Murfree, the American writer of novels and short stories in dialect (mainly in *Lippincott's* and the *Atlantic Monthly*) took her masculine name from that of the hero of an early story in *Appleton's Journal*. It was not until the year after the publication of her first collection of stories, *In the Tennessee Mountains* (1884), that the editor of the *Atlantic* discovered the author of the tales of mountaineers and their hard life to be in reality a frail, crippled spinster.

Gordon Craig : Edward Godwin Craig, the British stage actor, was the illegitimate son of the actress Ellen Terry and Edwin Godwin, an architect. He bore the name Edward Godwin until his mother married the actor Charles Wardell (1877), when he became Edward Wardell. His mother renamed him (1887) Henry, after Henry Irving, the great actor, and Gordon after her friend Lady Gordon. Craig came from the Scottish islet Ailsa Craig, a name which appealed to her: "What a magnificent name for an actress!"

Lucas Cranach : Lucas Cranach the Elder was born in Cranach, now Kronach, West Germany, as Lucas Müller. He first indicated his adoption of the name of his birthtown by signing a painting, *Rest on the Flight into Egypt* (1504), as "LC." His son, Lucas Cranach the Younger (1515-1586), kept the name.

Joan Crawford : The famed American film actress was born Lucille Le Sueur — "at a date variously placed between 1901 and 1908," said the *Times* obituary of her (May 12, 1977). She first appeared in a film (1925) under her real name ("Well, honey, you certainly picked a fancy one," a Hollywood producer is alleged to have commented, when she told him her name). She was soon to become Billie Cassin, however, Cassin being her stepfather's name. Later the same year (1925) she acquired her lasting stage name of Joan Crawford. This was as the result of a sponsored contest in *Movie Weekly*, with $1000 offered in prizes. The top prize of $500 would go to the person who could find a name "simple to pronounce," "euphonious," and one to match her personality — "energetic, ambitious and typically American." The contest closed on May 2, 1925. The winning name Joan Arden (nicely suggesting "ardent"), and Billie duly assumed the name. Only a week later, however, this was discovered to be the real name of an extra, so the second-prize name was chosen instead. Joan was not too keen on the surname, complaining that it sounded like "crawfish." Film actor William Haines commented: "You're lucky it isn't cranberry — you could be dished up every Thanksgiving with the turkey." But the name brought fame (Lucille Le Sueur had been thought "contrived" and "too theatrical") [Joan Crawford with Jane Kesner Ardmore, *A Portrait of Joan: The Autobiography of Crawford*, 1963].

Bing Crosby : When the "Old Groaner" was still a high-voiced lad, he delighted in the comic strip "Bingville Bugle," whose hero was a character named Bingo. Some say he even bore a resemblance to this personage. So "Bing" he was nicknamed, and as Bing Crosby, Harry Lillis Crosby grew up to delight or daunt the world with thousands of White Christmases.

Tony Curtis : Bernard Schwartz was the son of Jewish Hungarian immigrant parents. His name was changed by Hollywood producer Bob Goldstein, who said: "Schwartz ain't a name to get you into the big time — not even George Bernard Schwartz." Another Schwartz who changed his name was film comedian Andy Devine.

Dana : The popular singer from Northern Ireland born Rosemary Brown took her stage name from her nickname at school: in Irish *dana* means "mischievous," "naughty." It also happens to be both a forename (for both sexes) and a surname in its own right, as the film star Dana Andrews and the author of *Two Years Before the Mast* (1840) Richard Henry Dana. (Both the latter's father and his son were also Richard Henry Dana). In 1978 Dana married a Northern Ireland hotelier, Damien Scallon.

Clemence Dane : Winifred Ashton, the British novelist and playwright, took her name from the London church of St. Clement Danes (itself said to have been named after a former church on the site that was built on a Danish settlement). She first went on stage (1913) with the name Diana Cortis.

Bebe Daniels : Norma Jean Dougherty, the American film actress, made her first screen appearance at the age of seven (1908), when she was still a "baby." She grew up to marry Ben Lyon, who promptly changed her name (Bebe from "baby," and Daniels as simpler and sweeter than Dougherty) and took her to England where she appeared with him on radio and television [*The Guardian*, March 26, 1979]. (Other sources frequently give her original name as Virginia Daniels.)

Lisa Daniely : Elizabeth Bodington, the British film and television actress, used this name for what she defined as "sexy, undistinguished movies." She reverted to her real name (1970s) with "a new middleaged persona" (she was born in 1930).

Lorenzo Da Ponte : Emmanuele Conegliano was the librettist of several famous Mozart operas, including *Le Nozze de Figaro* (1786), *Don Giovanni* (1787), and *Così fan Tutte* (1790). He was born a Jew, the son of Geremia Conegliano. On conversion to the Roman Catholic faith he took the name of the bishop who baptized him, as was then customary, Monsignor Lorenzo da Ponte, Bishop of Ceneda.

Lawrence H. Davidson : Although resembling his real name, this early pseudonym of D.H. (David Herbert) Lawrence derived from Davidson Road School, Croydon, where the future novelist and short story writer taught for a brief period. He used it for a school textbook, *Movements in European History* (1921).

Skeeter Davis : Mary Frances Penick, the American country singer, took her name from that of her schoolfriend, Betty Jack Davis, with whom she formed (1953) the group the Davis Sisters and who was sadly killed that same year. Skeeter is a name favored by some popular musicians, presumably for its suggestion of "sting" or "bite" (it derives from "mosquito").

Doris Day : Doris Kappelhoff's new name was given her by Barney Rapp, a Cincinnati band leader. It was based on her well known song, *Day After Day*, and was also symbolic, to imply the dawn of "a new day."

Dave Dee : The British pop singer David Harman first used this name for his group Dave Dee and the Bostons — his stage surname itself being a school nickname (from David). This same group subsequently was renamed to incorporate the stage names — also originally school nicknames — of the other members, being thus called Dave Dee, Dozy, Beaky, Mick and Tich (viz., David Harman, Trevor Davis, John Dymond, Michael Wilson and Ian Amey).

Daniel Defoe : It is believed that the original name of the illustrious author of *Robinson Crusoe* (1719) was Daniel Foe (although it may indeed have been Defoe), and that the "De" derives from the fact that he was known as Mr. D. Foe to distinguish him from his father, James Foe. If this was so, it was a happy acquisition, since "de" implies an aristocratic ancestry. See Appendix II, page 335.

Theodore de la Guard : In choosing this name for *The Simple Cobler of Aggawam* (1647), the English poet and satirist Nathaniel Ward adopted the Greek version of his Christian name (they both literally mean "gift of God") and a French rendering of his surname. The same name, therefore — only different!

Della Crusca : This was the name assumed by Robert Merry, the English poet, and leader of the so called Della Cruscan school of poetry (described as "silly and pretentious" by the *Oxford Companion to English Literature*). Merry was himself a member of the Florentine "Accademia della Crusca" (literally "academy of the chaff"), founded 1582, which had the aim of purifying (by "sifting") the Italian language. Other members of the Della Cruscan school took similarly obscure names, such as Anna Matilda, The Bard, Edwin, Laura, Mit Yenda, Morosoph Este, and °Anthony Pasquin. The poets met in Florence around 1785.

Joseph Delorme : The French literary critic Sainte-Beuve used this name for his *Vie, Poésies et Pensées de Joseph Delorme* (1829), a collection of romantic autobiographical poems. "Joseph Delorme" was supposedly a friend of Sainte-Beuve who had died as a young medical student.

Billy de Wolfe : William Andrew Jones (Bill Jones) was told by a theatre manager that his real name would not do for a star. Jones, therefore, took the manager's own surname.

Fra Diavolo : The semilegendary Italian brigand chief was real enough, as Michele Pezza. His name, literally "Brother Devil," originated as a nickname, given him by victimized peasants on account of his ferocity. Rumor had it, moreover, that Pezza had actually once been a monk named Fra Angelo! The brigand was the subject of Auber's opera *Fra Diavolo* (1830).

Bo Diddley : Does this name, adopted by the American black jazz musician Ellas McDaniel, have a meaning? According to Leonard Chess of Chess-Checker Records, who chose it, it means "funny storyteller." But, like the jazz expressions "bebop" and "boop-a-doop," it would seem to be at least partly of imitative inspiration. (McDaniel was in fact born Ellas Bates. His mother, however, was too poor to raise him and he was adopted by his mother's first cousin, a Sunday school teacher in Chicago, whose surname he assumed.)

Marlene Dietrich : The German born singer and film actress derived her first name from the telescoping of her first two real names, Marie Magdalene. Her true surname is variously given as either von Losch or Dietrich. Researchers maintain that she is almost certainly the second daughter of Louis Erich Otto Dietrich, an officer in the Royal Prussian Police, and Wilhelmina Elisabeth Josephine Felsing, who came from a well-known family of Berlin jewelers. A year or two after Marie was born the family moved to Weimar where, shortly after the death of her father, her mother remarried Edouard von Losch, who served with the

Grenadiers. Either way — or both — accounts of her early childhood are somewhat confused [1. Charles Higham, *Marlene: The Life of Marlene Dietrich*, 1978; 2. Sheridan Morley, *Marlene Dietrich*, 1978].

Dito und Idem : This was the joint pseudonym assumed by °Carmen Sylva and °George Allan as coauthors. The words are respectively Italian, German, and Latin, and translate as "the same and the same," a touch of aristocratic humor.

Don Leucadio Doblado : Another mixed-language pen name, a blend of Greek and Spanish meaning "double white." Quite appropriate, when you consider that it was adopted by the British theological writer Joseph Blanco White. White was the son of an Irish Roman Catholic father and an Andalusian mother, and was actually born in Spain.

Q.K. Philander Doesticks, P.B. : Only a classic American humorist could choose a name like this! The author was Mortimer Neal Thomson, and the name simply a frivolous one — although P.B. was said to stand for "Perfect Brick."

Anton Dolin : The British ballet dancer was born Patrick Healey-Kay. He assumed the Russian-sounding name in 1921, when he joined Diaghilev's Ballets Russes. Anton is said to have been in homage to Anton Chekhov; Dolin was apparently suggested by a fellow ballet student. Chekhov in fact died in the year Healey-Kay was born (1904) and Dolin is a genuine Russian surname.

Diana Dors : The British film actress, born Diana Mary Fluck, was nearly called Diana Scarlett, a name that her agent Gordon Harbord (who also named °Laurence Harvey and °Adrienne Corri) had chosen for her. But Diana was not keen on this, and her final stage name came about as described in her autobiography: "To be born with the name of Fluck, particularly if one is a girl, can be nothing less than disastrous. Originally my reason for changing it was no more than a young girl's ambition to become a film star ... but when I was cast in my first film the director tried gently to explain that the second part of my name would have to be altered.... I was only fourteen and did not quite understand his well meant reasoning then, but as I wished to call myself something much more exotic anyway, I agreed willingly, and the search for a new surname was on! My agent had suggested Scarlett ... and I toyed with that for a while. My own fantasy of Diana Carroll also seemed a possibility, but my father was incensed that the family name was not to be used.... Finally my mother in a moment of brilliance decided that I *would* stick to a family name after all, and because my grandmother's maiden name had been Dors, she felt it sounded good to have two names with the same initial. So Dors it was and we were all happy!" [Diana Dors, *Behind Closed Dors*, 1979].

Fifi Dorsay : Angelina D'Sablon, the Canadian-born American actress, claims that her surname was adopted from a bottle of French perfume and that "Fifi" was what other girls called her when she was in the Greenwich Village Follies chorus in the 1920s. Fifi is a typical French "Folies Bergères" name, and belongs to more or less the same filly stable as Gigi, Lili, and Mimi. The "Quai d'Orsay" is to the French what Downing Street or Whitehall is to the British, and as such "D'Orsay" would be a prestige brand name suitable for a high-class perfume.

Kirk Douglas : Issur Danielovitch Demsky chose his new forename because it sounded "snazzy" and his surname out of admiration for °Douglas Fairbanks, Jr. Since his adoption of the name (in 1941), Kirk has caught on as something of a vogue Christian name, especially in the United States and Canada. The fact that it also happens to mean "church" gives its popularity an added rugged respectability.

Kent Douglass : Robert Douglas Montgomery, who also acted as Robert Douglas, changed his name to Kent Douglass since (a) there already was a Robert Montgomery and (b) there was already a Robert Douglas. Tricky!

M.B. Drapier : A "nonce" pseudonym adopted by Jonathan Swift, of *Gulliver's Travels* fame. He used the name for *The Drapier's Letters* (1724), written by Swift in the guise of a Dublin draper. A patent had been granted to the Duchess of Kendal for supplying copper coins for use in Ireland, and this she sold to one William Wood for £10,000. The profit on the patent would have been, it is said, around £25,000, and Swift published four letters prophesying ruin to the Irish if "Wood's halfpence" were admitted into circulation. The letters were effective, and the government was forced to abandon the plan and to compensate Wood.

Joanne Dru : During her short stage career, Joanne La Cock acted as Joanne Marshall. Later, when she entered films, director Howard Hawkes rightly indicated to her that she needed a new name and she chose that of Dru, after a Welsh ancestor.

Thomas du Clévier : This was the name used by the French humanist Bonaventure Des Périers for his *Cymbalum Mundi* (1537) — four satirical dialogues in the style of Lucian. (The title literally means "the cymbal of the world"). Du Clévier is an anagram of French *incrédule* ("unbeliever"), with Thomas referring to the biblical Doubting Thomas. The work was supposedly translated by du Clévier, who sent it to his friend Tryocan. But this, too, was a pseudonym of Des Périers, and an anagram of *croyant* ("believer").

Bob Dylan : Robert Alan Zimmerman, the rock musician, poet, and composer, allegedly chose his new name in homage to the Welsh poet Dylan Thomas, officially adopting it on August 9, 1962.

Jean Effel : The French cartoonist François Lejeune based his assumed surname on his initials F.L. (pronounced in French as in English), preceding this with the most popular of French forenames. He thus arrived at a handy, short name with which to sign his works. Compare °Erté, a similarly formed name.

Philippe Égalité : Louis Philippe Joseph, duc d'Orléans, assumed his (literally) egalitarian name in order to court the favor of the people when be became Deputy for Paris (1792) in the Convention Nationale. In the Convention he voted for the death of Louis XVI, his cousin — and was himself executed the following year.

George Egerton : Mary Chavelita Dunne, the Australian-born novelist, was married three times: first to H.H.W. Melville, who died the year after their marriage (1888), second to Egerton Clairmonte, who died in 1901, and third to Reginald Goldring Bright. Her pseudonym thus derives from the name of her second husband. Her father wrote as Hi-Regan.

Elia : Charles Lamb, the well known British writer, first used his pen name in his *Essays of Elia*, which appeared in *The London Magazine* in 1820-1823. The subject of the first essay was an Italian clerk named Elia who worked at South Sea House, headquarters of the East India Company, where Charles Lamb had worked and where his brother was still working at the time of the appearance of the *Essays*. The name was said to have been pronounced "Ellia."

George Eliot : Mary Ann (later Marian) Evans, the famous author of *The Mill on the Floss* (1860), took her male name from that of her lover, the philosopher and writer George Henry Lewes (who himself wrote as °Slingsby Lawrence). Her surname she chose because it was a "fully-mouthed, easily-pronounceable name." She first used her pen name in 1858 for her novel entitled *Scenes of Clerical Life*. Two years after the death of Lewes in 1878 Marian Evans married John Walter Cross, an American banker. She died that same year, but Cross lived on until 1924. Such is the generally accepted story behind her name. In his original book *Pribbles and Prabbles* (1906), however, Major-General Patrick Maxwell points out an unusual coincidence: that some time in the 1840s a young officer of the Bengal cavalry called George Donnithorne Eliot was accidentally drowned in a lake in the Himalayas. Not only does this officer's name contain the pen-name assumed by Marian Evans, but in her *Adam Bede* (1859) there is a character named Arthur Donnithorne. That the Bengal officer was, however, an early flame of Marian Evans seems unlikely, although the young authoress could have read about him.

Erté : In a similar manner to °Jean Effel, the Russian-born French costume designer Romain de Tirtoff used his initials for his pseudonym — R.T., pronounced (approximately) "air-tay."

Dr. Esperanto : Most people have heard of the famous artificial world language Esperanto, but perhaps not so many realize that the name of the language is the pseudonym of its inventor, Dr. Ludovik Zamenhof, a Polish physician. He used the name, which translates as "Dr. Hoping-one," for his book introducing the language, *Langue Internationale; Préface et Manuel Complet* (1887).

Partenio Etiro : We still do not know the real name of the Italian satirist who thus formed an anagrammatic pseudonym from his more familiar name Pietro Aretino. He used it for an edition of his satires that was published posthumously (1558), the change being necessary as he was already on the Vatican's list of banned authors, the *Index Librorum Prohibitorum*.

Eusebio : The Portuguese but Mozambiquan-born football player simply used his own Christian name, his full name being Eusebio Ferreira da Silva. Eusebio is the Portuguese form of Eusebius, more familiar to English-speakers as a rather remote saint's name. It actually derives from the Greek word for "pious."

Evoe : Edmund George Valpy Knox, the British essayist and humorist, was editor of *Punch* from 1932 to 1949. His pen name is a blend of the initials of two of his names and the Latin cry *evoe* (from Greek *euoi*) given as an exclamation of joy in Bacchic rites.

Philippe Fabre d'Églantine : The French playwright and revolutionary politician Philippe Fabre — who introduced the charming names of the months in the Revolutionary calendar (Vendémiaire, Brumaire, Germinal, Fructidor, etc.) and the purely functional names of the days of the week (Primidi, Duodi, Tridi, etc.) — assumed his pseudonym after winning the "Prix de l'Églantine" ("Wild Rose Prize") at the "Jeux Floraux" of Toulouse in his youth, a prize that some say he won under a false claim.

Fabulous Moolah : The champion American woman wrestler was born Lillian Ellison. She began her career in the ring at a tender age as *Slave Girl Moolah*, the "prop" of a wrestler called Elephant Boy. Her ring name originated as a nickname, from her announcement that she intended to wrestle for "all the moolah [money] I can get my hands on." She seems to have succeeded, since in the 1970s she was claiming to earn more than $100,000 a year.

Douglas Fairbanks : The film actor who was born Julius Ullman was the son of Hezekiah Charles Ullman and Ella Adelaide Marsh. When his parents divorced in the year after he was born (1884), his mother assumed the name of her first husband John Fairbanks. Douglas Fairbanks took this name legally in 1900 and of course passed it on to his son, Douglas Fairbanks, Jr.

Adam Faith : Terence Nelhams, the British pop singer, chose the name himself for the radio series *Six Five Special*, with Adam coming from the boys' section of a book of names for children, and Faith from the same book's girls' names. Nelhams commented on his choice: "I liked the sound of Adam. Adam, the first man. Short. Sweet. Easily memorised." Of Faith he said, "I liked the note of courage in it. Adam Faith. Yes, they seemed to match up" [Adam Faith, *Poor Me*, 1961].

Georgie Fame : Also a pop musician of the generation of Adam Faith (both born early 1940s). The name was given to Clive Powell by rock-'n'-roll producer Larry Parnes, who had said, "The next kid to walk through my door, I'm gonna call Georgie Fame."

Walli Farrad : This is one of the many names assumed by the Black Muslim leader Wallace D. Fard, who became prominent in the 1930s in America. He is now revered by Black Muslims as Master Wallace Fard Muhammad, and to him are assigned all the attributes of God (Allah), so that he is referred to as "Creator of Heaven and Earth, Most Wise, All Knowing, Most Merciful, All Powerful, Finder and Life-Giver, Master of the Day of Judgment." Understandably one of the criticisms leveled at the Black Muslims by orthodox Muslims is that they worship Wallace Fard rather than Allah of the "true" Islam. Among the other names used by Fard were: Professor Ford, Farrad Mohammed, F. Mohammed Ali, Wallace Fard Muhammad, and God (Allah). His divinity was reinforced by his mysterious disappearance around 1935.

Irving Fazola : The American jazz clarinettist Irving Henry Prestopnik concocted his new surname from the three musical notes *fa, so, la* (otherwise F, G, and A).

N. Felix : In quite a different world from Faith and Fame, N. Felix was a schoolmaster at Blackheath and a noted cricketer. For this most English of sports, the real name of the expert was an un-English one, Nicholas Wanostrocht. He used his pen name for his writings on cricket, including the primer *Felix on the Bat* — a book sometimes found in the natural history section of public libraries. Felix also invented the "catapulta," a mechanical bowler.

Fernandel : The mother-in-law of the French film comedian born Fernand-Joseph-Désiré Contandin used to refer to him as "Fernand d'elle," that is, *her* Fernand — meaning her daughter's, not her own.

Stepin Fetchit : The American black film actor Lincoln Theodore Perry derived his name from the playful request sometimes put to him meaning "go get it," the joke being that he was slow moving.

Michael ffolkes : Behind this idiosyncratic name lies the identity of the British cartoonist, Brian Davis. He explains how his name came about: "I've always had a kind of attraction for multiple identity. I got ffolkes from *Burke's Peerage*. As an unusual name it has been very valuable. It was about the time of Sprods and Trogs and Smilbys [see °Trog and Smilby]. I wanted a distinctive name. I don't think *Punch* knows, actually.... Originally I wanted to write and called myself Brian Chorister, horrible name. Then I tried using the name Dedalus, based on the James Joyce character.... I had just read Joyce. It shows a tendency to want to get away from the ordinariness of being Davis. Davis, plain Davis, is one of the commonest names in the country" [Michael Bateman, *Funny Way to Earn a Living*, 1966].

Gracie Fields : A theatrical agent advised that the surname of Grace Stansfield was too long to appear on a theatre, so the popular British singer's mother shortened it thus. For a time (1940-1950) "Our Gracie" was married to °Monty Banks.

W.C. Fields : William Claude Dukinfield adopted this as his most sober of stage names. All the many others ranged from the bizarre to the grotesque, and were in the best tradition of American humorous pseudonyms. (For a selection, see Chapter 6). As an appetizer, note the (admittedly rather tame) first name that he assumed when he started his career as a boy juggler (1891) this was simply "Whitey, the Wonder Boy." He first used W.C. Fields in 1893. Claude was a name that he had always hated; the villains in his films were often called Claude. Many of the names that he subsequently adopted were based on the names used by Charles Dickens, whose books he admired [Carlotta Monti with Cy Rice, *W.C. Fields and Me*, 1974].

Barry Fitzgerald : William Shields, the Irish film actor, started his career as a dual personality — he was a civil servant by day, and an actor by night. He adopted his stage name for fear of losing his job.

Bud Flanagan : Might the British comic, of Flanagan and Allen fame, have made it under his original name — his parents were Polish Jews — of Chaim Reuben Weintrop? He first trod the boards of the music hall as Fargo the Boy Conjuror. This was in London. At the age of 13 he emigrated with his family to the United States and, after a brief interlude as a boxer with the unlikely ring name of Luke McGluke, tried his fortune on the vaudeville stage as Bobby Wayne. Back in Britain again at the start of the First World War he joined the army as Driver Robert Winthrop. But why Flanagan? The name was inherited from his army years. Apparently a mean sergeant-major seemed to have it in for the future actor and singer, and when Driver Winthrop was wounded in 1918 and took his leave of the service, his last words to his sergeant-major were, "I'll remember your name as long as I live." Flanagan, thus, was the name he assumed when resuming his career on the stage. (Later the sergeant-major became a barman in London, and Bud and he were reconciled.) After Flanagan and Allen's famous song *Underneath the Arches* was published in 1932 the profits began to roll in handsomely. With his share, Bud bought a house in the village of Angmering, Sussex, and named it *Arches*. His actual first break in show business was given him by Florrie Forde — see this name! [Bill McGowran, "You See Him Everywhere," in *Late Extra: A Miscellany by "Evening News" Writers, Artists, and Photographers*, Associated Newspapers, c1952].

Fléchelles : Hugues Guéru, the classic French actor, used this name for tragedies. For comedies — actually coarse farces — he adopted the name Gaultier-Garguille. He worked with La Fleur and °Belleville as one of a trio.

Floridor : The 17th-century French actor Josias de Soulas, Sieur de Prinefosse, who assumed this name, was for a while associated with Filandre, otherwise Jean-Baptiste de Mouchaingre, an actor and manager who is said to have been Floridor's teacher. Floridor succeeded Bellerose, real name Pierre le Messier, as head of the Hôtel de Bourgogne theatre in Paris. The names of all three theatrical gentlemen are typical of the cool, classical fashion of the day, meaning respectively "golden flower," "lover of man," and "beautiful rose."

Florizel : A royal pseudonym — that assumed by George IV of England when Prince of Wales for his correspondence with Mrs. Robinson, the actress. Florizel is a character in Shakespeare's *A Winter's Tale* who falls in love with Perdita. When Mrs. Robinson first attracted the Prince's attention she was playing Perdita...

Joan Fontaine : Joan de Beauvoir de Havilland was born in Japan of English parents. In her teens she played small roles as Joan Burfield and Joan St. Joan. She adopted the name Joan Fontaine in 1937, following her mother's divorce and subsequent remarriage to George M. Fontaine. (Joan's elder sister, by one year, is Olivia de Havilland).

Margot Fonteyn : The British ballet dancer who married Roberto E. Arías, the Panamanian ambassador in London, was born Margaret Hookham. She first changed her name to Margot Fontes, based on her Brazilian mother's maiden name; then, on the advice of Ninette de Valois, changed this to Margot Fonteyn [Margot Fonteyn, *Autobiography*, 1975].

Ford Madox Ford : The British novelist and founder of the *English Review* (1908) was born Ford Hermann Hueffer. He added the Christian names Joseph Leopold Madox — he was the grandson of the Victorian painter Ford Madox Brown — and, embarrassed in the First World War by his German surname, changed his name by deed poll (1919) to Ford Madox Ford. On the title pages of his books his name alternated between Ford Madox Ford and Ford Madox Hueffer: he used the former for his sequence of war novels with the central character Christopher Tietgens as well as for travel books and reminiscences. For *The Questions at the Well; With Sundry Other Verses for Notes of Music* (1893) he had earlier used the name Fenil Haig.

Gerald Ford : The 38th President of the United States was born Leslie Lynch King. When he was a baby, his parents were divorced and his mother moved to Grand Rapids where she married Gerald R. Ford, Sr., who adopted him and gave him his name.

Forez : When working for the French Resistance, François Mauriac the novelist and poet wrote *Cahier Noir* (1943), choosing for this the name of the mountainous region in the Massif Central that Resistance workers found suitable for cover.

George Formby : The famous comedian, singer and ukelele player born George Hoy Booth (Hoy was his mmn) took the same stage name as his father, James Lawler Booth. How did Booth Senior come to acquire his name? As a young millworker, James would supplement his small wages by singing in the street, where he was "discovered" by a Mr. Brown, together with another boy who had teamed up with him, and sent to different Northern towns to earn a shilling or two for his "manager." Mr. Brown would pay James threepence a week and the other boy sixpence. To cut his expenses, Mr. Brown transported the boys in the traveling props basket, with the lid down, to avoid paying their train fares. "On one occasion, when they were travelling from Manchester to Bury, Jimmy happened not to be in the basket and sat watching coal wagons go by. A sign on one of the wagons showed that it came from Formby, Lancashire. The name appealed to him. He preferred it, in a theatrical sense, to his own name of Booth and decided there and then to make it his own. But Jimmy or James did not go with it. Beginning with the first letter of the alphabet he went through in his mind all the names he could think of and stopped when he got to 'G' and George. That was it — George Formby. It sounded right. It suited him. His change of name coincided with his desire to end the singing partnership" [Alan Randall and Ray Seaton, *George Formby*, 1974].

Susanna Foster : Susan Larson, the American film actress who starred as an opera singer in the 1940s, combined the names of Stephen Foster and the subject of his song, *Oh, Susanna*. There's a nice musical tribute. Foster's way with women resulted in more than one compliment: see also, for example, °Nelly Bly.

Fougasse : The British artist and cartoonist who was also editor of *Punch* (in succession to °Evoe) was born Cyril Kenneth Bird. He adopted the unusual name Fougasse so as to avoid confusion with another *Punch* artist named Bird, explaining later that "fougasse" was an old technical term used by sappers for a rough-and-ready landmine that might or might not go off. He presumably hoped that most of his pictorial and verbal quips *would* go off.

Redd Foxx : The rather extravagant name has a logical origin. John Elroy Sanford, the American comedian, was already nicknamed Chicago Red (for the Chicago baseball team), and to this he added an extra "d," taking his surname then from the great baseball player Jimmie Foxx (who at one stage played for Chicago).

Anatole France : The French novelist and writer Jacques Anatole François Thibault acquired his pseudonym not so much to emphasize his nationality as for the fact that his father, who owned a bookshop, was called by customers "Monsieur France" (instead of François).

Francis of Assisi : The great saint, founder of the Franciscan order, by origin an Italian monk and preacher, was born Giovanni di Pietro di Bernardone. His father, Pietro di Bernardone, was away on business in France at the time of his son's birth, and on his return changed the baby's name to Francesco (i.e., Francis) as a memorial to his visit.

Greta Garbo : That the Swedish born film star was originally Greta Lovisa Gustafsson there is little doubt. Exactly how she acquired her well known stage surname is rather more uncertain. The name is generally thought to have been given her by the Swedish film director Mauritz Stiller (although it is possible that someone other than Stiller was responsible for the name). But how did he devise it? One version says that he "toyed with Gabor after Gabor Bethlen, an ancient Hungarian king, then settled on the variation, Garbo" [Norman Zierold, *"Garbo,"* 1970].

One of the most detailed accounts of the origin of the name is given by Garbo's biographer, Robert Payne: "The name, which became so memorable, was the invention of Mauritz Stiller, who had long cherished it and was determined to bestow it on an actress worthy of it. In his imagination the name suggested fairyland, romance, beauty, everything he had associated in his childhood with the utmost happiness and the wildest dreams. Many explanations were later offered to explain the name. Someone wrote that he derived it from the first letters of a sentence he wrote describing Greta Gustafsson: *Gör alla roller berömvärt opersonligt* ("Plays all roles in a commendably impersonal fashion"). Others remembered that *garbo* in Spanish and Italian is a rarely used word describing a peculiar kind of grace and charm. Still others imagined it was derived from the name of Erica Darbo, a famous Norwegian singer of the time. A more plausible explanation can be found in the *garbon*, a mysterious sprite that sometimes comes out at night to dance to the moonbeams. This elfin creature was a descendant of the dreaded *gabilun* of Swedish and German folklore, who was killed by Kudrun. The *gabilun* breathed fire from its nostrils and could assume any shape at will, and some memory of his ancient power remained in the *garbon*, just as Robin Goodfellow retains some features of the Great God Pan. No one knows the true origin of the word. When asked about it, Stiller simply looked up in the air, smiled, and said, 'I really don't know. But it's right, isn't it?'" [Robert Payne, *The Great Garbo*, 1976].

Yet another theory, put forward by Frederick Sands and Sven Broman in their biography [*The Divine Garbo*, 1979], is that Greta had visited some relatives from time to time who live on a farm called "Garboda," and that this might perhaps be the explanation. The change was at any rate made officially on December 4, 1923. Finally, as if all this mystery was not enough, Garbo at times used other pseudonyms, if only to escape from a "Garbo"-saturated society. Among these other names were Harriet Brown (her favorite), Gussie Berger, Mary Holmquist, Jean Clark, Karin Lund, Miss Swanson, Emily Clark, Jane Emerson, Alice Smith, and the unexpected male name Karl Lund.

Judy Garland : Frances Ethel Gumm changed her name in 1934 or 1935, when she was still only 12, for a singing act that she performed with her sisters (as the Gumm Sisters, who were on one occasion wrongly billed as the Glum Sisters). Young? Well, yes. But then Frances Gumm was one of the greatest child film stars, playing Dorothy in *The Wizard of Oz* when she was still in her teens. Her new name was given her by her agent, George Jessel, who based it on the name of *New York Post* theatre critic Robert Garland and the song *Judy*, by Hoagy Carmichael. This was popular at the time and her favorite—especially the line that went, "If she seems a saint, and you find she ain't, that's Judy!"

Pearly Gates : Viola Billups, the black American popular singer, was so named by her manager Bruce Welch, who told her she had "better learn how to spell it." But how else could you spell such a heavenly name?

Paul Gavarni : The French illustrator and caricaturist was born Sulpice Chevalier. He acquired his "canvas name" by a curious mistake. He once sent his paintings to a Paris exhibition from the Pyrenean village of Gavarnie. When displayed, the pictures were erroneously labeled as being by "Gavarnie." In fact the exhibition was a success, and the previously unknown artist thus became known by the name of the remote mountain village – with a slight adjustment of spelling.

Noel Gay : When Reginald Armitage was director of music and organist at St. Anne's Church, Soho, London, he took to writing popular songs and subsequently became a music publisher of such songs. Not wishing to embarrass the church authorities – a church organist writing musicals, indeed! – he changed his name euphoniously and briefly to Noel Gay.

Genghis Khan : The great Mongol conqueror was originally named Temujin, or Temuchin. He adopted the title Genghis (or Chingis), meaning "perfect warrior" in 1206, adding the Khan to mean "lord" or "prince."

Geraldo : The British danceband leader Gerald Bright adopted this name after a visit to Brazil.

William Gerhardie : The Russian-born English writer was born William Gerhardi. During the 1960s he added a final "e" to his name, saying that Dante, Shakespeare, Racine, Goethe and Blake had "e's" so why not he? [*The Times*, July 16, 1977].

Domenico Ghirlandaio : Domenico di Tommaso Bigordi, the 15th-century Florentine painter, was famous for his frescoes. His new name was based on his father's skill in making garlands (Italian *ghirlanda*).

John Gilbert : There must be several instances where one person casts off a name, and another adopts it. This was so with John Pringle, the American film actor who became John Gilbert, and Aileen Bisbee, the American film actress, who became Aileen Pringle!

Gertie Gitana : The attractive alliterative name was adopted by the British music hall star Gertrude Mary Astbury, famous for her rendering of the song *Nellie Dean*. Her surname derives from the Spanish for "gypsy": the first troupe she played with wore gypsy costumes.

Gary Glitter : The British pop star was born Paul Gadd. His stage name would appear to have been a former nickname, although Glitter himself says it was "a name derived from a think-tank with some friends" [*Radio Times*, August 8, 1974]. For a time he used the name Paul Raven, and for one single, *Here Comes the Sun* (1967), he was Paul Monday.

Samuel Goldwyn : One of the greatest, "gold-winning" names of film production. The movie mogul was born in Poland, with his original American name of Goldfish (sic) being an immigration authority translation of his Polish name. In 1917 he and his two brothers Edgar and Arch Selwyn formed the Goldwyn Pictures Corporation — with Goldwyn thus being a blend of *Gold*fish and Sel*wyn*. (Changed the other way round he would have been Samuel Selfish!) He changed his name legally in 1919. See the epigraph at the head of Chapter 4 for a legal comment.

Maxim Gorky : The Russian writer was born Aleksei Peshkov. Early in his career he identified closely with the ordinary Russians and lived "among the people," sharing their poverty and daily struggle for existence. For many such folk life was hard — hence his name *Gorky*, Russian for "bitter." He first used the name for his story *Makar Chudra* (1892). The name had in fact been used by earlier writers, e.g., in the early works of the poet I.A. Belousov (1863-1930).

Jeremias Gotthelf : Albert Bitzius, the 19th-century Swiss novelist and short story writer was professionally a pastor, with strong Christian principles. He thus changed his name so as to express his ideal. Jeremias for the great Old Testament prophet, whose name means "May Jehovah raise up," and Gotthelf as the German for "God's help." Much more lofty than Albert Bitzius!

Sheilah Graham : The English writer and biographer and companion (1937-1940) to Scott Fitzgerald was born Lily Sheil. In 1927 she married Major John Graham Gillam and in the 1930s went to Hollywood where she became a gossip columnist. She once commented, "The name Lily Sheil, to this day, horrifies me to a degree impossible to explain." Her new name was presumably based on her original surname and her husband's second name.

Stewart Granger : James Lablache Stewart changed his name to avoid possible confusion with the American film actor James Stewart, born five years before him. Apart from this, as an English actor he was governed by the rules of Equity, the actors' union, which says that no two actors can have the same name.

Cary Grant : How did the British-born film actor Alexander Archibald Leach, who settled in America in 1921 and took his new name in 1942 when adopting American citizenship, come to choose this particular pseudonym? The story goes that a friend, Fay Wray, suggested he should use the name of the character he had played in the musical comedy "Nikki," Cary Lockwood. Alexander Leach liked Cary but not Lockwood. So, "someone rummaged in a desk and brought out a notebook filled with page after page of names.... They came up with 'Grant' ... I said it was fine" [Albert Govoni, *Cary Grant: An Unauthorized Biography*, 1973].

Ingahild Grathmer : The name became something of a literary *cause célèbre* in 1977, when the British Folio Society published an edition of J.R.R. Tolkien's *The Lord of the Rings* with "illustrations by Ingahild Grathmer: drawn by Eric Fraser." But who was Ingahild Grathmer? In its issue of October 6, 1977, *The Times* blew the story. It reproduced one of the illustrations from the book with the announcement that they had been "drawn by Queen Margrethe of Denmark" who "uses the pseudonym Ingahild Grathmer." Two days later, a letter to the editor of *The Times* appeared from John Letts, director of the Folio Society, stating, in part: "Some six years ago, Queen Margrethe drew a set of illustrations, out of private enthusiasm, and, with no thought of publication, sent them to Tolkien. Somewhat unexpectedly ... he approved these designs warmly. After his death, they were found among his files; and his literary heirs suggested that they, too, would approve their use in the new illustrated edition the Folio Society was already planning. Queen Margrethe ... kindly agreed to collaborate with Eric Fraser ... and the work was published under a pseudonym. Obviously we are sorry that the anonymity has been broken. But we imagine that the pseudonymous Ingahild Grathmer would also be sorry that you have published a reproduction from this first edition which gives no credit either to Eric Fraser, or to the publishers...." Astute readers will have spotted that the Danish queen's pseudonym is based on an anagram of her real name.

    Larry Grayson : The English TV entertainer born William White had his name changed by his agent Evelyn Taylor in 1956. Earlier (1950) he was appearing in shows in the Midlands as Billy Breen. The metamorphosis is not quite so radical: Larry is a name on the same lines as Billy, but more stylish, and Grayson must somehow be related to White!

    Beryl Grey : The famous ballerina was born Beryl Groom. Dame Ninette de Valois suggested the new name when Beryl was still a girl of 14. "I called her Beryl Grey because there was an easy flow to it. If she had remained Groom people would have called her Broom or something. It's not a ballet name." A few months later Dame Ninette suggested "Iris Grey," but Beryl resisted this. It took her about twenty years to get used to her new name [David Gillard, *Beryl Grey: A Biography*, 1977].

    Joel Grey : The American stage actor was born Noel Katz. His father formed a group called Mickey Katz and His Kittens. When the father changed this name to Mickey Kats and His Kosher Jammers, Joel went on the stage alone as Joel Kaye, later changing this to Joel Grey [*The Times*, May 15, 1976].

    Grey Owl : Archibald Belaney was known for his books on the Canadian Indians, especially the bestseller *Pilgrims of the Wild* (1935). Himself an Englishman, his father had married in America a woman alleged by him to be of Indian descent. Archibald's pen name was that of an Indian chief — in the native form, Wa-sha-quon-asin.

    Grock : The Swiss clown who began life as Adrien Wettach had originally been a partner of a clown named Brick, whose former partner had been Brock. Grock went well with Brick but was different from Brock. For similar clown pair-names see °Bim.

Guercino : A name that as with several painters derives from a nickname referring to a physical characteristic; it means "squint-eyed," which Giovanni Barbieri alas was. It did not seem to matter that such characteristics were undesirable for the nickname to become a pseudonym: compare °O Aleijadinho and the morally avoidable °Sodoma.

Che Guevara : Argentines have a verbal mannerism in that they punctuate their speech with the interjection ¡*che!* The word became the nickname of Ernesto Guevara de la Serna, the Argentine turned Cuban socialist revolutionary, who subsequently adopted it as a forename.

Johannes Gutenberg : The 15th-century German printer who invented printing by means of moveable type was understandably anxious to change his real name of Gensfleisch, which means "gooseflesh." He therefore adopted his mmn, which conveniently began with the same letter as his own surname.

Gyp : Sibylle Gabrielle Marie Antoinette, née de Riquetti de Mirabeau, comtesse de Martel de Janville, must feature somewhere in this book, if only as a record conversion from a lengthy real name to the briefest of pseudonyms. She was the French novelist who introduced the literary phenomenon known as the "enfant terrible," who first made his appearance in her *Petit Bob* (1882).

Haile Selassie : The name assumed by Ras Tafari Makonnen, the last of the emperors of Ethiopia, was actually a title, meaning "power of the Trinity." Even his real "forename" Ras is a title, meaning "prince." He adopted his new titular name in 1930, on assuming full authority as emperor. His original name was passed to the Rastafarians or "Rastas," the Jamaican cult who regard him as God.

Brett Halliday : The American author of "private eye" stories was born Davis Dresser. His new surname came from the name of the detective in his first novel. His publisher, however, had not liked the name Halliday and had changed it to Burke. The publisher's own name was Brett — and this was the one adopted by Dresser as his new forename. Among other names used by Dresser for pulp magazine short stories were Matthew Blood, Peter Shelley, Anthony Scott, Don Davis, Anderson Wayne, Hal Debrett (jointly with Kathleen Rollins), Asa Baker (for his first mystery), Sylvia Carson, and Kathryn Culver.

Emma Hamilton : This was the famous Lady Hamilton, Nelson's mistress. Her surname was not properly a pseudonym, although her Christian name was modified. She was born (1765) Amy Lyon. At the age of 16 she was calling herself Emily Hart when she began to live with the nephew of the man who was to become her husband, Sir William Hamilton. (The nephew was Charles Francis Greville.) At the time of her marriage (1791) she was thus 26 — and her husband 61.

Gail Hamilton : Mary Abigail Dodge was an American writer noted for her support for women's suffrage in the second half of the 19th century. Her new forename derives from her original middle name, with Hamilton from her home town in Massachusetts.

Cyril Hare : By profession, Alfred Clark was a lawyer and judge; by repute he was an author of crime novels. After his marriage (1933) he settled in Cyril Mansions, Battersea, London, being at the time employed at Hare Court, Temple. The two place-names provided his pseudonym as a writer.

Laurence Harvey : The actor who starred mainly in American films but also in some British movies was Lithuanian-born Larushka (originally Hirsch) Mischa Skikne. His name was changed by his agent, Gordon Harbord, who was also responsible for rechristening Adrienne Riccoboni as °Adrienne Corri and who wanted to rename Diana Fluck — who actually became °Diana Dors — as Diana Scarlett. Harbord usually tried to evolve a name from a person's relatives, especially his mother's maiden name. But Larry Skikne's mother's name had been Zotnik, which didn't help. Harbord therefore chose Harvey as "the most English name he could think of" (as in the Knightsbridge store Harvey Nichols). In a private letter the new "English" actor wrote, "Another regrettable thing has happened over which I have no control: this time it is something more personal — they have changed my name because it was suddenly decided by the distributors that it wasn't *commercial*, so I am now known as 'Laurence Harvey'. O, this too, too unfortunate society!" [Des Dickey and Gus Smith, *The Prince: Being the Public and Private Life of Larushka Mischa Skikne, a Jewish Lithuanian Vagabond Player otherwise known as Laurence Harvey*, 1975].

O. Henry : The famous American short story writer was born William Sydney (earlier Sidney) Porter. Be it noted here and now, incidentally, that his pen name is just so, not, as is sometimes seen, "O'Henry." Porter first used the name for his story *Whistling Dick's Christmas Stocking* (1899) written in prison at Columbus, Ohio, where he was serving a sentence for embezzlement (as a result of obtaining money for his sick wife). The pseudonym is sometimes said to have been taken from one of the prison guards, Orrin Henry, but the commonly accepted version of the origin says that it is presumed to be an abbreviation of the name of a French pharmacist, Etienne-Ossian Henry, found in the *U.S. Dispensatory*. This last was a reference work used by Porter when he was working as a prison pharmacist.

Audrey Hepburn : The pretty, "gamine" American film actress was originally Belgian-born Edda Hepburn van Heemstra. She is not related to Katharine Hepburn, although the latter actress was also involved in a name change — when she married Ogden Smith she insisted on changing his name to Ogden Ludlow so that she wouldn't become Kate Smith! Not that she even became Kate Ludlow… [*Village Voice*, January 10, 1977].

Aleksandr Herzen : The real surname of the Russian revolutionary writer, philosopher and publicist (whose assumed name is phonetically more correctly rendered as Gerzen) was Yakovlev. At least, that was his father's name. Aleksandr was an illegitimate child, with his mother a German, Luise Haag. The boy's new name, since he was a "love child," was invented by the father and based on the German for "heart" — *Herz*.

William Hickey : The name has become a kind of "house" name for the gossip columnists of the London *Daily Express*. The original William Hickey was the author of a number of diverting (even "racy") *Memoirs* (1749-1809), first published 1913-1925. The name was first used on the newspaper by the columnist and Member of Parliament, Tom Driberg, who was on the *Express* from 1928 to 1943. A well-known successor to the name was the author James Leasor, who was the paper's columnist from 1948 to 1955.

H.L.L. : Together with her sister, Sarah Borthwick Findlater, the Scottish hymnwriter Jane Maurie Borthwick made a series of translations (1854-62) from the German, entitling the work *Hymns from the Land of Luther*. Jane adopted the initials of the title as her pseudonym.

John Oliver Hobbes : This unremarkable male name in fact belonged to Pearl Richards — better known by her married name of Mrs. Craigie, the American novelist. (Pearl's family settled in England when she was very young — less than a year old). She chose the name Hobbes because it was "homely." So "hob" (by the hearth), "hobby" and "hob-nob" — that's what's in *this* name. For another homely name see °Evelyn Home.

Ho Chi Minh : The former president of North Vietnam was born Nguyen That Thanh. He first (in 1917) became an active socialist in France as Nguyen Ai Quoc ("Nguyen the patriot"). When he went to China (1924) he assumed the name Ly Thuy. In about 1940 he became Ho Chi Minh ("he who enlightens"). Before this, however, he had also used the names Song Man Tcho, Nguyen O Phap, and Nguyen Sinh Chin.

William Holden : A Paramount executive said that the film actor's real name, William F. Beedle, "sounds like an insect," so renamed him (1958) after a newspaper friend.

Evelyn Home : The popular British "agony columnist," whose long and honorable tenure of the office in the magazine *Woman* ran from 1937 to 1974, was born Peggy Carn. (She herself married after three years in this advisory capacity — her married name is Makins). The name was one she inherited on the magazine, and derives from Eve, symbolizing womanhood, and (obviously) Home, conjuring up domestic bliss. The name itself was first chosen by a German Jewish woman psychologist who was writing for *Woman* when Peggy Carn took over. Commenting on the name in her autobiography, the retired columnist was to write: "The 'Evelyn' contained Eve, the archetypal mother, the temptress, the sexy side of woman; the 'home' was what every woman is supposed to want. At the time I thought the name too phony to be taken seriously ever; I was totally mistaken" [Peggy Makins, *The Evelyn Home Story*, 1975]. When the post was assumed by Anna Raeburn (under her real name) in 1974, the pseudonym was abandoned.

Bob Hope : The American film comedian (actually British-born, although he left his native shores when he was four) was originally Leslie Townes Hope. It was "Leslie" that really prompted the change: in the first place it was ambiguous in gender (Leslie/Lesley), and secondly Les Hope was nicknamed "Hopeless" at school. So "Bob" came to the rescue. Would he have changed it if he had not entered a career on the stage?

Hedda Hopper : The American film actress and gossip columnist Elda Furry grew up to marry the comedian De Wolf Hopper in 1913. Her husband had been married four times already — and his wives had been called Ella, Ida, Edna, and Nella. In view of the similarity of these names, and of Elda's own resemblance to them, a numerologist was consulted. The recommendation given was that she should take the name Hedda. But was that really so different?

Harry Houdini : The American escapologist was keen to escape his real name of Erik Weisz. Houdini he assumed in admiration of the French illusionist Jean Robert Houdin, but where did Harry come from? One account maintains it, too, derives from a magician — the American Harry Kellar. But another explanation claims that it evolved gradually — from Erik to Ehrich to Ehrie to Erie to Harry! This seems much more like the emergence of an escapologist, slowly but surely, from his confinement.

Frankie Howerd : A subtle yet distinctive change of name. The popular British comedian was born Francis Howard. Frankie himself explains the reasoning behind the change in his autobiography: "It seems to me that there were too many Howards: among them Trevor, Sidney and Arthur. So how to stay Howard, yet alter it? I hit on the idea of a change of spelling: Howerd — which, I argued, would have the added advantage of making people look twice because they assumed it to be a misprint" [Frankie Howerd, *On The Way I Lost It*, 1976].

Rock Hudson : How did Roy Fitzgerald acquire this famed cinematic name? It was given him by a talent scout for Selznick Studios, Henry Willson, who "discovered" the actor in 1946 and named him after the Rock of Gibraltar and the Hudson River. (The story goes that he had considered Crash and Brick before settling for the rugged Rock). Years later Hudson said, "I blushed when I was given that name. I still haven't got used to it. So much so that I still have occasional difficulty pronouncing it."

Engelbert Humperdinck : Gerry Dorsey — formally Arnold George Dorsey — took his name from the German classical composer (1854-1921), best known for his opera *Hansel and Gretel*. It was suggested to Dorsey in 1965 when the British pop singer's manager, Gordon Mills, was looking through some old records of works by the German composer. Dorsey officially adopted the name the following year.

Kim Hunter : The American actress had her name changed by David O. Selznick, who told her that Janet Cole, her real name, could be anyone, but that Kim Hunter had individuality and with a name like this she would go far as an actress.

Betty Hutton : Elizabeth Thornburg's name was thus changed (1937) by Vincent Lopez, a Detroit bandleader, after a numerologist had been consulted. Betty's sister Marion also changed her surname to Hutton.

Michael Innes : John Innes Mackintosh Stewart, professionally a (now retired) university English lecturer, is best known under his pen name as a writer of detective novels. The pseudonym derives from the Christian names of two of his sons. On one occasion he was amused to find himself credited with being the father of Michael Stewart, the economist and author of *Keynes and After* (1967). J.I.M. Stewart has written critical studies under his real name.

Henry Irving : John Henry Brodribb was the first British actor to be knighted (1895) for his services to the theatre. He changed his name in order to avoid embarrassing his parents, who were ashamed of his profession. His new surname was a tribute to two real Irvings: Edward Irving, a popular Scottish religious writer, and Washington Irving, his favorite boyhood author.

Iskander : °Alexander Herzen, the Russian revolutionary writer, used the Turkish form of his first name as a pseudonym, first writing under it in 1940, for *Notes of a Young Man*. For a similarly derived name, see °Skanderbeg.

Jimmy James : James Casey, the English music hall comedian, changed his name when an agent, booking him to work in Wales, told him that the name Casey would not be popular there. One wonders why...

Kid Jensen : When the Canadian-born DJ was 18 he was nicknamed "Kid" at Radio Luxembourg, where he was working at the time. He took the name in preference to his real first name David.

Elton John : Reg Dwight changed his name by deed poll, adopting his new first name from Elton Dean, saxophonist for the soul group Bluesology, and his surname from Long John Baldry, the rock singer. The pop singer's *full* stage name is in fact Elton Hercules John, the middle name added later since, as he explained, "It gave me something to look up to and to remind me always to be strong." (Before changing his name Reginald Kenneth Dwight had expressed his view that it "sounded like a cement mixer!") [Gerald Newman with Joe Bivona, *Elton John*, 1976].

Al Jolson : The American singer Asa Yoelson was born in Srednik, Lithuania, of Jewish stock. He first changed his forename Asa to Al when his elder brother changed his own name, Hirsch, to Harry. Later (in 1899) Fred E. Moore, an electrician in New York's Dewey Theatre, suggested he join him in a singing act as Harry Joelson. Eventually (1903) the printer shortened Joelson to Jolson as it was "long, foreign sounding" [Michael Freedland, *Al Jolson*, 1972].

Jennifer Jones : The American film actress born Phyllis Isley was once asked by a reporter how she came by her name. She replied, "My mother must have been reading an English novel, but I suppose they'll change it once I get to Hollywood."

Père Joseph : François du Tremblay was a French friar and diplomat, better known as "L'Éminence Grise" in his role as friend and advisor to Cardinal Richelieu. His assumed name seems to be arbitrary — or perhaps biblical? — but his nickname (meaning "The Grey Eminence") was given in contrast to Richelieu's own nickname of "Eminence Rouge." ("Eminence" is the official form of address for a cardinal, and a cardinal's robes — as the title implies — are red).

Eden Kane : The English pop singer Richard Sarstedt, who in the 1970s was to sing with his brothers under his real name (the Sarstedt Brothers), took his initial stage name, apparently, from the film *Citizen Kane*. Possibly his first name also came from a film (as *East of Eden*)?

Karandash : The Russian clown born Mikhail Rumyantsev adopted a name that is the Russian word for "pencil." He took it (1934) when appearing in Leningrad, from the French cartoonist °Caran d'Ache — although one might have expected it to be the other way round. For the record, the word is not a native Russian one anyway, but is Turkish in origin, meaning "black stone." And here we have the makings of another suitable artist's pseudonym.

Boris Karloff : The film actor with the sinister Russian-sounding name — just right for the portrayer of the monster in *Frankenstein* (1931) — derived his name from one of his mother's ancestors. The whole name came to him on a train journey to Kamloops, the mining town northeast of Vancouver, Canada. "I dredged up 'Karloff' from Russian ancestors on my mother's side," said the British born actor whose real name was William Pratt, "and I picked 'Boris' out of the chilly, Canadian air."

Fred Karno : The British music-hall comedian was born Frederick Westcott. He adopted his name in 1887 when he and two gymnast colleagues filled in at a London music hall for a troupe called "The Three Carnos." His agent, Richard Warner, suggested they change the "C" to "K" [J.P. Gallagher, *Fred Karno, Master of Mirth and Tears*, 1971]. An early stage name used by Westcott was Alto.

Elia Kazan : The Turkish-born film director started life as Elia Kazanjoglou. He emigrated at the age of four to the United States, where his parents shortened their surname to Kazan. Later, when he was established in Hollywood, an attempt was made, unsuccessfully, to persuade him to change yet again to "Cezanne."

Buster Keaton : How exactly Joseph Francis Keaton came by his nickname, a common enough one anyway, is not certain. According to one authority (Clarke), he was so called by °Harry Houdini, who was in the same traveling show with him when Keaton was only three. Leonard Ashley suggests that there may be a link with the comic strip Buster Brown. Either way, the nickname is just right for one of the greatest clowns of the silent screen. He was no relation of the actress Diane Keaton, whose real name is Diane Hall.

Pamela Kellino : In a sense this is Pamela Ostrer's real name, since before her marriage to James Mason she was for a while married to Roy Kellino. She is therefore in the same category (retaining the surname of a former husband) as °Cyd Charisse.

Jomo Kenyatta : The former president of Kenya was born with the name Kamau, the son of Ngengi. He was baptised (1914) as Johnstone Kamau. Jomo is a pet form of Johnstone; Kenyatta derives from a Kikuyu word for a fancy belt, which he affected.

Orpheus C. Kerr : Robert Henry Newell was an American humorous journalist whose letters and verses were printed in daily papers from 1862 to 1871. His name is a pun on "office seeker," the reference being to those who sought office in Washington.

B.B. King : As a DJ in Memphis, Riley B. King used the radio name Beale Street Blues Boy, later shortening this to "B.B.".

Nosmo King : Another punning name. The British stage comedian Verson Watson went on stage through double doors on the left and right halves of which was a notice: NO SMOKING (five letters on the left door, four on the right!)

Sergey Kirov : The Russian statesman and Communist leader Sergey Kostrikov had a "party" name chosen for him in the office of the Vladikavkaz newspaper *Terek* by the selection of the rare Christian name Kir from a calendar. This was in 1912. Earlier he had signed himself "S. Mironov," from his patronymic, Mironovich, but this was thought to be not "secret" enough.

Klabund : The rather unusual name adopted by the German Expressionist poet and adaptor of Oriental literature Alfred Henschke derives from a blend of *Klabautermann*, "hobgoblin," and *Vagabund*, "vagabond." He felt such a name to be appropriate for the eternally seeking, wandering poet with whom he identified himself.

Klaxon : Commander Bower's adventure stories were often set in the submarine service, where the sound of the klaxon was often the signal for dangerous action. The word itself is the name of the American manufacturing company who made such hooters. (Commander Bower married Barbara Euphan Todd, creator of the children's radio and TV character, the scarecrow Worzel Gummidge.)

Diedrich Knickerbocker : Washington Irving, the great American humorist, devised a pen name that gave the English-speaking world first the breeches called knickerbockers and then the underwear called, mostly in Britain, knickers. But where did he get the name itself? Very likely from a Dutch family of this name who came to live in Albany county around 1674. (He used the name, as is well known, for the supposed Dutch author of the *History of New York*.) The family name — which may have been originally Knickerbacker — apparently means "baker of knickers," the latter being clay marbles. Irving's pseudonym became popular from the illustrations to the *History of New York* by George Cruikshank, showing Dutchmen in wide, loose knee-breeches.

Alexander Korda : The famous British movie director was born Sandro Kellner in Hungary 90 miles east of Budapest. At the age of 15 he migrated to the capital where he was befriended by a Catholic priest who got him a job on a local paper. Since the boy was too young by law to have a job, he had to find a pseudonym for himself, and as a compliment to his patron took the phrase "Sursum Corda" (Latin for "Lift up your hearts") from the Roman mass. This bore at least a faint resemblance to his real name [Michael Korda, *Charmed Lives*, 1980].

Kukryniksy : The joint pseudonym of the Russian artists and satirical cartoonists Mikhail *Ku*priyanov, Porfiry *Kry*lov, and *Nik*olay Sokolov, with the final "-y" being the Russian plural ending. All three were born at the turn of the century but their work can still be seen in current numbers of the Soviet satirical magazine *Krokodil*.

Louise Labé : The French poetess Louise Charly was nicknamed "La Belle Cordière" as her husband was a ropemaker (French *cordier*). Her pseudonym is an abbreviation of this nickname.

Frankie Laine : The American pop singer and film actor was born Frank Paul Lo Vecchio. When starting in show business he took the name Frankie Lane. Later, however, on discovering that there was a girl singer called Frances Lane, he added an "i" to avoid confusion.

Veronica Lake : Constance Ockleman, who made her debut as Constance Keane in *Sorority House* (1939), was given her famous name by the film producer Arthur Hornblow, Jr., in 1940, when she was 17, for the film *I Wanted Wings* (1941). The actress tells how the name was arrived at in her autobiography: "'Believe me' [said Hornblow], 'the right name, a name that the public can latch on to and remember can make all the difference. It isn't just a matter, though, of creating a name that can be remembered. If that were all it took, we'd just name you Maude Mudpie or Tilly Tits or something and they'd remember the name.... Picking a name involves coming up with something that associates in the fan's mind the person attached to that name. The name has to ... well, it has to be the person, or at least what the fan thinks that person is.... Connie, here's how I came to choose your new name. I believe that when people look into those navy blue eyes of yours, they'll see a calm coolness — the calm coolness of a lake.' The first thing that crossed my mind was that I was going to be named Lake something or other. That doesn't sound very outlandish these days with Tab and Rock, but in those days names stuck closer to the norm.... 'And your features, Connie, are classic features. And when I think of classic features, I think of Veronica.' Lake Veronica!

Oh! Veronica Lake. Of course. And then it hit me. My mother was some-
times called Veronica. Of all the goddam names in the world to choose....
I broke down and bawled like a baby into the couch cushions" [Veronica
Lake with Donald Bain, *Veronica*, 1969].

Hedy Lemarr : Hedwig Kiesler, the Austrian film actress
working in the United States, was so named by MGM's Louis B. Mayer after "the most beautiful star he had ever seen" — Barbara La Marr.

Mario Lanza : The stage name of Alfredo Cocozza, the Italian-
born opera singer and film actor, derives from the hero of his favorite
opera, Puccini's *Tosca* (in which the singer Floria Tosca falls in love with
the painter Mario Cavaradossi), and from his mmn, Lanza.

Larry : The British cartoonist was born Terence Parkes. The
name was originally a nickname given him by school pupils when he was
teaching in Peterborough. The nickname in turn came from the film then
showing locally, *The Al Jolson Story*, in which the actor Larry Parks
starred as Jolson.

Danny La Rue : How did Daniel Patrick Carroll, the Irish-born
British revue star and female impersonator, come to have this French-
style name? It was given him by the comedian and producer Ted Gatty
for his revue *Men Only* — allegedly because Carroll was said to have
looked "as long as a street" when wearing drag! [Peter Underwood, *Life's
a Drag! Danny La Rue and the Drag Scene*, 1974].

Slingsby Lawrence : Slingsby seems to have been something of
a vogue pseudonym among English writers in the 19th century. Slingsby
Lawrence was the name used by °George Eliot's partner and lover, George
Henry Lewes, for adaptations of French plays. Others of the name were
Jonathan Freke Slingsby (John Francis Waller), who adopted the
pseudonym for his contributions to the *Dublin University Magazine*, of
which he ultimately became the editor, and Philip Slingsby (Nathaniel
Parker Willis), the American poet, who used the name when in England
for a collection of sketches, *Inklings of Adventure* (1836). (His sister was
Fanny Fern). No doubt there was some mutual borrowing of the name,
but who started it? There is a village Slingsby in North Yorkshire, with
ruins of the 17th-century Slingsby Castle, but none of the writers seems to
have had any connections here.

John Le Carré : You can pick out the pseudonym from the letters of the spy storywriter's real name, David John Moore Cornwell. This
is not its origin, however. When starting his career as a writer, but still
working with the Foreign Office, Cornwell was advised to adopt another
name, since it would not have done for a serving diplomat to publish novels
under his own name. The story goes that one day, when riding on a London bus, Cornwall saw the name on a shopfront, and decided to take it.

Canada Lee : Leonard Canegata, the black American stage
and screen actor, adopted the name when an announcer, it is said, had
difficulty pronouncing "Lee Canegata."

Gypsy Rose Lee : The American stage and screen actress Rose Louise Hovick took the name Gypsy as suitable for her burlesque strip-tease acts, with Rose Lee based on her real first two names. (In addition, her stage mother was called Madam Rose). Gypsy's younger sister is June Havoc.

Peggy Lee : Yet another Lee. When Norma Egstrom, the night-club singer and film actress, was working on the radio station WDAY, manager Ken Kennedy called her Peggy Lee (1938), possibly, as Leonard Ashley suggests, after the singer of this name.

Vivien Leigh : Vivian Mary Hartley married Herbert Leigh Holman in 1932 and the same year adopted his middle name, changing the "a" of Vivian to an "e" for added distinction.

Sir Peter Lely : The Dutch-born portrait painter, who worked in England, was born Peter van der Faes, the son of a military captain — who was known by the nickname of Lely, from the lily prominent on the house where he was born. Or so the story goes. ("Origin uncertain," say several sources).

Lenare : The English society photographer Leonard Green opened his studio in 1924. Since in those days a French-sounding name was the fashion for dressmakers and photographers, he took the "Len" part of his name and added a "French" ending. When asked about the origin of this, he would point to his bald head and say, "Look, Len no 'air" [*Sunday Times Magazine*, November 13, 1977].

Leonid Lench : The Russian writer and dramatist was born Leonid Popov. His real surname he regarded as too ordinary, so a member of the editorial staff of the magazine where he worked — the Krasnodar *Krasnoye Znamya* — devised the name Lench from Lenchik, one of the diminutives of his first name.

Lenin : A much more widely known Russian, born Vladimir Ilyich Ulyanov. The origin of his name, famous though it is, is still uncertain. He first used it in 1901 — some time before the Revolution — for an article in the revolutionary journal *Iskra*, then published in Munich. The traditional explanation is that the name derives from the river Lena, Siberia, where there had been disturbances. Ulyanov had been exiled to Siberia, although not to the Lena but to the village of Shushenskoye, on the river Yenisey. So why this particular river? According to one authority, the choice was a more or less random one: he would have chosen a name based on the river Volga, but this was already "booked" (as Volgin) by the Marxist Plekhanov. He therefore took the next big river to the east [Louis Fisher, *The Life of Lenin*, 1966].

The uncertainty of the origin of the pseudonym is emphasized by the one person who should have known its derivation — Lenin's wife. In 1924, the year of his death, she wrote in a letter to the magazine *Komyacheyka*: "Dear Comrades, I don't know why Vladimir Ilyich took the name 'Lenin;' I never asked him about it. His mother was called Mariya

Aleksandrovna, his late sister Olga. The events on the river Lena happened after he took this pseudonym. He was never in exile on the Lena. Probably the name was chosen by chance" [Dmitriev, p. 44]. Another tentative explanation is that the name came from a girl classmate, Lena. The true origin may perhaps be revealed one day... (For the many pseudonyms adopted by Lenin, see Chapter 6.)

Joan Leslie : Like Shirley Broadbent (Amanda Barrie) and Dora Broadbent (°Dora Bryan), Joan Brodel changed her name to avoid the undesirable connotation of "broad."

Caroline Lewis : A satirical name for a threesome: two authors and an illustrator—Harold Begbie, M.H. Temple, and Stafford Ransome. The three used the pseudonym for *Clara in Blunderland* and *Lost in Blunderland*, political skits modeled on the stories by °Lewis Carroll. Even the innocent Alice would have easily spotted the source of the name.

Jerry Lewis : The former partner of °Dean Martin, born Joseph Levitch, used the same surname as the one adopted by his parents, who were also in show business. He commented, "How could anyone called Levitch get laughs?"

Thomas Little : This was the name adopted by the Irish-born poet and satirist Thomas Moore, alluding playfully to his small stature. He used it for his *Poetical Works* (1801) and was thus referred to by Byron in the latter's *English Bards and Scotch Reviewers* (1809). He used other pseudonyms on occasions, as Thomas Brown the Younger, One of the Fancy, and Trismegistus Rustifucius, D.D.

Little Tich : The British music-hall comedian, dwarfish in stature also, was born Harry Ralph. At the time of the so called Tichborne Case (1872)—the most famous impersonation case in English law, in which Arthur Orton, a butcher's son, claimed to be Roger Charles Tichborne, the heir to a lucrative baronetcy—Ralph was a pudgy four-year-old, resembling in corpulence the rotund claimant.

Lucy Vaughan Lloyd : An unexpected name used by the poet John Keats for an unfinished poem, *The Cap and Bells* (1820). The adoption of a pseudonym by the poet when he was already well established suggests that he intended the poem to be somehow directed against the Lake Poets. Robert Gittings points out that Lucy suggests Wordsworth (real person or not, Lucy was the subject of a number of Wordsworth's poems), while Charles Lloyd was a poet and neighbor of Wordsworth. Keats's poem written under the pseudonym was first published only in 1848, 26 years after his death [Robert Gittings, *John Keats*, 1968].

Jack London : The famous American author was the illegitimate son of William Henry Chaney, an itinerant astrologer, and Flora Wellman. Jack was born on January 12, 1876. On September 7 that year his mother married John London, a ruined farmer. Jack's surname was thus that of his stepfather.

Sophia Loren : The charismatic Italian-born actress was an illegitimate child, the daughter of Riccardo Scicolone and Romilda Villani. Her original name was thus Sofia Villani Scicolone. It would not be long, however, before people would be telling her that her real surname "sounded like a chunk of Italian sausage," and before she changed it to her famous present name. The choice of name is popularly supposed to have been made by Carlo Ponti, whom she married (in 1957). A biography of Loren suggests otherwise, however. Originally, it seems, a magazine editor had suggested the name "Sofia Lazzaro," from the New Testament story of Lazarus (with presumably a symbolic reference to a "rebirth"). Then the Italian producer, Goffredo Lombardo, who had been working with the Swedish actress Martha Toren, said that "Lazzaro" sounded more like a corpse than its resurrection and proposed a further change. Taking "Toren" as a basis, he worked through the alphabet, stopping at "Loren." "Yes," was his verdict, "Loren — it suits you..." Subsequently Sofia changed to Sophia, with the changed letters "adding a touch of class" [Donald Zec, *Sophia: An Intimate Biography*, 1975].

Pierre Loti : Louis-Marie-Julien Viaud was not only a noted French novelist but also a naval officer. His travels took him to Tahiti, where the native women nicknamed him "Loti," meaning "rose." How could he not adopt such a loving name?

Bessie Love : Juanita Horton, the American film actress who came to Britain, was renamed (1916) by Frank Woods, head of scenario for D.W. Griffith, right in front of the cast of her first film, *The Flying Torpedo*: "Bessie, because any child can pronounce it; and Love, because we want everyone to love her!" [*Sunday Times Magazine*, September 18, 1977].

Myrna Loy : The American film actress who was born Myrna Williams took her new name in 1932 as "the plain old Welsh name of Williams just didn't seem flossy enough."

Arthur Lucan : The English music hall comedian Arthur Towle was on tour (1913) at the Lucan Dairy, Dublin — this provided a handy stage name for the creator of *Old Mother Riley*.

Victoria Lucas : A little known pen name adopted by the American-born poet Sylvia Plath (who married Ted Hughes) for her semi-autobiographical novel *The Bell Jar* (1963), reissued later (1966) under her own name. Already suffering with sinusitis, and continually ill in the cold winter of 1962-1963, Sylvia was devastated when her pseudonym was penetrated in the year of publication of her novel. A few months later she took her own life [*The Times*, April 8, 1978].

Lulu : The popular Scottish singer was born with a real resounding Scottish name — Marie McDonald McLaughlin Lawrie. How did this condense to the little Lulu? It began as a nickname: when in her teens she was visiting a club with her lady manager, who recommended her to the club as "a lulu of a kid." The expression is an attractive one — the word is probably itself a pet form of the name Louise — for someone (or something) that is attractive and/or wonderful. What could be better?

Le Lycanthrope : This was the sinister name adopted by the French poet and horror story writer Petrus Borel. It means, via the Greek, "the wolf-man," and was no doubt chosen with reference to the saying, "Man is a wolf to man," as well as hinting darkly at vampires and eerie nocturnal metamorphoses.

Moura Lympany : The British concert pianist's original name was Mary Johnstone—later, upon marriage (both dissolved), Mary Defries, then Mary Korn. Her change of name was made at the suggestion of conductor Basil Cameron, so the pianist adapted her Cornish mmn, Limpenny, to the "more romantic" Lympany, at the same time modulating Mary to the softer Moura [*Telegraph Sunday Magazine*, June 10, 1979].

Vera Lynn : Vera Welch, the British popular singer, "The Forces' Sweetheart," explains how she arrived at her new name: "I ought to adopt a more comfortable name than Vera Welch. My main concern was to find something that was short, easily remembered, and that would stand out on a bill—something that would allow for plenty of space round each letter. We held a kind of family conference about it, and we found the answer within the family too. My grandmother's maiden name had been Lynn; it seemed to be everything a stage name ought to be, but at the same time it was a real one. From then on, I was to be Vera Lynn" [Vera Lynn, *Vocal Refrain: An Autobiography*; 1975].

Hugh MacDiarmid : The Scottish dialect poet's true name was Christopher Murray Grieve. The origin of his pen name remains a mystery. He first adopted it in 1922, and his only comment on it was quoted by *The Times* in its September 11, 1978, obituary notice of him: "It was an immediate realization of this ultimate reach of the implications of my experiment writing in Scots which made me adopt, when I began writing Scots poetry, the Gaelic pseudonym of Hugh MacDiarmid (Hugh has a traditional association and essential rightness in conjunction with MacDiarmid)."

Fiona Macleod : The Scottish author William Sharp adopted the female pseudonym which he consistently declined to acknowledge throughout his lifetime. Fiona—now a popular girls' name, especially in Scotland—was invented by him. It derives from the Gaelic meaning "fair," "white" (as does Welsh Gwyn), and for this reason George R. Stewart, in his *American Given Names* (1979) feels that there might be a pun somewhere on the lines of "white cloud" in the name as a whole. The true origin of the pseudonym otherwise remains as obscure as that of his fellow Scots author in the previous entry.

Butterfly McQueen : The surname is real enough, but the American Negro actress began life as Thelma McQueen. Early in her career (1938) she played the part of Butterfly in *Brown Sugar*, and the name stuck as a nickname. As Leonard Ashley points out, it is just right to indicate comic flightiness.

Maharaj Ji : The Indian guru who traveled the world as a spiritual leader when he was still only 16 (1973) was born Pratap Singh Rawat. His assumed name is really a title, meaning "perfect master."

Marjorie Main : The American film actress born Mary Krebs, famous for her role as "Ma Kettle," took her name from the title of Sinclair Lewis's novel *Main Street*.

Archbishop Makarios : The Cypriot leader who was president of Cyprus from 1959 until his death in 1977 was actually Mikhail Khristodolou Mouskos. His religious name—he was officially Makarios III—is the Greek word "blessed."

Louis Malone : This was an early pseudonym used by the Irish poet Louis MacNeice. He derived it from Malone Road, Belfast, where he was born.

Jayne Mansfield : Vera Jayne Palmer was already married in her teens, as Jayne Mansfield (her husband's name), when she was "discovered." So her stage name was really her own. (Compare °Cyd Charisse and °Pamela Kellino). Halliwell gives her original middle name with the spelling Jane.

Le Mapah : The real surname of the French founder of the quasireligion *Évadisme* was Ganneau. Évadisme exalted the standing of woman and preached equality of the sexes. Its name is based on the first syllables of "Eve" and "Adam," while Ganneau's own assumed name is devised from the first two letters of Latin *mater* and *pater*, "mother" and "father." This gallant attempt at women's liberation was founded about 1835, but today remains more a curiosity than a moving spirit.

Frederic March : Frederick Bickel changed his name at the suggestion of film director John Cromwell, who commented that the American actor's real name sounded like "pickle." So the star of *A Star Is Born* adapted his mother's maiden name of Marcher. Some years later he said, "I wish I'd left it as it was—after all, Theodore Bickel did all right."

Joseph Arthur Markham : Who assumed such an ordinary name? The answer—and he adopted it just because it *was* so ordinary—is the British M.P. John Stonehouse. He used the name, a genuine one—that of a person his own age who had died in hospital—for his passport and international vaccination certificate when entering Australia (1974) after his faked disappearance on Miami Beach. (The main aim in this mysterious affair was to develop a second personality.) When actually in Australia Stonehouse equipped himself with a birth certificate in the name of Donald Clive Mildoon, a name of similar provenance, and then ran bank accounts in both of these names [John Stonehouse, *My Trial*, 1976].

William Marshall, Gent. : This was the name taken by the author Horace Walpole for the first publication of his Gothic horror tale *The Castle of Otranto* (1764). William Marshall, gent or not, was said to be the translator of a rare Italian work written in 1529 by one Onuphrio Muralto.

Dean Martin : The American film actor, teaming with Jerry Lewis until 1957, was born Dino Crocetti. He was first billed as "Dino Martini — Nino Martini's cousin" (Nino Martini was a popular singer of the time). Soon after (1939) he changed this to the more anglicized form of Dean Martin.

Ik Marvel : The American essayist Donald Grant Mitchell adopted (1846) the name J.K. Marvel for his contributions to the *Morning Courier and New York Enquirer*. This was misprinted as Ik Marvel, and he stuck with it.

Chico Marx (and splendid company) : In order of appearance, the Marx Brothers' cast was as follows: Chico (born Leonard), Harpo (Arthur), Groucho (Julius), Gummo (Milton), and Zeppo (Herbert). Chico, it seemed, had a reputation for always being "after the chicks"; Harpo, of course, played the harp; Groucho "had a naturally caustic view of life" (and according to another theory was characterized by the grouch-bag or briefcase in which he carried his stage equipment); Gummo always had holes in his shoes and wore rubbers, or gumshoes, over them; Zeppo — although nobody is quite sure — was born around the time the first Zeppelin was built. The names grew out of their characters. In a television interview (reported in *The Listener* of August 16, 1979) Groucho said of his name: "I always had a grim visage, because I handled the money, and the others didn't have too much confidence in me, and it became Groucho, and it was a nice name."

Massachusettensis : This impressive pseudoclassical name was used by the American Loyalist writer Daniel Leonard for a series of contributions to *The Massachusetts Gazette and Post Boy* (1774-5). These were replied to by Novanglus.

Léonide Massine : A slight adjustment — more a Frenchification — of the name of the Russian dancer and choreographer Leonid Fedorovich Miassin (or Myasin). Most unromantically, his surname derives from the Russian word for "meat." His son Lorca Massine, following quite literally in his father's footsteps, kept the version of the name.

Mata Hari : The famous *femme fatale* was a Dutch-born dancer whose name for her exotic Eastern temple performance on the French stage derived from the Malay for "eye of the day," i.e., the sun. Before her arrival in Paris in 1904, Gertrud Margarete Zelle had been married briefly to a Dutch Colonial officer, Rudolph MacLeod, and with him had stayed, equally briefly, in the Dutch East Indies. She had retained enough of the language to invent the name for her new life in the theatre. Accused of spying for the Germans in the First World War, Mata Hari's days came to an end in 1917 at the age of 41, when she was executed by the French.

Anna Matilda : The name had two users of note. Mrs. Hannah Cowley, English dramatist and poet, called herself so in her poetical correspondence in the *World* with °Della Crusca. Another associate of the

Della Cruscans also adopted the name. This was Mrs. Hester Piozzi, a friend of Dr. Johnson. She had been called Matilda by William Gifford in his two satires *The Baviad* (1794) and *The Maeviad* (1795), both directed against the Dellacruscan school. Hester Piozzi was also known as Mrs. Thrale, from the name of her first husband.

Walter Matthau : The American film actor was the son of a Catholic Eastern Rite Orthodox priest who had fallen afoul of the authorities. His original surname is such a Slavonic mouthful and printer's nightmare that no two single sources seem able to agree as to its exact spelling. It would seem, however, to be not far short of Mataschanskayasky.

André Maurois : The French writer Émile Herzog first used the name in World War I for *Les Silences du Colonel Bramble* (1918), in which he desribed typical English officers in their mess. His pseudonym is said to be derived from a small front line village named Maurois and the first name of his cousin André who had been killed in the war [Dmitriev, p. 86].

Virginia Mayo : The movie star's real name was Virginia May Jones, and her stage name is probably derived from this. However, Leonard Ashley quotes an old Hollywood joke that gives a more imaginative origin: "It seems that she had attracted no attention whatsoever as just another Jones girl and was in a bus station in Hollywood ... just having a sandwich preparatory to going back home, totally discouraged. She ordered "a ham sandwich with mayonnaise." The counterman called to the cook "virginia, mayo" and Miss Jones cried triumphantly: 'That's it!'" [Ashley, p. 238, n24].

Golda Meir : The Russian-born Jewish prime minister and founder of the state of Israel started life as Golda Mabovitch. Having emigrated to the United States at the age of eight, Golda met (1917) Morris Myerson, a Russian Jewish immigrant, whom she later married. Back with her husband in Palestine, Golda changed her name to Meir at the insistence of David Ben Gurion when she was appointed (1956) Israeli foreign minister. She went as close to Myerson as she could, but compromised knowing that Meir means "illuminate." (Her marriage had in fact broken up some years before, in 1945).

Melanchthon : One of the Renaissance classical renderings – the original name of the German humanist and theologian was Philip Schwarzerd. His surname translates as "black earth," in Greek Melanchthon. (If this suggests "melancholy" it's because this word literally means "black bile.")

Dame Nellie Melba : Helen Armstrong, née Mitchell, the Australian operatic soprano, took her name from Melbourne, near which capital city she was born. She first used the name in Brussels (1887), for her debut as Gilda in *Rigoletto*. Named after her are peach Melba and Melba toast. Unkind wits say an excess of the first, which she adored, led to a diet of the second, which she cultivated.

Sebastian Melmoth : This was the name adopted by Oscar Wilde after his release from Reading Gaol in 1897. It comes from the hero of a novel, *Melmoth the Wanderer*, written by Charles Maturin, a remote ancestor on Wilde's mother's side. The first name Sebastian was apparently suggested by the arrows on his prison uniform. The reference is to classic paintings showing St. Sebastian being shot to death by arrows.

Adah Isaacs Menken : Dolores Adios Fuertes, the American actress and poet, married (1856) Alexander Isaacs Menken (not to be confused with Henry Louis Mencken, the editor and writer on language) and then, under the impression she was divorced, the boxer John Carmel Heenan (1859). Menken was a Jew, and this may have prompted her to change her first two names to something more specifically Jewish, although she herself was already the daughter of a Spanish Jew. She kept her name through subsequent marriages – she is said to have been married four times, one further husband being °Orpheus C. Kerr – and gained great popularity for her role on the London stage as Mazeppa (1864) in a dramatization of Byron's poem. Her original name is given in some sources as Adelaide McCord.

Mary Merrall : Mary Lloyd, the English stage and film actress, may have been prompted to change her name for fear of confusion with Marie Lloyd. She made her first stage appearance (1907) as Queenie Merrall.

Pietro Metastasio : A name that like that of °Lorenzo da Ponte is associated with Mozart, since its bearer, born Pietro Trapassi, wrote the libretto for *La Clemenza di Tito* (1732) which Mozart set to music in 1791. One is tempted to seek some kind of allegorical explanation in his name, for Greek *metastasis* means "change of place" and indeed the Italian poet and musician was called to Vienna in 1730 to be court poet to the Holy Roman Emperor, Charles VI. The actual origin of his name is in fact a translation, but not this one: at the age of 10 Pietro was made the heir adoptive of a man of letters, Gian Vincenzo Gravina, who graecized his surname, Italian *trapasso* meaning literally "passage," "transfer."

Ray Milland : Long established in the United States, the British film actor was born Reginald Truscott-Jones in Wales. His first change of name was to Mullane, the surname of his stepfather after his mother's second marriage. Later, a studio publicity man suggested a further change, and recommended the name Percival Lacy. (Could he really have been serious? Even Polesden Lacy, the name of a country house in Surrey, would have had greater charisma). Ray (or Reg), however, was nostalgically thinking back to the rural beauty of his Welsh childhood, and proposed "Mill-land." The publicity man, more reasonably this time, advised that a name with three "l" 's might present difficulties, whereupon the actor modified it to the form in which we now know it [Ray Milland, *Wide-eyed in Babylon*, 1975].

Joaquin Miller : Cincinnatus Hiner Miller, the 19th-century American poet, had the ambition of being "the American Byron." His changed forename was originally a nickname, as his earliest writing was a defense of the Mexican bandit Joaquin Murietta. He later preferred to alter his middle name to the spelling "Heine" — presumably as this was more poetic.

Max Miller : No doubt Harold Sargent was not aware of the American writer Max Miller when he changed his name. Whatever its origin, however, it seemed just right for the music hall comedian who embodied the role of "the Cheeky Chappie" (more alliteration), and moreover his name lives on in that of °Max Bygraves.

Cardinal Mindszenty : The Hungarian archbishop who was sentenced to life imprisonment (1949) by the Communists on a charge of treason was born Joszef Pehm. He had adopted the Magyar name after his native village of Szehimindszenty as a protest against Hungary's pro-Hitler stand in the 1930s. The Cardinal was released from prison in 1956 and given asylum in the U.S. Legation in Budapest.

Carmen Miranda : A name admirably suitable for the Portuguese-born American singer Maria de Carmo Miranda de Cunha. Even though it evolved from her middle names, it nicely conjures up Bizet's *Carmen* and a "wonderful song," to say nothing of the romantic heroine of Shakespeare's *The Tempest*.

Mistinguett : The French music-hall artiste, born Jeanne-Marie Bourgeois, was originally billed as "Miss Tinguette," from a song in the musical show, *Miss Helyett*. The name was apparently suggested by her supposedly English-looking protruding front teeth.

Gabriela Mistral : The Chilean poet Lucila Godoy de Alcayaga derived her name not from "mistral," the north wind, but from two poets, the Italian Gabriele d'Annunzio and the Provençal Frédérick Mistral. She began to use Mistral's name soon after his death (1914). Thirty years later she was awarded the Nobel prize for literature, as he had been.

Guy Mitchell : Al Cernick, the American pop singer and film actor, was discovered (in 1948) by Mitch Miller, who asked him to change his name. Cernick couldn't think of a name, so Miller said, "Look, you're a nice *guy*, and my name is *Mitchell*, so how about Guy Mitchell?" Al was not too keen on this. "You wouldn't like to end up being someone else, would you?" he complained.

M. le ch. X. o. a. s. s. d. s. M. S. : A pseudonym like this must surely mean something! It does. The initials stand for "Monsieur le chevalier Xavier, officier ancien sur service de sa Majesté Sardinienne" — otherwise, "Sir Knight Xavier, former officer in the service of His Sardinian Majesty," the cumbersome yet rather impressive name chosen by the French novelist Xavier de Maistre for his *Voyage Autour de Ma Chambre* ("Journey Round My Room") (1794). This was no ordinary journey round no ordinary room, since at the time he was temporarily imprisoned in his quarters in Turin when in the service of the Piedmontese army. The unusual book has the theme that it is not our surroundings that make us happy, for we can find happiness within ourselves.

President Mobutu : The African statesman and politician, president of Zaïre from 1965, was christened Joseph-Désiré Mobutu. In 1972 he dropped his Christian name and expanded his surname to become Mobutu Sese Seko Kuku Ngdenda Wa Za Banga. According to the *Sunday Times Magazine* of March 7, 1972 this is alleged to mean "invincible warrior cockerel who leaves no chick intact."

Molière : This classic pseudonym is also a classic mystery. How *did* the great French dramatist Jean-Baptiste Poquelin acquire his new name? We do know that he must have first used it in 1643 or 1644, for it is found in a document dated June 28, 1644. It at least has a much more theatrical ring than Poquelin, which to a Frenchman suggests either *poquet*, "seed-hole," or *poquer*, a verb meaning "to throw one's ball in the game of *boules* in such a way that it stops still where it lands." As for the name Molière, it did in fact also belong to a second-rank writer who died in the same year that Jean-Baptiste was born (1622). But the commonly held theory is that he derived it not from his lesser codramatist, but from a place of this name — or something like this name — that was visited by the touring company to which young Poquelin belonged. (There are several villages named Molières, for example, and at least one called Molères.)

Vyacheslav Molotov : The Russian diplomat, born Skryabin (like the composer), assumed his name, a "party" one, in 1906, when he became a Bolshevik. It is a typically symbolic Bolshevik name, meaning "hammer." Compare other meaningful names of this type such as °Stalin and Kamenev.

Marilyn Monroe : Norma Jean Baker (originally Mortenson) was named by Ben Lyon, the casting director of 20th-Century Fox, after Marilyn Miller, with Monroe being the famous film actress's mmn [BBC-1, "Hollywood Greats," August 24, 1979].

Nicholas Monsarrat : The English novelist's name had been incorrectly registered at his birth, with a spelling that was preferred by his mother, who claimed that the family went back to a French nobleman, the Marquis de Montserrat. In his autobiography, Monsarrat recalls that the discrepancy between spellings was to embarrass him both at school and later on joining the Navy [Nicholas Monsarrat, *Life Is a Four-Letter Word*, 1966].

Yves Montand : A French name that looks quite natural. It was adopted by the Italian-born film actor and singer Ivo Levi (who married Simone Signoret). The story behind his stage name is that his mother, when summoning him (in Italian), was often heard calling, "Ivo, monta!" ("Ivo, come up!").

Moondog : The blind American composer, famous for his unusual "popular-classical" works, is actually named Louis Hardin. He explained, "I began using Moondog as a pen name in 1947, in honor of a dog I had in Hurley, who used to howl at the moon more than any dog I knew of" [Jacket notes of record "Moondog," Poseidon Productions/CBS Records, 1969].

Garry Moore : Thomas Murfit, the American TV comic, got tired of people's mispronouncing his surname. A contest was therefore held (in 1940) to select a name. A Pittsburgh woman suggested Garry Moore and won the prize of $50 and a trip to Chicago.

Eric Morecambe : The popular British comedian, teaming with Ernie Wise, was born as Eric Bartholomew in the seaside town of Morecambe, Lancashire. Ernie Wise was born in Leeds, and early in their dual career the two comics considered calling themselves "Morecambe and Leeds" but rejected this as it sounded too much like a railway route.

Jelly Roll Morton : The American jazz composer and pianist's original surname was La Menthe. To this he added the name of the porter who married his mother after her husband left her. Jelly Roll, says Clarke, "suggests sexual prowess."

Mickie Most : Michael Hayes, the English record company director and promoter, originated his name for a skiffle double act, the Most Brothers, formed with his school friend Alex Murray in the late 1950s [*TV Times,* June 17, 1976].

Lord Louis Mountbatten : The British military leader who was the great-grandson of Queen Victoria was christened Louis Francis Albert Victor Nicholas of Battenberg. When his father, Louis Alexander Mountbatten, relinquished the title of Battenberg in 1917 (he was a naturalized British subject) at the request of George V, he and other members of his royal branch of German counts living in England adopted the partly translated name of Mountbatten (the German *Berg* meaning "mountain"). The assassination of Lord Louis in 1979 by Irish patriotic extremists shocked Britain and much of the English-speaking world.

Elijah Muhammad : The American Black Muslim leader was born Elijah (or possibly Robert) Poole. His meeting with °Walli Farrad started him on a career which led him to the top of the Black Muslim movement. He it was who converted, and named, °Malcolm X and °Muhammad Ali.

Multatuli : The Latin pseudonym adopted by the Dutch novelist Eduard Dekker means literally "I have borne much," i.e., I have suffered much. His suffering was perhaps more social than physical or spiritual, with his most important work *Max Havelaar* (1860) making a plea for justice to the natives in Java by the Dutch authorities. His main work, however, *Ideeën* ("Ideas") (1862-1877), shows him to have been an uncompromisingly radical thinker on many subjects, from the role of women in society to roulette. "Multatuli," therefore, is a name that is a clue to his intolerant and impatient nature.

Baron Münchhausen : It is usually known that the real name of the German author of the fantastic *Marvellous Travels and Campaigns in Russia* (1785) which the Baron supposedly undertook was Rudolfe Erich Raspe. What is not so widely known is that there was a real Baron Münchhausen on whose tales Raspe based his own stories. This was Karl Friedrich Hieronymus, born 17 years before Raspe (1720), who wrote embellished accounts of his adventures in the Russian war against the Turks.

Eadweard Muybridge : The English-born American photographer Edward James Muggeridge modified his name thus, believing this to be the original Anglo-Saxon form of his real name. If anything, the surname Muggeridge actually derives from a place in Devon, Mogridge, in turn taking its name from one Mogga who held a ridge there. Edward, on the other hand, was indeed spelled Eadweard in Old English.

Nadar : Felix Tournachon, the French photographer, illustrator and writer, adopted a name explained as follows: "He had also found his name: from Tournachon to Tournadard, an obscure epistemological gallic joke, referring either to his satirical *sting*, or else to the tongue of *flame* (also *dard*) above his brow; and thence to the more economical, and generally more marketable, Nadar. This signature now began to appear below little matchstick drawings, and at the age of 27, Nadar published a first caricature on the inside page of *Charivari...*" [*The Times*, October 12, 1974].

Donald Neilson : The British criminal, born Donald Nappey, was sentenced to life imprisonment (1976) for multiple murder. He had adopted his name from an ice cream van, mainly as he had never liked his original name but also to avoid future embarrassment for his daughter [BBC-1, "Reporting North," July 21, 1976].

Nadia Nerina : The South African ballet dancer who began life as Nadine Judd (her Russian mother's first name was Nadezhda) took her stage name from a red lily, Nerine (pronounced ne-rye-nee), that grows around Cape Town, her native city. She had earlier tried out the name Nadio Moore.

Nero : The famous Roman emperor — who apparently did anything *but* fiddle while Rome burned, although a man who can put his own mother to death and play pregnant women on the stage is capable of anything — was born Lucius Domitius Ahenobarbus. When he was 13 his mother married her uncle, Tiberius Claudius Drusus Nero Germanicus, otherwise just Emperor Claudius, who adopted him and renamed him as Nero Claudius Caesar Drusus Germanicus. Nero was thus a Roman surname, apparently originally meaning not "black," as one might expect, but "strong," "warlike." After Nero's suicide at the age of 31, however, the name became synonymous with tyranny and cruelty.

Pablo Neruda : The Chilean poet Ricardo Reyes Neftalí began using his pen name in 1920 so as not to annoy his father, a railway worker. He took the name from the 19th-century Czech writer Jan Neruda, whose story *By the Three Lilies* he had greatly admired. Neruda legally adopted the name in 1946.

Jimmy Nervo : James Holloway began his career as a circus artiste, whose speciality was balancing and buffoonery — and therefore falling and fractures. Anyone else would indeed have needed "nerve" to carry out the capers he performed with such gusto. Later, on teaming with his friend Teddy Knox and becoming a member of the Crazy Gang, he kept his circus name, even though he had now switched to a more verbal type of humor.

Nimrod : The 19th-century English sporting writer Charles James Apperley adopted the name of the biblical Nimrod, "the mighty hunter" (Genesis 19, ix).

Red Nirt : Tommy Trinder, the British comedian, used this reversal of his surname only early in his career, after which he performed under his own name. On one occasion, when opening a cabaret at the Embassy Club, he introduced himself to Orson Welles with the words, "Trinder's the name!" Welles replied, "Well, why don't you change it?" (Trinder's rejoinder was, "Is that a proposal of marriage?")

Nobody : The ultimate in self-effacing names! It was used by the English biographer William Stevens, and led to the founding (around 1800) of the "Society of Nobody's Friends." The name is of honorable, if literary, vintage. Odysseus, asked his name by the Cyclops, first plied the monocular monster liberally with wine, then replied, "My name is Nobody. That is what I am called by my mother and father and by all my friends" (the Cyclops cruelly quipped, "Of all his company I will eat Nobody last, and the rest before him") [Homer, *The Odyssey*, transl. by E.V. Rieu, 1973].

Jeremiah Noon : John Calvin, the 19th-century English boxer, based his name on that of Anthony Noon, killed in a fight against Owen Swift (1834).

Noor al-Hussein : When Elizabeth Halaby, a 27-year-old American businesswoman, married King Hussein of Jordan (1978), several society eyebrows were raised. In accordance with tradition, however, she assumed an Arabic name, hers meaning "light of Hussein." (Visitors to the Tower of London can see the Koh-i-Noor, the fabulous diamond presented to Queen Victoria, with its name meaning "mountain of light").

Max Simon Nordau : A swing of polarity here, since the original surname of the Hungarian-German writer was Südfeld, meaning "southern field," and his new name was German for "northern meadow." He made two radical changes in his own life, emigrating from Budapest to Paris and switching from medicine to literature.

Charles Norden : An early pseudonym adopted by Lawrence Durrell for his novel *Panic Spring* (1937). This was in fact his second novel, but as his first, *Pied Piper of Lovers* (1935), had been a failure, his publishers, Faber & Faber, suggested that the adoption of a pseudonym might be a wise precaution. With the huge success of *The Alexandria*

Quartet (1957-1960) the days of precautionary pen names were a thing of the past.

Captain George North : This was the name under which Robert Louis Stevenson wrote *Treasure Island* when it appeared serially in the magazine *Young Folks* (1881-1882). He used his real name a year later when the novel was published in book form. As a Scot, Stevenson of course came from North of the Border. Possibly his choice of pseudonym was suggested by that of John Wilson, who as as Edinburgh writer and critic used the name Christopher North.

Kim Novak : Marilyn Novak adopted a first name that she felt went well with her surname. Among names proposed for her, and thankfully rejected, were Kavon Novak, Iris Green, and Windy City. The first might have brought her success, but is over-esoteric; the second is unspeakable (apologies to any real Iris Greens, who I hope will know what I mean); the third is plain ridiculous.

Novalis : Friedrich Leopold von Hardenberg took his pseudonym from the traditional name of certain acres on his father's estate. The name is a fairly common one, in one form or another, for untilled or virgin land — in Scots law, for example, newly reclaimed waste lands are still known as *novalia* — and the German writer's family had been called "de Novali" as far back as the 13th century. Ultimately, of course, the word derives from the Latin for "new."

Ivor Novello : How did the famous Welsh actor-manager, dramatist and composer David Ivor Davies come to adopt his Italian name? Directly, he inherited it from his mother, Clara Novello Davies, née Davies, whose own Christian name had been given her by her father in admiration of the great singer Clara Anastasia Novello — to whom, incidentally, she was not related, as is sometimes stated, and who was also not her godmother. Clara Novello, otherwise Countess Gigliucci, sang the soprano part in Beethoven's *Missa Solemnis* when she was only 14 (1832), and was praised by Mendelssohn and Schumann. She was the daughter of Vincent Novello, an English organist and composer of sacred music, who himself in turn was the son of an Italian father and English mother. David Davies's pseudonym thus arrived by a somewhat devious route.

Jack Oakie : The film comedian Lewis Delaney Offield was born in Sedalia, Missouri, but later his family moved to Muskogee, Oklahoma, where his schoolfriends nicknamed him "Oakie." To this he added Jack to fit himself up with a satisfactory stage name.

Annie Oakley : °Buffalo Bill's Wild West Show would not have been complete without this crack markswoman, who began life as Phoebe Anne Oakley Moses. As a girl she had tried out the name Annie Mozee, but settled for a more conventional adaptation of her two middle names.

Merle Oberon : The film actress who was born (in Tasmania) Estelle Merle O'Brien Thompson came to Britain (1928) as dancer Queenie O'Brien. In 1939 she married Alexander Korda, and he it was who changed her middle names to Merle Oberon. He had intended to change them to Merle Auberon, but it turned out that there was a Bond Street hairdresser of this name and because of his protests "Auberon" was modified to "Oberon." It is thus only a coincidence, if a fortuitous one, that "Oberon" is a partial anagram of O'Brien, and that Oberon was the name of the king of the fairies.

Sean O'Casey : The Irish dramatist John Casey first wrote (in 1918) under an Irish version of his name, Sean O'Cathasaigh. Later (in 1923), when his first plays were produced at the Abbey Theatre, Dublin, he reverted in part to an anglicized form of this.

Jehu O'Cataract : There are several whimsical pseudonyms beginning with "O'..." This one began as a nickname, given the American romantic novelist and poet John Neal for his impetuosity. His feverish literary career suited him, apparently, for he lived to the respectable old age of 83.

Maria del Occidente : The American poet Maria Gowen Brooks was dubbed "Maria of the West" by Southey, who held her in high regard. She italianized this nickname to form her pseudonym. But why "West?" She in fact came from an eastern state, Massachusetts. (Her real name is usually quoted as given here, but it was in fact her married name, from her husband John Brooks, a Boston merchant. Her maiden name was Gowen.)

Dawn O'Day : A twee name for the child film star Dawn Paris. She later acted as Anne Shirley.

Jacques Offenbach : The father of Jakob Eberst, the German-born French operetta composer, was born in Offenbach-am-Main, and was known as "Der Offenbacher." The family moved to France when the boy was 14, and he subsequently adopted his father's nickname and modified his first name to its French equivalent.

Ambrosio O'Higgins : The Irish soldier and administrator prefixed his name with O' when captain-general of Chile (1789-96). His name is commemorated to this day in that country in a mountain and one of the central provinces — somewhat incongruous place-names among the many Spanish ones.

Old Block : The name was adopted by the American playwright and humorist Alonzo Delano. He first used it, perhaps somewhat predictably, for *Penknife Sketches, or Chips of the Old Block* (1853.)

Oliver Oldstyle : James Kirke Paulding, the American satirist who was a friend of Washington Irving and wrote a portion of *Salmagundi* took his pen name from that of Irving — Jonathan Oldstyle. Paulding's sister had married Irving's brother William.

Patrick Albert O'Leary : This Irish-style name was adopted (1940) by Albert Guerisse, a Belgian army officer, when he became first officer of the "Q" ship *HMS Fidelity*, with the rank of lieutenant commander, while serving with the British Navy. He was awarded the DSO

(1942) with this name, and later the Grand Cross (1946). On demobilization from the Royal Navy he rejoined the Belgian Army.

Ole Luk-Oie : Another military name. This unusual pseudonym—a Danish term meaning roughly "Olaf Shut-Eye"—was assumed by the British army officer and military history professor Sir E.D. Swinton for his book of short stories *The Green Curve* (1909) and other writings. Swinton was the originator of the name "tank" for the original self-propelled armored gun-carrying tracked vehicles when these were disguised for security reasons as railway wagons carrying fuel (tank-wagons) in the First World War. A lesser known pen name used by Swinton was Backsight-Forethought.

Omar Khayyám : The Persian poet best known to English speakers for his *Rubáiyát* (in the version published (in 1859) by Edward FitzGerald) was properly Gheyas od-Din Abu ol-Fath Umar ebna Ebrahim ol-Khayyami. His better-known name can be detected in this, so perhaps is not a true pseudonym. "Khayyam" means "tentmaker," in fact. This was his father's trade.

George Orwell : The famous author of *Animal Farm*, *1984* and a number of other still controversial novels was born Eric Arthur Blair. He first used his pen name for *Down and Out in Paris and London* (1933). He felt that Eric was too "Norse" and Blair too Scottish—a more suitable English name was one composed of the name of the patron saint of England and that of the river in Suffolk on whose banks he had lived. He also said that he wished to avoid embarrassing his parents—although friends felt that perhaps he was really seeking to escape from his genteel middleclass background. Somewhat mixed motives, therefore, seem to have led to his decision on a new name. (Another authority claims that the specific choice of George Orwell was made by Victor Gollancz, his publisher.) Blair had also considered other names, among them P.S. Burton, Kenneth Miles, and H. Lewis Allways [Bernard Crick, *George Orwell: A Life*, 1980].

Osman Pasha : Jan Willem, Duke of Ripperda, was a Dutch adventurer in the Spanish diplomatic service and a worthy rival of the Vicar of Bray. First a Protestant, then a Catholic, then a Protestant again, he finally adopted his new name when he became a follower of Islam.

Gilbert O'Sullivan : The Irish pop star born Raymond O'Sullivan originally intended to call himself simply Gilbert, but Gordon Mills—also responsible for the name of °Engelbert Humperdinck—suggested that he keep his surname, no doubt bearing in mind the association with the comic opera team of Gilbert and Sullivan.

Ouida : The English novelist Marie Louise de la Ramée adopted her pen name from her own pronunciation, as a child, of her name Louise. Born of Anglo-French parentage, the authoress of the gushingly romantic novel *Under Two Flags* (1867)—now a half-forgotten period piece—was originally Maria Louisa Rame [Eileen Bigland, *Ouida: The Passionate Victorian*, 1950].

Philo Pacificus : This was the name adopted by the American clergyman and pacifist Noah Worcester for *A Solemn Review of the Custom of War* (1814), as well as some other works. It is mock-classical for "peace-lover."

Patti Page : It is possible that the first name adopted by Clara Ann Fowler, the American popular singer, was taken from the surname of the singer of a hundred years earlier, Adelina Patti. Her surname was given her by the Page Company, a dairy in Tulsa, Oklahoma, when she appeared in their radio commercials.

Janis Paige : The American film actress's real name is Donna Mae Jaden. She derived her new first name from Elsie Janis, and her surname Paige from a grandparent.

Palinurus : A symbolic classical name used as a pseudonym by the British critic and novelist Cyril Connolly for *The Unquiet Grave* (1944), which he described as "a word-cycle in three or four rhythms: art, love, nature and religion." In mythology, Palinurus was the pilot of Aeneas's ship, in Virgil's *Aeneid*, famed for his fall from the ship to the sea. Connolly thought that Palinurus fell through the typically modern will to failure.

Paracelsus : An impressive name, clinically classical, that was assumed by a man with a possibly even more impressive real name: Philippus Aureolus Theophrastus Bombast von Hohenheim, a Swiss-German doctor of the time of the Renaissance. Von Hohenheim regarded himself as "para-Celsus," i.e. "beyond Celsus." Celsus was a first-century Roman physician, and von Hohenheim indeed outdid Celsus in the sense that he was not merely a physician but a noted alchemist. In addition he was one of the most outrageous and extraordinary men of the Renaissance, a unique blend of cunning charlatan and medical genius.

Parkyakarkus : Anything but a classical name. It was assumed by the American radio comedian Harry Einstein, working early in his career as Harry Parke. He reckoned it would be a name easily remembered and pronounced by Americans, who would recognize it as an invitation to take a seat — "park your carcass!"

Peter Parley : A name — suggesting a chatterer or tale-teller — that originally belonged to Samuel Goodrich, the American author of moral tales for children, for *The Tales of Peter Parley about America* (1827). These tales, actually a series of books, were widely imitated, so that there were other Peter Parleys, including seven English ones (among them George Mogridge, who was also Old Humphrey and Ephraim Holding, John Bennet, William Martin, and William Tegg).

Mrs. Partington : Benjamin Shillaber, the 19th-century American humorist, created this lady as a kind of Mrs. Malaprop for his *Life and Sayings of Mrs. Partington* (1854) and other books in which Mrs. Partington chats pleasantly yet ignorantly on a whole range of topics. There had been a real Mrs. Partington, it seems, who during a storm at

Sidmouth, England, (in 1824) had tried to brush back the sea with her mop. References to her abortive effort became legendary and metaphorical, so that the House of Lords had been compared to her in a speech (1831) attacking that body's opposition to the progress of reform. Shillaber admitted that he borrowed his own character from the English archetype. He originally used her in 1847 for a newspaper on which he was employed.

Anthony Pasquin : This was the pseudonym adopted by the English critic and satirist John Williams, who settled in America at the end of the 18th century. He took the name from the statue called Pasquin in Rome. This was unearthed in 1501 as an incomplete Roman bust, and a habit became established of attaching satirical Latin verses to it on St. Mark's Day. From this practice came the term "pasquinade" to apply to any brief but anonymous satirical comment. (It is not certain how the statue acquired its name: one theory is that it was named after a local shopkeeper whose premises were near the site where it was discovered.)

Ted Pauker : This is the standard pen name of the British editor and writer Robert Conquest. Its exact origin is not clear, although *Pauker* is German for "kettle-drummer," as well as having a slang meaning "school-teacher," "crammer." Conquest is also a poet, and as Ted Pauker had some of his verse included in *The New Oxford Book of Light Verse* (1978), edited by Kingsley Amis. Shortly before his collection of poems there appears in the book a selection of limericks by one Victor Gray. Gray is given the same birth year as Pauker (1917). A columnist on the *Sunday Times*, in an informal review of the book (June 4, 1978), pointed out that Conquest's full name is George Robert Acworth Conquest, and that if you take the initials of his first three names and precede the name of the unknown rhymster by them you get G.R.A. Victory, otherwise an anagram of Victor Gray, with a victory of course being a conquest! This sleuthwork can hardly have pleased the venerable Oxford University Press.

Saint Paul : When the Christian disciple and missionary was still a Jew he was known by the name Saul. After his dramatic conversion he took the Roman name Paul, which he used for preference as a proud Roman citizen. (The actual changeover is alluded to in Acts 13, ix — "Saul, also called Paul.") This is thus one of the earliest well known name changes in history. Why did the Jew Saul choose the name Paul specifically? In Hebrew "Saul" means "asked for"; in Latin "Paul" (Paulus) means "little," and as such was a standard Roman name. The meaning of the new name may perhaps have been significant in some way, but perhaps the theologian chose the name simply because it was close in sound to his previous name. It certainly marked a transition: both from Jew to Christian, and to Paul's new role as leader when Barnabas, formerly the leader, handed over to him. See two entries down for Paul's associated saint, Peter.

Pelé : The Brazilian footballer born Edson Arantes do Nascimento claims that he doesn't know the meaning of his "game name," and that it doesn't mean anything in any language known to him. He apparently was first so called (or nicknamed) when he was only seven. At least, as he points out, it's easy to say — in many languages [Pelé and Robert L. Fish, *My Life and the Beautiful Game*, 1977].

Saint Peter : The early Christian leader who was the first pope was originally named Simon (or Simeon). As leader of the Disciples, he was given the name Peter more or less as a nickname by Jesus: "Thou art Peter, and upon this rock I will build my church" (St. Matthew 16, xviii). The name is a play on words since in Greek *Petros*, in Latin *Petrus*, and in Aramaic (which was Christ's vernacular tongue) *Cephas* all mean "rock," "stone." The popularity of the name as a Christian name stems entirely from this biblical origin. (However, Simon is not such a bad name. It means "hearkening" or "one who hears.")

Philidor : This was the assumed surname of the French musicians, *père et fils*, André and François-André Danican. Their ancestor Michel Danican (died about 1659) had been nicknamed Philidor, after an Italian musician of this name, by Louis XIII as a compliment to his skill.

Esther Phillips : Esther May Jones, the American pop singer, first appeared as Little Esther. Then, seeking a more dramatic change of name, she spotted Phillips on a gas station sign and adopted that. Maybe if she had traveled another hundred yards or so she could have found something a little more original.

Phiz : One of the most famous illustrators of the works of Surtees and Dickens was the artist Hablot Knight Brown. Early in his career he used the partly facetious name *Nemo* (Latin for "nobody") to illustrate some plates for *Pickwick Papers*. Later he chose a name designed to match Dickens's own pseudonym of °Boz. At the same time, "phiz" is a slang term in its own right for "face" (from "physiognomy"), also suitable for a portrayer of facial expressions.

Edith Piaf : Tania, Denise Jay, and Hugette Hélia were early stage names used by the famed French singer and entertainer Edith Gassion before she became Edith Piaf. Her new name was given her (1935) by nightclub owner Louis Leplée. He wanted to call her "Moineau," French for "sparrow," but this name was already being used, as La Môme Moineau ("Kid Sparrow"), by Lucienne Garcia, so he had to think of something else. The nearest suitable alternative was the French slang word for "sparrow," *piaf*, so that was what the "little sparrow of Paris" came to be called [Edith Piaf, *The Wheel of Fortune*, 1965].

Nova Pilbeam : Margery Pilbeam, the British film actress, had the same Christian name as her mother, so she changed her first name to Nova for her mother's family associations with Nova Scotia.

Peter Pindar : The name was adopted by more than one writer, notably by the English satirist John Wolcot. Pindar was actually a Greek lyric poet of the 4th century B.C., and in his first publication, *Lyric Odes to the Royal Academicians for 1782*, Wolcot described himself as "a distant relation to the poet of Thebes." Doubtless Paul Pindar, the English antiquary who was secretary to William Cobbett, based his name on this. Most of the Peter Pindars were imitators of Walcot, notably C.F. Lawler, described by the *Biographical Dictionary* in 1816 as "a poetaster of little or no art."

Pintoricchio : A somewhat pleasanter nickname than that given to other classical painters. Bernardino di Betti was so called because he was small in stature: the word is Italian for "little painter." Compare Botticelli ("little barrel") and Masolino ("little Tom").

Pocahontas : The real name of the daughter of the American-Indian chief Powhatan was Matoaka. Her nickname-cum-assumed name means "sportive." Little might have been heard of her had she not married (1614) the English colonizer John Rolfe and gone with him (1616) to England, where she died the following year. All these names (Pocahontas, Powhatan, Matoaka, Rolfe) live on in the place names of various habitations in the United States.

Boris Polevoy : Many English-speaking moviegoers have seen the Russian classic film *Story of a Real Man*, based on the novel (1946) by Boris Polevoy. Polevoy's original surname was Kampov, but this was changed by the editor of *Tverskaya Pravda*, in which he had had an article published (under the pseudonym B. Ovod) as a 14-year-old schoolboy. Kampov, thought the editor, was too "Latin," so he changed it to the Russian equivalent — i.e., from Latin *campus* (field) to Russian *pole* (field).

Pont : Graham Laidler, the British cartoonist, originally intended to take up a career as an architect, and adopted the name Pontex Maximus, Latin for "great builder," which was already a family nickname after he had paid an early visit to Italy. This later became abbreviated to Pont, subsequently a famous name in the pages of *Punch*. He thus did not adopt his name from Pont Street, London, as has been conjectured [R.G.G. Price, *A History of Punch*, 1957].

Father Prout : Francis Mahoney, the 19th-century Irish humorist, adopted this name for his *Prout Papers* (1834-6), which purported to be the autobiography of a rural Irish priest. Mahoney had himself abandoned the priesthood for literary pursuits after being expelled from the Jesuits (1830). He also used the pseudonyms Jeremy Savonarolo (for *Facts and Figures from Italy*, 1847, addressed to Charles Dickens), Matthew Stradling, and Oliver Yorke.

Kozma Prutkov : A joint pseudonym for the Russian author A.K. Tolstoy and his cousins A.M. and V.M. Zhemchuzhnikov, poets. They used the name from 1853 to 1863 for satirical, humorous and nonsense verse. The name used was that of the Zhemchuzhnikov brothers' valet.

M. Quad : An "em" is a unit of measurement used in spacing type when typesetting; a "quad" is the name of the piece of typemetal used in this spacing. Such a pseudonym could only be assumed by a printer, as indeed it was — the American printer, journalist and humorist Charles Lewis.

Ellery Queen : This is the joint pseudonym of the American crime novelists whose names are usually given as Frederic Dannay and Manfred B. Lee — originally Daniel Nathan and Manford Lepofsky. The pseudonym is well known as the name of the private detective in the novels of these two writers, and was itself based on the name of a boyhood friend of theirs, Ellery. (They had also considered James Griffen and Wilbur See.) In choosing the detective's name for their own pen name, Dannay and Lee felt that readers would be likely to remember Ellery Queen since it appeared throughout the books and was, they judged, unusual and memorable anyway. See also °Barnaby Ross.

Patrick Quentin : More American detective fiction writers hide behind this name. It was used, as was Q. Patrick and Jonathan Stagge, for a group of novelists active in the 1920s and 1930s. There were basically four in the group — Richard Webb, Hugh Wheeler, Martha Kelly, and Mary Aswell — and the name was used either by these four or by one of the four with any one or more of the other three, a suitably convoluted procedure for crime story authors!

Marie Rambert : The real name of the Polish-born English ballet teacher and founder of the Ballet Rambert (1930) is usually given as Myriam Ramberg. Her birth certificate however gives her first name as Cyvia. Myriam, therefore, was originally a nickname, given her by her French poet friend, Edmée Delebecque. Myriam's father's family name was Rambam, and her father and his brothers had this name changed to make them seem only children (and thus escape military service), so one son retained the name Rambam, one (her father) took the name Ramberg, one took Rambert, as Myriam herself did, and the fourth, to represent their Polish nationality, assumed the name Warszawski ("from Warsaw") [Marie Rambert, *Quicksilver: An Autobiography*, 1972].

Rasputin : The infamous Russian monk who was the favorite of Czar Nicholas II and his wife Alexandra Fyodorovna was born into the family of the peasant Yefim Novykh, at Pokrovskoye, Siberia. His original name was thus Gregory Yefimovich Novykh. As a religious fanatic he led a dissolute life and was given the nickname Rasputin (Russian *rasputny*, "debauched" or "dissolute"), which he subsequently adopted as a surname. An earlier uncomplimentary nickname had been Varnak, a Siberian word meaning "vagabond" or "runaway thief;" Rasputin was the son of a horse-stealer and one himself, and thus established his notorious reputation while still quite young [Prince Yousoupoff, *Rasputin*, 1974].

Man Ray : The American surrealist painter and photographer was of Jewish Russian stock, born Emmanuel Rudnitsky. He changed his name when at art school in Manhattan to avoid the taunts of his fellow students. Many sources (e.g., *Encyclopaedia Britannica,* Clarke) state that his real name is "unknown." It was revealed, however, in a report of his death (1976) in the American Russian émigré newspaper *Novoye Russkoye Slovo.*

Ted Ray : Both the original name and true date of birth of the well known English comedian are on the uncertain side. His surname at birth seems to have been Alden, changed by his parents when he was still a boy to Olden. As for his date of birth, it varies between about 1906 and 1910. We do at least know that Charles Olden appeared early in his career as Nedlo (his surname reversed) and also as a comic violinist named Hugh Neek ("unique!"). Not long after he selected his permanent stage name — adopting it from a noted golfer of the day, Ted Ray, who was the British winner of the U.S. Open Golf Championship of 1920. And what could be better than a brief, bright name like this for a snappy comic?

Ronald Reagan : Something of a curiosity. When the American President was a film actor, he pronounced his name "Reegan." On abandoning the screen for politics (in 1966) he changed the pronunciation to "Raygen." The spelling of the name remained the same for both roles. This is the only name-change recorded in this book that is a change in pronunciation only, and Ronald Reagan is thus the only name appearing in the Who's Who and Index with identical spellings for both the real name and the "pseudonym."

Mary Renault : The English novelist, famous for her series of books based on the Theseus legend, was born Mary Challans. She began to write when a nurse before the Second World War — when her writing had to be kept secret from Matron, her "presiding deity" in the hospital, who might not have approved! She chose the name from Froissart, the French 14th-century historian and poet. "I never thought of the car!" she said.

Debbie Reynolds : The American film actress was not even a Deborah, but Mary Frances Reynolds. Her new first name was given her when she was beginning her career (1948) by Jack Warner, of Warner Brothers. She is said to dislike it to this day. By adopting it, however, she at least started something of a fashion for the name and boosted similarly abbreviated girls' names (Mandy, Sandy, Katie, Vicky, Lindy and the like).

Ruggiero Ricci : The American virtuoso violinist indeed had Italian ancestors, but he himself began life as Woodrow Wilson (later Roger) Rich. His father italianized "Roger Rich" (strictly speaking, Roger should be "Ruggero" in Italian) in the hopes that such a "classical" name would be a propitious one — and doubtless a prophetic one ("rich"). His hopes were fulfilled.

Craig Rice : This does seem to be one pseudonym whose

origin is unknown. It belonged to Georgiana Ann Randolph, the American mystery novelist and film script writer. Also unknown is the exact number of husbands that she had.

Elmer Rice : Elmer Reizenstein, the American playwright and novelist, simplified his name thus (in 1914) since he was so often misunderstood on the telephone. Well, *everyone* can spell "rice"...

Cliff Richard : Harold Webb is probably not such an exciting name for a pop star and film actor. How did the change come about? Harold, at the start of his career, felt he needed a new name and had always liked Richard but found the choice of a surname difficult. (He toyed with Richard Webb, but rejected it.) The manager of his group, The Drifters, agreed that a change of name was desirable, and one member of the group proposed Russ Clifford. Harry Webb thought about it, felt it was too "soft-spoken," and hazarded Cliff Russard. Almost there. But meanwhile an earlier manager, Johnny Foster, had come up with Cliff Richard — "Not Richards, but without the 's'. It's just the name we're looking for. Everybody will call him Cliff Richards and then we can correct them — that way they'll never forget his name." So Cliff Richard he became — the name first being used at the public appearance of Cliff Richard and The Drifters at a ballroom in Derby (in 1958) [David Winter, *New Singer, New Song: The Cliff Richard Story*, 1967].

John Ringling : The name of the circus impresario is almost his own, since his father, a German was August Rüngeling. To anglicize it slightly was, perhaps coincidentally, to create a name that sounds just right for the head of a circus!

Larry Rivers : Yitzroch Loiza Grossberg, the American painter, started his career as a jazz musician and formed his own group, "Loiza Grossberg and his Combo." A nightclub musician suggested that he should change this to "Larry Rivers and his Mudcats."

Edward G. Robinson : How did the Romanian-born American film actor change from Emanuel Goldenberg to Edward G. Robinson? The exact process is described in interesting detail in his autobiography. Given the need for a change, since Emanuel Goldenberg was "not a name for an actor ... too long, too foreign and ... too Jewish," "The obvious ploy was translation, but Emanuel Goldenhill didn't work and Goldenmount was too pretentious.... I continued to debate lists of names in the phone book, catalogs, and encyclopedias I picked up in the Astor Place Library ... and none would satisfy me. Then one night I went to see a play, a highly urbane English drawing room comedy, and from my perch in the rear of the second balcony I heard a butler on stage announce to a lady (could it have been Mrs. Fiske?), 'Madam, a gentleman to see you — a Mr. Robinson.'"

"Mr. Robinson! I liked the ring and strength of it. And, furthermore, it was a common change. I knew many Rosenbergs, Rabinowitzes, and Roths who'd switched to Robinson. Yes, that was it. From this time forward I would be Robinson—Emanuel Robinson. That decision was greeted at the Academy with something less than enthusiasm. Emanuel and Robinson were an odd coupling. What other names began with *E*? Edgar? Egbert? Ellery? Ethan? Edward? Why not Edward, then King of England?... Edward Robinson. But I could not desert the Goldenberg entirely. That became the *G*, my private treaty with my past. But that wasn't enough. Some managers didn't like the *G*, and quite arbitrarily one of them translated it to Gould. And so, if you ever look at the early programs, you will see me billed as Edward Gould Robinson..." [Edward G. Robinson with Leonard Spigelgass, *All My Yesterdays: An Autobiography*, 1974].

Sugar Ray Robinson : There was another boxer Ray Robinson, and early in his career Walker Smith used one of his amateur certificates to qualify for a bout—all part of the game!

Rob Roy : The real name of the Scottish Highland outlaw was Robert Macgregor. The usual explanation behind his name is that he signed himself thus, meaning "red Rob," with reference to his dark red hair. However, the motto of the Macgregors was "My tribe is royal," and "Roy" could have derived from this.

Ginger Rogers : A name quite different from Virginia McMath. Ginger was apparently a childhood nickname of the future actress. Also in her childhood her parents separated, and when her mother married John Rogers (1920), Virginia ("Ginger") took his surname as well.

Roy Rogers : The name chosen by the famous cowboy movie star born Leonard Slye seems to have been an arbitrary one, vaguely attractive, but certainly an improvement on his true name. Early, when singing with the group the Pioneer Trio, he called himself Dick Weston (1930). Of course, he might have been influenced by °Ginger Rogers or even Will Rogers, who had been a cowboy. By his two wives he had 10 children, two boys and eight girls: Roy, Jr., and John; Robin, Cheryl, Linda Lou, Marion, Scottish Ward, Mary, Little Doe, and Deborah Lee.

Sax Rohmer : The British writer of oriental mystery stories having the central character Fu Manchu was born Arther Henry Ward, changing Henry to Sarsfield when a boy of 15. His name derives, somewhat esoterically, from Anglo-Saxon: *sax* meaning "blade" (from which maybe the Saxons came to be so called), and *rohmer* meaning "wandering." In other words, a "wandering blade"—otherwise a freelance! He also wrote as Michael Furey.

Michael Romanoff : Here was the noblest impostor of them all. The Lithuanian-born American restaurateur and film actor born Harry Gerguson posed (to 1958) as His Imperial Highness Prince Michael Alexandrovitch Dmitry Obolensky Romanoff. Any émigré Russian will tell you what weight such names carried in the ancien régime. (Earlier, he had used the try-out noble names of William Wellington, Arthur Wellesley, and Count Gladstone.) When once at a party in his role of royal Russian, someone spoke Russian to him. He turned away and said to a friend, "How vulgar, we only spoke French at court." We shall not often see his like again...

Mickey Rooney : Joe Yule, Jr., first appeared as Mickey McGuire (1926). Six years later he switched to the name that brought him movie fame. Why Mickey Rooney? No one seems quite sure. Perhaps the reference was to the song *Little Annie Rooney*, bearing in mind the actor's small stature. Another theory maintains that his mother had suggested his name should be Mickey Looney and his modification of this was the result.

Milton Rosmer : Arthur Milton Lunt, the English actor and director, adopted his surname from the character of this name in Ibsen's play *Rosmersholm* (1886). In this respect compare °Rebecca West.

Barnaby Ross : Another well known name used by the crime novelists Frederick Dannay and Manfred B. Lee (see °Ellery Queen) — this one being for the stories that featured a detective named Drury Lane. (London theatregoers will recognize this.) The name Barnaby Ross comes from the Ellery Queen book *The Roman Hat Mystery*, in which there is a reference to the "Now-ancient Barnaby Ross murder case."

Martin Ross : The Irish author Violet Florence Martin, together with her cousin Edith Somerville, wrote a number of stories and novels telling of Irish life under the name "Somerville and Ross." Violet Martin's name derived from the house where she was born, Ross House in County Galway.

T.E. Ross : This was the name under which T.E. (Thomas Edward) Lawrence, popularly known as "Lawrence of Arabia," the British soldier, archaeologist and writer, enlisted in the Royal Air Force in 1922. His true identity soon became known, so the following year he transferred to the Tank Corps as T.E. Shaw, a name chosen out of respect for George Bernard Shaw. In 1925 he returned to the RAF and two years later adopted the name Shaw by deed poll.

Samuel Roxy : A pseudonym interesting not so much for its origin (which would appear to be arbitrary) but for its subsequent associations: Samuel L. Rothafel, the American film distributor, had chosen a name which passed to the first magnificent "picture palaces." This, therefore, is the origin of the Roxy Cinema and in turn of the pop group Roxy Music (formed 1970), who picked the cinema name to suggest both a kind of nostalgic glamour and "rock."

Titta Ruffo : Here we have an unusual example of a professional name derived, albeit indirectly, from a family pet. Oresta Titta had a dog named Ruffo of whom he was very fond. One day, while hunting with his master, Ruffo was accidentally shot and killed. Titta was grief-stricken, and later, when his son was born, named the child Ruffo in memory of the dog. In time, however, when the boy grew up and started on the career that was to make him one of Italy's best-known baritone singers, he came to dislike his canine-derived name. Not wishing to offend his father, though, he did not change his name completely but simply switched his two names round: Ruffo Titta became Titta Ruffo!

Fred Russell : The English ventriloquist and variety artiste Thomas Frederick Parnell changed his name because, as a young man, there could have been undesirable political associations with the name of the Irish president of the Nationalist Party, Charles Stewart Parnell.

Françoise Sagan : The French author of *Bonjour Tristesse* began life as Françoise Quoirez. She took her pen name from Princesse de Sagan, a character in Proust's *A la Recherche du Temps Perdu*.

Saki : Hector Hugh Munro, the British short-story writer, first used his pen name for the short story collection *Reginald* (1904). According to his sister, the pseudonym comes from a line in Fitzgerald's translation of *The Rubaiyat of Omar Khayyam* — "And when like her, O Saki, you shall pass" — but another theory maintains that the name is a contraction of Sakya Muni or Skyamuni, one of the names of the Buddha.

Soupy Sales : The American TV entertainer and film actor Milton Hines was called Soupy when a child since "Hines" sounded like "Heinz." He changed his name to this in 1952, when he was 26.

George Sand : One of the most famous of literary pseudonyms. The French novelist Amandine-Aurore-Lucile Dudevant derived it from her liaison with the writer Jules Sandeau. (George, it seems, comes from the fact that Sandeau first advised her to write independently, without his assistance, on St. George's Day.) Mme Dudevant first used the name in 1831 for writing done jointly with Sandeau: some articles for *Le Figaro* and their first joint novel *Rose et Blanche*. She herself first used the name independently the following year, for her novel *Indiana*. Earlier she had used the name Blaise Bonnain, taken from a carpenter she had known as a girl. Note that "George" is so spelled — not in the French manner with an 's'. The abbreviated form "Sand" was devised by Jules, and used both by him (as Jules Sand) and Maurice Sand, the son of George Sand and her husband the baron Dudevant.

Sapper : The English creator of "Bulldog Drummond," Herman (sometimes recorded as Hector) McNeile adopted his pseudonym, the army term for a military engineer, when he was an officer in the Royal Engineers. (Bulldog Drummond? He was the ex-army officer who foils the activities of the international crook, Carl Peterson!) The name was devised for him by Lord Northcliffe, since no regular serving officer could write under his own name. McNeile attempted to write under his own name after World War One, but the public would have none of it [*The Times*, December 14, 1974].

Leo Sayer : The rock singer was born Gerard Hughes Sayer. When Adam Faith's wife first met him she said, "Hey, he's like a little lion" (Sayer had a long mane of hair at the time). The name appealed, and stuck [*Reveille*, January 12, 1979].

Scaeva : A grisly story lies behind the name. John Stubbes, a 16th-century Puritan zealot, published a pamphlet entitled *The Discovery of a Gaping Gulf* (1579), condemning Queen Elizabeth's proposed marriage with Henry, Duke of Anjou. For this traitorous act, his right hand was ordered to be cut off. *Scaeva* is Latin for "left-handed."

Dr. Schmidt : A "cover" name, presumably an arbitrary one, chosen by the great German poet and playwright Johann von Schiller when fleeing his employer (1782), the Duke of Württemberg. Schiller was originally a surgeon in a Württemberg regiment, and went absent without leave to be present at a performance of his first play *Die Räuber* (1781). He was arrested by the Duke of Württemberg and condemned to publish nothing but medical treatises. He escaped from Württemberg under this assumed name and spent several years — the so-called *Wanderjahre* — outside the country.

Sir Walter Scott : More than one author was tempted to take advantage of the success of the great Scots novelist and poet. One noted example was that of the American writer James Kirke Paulding, the close friend of Washington Irving (see p. 20), who in 1813 published under this name *The Lay of the Scotch Fiddle, a Tale of Havre de Grace*. This of course was plain plagiary, and a real Scotch fiddle! Scott's novels were very much to the German taste, and one German author who assumed the novelist's name for a work of his own, purportedly translated freely from the English ("*frei nach dem Englischen*"), was Willibald Alexis. His "Scottish" novel *Walladmor* appeared in Berlin in 1824. A year later, a version of this was published in London ("freely translated into German from the English of Sir Walter Scott, and now freely translated from the German into English"), and *this* was translated into French and was published in Paris, the same year, in three volumes.

Martinus Scriblerus : A jokey name for the members of the so-called "Scriblerus Club," formed about 1713, and including such well-known authors as Pope, Swift, and Arbuthnot. They undertook the production of the *Memoirs of Martinus Scriblerus*, printed in the second volume of the works of Pope in 1741. Henry Fielding cashed in on the name in slightly modified form, H. Secundus Scriblerus, for *The Tragedy of Tragedies; or, The Life and Death of Tom Thumb the Great* (1731).

David Seville : The name assumed by Ross Bagdassarian, creator of the Chipmunks, calls for little comment — it is simply a suitable English name to replace his un-English one. It is worth noting, however, that the names of the Chipmunks, Simon, Theodore, and Alvin, were the real first names of executives of the Liberty Record Company.

Lynn Seymour : The Canadian ballet dancer was born Lynn Springbett. In spite of the possible suitability of such an agile name for a ballerina (although it does also suggest "bedsprings"), choreographer Kenneth MacMillan advised Lynn to change it to Seymour. There seems to be a certain magic in this name, that of Henry VIII's third wife, since several other people have adopted it, including Jane Seymour, of course. But no one seems to have wished to change to Anne Boleyn.

Omar Sharif : The Egyptian-born film star, of Syrian-Lebanese descent, was born Michel Shalhoub. He explains in his autobiography how he arrived at his stage name: "I'd changed my name to do 'The Blazing Sun.' At birth, I was Michael Shalhoub. My first name, Michael, annoyed me. Anybody could be a Michael. I'd tried to come up with something that sounded Middle Eastern and that could still be spelled in every language. Omar! Two syllables that had a good ring to them and reminded Americans of General Omar Bradley. Next I thought of combining Omar with the Arabic Sherif, but I realised that this would evoke the word 'sheriff,' which was a bit too cowboyish. So I opted for a variant — I became Omar Sharif..." [Omar Sharif with Marie-Thérèse Guinchard, *The Eternal Male*, 1977]. (A footnote by the translator of the book from the French, Martin Sokolinsky, points out that the Arabic word *sherif* is a form of title applied to one of noble ancestry in a Middle Eastern country.)

Jack Sharkey : The American heavyweight boxer Joseph Zukauskas derived his name not from an anglicization of his surname but from a former leading heavyweight, Sailor Tom Sharkey.

Luke Sharp : A name that for a writer of detective stories (Robert Barr) provokes a similar groan to that caused by Justin Case.

N. Shchedrin : If English-speaking readers are at all familiar with any work of the Russian author born Mikhail Yevgrafovich Saltykov, who is also often called Saltykov-Shchedrin, it will probably be with his famous novel describing the decay of the provincial gentry *The Golovlëv Family* (1872-6), translated by Natalie Duddington, among others. Saltykov's son has explained how his father came by his pseudonym, which is based on the Russian word *shchedry*, "generous": "It was like this. When he was in government service, he was advised that it was not done to sign one's work with one's real name. So he had to find a pen name, but could not hit on anything suitable. My mother suggested that he should choose a pseudonym based on the word 'shchedry,' as in his writings he was extraordinarily generous with any kind of sarcasm. My father like his wife's idea, and from then on he called himself Shchedrin." It is possible, however, that the name could have come from a servant in the employ of Saltykov's family, or from a local merchant T. Shchedrin, or some acquaintance of Saltykov, or it could even derive from the word *shchedrina*, "pockmarks," with reference to the "pockmarks" on the face of Russia at the time (1870s) [Dmitriev, pp. 58-9].

Dinah Shore : Did Frances Rose Shore, the American actress, ever consider that her new name might suggest "dinosaur?" The change was initially prompted by "everyone down in Nashville" changing her name Frances to Fanny and quipping: "Fanny sat on a tack. Fanny Rose. Fanny Rose sat on a tack. Did Fanny rise?" "I had to do something," explained Frances — so she changed Frances Rose to Dinah, from the song of that name.

The Silent Traveller : Chiang Yee, the Chinese-born writer, famous for his travel books in English — *The Silent Traveller in*... London, Oxford, New York, Edinburgh, among other places — derived his name from his Chinese pseudonym meaning "dumb walking man."

Georges Sim : An obvious contraction of the real name of the famous Belgian-born writer of detective fiction (featuring Maigret) Georges Simenon. He once stated that he has written under 17 pen names. Among others he used were Christian Brule (based on his mother's maiden name), Orson, Aramis (one of the "Three Musketeers") and Jean du Perry. The pen name Georges Sim must not be confused with the real name George Sim — that of an English poet, novelist and playwright who was born half a century before Simenon (in 1847).

Nina Simone : Eunice Waymon, the American jazz musician, had changed her name to avoid embarrassing her parents when she worked (as a singer) at the Midtown Bar, Atlantic City, New Jersey. Nina was a name she had been called when a child; Simone simply seemed to go well with it.

Simplicissimus : A name adopted for a while by the Russian socialist Plekhanov, who also wrote as Volgin (see °Lenin). It derives from the title of a 1669 book by the 17th-century German author Hans Jakob Christoffel von Grimmelshausen, in full: *Der Abenteuerliche Simplicissimus Teutsch, das ist: Beschreibung des Lebens eines Seltzamen Vagantens Genannt Melchior Sternfels von Fuchshaim* ("The Adventurous German Simpleton, that is: Description of the Life of a Strange Wanderer Named Melchior Sternfels von Fuchshaim"). Canny readers will have noticed that the name of the hero is an anagram of that of the author; moreover, the book was supposedly published by one Hermann Scheifhaim von Sulsfort, a similarly anagrammatic name. And as if this wasn't enough, the author purported to be a certain Samuel Greifensohn von Hirschfeld! The book itself is a picaresque novel about the adventures of a simple youth in various guises (soldier, robber, slave, and the like) and gives a vivid picture of the havoc wrought in Germany by the Thirty Years' War (1618-1648).

Sirin : This was an early pseudonym used by Vladimir Nabokov, author of *Lolita* (1955), when he was still writing in Russian, although in emigration in the United States (from 1919). The name is that of a legendary bird of paradise in Russian folklore. Nabokov chose it so that he would not be confused with his father, Vladimir Dmitriyevich Nabokov, a criminologist and political figure (he was one of the founders of the "Kadets," the Constitutional Democratic Party led by Milyukov).

Skanderbeg : George Kastrioti, the 15th-century Albanian national hero, adopted this name when, as Iskander, after Alexander the Great, he was converted to Islam with the rank of bey — i.e. "Skanderbeg."

Smectymnuus : A rather unattractive joint pseudonym for no less than five English 17th-century Presbyterian ministers for a pamphlet (1641) attacking Bishop Joseph Hall's claim of divine right for the episcopacy. The name comes from the initials of the five just men: Stephen **M**arshall, **E**dmund **C**alamy, **T**homas **Y**oung, **M**atthew **N**ewcomen, and William Spurstow (the latter's "W" producing the "double u").

Smokey Joe : The English gunslinger and director of the British Fast Draw Association was in the news in the spring of 1978. The sad fact was that Joseph Sewell, of Kensal Green, London, was unable to obtain a firearms certificate permitting him to have a deactivated gun in order to take part in competitions. In spite of Smokey's four applications, Scotland Yard refused him a certificate because, they said, to grant one would be "a way of bringing lethal weapons into circulation." Smokey Joe appealed against this decision, but lost. "It's tough trying to be a gunslinger without a gun," he sighed [*Sunday Times*, March 19, and *The Times*, April 8, 1978].

Sir Henry F.R. Soame : There seems to be a case of mistaken identity here. This name is usually given as the pseudonym of the soldier, historian, and Member of Parliament Sir Henry Edward Bunbury. The *Dictionary of National Biography* points out, however, that it is the *real* name of Sir Henry Bunbury's cousin, Henry Francis Robert Soame, born ten years earlier (1768). To the 20th century neither gentleman may seem particularly significant, but the instance is an example of the shaky historical foundation some pseudonyms can have.

Sodoma : It seems somewhat perverse of the 16th-century Italian painter Giovanni Bazzi to deliberately choose to adopt his forthrightly descriptive nickname as a pseudonym, but presumably he knew best. A reputed homosexual he may have been, but he was also a highly gifted fresco painter, and a worthy rival of the master of the fresco, Raphael, who superseded him in 1509 in his position of painter to pope Julius II.

Lydia Sokolova : Born plain Hilda Munnings, the English ballet dancer was given her new name by Diaghilev himself: "I have signed your photograph ... with the name Lydia Sokolova, and I hope you will live up to the name of Sokolova, as it is that of a great dancer in Russia" [Richard Buckle, *Dancing for Diaghilev; The Memoirs of Lydia Sokolova*, 1960].

Sonny : The American pop singer and writer Salvatore Bono teamed with Cher and married her in 1964 (although the pair were to separate ten years later). Earlier he had recorded as Don Christy, a name derived from those of his first wife, Donna, and daughter, Christy.

Jean Sorel : Leonard Ashley suggests that the name adopted by Jean de Rochbrune, the French film actor, may have been taken from that of Julien Sorel, the hero of °Stendhal's *Le Rouge et le Noir.*

Suzi Soul : This was the name used by the American pop singer Suzi Quatro when she was a television go-go dancer at the age of 14, and the following year for her group Suzi Soul and the Pleasure Seekers. Quatro is sometimes thought to be a stage name, but it is her real one, of Italian origin. Suzi was extensively promoted in Britain by °Mickie Most.

Dusty Springfield : Mary O'Brien, the British pop singer, took her name from an early group, The Springfields, of which one member was Tom Field. Dusty originated as a nickname.

Spy : This was the name selected for his work by the English cartoonist and caricaturist Leslie (from 1918 Sir Leslie) Ward, who made many famous contributions to the topical illustrated magazine *Vanity Fair* founded in 1868 as a periodical designed to "display the vanities of the week." Ward was asked to choose a pen-name by the magazine's editor, Thomas Gibson Bowles, and did so by opening a copy of Dr. Johnson's Dictionary at random and selecting the first word his eye fell on. This was "spy" — a highly apt name for a man whose professional job was to "spy" on society and produce his observations in pictorial form. Other artists contributing to *Vanity Fair* were °Ape, Sir Max Beerbohm (as Ruth, Sulto, and Max) and Walter Sickert (as Sic). (Editor Bowles wrote as Jehu Junior, a name retained by his successors until the magazine closed in 1929.) [1. Leslie Ward, *Forty Years of "Spy"*, 1915; 2. John Arlott, "Ape, Spy, and Jehu Junior," in *Late Extra: A Miscellany by "Evening News" Writers, Artists, and Photographers*, 1952].

Stainless Stephen : The English music hall comedian Arthur Baynes was born in Sheffield, a city long famous for its stainless steel. The London-Sheffield express train is still called "The Master Cutler."

Joseph Stalin : Iosif Vissarionovich Dzhugashvili, the Soviet Communist leader, did not adopt his pseudonym — basically meaning "steel" — all at once. It took some evolving. He was contributing to Bolshevik magazines such as *Zvezda* ("The Star") under the name K.S. and K. Salin, for example, two or three years before he first used his familiar pseudonym of Stalin (in 1913). Opinions seems divided as to the symbolic intention of the meaning of the name. Undoubtedly Russian *stal'* means "steel," and certainly, after repeated arrest, banishment and imprisonment in czarist days Dzhugashvili's spirit was unbroken, but it is unlikely that the name was given him by °Lenin, as legend has it, because of his seeming "steel-like" nature. Another early favorite pseudonym of the Bolshevik activist was Koba — said to be Turkish for "fearless" — and at one time he used the name Kato, perhaps with reference to the forthrightness of Cato the Elder. And these were not all. Among other names favored by the revolutionary were David Bars, Gayoz Nizheradze, I. Besoshvili, Zakhar Gregoryan Melikyants, Ogoness Vartanovich Totomyants, K. Solin (perhaps suggesting Russian *sol'*, "salt"), and K. Stefin. Some of these names are reminiscent of his own real Georgian name [Robert Payne, *Stalin*, 1966].

Sir Henry Morton Stanley : It comes as something of a surprise to discover that the famous English explorer was born in Wales as

John Rowlands, the illegitimate son of John Rowlands and Elizabeth Parry. When John was in America at the age of 18 (in 1859) he was adopted by a New Orleans merchant, Henry Morton Stanley, who gave him his own name.

Alvin Stardust : The individualistic English pop singer born Bernard Jewry started his career as Shane Fenton. His permanent stage name he took from his favorite singers, Elvis Presley and Gene Vincent ("El-" from one, "Vin-" from the other), and added Stardust as he thought it more "1974."

Ringo Starr : The former Beatle, Richard Starkey, changed his name in 1961, when he was appearing with °Rory Storm. His second name is an adaptation of his real surname, with "Ringo" the nickname given him by his mother, as he was fond of wearing rings.

Henry Engelhard Steinway : The German piano manufacturer Heinrich Engelhardt Steinweg settled in the United States (in 1851) and with his sons founded a piano factory in New York (in 1853). He changed his name legally to an anglicized version in 1864.

Stendhal : One of the many and varied pseudonyms adopted by the famous French novelist Marie-Henri Beyle, this is the one by which he is best known. It comes from the name of a small Prussian town, the birthplace of J.J. Winckelmann, a German art critic admired by Beyle, and was first used for his travel account *Rome, Naples et Florence* (1817-1826). Altogether he used up to 200 pseudonyms, many of them Italian. From among them, and to give an idea of their diversity, we may note: Dominique, Salviati (names intended to charm), Cotonnet, Chamier, Baron de Cutendre, William Crocodile (for sheer amusement), Lizio and Viscontini. His first book, *Vies de Haydn, de Mozart et de Métastase* (1814) he wrote as L.-A.-C. Bombet. For his autobiography, published posthumously (1890), he chose the name Henri Brulard, with reference to his passionate nature (French *brûler* means "to burn").

Daniel Stern : Marie Catherine Sophie de Flavigny, comtesse d'Agoult, was the mistress of Liszt as well as a noted writer. In 1854 her novel *Nélida* appeared, which pictured her relations with the composer. The novel was published under this pseudonym, whose first name is an anagram of the novel's title.

Leopold Stokes : Was or was not the great conductor Leopold Stokowski at one stage known by this English version of his name? His father was Polish, and his mother Irish, and in his obituary notice in *The Times* (1977) mention was made of the fact that it was his father who had so anglicized his name to 1905, from which year the conductor worked mainly in the United States under his more familiar Polish name. However, a few days later (September 24, 1977), *The Times* printed a correction, which ran as follows: "We have been asked to point out that Leopold Stokowski was registered at birth under that name and not under that of Stokes; and that, similarly, he studied at the Royal College of

Music under the name of Stokowski." Leopold Stokes would thus appear to have been very short-lived — if he ever lived at all.

Tom Stoppard : The Czech-born English dramatist and critic was the son of Eugene Straussler. When he was still only nine (1946), his mother remarried Major Kenneth Stoppard. See also °William Boot.

Rory Storm : Alan Caldwell tried out the name Jet Storme early in his career as a pop singer. °Ringo Starr was the drummer of his group (1961) before joining the Beatles.

Leslie Stuart : Thomas Barrett is today remembered not as a church organist in Salford, just outside Manchester, which is where he began his career (under his real name), but as the composer of such popular songs as *Tell Me Pretty Maiden* and *Lily of Laguna* (under his pseudonym). It just wouldn't have done, at the turn of the century, for a man in his serious profession to be found to have active links with the music hall — hence the name-change. (He first made a change to Lester Thomas.)

Poly Styrene : Someone was presumably bound to come up with this name sooner or later. It was selected by the English punk rock singer Marion Elliott, who formed the band X-Ray Spex. There is in fact a degree of symbolism in the name, which its bearer felt was suitable for the plastic culture and values of the 1970s.

Eugène Sue : The French novelist began life as Marie-Joseph Sue. His new first name came from Prince Eugène de Beauharnais, who was one of his patrons.

Felix Summerly : How did Sir Henry Cole, English 19th-century public servant, art patron and educator, come to assume this name? He won (in 1845) a competition organized by the Society of Arts with "Summerly's" (i.e., his) tea service, manufactured by Minton's pottery works. Two years later he founded Summerly's Art Manufactures.

Surfaceman : The Scottish poet Alexander Anderson had worked both as a quarryman and on the railway as a "surfaceman," a track layer.

Italo Svevo : The real name of the Italian novelist and short story writer was Ettore Schmitz. His pen name, meaning literally "Italus the Swabian" (i.e. the Italian-Swabian), was one he chose when publishing his first novel. It expressed his feeling of being a hybrid: Italian by language, Austrian by citizenship, and German by ancestry and education [P.N. Furbank, *Italo Svevo: The Man and the Writer*, 1966].

Gloria Swanson : This *must* be a propitious name. Josephine Swenson was born in 1897 and in the 1970s was still making fine film appearances — indeed a glorious swansong!

Taffrail : Captain Henry Taprell Dorling was a noted writer of books on the sea and on naval affairs. His pseudonym, based on his middle name, is an actual naval term for the upper part of a ship's stern timbers.

Taffy : Nadezhda Buchinskaya was a Russian short story writer and poet who emigrated to France (1920). She took her pen name from the character so called in *How the Alphabet Was Made*, one of Kipling's *Just So Stories*.

Talvj : The German author (also writing in English) Therese Robinson derived her pseudonym from the initials of her full maiden name — Therese Albertine Louise von Jakob. She pronounced the name to rhyme with "Calvey." (Her husband was Professor Edward Robinson, the American biblical scholar.)

Tania : Haydee Tamara Bunke was the daughter of German Communists — herself Argentinian born — and was a Soviet agent working, and cohabiting, with °Che Guevara. When in Havana she used the cover name Laura Gutierrez Bauer. Earlier (1964) when leaving Cuba for Europe she was to become either Vittoria Pancini, and the daughter of German parents living on the Italian-German border, or Marta Iriarte, an Argentinian. Her Cuban cover name above was the outcome: an Italian-Argentinian-German compromise. She was killed, aged 29, in Bolivia when Bolivian forces ran °Che Guevara to earth. Tania (or Tanya) had for some time become a popular Soviet or revolutionary cover name, used before her by the Russian girl partisan and heroine Zoya Kosmodemyanskaya, and after her by the Symbionese Liberation Army agent (who adopted the name in Haydee's honor) Patricia Hearst [1. *Sunday Telegraph*, July 21, 1968; 2. Marta Royas and Mirta Rodriguez Calderon, *Tania*, 1973; 3. David Boulton, *The Making of Tania: The Patty Hearst Story*, 1975].

Jacques Tati : The French comic film actor was the grandson of Count Dmitri Tatischeff, an attaché at the Russian Embassy in Paris who had married a Frenchwoman. His screen name is simply a shortening of this, and at the same time sounds engagingly affectionate in French.

Laurette Taylor : No doubt, as Leonard Ashley suggests, Laurette Cooney felt that her real name had an association of "coon" or "raccoon."

Robert Taylor : The real name of the famous film actor is more striking than his screen name, which was given him (1934) by MGM head Louis B. Mayer. It was Spangler Arlington Brough.

Paul Temple : The two crime fiction writers Francis Durbridge and James McConnell used this name for mystery novels which did *not* feature the detective Paul Temple created by Durbridge. But you must expect some confusion in the world of mystery fiction.

Tammi Terrell : Tammy Montgomery, the American pop singer, chose this nicely alliterative name from her first husband, the boxer Ernie Terrell, to whom she was briefly married. It is therefore, like °Cyd Charisse, actually a true name.

Terry-Thomas : The British comic stage and film actor Thomas Terry Hoar-Stevens started in show business as Mot Snevets (compare Red

Nirt), then tried Thomas Terry. People started to link him, wrongly, with the theatre family Terry (Ellen Terry, for example), so he reversed the names. He added the hyphen around 1947, saying "The hyphen's the gap between my teeth."

Dame Maggie Teyte : The British soprano was born Margaret Tate. When she went to Paris at the age of 20 (in 1908) she changed the spelling of her name to ensure correct pronunciation of "Tate" by the French. In a doggerel commentary on this change, an American wrote: "Tell us ere it be too late/ Art thou known as Maggie Tayte?/ Or, per contra, art thou hight/ As we figure, Maggie Teyte?"

Octave Thanet : It is possible that the American novelist Alice French may have been influenced in her choice of pseudonym by the name of Octave Chanute, the French aviation pioneer who went to America in 1872 (when she would have been 22).

Theodosia : Presumably Anne Steel, the English writer of hymns and religious verse, chose the name for its religious meaning, "God-given." She used it for *Poems on Subjects Chiefly Devotional*, published in two volumes (1760). Her fiancé had earlier tragically drowned on the day she was to have married. (Was this fate somehow reserved for hymn-writers? It befell Joseph Medlicott Scriven, the 19th-century writer, whose fiancée was drowned the day *before* he was due to marry.)

James Thomson, B.V. : An unusual form of pseudonym, derived by placing two initials after one's real name. The initials were added to the name of the 19th-century Scottish poet James Thomson, who resorted to the device in order to be distinguished from the 18th-century poet of the same name. The letters stood for Bysshe Vanolis: the first of these names being the middle name of Percy Bysshe Shelley, and the second being an anagram of °Novalis. Both writers were greatly admired by Thomson.

General Tom Thumb : It is perhaps worth remembering that this name did not originate with the famous American midget, really Charles Sherwood Stratton, but was the name of an old nursery hero popular in the 16th century.

Henry T. Thurston : Francis Palgrave, the English 19th-century poet and critic, was the son of (Sir) Francis Palgrave, whose original name was Meyer Cohen. (He changed it by royal permission in 1823.) Francis Palgrave the younger used the name Thurston for *The Passionate Pilgrim; or, Eros and Anteros* (1858).

Vesta Tilley : This is the name by which the popular British music-hall artiste and male impersonator is best known. She began life (in 1864) as Matilda Alice Powles, and was first billed, at the age of six, as Little Tilley (this being a pet form of Matilda) at the Star Music Hall, Gloucester, where her father — who had the stage name Harry Ball — was manager. No doubt with a reference to the name "Star," and because she was an already famous child star, her father added "Vesta" in 1873. (The minor planet Vesta, the only one ever visible with the naked eye, had been discovered in 1807. It is the brightest of all the minor planets.)

Tintoretto : The name means "little dyer." Jacopo Robusti, the 16th-century Italian painter, was the son of a dyer, for which the Italian is *tintore*. The name, a direct descriptive one, is typical of Renaissance painters.

Michael Angelo Titmarsh : William Makepeace Thackeray, the novelist, used this name for *The Paris Sketch-Book* (1840) and *The Great Hoggarty Diamond* (1841), both printed in *Fraser's Magazine*, and subsequently for various other tales. The pen name is said to have been based on a nickname given Thackeray — "Michael Angelo" — by a friend who admired his head and shoulders. To this, by way of absurd contrast, Thackeray himself added "Titmarsh."

Josip Tito : Josip Broz, the Yugoslav soldier and statesman, adopted his name in the Partisan War (1934). It is said to originate from the Serbocroat *ti to*, literally "you this" — i.e., "you do this" — Tito was always saying "You do this," "You do that" — but the leader himself said that the name simply occurred to him after reading a book by two Serbocroatian writers who had Tito as their first name. In the world of partisan warfare Tito had several underground names, but in Comintern communications was always known as Comrade Walter. The hazardous conditions of guerrilla combat sometimes necessitated a change of cover name three times a *day* [Jules Archer, *Red Rebel: Tito of Yugoslavia,* 1968].

Toby, M.P. : This was the name assumed by Sir Henry Luce for humorous and satirical articles contributed by him (1881-1916) to *Punch*. Toby, of course, is the name of Punch's dog in the traditional puppet show *Punch and Judy*; M.P. stands for Member of Parliament. Sir Henry was not in fact an M.P. but a J.P. — a Justice of the Peace.

Ann Todd : The American film actress born Ann Todd Mayfield (in 1932) and a child star in the 1930s, must not be confused with Ann Todd, the British film actress born Ann Todd (in 1909)! The American film producer °Mike Todd (born in 1907) was related to neither of them.

Mike Todd : One of the many Todds in the film world. His real name was Avrom Goldbogen. When his father died (1931) Avrom assumed the first name of his son, Michael, and changed both their surnames to Todd, from his own nickname, Toat.

Tom and Gerry : Art Garfunkel and Paul Simon, the American pop singers and composers, called themselves thus for the four years 1956-1959, having started in show business as, respectively, Tom Graph and Jerry Landis. In 1959 they vanished from the musical scene until 1964, when they re-emerged under their own names (Simon and Garfunkel), subsequently splitting in 1970. The popular pair name Tom and Jerry goes back a good deal further than the well-known cartoon cat and mouse: in 1821 Pierce Egan, an English sports writer, published *Life in*

London; or, The Day and Night Scenes of Jerry Hawthorn, Esq., and his Elegant Friend Corinthian Tom, and the names came to typify a couple of roistering young men-about-town.

Maurice Tourneur : Did Maurice Thomas, the French film director, feel that his surname was not French enough? It may be no coincidence, too, that French *tourner* means "to shoot a film."

Sir Herbert Beerbohm Tree : Herbert Beerbohm, the English actor-manager, was the son of Julius Beerbohm, a naturalized English grain merchant of German origin. By taking the name Tree he was combining two pseudonymous devices: not only translating the second element of his surname Beerbohm (the original version of the German word meaning "pear-tree" that is now *Birnbaum*), but adding his new name to his existing one.

Trog : The Canadian-born cartoonist Wally Fawkes, creator of "Flook" in the London *Daily Mail,* took his name from the jazz group The Troglodytes of which he was formerly a member. The group played in a cellar, as their name suggests.

Leon Trotsky : There has been a good deal of controversy as to the precise origin of this famous (or infamous) name, adopted by the Russian revolutionary born of Jewish parents as Lev Davidovich Bronstein. A popular theory is that he picked it at random — writing it in a blank passport handed him by friends — when emerging from exile in Siberia (1902). It is known, however, that Trotsky had been the name of a jailer in the prison of Odessa, where the young Bronstein had been before this. Trotsky is certainly not an invented Russian name, but one that exists in its own right. Even so, with his knowledge of German, Bronstein may have been consciously or unconsciously thinking of the German word *Trotz,* with its symbolic meaning of "defiance, insolence, intrepidity." Certainly, some of his other pseudonyms seem to have been meaningfully selected. At one stage he was Antid-Oto, a word found (*antidoto*) in an Italian dictionary when he started to weight up different pen names, and seen by him as suitable since he "wanted to inject a Marxist antidote into the legal press." At another time (1936) he was Crux, a name he used for articles in the *Bulletin of the Opposition.* At various times he had also been Ensign, Arbuzov, Mr. Sedov (when leaving incognito for Europe in 1932), Pyotr Petrovich (to local Petersburg revolutionaries), Vikentyev (his "official" name in Petersburg in 1905), and Yanovsky (derived from Yanovka Farm, itself named after the colonel who had sold it to his father) [1. Joel Carmichael, *Trotsky: An Appreciation of His Life,* 1975; 2. *The Observer Colour Magazine,* October 21, 1979].

H. Trusta : This was the name adopted by the American novelist Elizabeth Stuart Phelps for her two semiautobiographical novels, *A Peep at Number Five* (1851), and *The Angel Over the Right Shoulder* (1851). It is formed from letters from her real name.

Sojourner Truth : A fine puritanical name. It was the one taken by the American Black evangelist and reformer Isabella Van Wagener in 1843 when she left New York to "travel up and down the land" singing and preaching. Isabella was originally a slave, and her legal name was taken from the family who bought her then set her free just before the abolition of slavery in New York state (in 1827).

Yevgeniya Tur : The real name of the Russian 19th-century writer who became Yevgeniya Tur or Eugenie Tour was Yelizaveta Vasilyevna Salias-de-Turnemir. She is little known in the Western world, and indeed many Russians will not have heard of her (she wrote a number of popular children's books), but her son has given an illuminating account of how she came by her name. This will be of interest both to pseudonymists and admirers of the Russian classic writers: "They have said that 'Yevgeniya Tur' was 'Turgenev' turned round. By sheer coincidence this is so, and you get an almost complete anagram. But there is no secret in this: the stories about my mother's affair with Turgenev are complete nonsense. My mother was called Yelizaveta, but she was extremely fond of the names 'Yevgeny' and 'Yevgeniya.' She was a passionate admirer of Pushkin and of *Eugene Onegin* in particular. That's where I get my own name of Yevgeny from.... The way her pen name came about is as follows: 'Yevgeniya' was chosen with little hesitation. Then the search began for a surname. 'Yevgeniya Sal' was an abbreviation of 'Salias,' but *sale* in French is 'dirty.' 'Yevgeniya Lias' doesn't sound well, 'Yevgeniya Nemir' is too long.... Everyone liked 'Yevgeniya Tur'" [Dmitriyev, p. 53].

Mark Twain : Almost everyone knows that the real name behind this famous pseudonym was Samuel Langhorne Clemens. Most people will know, too, that the great American novelist derived his pen name from the call, "Mark twain!", of pilots on the Mississippi River when they wanted a depth sounding (i.e., "mark two fathoms"). But perhaps it is less well known that there was an elderly writer whom Clemens began by satirizing called Mark Twain—his real name being Isaiah Sellers (born possibly in 1802, died in 1864)—and that conceivably *this* was the origin of his pseudonym. Be that as it may, Clemens first used the name, as far as is known, for a contribution to the Virginia City *Territorial Enterprise* (1863). Mencken points out that in the United States the name Mark Twain has become a registered trade name, which may not be used on the jacket, cover, or title page of a book without permission of the Mark Twain Company, through its agents, the publishers Harper & Row.

Helen Twelvetrees : The unusual surname adopted by the film actress Helen Jurgens is a real one, and was that of her first husband, Charles Twelvetrees. (As a surname, it is believed to have originated from a person who lived near a clump of trees, arbitrarily rounded to twelve in number.)

Twiggy : An obvious nickname for a slim or skinny person.

When the British fashion model so known was at school she was nick-named "Sticks." Twiggy was a subsequent nickname, which her future husband Justin de Villeneuve suggested (in 1964) she should adopt professionally. The real owner of the boyish figure was Lesley Hornby. After her success as a model in the sixties, Twiggy blossomed into something of a film actress (*The Boy Friend*, 1971) and popular singer.

Conway Twitty : Harold Jenkins, the popular American folk singer, has explained how he got his name: "So we started thinking about all kinds of names, and to make a long story short, what I finally wound up doing was, I got the map out and there's a place called Twitty, Texas. Then I thought if I could get something different to go with this, it might be something. I finally got the map of Arkansas and started looking through that, and there're towns in Arkansas like Baldknob, Walnut Creek, Smackover, and all kinds of crazy names like that. But right out-side of Little Rock there's a town called Conway, and that's how it came about — Conway, Arkansas, and Twitty, Texas. So we all agreed that that was an unusual name, and my first record was ... under the name of Conway Twitty. I didn't agree with the idea first because my main in-terest was I was worried about the people in my hometown that wouldn't know who Conway Twitty is, and I wanted them all to know I had a new record out.... But I finally realized what the fellow was talking about and I decided he was right, so we went with Conway Twitty" [Shestack, p. 285].

Paolo Uccello : The painter Paolo di Dono was nicknamed "Uc-cello," Italian for "bird," not because he resembled one, presumably, but doubtless because of his fondness for painting them.

Sylvanus Urban : The name was adopted by Edward Cave, the printer, who founded *The Gentleman's Magazine* (1731). (It lasted until 1914.) The quasiclassical pseudonym was intended to typify Cave's dual interest in both town and country affairs — "urban" and "sylvan."

Maurice Utrillo : How did the popular French painter come to have this un-French surname? He was in fact the son of Suzanne Valadon and a painter named Boissy. When he was eight years old, Maurice was formally adopted by a Spanish art critic named Miguel Utrillo, who gave him his own name. Suzanne Valadon had undergone a name change, too. She was originally Marie-Clementine Valadon — and a model for Renoir, Toulouse-Lautrec and Degas. She started to draw in the year her son was born (1883, when she was 18), and was persuaded by Degas and Lautrec to change her career from model to artist. At this point she changed her name from Marie-Clementine to Suzanne.

Rudolph Valentino : The great romantic hero of the silver screen evolved his stage name from his mellifluous full name: Rodolpho Alfonzo Raffaelo Pierre Filibert Guglielmi di Valentina d'Antonguolla.

S.S. Van Dine : Willard Huntington Wright, the American critic and writer who created the detective Philo Vance, derived his pseudonym from an old family name, Van Dyne, with S.S. standing, as commonly in another naming system, for "steamship."

Comte Paul Vasili : The bearer of this name was not a count but a commoner, not Russian but French, and not even male! She was Juliette Adam, famous for founding *La Nouvelle Revue* (1879-1926).

Vera : This was the name used by Lady Colin Campbell, arts critic and author. Her pen name is comparatively unremarkable, but her surname has something of a history. Her husband Colin Campbell (born in 1792, died in 1863) was a Scottish-born military commander. His original surname was Macliver. This was changed (in 1807) to Campbell through an error: when Macliver met his commander-in-chief, the Duke of York, the latter mistakenly recorded his name. Duly registered as Campbell, Macliver was obliged to adopt this name.

Vercors : Jean Bruller, the French writer, used this name for his secretly distributed *Le Silence de la Mer* (1942). The pseudonym derives from the name of an Alpine plateau which was one of the centers of the French resistance in World War II. For a similar name, see °Forez.

Madame Vestris : Yet another name from an early husband. Lucia Mathews, née Bartolozzi, the English actress and singer, had married Auguste-Armand Vestris at the age of 16. He left her four years later. Not until she was 35 (in 1838) did she marry Charles James Mathews, an actor and playwright.

Vetus : Again, a name with a connected history. Vetus was Edward Sterling, and a veteran (or inveterate) writer of letters to *The Times* (1812-1813). He later became a member of the newspaper's staff and, in effect, its editor, and was nicknamed "The Thunderer" for his forthright articles. This nickname (actually bestowed by Thomas Carlyle) was subsequently transferred to the paper itself. The pseudonym Vetus, as hinted above, is actually Latin for "old" or "longstanding."

Sid Vicious : The archetypal punk rock star John Beverley, member of the group Sex Pistols, received his name, apparently, after a violent chain attack on a journalist. He died in 1979 of a drug overdose in the United States following a murder charge [*Sun*, January 13, 1978].

François Villon : Some uncertainty remains about the real name of the 15th-century French poet, and his date of death is also not accurately recorded. He seems to have been born as either François de Montcorbier or François des Loges, these two "surnames" being respectively the name of a village on the borders of Burgundy where his father was born and, probably, the name of his father's farm. The name by which we know him is that of the man who adopted him, Guillaume de Villon, a Paris chaplain. Villon used other pseudonyms, among them Michel Mouton ("Michael Sheep!").

Vitalis : The Latin name taken by the Swedish poet Erik Sjöberg means literally "life [is a] struggle." He died when only 31, the struggle having been too much.

Voltaire : Possibly the best known of all pseudonyms — and of all pseudonyms, the most uncertain in origin. The commonly held theory is that the name is an anagram of the surname of the great French philosopher and writer François Marie Arouet, with "l.j." standing for *le jeune* (i.e. "The Young") added. (One must also, with this derivation, allow that the 'u' of Arouet becomes 'v', and the initial 'j' shifts to 'i'.) But the name may have been taken from the village of Volterre. Qui sait? We do at least know that the name was first used on the release of its illustrious bearer from the Bastille in 1718. Appendix I gives a complete list of his 173 pseudonyms.

Samuel Greifensohn von Hirschfeld : If ever there was a man who reveled in anagrammatic pseudonyms, it was Hans Jakob Christoffel von Grimmelshausen, the 17th-century German writer. He must have spent hours devising such a neat one from such a long name. He also wrote as Erich Stainfels von Grufensholm, Israel Fromschmit von Hugenfels, Filarhus Grossus von Trommenhaim, among others, and to cap it all, signed himself on the title page of *Das wunderbarliche Vogelnest* ("The wondrous bird's nest") (1672) as A.c.eee.ff.g.hh.ii.ll.-mm.nn.oo.rr.sss.t.uu, which must be one of the most off-beat pen names of all time. (Readers anxious for more should refer to the entry on his best known pseudonym, °Simplicissimus.)

Max Wall : The Scottish-born actor Maxwell Lorimer derived his stage name not so much from his first name alone as from a combination of the first half of it followed by the first half of his stepfather's name, Wallace.

Edgar Wallace : The British novelist was born Richard Edgar, son of Polly Richards and Richard Horatio Edgar, an actor. His name was invented by Polly, who registered his father as "William Wallace." Later, he was adopted by a fishporter George Freeman and his wife and called Dick Freeman, but the future thriller writer abandoned this name when joining the army (in 1893) as Richard Edgar Wallace.

Artemus Ward : Charles Farrar Browne, the American humorous writer, is said to have adopted his pen name from that of an eccentric showman known by him. The name was first used for a character who gave illiterate "commentaries" on various subjects in his letters. In 1861 Browne took to lecturing as Artemus Ward. By a coincidence, there had earlier (1727-1800) been an American Revolutionary commander named Artem*as* Ward, and Artemas Ward was also the name of the advertising manager who gave King C. Gillette valuable advice about hard-hitting advertising when the now famous inventor of the disposable razor blade visited London in the 1880s. No doubt yet more Artemas — or Artemus — Wards are still alive and well and flourishing in the English-speaking world even today.

Peter Warlock : The name assumed (about 1921) by the English composer and writer Philip Arnold Heseltine, who used his real name for literary and editorial work. It was intended to signify a change to a new, aggressive personality, one of "wine, women and song." A warlock, after all, is a wizard, a practicer of black magic. Heseltine had first used the name in 1919, after the failure of his early work and a number of rejects. Reviewing a new book on Warlock in the *Times Literary Supplement* (July 11, 1980), Eric Sams points out that the assumed name may be even more meaningful, since Heseltine is said to derive from "hazel," and thus, by means of an associative switch, via "witch hazel," and a sex-change ("witch" to "warlock"), the composer arrived at his new name. One literary pseudonym Warlock did use was Rab Noolas (1929), for *Merry-Go-Down: A Gallery of Gorgeous Drunkards Through the Ages.* This name is best seen from a tippler's back-to-front point of view.

Jack Warner : The British stage, film and TV actor, famous as "Dixon of Dock Green," was originally Jack Waters. He is not to be confused with Jack L. Warner, born two years before him (1892), one of the original Warner Brothers (the others were Albert, Harry M., and Sam).

John Wayne : It always comes as something of a shock to discover that this craggy hero of the Wild West movie world was born Marion Michael Morrison (or possibly Marion Robert Morrison, the name that was apparently recorded on his birth certificate). His name change was prompted by head of production Sheehan for the film *The Big Trail* (1930), Sheehan commenting, "I don't like this name, Duke Morrison, it's no name for a leading man." (Earlier Morrison had adopted the first name Duke. This was in fact the name of his Airedale, and the nickname used by firemen in a nearby fire station when young Morrison and dog went past.) Director Raoul Walsh, who admired Mad Anthony Wayne, a general of the American Revolution, suggested Anthony Wayne. Sheehan said that this "sounded too Italian." "Then Tony Wayne," countered Walsh. Here Sol Wurtzel, head of production at Fox, protested that this "sounds like a girl." So Sheehan decreed, "What's the matter with just plain John? John Wayne." Wurtzel approved, "It's American" [Maurice Zolotow, *John Wayne: Shooting Star*, 1974].

Arthur Weegee : The Polish-born American photographer, of Jewish origin, started his career as Arthur (or Usher) H. Fellig. His unusual name began as a nickname, Ouija, otherwise "Weegee," for his ability to sniff out a good potential story — i.e., for his apparent "psychic" sense [*Camera User*, June 1979].

Kitty Wells : The first "queen of country music," Muriel Deason, had her name chosen for her by her husband Johnny Wright, who when courting her recalled the song made popular by the Carter Family, *I'm A-Goin' to Marry Kitty Wells.*

Rebecca West : The real name of the talented British novelist and critic is Cicily Isabel Fairfield. She took her pen name from the character so called in Ibsen's *Rosmersholm*, since Rebecca West stood for Rights of Women, her own cause, and she had also played this role in

London as an actress. She also used the name Lynx for *Lions and Lambs* (1929), written in collaboration with Low. This was a set of literary sketches designed to accompany Low's portraits of living celebrities. The name Rebecca West she first used in 1911.

Mr. Whatsisname : *The Times*, in its issue of January 21, 1978, had a two-column headline, "Mr. Whatsisname Fined £150 in Property Conveyancing Case." The report began, "Mr. Francis Whatsisname (formerly Reynolds)...," thus reminding readers who Mr. Whatsisname had been and telling them what he was now up to. In brief, Mr. Whatsisname had challenged the Law Society, the solicitors' trade union, by preparing conveyancing instruments (documents for buying and selling property) when not being himself a solicitor. Furthermore, he had been offering cut-price transactions. His contention, shared by a number of supporters, was that it was unfair for solicitors to have a monopoly of a number of common legal transactions, especially the conveyancing of property and matters of probate (the authenticating of wills). He took his name from a series of advertisements run by the Law Society in which a character called Mr. Whatsisname attempted to undertake legal tasks that should be properly be assigned to a solicitor [*The Times*, January 21 and June 2, 1978].

Chris White : In 1978 a strange autobiography was published. It was entitled *Eve*, and the author was Chris Sizemore. In it, the writer describes how she developed into that weird psychiatric phenomenon, a multiple personality. It was the story of how one woman became, in effect, 12 different personalities, all existing within the body of a single human being. Naturally, the personalities assumed different names: with Chris White, a "sad, dowdy woman," Chris Costner, a "flamboyant party-goer," and Jane Doe, a "well-bred, refined Southern lady" as the three main women, whose experiences were told in the book, and the film, that swept the United States — *The Three Faces of Eve* (film 1957). The third of these names was the one she used when marrying Don Sizemore, so that the subject of it all has a real name that incorporates her maiden name (Costner) and her married name (Sizemore): Chris Costner Sizemore.

Joseph Blanco White : The Spanish-born English churchman and writer started life as José María Blanco y Crespo. He fled to England as a Roman Catholic priest (in 1810) later taking Anglican orders and anglicizing his name thus with a kind of bilingual version. (Later still he left the Church of England and became a Unitarian.) See also °Don Leucadio Doblado.

Slim Whitman : Otis Dewey, the American country singer and yodeller, was a self-styled protégé of Montana Slim.

Tennessee Williams : Thomas Lanier Williams, the famous American dramatist, was not born in Tennessee but in Mississippi. His father, however, was directly descended from John Williams, first senator of Tennessee, from the brother Valentine of Tennessee's first governor

John Sevier (whose own name was itself changed from Xavier by the Huguenots), and from Thomas Lanier Williams I, first chancellor of the Western Territory, as Tennessee was called before it became a state. So "I've just indulged myself in the Southern weakness for climbing a family tree," explained the author of *A Streetcar Named Desire* [Tennessee Williams, *Memoirs*, 1976].

Sonny Boy Williamson : In order to gain greater popularity, the American blues harmonica player and singer Rice Miller (1897-1965) claimed to be *the* Sonny Boy Williamson (1914-1948), who was officially John Lee Williamson.

Barbara Windsor : Barbara Anne Deeks, the British film and TV actress and singer, was once asked why she changed her name to Windsor. It turned out that not only was Windsor the name of a favorite aunt, but also the name of the royal family. "I'm very, *very* pro-Royal," said Miss Windsor, adding, somewhat imprecisely, that she had made the change when "it was the time of Princess Elizabeth getting married, or was it the Coronation?" (If the former, this would have been 1947, when she was only 10; if the latter, in 1953.) By another coincidence, "Barbara" is said to be the nickname of Queen Elizabeth within the royal family circle.

Googie Withers : The British actress was christened Georgina Withers. Miss Withers has also stuck by the story that the name Googie was given her by her Indian nurse during her childhood in Karachi, and that it derives either from a Punjabi word meaning "dove" or a Bengali word meaning "clown." But could the truth perhaps have been that this was the nurse's merely random or pet version of Georgina?

Stevie Wonder : The blind American black "Motown" singer was born Stephen Judkins (otherwise, after his mother's remarriage, Stephen Morris). He became a singing star when he was only 12 (in 1962), when he was called "Little Stevie Wonder." Two years later, when still only 14, he had grown to six feet tall, so he dropped the "Little" [Constance Elsner, *Stevie Wonder*, 1977].

Natalie Wood : Natasha Gurdin was the daughter of Russian immigrants to America. Her name was changed when she was still only an eight-year-old child film star for the film *Tomorrow Is Forever* (1946). The change was made by production executives William Goetz and Leo Spitz in memory of director Sam Wood.

Henry Woodhouse : The Italian authority on aeronautics, Mario Casalegno, had a name that perfectly lent itself to translation when he emigrated to the United States (1904), became naturalized, and legally changed his name (1917).

Flying Officer X : The English novelist H.E. Bates used this pseudonym for short stories about the Royal Air Force (in which he was serving as an officer) in *The Greatest People in the World* (1942) and *How Sleep the Brave* (1943).

Malcolm X : The American Black Muslim member and campaigner for Negro rights was born Malcolm Little. He received the conventional Muslim 'X' from °Elijah Muhammad in 1952. As he explained, "The Muslim's 'X' symbolized the true African family name that he could never know. For me, my 'X' replaced the white slavemaster name of 'Little' which some blue-eyed devil named Little had imposed upon my paternal forebears.... Mr. Muhammad taught that we would keep this 'X' until God Himself returned and gave us a Holy Name from His own mouth" [*The Listener*, August 8, 1974]. See also °Michael X and °Muhammad Ali.

Michael X : The Trinidad-born black power leader was the son of a black mother and Portuguese father, and was originally named Michael de Freitas. This later became Michael Abdul Malik and subsequently Michael X on his conversion to the Muslim religion. He was sentenced to death (in 1972) for the murder of Joseph Skerritt in Trinidad and was executed three years later [*Evening News*, May 16, and *The Times*, May 17, 1975].

Ximenes : Perhaps one of the most imposing and suitable of all pseudonyms, in view of the significant capital letter. It belonged to Derrick Macnutt, professionally a teacher of classics, but a renowned crossword compiler, notably the "Everyman" (to 1963) and harder "Ximenes" ones in *The Observer* (from 1939). He assumed the name in 1943 — it was that of the 15th-century Spanish Cardinal and Grand Inquisitor Ximenes — when he succeeded to the compilership vacated by the doyen crosswordist Torquemada. In the 1930s Macnutt had contributed some crosswords to *The Listener* as Tesremos, his middle name reversed.

Gig Young : Byron Barr, the American actor, took his stage name from the character so called in the film *The Gay Sisters* (1942) played by him. He also earlier used the name Bryant Fleming.

Zouzou : Danielle Ciarlet, the French film actress, adopted her screen name from a childish nickname given her, one of the typically French "endearment" names. (Compare °Fifi Dorsay.)

"Stephen Sly, and old John Naps of Greece,
And Peter Turf, and Henry Pimpernell,
And twenty more such names and men as these,
Which never were nor no man ever saw."
(The Taming of the Shrew)

Name Lists

The 40 lists that follow are a categorized arrangement of most, but not all, of the names given in the Who's Who. They are presented numerically in virtually the same order as the treatment of their categories in the six main chapters, that is, lists 1-13 deal broadly with the motives leading to a new name (*why* a name is changed), and lists 14-32 deal with the methods of assuming a new name (*how* a name is changed). The final eight lists (33-40) are more specialized in character, and illustrate such aspects as humorous names, rare or "nonce" names, papal names, and alliterative names.

On the whole, the length or brevity of any given list is testimony to that particular category's popularity or frequency. List 1, for example, is one of the longest, and is even subdivided, since one of the most common general motives for a name change is the unsuitability of a real name for a person's public activity (usually acting or writing). List 27 (names evolved as the result of a mistake) is the shortest, as not many pseudonyms came about thus — which is no doubt a sign that most people like to feel there was some active creative element in the formation of their pseudonym, however or by whomever it was devised.

The aim of the lists is to inform and interest. A brief preamble to each list will point out any features of particular interest, and the lists as a whole are reasonably "browsable," enabling the reader to trace a common theme through a set of names.

Most lists show in one column the real names and in a second the pseudonyms. The order in which these are given depends on the emphasis of the list: real names tend to be given first in lists 1-13, and pseudonyms first in lists 14-32. The information provided in some of the later lists varies: List 39, for example, gives four items of information, but the final List 40 has simply a single run of names (although printed in two columns) for pure browsing.

Both real names and pseudonyms are usually given in their short or common form — that is, just forename and surname (where this applies).

159

Titles, too, receive no special treatment. The full names, dates, and identities of the bearers of the names can of course be found in the Who's Who.

Inevitably, in some lists the concise information given will overlap with the fuller account made in the Name Stories. On the other hand, very many names not explained in the Name Stories will have their background given, or will be specially considered, in one or more of the lists. (Origins are specifically dealt with in lists 21, 22, 23, 24, 26, 27, 28, 32, and 37.)

1. UNSUITABLE NAMES

This first list is one of the longest, and is subdivided into "common names," "awkward names," "embarrassing names," and "lengthy names."

Common names are names such as Smith, Cole, and Johnson that are perfectly respectable and reasonable names, but are not particularly memorable on account of their "ordinariness." The bearers of such names usually change their surname, and occasionally their forename, to a name that is thus more memorable and individualistic. The change may be only a small one, but is enough to make the name stick in the mind: Brown to Browne, Howard to Howerd, Lowe to Loder, and Tate to Teyte.

Awkward names are names that are anything *but* "common," and which may even cause mirth or embarrassment (although not in the sense of the next category). They are names that sound odd or "funny," and which are therefore best changed to something a little more conventional, yet at the same time memorable. Thus Hinkle becomes Ayres, Piff turns into Kay, and Millsop is improved to Lee. A number of "difficult" Scottish and Irish names come into this category, names such as McMinn, McGonegal, McKeown and McLaughlin. Such names can be both difficult to say and to spell, so are better changed or at least simplified.

Embarrassing names are names that can cause personal embarrassment to their bearer since they resemble "taboo" words, usually of a sexual, scatalogical, or at least a morally undesirable nature. Most of these are obvious, from the unfortunate Belcher to the mishearable Hunt or Ficker. The surname Broadbent is unwelcome for an actress since it suggests "broad." (In origin it means, wholesomely enough, "dweller by the broad grassy plain": but that is not the association that most people will make, alas.) As undesirable for a male actor is the name Pratt, which may be used as an equivalent of "ass" in the American sense.

Lengthy names are just that: names that are not only laboriously long to say and write, but undesirably lengthy when put on billboards. Double-barrelled (hyphenated) names often lose their longer element or are changed altogether.

Most of the names in this list are those of actors and actresses, and doubtless the browser will be able to spot a number of stage and screen personalities in each of the four categories.

Common names (real names in left column, pseudonyms right)

Donald Smith	Robert Armstrong
Charles Smith	Bill Arp
Gladys Greene	Jean Arthur
Anne Lloyd	Anne Aston
Barnet Isaacs	Barney Barnato
Maud Barlow	Ida Barr
Merig Jones	David Barry
Susan Black	Susan Beaumont
Doris Collier	Josephine Bell
Vivienne Stapleton	Vivian Blaine
David Butterfield	David Blair
Coral Brown	Coral Browne
Thomas Connery	Sean Connery
Frank J. Cooper	°Gary Cooper
Marilyn Watts	Mara Corday
Claude Cowan	Claude Dampier
Margaret Symonds	Nuna Davey
William Davis	David Davis
Peggy Middleton	Yvonne de Carlo
Derek Harris	John Derek
James Sadler	Jerry Desmonde
David Wighton	David Devant
Nigel Davies	Justin de Villeneuve
Merle Johnson	Troy Donahue
Charles Springall	Charlie Drake
Edna Durbin	Deanna Durbin
David Cook	David Essex
Frances Smith	Dale Evans
Maurice Cole	Kenny Everett
Emily Judson	Fanny Forester
Henry Herbert	Frank Forester
Frederick Hargate	Freddie Frinton
Lucy Johnson	Ava Gardner
Frances Clarke	Sarah Grand
Dorothy Gatley	Ann Harding
Donella Donaldson	Julie Haydon
Edythe Marriner	Susan Hayward
Leslie Stainer	Leslie Howard
Francis Howard	°Frankie Howerd
Elizabeth Ward	Fay Inchfawn
Arthur Adams	James James
James Carey	°Jimmy James
Diane Hall	Diane Keaton
Harold Keel	Howard Keel
Mary Moss	Laura Keene
William Grimston	William Kendal
Frieda Harrison	Susy Kendall
Frederick Keen	Frederick Kerr
Frederick Heath	Johnny Kidd
William Ashton	Bill J. Kramer
Dorothy Milligan	Lola Lane
John Lowe	John Loder
Myrna Williams	Myrna Loy

Violet Watson	Viola Lyel
Kathleen Smith	Kathleen Michael
Norma Baker	°Marilyn Monroe
Edward Muggeridge	°Eadward Muybridge
John Casey	°Sean O'Casey
Agnes Higginson	Moire O'Neill
Donna Jordan	°Janis Paige
Dorothy Buckley	Dorothy Primrose
Harriet Lake	Ann Sothern
Thomas Hicks	Tommy Steele
Violet Turner	Prudence Summerhayes
Margaret Tate	°Maggie Teyte
Colin Williams	Colin Welland
Reginald Smith	Marty Wilde
Brenda Wright	Belinda Wright
Wynette Pugh	Tammy Wynette

Awkward names (real names in left column, pseudonyms right)

Patricia Bigg	Patricia Ainsworth
Daphne Scrutton	Daphne Anderson
Arthur Porges	Peter Arthur
Mary Cragg	Mary Ault
Cora Colhoun	Lovie Austin
Agnes Hinkle	Agnes Ayres
Thomas Budges	Christopher Beck
Elizabeth Mahony	Bessie Bellwood
Jules Paufichet	Jules Berry
Oscar Pelicori	Ernesto Bianco
Elizabeth Bryer	Betsy Blair
Marth Lafferty	Janet Blair
Joyce Ogus	Joyce Blair
Leon-Émile Petitdidier	Émile Blémont
Peter Huggins	Jeremy Brett
Lea Bregham	Lea Brodie
Marden McBroom	David Bruce
Phyllis Bickle	°Phyllis Calvert
Maryse Mourer	Martine Carole
Ann La Hiff	Nancy Carroll
Robert Wyckoff	Robert Fletcher
Gwyllyn Ford	Glenn Ford
Katherine Feeney	Sally Forrest
Chloe Cawdle	Chloe Gibson
John Pringle	John Gilbert
Lily Sheil	°Sheilah Graham
Angela Williams	Mary Grant
Robert Caffin	Barry Gray
Reed Herring	Reed Hadley
Jonathan Hatley	Jonathan Hate
Charles Hartree	Charles Hawtree
Mildred Herman	Melissa Hayden
Gladys Gunn	Gladys Henson
James Ahern	James A. Herne
Johanna Eckert	Hanya Holm

Katherine Gribbin	Renée Houston
Walter Houghston	Walter Huston
Burl Ivanhoe	Burl Ives
Ursula McMinn	Ursula Jeans
Alfred McGonegal	Allen Jenkins
Paul Pond	Paul Jones
William Aytoun	T. Percy Jones
Charles Piff	Charles Kay
Malcolm Knee	Malcolm Keen
Justine McCarthy	Kay Kendall
Edith Keck	Edith King
Francis Cunyinghame	Julian Kingstead
Louise Jelly	Louise Kirtland
Agnes Dunlop	Elisabeth Kyle
Frances Leach	Jane London
Harry Albertshart	Allan Lane
Rosetta Jacobs	Piper Laurie
Dickey Lipscomb	Dickey Lee
Marjorie Millsop	Dorothy Lee
Augusta Apple	Lila Lee
Winifred Moule	Vanessa Lee
Hugh Corcoran	Tommy Lorne
Geraldine McKeown	Geraldine McEwan
Charles McLaughlin	Charles Macklin
Florence Friend	Mary Mannering
Hugh Hipple	Hugh Marlowe
Pierre Cuq	Pierre Mondy
Helen Koford	Terry Moore
Donald Nappey	°Donald Neilson
Nadine Judd	°Nadia Nerina
William Parrot	Talbot O'Farrell
Nigel Wemyss	Nigel Patrick
Aileen Bisbee	Aileen Pringle
Yvonne Wigniolle	Yvonne Printemps
Kathleen Corkrey	Carol Raye
Septimus Ryott	Stewart Rome
Arthur Ropes	Adrian Ross
Morton Stubbs	Morton Selten
Michael Sinnott	Mack Sennett
Brian Earnshaw	Brian Shaw
Dorothy McNulty	Penny Singleton
Ronald Squirl	Ronald Squire
George Stitch	Ford Sterling
Alfred Arrington	Charles Summerfield
Josephine Swenson	°Gloria Swanson
Laurette Cooney	Laurette Taylor
Virginia McSweeney	Virginia Valli
Carol Friday	Caroline Villiers
Arnold Cream	Jersey Joe Walcott
Joan Deery	Joan Wetmore
Jeremiah Colbath	Henry Wilson
Claire Cronk	Claire Windsor
Donald Woolfitt	Donald Wolfit
John Suckling	John Wyckham
Patrick Cheeseman	Patrick Wymark

Embarrassing names (real names in left column, pseudonyms right)

Julie Lush	Julie Anthony
Lena Pocock	Lena Ashwell
Lucille Hunt	Lucille Ball
Shirley Broadbent	Amanda Barrie
Lina Belcher	Lina Basquette
Jean Conneau	André Beaumont
George Beldam	Rex Bell
Margaret Philpott	Madge Bellamy
Dora Broadbent	°Dora Bryan
Joan Felt	°Joan Carroll
Jean Shufflebottom	Jeannie Carson
Eleanor Hunt	Joyce Compton
Edward Haddakin	A.V. Coton
Ernest Brimmer	Richard Dix
Diana Fluck	°Diana Dors
Joanne La Cock	°Joanne Dru
Gilbert Pottle	Gilbert Emery
Roberta Ficker	Suzanne Farrell
Edwige Cunati	Edwige Feuillère
Fletcher Pratt	George V. Fletcher
Leon Pott	Harry Fragson
David Pilditch	David Hamilton
Pamela Ripman	Caryl Jenner
William Pratt	°Boris Karloff
Joan Brodel	Joan Leslie
Lois Hooker	Lois Maxwell
Samuel Pratt	Courtney Melmoth
Ralph Shotter	Ralph Michael
Bill Rowbotham	Bill Owen
Sally Rutter	Gale Page
Robert Higgenbotham	Tommy Tucker
Charles Lickfold	Charles Warner
Antonia Botting	Antonia White
Sarah Fulks	Jane Wyman
Dorothy Cox	Diana Wynyard

Long names (real names in left column, pseudonyms right)

Frances Anderson-Anderson	Judith Anderson
Michael Dumble-Smith	Michael Crawford
Isabel Hodgkinson	Isabel Dean
Carl Henty-Dodd	Simon Dee
Grace Stansfield	°Gracie Fields
Katherine Grandstaff	Kathryn Grant
Constance Stevens	Sally Gray
Joan Haythornthwaite	Joan Haythorne
Jane Cunningham	Jennie June
William Gislingham	Will P. Kellino
Deborah Kerr-Trimmer	Deborah Kerr
Albert Cromwell-Knox	Teddy Knox
Clementine Campbell	Cleo Lane
Sally Harrington	Sara Leland

Maureen Rippingale	Carole Lesley
Cornelius McGillicuddy	Connie Mack
Jill Melford-Melford	Jill Melford
Ioannes Papadiamantopoulos	Jean Moreas
Roger Ollerearnshaw	Roger Shaw

2. FOREIGN TO ENGLISH

These are cases where a more or less standard English name has been adopted in place of a foreign one, with no adaptation or respelling — in fact, the two names, foreign original and English replacement, are quite unalike.

Real name	*Pseudonym*
Max Showalter	Casey Adams
Elizabeth Enke	Edie Adams
Max Bor	Max Adrian
Harvey Matusov	Gordon Allenby
Ella Geisman	June Allyson
Leon Waycoff	Leon Ames
Joseph Deuster	Joseph Anthony
Dikran Kuyumjian	Michael Arlen
Cornelius Van Mattimore	Richard Arlen
Guenther Schneider	Edward Arnold
John Heiss	Oscar Asche
Lucille Langehanke	Mary Astor
Vladimir Vujoric	Michel Auclair
Maxine Hecht	Maxine Audley
Eugene Klass	Gene Barry
Okon Asuquo	Hugan Bassey
Dora Goldberg	Nora Bayes
Herman Brix	Bruce Bennett
Vic Cohen	Vic Berton
Michael Gubitosi	Robert Blake
Elizabeth Jung	Sally Blane
Helene Lipp	Helene Bliss
Benjamin Bernstein	Ben Blue
Marc Feld	°Marc Bolan
Caterina di Francavilla	Katie Boyle
Henry Kleinbach	Henry Brandon
Romulo Larralde	Romney Brent
Louise Dantzler	Mary Brian
Barbara Czukor	Barbara Britton
Geraldine Stroock	Geraldine Brooks
Lesli Gettman	Leslie Brooks
Phyllis Weiler	Phyllis Brooks
Lillian Klot	Georgia Brown
Smylla Brind	Vanessa Brown
Leonard Schneider	°Lenny Bruce
Noah Brusso	Tommy Burners
Henry Schroeder	William Butterworth

Etienne de Bujac	Bruce Cabot
Samile Friesen	Dyan Cannon
Catherine Holzman	Kitty Carlisle
Evelyn Lederer	Sue Carol
Elisabeth Pfister	Elisabeth Carroll
Janis Dremann	Janis Carter
Ira Crossel	Jeff Chandler
Ina Fagan	Ina Claire
Evelyn Gordine	Lucie Clayton
Clayton Heermanse	Bud Collyer
Dorothy Heermanse	June Collyer
Kreker Ohanian	Michael Connors
Harold Neberroth	Alan Curtis
Stuart Zonis	Stuart Damon
Violet Flugrath	Violet Dana
James Ercolani	James Darren
Florian Drosendorf	Florian Deller
Jeremiah Schwartz	Andy Devine
Walter Fleischmann	Anthony Dexter
Melvyn Hesselberg	Melvyn Douglas
Alfredo Capurro	Alfred Drake
Rita Novella	Dona Drake
Irma Grimme	Irma Duncan
Barbara Huffmann	Barbara Eden
Paul Ernst	George Edson
Ellen Cohen	Cass Elliott
Baldemar Huerta	Freddy Fender
Chaim Weintrop	°Bud Flanagan
Arif El-Michelle	Herbert Flemming
Ford Hueffer	°Ford Madox Ford
William Friedman	William Fox
Jacob Leibowicz	Jacob Frank
Lou Gitlotz	Lou Gilbert
Marion Levy	Paulette Goddard
Marianna Michalska	Gilda Gray
Zelma Hedrick	Kathryn Grayson
Noel Katz	°Joel Grey
Jean-Philippe Smet	Johnny Halliday
Jules Israel	Jules Irving
Elsie Bierbower	Elsie Janis
Betty Leabo	Brenda Joyce
George Duryea	Tom Keene
Francis Steegmuller	David Keith
Jan Kowsky	Leon Kellaway
Merna Kahler	Merna Kennedy
Barry Sautereau	Barry Kent
Arnold Kaiser	Norman Kerry
Avice Spitta	Avice Landon
Eugene Orowitz	Michael Landon
June Vlasek	June Lang
Paula de Lugo	Paula Laurence
Gertrude Klasen	Gertrude Lawrence
Lee Yuen Kam	Bruce Lee
Michele Dusiak	Michele Lee

Joan Brodel	°Joan Leslie
Theodore Friedman	Ted Lewis
Harold Lipshitz	Hal Linden
Gabriel Leuvielle	Max Linder
Margaret Kies	Margaret Lindsay
John Yusolfsky	Gary Lockwood
Mariska Megyzsi	Mae Madison
Nathaniel Moscovitch	Noel Madison
Malden Sekulovich	Karl Malden
Feike Feikema	Frederick Manfred
Rauff Acklom	David Manners
Hana Smekalova	Florence Marly
Violet Krauth	Marian Marsh
Leona Flugrath	Shirley Mason
Ian Hoch	Robert Maxwell
Ralph Rathgeber	Ralph Meeker
Evert Duychinck	Felix Merry
Samuel Messer	Robert Middleton
Rubye Blevins	Patsy Montana
Francis Wuppermann	Frank Morgan
Harry Bratsburg	Harry Morgan
Marie Koenig	Mae Murray
N. Richard Nusbaum	N. Richard Nash
Nathalie Belaieff	Nathalie Nattier
Gene Berg	Gene Nelson
Michael Peschkowsky	Mike Nichols
Norman Levison	Norman Norell
Nedra Gullette	Nedra Norris
Hugh Krampke	Hugh O'Brien
Albert Guerisse	Patrick O'Leary
Leon Blouet	Max O'Rell
Harry Kurnitz	Marco Page
Cecil Schwabe	Cecil Parker
Dorothy Rothschild	Dorothy Parker
Worster van Eps	Willard Parker
Donna Mullenger	Donna Reed
George Besselo	George Reeves
Yitzroch Grossberg	°Larry Rivers
Emanuel Goldberg	°Edward G. Robinson
Alfred Corn	Alfred Ryder
Ross Bagdassarian	David Seville
Patsy Sloots	Susan Shaw
Ramon Estevez	Martin Sheen
Robert Van Orden	John Smith
Paul Hornig	Paul Streeten
Ricardo Metzetti	Richard Talmadge
Louis Weiss	Kent Taylor
Juan Mundanschafftner	Carlos Thompson
Harriet Katzman	Harriet Toby
Claire Wemlinger	Claire Trevor
Sophia Abuza	Sophie Tucker
Charles Goldblatt	Charles Vance
Frank Abelsohn	Frankie Vaughan
Ingabor Klinckerfuss	Karen Verne

Harry Eichelbaum	Harry Warner
Daniel Grossman	Daniel Williams

3. Foreign to Anglicized

Unlike the names in List 2, the English names here are all adaptations or respellings of some kind of the foreign original. Normally both forename and surname modify in this way, although an already existing English forename may be retained (as with Richard Baer, Mary Elsas, and Sidney Kieschner). Many of the English surnames are noticeably shorter than the foreign surnames from which they derive.

Real name	*Pseudonym*
Nicholas Adamschock	Nick Adams
Spiro Anagnostopoulos	Spiro Agnew
Hardig Albrecht	Hardie Albright
Max Aronson	G.M. Anderson
Hymen Arluck	Harold Arlen
Renée Ascherson	Renée Asherson
Lewis Ayer	Lew Ayres
Mario Bianchi	°Monty Banks
Richard Baer	Richard Barr
Sacha Boraniev	Sy Bartlett
Alexander Bliedung	John Beal
Riccardo Benedetto	Richard Benedict
Claire Blume	Claire Bloom
Ivan Blieden	Larry Blyden
Fannie Barach	°Fanny Brice
Elaine Bookbinder	Elkie Brooks
Nathan Birnbaum	George Burns
Edward Breitenberger	Edd Byrnes
Miriam Bilenkin	Marion Byron
Stanford Kadinsky	Stanford Cade
Martin Caliniff	Michael Callan
Florencia Cardona	Vikki Carr
Józef Korzeniowski	Joseph Conrad
Marion Dousas	Marion Davies
Gabriel del Vecchio	Gabriel Dell
Louis Denninger	Richard Denning
Peggy Varradow	Peggy Dow
Vladimir Dukelsky	Vernon Duke
Mary Elsas	Mary Ellis
Geoffrey Ehrenberg	Geoffrey Elton
Sophie Feldman	Totie Fields
Sean O'Fearna	John Ford
Lukas Fuchs	Lukas Foss
Constance Franconero	Connie Francis
Julius Garfinkle	John Garfield
Francesca von Gerber	Mitzi Gaynor
Wolfgang Grajonca	Bill Graham
Ara Heditsian	David Hedison

Asa Yoelson	°Al Jolson
Philip Karlstein	Phil Karlson
David Kaminsky	Danny Kaye
Nora Koreff	Nora Kaye
Sidney Kieschner	Sidney Kingsley
Gertrude Konstam	Gertrude Kingston
Phyllis Kierkegaard	Phyllis Kirk
Joseph Lichtman	Joe Layton
Jeanne Loiseau	Daniel Lesueur
Otto Linkenholter	Elmo Lincoln
Bambi Linnemeier	Bambi Linn
Dolores Loehr	Diana Lynn
Emil Bundsman	Anthony Mann
David Liebermann	Hank Mann
Theodore Goldman	Theodore Mann
Ronal Moodnick	Ron Moody
Barbara Nicekraues	Barbara Nichols
Johnny Veliotes	Johnny Otis
Joseph Papirofsky	Joseph Papp
Emmanuel Rudnitsky	°Man Ray
Elmer Reizenstein	°Elmer Rice
Laura Reichenthal	Laura Riding
John Ramistella	Johnny Rivers
Jerome Rabinowitz	Jerome Robbins
Edward Aarons	Edward Ronns
William Rosenberg	Billy Rose
Philip Rosenberg	Philip Rose
Joseph Sauer	Joseph Sawyer
Jack Scafone	Jack Scott
Arthur Arshawsky	Artie Shaw
Alfred Schoenberg	Al Shean
Paul Schouvalov	Paul Sheriff
Beverly Silverman	Beverly Sills
Elsy Steinberg	Elaine Stewart
Adolf Wohlbruck	Anton Walbrook
Nathan Weinstein	Nathaniel West
George Wenzlaff	George Winslow
Herbert Weisz	Herbert Wise

4. Foreign to Simplified

This list instances names that still appear foreign or un-English in their modified version, but at the same time are mostly simpler and shorter than the foreign original surname. Forenames are sometimes also simplified and shortened, but in many cases remain unchanged in the pseudonym.

Real name	*Pseudonym*
Dominic Amici	°Don Ameche
James Aurness	James Arness
Kridur Aslanian	Gregoire Aslan

Mischa Ounskowsky	Mischa Auer
Francis Avallone	Frankie Avalon
Charles Aznavurgan	Charles Aznavour
Georgy Balanchivadze	George Balanchine
Gyozo Braun	Victor Barna
Raymond Barallobre	Ray Barra
Lionel Begleiter	Lionel Bart
Neilli Burgini	Polly Bergen
Ludwig Bamberger	Ludwig Berger
Mendel Berlinger	Milton Berle
Derek Van den Bogaerde	Dirk Bogarde
James Bruderlin	James Brolin
Cecilia Kalegeropoulos	°Maria Callas
Konstantinos Kavaphes	C.P. Cavafy
Walter Annichiarico	Walter Chiari
Louis Cristillo	Lou Costello
Morton Da Costa	Morton Tecosky
Harold Silverblatt	Howard Da Silva
Rick Zehringer	Rick Derringer
Romain Kacewgary	Romain Gary
Jacob Gershvin	George Gershwin
June Hovick	June Havoc
Gisele Schiltenhelm	Brigitta Helm
Elra Kazanjoglou	Elia Kazan
Stanislaus Kiecal	Stanley Ketchel
Edward Knoblauch	Edward Knoblock
Hermann Kosterlitz	Henry Koster
Irving Lahrhelm	Bert Lahr
Dorothy Kaumeyer	Dorothy Lamour
Elizabeth Zanardi-Landi	Elissa Landi
Leonard Canegati	°Canada Lee
Franz van Strehlenau	Nikolas Lenau
Roza-Maria Lubienska	Rula Lenska
Vladimir Leventon	Val Lewton
Laszlo Lowenstein	Peter Lorre
Paul Lugacs	Paul Lukas
Rocco Marchegiano	Rocky Marciano
Walter Matuschanskayasky	°Walter Matthau
Jean Mokiejeswki	Jean-Pierre Mocky
Hildegarde Knef	Hildegarde Neff
Federico Nobile	Fred Niblo
Max Oppenheimer	Max Ophuls
Felicia Riese	Patricia Roc
Harry Rubinstein	Harry Ruby
Felia Salzmann	Felix Salten
Elke Schletz	Elke Sommer
David Solberg	David Soul
Peter Torkelson	Peter Tork
Pirson Aldabaldetrecu	Pirmin Trecu

5. NAMES TO DISTINGUISH

These are the names deliberately chosen in order to distinguish:

either a literary activity (often the writing of detective novels) from a professional career (as a lawyer, lecturer, or doctor, for example), or a single literary work, or literary genre or period, from other writing (as a one and only novel, or magazine contributions distinguished from a novelist's usual output). It is not so much the names themselves that are important here but their distinguishing function. Against each pair of names (real and assumed) is given the person's main activity, whether already a writer or not. Where he is not a writer, his pseudonym will serve, of course, to distinguish his literary work from his profession. In a couple of cases the "writing" is very specialized (Noel Gay, popular song writer, and Ximenes, who compiled crosswords), but these two did at least write something.

Real name (with Pseudonym)	*Main activity*
Charles Oursler (Anthony Abbot)	writer
Emile-Auguste Chartier (Alain)	philosopher
Alfred George Gardiner (Alpha of the Plough)	essayist
Paul Bourguin (Richard Amberley)	writer
Ronald Beckett (John Anthony)	lawyer
Heinrich Fruenkel (Assiac)	historian
Ezra Pound (William Atheling)	poet
George Tucker (Joseph Atterley)	philosopher
Bernard De Voto (John August)	writer
Edmund Cooper (Richard Avery)	writer
Francis Bickerstaffe-Drew (John Ayscough)	priest
Cedric Simpson (Guy Bailey)	pathologist
William Godwin (Edward Baldwin)	writer
Bruce Cummings (°W.N.P. Barbellion)	writer
Harold Blundell (George Bellairs)	banker
Bernard Newman (Don Betteridge)	novelist
James Lowell (Hosea Biglow)	professor of literature
James Hannay (George A. Birmingham)	priest
Cecil Day-Lewis (°Nicholas Blake)	poet
Peter de Rosa (Neil Boyd)	writer
Osbourne Mavor (James Bridie)	doctor
John Wilson (Anthony Burgess)	writer
Victor Purcell (Myra Buttle)	writer
Ronald Chatwynd-Hayes (Angus Campbell)	writer
Evelyn Vivian (Charles Cannell)	writer
Rosalind Wade (Catherine Carr)	writer
Peter Brooke (Anthony Carson)	writer
Richard Hough (Bruce Carter)	writer
Evelyn Blackburn (Frances Castle)	writer
Christopher Sprigg (Christopher Caudwell)	writer
Henry Jones (Cavendish)	doctor
Alfred Stewart (John Jervis Connington)	professor of chemistry
Robert Montgomery (Edmund Crispin)	musician
Chaim Raphael (Jocelyn Davey)	civil servant
Jean Bowden (Belinda Dell)	writer
Carmen Conde (Florentina del Mar)	poet
Geoffrey Howard (Marmaduke Dixey)	barrister
Joseph Macleod (Adam Drinan)	writer

William Aytoun (Augustus Dun-Shunner)	poet
John Squire (Solomon Eagle)	writer
Erle Gardner (A.A. Fair)	writer
Kathleen Freeman (Mary Fitt)	lecturer in Greek
William Shields (Barry Fitzgerald)	civil servant
James Farrell (Jonathan Lituleson Fogarty)	writer
Leslie Forse (Fortis)	journalist
Charles Briggs (Harry Franco)	journalist
Reginald Armitage (Noel Gay)	organist
James Mitchell (Lewis Gibbon)	writer
Brian O'Nolan (Myles na Gopaleen)	novelist
Cecil Fitzgerald (Janet Gordon)	writer
Gordon Ostlere (Richard Gordon)	doctor
Arrigo Boito (Tobio Gorria)	musician
Albert Bitzius (°Jeremias Gotthelf)	pastor
Roderick Jeffries (Rodney Graeme)	lawyer
Ray Baker (David Grayson)	essayist
Benjamin Shepard (Francis Grierson)	musician
Henry Wise (Harry Gringo)	naval officer
Richard Clayton (William Haggard)	civil servant
Alfred Clark (Cyril Hare)	lawyer
James Abraham (James Harpole)	surgeon
Ruth France (Paul Henderson)	writer
James Wight (James Herriot)	veterinary surgeon
Anthony Hawkins (Anthony Hope)	barrister
Richard Sampson (Richard Hull)	chartered accountant
John Stewart (°Michael Innes)	lecturer in English
Gilbert Seldes (Foster Johns)	journalist
Adrian Rouquette (E. Junius)	writer
Milward Burge (Milward Kennedy)	civil servant
James Gilmore (Edmund Kirke)	businessman
Alfred Harbage (Thomas Kyd)	educationalist
George Darley (John Lacy)	writer
Patrick Gilmore (Louis Lambert)	bandmaster
Eleanor Jourdain (Miss Lamont)	college principal
George Lewes (°Slingsby Lawrence)	philosopher
David Cornwell (°John Le Carré)	diplomat
Henry Carter (Frank Leslie)	publisher and engraver
John Kennedy (Mark Littleton)	politician
Ben Redman (Jeremy Lord)	journalist
Henry Harland (Sidney Luska)	writer
John Watson (Ian Maclaren)	minister of religion
Patrick Connor (Peter Malin)	writer
Harold Sebag-Montefiore (Marco II)	barrister
Rene Oppitz (J.-J. Marine)	poet and critic
Ralph Mottram (J. Marjoram)	novelist
Lucy Malleson (Anne Meredith)	writer
Hugh Scott (Henry Seton Merriman)	insurance clerk
John Lockhart (Peter Morris)	writer
Lydia Fraser (Harriet Myrtle)	writer
Raymond Chapman (Simon Nash)	writer
Eric Hobsbawm (F. Newton)	economist and historian
Ernest Swinton (°Ole Luk-Oie)	army officer
Henry Fuller (Stanton Page)	writer

Gilbert Hudlestone (Philip Roger Pater)	priest
Julian Ralph (Percival)	journalist
Charles Spurgeon (John Ploughman)	Baptist preacher
Paul Adam (Jacques Plowert)	writer
Michael McConville (Patrick Plum)	civil servant
John Irving (John Quod)	writer
Elizabeth Robins (C.E. Raimond)	actress
Jean-Raymond de Kremer (Jean Ray)	writer
Ronald Reagan (°Ronald Reagan)	film actor
Benjamin Franklin (Richard Saunders)	statesman
Leslie Truss (George Selmark)	writer
David Unwin (David Severn)	writer
Nevil Norway (Nevil Shute)	engineer
Dominic Wyndham Lewis (Timothy Shy)	writer
Nathaniel Tucker (Edward Sidney)	professor of law
Ruth Fulton (Anne Singleton)	anthropologist
George Rose (Arthur Sketchley)	priest
Ann Stephens (Jonathan Slick)	writer
John Waller (Jonathan Slingsby)	journalist
Alistair Maclean (Ian Stuart)	writer
Frank Slaughter (C.V. Terry)	writer
Andrey Sinyavsky (Abram Tertz)	writer
Josiah Holland (Timothy Titcomb)	writer
Margaret Todd (Graham Travers)	doctor
Francis Slater (Jan Van Avond)	writer
Grace Stone (Ethel Vance)	writer
Lester del Rey (Erik Van Lhin)	writer
Walter Campbell (Stanley Vestal)	writer
Christopher Logue (Count Palmiro Vicarion)	writer
Henrietta Palmer (Violet Whyte)	writer
John Oldmixon (Charles Wilson)	historian
Philip Mason (Philip Woodruff)	writer
Derrick Macnutt (°Ximenes)	classics teacher

6. NAMES TO DIFFERENTIATE

These are names adopted in order to differentiate the bearer from another person similarly or identically named. Sometimes the other person may be one's own parents; sometimes there is simply a confusion of identity, especially where two people are both active in the same field. The list shows the person or persons who motivated the change. Within a family, such a change may have been prompted by parental disapproval of the activity of the son or daughter.

Real name : Changed to	Because of
Anna Gorenko : °Anna Akhmatova	father
Henri-Alban Fournier : Alain-Fournier	writer Édouard Fournier
David Hayward-Jones : °David Bowie	pop musician David Jones
Melvin Kaminsky : °Mel Brooks	trumpeter Max Kaminsky
Roy Charles Hammond : Roy C.	1 pop musician Roy Hamilton, 2 Ray Charles

Ray Charles Robinson : Ray Charles   °Sugar Ray Robinson
Robert Montgomery : Robert Douglass   Robert Douglas
Henry Smith : Henry Durant   many other Smiths
Cyril Bird : °Fougasse   another *Punch* artist named Bird

Adrien Wettach : °Grock   another clown Brock
Henry Brodribb : °Henry Irving   parents
Frank lo Vecchio : °Frankie Laine   female singer Frances Lane
Neftalí Reyes : °Pablo Neruda   father
Margery Pilbeam : °Nova Pilbeam   mother Margery Pilbeam
William Pole : William Poel   father
Thomas Parnell : °Fred Russell   Irish politician Charles Stewart Parnell

Michael Sadler : Michael Sadleir   father Sir Michael Sadler
Secondo Tranquilli : Ignazio Silone   family
Eunice Wayman : °Nina Simone   parents
Vladimir Nabokov : °Sirin   father Vladimir Dmitriyevich Nabokov

Thomas Terry Hoar-Stevens : °Terry-Thomas   actor family Terry
James Thomson : °James Thomson, B.V.   18th-century poet James Thomson

Patricia White : Patricia Wilde   sister Nora White, also a ballet dancer

7. MULTIPLE PSEUDONYMS

This list is rather different. Many people, especially writers, use not one pseudonym but two or three. Some use even more. There follow the real names of 19 writers of different periods and genres, and the pen names that they used or use. Note the fairly conventional names devised by John Creasey, the anagrams of Robert Fanthorpe, the multilingualism of Richard Bickers (including the Italian translation of his first and third names), the wordplay of Jonathan Swift, and the good humor of Thackeray. Note, too, the predominant masculinity of the names selected by Gabrielle Long, as well as the alliterations of Scott. And do not miss the name under which °Lenin came to England as a British subject — William Frey.

Real name	*Pseudonyms*
Christine Thomson (b. 1897)	Dair Alexander
English light fiction writer	Molly Campbell
	Christine Hartley
	Flavin Richardson
John Creasey (1908-1973)	Gordon Ashe
English crime novelist	M.E. Cooke
	Margaret Cooke
	Henry St. John Cooper
	Norman Deane

Elise Fecamps
Robert Caine Frazer
Patrick Gill
Michael Halliday
Charles Hogarth
Brian Hope
Colin Hughes
Kyle Hunt
Abel Mann
Peter Manton
J.J. Marric
James Marsden
Richard Martin
Rodney Mattheson
Anthony Morton
Ken Ranger
William K. Reilly
Tex Riley
Jeremy Yorke

Robert Fanthorpe (b. 1935)
English writer of horror stories

Othello Baron
Erle Barton
Lee Barton
Thornton Bell
Lee Brett
Bron Fane
Oben Lerteth
John E. Muller (house name)
Elton T. Neef
Phil Nobel
Peter O'Flinn
Lionel Roberts
Rene Rolant
Deutero Spartacus
Robin Tate
Neil Thanet
Trebor Thorpe
Pel Torro
Olaf Trent
Karl E. Zeigfried (house name)

Henry Bedford-Jones (1887-1949)
Canadian-born American
    writer of historical
    adventures

Donald Bedford
Montague Brissard
Cleveland B. Chase
Paul Ferval
Michael Gallister
Allan Hawkwood
Gordon Keyne
M. Lassez
George Souli de Mourant
Lucian Pemjean
Margaret Love Sangerson
Charles George Souli
Gordon Stuart

Elliott Whitney
John Wycliffe

Richard Leslie Townshend Bickers
  (b. 1917)
English RAF pilot and writer of war
  stories

Richard Townshend Bickers
Mark Charles
Ricardo Cittafino
Philip Dukes
Paul Kapusta
Burt Keene
Fritz Kirschner
Gui Lefevre
Gerhardt Muller
David Richards
Richard Townshend

Honoré Balzac (1799-1850)
French novelist and short story writer

Alexandre de B...
Henri B.
°Honoré de Balzac
Alfred Coudreux
Felix Davin
Eugène Morrisot
Lord R'hoone
Horace de Saint-Aubin

Ray Bradbury (b. 1920)
American science fiction and general
  writer

Edward Banks
Leonard Douglas
William Elliott
Don Reynolds
Leonard Spaulding

Eliza Louisa Moresby Beck (d. 1931)
English novelist

E. Barrington
Lily Adams Beck
Louis Moresby

Jonathan Swift (1667-1745)
Irish writer and satirist

Isaac Bickerstaff
M.B. Drapier
Jack Frenchman
T. Fribble
Lemuel Gulliver
Gregory Miso-Sarum
M. Flor O'Squarr
A Person of Honour
T.N. Philomath
Presto
Abel Roper
A Shoeboy
S.P.A.M.
Student of Astronomy
T. Tinker
Dr. Andrew Tripe
Simon Wagstaff, Esq.

Gabrielle Margaret Vere Long,
  née Campbell (1886-1952)

Marjorie Bowen
Margaret Campbell

English novelist and biographer

Robert Paye
George R. Preedy
Joseph Shearing
John Winch

Frederick Schiller Faust (1892-1944)
American writer of westerns and the
  "Dr. Kildare" series

Frank Austin
George Owen Baxter
Lee Bolt
Walter C. Butler
George Challis
Peter Dawson
Martin Dexter
Evin Evan
Evan Evans
John Frederick
Frederick Frost
Dennis Manning
David Manning
Peter Henry Morland
Hugh Owen
Nicholas Silver
Henry Uriel
Peter Ward

William Makepeace Thackeray
  (1811-1863)
English novelist

Mr. Brown
Growley Byles
Folkstone Canterbury
John Corks
Fitzroy Clarence
Jeames de la Pluche
Frederick Haltamont de
  Montmorency
Henry Esmond, Esq.
Boldomero Espartero
The Fat Contributor
George Savage Fitz-Boodle,
  Esq.
Major Goliah Gahagan
A Gentleman in Search of a
  Man-Servant
M. Gobemouche
Leontius Androcles Huggle-
  stone
Jeames of Buckley Square
Theresa MacWhorter
Master Molloy Molony
Mulligan of Kilballymulligan
One of Themselves
Arthur Pendennis
Peter Perseus
Harry Rollicker
The Honorable Wilhelmina
  Amelia Skeggs
Ikey Solomons, Esq., Junior

Miss Tickletoby
°Michael Angelo Titmarsh
Lancelot Wagstaff
Theophile Wagstaff
Charles James Yellowplush

Irene Maude Swatridge, née Mossop
  (b. ca. 1905)
English novelist

Fay Chandos
Irene Mossop
Virginia Storm
Jan Tempest

Washington Irving (1783-1859)
American humorist

Friar Antonio Agapida
Geoffrey Crayon
Anthony Evergreen
°Diedrich Knickerbocker
Launcelot Langstaff
Jonathan Oldstyle

Ursula Bloom (b. 1892)
English novelist

Sheila Burnes
Mary Essex
Rachel Harvey
Deborah Mann
Lozania Prole
Sara Sloan

Eleanor Alice Burford Hibbert
  (b. 1906)
English historical novelist

Eleanor Burford
Philippa Carr
Elbur Ford
Victoria Holt
Kathleen Kellow
Jean Plaidy
Ellalice Tate

Charles Hamilton (1875-1961)
English author of school stories

Winston Cardew
Martin Clifford
Owen Conquest
Ralph Redway
Frank Richards
Hilda Richards

Vladimir Ilyich Ulyanov (1870-1924)
Russian Communist leader and head
  of state

Bolshevik
William Frey
Konstantin Petrovich Ivanov
N. Karpov
B.V. Kuprianov
N. Lenin
°Vladimir Ilyich Lenin
A. Linitsch
Meyer
Iv. Petrov
A Reader
Russian Communist
K. Tulin

[Sir] Walter Scott (1771-1832)
Scottish poet and novelist

°Jedediah Cleishbotham
Captain Cuthbert Clutterbuck
Chrystal Croftangry
The Rev. Dr. Dryasdust
Malachi Malagrowther
Peter Pattieson
Paul
Laurence Templeton

8. FEMALE TO MALE

Some of the names to which feminine writers changed in this list are not so much overtly male as ambiguous. A name beginning with initials (C.L. Anthony, or M.J. Farrell, for example) can obviously be either male or female, but there are also names with a "bisexual" forename, such as Billie Burke, Dormer Creston, °Clemence Dane, and of course the three Brontës.

Real name	*Pseudonym*
Victoria Benedictssohn	Ernst Ahlgren
Mite van Bardeleben	George Allen
Karen Dinesen	Pierre Andrezel, Izak Dinesen
Dodie Smith	C.L. Anthony
Anne Brontë	Acton Bell
Charlotte Brontë	°Currer Bell
Emily Brontë	Ellis Bell
Mary Burke	Billie Burke
Olive Tilford	Fielding Burke
Janet Caldwell	Taylor Caldwell
Mary Murfree	Charles Craddock
Dorothy Colston-Baynes	Dormer Creston
Harriet Beecher Stowe	Christopher Crowfield
Jean Bowden	Avon Curry
Norah Robinson	Peter Curtis
Julia Frankau	Frank Danby
Winifred Ashton	°Clemence Dane
Marjorie Huxtable	Simon Dare
Elizabeth Mackintosh	Gordon Daviot
Joan Aiken	Nicholas Dee
Clotilde Graves	Richard Dehan
Isbella van Servoskerken	Abbé de la Tour
Delphine Gay	Charles de Launey
Helen Rhoder	Guy D'Hardelot
Joyce Muddock	Dick Donovan
Mary Dunne	°George Egerton
Mary Anne Evans	°George Eliot
Sydney Tapping	Sydney Fairbrother
Margaret Barber	Michael Fairless
Mary Skrine	M.J. Farrell

Dorothy Fielding	A. Fielding
Constance Fletcher	George Fleming
Zenith Jones	Leslie Ford, David Frome
Lucy Malleson	Anthony Gilbert
Laura Redden	Howard Glyndon
Alice Fleury	Henry Greville
Hilda Grieg	Sidney Grier
Zoe Gisling	Martin Hare
Ellen Olney	Henry Hayes
Elizabeth Smith	Ernest Helfenstein
Ruth France	Paul Henderson
Pearl Richards	°John Oliver Hobbes
Gladys Mitchell	Stephen Hockaby
Helen Jackson	Saxe Holm
Julia Davies	Cecil Home
Jessie Hope	Graham Hope
Adela Cory	Laurence Hope
Iris Wilkinson	Robin Hyde
Olive Schreiner	Ralph Iron
Rosalie Muspratt	Jasper John
Grace Johnston	Leslie Keith
Edith Lyttleton	G.B. Lancaster
Gertrude Horn	Frank Lin
Ellen Price	Johnny Lardlow
Annie Susan	David Lyall
Helen Mathers	David Lyall
Emma van Deventer	Lawrence L. Lynch
Charlotte Stewart	Allan M'Aulay
Mary Kingsley	Lucas Malet
Eliza Beck	Louis Moresby
Pamela Frankau	Eliot Naylor
Emily Symonds	George Paston
Gabrielle Campbell	Robert Paye, Joseph Shearing, John Winch
Agnes Weekes	Anthony Pryde
Jane Taylor	Q.Q.
Anne Puddicombe	Allen Raine
Alice Brown	Martin Redfield
Georgiana Randolph	Craig Rise
Ethel Richardson	Henry Handel Richardson
Eileen Robertson	E. Arnot Robertson
Violet Martin	Martin Ross
Helen Wallace	Gordon Ray
Frances Marshall	Alan St. Aubyn
Marguerite Jervis	Oliver Sandys
Ann Stephens	Jonathan Slick
Marie de Flavigny	°Daniel Stern
Gladys Mitchell	Malcolm Torrie
Charlotte Cowan	F.G. Trafford
Margaret Todd	Graham Travers
Elizabeth Phelps	°H. Trusta
Juliette Lamber	Comte Paul Vasili
Mary Braddon	Babington White
Henrietta Palmer	John Strange Winter
Mary Linskill	Stephen Yorke

9. MALE TO FEMALE

A list that is, understandably, only one fifth the length of List 8. No male writer, either, seems inclined to change to an ambiguous ("bisexual") name — except perhaps Alister McAllister.

Real name	Pseudonym
Donald Rowland	Annette Adams
Desmonde Coke	Belinda Blinders
Alister McAllister	Lynn Brock
Charles Edward Stuart	Betty Burke
Victor Purcell	Myra Buttle
Henry Adams	Frances Snow Crampton
Vince Furnier	°Alice Cooper
Stephane Mallarme	Madame Marguerite de Ponti
Charles Gibson	Barbara Gilson
Charles Radcliffe-Cooke	Angelina Gushington
Septimus Winner	Alice Hawthorne
Osborne Stratemeyer	Carolyn Keene
William Sharp	°Fiona Macleod
Benjamin Shillaber	°Mrs. Partington
Frederick Stephens	Laura Savage
Paul Feval	Frances Trollope

10. ENGLISH TO FOREIGN

These names are the exact opposite of those in lists 2 and 3. In some cases an English name is replaced by a foreign name quite unlike it; in others the foreign version is an adaptation of the English name (as Hilda Butsova). Names of this latter type usually turn out to be those of ballet dancers.

Real name	Pseudonym
Richard Adams	Richard Adama
Elizabeth McLauchlan	Babette
Charles Leland	Hans Breitmann
Hilda Boot	Hilda Butsova
Henry Higgins	°Cañadas
Bonar Sullivan	Bonar Colleano
Edris Stannus	Ninette de Valois
Patrick Healey-Kay	°Anton Dolin
Barry Walls	El Hakim
William Anderson	Leif Erickson
Celia Franks	Celia Franca
Evelyne Cournand	Anna Galina
Romayne Austin	Romayne Grigorova
Walter Smith	Hermann Kunst
Ethel Liggins	Ethel Leginska
Lilian Marks	Alicia Markova
Lillian Norton	Lillian Nordica

11. ARISTOCRATIC OR LOWLY

This list gives names that have been socially enhanced, either by the addition of a title (as Baron Corvo) or by the use of an "aristocratic" particle such as *de*. In four cases (asterisked) persons who were already aristocrats adopted suitably lowly names, two of them for purposes of correspondence.

Real name	*Pseudonym*
Honoré Balzac	°Honoré de Balzac
Marguerite Jervis	Countess Barcynska
Pierre-Auguste Caron	Pierre-Auguste de Beaumarchais
Frederick Rolfe	°Baron Corvo
Daniel Foe	°Daniel Defoe
Thomas Quincey	Thomas De Quincey
Andreas Toth	André de Toth
Edris Stannus	Ninette de Valois
Nigel Davies	Justin de Villeneuve
Robert Hery	Robert Dhery
Philippe Fabre	°Philippe d'Églantine
Sarah Churchill, Duchess of Marlborough	Mrs. Freeman*
William Gerhardi	°William Gerhardie
Clement Dominguez	Gregory XVIII
Edward Everett Hale	Colonel Frederic Ingham
Mary Braddon	Lady Caroline Lascelles
Queen Anne of England	Mrs. Morley*
Sarah Aust	The Honourable Mrs. Murray
Baron de Tabley	George F. Preston*
King George III of England	Ralph Robinson*

12. COVER-UP NAMES

All the names in this list were adopted for some secretive, but not necessarily criminal, purpose—flight, evasion, enlistment, espionage, propaganda, reconnaissance, satire, and sheer expediency among them. Guy Fawkes, for example, passed himself off as a porter named John Johnson, and the poet Samuel Taylor Coleridge enlisted in the dragoons in 1793 as Silas Tomkyn Comberback, thus retaining his initials.

Pseudonym	*Real name*
Major E.J. Allen	Allan Pinkerton
Imamu Amiri Baraka	Le Roi Jones
David Ben-Gurion	David Gruen
Levi Blodgett	Theodore Parker
Father Bonaventura	Charles Edward Stuart
°Willy Brandt	Herbert Frahm
Colonel Britton	Douglas Ritchie

Geffery Broadbottom	Philip Stanhope
°Charles Bronson	Charles Buchinsky
Thomas Brown the Younger	Thomas Moore
Betty Burke	Charles Edward Stuart
Count Alessandro di Cagliostro	Giuseppe Balsamo
Colonel Tony Callan	Costas Giorgiou
Carlos	Illich Sánchez
°Butch Cassidy	Robert Parker
Céline	Odette Sansom
John Clarke	Richard Cromwell
Silas Tomkyn Comberback	Samuel Taylor Coleridge
Cuthbert Comment	Abraham Tucker
Doleman	Robert Parsons
Thomas du Clevier	Bonaventure Desperiers
Mlle Dumesnil	Davy de la Pailleterie
Étienne	Lev Manevich
°Partenio Etiro	Pietro Aretino
°Forez	François Mauriac
Gilderoy	Patrick Macgregor
Caius Gracchus	François-Émile Babeuf
Père Hyacinthe	Charles-Jean-Marie Loyson
Frank Jacson	Ramon Mercader
John Johnson	Guy Fawkes
John Paul Jones	John Paul
W. Kinsayder	John Marston
°Sergey Kirov	Sergey Kostrikov
Edward Knott	Matthias Wilson
Vasily Komarov	Vasily Korzh
Major Le Caron	Thomas Beach
Gordon Lonsdale	Konon Molody
Malcolm Macgregor	William Mason
Richard McGrory	Keith May
Madeleine	Noor Imayat Khan
°Joseph Markham	John Stonehouse
L. Martov	Yuly Tsederbaum
Mary of Arnhem	Helen Sensburg
Thomas Matthew	John Rogers
Thomas Neill	Thomas Cream
Aristarchus Newlight	Richard Whately
Darleen O'Connor	Joyce McKinney
Vladimir Petrov	Afanasy Shokhorov
Abbé Pierre	Henri Groues
Peter Plymley	Sydney Smith
Popski	Vladimir Peniakoff
Hanna Puttick	Astrid Proll
Mr Robinson	Henry Crippen
Master Robinson	Ethel le Neve
Michael Romanoff	Harry Gerguson
Dr. Schmidt	Johann von Schiller
°Tania	Haydee Bunke
Tanya	Zoya Kosmodemyanskaya
Léo Taxil	Gabriel Pagès
Guy de Valmont	Guy de Maupassant
°Vercors	Jean Bruller

Baron Arminius von Thunder-
Ten-Tronckh   Matthew Arnold
Curt Von Veltheim   Ludwig Kurtze
Matthew White   William Prynne
°Sonny Boy Williamson   Rice Miller

13. RELIGIOUS NAMES

The list gives a brief selection of typical religious names and titles, both Christian and non-Christian. The Christian religious names derive either from the person's own forename (Christian name) or from the forename of some earlier saintly or scholarly person. Defining attributes apart (as "... of Calcutta"), not a single name in the list is of course unique, Buddha included.

Lay name	*Religious name*
Sergei Vladimir Simansky	Alexis
Rose Hawthorne	Mother Alphonsa
Ann Lee	Mother Ann
Pierre de Guibours	Père Anselme
Andrew Borisovich Bloom	Anthony
William Everson	Brother Antoninus
Marie-Bernarde Soubirous	St. Bernadette
Siddhartha Gautama	Buddha
Joseph Damien de Veuster	Father Damien
Vasily Mikhaylovich Drozdov	Filaret
Frances Ball	Mother Frances Mary Theresa
Ras Tafari Makonnen	°Haile Selassie
Joseph Leycester Lyne	Father Ignatius
Juan de Yepis y Alvarez	Saint John of the Cross
François Leclerc du Tremblay	Père Joseph
Pratap Singh Rawat	°Maharaj Ji
Mikhail Khristodolou Mouskos	°Makarios III
Mary Maud Morant	Sister Mary Regis
Boris Georgiyevitch Rotov	Nikodim
Nikita Minov	Nikon
Jan Willem	°Osman Pasha
Ivan Nikolayevich Starogorodsky	Sergius
Agnes Gonxa Bojaxhiu	Mother Teresa of Calcutta
Marie-François-Thérèse Martin	Saint Thérèse de Lisieux

14. OMISSION OF SURNAME

A lengthy list but a straightforward one: those people who changed their name by the simple expedient of dropping their surname. Note that in many cases the resulting "surname," originally a middle name, is often a mother's maiden name (mmn) and was therefore a surname anyway in the first place. Note also that in some cases the forename is also dropped, and the new name formed exclusively from middle names (as with Louis Moresby). Owners of double-barrelled names frequently shorten their name by omitting one half of the double surname.

Pseudonym	*Real name*
Iris Adrian	Iris Adrian Hostetter
Eddie Albert	Eddie Albert Heimberger
[Sir] George Alexander	George Alexander Gibb-Samson
Elizabeth Allen	Elizabeth Allen Gillease
Robert Alton	Robert Alton Hart
Annie Amelia	Annie Amelia Garrett
Ellen Amelia	Ellen Amelia Garrett
Fern Andra	Fern Andra von Weichs
Thomas Andrew	Edward Thomas Andrulewicz
[Sir] Norman Angell	Ralph Norman Angell Lane
Muriel Angelus	Muriel Angelus Findlay
Piers Anthony	Piers Anthony Billingham Jacob
Guillaume Apollinaire	Guillaume Apollinaire de Kostrowitsky
George Arliss	George Augustus Andrews
Anthony Armstrong	George Anthony Armstrong Willis
George K. Arthur	George K. Arthur Brest
Robert Arthur	Robert Arthur Feder
Edward Ashley	Edward Ashley Cooper
[Sir] Felix Aylmer	Felix Edward Aylmer-Jones
Angela Baddeley	Madeleine Angela Clinton-Baddeley
Hermione Baddeley	Hermione Clinton-Baddeley
Patricia Barnes	Patricia Barnes Abercrombie
Rutland Barrington	George Barrington Rutland Fleet
Dan Barry	Donald Barry d'Acosta
Michael Barry	James Barry Jackson
Keith Baxter	Keith Baxter-Wright
Janet Beecher	Janet Beecher Meysenbury
Busby Berkeley	William Berkeley Enos
Billy Bevan	William Bevan Harris
Dinna Bjorn	Dinna Bjorn Larsen
Betty Blythe	Elizabeth Blythe Slaughter
William Bolitho	William Bolitho Ryall
Sherwood Bonner	Katherine Sherwood Bonner Macdowell
Ernest Bramah	Ernest Bramah Smith
George Brent	George Brent Nolan
Jonathan Burn	Henry Jones Jonathan Burn-Forti
Henry Cecil	Henry Cecil Leon
Ray Charles	Ray Charles Robinson
Leslie Charteris	Leslie Charles Bowyer Yin
Peter Cheyney	Reginald Evelyn Peter Southouse-Cheney
Hal Clement	Harry Clement Stubbs
E. Clerihew	Edmund Clerihew Bentley
Sam Collins	Samuel Thomas Collins Vegg
Albert Conti	Albert de Conti Cedassamare
Gloria Contreras	Carmen Gloria Contreras Rueniger
Kathryn Crawford	Kathryn Crawford Moran
Richmal Crompton	Richmal Crompton Lamburn
Claudia Dell	Claudia Dell Smith

George Douglas	George Douglas Brown
Robert Douglas	Robert Douglas Finlayson
Fabia Drake	Fabia Drake McClinchy
Vince Edwards	Vincent Edwards Zorrio
James Ellison	James Ellison Smith
Judith Evelyn	Judith Evelyn Allen
Martha Farquharson	Martha Farquharson Finley
José Ferrer	José Vincente Ferrer Otero y Cintrón
Walter Fitzgerald	Walter Fitzgerald Bond
Paul Ford	Paul Ford Weaver
Bruce Forsyth	Bruce Joseph Forsyth Johnson
Sydney Fowler	Sydney Fowler Wright
Daniel George	Daniel George Bunting
[Sir] Edward German	Edward German Jones
Rodney Graeme	Roderic Graeme Jeffries
Gloria Grahame	Gloria Grahame Hallward
Ruth Hall	Ruth Hale Ibáñez
Walter Hampden	Walter Hampden Dougherty
Rolf Harolde	Rolf Harolde Wigger
Ian Hay	John Hay Beith
Hy Hazell	Hyacinth Hazel O'Higgins
Ian Holm	Ian Holm Cuthbert
Anthony Hope	[Sir] Anthony Hope Hawkins
Claude Houghton	Claude Houghton Oldfield
George Irving	George Irving Sheasky
Jean Paul	Jean Paul Friedrich Richter
Gloria Jean	Gloria Jean Schoonover
Evan John	Evan John Simpson
John Paul Jones	John Paul
Leatrice Joy	Leatrice Joy Zeilder
Anna Karina	Hanne Karin Beyer
Hugh Kingsmill	Hugh Kingsmill Lunn
Rudolf van Labon	Rudolf Laban de Varaljas
Rod la Rocque	Roderick la Rocque de la Rour
Richard Llewellyn	Richard Dafydd Vivian Llewellyn Lloyd
Charles Lloyd	[Sir] Charles Lloyd Birkin
Marian Lorne	Marian Lorne MacDougal
Joe Louis	Joseph Louis Barrow
Anita Louise	Anita Louise Fremault
Robert Lowery	Robert Lowery Hanks
Bela Lugosi	Bela Lugosi Blasko
Barbara Lynn	Barbara Lynn Ozen
Katherine Mansfield	Kathleen Mansfield Murray
Tully Marshall	Tully Marshall Phillips
°Carmen Miranda	Maria de Carmo Mirando de Cunha
George Montgomery	George Montgomery Letz
Louis Moresby	Eliza Louisa Moresby Beck
Leonard Mudie	Leonard Mudie Cheetham
Jean Muir	Jean Muir Fullerton
Owen Nares	Owen Nares Ramsay
Francis Nesbitt	Francis Nesbitt McCron
Annie Oakley	Phoebe Anne Oakley Moses
Vic Oliver	Viktor Oliver von Samek
James Otis	James Otis Kaler

John Patrick	John Patrick Goggan
Edward Percy	Edward Percy Smith
Jessie Ralph	Jessie Ralph Chambers
Moira Shearer	Moira Shearer King
Nevil Shute	Nevil Shute Norway
Henry Stephenson	Henry Stephenson Garroway
Ed Stewart	Edward Stewart Mainwaring
Kylie Tennant	Kylie Tennant Rodd
Ann Todd	Ann Todd Mayfield
Arthur Treacher	Arthur Treacher Veary
William Trevor	William Trevor Cox
C.C. Fraser Tytler	Christina Catherine Fraser-Tytler Liddle
Roger Vadim	Roger Vadim Plemiannikow
°Rudolph Valentino	Rudolpho Alfonzo Raffaelo Pierre Filibert Guglielmi di Valentina d'Antonguolla
Gene Vincent	Eugene Vincent Craddock
Erich Von Stroheim	Erich von Stroheim von Nordenwall
Bruno Walter	Bruno Walter Schlesinger
Lavinia Warren	Mercy Lavinia Warren Bumpus
Dennis Wayne	Dennis Wayne Wendelken
Bransby Williams	Bransby William Pharez
David Wilson	David Wilson MacArthur

15. FORENAME ALONE

A nice straightforward list, in which a pseudonym is formed by using the first name or a middle name on its own. Occasionally this is preceded by a "title," such as Mrs. or Mlle. It may also at the same time be slightly modified (as with Geraldo or Vicky).

Pseudonym	*Real name*
Anatoli	Anatoli Kuznetsov
Annette	Annette Funicello
Ann-Margret	Ann-Margret Olson
Antoine	Antek Cierplikowski
Anton	Beryl Botterill Antonia Yeoman
Antonio	Antonio Ruiz Soler
Arletty	Arlette Léonie Bathiat
Armand	Friedrich Armand Strubberg
Mlle Augusta	Caroline Augusta Josephine Theresa Fuchs
Babette	Elizabeth McLauchlan
Fra Bartholommeo	Bartolommeo di Pagolo del Fattorino
°Jack Benny	Benjamin Kubelsky
Bhaskar	Bhaskar Roy Chowdhury
May Britt	Maybritt Wilkens
Carlota	Marie-Charlotte-Amélie-Augustine-Victoire-Clémentine-Léopoldine
[Saint] Catherine	Caterina de Ricci
[Saint] Catherine of Bologna	Caterina de Vigri
[Saint] Catherine of Genoa	Caterina Fieschi Adorno

[Saint] Catherine of Siena	Caterina Benincasa
Cher	Cherilyn Sarkasia Lalier
Mlle Clairon	Claire Josephe Hippolyte Leris
Donovan	Donovan P. Leitch
Douglas	Douglas England
°Eusebio	Eusebio Ferreiro da Silva
Fabian	Fabian Forte Bonaparte
Felix	Felix Fernández García
°Geraldo	Gerald Bright
Manolete	Manuel Laureano Rodriguez Sánchez
Matteo	Matteo Marcellus Vittucci
Melanie	Melanie Safka
Michelangelo	Michelagniolo di Lodovico Buonarroti Simoni
Miroslava	Miroslava Stern
Odetta	Odetta Felious
Odette	Odette Brailly
Oliver	William Oliver Swofford
Jean Paul	Jean Paul Friedrich Richter
Perley	Benjamin Perley Poore
Raymond	Raymond Pietro Carlo Bessone
Sabu	Sabu Dastagis
Solomon	Solomon Cuttner
Speranza	Jane Francisca Speranza-Wilde
Sylvia	Sylvia Vanderpool
Teresa	Teresa Viera-Romero
Vera-Ellen	Vera-Ellen Westmeyr Rohe
Vicky	Victor Weisz
Xavier	Joseph Xavier Boniface Saintine
Zander	Alexander Robins

16. Surname Alone

To use your surname alone is hardly to acquire a pseudonym. However, eight examples of such a use are given here, with three minor variations.

Pseudonym	*Real name*
Adrian	Gilbert Adrian
Mrs. Beeton	Isabella Beeton
Giles	Carl Giles
Lekain	Henri-Louis Cain
Liberace	Wladziu Liberace
Low	David Low
Noël-Noël	Lucien Noël
Topol	Chaim Topol

17. Anagram

Most of the names in this list are pure anagrams, that is, all the letters in the original name are rearranged to form another name of exactly the same length. There are one or two near-anagrams, however, such as Barry Cornwall and Max Terpis, and rather more instances when a new name has been formed on the basis of an anagram of some, but not all, of the letters in the real name, as with Nuitter and H. Trusta. Sydney Yendys combines half his real name with its reversal.

Pseudonym	*Real name*
Arthénice	Catherine de Vivonne, marquise [Madame] de Rambouillet
C.W. Ceram	Kurt W. Marek
Barry Cornwall	Bryan Waller Procter
°Partenio Etiro	Pietro Aretino
R.E.H. Greyson	Henry Rogers
Olphar Hamst	Ralph Thomas
Leon Ladulfi	Noel du Fail
Edna Lyall	Ada Ellen Bayly
Mit (or Mot) Yenda	Timothy (or Thomas) Adney
°Red Nirt	Tommy Trinder
T.R. Noon	Olive Marion Norton
Nuitter	Charles Truinet
Philothée O'Neddy	Théophile Dondey
Rudolf Otreb	Robert Fludd
Jules Pascin	Julius Pincas
Raimu	Jules Muraire
Lord R'hoone	°Honoré de Balzac
G.A. Sekon	George Augustus Nokes
P.F. Stern	P.F. Ernst
J. Telio	Charles Joliet
Max Terpis	Max Pfister
°H. Trusta	Elizabeth Stuart Phelps
°Voltaire	François Marie Arouet
Henry Wenman	Henry Newman
Sydney Yendys	Sydney Dobell

18. "Juggling"

This list contains a few names with which liberties have been taken. They have been transposed (Carr Dickson), respelled (Rearden Conner), desegmented (Pier Angeli), or otherwise rearranged, but never so completely as to qualify them for admission to the anagrams of List 17.

Pseudonym	*Real name*
Pier Angeli	Anna Maria Pierangeli
Korney Ivanovich Chukovsky	Nikolay Vasilyevich Korneychuk
Lee J. Cobb	Leo Jacob
Rearden Conner	Patrick Reardon Connor
Con Conrad	Conrad K. Dober
Julian d'Albie	D'Albiac Luard

Dalida	Gigliotta Lolande
A. De Burgh	Edward Morgan Alborough
Carr Dickson	John Dickson Carr
Carter Dickson	John Dickson Carr
W. Scott King	William Kingscote Greenland
Frank Lin	Gertrude Franklin Atherton
E.C.R. Lorac	Edith Caroline Rivett
Ross Martin	Martin Rosenblatt
W.B. Rainey	Wyatt Rainey Blassingame
Gene Raymond	Raymond Guion
Ernest Thompson Seton	Ernest Seton Thompson

19. ABBREVIATIONS

These are the truncated names—names formed from a single syllable or even just initials. In one or two cases an original name has been altered a little (Max Greene, Lew Grade), but in every case the new name is significantly briefer than the old, true name.

Pseudonym	Real name
Afrit	Alistair Ferguson Ritchie
Alan Alda	Alphonso D'Abruzzo
G.R. Aldo	Aldo Graziati
Artemas	Arthur Telford Mason
Batt	Oswald Barrett
Jon Bee	John Badcock
Marie Bell	Marie-Jeanne Bellon-Downey
°Coco	Nikolai Poliakov
Diz	Edward Ardizzone
°Jean Effel	Francois Lejeune
Eha	Edward Hamilton Aitken
Ziggy Elman	Harry Finkelman
Emmwood	John Musgrove-Wood
°Erté	Romain de Tirtoff
°Evoe	Edmund George Valpy Knox
Lew Fields	Lewis Shanfields
°W.C. Fields	William Claude Dukinfield
Gath	George Alfred Townsend
Lew Grade	Louis Winogradsky
Max Greene	Mutz Greenbaum
Gus	George W. Smith
H.B.	Hilaire Belloc
H.D.	Hilda Doolittle
Van Heflin	Emmett Evan Heflin
Herblock	Herbert Block
Hergé	Georges Remi
H.H.	Helen Hunt Jackson
Jak	Raymond Jackson
W.M.L. Jay	Julia L.M. Woodruff
Jon	W.P. John Jones
J.S. of Dale	Frederic Jesup Stimson

Eff Kaye	F. Konstam
Kem	Kimon Evan Marengo
Krik	Henry G. Crickmore
Simon Lack	Simon Macalpine
Arthur Lake	Arthur Silverlake
La Meri	Russell Meriwether Hughes
L.E.L.	Letitia Elizabeth Landon
Margo	María Marguerita Guadelupe Boldao y Castilla
Mehboob	Ramjankhan Mehboobkhan
Jesse Owens	John Cleveland Owens
Poy	Percy Hutton Fearon
S.Z. Sakall	Eugene Gero Szakall
Jules Sand	Leonard Sylvain Jules Sandeau
Sigma	Douglas Straight
Jan Struther	Joyce Anstruther
Tad	Thomas Aloysius Dorgan
°Talvj	Therese Albertine Louise von Jakob
Phillida Terson	Phyllis Neilson-Terry
°Yevgenia Tur	Yelizaveta Salias-de-Turnemir
Bobby Vee	Robert Velline
Willy	Henri Gauthier-Villars
Ernie Wise	Ernest Wiseman
Woon	Ralph Wotherspoon
Zim	Eugene Zimmerman

20. TRANSLATION OR RENDERING

In some cases, it is possible to translate a name (usually a surname) literally, so that German Stein becomes Stone in English, and Italian Casalegno (*casa*, "house," *legno*, "wood") becomes Woodhouse. In others a name can be rendered into its foreign language equivalent, as John Phelan, the English name, is represented in its Irish form, Sean O'Faiolain. This list gives examples of both types, with literal translations predominating.

Pseudonym	*Real name*
Johannes Agricola	Johannes Schneider
Jacobus Arminius	Jakob Harmensen
Balthasar de Beaujoyeux	Baldassare di Belgiojoso
°Martin Bucer	Martin Kuhhorn
William Castle	William Schloss
Jan Amos Comenius	Jan Amos Komensky
°Confucius	K'ung Fu-tzu
E.M. Delafield	Elizabeth Monica de la Pasture
°Don Leucadio Doblado	°Joseph Blanco White
Carolus Duran	Charles-Auguste-Émile Durand
Thomas Erastus	Thomas Lieber
Georg Fabricius	Georg Goldschmied
Judy Holliday	Judith Tuvim

°Iskander	°Aleksandr Herzen
Orlando di Lasso	Roland Delattre
Carolus Linnaeus	Carl von Linne
Jean-Baptiste Lully	Giovanni Battista Lulli
Seosamh MacCathamhaoil	Joseph Campbell
Siobhan McKenna	Siobhan Giollamhuire nic Cionnaith
°Melanchthon	Philip Schwarzerd
Gerhardus Mercator	Gerhard Kremer
°Pietro Metastasio	Pietro Trapassi
°Louis Mountbatten	Louis of Battenberg
Nauticus	Owen Seaman
Sean O'Faiolain	John Phelan
°Boris Polevoy	Boris Kampov
Michael Praetorius	Michael Schultheiss
William Rabbit	Katay Don Sasorith
Sagittarius	Heinrich Schutz
Alexander Sakharoff	Alexander Zuckermann
George E. Stone	George Stein
°Herbert Beerbohm Tree	Herbert Beerbohm
°Joseph Blanco White	José María Blanco y Crespo
Frances Winwar	Francesa Vinciguerra Grebanier
Henry Woodhouse	Mario Terenzio Enrico Casalegno
Xanrof	Léon Fourneau

21. NICKNAME-BASED

This list instances names adopted as the result of a nickname. The meaning or origin of the nickname is also given. (For the original names of the nicknamed persons in this list, see the Who's Who.)

Pseudonym	*Meaning or origin of nickname*
Vladimir Bill-Belotserkovsky	attempts by Americans to say "Belotserkovsky"
Sandro Botticelli	"little barrel"
°Boz	"Moses"
°Buffalo Bill	association with buffalo
°Red Buttons	red-headed "buttons" (bell-boy)
°Michael Caine	"Mike" (see also list 24)
Caligula	"little boots"
Canaletto	"little Canale"
°Jasper Carrott	school nickname (Jasper)
°Cyd Charisse	"sister"
°Chubby Checker	after Fats Domino
Antosha Chekhonte	school nickname (given by scripture teacher)
°Cimabue	"top of the oxen" (*cima*, "peak," *bue* "ox") — i.e., "biggest dunce"
Clio [2]	for precocity in poetry and history
°Bing Crosby	comic strip character Bingo
°Dana	school nickname ("naughty")
°Bebe Daniels	"baby"
°Dave Dee	school nickname
°Fra Diavolo	"father Devil" (by victimized peasants)

°Fifi D'Orsay	"Fifi" (by fellow chorus-girls)
°Fernandel	"Fernand d'elle" = *her* Fernand (i.e., his mother's)
°Redd Foxx	"Chicago Red"
Giorgione	"big George"
°Guercino	"squint-eyed"
°Che Guevara	habit of interjecting ¡che!
His Nibs	so called in *The Times*
°Kid Jensen	Radio Luxemburg's youngest ("kid") DJ
Buster Keaton	so called (Buster) by °Harry Houdini, with whom shared stage act
Kempferhausen	(literary) in *Noctes Ambrosianae*
°Jomo Kenyatta	from "Johnstone," plus Kikuyu word "fancy belt"
°B.B. King	from DJ name "Beale Street Blues Boy"
°Louise Labé	"La Belle Cordière"
°Larry	for Larry Parks
Laura	(literary) in Gifford's *Maeviad* (1795)
°[Sir] Peter Lely	for father, so nicknamed
°Little Tich	from claimant in Tichborne Case
°Pierre Loti	Tahitian "rose"
°Lulu	"lulu of a kid" (by manager)
Masaccio	"Huge Tom"
Masolino	"Little Tom"
Maxim the Greek	for nationality
°Joaquin Miller	for support for Mexican bandit, Joaquín Marietta
Zero Mostel	school nickname (for zero marks)
°Jack Oakie	school nickname (for native state, Oklahoma)
°Jehu O'Cataract	for impetuosity
°Maria del Occidente	"Maria of the West" (so called by Southey)
°Omar Khayyam	*khayyam* means "tentmaker," his father's trade
°Ouida	"Louise"
°[Saint] Peter	Greek *petros* = "rock"
°Edith Piaf	French slang *piaf* = "sparrow"
°Pintoricchio	"Little painter" (for small stature)
°Pocahontas	"sportive"
Antonio Pollaiuolo	"little chicken" (as a younger brother)
°Pont	Latin *pontifex* = "builder"
°Rasputin	"dissolute"
°Ginger Rogers	childhood nickname (Ginger)
Andrea del Sarto	"tailor" (father's trade)
°Leo Sayer	for long mane of hair (Leo)
°Sodoma	"the sodomite"
°Ringo Starr	for fondness for wearing rings (so called by mother)
°Vesta Tilley	"Little Tilley" (at age 6, on stage)
°Tintoretto	"little dyer" (father's trade)
°Mike Todd	"Toat" (nickname)
°Twiggy	thin appearance
°Paolo Uccello	"bird" (from fondness of painting them)
°Sid Vicious	for attack on journalist with a chain
Fats Waller	for plump appearance
William Wastle	"Willie Wastle" (from Robert Burns poem)
°Arthur Weegee	"ouija" (for "psychic" ability to track down a story)
°Googie Withers	Indian word = "love" or "clown" (so called by Indian nurse)
°Zouzou	childhood nickname

22. FAMILY-BASED

A fairly lengthy list of names derived from a member of the family, however close or remote. Not surprisingly, many names derive directly from a person's mother's maiden name—designated here as *mmn*. In a few cases, a name is adopted from a family pseudonym, as with Jean Gabin, for example.

Pseudonym	*Origin*
Maud Adams	mmn
Martha Albrand	great-grandfather
Mrs. Alexander	husband's first name
F.M. Allen	wife's maiden name
Ronald Allen	wife's maiden name (Christine Roland)
Julie Andrews	step-father
Madame d'Arblay	French husband
°Lauren Bacall	mmn (modified)
Ethel, John, Lionel Barrymore	father's pseudonym
Sarah Bernhardt	adoptive parents
°Nicholas Blake	younger son (Nicholas) + mother's middle name
James Bridie	grandmother
Lea Brodie	husband's (former) pseudonym
°Mel Brooks	mmn (Brookman)
Mary Calvert	own married name
Marie Camargo	Spanish mmn
Judy Campbell	father's pseudonym (John Arthur Campbell
Mrs. Patrick Campbell	husband
Henry Campbell-Bannerman	mmn added to own surname
Denis Cannan	mmn
Truman Capote	stepfather
Anna Carteret	mmn
Pamela Charles	father's first name
Geoffrey Chater	father's middle name
Sylvia Burton Christopher	2 successive husbands: °Richard Burton, Jordan Christopher
°Le Corbusier	mmn (or cousin)
°Elvis Costello	father's (occasional) pseudonym (Costello) (see also list 23)
Richard Cromwell [1]	mmn
Constance Cummings	mmn
°Diana Dors	grandfather
Stephen Douglass	mmn
Eddie Dowling	father's middle name (or mmn)
°Joanne Dru	Welsh ancestor
Frank Duveneck	stepfather
Ann Dvorak	mmn
°George Egerton	2nd husband's first name
Avril Elgar	father's 3rd name
Tom Ewell	from mmn (Yeuell)

°Douglas Fairbanks	mother's first husband
Douglas Fairbanks, Jr.	father's pseudonym
Elizabeth Ferrars	mmn
Gabriel Fielding	mmn (Fielding-Smith)
°Joan Fontaine	mother's 2nd husband
°Margot Fonteyn	mmn (Fontes)
Brenda Forbes	mmn
°Gerald Ford	stepfather (Gerald R. Ford, Sr.)
Paul Ford	mmn
°George Formby	father's pseudonym
°Anatole France	from father's 1st name (François)
Frederick	grandfather
Christopher Fry	mmn and grandfather
Jean Gabin	father's pseudonym
°Samuel Goldwyn	from 2 brothers Edgar and Arch Selwyn
Joan Grant	first husband (Arthur Leslie Grant)
Dulcie Gray	mmn
Linda Gray	mmn
Rachel Gurney	father's middle name
William Haggard	mmn
Cosmo Hamilton	mmn
Paul Hamlyn	from mmn (Hamburg)
Kay Hammond	mother's pseudonym
Jean Harlow	mmn (both mother's names)
Alice Hawthorne	from ancestor on mother's side Nathaniel Hawthorne
Helen Hayes	mmn
Patricia Highsmith	adoptive parents
Wendy Hiller	mmn
Antony Hopkins	mmn
Elizabeth Jane Howard	mmn
Hazel Hughes	mmn
Michael Innes	from forenames of 2 sons
Anne Jeffreys	mmn
°Boris Karloff	maternal ancestor
Maria Karnilova	from mmn (Karnilovich)
Viola Keats	mmn
Jeremy Kemp	mmn
Joan Kemp-Welch	mmn
Dennis King	mmn
David Knight	mmn
Elsa Lanchester	mmn
Jane Lane	grandmother's maiden name
°Mario Lanza	mmn
Steve Lawrence	first names of 2 nephews
°Vivien Leigh	husband's middle name (Herbert Leigh Holman)
André Léo	first names of 2 sons
°Jerry Lewis	parents' pseudonyms
°Jack London	stepfather (John London)
°Moura Lympany	from mmn (Limpenny)
°Vera Lynn	grandmother's maiden name
Ross Macdonald	father's middle name
Shirley Maclaine	from mmn (Maclean)

Fredric March	from mmn (Marcher)
Anthony Marlowe	mmn
Garry Marsh	father's middle name
°André Maurois	cousin's first name
°Adah Isaacs Menken	first husband's name
Owen Meredith	remote ancestors
Karin Michaelis	husband's name
Mary Millar	from mmn (Mellow)
Joni Mitchell	husband's name
Yvonne Mitchell	mmn
Mlle Montansier	aunt who brought her up
Brian Murray	mmn
Anna Neagle	mmn
°Novalis	family name in 13th century (de Novali)
°Ivor Novello	mother's 2nd name
Frank O'Connor	mmn
°Jacques Offenbach	father's nickname ("Der Offenbacher")
Annette Page	mmn
°Janis Paige	grandparent
Pesellino	from grandfather who brought him up (Giuliano il Pesello)
°François-André Philidor	nickname of ancestor Michel Danican
Mary Pickford	family name
Augustus Henry Pitt-Rivers	from great-uncle (George Pitt, 2nd Baron Rivers)
Bobby Purify	cousin (James Purify), with whom teamed
C.E. Raimond	from brother (Raymond)
Marjorie Reynolds	husband's name
°Ginger Rogers	mother's 2nd husband (John Rogers)
Maurice Sand	mother's pseudonym (°George Sand)
Romy Schneider	mmn
George Scrope	wife's name
Simone Signoret	mmn
John Standing	maiden name of 1st wife (Kay Hammond)
°Henry Stanley	adoptive parents
Oswald Stoll	stepfather
°Tom Stoppard	mother's 2nd husband (Major Kenneth Stoppard)
Preston Sturges	mother's 2nd husband (Solomon Sturges)
Marie Tempest	husband's name
°Tammi Terrell	husband's name
Josephine Tey	great-great-grandmother
Danny Thomas	first names of two brothers
Frank Thornton	mmn
Linda Thorson	from husband (Barry Bergthorson)
°Mike Todd	son Michael
Helen Twelvetrees	1st husband Charles Twelvetrees
Michael Underwood	mmn
°Maurice Utrillo	adoptive parents
°S.S. Van Dine	old family name (Van Dyne)
°Madame Vestris	1st husband Auguste-Armand Vestris
°François Villon	adoptive father
Jacques Villon	half brother Raymond Duchamp-Villon
Harry Von Tilzer	from mmn (Tilzer)

Henry Wade	mmn
°Max Wall	from stepfather (Wallace)
°Edgar Wallace	from father (Richard Edgar)
Richard Waring	mmn
Raquel Welch	first husband James Welch
Antonia White	mmn
°Barbara Windsor	aunt
Shelley Winters	mmn

23. FROM SOMEONE ELSE

One important category of "ready-made" names are those taken deliberately, or almost randomly, from another person.

Pseudonym	*Name derived from...*
°Muhammad Ali	°Elijah Muhammad
°Fred Allen	soldier and frontiersman Ethan Allen
°Elizabeth Arden	Elizabeth (see also list 24)
°Eve Arden	°Elizabeth Arden
°Azed	Spanish grand inquisitor Diega de Deza
Busby Berkeley	actress Amy Busby
Dave Berry	Chuck Berry
Joey Bishop	his roadie, Glenn Bishop
Edwina Booth	stage actor Edwin Booth
°Bos	°Boz
Nicolas Boulanger	philosopher Nicolas-Antoine Boulanger
°Richard Burton	his schoolteacher and benefactor Philip Burton
°[Sir] Alexander Bustamente	Cuban lawyer Sánchez de Bustamente y Sirven
°Max Bygraves	°Max Miller
°Chung Ling Soo	Chinese conjuror Ching Ling Foo
Paul Cinquevalli	his tutor Cinquevalli
°Mara Corday	perhaps Swiss actress Paule Corday rather that French assassinator of Marat, Charlotte Corday
°Elvis Costello	1. Elvis Presley, 2. father's pseudonym Ross Costello
Cynddelw	12th-century poet Cynddelw
°Lorenzo da Ponte	bishop who baptized him, Msgr. Lorenzo da Ponte
°Skeeter Davis	her schoolfriend Betty Jack Davis
Laraine Day	her drama teacher Elias Day
°Billy de Wolfe	his theatre manager de Wolfe
Lonnie Donegan	pop musician Lonnie Johnson
°Kirk Douglas	Douglas Fairbanks, Jr.
Maria Theresa Duncan	dancer Isadora Duncan, with whom worked
°Bob Dylan	Welsh poet Dylan Thomas
°Elia	former Italian clerk at workplace Elia
Carlo Farinelli	benefactors brothers Farina

°Susanna Foster	songwriter Stephen Foster (see also list 24)
°Redd Foxx	baseball player Jimmy Foxx
°Grey Owl	Canadian Indian chief Grey Owl (native name Wa-sha-quon-asin)
°Grock	clown Brock
°Brett Halliday	his publisher Brett (see also list 24)
Robert Heller	perhaps Robert Houdin
°O. Henry	either French pharmacist Étienne-Ossian Henry or his prison guard Orrin Henry
H.H. Holmes	murderer H.H. Holmes
°Harry Houdini	Robert Houdin
°Engelbert Humperdinck	French composer Engelbert Humperdinck
°[Sir] Henry Irving	Scottish writer Edward Irving and American writer Washington Irving
°Elton John	1. saxophonist Elton Dean, 2. rock singer Long John Baldry
Junius Americanus	Junius
°Karandash	°Caran d'Ache
°Fred Karno	music hall troupe "The Three Carnos"
Bogomir Korsov	his Italian teacher G. Corsi
°Gypsy Rose Lee	her stage manager's pseudonym Madam Rose
°Peggy Lee	singer Peggy Lee
°Caroline Lewis	°Lewis Carroll
Marie Lloyd	*Lloyd's Weekly News*
Curzio Malaparte	Napoleon Bonaparte (or Buonaparte)
°Joseph Arthur Markham	deceased man Joseph Arthur Markham
°Dean Martin	popular singer Nino Martini
Ilona Massey	probably Canadian film actor Raymond Massey
Jean Mirabeau	secretary of French Academy Jean Mirabeau
°Gabriela Mistral	1. Gabriele d'Annunzio, 2. Provençal poet Frédéric Mistral
°Guy Mitchell	his "discoverer" Mitch Miller
°Baron Munchhausen	storyteller Karl Friedrich Hieronymus, Baron Munchhausen
°Pablo Neruda	Czech writer Jan Neruda
°Jeremiah Noon	boxer Anthony Noon
Darleen O'Connor	an earlier Mormon — Darleen O'Connor
°Gilbert O'Sullivan	presumably comic opera writers W.S. Gilbert and Arthur Sullivan
°Patti Page	1. perhaps Italian-born opera singer Adelina Page, 2. Page Company dairy
°Janis Paige	Elsie Janis (see also list 22)
Piero di Cosimo	his master Cosimo Russelli
Paul Pindar	presumably °Peter Pindar
°Ellery Queen	their boyhood friend Ellery (see also list 24)
Quevedo Redivivus	17th-century Spanish poet and satirist Quevedo
°Ted Ray	golfer Ted Ray
°Sugar Ray Robinson	boxer Ray Robinson
°Rob Roy [2]	°Rob Roy [1]
Jimmy Rodgers	popular singer Jimmie Rodgers (the "singing brakeman")

°George Sand	Jules Sand
Jacopo Sansovino	his master Andrea Sansovino
°Sir Walter Scott	Scottish poet and novelist Sir Walter Scott
The Scout	predecessor Cyril Luckman's pseudonym The Scout
H. Secundus Scriblerus	presumably °Martinus Scriblerus [1]
Jane Seymour	presumably 3rd wife of Henry VIII Jane Seymour
°Jack Sharkey	boxer Sailor Tom Sharkey
T.E. Shaw	Irish playwright George Bernard Shaw
Bob Short [1]	presumably Bob Short [2]
°Skanderbeg	Alexander (Turkish = Iskender) the Great
°Lydia Sokolova	Russian ballet dancer Sokolov
Fyodor Sologub	writer Count V.A. Sollogub
°Dusty Springfield	pop group the Springfields (of which one member was Tom Field)
°Alvin Stardust	singers Elvis Presley and *Gene Vincent* (*i.e.*, *Elv*is + *Vin*cent)
°Eugène Sue	patron Prince Eugène de Beauharnais
Tania [2]	°Tania [1]
Harry Tate	sugar refiner Henry Tate (of Tate and Lyle) with whose firm had worked
Little Johnny Taylor	soul singer Ted Taylor
°Josip Tito	possibly Serbo-Croat writers with forename Tito
Jacob Tonson	18th-century bookseller Jacob Tonson
Torquemada	Spanish grand inquisitor Tomás de Torquemada
Frances Trollope	English writer Frances Trollope, mother of novelist Anthony Trollope
°Leon Trotsky	perhaps his prison guard in Odessa
Andrea del Verrocchio	his master, goldsmith Verrochio
°Artemus Ward	reputedly an eccentric showman Artemus Ward known by him
°John Wayne	Revolutionary War general "Mad" Anthony Wayne
°Slim Whitman	his teacher Wilf Carter ("Montana Slim")
°Natalie Wood	film director Sam Wood
°Ximenes	Spanish grand inquisitor Ximenes (Jimenez de Cisneros)

24. From Fiction

As will be seen, "fiction" here means more than literature, since it includes names taken from songs, films, and pop groups (where the name is either a random one or in turn taken from fiction).

Pseudonym	*Source*
Annabella	Edgar Allan Poe's *Annabel Lee*
°Elizabeth Arden	Tennyson's *Enoch Arden* (see also list 23)
Elizabeth Ashley	Ashley Wilkes, played by Leslie Howard in film *Gone with the Wind*

°Azorín	hero of own novel *António Azorín* (1903)
Florence Bates	Miss Bates in stage adaptation (1935) of Jane Austin's *Emma*
°Demyan Bedny	character in own poem *On Demyan Bedny, the Harmful Peasant*
Ivan Petrovich Belkin	supposed narrator of own *Tales of the Late Ivan Petrovich Belkin* (1831)
°N. Beltov	hero of Alexander Herzen's novel *Whose Fault?*
Bilitis	supposed Greek poetess author of own "translations" — *Chansons de Bilitis* (1894)
°Nelly Bly	character in song by Stephen Foster
°William Boot	hero of Evelyn Waugh's novel *Scoop*
Neil Boyd	Roman Catholic curate in own novels
°Michael Caine	film *The Caine Mutiny* (see also list 21)
°Nick Carter	own detective hero
Nat King Cole	group King Cole (in turn from nursery character)
°Charles Egbert Craddock	hero of own early story in *Appleton's Journal*
Captain Crawley	Sir Pitt Crawley in Thackeray's *Vanity Fair*
Jane Darwell	"a character in fiction"
Frank Fairleigh	hero of own novel *Frank Fairleigh* (1850)
°Florizel	character in Shakespeare's *A Winter Tale*
°Suzanna Foster	character in Stephen Foster's song *Oh, Susannah*
Greta Gynt	perhaps hero of Ibsen's play *Peer Gynt*
Brett Halliday	detective Halliday in 1st novel (see also list 23)
Martin Hewitt	hero of own detective stories
Margaret Howth	heroine of own novel *Margaret Howth* (1862)
Idris	presumably Idris, figure in Islamic legend
Tom Jones	reputedly from hero of filmed version (1963) of *Tom Jones*
°Eden Kane	reputedly from (deceased) hero of film *Citizen Kane* (1941)
Michael Kidd	hero of Aaron Copland's ballet *Billy the Kid* (1938), in which first danced
Tristan Klingsor	Klingsor, evil magician in medieval German legend
°Mario Lanza	Mario, hero of Puccini's opera *Tosca* (see also list 22)
Conte de Lautréamont	hero of °Eugène Sue's novel *Lautréamont*
Malachi Malagrowther	Sir Mungo Malagrowther in own novel *The Fortunes of Nigel* (1822)
°Sebastian Melmoth	hero of Charles Maturin's novel *Melmoth the Wanderer*
Merlin	character in Tennyson's *Idylls of the King*
°Mistinguett	character in song in musical *Miss Helyett*
°Mickie Most	skiffle duo Most Brothers (himself and schoolfriend Alex Murray)
°Nimrod	biblical character (Genesis 10, ix) ("the mighty hunter")

Pansy	children's magazine *Pansy*, of which was editor (1873-1896)
Peter Parley [2, 3, 4, 5]	°Peter Parley [1]
°Anthony Pasquin	Pasquin, popular name of statue unearthed in Rome (1501)
Peregrine Pickle	hero of Tobias Smollett's *The Adventures of Peregrine Pickle*
°Ellery Queen	hero of detective novels (see also lists 23, 42)
Peter Quince 1)	character in Shakespeare's *A Midsummer Night's Dream*
°Mickey Rooney	perhaps from song *Little Annie Rooney*
°Milton Rosmer	character in Ibsen's play *Rosmersholm*
°Françoise Sagan	Princesse de Sagan, character in Proust's *À la Recherche du Temps Perdu*
°Saki	perhaps character in *Rubaiyat* of °Omar Khayyam
°Dinah Shore	character in song *Dinah*
°Simplicissimus	hero of German novelist von Grimmels- hausen's *Simplicissimus*
°Sirin	legendary bird in Russian folklore
Ally Sloper	hero of comic paper (1890s)
°Jean Sorel	Julien Sorel, hero of °Stendhal's *Le Rouge et le Noir*
°Daniel Stern	heroine of own novel *Nélida* (1854) (as anagram)
Colonel Surry	own character, fictitious side of Stonewall Jackson
°Taffy	character in Kipling's "Just So" story, *How the Alphabet Was Made*
°Paul Temple	Durbridge's own detective novel
°General Tom Thumb	16th-century nursery tale hero
Dick Tinto	supposed relater in Walter Scott's *Bridge of Lammermoor*
Kilgore Trout	fictitious science fiction writer in stories by Kurt Vonnegut, Jr.
Edward Bradwardine Waverley	Edward Waverley and the Baron of Bradwardine, characters in Walter Scott's *Waverley*
Samuel Weller	character in Dickens's *Pickwick Papers*
°Kitty Wells	song *I'm A-Goin' to Marry Kitty Wells* popularized by singing Carter family
°[Dame] Rebecca West	character in Ibsen's *Rosmersholm*
°Gig Young	character played by him in film *The Gay Sisters* (1942)

25. CLASSICAL

Names in this list are either genuine classical ones (as °Cassandra) or pseudoclassical (as Sylvanus Theophrastus). They are almost all of Latin or Greek origin or inspiration — the exceptions being the first and last names, Afrit and Zadkiel.

Real name	Pseudonym
Alistair Ritchie	Afrit
Albert, Margrave of Brandenberg	Alcibiades
George Villiers, Duke of Buckingham	Alcibiades
George Chesterton	Arion
William Falconer	Arion
Mary Montague	Artemisia
Angelo Siciliano	Charles Atlas
William Connor	°Cassandra
Adolphe Mouron	Cassandre
Michael Foot	Cassius
Agnes Craig	°Clarinda
Emma Embury	Ianthe
Johann von Dollinger	Janus
Robert le Bonnieres	Janus
Johannes Friedrich	Janus
Alfred Austin	Lamia
Frederick Rose	Martius
Charles Morgan	Menander
Charles Eliot	Odysseus
Katherine Fowler	Orinda
Cyril Connolly	°Palinurus
Philippus von Hohenheim	°Paracelsus
Charles Gerault	Pertinax
Elizabeth Rowe	Philomela
John Welcot	°Peter Pindar
Charles Cotterell	Poliarchus
Johann von Dollinger	Quirinus
Karl Liebknecht	Spartakus
Robert Burns	Sylvander
Anne Steel	°Theodosia
John Thelwall	Sylvanus Theophrastus
Richard Morrison	Zadkiel

26. ARBITRARY

The names here are real enough but come from random sources, such as shop signs, telephone books, and playbills. A few are genuine random names, with no known point of reference.

Real name (with Pseudonym)	Source
Herbert Blythe (°Maurice Barrymore)	old playbill
William Thompson (°Bendigo)	Abednego (biblical character)
Paul Thiry, baron d'Holbach (L'Abbé Bernier)	invented
Jonathan Swift (°Isaac Bickerstaff)	Smith's sign
David Hayward-Jones (°David Bowie)	perhaps Bowie knife
Mario Moreno (°Cantinflas)	meaningless

Andrei Friedmann (°Robert Capa)	imaginary American photographer
Richard Pitchford (Cardini)	perhaps "cards" and Houdini
Kate Williams (Madame Cariba)	traditional
Robert Cassotto (Bobby Darin)	found in phone book
Charles-Augustin Sainte-Beuve (°Joseph Delorme)	imaginary friend
Terence Nelhams (°Adam Faith)	book of boys' and girls' names
Clive Powell (°Georgie Fame)	random "image" name
Irving Prestopnik (°Irving Fazola)	3 musical notes *fa, so, la* (F, G, A)
Brian Davis (°Michael ffolkes)	*Burke's Peerage*
Ronald Wycherly (Billy Fury)	random "image" name
Alexander Leach (°Cary Grant)	studio stock name list
David Cornwell (°John Le Carré)	shop front
Christopher Grieve (°Hugh MacDiarmid)	apparently random
Donald Nappey (°Donald Neilson)	ice cream van
Edson do Nascimento (°Pelé)	apparently random
Esther Jones (°Esther Phillips)	gas station
Margaret Reed (Martha Raye)	telephone book
Henry Cole (°Felix Summerly)	"Summerly's" tea service

27. MISTAKE

Of the seven names listed here, four resulted from "typos," and the other three by a form of written error.

Real name (with Pseudonym)	*Nature of mistake*
Thomas Anstey Guthrie (F. Anstey)	printer's error (for "T. Anstey")
Israel Baline (°Irving Berlin)	printer's error on music sheet
Charles Gordon (°Ralph Connor)	"Connor" instead of intended "Cannor"
Matthias Nithardt (Matthias Grünewald)	"Grünewald" instead of original Gothardt
Percy Thompson (Percy Honri)	printer's error (for "Henry") on handbill
Donald Mitchell (°Ik Marvel)	printer's error (for "J.K. Marvel")
Nicholas Montserrat (°Nicholas Monsarrat)	error on birth certificate ("Monsarrat" for "Montserrat")

28. FROM PLACE-NAMES

A list as long as 27 was short. Several pseudonyms originated from place-names, which provide a handy and often appropriate source of name.

Real name (with Pseudonym)	Place-name origin
Benjamin Brierley (°Ab-o'-th'-Yate)	"The Yate" (= "the street"), north England
Alexander Witkins (Afrique)	Africa
Maria Coronel (Mariade Agreda)	Agreda, Spain
? (Pietro Aretino)	Arezzo, Italy
Antonia Merce y Luque (La Argentina)	Argentina
Encarnación Julves (La Argentinita)	Argentina
Pierre-Augustin Caron (Pierre-Augustin de Beaumarchais)	Beaumarchais' 1st wife's property
Jerom van Aeken (Hieronymus Bosch)	's Hertogenbosch, Netherlands
Robert S. Coffin (Boston Bard)	Boston, Mass.
George Sturt (George Bourne)	Lower Bourne, Surrey
Gyula Halesz (°Brassaï)	Brassó, Hungary (now Braşov, Romania)
Annie Ellerman (Bryher)	Bryher, Isles of Scilly
Michelangelo Merisi (Caravaggio)	Caravaggio, Italy
Claude Gellée (Claude Lorrain)	Lorraine, France
Joseph Addison (Clio [1])	Chelsea, London, Islington, the Office
Colin McCallum (Charles Coburn)	Coburn Road, Bow, London
Carlo Lorenzini (°Carlo Collodi)	Collodi, Italy
Manuel Perez (°El Cordobés)	Córdoba, Spain
Antonio Allegri (Correggio)	Correggio, Italy
Henry Terry (°Gordon Craig)	Ailsa Craig rock, Scotland
Lucas Müller (°Lucas Cranach)	Cranach, now Kronach, West Germany
Winifred Ashton (°Clemence Dane)	St. Clement Danes Church, London
D.H. Lawrence (°Lawrence H. Davidson)	Davidson Road School, Croydon
Gabriel Tellez (Tirso de Molina)	"The Mill" (Spanish molina)
Blaise Pascal (Louis de Montalte)	Latin rendering of Puy de Dôme, France
Marianne Hearn (Marianne Farningham)	Farningham, Kent
Frederick Horner (Martyn Field)	St. Martin-in-the-Fields Church, London
François Mauriac (°Forez)	Forez Mountains, France
John Jones (Jac Glan-y-Dors)	Glan-y-Dors, Clwyd, Wales
Mary Dodge (°Gail Hamilton)	Hamilton, Mass.
Alfred Clark (°Cyril Hare)	1. Cyril Mansions, Battersea, London, 2. Hare Court, Temple, London

Roy Fitzgerald (°Rock Hudson)	1. Rock of Gibraltar, 2. Hudson River
James Hildyard (Ingoldsby)	Ingoldsby, Lincolnshire
Richard Barham (Thomas Ingoldsby)	Ingoldsby, Lincolnshire
Ioann Sergiev (John of Kronshtadt)	Kronshtadt, Russia
Emile Dillon (E.B. Lanin)	Dublin ("Eblana" in imprints)
Arthur Towle (°Arthur Lucan)	Lucan Dairy, Dublin
Lucas Hugensz (Lucas van Leyden)	Leyden, Netherlands
Louis MacNeice (°Louis Malone)	Malone Road, Belfast
Elizabeth Cartwright (Mrs. Markham)	Markham, Nottinghamshire
Daniel Leonard (°Massachusettensis)	Massachusetts
Émile Herzog (°André Maurois)	Maurois, France
Helen Mitchell (°Nellie Melba)	Melbourne, Australia
Joszef Pehm (°Joszef Mindszenty)	Szehimindszenty, Hungary
Eric Bartholomew (°Eric Morecambe)	Morecambe, Lancashire
Friedrich Plumpe (Friedrich Murnau)	Murnau, West Germany
Emil Hansen (Emil Nolde)	Nolde, West Germany
Friedrich von Hardenburg (°Novalis)	ancient name for section of father's estate
Wilfred Whitten (John O'London)	London
Walter Smith (Orwell)	Orwell, Kinross, Scotland
Eric Blair (°George Orwell)	Orwell River, Suffolk
Francis Trench (Oxoniensis)	Oxford
Giovanni Drughi (Giovanni Pergolesi)	Pergola, Italy
Pietro Vanucci (Pietro Perugino)	Perugia, Italy
Jacopo Carrucci (Pontormo)	Pontormo, Italy
Marcel Jouhandeau (Marcel Provence)	Provence, France
Georg von Lauchen (Rhäticus)	Raetia (Roman province), Austria
Gilles Personne (Gilles Roberval)	Roberval, France
Violet Martin (°Martin Ross)	Ross House, County Galway, Ireland
Frances Marshall (Alan St. Aubyn)	St. Aubyn's, Tiverton, Devon
Stephen Critten (Stephen Southwold)	Southwold, Suffolk
Georg Burkhardt (Georg Spalatin)	Spalt, West Germany
Arthur Baynes (°Stainless Stephen)	Sheffield, U.K. (famous for stainless steel
Marie-Henri Beyle (°Stendhal)	Stendhal (now Stendal), East Germany
William Lewin (William Terriss)	Adelphi Terrace, London
Harold Jenkins (°Conway Twitty)	1. Conway, Arkansas, 2. Twitty, Texas
David Myrick (T. Texas Tyler)	Texas
Jean Bruller (°Vercors)	Vercors plateau, France
Paolo Cogliari (Paolo Veronese)	Verona, Italy
Philip Örtel (W.O. Von Horn)	Horn, East Germany

Thomas Williams (°Tennessee Williams)	Tennessee
George Slaney (George Woden)	Wednesbury, West Midlands
Alfred Smith (Brenton Wood)	Brenton Wood, U.S.

29. WORD INTO NAME

In this list can be found some of the more interesting and original pseudonyms, all concocted from ordinary words. As can be seen, most of these have their origins explained in the Name Stories. The last two names were included since "X" has virtually the significance that a word has.

Pseudonym	Real name
Ahad Ha'am	Asher Ginzberg
°Shalom Aleichem	Solomon Rabinowitz
Andrea del Sarto	Andrea d'Agnolo
°Henry Armstrong	Henry Jackson
°Theda Bara	Theodosia Goodman
°Marti Caine	Lynn Sheppard
°Caran d'Ache	Emmanuel Poiré
Felix Carmen	Frank Sherman
Cheiro	Louis Hamm
°Upton Close	Josef Hall
°Della Crusca	Robert Merry
Jimmy Driftwood	James Moris
°Dr. Esperanto	Ludovik Zamenhof
Fiore della Neve	Martinus van Loghem
Dion Fortune	Violet Furth
°Gertie Gitana	Gertrude Astbury
°Gary Glitter	Paul Gadd
°Maxim Gorky	Aleksei Maksimovich Peshkov
Harry Hieover	Charles Bindley
Lev Kamenev	Lev Rosenfeld
°Nosmo King	Vernon Watson
°Klabund	Alfred Henschke
La Fleur	Robert Guérin
°Veronica Lake	Constance Ockleman
°Danny La Rue	Daniel Carroll
Holm Lee	Harriet Parr
°Thomas Little	Thomas Moore
Kazak Lugansky	Vladimir Dal'
Manchecourt	Henri Lavedan
°Mata Hari	Gertrud Zelle
°Ray Milland	Reginald Truscott-Jones
°Vyacheslav Molotov	Vyacheslav Skryabin
A.A. Nadir	Achmed Abdullah
Christopher North	John Wilson
Aleksey Novikov-Priboy	Aleksey Novikov
°Dawn O'Day	Dawn Paris
Dita Parlo	Gerthe Kornstadt

Pasionaria	Dolores Ibárruri
°Ted Pauker	Robert Conquest
°[Saint] Paul	Saul
Jack Riskit	John Evans
°Rob Roy	Robert Macgregor
°Omar Sharif	Michael Shalhouz
°N. Shchedrin	Mikhail Saltykov
°Joseph Stalin	Iosif Dzhugashvili
Patience Strong	Winifred May
°Poly Styrene	Marion Elliott
°Italo Svevo	Ettore Schmitz
Talis Qualis	Carl Strindberg
°Josip Tito	Josip Broz
Martello Tower	Commander F.M. Norman
Ben Trovato	Samuel Lover
°Mark Twain	Samuel Clemens
°Peter Warlock	Philip Heseltine
Muddy Waters	McKinley Morganfield
°Malcolm X	Malcolm Little
°Michael X	Michael Malik

30. Descriptive Names and Titles

Most of the names or titles in this list are self-explanatory. Those in a foreign language are translated for ease of appreciation.

Pseudonym (with meaning, if not obvious)	*Real name*
°An Craoibhín Aoibhinn ("the fair maiden" Gaelic)	Douglas Hyde
Angelus a Sancto Francisco ("St. Francis' Angel" Latin)	Richard Mason, D.D.
Annalist	Frances Gerard
°Apex	Eric Chalkley
The Bard	Edward Jerringham
Baron	[Baron] de V. Nahum
El Baron	Horatio McFerrin
Beachcomber	1. Dominic Wyndham Lewis, 2. J.B. Morton
Big Bopper	J.P. Richardson
Big Daddy	Shirley Crabtree
Blondin	Jean-François Gravelet
The Bystander	Goldwin Smith
A Cambridge Graduate	[The Rev.] W. Begley
The Citizen of the World	Oliver Goldsmith
Civis ("citizen" Latin)	[Sir] Harry Russell
Clarín ("bugle" Spanish)	Leopoldo Alas
Coldstreamer	Harry Graham
Coram ("openly," "in public" Latin)	Thomas Whitaker
The Curé d'Ars	Joan-Baptiste Vianney
The Czar of Muscovy	Archibald Constable
Diplomat	John Carter

Discobolus ("discus thrower" Latin)	Donald Aldous
The Druid	Henry Dixon
An English Opium-Eater	Thomas de Quincey
Ephemera	Edward Fitzgibbon
Barent Fabritius	Barent Pieterz
Carel Fabritius	Carel Pieterz
Fieldfare	[Sir] Alexander Valentine
Filarete	Antonio di Pietro Averlino
Fin-Bec ("gourmet" French)	William Jerrold
Fleury	Abraham-Joseph Benard
°Floridor	Josias de Soulas
A Gentleman who has left his lodgings	[Lord] John Russell
A Gentleman with a Duster	Harold Begbie
El Greco ("The Greek" Spanish)	Domenikos Theo-tokopoulos
Giant Haystacks	Luke McMasters
Homo Novus ("new man" Latin)	William Courthope
Iconoclast	1. Mary Hamilton, 2. Charles Bradlaugh
The Impenitent	Henry Lowry
Ionicus ("Ionian" Latin)	J.C. Armitage
The Khalifa	Abdullah et-Taaisha
°Klaxon	[Commander] J.G. Bower
A Layman	1. [Dr.] William Falconer, 2. Walter Scott, 3. [Lord] Houghton
Linesman	[Captain] Maurice Grant
London Antiquary	Frederick Fairholt
Looker-On	1. David Meldrum, 2. J. Stainton
Magpie	W. Lotinga
Maori	James Inglis
°Le Mapah	Ganneau
The Master	John Corlett
Merlinus Anglicus ("the English Merlin" Latin)	William Lilly
A Ministering Friend	°Daniel Defoe
A Minute Philosopher	Charles Kingsley
Monitor	Arthur Lee
°Multatuli ("I have suffered much" Latin)	Eduard Dekker
Le Myosotis	Hégésippe Moreau
°Nadar	Félix Tournachon
Nauticus	[Sir] William Clowes
A New Writer	[Sir] Lewis Morris
Nomad	1. Norman Ellison, 2. Adele Grafton-Smith
°Noor al-Hussein ("light of Hussein" Arabic)	Elizabeth Halaby
Northerner	William Hughes
Nostalgia	James Bentley

Novanglus ("New Englander" new Latin)	John Adams
Nunquam ("never" Latin)	Robert Blatchford
An Octogenarian	James Roche
Le Prieur Ogier ("Prior Ogier" French)	Jean Louis Guez
°Ole Luk-Oie ("Olaf Shut-Eye" Danish)	[Sir] Ernest Swinton
°Omar Khayyam ("Omar the tentmaker" Persian)	Gheyas ol-Khayyami
One of the Boys	Percy Fitzgerald
Onlooker	G.W.E. Russell
Pacificus ("peacemaking" Latin)	Alexander Hamilton
°Philo Pacificus ("friend of Pacificus" mock Latin)	Noah Worcester
Pellerin ("pilgrim" French)	[Baron] Friedrich de la Motte-Fouqué
Phantasus	Joseph Maximilian
Alazonomastix Philalethes ("impostor Philalethes" mock Greek)	[Dr.] Henry More
Eugenius Philalethes ("noble-born stone-lover" mock Greek)	Thomas Vaughan
Phil Anglus ("friend of England" mock Latin)	William Penn
Phileleutharus ("Norfolk freedom-lover" mock Greek & Latin)	[Dr.] Samuel Parr
Philenia	Sarah Morton
The Philistine	John Spender
Philo-Criticus	Francis Hare
°Phiz	Hablot Knight Browne
Pictor Ignotus ("an unknown painter" Latin)	William Blake
Piscator ("fisherman" Latin)	1. Robert Lascelles, 2. Thomas Lathy
Pitcher	Arthur Binstead
Porte-Crayon ("pencil-holder" French)	David Strother
The Prig	T. Longueville
Quiz	1. [Sir] Max Beerbohm, 2. Charles Dickens
The Ranger	[Captain] Flack
The Redeemed Captive	John Williams
Romany	George Evens
Rover	Alfred Gibson
The Roving Englishman	E.C. Grenville-Murray
Sagittarius ("archer" Latin)	Olga Miller
Saladin	William Russ
°Sapper	Herman McNeile
°Scaeva ("left-handed" Latin)	John Stubbes
A. Scholar	Samuel Wesley
Scrutator ("searcher," "examiner" Latin)	[Sir] Robert Ensor
Sealion	Geoffrey Bennett
Senior	[The Rev.] John Penrose
°The Silent Traveller	Chiang Yee
Silver Pen	Eliza Meteyard
A Son of the Soil	Joseph Fletcher
Spectator	Arthur Walkley
Staccato	A. Kalisch
Stet ("let it stand" Latin)	Thomas Welby
The Stonesman of Cromarty	Hugh Miller

°Surfaceman	Alexander Anderson
°Taffrail	[Captain] Henry Dorling
Chief Thundercloud	Victor Daniels
°Trog	Wally Fawkes
°Sojourner Truth	Isabella Van Wagener
Ubique ("everywhere" Latin)	[Colonel Parker Gilmore
°Sylvanus Urbanus ("of the woods" [and] "of the city" Latin)	Edward Cave
°Flying Officer X	H.E. Bates

31. NAMES WITH QUALIFIERS

A short list of pseudonyms formed from a real name (usually a real forename) with a qualifying word such as an adjective or a noun. Many such qualifiers are either a word denoting a relationship or "Big" or "Little." "Little" may indicate small stature or size, but may equally be a sign of deference to a "big" original.

Pseudonym	*Real name*
Woody Allen	Allen Stewart Konigsberg
°Mustafa Kemal Atatürk	Mustafa Kemal [Pasha]
°Wilkie Bard	William Augustus Smith
Widow Bedott	Frances Whitcher
Big Maybelle	Mabel Smith
Haywire Mac	Harry Kirby McClintock
Josiah Allen's Wife	Mariette Holley
Cousin Kate	Catherine Bell
Little Eva	Eva Boyd
Little Milton	Milton Campbell
Little Richard	Richard Peeniman
Little Walter	Marion Walter Jacobs
Aunt Lucy	Lucy Bather
Uncle Mac	Derek McCulloch
Magic Sam	Sam Marghett
Maître Adam	Adam Billaut
Johnny Rotten	John Lydon
°Smokey Joe	Joseph Sewell

32. NAMED BY ANOTHER

This list shows who, exactly, named several of the pseudonymous people who feature in this book. Such namers range from professional nomenclators such as producers, directors, agents, and editors to a more homely spouse or parent. One or two names were devised more impersonally, as the result of a contest.

Real or former name (with Pseudonym)	*Namer*
Anne Italiano (°Ann Bancroft)	producer Darryl F. Zanuck
Boris Bugayev (Andrey Bely)	editor M.S. Solovyov
Priscilla White (Cilla Black)	feature writer in magazine *Merseybeat*
David Cohen (David Blue)	°Bob Dylan
Elizabeth Seaman (°Nelly Bly)	editor of *Pittsburgh Dispatch*
Wynfrith (°Boniface)	pope Gregory II
William Cody (°Buffalo Bill)	°Ned Buntline
Li Yun-ho (°Chiang Ch'ing)	husband Mao Tse-tung
Adrienne Riccoboni (°Adrienne Corri)	agent Gordon Harbord
Lucille Le Sueur (°Joan Crawford)	*Photoplay* contest
Bernard Schwartz (°Tony Curtis)	producer Bob Goldstein
Florence Dawson (Florence Desmond)	matron overseeing child dancers
Elias McDaniel (°Bo Diddley)	record company executive Leonard Chess
Patrick Healey-Kay (°Anton Dolin)	fellow student
Jessie Dermot (Maxine Elliott)	Dion Boucicault
Clive Powell (°Georgie Fame)	producer Larry Parnes
Grace Stansfield (°Gracie Fields)	mother
Ronald Wycherly (Billy Fury)	producer Larry Parnes
Greta Gustafsson (°Greta Garbo)	director Mauritz Stiller
Frances Gumm (°Judy Garland)	agent George Jessel
Viola Billups (°Pearly Gates)	manager Bruce Welch
Elliott Goldstein (Elliott Gould)	mother
William White (°Larry Grayson)	agent Evelyn Taylor
Beryl Groom (°Beryl Grey)	Ninette de Valois
Larushka Skikne (°Laurence Harvey	agent Gordon Harbord
Marguerita Cansino (Rita Hayworth)	husband Edward Judson
Aleksandr Yakovlev (°Aleksandr Herzen)	father I.A. Yakovlev
William Beedle (°William Holden)	film company executive
Roy Fitzgerald (°Rock Hudson)	talent scout Henry Wilson
Gerry Dorsey (°Engelbert Humperdinck)	manager Gordon Mills
Janet Cole (°Kim Hunter)	producer David O. Selznick
Martin Fuss (Ross Hunter)	casting director Max Arnow
Elizabeth Thornburg (°Betty Hutton)	bandleader Vincent Lopez
Thomas Woodward (Tom Jones)	manager Gordon Mills
Sergey Kostrikov (°Sergey Kirov)	editorial staff
Hedwig Keisler (°Hedy Lamarr)	producer Louis B. Mayer
Daniel Carroll (°Danny La Rue)	producer Ted Gatty
Norma Egstrom (°Peggy Lee)	manager Ken Kennedy
Leonid Popov (°Leonid Lench)	editorial staff
Sofia Scicolone (°Sophia Loren)	producer Goffredo Lombardo
Juanita Horton (°Bessie Love)	scenario head Frank Woods
Mary Johnstone (°Moura Lympany)	conductor Basil Cameron
Frederick Bickel (°Fredric March)	director John Cromwell
Pietro Trapassi (°Pietro Metastasio)	adoptive father Gian Vincenzo Gravina
Thomas Morfit (°Garry Moore)	contest
Estelle Thompson (°Merle Oberon)	husband Alexander Korda
Eric Blair (°George Orwell)	publisher Victor Gollancz

Clara Fowler (°Patti Page)   dairy Page Company
Edith Gassion (°Edith Piaf)   nightclub owner Louis
                                                 Leplée
Gladys Smith (Mary Pickford)   producer David Belasco
Cyril Rotenberg (Cyril Ray)   father
Mary Reynolds (°Debbie Reynolds)   producer Jack L. Warner
Harold Webb (°Cliff Richard)   manager Johnny Foster
Herman McNeile (°Sapper)   newspaper proprietor Lord
                                                 Northcliffe
Lynn Springbett (°Lynn Seymour)   choreographer Kenneth
                                                 MacMillan
Hilda Munnings (°Lydia Sokolova)   impresario Serge Diaghilev
Esther Johnson (Stella)   correspondent Jonathan
                                                 Swift
Spangler Arlington Brough (°Robert
   Taylor   producer Louis B. Mayer
Muriel Deason (°Kitty Wells)   husband Johnny Wright
Natasha Gurdin (°Natalie Wood)   production executives
                                                 William Goetz and Leo
                                                 Spitz
Malcolm Little (°Malcolm X)   Black Muslim leader
                                                 Elijah Muhammad

33. Masculine Names

This is a select list of names of males that would appear to possess a
particular masculinity. Many of them are of "he-man" or "tough-guy"
film stars. The curt, concise forenames at any rate often suggest strength,
toughness, energy, or resilience (especially ones such as Tex, Dirk, Rock,
Tab, Sax, and Mark), or youth and agility (Gary, Lee, Kid, Rob, Mike,
Sonny, Marty). Note the favorable associations of many of the surnames
(Hunter, Kidd, Majors, Steele, Temple, Wilde), with others conjuring up
the required degree of manliness (Brady, Forest, Hudson, Rogers, Taylor,
Todd). Unlike feminine names (see List 34), alliteration is not resorted to
for effect. What does seem desirable, however, is the combination of a
monosyllabic forename and mono- or bisyllabic surname. The letters "k"
and "x" appear popular (Tex, Rex, Rock, Sax, Mike, Mark, Jack), doubtless suggesting a masculine conciseness and resolve (a snap decision, instant action). Forenames ending in "y" are on the whole avoided, since
they often suggest undue youth or immaturity – "John" is more mature
and manly than "Johnny." A double consonant in the forename can
strengthen it for added visual impact as with Scott, Jeff, Glenn, Ross.

Charles Atlas   Ben Blue
John August   Dirk Bogarde
Tex Avery   Scott Brady
Lew Ayres   °Red Buttons
Rex Bell   Jeff Chandler

°Gary Cooper
Glenn Ford
Mark Forest
Lee Grant
°Rock Hudson
Ross Hunter
Tab Hunter
°Jimmie James
Johnny Kidd
Kid McCoy
Earl Majors
°Ted Ray

°Rob Roy
°Roy Rogers
°Sax Rohmer
Tommy Steele
°Robert Taylor
°Paul Temple
°Mike Todd
Sonny Tufts
°Mark Twain
°Jack Warner
°John Wayne
Marty Wilde

34. Feminine Names

This list is the female counterpart of List 33. Feminine pseudonyms are on the whole more widespread than masculine ones, and their characteristics are more clear cut. In general, most effective feminine names consist of a bisyllabic forename and surname, and possibly the impact of both names together is greater than that of the forename alone (as with masculine names). Other features of feminine names may be distinguished as follows:

(1) A predilection for foreign, and hence exotic names (French Renée Adorée, Spanish Florentina del Mar, Russian Marina Vlady).

(2) Alliteration can be alluring (Anouk Aimée, °Brigitte Bardot, Corinne Calvet, °Jennifer Jones, Virginia Valli, and many more — see List 40).

(3) Many forenames have the diminutive or "pet" ending -y or -ie or the more exotic -i (Wendy, Fanny, Sally, Tammy; Dulcie, Stefanie, Bonnie; Kiki, Patti). Names ending in -e or -a look good, too (Brigitte, Corinne, Suzanne, Carole, Françoise; Gloria, Julia, Veronica, Monica, Loretta, Rula).

(4) Double consonants are particularly popular, in both forenames and surnames (Brigitte, Corinne, Suzanne, Bonnie, Shelley, Loretta; Barrie, Farrell, Forrest, Hazell, Holliday, Lamarr, Valli, Wynette). Some names have double consonants in both forename and surname (Suzanne Farrell, Sally Forrest, Tammy Wynette).

(5) The letter "y" seems popular in feminine names, no doubt because of its association with diminutives or affectionate names (Crystal Gayle, Judy Holliday, Sandy Posey, °Lynn Seymour, Tammy Wynette). (Compare point 3 above.)

(6) Meaning associations do not seem to be quite so important as for masculine names, although some are suggestive enough: °Eve Arden (basic woman + forest or "ardent"), Belinda Dell ("belle," "bell"), Hy Hazell (hazel + catkins), Stefanie Powers (gentleness and resilience combined), Gale Storm (obviously a feminine name, but an impetuous or

fiery one), Virginia Valli (maidenly innocence and the countryside), Penny Singleton (simplicity and wistful loneliness combined), and so on.

(7) Many feminine names are pleasant, even musical, to say and hear. Notice the labials (evoking kisses!) of °Brigitte Bardot, °Marilyn Monroe, °Patti Page, °Barbara Windsor. (Labials are letters involving the closure of the lips, such as "b," "f," "m," "p," "v," "w.") Most feminine names are "softer" than their rugged masculine opposite numbers.

Renée Adorée	Rula Lenska
Anouk Aimée	Carole Lesley
°Eve Arden	Julia Marlowe
°Brigitte Bardot	°Carmen Miranda
Wendy Barrie	°Marilyn Monroe
Corinne Calvet	°Nadia Nerina
Sue Carol	°Merle Oberon
Linda Christian	°Patti Page
Claudette Colbert	Sandy Posey
Linda Cristal	Stefanie Powers
Kiki Dee	Carol Raye
Belinda Dell	Fiona Richmond
Florentina del Mar	Françoise Rosey
Suzanne Farrell	Susan Saint James
Fanny Fern	Jane Seymour
Sally Forrest	°Lynn Seymour
°Judy Garland	Penny Singleton
Crystal Gayle	Kay Starr
Gloria Grahame	Gale Storm
Dulcie Gray	Lesley Storm
Hy Hazell	°Gloria Swanson
Judy Holliday	Bonnie Tyler
°Evelyn Home	Virginia Valli
Gloria Jean	Monica Vitti
°Jennifer Jones	Marina Vlady
Kay Kendall	°Barbara Windsor
Suzy Kendall	Claire Windsor
Veronica Lake	Shelley Winters
°Hedy Lamarr	Tammy Wynette
Piper Laurie	Loretta Young

35. HUMOROUS NAMES

A selection of enjoyable names, including puns, pleasantries, and general eccentricities. It is worth noting that some of the most frivolous of names mask a serious intent — that of satire and the stinging response (what we might call the "retort caustic"). Richard Whately, for example, archbishop of Dublin, chose the name Aristarchus Newlight for a work written in ridicule of German neologism, and Siful Sifadda was the name chosen by Henrik Wergeland, the Norwegian poet, for satirizing Johann Welhaven who had attacked his ornate style of writing.

Pseudonym	*Real or best-known name*
R. Andom	Alfred Barratt
Samuel A. Bard	Ephraim Squier
°Orson Bean	Dallas Burroughs
Josh Billings	Henry Shaw
Bourvil	André Raimbourg
°Ned Buntline	Edward Judson
Augustus Carp	[Sir] Henry Bashford
Christopher Caustic	Thomas Fessenden
Colon	Joseph Dennie
Christopher Columbus	Joseph Morris
Chester Conklin	Jules Cowles
°Corno di Bassetto	George Bernard Shaw
George Crayon	Washington Irving
Otis Criblecolis	°W.C. Fields
Rann Daly	Edward Palmer
Dangle	Alexander Thompson
Comtesse Dash	[Marquise] Gabrielle Saint-Mars
Dan De Quille	William Wright
°Bo Diddley	Elias McDaniel
°Q.K. Philander Doesticks, P.B.	Mortimer Thomson
Doggerel Drydog	Charles Clark
Gus Elen	Ernest Augustus
Erratic Enrique	Henry Lukens
Eutrapel	Noel du Fail
°Stepin Fetchit	Lincoln Perry
George Savage Fitz-Boodle	William Thackeray
Flotsam	B.C. Hilliam
°Fougasse	Kenneth Bird
Adam Fouleweather	Thomas Nash
Sir Gregory Gander	George Ellis
Lemmie B. Good	Limmie Snell
Will B. Good	Rosco ("Fatty") Arbuckle
Gabbler Gridiron	Joseph Haselwood
Nathaniel Gubbins	Edward Mott
Impulsia Gushington	Helena Sheridan
Ironquill	Eugene Ware
Mahatma Cane Jeeves	°W.C. Fields
°Orpheus C. Kerr	Robert Newell
Mme Kinkel	Elizabeth Sheppard
°Diedrich Knickerbocker	Washington Irving
°Lenare	Leonard Green
Professor Longhair	Henry Bird
Mike McGear	Michael McCartney
Fibber McGee	James Jordan
Medium Tem Plum	Mostyn Piggot
T. Merchant	Thomas Dibdin
Mont Blong	Montague Blatchford
Marmaduke Myrtle	[Sir] Richard Steele
Petroleum Vesuvius Nasby	David Ross Locke
°Jimmy Nervo	James Holloway
Aristarchus Newlight	Richard Whately
Sir Nicholas Nipclose, Bart.	David Garrick

Cedric Oldacre of Saxe Normanby	[The Rev.] John Warter
°Old Block	Alonzo Delano
Jonathan Oldstyle	Washington Irving
Oliver Optic	William Adams
Mona K. Oram	Mrs. Arthur Grenville
Miles O'Reilly	Charles Halpine
°Parkyakarkus	Harry Einstein
Wally Patch	Walter Vinnicombe
K.N. Pepper	James Morris
Philemon Perch	Richard Johnson
Paul Periwinkle	Percy St. John
Peregrine Persic	James Morier
Peter Porcupine	William Cobbett
°Father Prout	Francis Mahoney
°M. Quad	Charles Lewis
Seeley Regester	Metta Victor
Reginald Reverie	Grenville Mellen
Monte Rey	James Fyfe
John Rhode	Cecil Street
°Sax Rohmer	Arthur Ward
°Luke Sharp	Robert Barr
Sandie Shaw	Sandra Goodrich
Abel Shufflebottom	Robert Southey
Siful Sifadda	Henrik Wergeland
Skitt	Harden Taliaferro
Sam Slick	Thomas Haliburton
Mark Spade	Nigel Balchin
Spondee	Royall Tyler
Squibob	George Derby
Stanelli	Edward Stanley de Groot
Swears	Ernest Wells
Miss Teerius	Mrs. Frederick Horner
Paul Tell-truth	George Carey
Madison Tensar, M.D.	[Dr.] Henry Lewis
°Toby, M.P.	[Sir] Henry Lucy
Rip Torn	Elmore Torn
Vera Vague	Barbara Allen
Count Palmiro Vicarion	Christopher Logue
William and Robert Whistlecraft	John Frere
Norman Wisdom	Norman Wisden
The Wizard	J. Corlett
Woon	Ralph Wotherspoon

36. "E Pluribus Unum"

With the possible exception of °Kukryniksy, which has a Russian plural ending, none of the names in this list indicates its plurality — that it is a single name shared by two or more persons. In a number of cases, such names are devised from a combination of the names of both or all parties, but this is certainly not always so. The usual number of partners sharing a name is two, but °Smectymnuus is the name of a quintet. A name that is the exact opposite of this type—i.e., an apparently plural name for a single person—is William and Robert Whistlecraft. For the identity of these two gentlemen, see the Who's Who.

Pseudonym	*Real names*
Edward Sidney Aarons	Paul Ayres + Edward Ronns
Peter Anthony	Peter Shaffer + Anthony Shaffer
Clifford Ashdown	R. Austin Freeman + John James Pitcairn
°Francis Beeding	John Leslie Palmer + Hilary Saunders
Judith M. Berrisford	Clifford Lewis + Mary Lewis
°A Citizen of New York	Alexander Hamilton + James Madison + John Jay
Manning Coles	Adelaide Manning + Cyril Coles
Alfred Crowquill	Alfred Forrester + Charles Forrester
Clark Darlton	Walter Ernsting + Karl Scheer
Sir Iliad Doggrel	[Sir] Thomas Burnet + George Ducket
Dolbokov	Hannes Bok + Boris Dolgov
Michael Field	Katherine Bradley + Edith Cooper
Peter Goldsmith	J.B. Priestley + George Billam
Clifford Halifax	[Dr.] E. Beaumont + L.T. Meade
Francis Herbert	William Bryant + Gulian Verplanck + Robert Sands
Historicus	George Grote + [Sir] William Harcourt
Lorin Kaye	Lorin Lathrop + Miss F. Kostam
°Kukryniksy	Mikhail Kupriyanov + Porfiry Krylov + Nikolai Sokolov
Launcelot Langstaff	Washington Irving + William Irving + James K. Paulding
Emma Lathen	Mary Latsis + Martha Hennissart
John Le Breton	Miss M. Harte-Potts + T. Murray Ford
°Caroline Lewis	Harold Begbie + M.H. Temple + Stafford Ransome
Martin Marprelate	John Penry + John Udall + Henry Barrow + Job Throckmorton
Alan Longdon Martin	Grace Bailey + Jane Murfin
Wade Miller	Robert Wade + Bill Miller
David Pilgrim	John Leslie Palmer + Hilary Saunders
°Kozma Prutkov	A.K. Tolstoy + A.M. Zhemchuzhnikov + V.M. Zhemchuzhnikov
°Ellery Queen	Frederic Dannay + Manfred B. Lee
°Patrick Quentin	Richard Webb + Hugh Wheeler + Martha Kelly + Mary Aswell
Philip Reid	Richard Reid Ingrams + Andrew Osmond
J.H. Rosny	Joseph Boex + Séraphin Boex
°Barnaby Ross	Frederick Dannay + Manfred B. Lee
°Martinus Scriblerus	Alexander Pope + Jonathan Swift (+ others)
°Smectymnuus	Stephen Marshall + Edmund Calamy + Thomas Young + Matthew Newcomen + William Spurstowe
A Son of the Marshes	Mrs. Owen Visgar + Denham Jordan
Herbert Strang	George Herbert Ely + Charles L'Estrange
°Paul Temple	Francis Durbridge + James McConnell
Patry Williams	M. Patry + D.F. Williams

37. Initials

This short list is of names comprised of initials only – and moreover that are not the initials of the person's real name. Where known, the interpretation of the initials is given.

Initials (with real name) — *Meaning (where known)*

°Æ (George William Russell) — Æon
A.L.O.E. (Charlotte Maria Tucker) — A Lady of England
°BB ([1] Denys Watkins-Pitchford, [2] °Lewis Carroll) — [1] (shot size)
G.G. (H.G. Harper) — perhaps "gee-gee" (i.e., horse)
°H.L.L. (Jane Laurie Borthwick) — Hymns from the Land of Luther
°M. le. ch. X.o.a.s.s.d.s.M.S. (Xavier de Maistre) — (see Name Stories)
Q.Q. (Jane Taylor)
S.B. (H.G. Wells) — Scientiae Baccalaureus
T.B. (A.C. Benson)
V (Caroline Clive)
X (Eustace Budgell)
X.L. (Julian Field) — perhaps "excel"
Y.Y. (Robert Lynd) — perhaps "wise" (or "too wise")
Z.Z. (Louis Zangwill)

38. Early, Rare, or Occasional Names

In this, the longest list of all, the real names will be mostly familiar, but the pseudonyms less well known. The latter are mostly names used early, then dropped, or names used for a single work or on a single occasion. Readers may like to try their hand at "cracking" some of the more meaningful names, perhaps starting with Droch and Walter Ramal.

Pseudonym — *Real name or better known pseudonym*

Mozis Addums — Moses Adams
Alcibiades — Alfred [Lord] Tennyson
Ronald Allen — Alan Ayckbourn
Ellen Alleyne — Christina Rossetti
Alma — Charlotte Mary Yonge
V. Alov — Nikolay Gogol
Battista Angeloni — John Shebbeare
Dr. Pessimist Anticant — Thomas Carlisle
Ariosto — [The Rev.] Edward Issing
Robert Arvill — Robert Boote
Nikolay Arzhak — Yury Daniel
Asper — Samuel Johnson
James Aston — T.H. White
William Atheling — Ezra Pound
Backsight-Forethought — [Sir] Ernest Swinton

Clara Balfour
D.R. Banat
David Baron
Maurice Barrington
Louis Barsac
Beatrice
Mrs. Belfour
Paul Bell
W. Bird
Brynjolf Bjarme
Kid Blackie
Reginald Bliss
°William Boot
A. Bostonian
Benjamin Bounce
B. Bouverie
Edgar Box
Nancy Boyd
Billy Breen
James Brian
Mr. Brown
Harry Brown
Henri Brulard
Katherine Burns
Burton Junior
The Busy-Body
James Byrne
°Cadenus
John Cameron
S. Carrol
Rita Casino
Billie Cassin
Pigistratus Caxton
Daniel Chaucer
Antosha Chekhonte
Alice Cholmondeley
Don Christy
The Citizen of the World
°The Rev. T. Clark
Mrs. Mary Clavers
Dorothy Clyde
Pindar Cockloft
Joshua Coffin
Silas Tomkyn Comberback
Comus
Will Conroy
°Corno di Bassetto
Peregrine Courtenay
Christopher Crowfield
Victor d'Auverney
°Lawrence H. Davidson
Frances Dean
Jean de I'Isle
°Joseph Delorme

Felicia Hemans
Ray Bradbury
Harold Pinter
[Sir] Denis Brogan
Ernest Oldmeadow
Anne Manning
[Lady] Bradshaigh
Henry Chorley
Jack Butler Yeats
Henrik Ibsen
Jack Dempsey
H.G. Wells
°Tom Stoppard
Edgar Allan Poe
Henry Carey
William Gladstone
Gore Vidal
Edna Millay
°Larry Grayson
A.G. Street
W.M. Thackeray
Vic Oliver
°Stendhal
Katherine Hepburn
Charles Lamb
Benjamin Franklin
Edward Garnett
Jonathan Swift
Archibald Macdonell
Susanna Centlivre
Rita Hayworth
°Joan Crawford
[Lord] Lytton
°Ford Madox Ford
Anton Chekhov
[Countess] Russell
Sonny
Oliver Goldsmith
John Galt
Caroline Kirkland
Fay Holden
William Irving
H.W. Longfellow
Samuel Taylor Coleridge
R.M. Ballantyne
Harry Champion
George Bernard Shaw
Winthrop Praed
Harriet Beecher Stowe
Victor Hugo
D.H. Lawrence
Betty Grable
Alphonse Daudet
Charles-Augustin Sainte-Beuve

Delta — Benjamin Disraeli
Democritus Junior — Robert Burton
Madame Marguerite de Ponti — Stéphane Mallarmé
Dick Distich — Alexander Pope
°M.B. Drapier — Jonathan Swift
Sir Alexander Drawcansir — Henry Fielding
Droch — Robert Bridges
Sieur du Baudrier — Jonathan Swift
Edward Eastaway — Philip Thomas
Sir John Edgar — [Sir] Richard Steele
Don Miguel Alvarez Espriella — Robert Southey
Robert Eton — Laurence Meynell
An Eye-Witness — Charles Lamb
Frederick Fag — [Dr.] James Johnson
Shane Fenton — °Alvin Stardust
Sir Thomas Fitzosborne — William Melmoth
John Fitzvictor — P.B. Shelley
Arthur Francis — Ira Gershwin
Paul French — Isaac Asimov
Major Gahagan — W.M. Thackeray
Ganconagh — W.B. Yeats
Gaston-Marie — Alphonse Daudet
A Gentleman of the University
of Oxford — P.B. Shelley
Sirak Goryan — William Saroyan
A Graduate of Oxford — John Ruskin
Ennis Graham — Mary Louisa Molesworth
°Ingahild Grathmer — [Queen] Margrethe II
Dod Grile — Ambrose Bierce
Albert Haddock — A.P. Herbert
Fenil Haig — °Ford Madox Ford
Walter Maurice — [Sir] Walter Besant
°Sebastian Melmoth — Oscar Wilde
Menander — Charles Morgan
Merlin — Alfred, [Lord] Tennyson
Queenie Merrall — °Mary Merrall
Tristram Merton — Thomas Macaulay
Miles — Neil Bell
Martin Mills — Martin Boyd
A Ministering Friend — °Daniel Defoe
A Minute Philosopher — Charles Kingsley
A. Modus — Jonathan Swift
Andrew Moreton — °Daniel Defoe
Charles Morin — [Sir] Winston Churchill
Marmaduke Myrtle — [Sir] Richard Steele
Alcofribas Nasier — François Rabelais
Eliot Naylor — Pamela Frankau
Nemo — °Phiz
F. Newton — [Professor] Eric Hobsbawn
Sir Nicholas Nipclose, Bart. — David Garrick
°Red Nirt — Tommy Trinder
°Charles Norden — Lawrence Durrell
Normy — Norman Douglas
°Captain George North — Robert Louis Stevenson

Flann O'Brien	Myles na Gopaleen
Dermot O'Byrne	[Sir] Arnold Bax
°Dawn O'Day	Dawn Paris
Gavin Ogilvy	J.M. Barrie
An Old Boy	Thomas Hughes
John Oldcastle	Wilfred Meynell
Old Humphrey	George Mogridge
John Pickard Owen	Samuel Butler
Harry Parke	Harry Einstein
Pax	Mary Cholmondeley
Robert Paye	Gabrielle Lang (Mrs. Campbell)
A. Pen, Esq.	John Leech
Edgar A. Perry	Edgar Allan Poe
Le Petit Homme Rouge	Ernest Vizetelly
Pictor Ignotus	William Blake
Benjamin Place	[The Rev.] Edward Thring
Paul Prendergast	Douglas Jerrold
Private 19022	Frederic Manning
Joseph Prunier	Guy de Maupassant
Quevedo Redivivus	[Lord] Byron
Quiz	Charles Dickens
Richard Quongti	Thomas Macaulay
Walter Ramal	Walter de la Mare
Lord R'hoone	°Honoré de Balzac
A. Riposte	Elinor Maudaunt
Runnymede	Benjamin Disraeli
Sarah Russell	Marghanita Laski
Mark Saltmarsh	David Markham
S.B.	H.G. Wells
Dr. Schmidt	Johann van Schiller
John Shadow	John Byron
Reuben Shapcott	Mark Rutherford
Bob Short	Alexander Pope
Abel Shufflebottom	Robert Southey
John Sinjohn	John Galsworthy
Mace Sloper	Hans Breitmann
Gamaliel Smith	Jeremy Bentham
Johnston Smith	Stephen Crane
°Suzi Soul	Suzi Quatro
Mark Spade	Nigel Balchin
Godfrey Sparks	Charles Dickens
Speranza	[Lady] Jane Francisca Speranza Wilde
Byron Steel	Francis Steegmuller
Ellalice Tate	Eleanor Hibbert
T.B.	A.C. Benson
Launcelot Temple	John Armstrong
Phillida Terson	Phyllis Neilson-Terry
Denis Thevenin	Georges Duhamel
Henry T. Thurston	F.T. Palgrave
Jacob Tonson	Arnold Bennett
Charles Townshend	Charlotte Brontë
F.G. Trafford	Charlotte Riddell
Glen Trevor	James Hilton

Sven Trost
Baron Arminius von Thunder-
    Ten-Thronckh
Simon Wagstaff, Esq.
Joseph Walton
Mary Westmacott
James Willington
Alfred Willmore
Nicholas Worth
Mr. Yorick

[Count] Carl Snoilsky

Matthew Arnold
Jonathan Swift
Joseph Losey
[Dame] Agatha Christie
Oliver Goldsmith
Micheál MacLiammóir
Walter Page
Laurence Sterne

39. Popes

This list is purely for reference, so that readers can see at a glance what the lay names of the popes were, when they pontificated, and what their nationalities were (mostly, of course, Italian). It also provides an overview of when a particular papal name was most in favor: Clement, for example, is essentially a name of the 17th and 18th centuries, while John was revived in 1958 after a gap of over six centuries by Angelo Roncalli, to be taken up by two of his successors, John Paul I and John Paul II. It is always interesting to speculate on the name of a new pope: will he select the name (or names) of a predecessor, or will he introduce an entirely original papal name?

Papal name (with Pontificate)	*Lay name (with Nationality)*
Adrian IV (1154-59)	Nicholas Breakspear (Eng.)
Adrian V (1276)	Ottobono Fieschi (It.)
Adrian VI (1522-23)	Adriaan Dedel (Du.)
Alexander III (1159-81)	Rolando Bandinelli (It.)
Alexander IV (1254-61)	Rinaldo (It.)
[Antipope] Alexander V (1409-10)	Pietro di Cardia (It.)
Alexander VI (1492-1503)	Rodrigo de Borja y Doms (Sp.)
Alexander VII (1655-67)	Fabio Chigi (It.)
Alexander VIII (1689-91)	Pietro Vito Ottoboni (It.)
Benedict XI (1303-04)	Niccolò Boccasini (It.)
Benedict XII (1334-42)	Jacques Fournier (Fr.)
Benedict XIII (1724-30)	Vincenzo Maria Orsini (It.)
Benedict XIV (1740-58)	Prospero Lambertini (It.)
Benedict XV (1914-22)	Giacomo della Chiesa (It.)
Boniface VIII (1294-1303)	Benedetto Caetani (It.)
Boniface IX (1389-1404)	Pietro Tomacelli (It.)
Calixtus II (1119-24)	Guido di Borgogne (Fr.)
Calixtus III (1455-58)	Alfonso de Borgia (Sp.)
Celestine II (1143-44)	Guido di Città di Castello (It.)
Celestine III (1191-98)	Giacinto Bobo-Orsini (It.)
Celestine IV (1241)	Goffredo Castiglioni (It.)
[Saint] Celestine V (1294)	Pietro da Morrone (It.)
Clement II (1046-47)	Suidger (Ger.)
Clement III (1187-91)	Paolo Scolari (It.)
Clement IV (1265-68)	Guy le Gros Foulques (Fr.)

Clement V (1305-14)	Bertrand de Got (Fr.)
Clement VI (1342-52)	Pierre Roger (Fr.)
Clement VII (1523-34)	Giulio de' Medici (It.)
Clement VIII (1592-1605)	Ippolito Aldobrandini (It.)
Clement IX (1667-69)	Giulio Rospigliosi (It.)
Clement X (1670-76)	Emilio Altieri (It.)
Clement XI (1700-21)	Giovanni Albani (It.)
Clement XII (1730-40)	Lorenzo Corsini (It.)
Clement XIII (1758-69)	Carlo Rezzonico (It.)
Clement XIV (1769-74)	Giovanni Ganganelli (It.)
Eugenius III (1145-53)	Bernardo Paganelli (It.)
Eugenius IV (1431-47)	Gabriele Condolmieri (It.)
[Saint] Gregory VII (1073-85)	Hildebrand (It.)
Gregory VIII (1187)	Alberto de Morra (It.)
Gregory IX (1227-41)	Ugo di Segni (It.)
Gregory X (1271-76)	Teobaldo Visconti (It.)
Gregory XI (1370-78)	Pierre-Roger de Beaufort (Fr.)
Gregory XII (1406-15)	Angelo Corrario (It.)
Gregory XIII (1572-85)	Ugo Buoncampagni (It.)
Gregory XIV (1590-91)	Niccolò Sfondrato (It.)
Gregory XV (1621-23)	Alessandro Ludovisi (It.)
Gregory XVI (1831-46)	Bartolommeo Cappellarri (It.)
Honorius II (1124-30)	Lamberto Scannabecchi (It.)
Honorius III (1216-27)	Cencio Savelli (It.)
Honorius IV (1285-87)	Giocomo Savelli (It.)
Innocent II (1130-43)	Gregorio Papareschi dei Guidoni (It.)
Innocent III (1198-1216)	Giovanni Lotario de Conti (It.)
Innocent IV (1243-54)	Sinibaldo (de) Fieschi (It.)
Innocent V (1276)	Pierre de Tarenlaise (Fr.)
Innocent VI (1352-62)	Etienne Aubert (Fr.)
Innocent VII (1404-06)	Cosimo Gentile de Migliorati (It.)
Innocent VIII (1484-92)	Giovanni Battista Cibo (It.)
Innocent IX (1591)	Giovanni Facchinetti (It.)
Innocent X (1644-55)	Giovanni Battista Pamfili (It.)
Innocent XI (1676-89)	Benedetto Odescalchi (It.)
Innocent XII (1691-1700)	Antonio Pignatelli (It.)
Innocent XIII (1721-24)	Michelangiolo Conti (It.)
John II (533-35)	Mercurius (It.)
John III (561-74)	Catelinus (It.)
John XII (955-64)	Octavian (It.)
John XIV (983-84)	Pietro Canepanova (It.)
John XVII (1003)	Giovanni Siccone (It.)
John XVIII (1004-09)	Giovanni Fasano (It.)
John XXI (1276-77)	Peter Juliani (It.)
John XXII (1316-34)	Jacques d'Euse (Fr.)
John XXIII (1958-63)	Angelo Roncalli (It.)
John Paul I (1978)	Albino Luciani (It.)
John Paul II (1978-)	Karol Wojtyla (Pol.)
Julius II (1503-13)	Giuliano della Rovere (It.)
Julius III (1550-55)	Giammaria Ciocchi del Monte (It.)
[Saint] Leo IX (1049-54)	Bruno of Egisheim (Fr.)
Leo X (1513-21)	Giovanni de' Medici (It.)
Leo XI (1605)	Alessandro de' Medici (It.)
Leo XII (1823-29)	Annibale della Genga (It.)
Leo XIII (1878-1903)	Vincenzo Pecci (It.)

Lucius II (1144-45)	Gherardo Caccianemici (It.)
Lucius III (1181-85)	Ubaldo Allucingoli (It.)
Martin IV (1281-85)	Simon de Brie (Fr.)
Martin V (1417-31)	Oddone Colonna (It.)
Nicholas II (1058-61)	Gerard (Fr.)
Nicholas III (1277-80)	Giovanni Gaetano Orsini (It.)
Nicholas IV (1288-92)	Girolamo Masci (It.)
Nicholas V (1447-56)	Tommaso Parentucelli (It.)
Paschal II (1099-1118)	Ranierus (It.)
Paul II (1464-71)	Pietro Barbo (It.)
Paul III (1534-49)	Allessandro Farnese (It.)
Paul IV (1555-59)	Gian Pietro Carafa (It.)
Paul V (1605-21)	Camillo Borghese (It.)
Paul VI (1963-78)	Giovanni Battista Montini (It.)
Pius II (1458-64)	Enea Silvio de Piccolomini (It.)
Pius III (1503)	Francesco Todeschini Piccolomini (It.)
Pius IV (1559-65)	Giovanni Angelo de' Medici (It.)
[Saint] Pius V (1566-72)	Michele Ghislieri (It.)
Pius VI (1775-99)	Giovanni Braschi (It.)
Pius VII (1800-23)	Gregorio Chiaramonti (It.)
Pius VIII (1829-30)	Francesco Castiglioni (It.)
Pius IX (1846-78)	Giovanni Mastai-Ferretti (It.)
[Saint] Pius X (1903-14)	Giuseppe Sarto (It.)
Pius XI (1922-39)	Achille Ratti (It.)
Pius XII (1939-58)	Eugenio Pacelli (It.)
Sergius IV (1009-12)	Peter Buccaporci (It.)
Sixtus IV (1471-84)	Francesco della Rovere (It.)
Sixtus V (1585-90)	Felice Peretti (It.)
Stephen IX (or X) (1057-58)	Frederick of Lorraine (Fr.)
Urban II (1088-99)	Odo of Lagery (Fr.)
Urban III (1185-87)	Uberto Crivelli (It.)
Urban IV (1261-64)	Jacques Pantaleon (Fr.)
Urban V (1362-70)	Guillaume de Grimoard (Fr.)
Urban VI (1378-89)	Bartolomeo Prignani (It.)
Urban VII (1590)	Giambattista Castagna (It.)
Urban VIII (1623-44)	Maffeo Barberini (It.)

40. ALLITERATIVE NAMES

As mentioned in List 34 (feminine names), alliteration is often felt to be a desirable feature of a pseudonym, especially a pen name or stage name. This list singles out some of the most striking examples. A few names consisting of a forename and surname that begin with the same sound as distinct from letter are also included, such as Carolyn Keene and Carole King.

Anthony Abbot	Anouk Aimée
Achmed Abdullah	°Anna Akhmatova
Alice Acland	Antony Alban
Andy Adams	Alan Alda
Annette Adams	Adair Aldon

Alfred Allendale
Alan Allyson
Arthur Amyand
Anthony Armstrong
Anne Aston
°Brigitte Bardot
Barney Barnato
Binnie Barnes
Beryl Baxter
Bruce Bennett
Busby Berkeley
Billy Bevan
Betsy Blair
Belinda Blinders
Ben Blue
Betty Blythe
Benjamin Bounce
Bonar Bridge
Barbara Britton
Betty Burke
°Billie Burke
Corinne Calvet
Catherine Carr
Christopher Caudwell
Christopher Caustic
Charlie Chase
°Chubby Checker
Claudius Clear
Colin Clive
Captain Coe
Claudette Colbert
Constance Collier
°Carlo Collodi
Cuthbert Comment
Captain Crawley
Chrystal Croftangry
Christopher Crowfield
Constance Cummings
David Davis
°Doris Day
Dave Dee
°Daniel Defoe
Danielle Delorme
David Devant
Dick Distich
Dorothy Dix
Dick Donovan
°Diana Dors
Donald Douglas
Doggerel Drydog
Deanna Durbin
Edward Eastaway
Erratic Enrique
Frederick Fag

Freddy Fender
Fanny Fern
Francis Flagg
Francis Ford
Florrie Forde
Fanny Forester
Freddie Frinton
Francis Fullwood
Sir Gregory Gander
°Greta Garbo
Gene Gerrard
°Gary Glitter
Gloria Grahame
Gilda Gray
Grace Greenwood
Greta Gynt
Hugh Haliburton
Holworthy Hall
Hugh Halliburton
Hugh Hastings
Helen Haye
Helen Hayes
Hy Hazell
Holmes Herbert
Harrington Hext
Harry Hieover
Headon Hill
Hanya Holm
°Hedda Hopper
°Harry Houdini
Hazel Hughes
James Joyce
°Jimmy James
Jasper John
°Jennifer Jones
Jennie June
Cousin Kate
Carolyn Keene
Kathleen Kellow
Kay Kendall
Carole King
Kennedy King
Louis Lambert
Lew Landers
Lola Lane
Lupino Lane
Lillie Langtry
Lars Lawrence
Lila Lee
°Leonid Lench
Lotte Lenya
Leonard Lyons
Maarten Maartens
Marie McDonald

Murray Macdonald
Malcolm Macgregor
Mae Madison
Marjorie Main
Malachi Malagrowther
Miles Mander
Mary Mannering
Marcel Marceau
Mona Mavis
Moore Marriott
Marian Marsh
Mary Merrall
Mary Millar
Marilyn Miller
°Max Miller
Martin Mills
°Marilyn Monroe
Maria Montez
°Mickie Most
Minnie Myrtle
Nathalie Nattier
°Nadia Nerina
Noël-Noël
Norman Norell
°Oliver Oldstyle
Oliver Optic
°Patti Page
°Peter Parley
Pip Pepperpod
Paul Periwinkle
Peregrine Persic
Peregrine Pickle
Paul Pindar
°Peter Pindar
Patrick Plum
Peter Plymley
Peter Porcupine

Paul Prendergast
Paula Prentiss
P.J. Proby
Ralph Redway
Reginald Reverie
Ralph Robinson
°Rob Roy
°Roy Rogers
Susan Saint James
°Soupy Sales
Simon Scribe
Sandie Shaw
Susan Shaw
Sylvia Sidney
Simone Signoret
Sam Slick
Sam Smiff
Stevie Smith
°Suzi Soul
Stephen Southwold
°Stainless Stephen
°Tammi Terrell
°Terry-Thomas
Tiny Tim
Timothy Titcomb
Tommy Tucker
Tom Tyler
Vera Vague
Virginia Valli
Violet Vanbrugh
Victor Varconi
Violette Verdy
Victoria Vetri
William Wastle
Wylie Watson
Warren William

Who's Who and Index

This is the most extensive section of the book, and it aims, basically, to identify the true person behind the pseudonymous mask — to say who he or she really was or is. It is essentially an informative section, giving (in this order) the person's pseudonym, then real name, then dates of birth and death, then nationality, main occupation, professional or otherwise, and, in a few cases, nickname.

Some persons are entered more than once, especially when their several pseudonyms are equally well known. On the whole, however, each entry deals with a person once only, and readers who wish to see examples of one person's many pseudonyms are referred to Name List 7 or, uniquely, Appendices I and II.

I have tried to make the handling of each entry consistent, as follows:

The pseudonym is given in its normal form, with the spelling as given in the source from which it was taken (or from another source if the spelling seemed suspect), and with pseudonyms comprised of more than one name in the normal order (not surname first).

To locate a pseudonym alphabetically, look for the surname or first main word of "phrase" names (as *A Ministering Friend.*) Thus *Clive Exton* will be found near the end of letter "E," and *An Eye-Witness* will follow him, rather than come under the letter "A." Traditional titles, ranks, relationships and the like do not count for alphabetical purposes, so that *Mr. Yorick* is under "Y," not "M," °*Flying Officer X* is under "X," not "F," and *Uncle Harry* is under "H," not "U." On the other hand, *Ex-Private X* is under "E," not "X," since "Ex-Private" is a special name, not a traditional accepted rank. In some cases it is difficult to decide whether a first name counts as a forename or as an ordinary word. Should °*Red Buttons* thus be under "B" or "R"? The guiding principle here is that if the first part of the name could be used as a forename or nickname, the pseudonym will be listed alphabetically under its last name. So °*Red Buttons* will be found under "B" and even *Giant Haystacks* under "H," but *Poor Richard* is under "P," since "Poor" could never have been used as a forename or nickname on its own.

Names beginning with "A" or "The" will always be found under

227

the first letter of the next word, while names beginning "De" (and surnames beginning thus) will usually be found under "D" unless this is
clearly a linking particle. Similarly, names beginning with a foreign form
of "A" or "The" (as French *Le*, Italian *Il*, Spanish *El* and German *Der*)
will be found under the next word. Names starting with a form of "Mac"
(as *Mc* or *M'*) are alphabetized as "Mac," rightly or wrongly, as is the
practice in telephone directories. A title in square brackets preceding a
pseudonym (mostly "Sir" or "Saint") is a genuine honorific, and not part
of the pseudonym. If it is *not* in brackets, it is a pseudonymous title, as *Sir
Iliad Doggrel*.

The real name is normally given in its full form, where known,
although very well known names are given simply as forename and surname (so Charles Dickens, rather than Charles John Huffam Dickens). In
a few cases I have not been able to discover the names for which initials
stand, so such initials must suffice. In a very few instances I have not been
able to discover a forename (as with Gluck), and so have left a blank.
Titles such "The Rev." (without the "The") and "Sir" are enclosed in
square brackets, lest they be thought an actual name. (This could happen
with such a title as "Lady.") Alternative names are given in round
brackets, preceded by the word "or". I have given a married woman's
maiden name when it seemed relevant or interesting to do so: this appears
after the married surname preceded by the word *née*. Occasionally instead of a real name a cross reference to a pseudonym will be made. This
happens when the entry gives a rare or nonce pseudonym used by a person
normally known by another pseudonym. See for example, *Fenil Haig*,
better known as *Ford Madox Ford*.

The dates proved to be one of the more difficult information items
to determine accurately. They are the years of birth and death, with a gap
after the hyphen indicating either (and usually) that the person is still
living, or that regrettably I have failed to find the year of death. John
Ackworth, for example, devout believer that he was, could not possibly
have survived in his earthly life to the present year. Where a year of birth
is generally unknown or uncertain, as with some of the early popes, a
question mark is inserted (e.g., for Adrian V). An approximate year of
birth is preceded by "*c.*" (Latin *circa*, "about") and a hazarded year of
birth, or a calculated one based on secondary dates, is preceded by a
question mark.

The birth years of very many film actresses, and a number of actors, are notoriously difficult to pin down. The ladies in question are
either coy about their age or fail to reveal it. All one can go on here is
what other biographers and researchers have managed to find out, and I
have operated on the basis followed by Halliwell, that the earliest date
given by an authority is likely to be the most accurate. The same principle
applies to writers, and indeed to anyone of uncertain age.

In a few cases I have been unable to discover any dates at all, so
have left two blanks.

The nationality is given in abbreviated form for the most part, and although most of the abbreviations are obvious their full forms are given in the list that precedes the Who's Who. "U.S." means "United States of America." There is a rather unsatisfactory distinction between "Eng." and "Br." The latter will very likely also turn out to denote an English (as opposed to a Scottish) subject, whereas "Eng." *will* be English and not Scottish, Irish or Welsh. The addition of "-born" (as "Ger.-born") means that the true nationality of birth is German, with the assumed or adopted nationality given as in the next word. Thus Renée Adorée was (one might also say "is") French in origin, but an American citizen. Dual nationalities are given in the form "Russ.-Eng." (which will usually mean one Russian parent and one English). Where it has a bearing on a pseudonym, the nationality of a subject's parents is also given (see, for example, Charles Aznavour).

The occupation of the subject is given in the broadest terms, and is chiefly designed to "place" the person as an actor, writer, spy, or whatever. Since actors and writers predominate, however, a little further guidance is given. For an actor, an indication is given for either stage, screen (film), or TV — although this distinction is obviously not made pre-1900 — and for a writer, his or her particular genre (novels, short stories, plays, poems, etc.) is usually stated. Similarly, a musician's field is given, as classical or pop, for example. With regard to the latter, I have tried to make a distinction between a popular singer and a pop singer. A popular singer is usually someone of an older generation whose music is "light" or "easy listening." A pop singer will normally be a younger person whose product is rock music or some derivative of it.

It will be appreciated that only the main occupation or profession is given, and in particular the one, or the ones, relating to the choice of pseudonym. Edward Powys Mathers, for instance, was a poet and translator of some distinction, even rendering a long, elegiac Sanskrit love poem into English, but he is most popularly known as Torquemada the crossword compiler.

In a number of cases people will have settled in another country to realize their life's main work — this particularly applies to Europeans settling in America — and in many such instances the country of adoption is given in the formula "working in U.S." Such an emigration will frequently, of course, have a direct bearing on the choice or form of pseudonym.

Where is it relevant or memorable I have also added a person's nickname or epithet, in particular where it neatly sums up the subject. Such nicknames are either widely known ("Bronco Billy" for G.M. Anderson, the "Oomph Girl" for Ann Sheridan) or less well known but effective (Pietro Aretino is the "scourge of princes"; Ann Candler is the "Suffolk Cottager").

An additional piece of information is sometimes given following the occupation. This is a person's relationship with a fellow Who's Who subject. Such a relationship (parent, sibling, spouse and the like) will often link two identical names, and in the case of "single for plural" pseudonyms (a single name for two or more people, as in Name List 36), will frequently provide an explanation for the choice of name. The relationship of partners working under a single pseudonym is usually given as a matter of course.

In those few cases where a pseudonymous person's true name is not known, then of course all information (apart from the pseudonym itself) will usually be lacking. Such names are anyway dealt with in the Name Stories.

The usual "degree" symbol (°) precedes the name of any person whose pseudonym is treated more fully in the Name Stories.

The Who's Who is also an Index, and a page number is given against a name where it has been mentioned or dealt with in some way earlier in the book. Such a page, however, will be only in the main six chapters, and not in the Name Lists or Name Stories, since in the case of the former the referral is really the other way round (names in the Lists can be mostly found in the Who's Who in their alphabetical place), and in the case of the latter the "degree" sign will indicate a treatment.

Numbered real names indicate the different individuals who used the pseudonym given. (See, for example, Alceste or Alcibiades.) Real names preceded by a plus sign (+) indicate that the pseudonym given is a joint one for all such persons so linked. See, for example, °Smectymnuus, where all five real names are so cumulatively linked.

The Who's Who is as accurate as I have been able to make it. Allowing, however, both for the instability and disparity of source materials and the frailties of human nature, errors and inconsistencies there will almost certainly be. While sincerely hoping that they will be minimal, I would be most grateful if readers having access to specific information on an incomplete or inaccurate entry would be kind enough to notify me, so that I can rectify the shortcoming in a future edition of the book. Especially, as Miss Mansfield said, if I haven't spelled the name right.

Abbreviations

Austr.	Austrian	Fr.	French
Belg.	Belgian	Ger.	German
Br.	British	Gk.	Greek
Bulg.	Bulgarian	Hung.	Hungarian
Can.	Canadian	Ir.	Irish
Dan.	Danish	It.	Italian
DJ	disc jockey	Norw.	Norwegian
Du.	Dutch	N.Z.	New Zealand
Eng.	English	Pol.	Polish

Port.	Portuguese	Sp.	Spanish
Rom.	Romanian	Swe.	Swedish
Russ.	Russian	Turk.	Turkish
S.A.	South African	TV	television
Sc.	Scottish	U.K.	United Kingdom
SF	science fiction	U.S.	United States

A

A.A.: Anthony Armstrong (*q.v.*)

Anthony **Abbot**: Charles Fulton Oursler (1893-1952) U.S. journalist, playwright, novelist

John **Abbot**: Vernon John (1896-1943) U.S. music hall singer [63]

Bud **Abbot**: William A. Abbott (1895-1974) U.S. film comedian

Achmed **Abdullah**: Alexander Nicholayevitch Romanoff (1881-1945) Russ.-Eng. mystery story writer

Johann Philip **Abelin**: Johann Ludwig Gottfried (*c.* 1600-1634) Ger. historian

°**Ab-o'-th'-Yate**: Benjamin Brierley (1825-1896), Eng. dialect writer

Acanthus: H. Frank Hoar (1909-1976) Eng. cartoonist

Johnny **Ace**: John Marshall Alexander, Jr. (1929-1954) U.S. black rock musician

John **Ackworth**: [Rev.] F R Smith (1854-) Eng. novelist, religious writer

Acquanetta: Burnu Davenport (1920-) U.S. film actress

Richard **Adama**: Richard Adams (1928-) U.S. ballet dancer [32, 33]

Casey **Adams**: Max Showalter (1917-) U.S. film actor [27, 63]

Don **Adams**: Donald James Yarmy (1927-) U.S. TV comedian

Edie **Adams**: Elizabeth Edith Enke (1929-) U.S. film actress, singer

Maude **Adams**: Maude Kiskadden (1872-1953) U.S. stage actress

Moses **Adams**: George William Bagby (1828-1883) U.S. humorist, lecturer

Nick **Adams**: Nicholas Adamschock (1932-1968), U.S. film actor

Stephen **Adams**: Michael Maybrick (1844-) Eng. composer, singer

Max **Adeler**: Charles Heber Clark (1847-1915) Ger.-born U.S. humorous writer

Renée **Adorée**: Jeanne de la Fonte (1898-1933) Fr.-born U.S. film actress [63]

Adrian: Gilbert Adrian (1903-1959) U.S. film costume designer

Adrian IV: Nicholas Breakspear (c. 1100-1159) Eng. pope

Adrian V: Ottobono Fieschi (?-1276) It. pope

Adrian VI: Adriaan Dedel (1459-1523) Du. pope [52]

Iris **Adrian**: Iris Adrian Hostetter (1913-) U.S. film actress

Max **Adrian**: Max Bor (1903-1973) Ir.-born Eng. stage actor

°**Æ** (or AE, A.E.): George William Russell (1867-1935) Ir. poet, artist

°**Affable Hawk**: [Sir] Desmond MacCarthy (1878-1952) Br. dramatic, literary critic

Afrique: Alexander Witkins (1907-) S.A. music hall singer

Afrit: Alistair Ferguson Ritchie (1887-1954) Br. crossword compiler [31]

Luigi **Agnesi**: Louis Ferdinand Léopold Agniez (1833-1875) Belg. bass opera singer

Spiro **Agnew**: Spiro Theodore Anagnostopoulos (1918-) U.S. pol. [26]

Shmuel Yosef **Agnon**: Samuel Josef Czaczkes (1888-1970) Hebrew novelist, short story writer

Orme **Agnus**: John C Higginbotham (?-1919) Eng. novelist

Mariade **Agreda**: María Fernandez

Coronel (1602-1665) Sp. abbess, mystic

Johannes **Agricola**: Johann Schneider (or Schnitter) (1494-1566) Ger. Lutheran theologian [31, 32]

Ahad Ha'am: Asher Ginzberg (1856-1927) Russ. Zionist leader

Ernst **Ahlgren**: Victoria Benedictsson (1850-1888) Swe. writer

Juhani **Aho**: Johannes Brofeldt (1861-1921) Finnish author

Gustave **Aimard**: Olivier Gloux (1818-1883) Fr.-born U.S. romantic novelist

Anouk **Aimée**: Françoise Sorya (1932-) Fr. film actress [63]

Patricia **Ainsworth**: Patricia Nina Bigg (1932-) Australian writer

Ruth **Ainsworth**: Ruth Gilbert (1918-) Br. writer

Catherine **Aird**: Kinn Hamilton McIntosh (1930-) Eng. mystery writer

Catherine **Airlie**: Jean Sutherland MacLeod (1908-) Sc. writer

°Anna **Akhmatova**: Anna Andreyevna Gorenko (1889-1966) Russ. poet

Alain: Émile-Auguste Chartier (1868-1951) Fr. philosopher, essayist, teacher

Alain-Fournier: Henri-Alban Fournier (1886-1914) Fr. novelist

A.J. **Alan**: Leslie Harrison Lambert (1883-1940) Br. broadcaster, storyteller [64]

Jane **Alan**: Lillian Mary Chisholm (1906-) Eng. short story writer

Antony **Alban**: Antony Allert Thompson (1939-) Br. author

Mme **Albani**: Marie Louise Emma Cécile Lajeunesse (1847-1930) Can. opera singer

°Eddie **Albert**: Eddie Albert Heimberger (1908-) U.S. stage, film, TV actor

Martha **Albrand**: Heidi Huberta Freybe Loewengard (1912-) Ger.-U.S. spy novelist

Hardie **Albright**: Hardy Albrecht (1903-) U.S. film actor [26]

Alceste: [1] Alfred Assolant (1827-1886) Fr. writer. [2] Hippolyte de Castille (-) Fr. writer. [3] Louis Belmontet (1799-1879) Fr. writer [4] Édouard Laboulaye (1811-1883) Fr. writer

Alcibiades: [1] Albert, Margrave of Brandenburg (1522-1557) Ger. prince. [2] Alfred Tennyson (1809-1892) Eng. poet. [3] George Villiers [Duke of Buckingham] (1627-1688) Eng. courtier

Baron de M. **Alcide**: Alfred de Musset (1810-1857) Fr. poet

Alan **Alda**: Alphonso D'Abruzzo (1936-) U.S. stage actor

Frances **Alda**: Frances Davies (1883-1952) N.Z. opera singer

Robert **Alda**: Alphonso Giovanni Giuseppe Roberto D'Abruzzo (1914-) It.-born U.S. film actor

Mark Aleksandrovich **Aldanov**: Mark Aleksandrovich Landau (1889-1957) Russ. writer

G.R. **Aldo**: Aldo Graziati (1902-1953) It. cinematographer

Adair **Aldon**: Cornelia Lynde Meigs (1884-1973) U.S. educator, author, playwright

Louis **Aldrich**: Louis Lyon (1843-1901) U.S. stage actor

°Shalom **Aleichem**: Solomon J. Rabinowitz (1859-1916) Russ.-born Jewish novelist, short story writer

°O **Aleijadinho**: António Francisco Lisbôa da Costa (?1730-1814) Brazilian sculptor, architect

Alexander **Alekhine**: Aleksandr Aleksandrovich Alyokhin (1892-1946) Russ. chess player

Aleksandr Nikolayevich **Aleksan**-Aleksandr Nikolayevich Fedotov (1901-1973) Russ. circus artiste

Grigory Vasilyevich **Aleksandrov**: Grigory Vasilyevich Mormenko (1903-) Russ. film director

Vladimir Borisovich **Aleksandrov**: Vladimir Borisovich Keller (1898-1954) Russ. literary critic

°Jean Le Rond d'**Alembert**: Jean-Le-Rond Destouches (1717-1783) Fr. mathematician

Alexander **III**: Rolando Bandinelli (c. 1105-1181) It. pope

Alexander **IV**: Rinaldo [Count] of Segni (1199-1261) It. pope

Alexander **V**: Pietro di Candia (c. 1339-1410) It. antipope

Alexander **VI**: Rodrigo de Borja y Doms (1431-1503) Sp.-born It. pope

Alexander VII: Fabio Chigi (1599-1667) It. pope

Alexander VIII: Pietro Vito Ottoboni (1610-1691) It. pope

Mrs. Alexander: Annie Hector, née French (1825-1902) Ir.-born Br. popular novelist

Ben Alexander: Nicholas Benton Alexander (1911-1969) U.S. film actor

Dair Alexander: Christine Campbell Thomson (1897-) Eng. writer

[Sir] George Alexander: George Alexander Gibb Samson (1858-1918) Br. stage actor, theatre manager

Joan Alexander: Joan Pepper (1920-) Br. author

John Alexander: Jeremy Taylor (1613-1667) Eng. bishop, author

Alexis: Sergei Vladimirovich Simansky (1877-1970) Russ. churchman, patriarch of Moscow and All Russia

Willibald Alexis: Georg Wilhelm Heinrich Haring (1798-1871) Ger. historical novelist

Claudie Algeranova: Claudie Leonard (1924-) Br. ballet dancer

°Muhammad Ali: Cassius Marcellus Clay (1942-) U.S. black boxer

Alien: Louise Alien Baker (1858-) U.S. novelist

Alkan: Charles-Henri Valentin Morhange (1813-1888) Fr. pianist, composer

°George Allan: Mite (or Marie) Kremnitz, née Marie von Bardeleben (1852-1916) Ger. writer

°Paula Allardyce: Ursula Torday (-) Br. thriller writer

Chesney Allen: William E. Allen (1896-) Br. music-hall comedian, teaming with °Bud Flanagan

°Dave Allen: David Tynan O'Mahoney (1936-) Ir. TV entertainer

Major E.J. Allen: Allan Pinkerton (1819-1884) Sc.-born U.S. detective

Elizabeth Allen: Elizabeth Allen Gillease (1934-) U.S. stage, film actress [28]

F.M. Allen: Edmund Downey (1856-1937) Ir. humorous writer

°Fred Allen: John F. Sullivan (1894-1956) U.S. radio comedian, film ac-actor

Ronald Allen: Alan Ayckbourn (1939-) Eng. playwright

Woody Allen: Allen Stewart Konigsberg (1935-) U.S. stage, film comedian, playwright [46]

Alfred Allendale: Theodore Edward Hook (1788-1841) Eng. novelist

Mary Allerton: Mary Christine Govan (1897-) U.S. author

Ellen Alleyne: Christina Georgina Rossetti (1830-1894) Eng. poet

Claude Allister: Claud Palmer (1891-1970) Eng. film actor

June Allyson: Ella Geisman (1917-) U.S. dancer, singer, film actress [63]

Alma: Charlotte Mary Yonge (1823-1901) Eng. novelist

E.M. Almedingen: Martha Edith von Almedingen (1898-1971) Russ.-born Eng. novelist, poet, biographer

A.L.O.E.: Charlotte Maria Tucker (1821-1893) Br. writer, children's author

Alicia Alonso: Alicia Martinez (1909-) Cuban ballet dancer

V. Alov: Nikolay Vasilyevich Gogol (1809-1852) Russ. novelist, playwright

Alpha of the Plough: Alfred George Gardiner (1865-1946) Br. essayist

[Mother] Alphonsa: Rose Hawthorne (1851-1926) U.S. author, nun, medical worker

Peter Altenberg: Richard Engländer (1859-1919) Austr. writer

Robert Alton: Robert Alton Hart (1903-1957) U.S. film director

Alun: John Blackwell (1797-1840) Welsh poet and prose writer

Don Alvarado: José Paige (1900-1967) U.S. film actor

Albert Alvarez: Raymond Gourron (1861-1933) Fr. opera singer

Giuseppe Amato: Giuseppe Vasaturo (1899-1964) It. film producer

Richard Amerley: Paul Bourquin (1916-) Br. writer [63]

Simon Amberley: Peter Hoar (1912-) Br. author

°Don Ameche: Dominic Felix Amici (1908-) U.S. film actor

Jennifer Ames: Maysie Sopoushek, née Greig-Smith (1901-1971) Australian-born romantic novelist

Leon **Ames**: Leon Waycoff (1903-)
U.S. stage, film, TV actor [27]

Arthur **Amyand**: [Major] Andrew
Charles Parker Haggard (1854-
?1923) Br. novelist, historian, poet

Anatoli: Anatoli Kuznetsov (1930-
1979) Russ. émigré writer, working
in U.K.

Dulce **Anaya**: Dulce Esperanza
Wöhner de Vega (1933-) Cuban
ballet dancer

°**An Craoibhín Aoibhinn**: Douglas
Hyde (1860-1949) Ir. writer and
statesman

Daphne **Anderson**: Daphne Carter,
née Scrutton (1922-1977) Eng. stage
and film actress

G.M. **Anderson**:Max Aronson (1882-
1972) U.S. film actor ("Bronco
Billy")

[Dame] Judith **Anderson**: Frances
Margaret Anderson-Anderson
(1898-) Australian stage actress [14]

R. **Andom**: Alfred Walter Barratt
(1869-) Eng. humorist [45]

Fern **Andra**: [Baroness] Fern Andra
von Weichs (-) U.S. film actress

Andrea del Sarto: Andrea d'Agnolo
(1486-1531) It. painter

Stephen **Andrew**: Frank G Layton
(1872-1941) Eng. novelist

Thomas **Andrew**: Edward Thomas
Andoulewicz (1932-) U.S. ballet
dancer and choreographer [28]

°Julie **Andrews**: Julia Elizabeth Wells
(1935-) Eng. film actress

Tige **Andrews**: Tiger Androwaous
(?1923-) Gk.-born U.S. film actor

Pierre **Anrezel**: Karen Blixen, née
Dinesen (1885-1962) Dan. novelist

Pier **Angeli**: Anna Maria Pierangeli
(1932-1971) It. film actress

°**Angelico**: [Fra] Giovanni da
Fiesole (1387-1455) It. painter

Angelina: Harriet Martineau (1802-
1876) Eng. author

[Sir] Norman **Angell**: Ralph Norman
Angell Lane (1872-1967) Eng.
writer

Battista **Angeloni**: John Shebbeare
(1709-1788) Eng. political writer

Muriel **Angelus**: Muriel Angelus Findlay (1909-) Sc. film actress

Angelus à Sancto Francisco: Richard

Mason (1601-1678) Eng. Franciscan
priest

Margit **Angerer**: Margit von Rupp
(1905-1978) Hung.-born Austr.
opera singer

[Mother] **Ann**: Anne Lee (1736-1784)
U.S. mystic

Annabella: Suzanne Charpentier
(1909-) Fr. film actress

Annalist: Frances A Gerard (-) Eng.
writer

Annette: Annette Funicello (1947-)
U.S. film actress

Ann-Margret: Ann-Margret Olson
(1941-) Swe.-born U.S. film actress
[29]

°**Anodos**: Mary Elizabeth Coleridge
(1861-1907) Eng. poet

°**Another Lady**: Marie Dobbs, née
Catton (-) Australian author

Dr. Pessimist **Anticant**: Thomas
Carlyle (1795-1881) Sc. philosopher,
writer

[Père] **Anselme**: Pierre de Guibours
(1625-1694) Fr. genealogist, friar

F. **Anstey**: Thomas Anstey Guthrie
(1856-1934) Eng. novelist [40]

[Archbishop] **Anthony**: Andrew
Borisovich Bloom (1914-) Swiss-
born Russ. churchman

C.L. **Anthony**: Dorothy Gladys Smith
(1896-) Eng. playright, novelist

John **Anthony**: Ronald Brymer Beckett
(1891-) Eng. writer

Joseph **Anthony**: Joseph Deuster
(1912-) U.S. stage actor, director

Julie **Anthony**: Julie Nutt, née Lush
(1952-) Australian cabaret singer,
dancer

Piers **Anthony**: Piers Anthony Dilling-
ham Jacob (1934-) Eng.-born Am.
SF writer

Antoine: Antek Cierplikowski (1884-)
Pol.-born Fr. hairdresser

Anton: Beryl Botterill Antonia Yeoman
(?1914-1970) Australian-born Br.
cartoonist [29]

[Brother] **Antonius**: William Everson
(1912-) U.S. poet, Dominican lay
brother

[Saint] **Antonius**: Antonio Pierozzi
(1389-1459) It. Dominican friar

António: António Ruíz Soler (1921-)
Sp. dancer

Peter **Antony**: Peter Levin Shaffer (1926-) Eng. playwright + Anthony Joshua Shaffer (1926-) Eng. playwright, his twin brother

Christopher **Anvil**: Harry C Crosby (-) U.S. SF writer

°**Ape**: Carlo Pellegrini (1839-1889) It. cartoonist working in England

°**Apex**: Eric Chalkley (1917-) Eng. crossword compiler

Guillaume **Apollinaire**: Guillaume Apollinaire de Kostrowitsky (1880-1918) Fr. poet

°Johnny **Appleseed**: John Chapman (1774-1847) U.S. orchardist

Thoinot **Arbeau**: Jehan Tabourot (1519-1595 or 6) Fr. author of books on dancing

Madame d'**Arblay**: Frances (or "Fanny") Burney (1752-1840) Eng. novelist

John **Archer**: Ralph Bowman (1915-) U.S. film actor

Archimedes: [Sir] James Edward Edmonds (1861-1956) Eng. military historian

°Elizabeth **Arden**: Florence Lewis, née Graham (1884-1966) Can. cosmetician

°Eve **Arden**: Eunice West, née Quedens (1912-) U.S. comic film actress

Pietro **Aretino**: ? (1492-1556) It. satirist, dramatist (the "scourge of princes") [66, 67]

La **Argentina**: Antonia Mercé y Luque (1888-1936) Argentinian-born Sp. ballet dancer

La **Argentinita**: Encarnación Lopez Julves (1895-1945) Argentinian-born Sp. ballet dancer

Pearl **Argyle**: Pearl Wellman (1910-1947) Br. ballet dancer, stage actress

Carina **Ari**: Carina Janssen (1897-1970) Swe. ballet dancer

Arion: [1] George Loval Chesterton (1856-) Eng. sporting correspondent. [2] William Falconer (1732-1769) Eng. "sailor-poet"

Ariosto: [Rev.] Edward Irving (1792-1834) Sc. clergyman, founder of Holy Catholic Apostolic Church

Harold **Arlen**: Hyman Arluck (1905-) U.S. composer of musicals

Michael **Arlen**: Dikran Kuyumjian (1895-1956) Bulg.-born Br. novelist of Armenian parentage

Richard **Arlen**: Cornelius Van Mattimore (1899-1976) U.S. film actor

Arletty: Arlette-Léonie Bathiat (1898- Fr. stage, screen actress

George **Arliss**: George Augustus Andrews (1868-1946) Eng. stage and film actor [28]

Armand: Friedrich Armand Strubberg (1806-1889) Ger.-born author, working in U.S.

Jacobus **Arminius**: Jakob Harmensen (1560-1609) Du. Protestant churchman [31]

Anthony **Armstrong**: George Anthony Armstrong Willis (1897-1976) Can.-born Br. humorist, novelist [28]

°Henry **Armstrong**: Henry Jackson (1912-) U.S. boxer

Robert **Armstrong**: Donald Robert Smith (1890-1973) U.S. film actor

Dudley (or Ernest) **Armytage**: William Edward Armytage Axton (1846-) Eng. journalist and author

Desi **Arnaz**: Desiderio Alberto Arnaz y de Acha (1915-) Cuban-born U.S. film, TV actor

James **Arness**: James Aurness (1923-) U.S. film, TV actor

Peter **Arno**: Curtis Arnous Peters, Jr. (1906-1968) U.S. cartoonist, illustrator

Sig **Arno**: Siegfried Aron (1895-1975) Ger. film comedian, working in U.S.

Edward **Arnold**: Guenther Schneider (1890-1956) U.S. film actor

Françoise **Arnoul**: Françoise Annette Gautsch (1931-) Algerian film actress in Fr. films

Sonia **Arova**: Sonia Errio (1927-) Bulg.-born Br. ballet dancer

Bill **Arp**: Charles Henry Smith (1826-1903) U.S. humorist

Artemas: Arthur Telford Mason (-) Br. author [30, 31]

Artemisia: [Lady] Mary Wortley Montagu (1689-1762) Eng. writer of letters, poems [39]

Arthénice: Catherine de Vivonne [Marquise (Madame) de Rambouillet] (1588-1665) Fr. social leader

George K. **Arthur**: George K. Arthur Brest (1899-) Sc. film actor

Jean **Arthur**: Gladys Georgianna Greene (1908-) U.S. film actress

Julia **Arthur**: Ida Lewis (1869-1919) Can. stage actress

Peter **Arthur**: Arthur Porges (1915-) U.S. writer of detective stories, SF, horror fiction

Robert **Arthur**: [1] Robert Arthur Feder (1909-) U.S. film producer [2] Robert Arthaud (1925-) U.S. film actor, former radio announcer

Robert **Arvill**: Robert Edward Boote (1920-) Eng. director of Nature Conservancy Council

Nikolay **Arzhak**: Yury Daniel (1925-) Russ. dissident writer

Oscar **Asche**: John Stanger Heiss (1871-1936) Br. stage actor

Clifford **Ashdown**: Richard Austin Freeman (1862-1943) Eng. mystery writer. + John James Pitcairn (1860-1936) Eng. mystery writer

Gordon **Ashe**: John Creasey (1908-1973) Br. crime novelist

Renée **Asherson**: Renée Ascherson (1920-) Eng. stage actress

Daisy **Ashford**: Margaret Mary Ashford (1881-1972) Eng. child author

Edward **Ashley**: Edward Ashley Cooper (1904-) Br. film actor working in U.S. [28]

Elizabeth **Ashley**: Elizabeth Cole (1939-) U.S. film actress [37, 38]

Sylvia **Ashton-Warner**: Sylvia Henderson (-) N.Z. writer, novelist

Lena **Ashwell**: Lena Margaret Pocock (1872-1957) Br. stage actress, producer

Grégoire **Aslan**: Kridor Aslanian (1908-) Fr.-Turk. film actor

Asper: Samuel Johnson (1709-1784) Eng. lexicographer, critic

Assiac: Heinrich Fraenkel (1897-) Ger.-born Eng. writer on Nazi Ger. history

°Fred **Astaire**: Frederick Austerlitz (1899-) U.S. dancer, stage, film actor

Anne **Aston**: Anne Lloyd (1948-) Sc. TV hostess

James **Aston**: Terence Hanbury White (1906-1964) Br. novelist

Mary **Astor**: Lucille Langehanke (1906-) U.S. film, TV actress of Ger. parentage

°**Mustafa** Kemal **Atatürk**: Mustafa Kemal [Pasha] (1881-1938) Turk. soldier, statesman

William **Atheling**: Ezra Pound (1885-1972) U.S. poet

Charles **Atlas**: Angelo Siciliano (1893-1972) U.S. body builder

Joseph **Atterley**: George Tucker (1775-1861) U.S. essayist, satirist

Atticus: [1] Joseph Addison (1672-1719) Eng. poet, dramatist. [2] Junius (*q.v.*) [3] Richard Hebes (1773-1833) Eng. bibliomaniac. [4] Anthony Holden (1947-) Eng. newspaper columnist [39, 40]

Cecile **Aubry**: Anne-José Benard (1929-) Fr. film actress

Michel **Auclair**: Vladimir Vujoric (1922-) Fr. film actor

Maxine **Audley**: Maxine Hecht (1923- Eng. stage actress

Mischa **Auer**: Mischa Ounskowsky (1905-1967) Russ.-born U.S. film actor

John **August**: Bernard Augstine De Voto (1897-) U.S. novelist

Mlle **Augusta**: Caroline Augusta Josephine Thérèse Fuchs [Comtesse] de Saint-James (1806-1901) Fr. ballet dancer [29]

Marie **Ault**: Mary Cragg (1870-1951) Br. stage and film actress

Jean-Pierre **Aumont**: Jean-Pierre Salomons (1909-) Fr. film actor, working in U.S.

Charles **Austin**: Charles Reynolds (1879-1942) Eng. music hall comedian

Lovie **Austin**: Cora Calhoun (1895-) U.S. black jazz pianist

Florence **Austral**: Mary Wilson (1894-1968) Australian opera singer

Frankie **Avalon**: Francis Avallone (1939-) U.S. pop singer and film actor

Richard **Avery**: Edmund Cooper (1926-) Eng. SF writer and reviewer

Tex **Avery**: Fred Avery (1907-) U.S. film animator

Catherine **Aydy**: Emma Tennant (c.

1935-) Br. novelist, journalist, literary magazine editor

[Sir] Felix **Aylmer**: Felix Edward Aylmer-Jones (1889-1979) Br. stage, film actor [28]

Allan **Aynesworth**: Edward Abbot-Anderson (1864-1959) Eng. stage actor

Agnes **Ayres**: Agnes Hinkle (1896-1940) U.S. film actress

Lew **Ayres**: Lewis Ayer (1908-) U.S. film actor

John **Ayscough**: Francis Browning Drew Bickerstaffe-Drew (1858-1928) Eng. writer of religious novels

°**Azed**: Jonathan Crowther (1942-) Eng. crossword compiler

Charles **Aznavour**: Charles Aznavurjan (1924-) Fr. film actor of Armenian parentage

°**Azorín**: José Martínez Ruíz (1873-1967) Sp. author, literary critic

B

Babette: Elizabeth McLauchlan (1925-) Sc. music hall dancer [33]

Jean **Babilée**: Jean Gutman (1923-) Fr. ballet dancer, choreographer, actor

°**Lauren Bacall**: Betty Joan Perske (1924-) U.S. stage, film actress

Backsight-Forethought: [Sir] Ernest Dunlop Swinton (1868-1951) Br. army officer, writer

Angela **Baddeley**: Madeleine Angela Byam Shaw, née Clinton-Baddeley (1904-1976) Eng. stage, film actress [28]

Hermione **Baddeley**: Hermione Willis, née Clinton-Baddeley (1906-) Eng. stage, film actress

Baha'u'llah: [Mirza] Husayn Ali (1817-1892) Persian religious leader, founder of Baha'i faith

Guy **Bailey**: [Professor] Cedric Keith Simpson (1907-) Eng. pathologist, forensic expert

Leon **Bakst**: Lev Samoylovich Rosenberg (1866-1924) Russ. theatrical designer, scenic artist

George **Balanchine**: Georgy Melitonovich Balanchivadze (1904-) Russ.-

born U.S. ballet dancer

Edward **Baldwin**: William Godwin (1756-1836) Eng. philosopher, novelist, miscellaneous writer

Neil **Balfort**: Robert Lionel Fanthorpe (1935-) Eng. writer of horror stories

Clara **Balfour**: Felicia Dorothea Hemans, née Browne (1793-1835) Eng. poet

Ina **Balin**: Ina Rosenberg (1937-) U.S. film actress

Harry **Ball**: William Henry Powles (?-1888) Eng. music hall singer, father of °Vesta Tilley

Lucille **Ball**: Lucille Hunt (1911-) U.S. stage, TV actress, comedienne

Kaye **Ballard**: Catherine Balotta (1926-) U.S. film comedienne

Balthus: Balthasar Klossowski de Rola (1908-) Fr. painter, of Pol. parentage

Micah **Balwhidder**: John Galt (1779-1839) Sc. novelist

°Honoré de **Balzac**: Honoré Balzac (1799-1850) Fr. novelist

D.R. **Banat**: Raymond Douglas Bradbury (1920-) U.S. SF writer

°Anne **Bancroft**: Anna Maria Italiano (1931-) U.S. stage, film actress

°Monty **Banks**: Mario Bianchi (1897-1950) It. film actor, director

Vilma **Banky**: Vilma Lonchit (1902-) Austr.-Hung. film actress, working in America

Margaret **Bannerman**: Margaret Le Grand (1896-) Can. stage actress

Baptiste: Nicolas Anselme (1761-1835) Fr. sentimental comedy actor

°Theda **Bara**: Theodosia Goodman (1890-1955) U.S. stage, film actress

Imamu Amiri **Baraka**: Everett Leroi Jones (1934-) U.S. black playwright, poet, novelist

°W.N.P. **Barbellion**: Bruce Frederick Cummings (1889-1919) Eng. essayist, diarist, naturalist

Barbette: Van der Clyde Broodway (1899-1972) U.S. female impersonator in the music hall

Gabriel **Barclay**: Manly Wade Wellman (1903-) U.S. SF, fantasy, mystery writer

Countess **Barcynska**: Marguerite Florence Hélène Evans, née Jervis (1894-

1964) Br. writer

The **Bard**: Edward Jerringham (1727-1812) Eng. poet, dramatist of Della Cruscan School

Samuel A. **Bard**: Ephraim George Squier (1821-1888) U.S. archaeologist, traveler, author

°Wilkie **Bard**: William Augustus Smith (1870-1944) Eng. music hall comedian

°Brigitte **Bardot**: Camille Javal (1934-) Fr. film actress

Lynn **Bari**: Marjorie Bitzer (or Fisher) (1915-) U.S. film actress

Victor **Barna**: Győző Braun (1911-1972) Hung.-born Eng. table tennis player

Barney **Barnato**: Barnett Isaacs (1852-1897) Eng. financier, diamond magnate, former vaudeville artiste

Louis **Barnaval**: Charles De Kay (1848-1935) U.S. editor, writer

Binnie **Barnes**: Gitelle Barnes (1905-) Eng. film actress

Apothecary Esdras **Barnivelt**: Alexander Pope (1688-1744) Eng. poet or John Arbuthnot (1667-1735) Sc. physician, writer

Baron: Baron de V Nahum (1906-1956) Eng. photographer

André **Baron**: André Boyron (1600-1655) Fr. actor

E.L. **Baron**: Horatio McFerrin (c.1920-) U.S. black jazz trumpeter

Ida **Barr**: Maud Barlow (1882-1967) Eng. music hall comedienne

Richard **Barr**: Richard Baer (1917-) U.S. stage director, producer

Ray **Barra**: Raymond Martin Barallobre (1930-) U.S. ballet dancer

Amanda **Barrie**: Shirley Ann Broadbent (1939-) Eng. stage, film, TV actress

Mona **Barrie**: Mona Smith (1909-) Australian film actress

Wendy **Barrie**: Wendy Jenkins (1912-1978) Br. film actress

E. **Barrington**: Eliza Louisa Moresby Beck (-1931) Br. romantic, historical novelist

Maurice **Barrington**: [Sir] Denis William Brogan (1900-1974) Br. historian, political science professor

Rutland **Barrington**: George

ton Rutland Fleet (1853-1922) Eng. actor, singer [28]

David **Barry**: Merig Wyn Jones (1944-) Eng. TV actor

Don **Barry**: Donald Barry d'Acosta (1212-) U.S. film actor

Gene **Barry**: Eugene Klass (1921-) U.S. film, TV actor [27]

John **Barry**: John Barry Prendergast (1933-) Eng. rock composer

Michael **Barry**: James Barry Jackson (1910-) Eng. musician, writer [28]

Ethel **Barrymore**: Ethel Blythe (1879-1959) U.S. stage, film actress

John **Barrymore**: John Blythe (1882-1942) U.S. stage, film actor

Lionel **Barrymore**: Lionel Blythe (1847-1905) U.S. stage, film actor

°Maurice **Barrymore**: Herbert Blythe (1847-1905) Eng. actor, father of Lionel, Ethel, John Blythe

Louis **Barsac**: Ernest James Oldmeadow (1867-1949) Br. journalist, writer

Lionel **Bart**: Lionel Begleiter (1930-) Br. lyricist, composer [27]

Freddie **Bartholomew**: Frederick Llewellyn (1924-) Eng. child film actor, working in U.S.

Bartimeus: Lewis Anselmo da Costa Ricci (1886-1967) Br. author of stories of naval life

Sy **Bartlett**: Sacha Baraniev (1909-1978) U.S. screenwriter, film producer

Eva **Bartok**: Eva Sjöke (1926-) Hung. film actress

Fra **Bartolommeo**: Bartolommeo di Pagolo del Fattorino (or Baccio della Porta) (1472-1517) It. painter

Count **Basie**: William Basie (1904-) U.S. pianist, jazz composer

Ivan **Baskoff**: Henri Meilhac (1832-1897) Fr. dramatist, author

Lina **Basquette**: Lina Belcher (1907-) U.S. film actress

Hogan Kid **Bassey**: Okon Bassey Asuquo (1932-) Nigerian boxer

Florence **Bates**: Florence Rabe (1888-1954) U.S. film actress

Batt: Oswald Barrett (-) Br. cartoonist

Battling Siki: Louis Phal (1897-1925) Senegalese boxer, working in U.S.

Beryl **Baxter**: Beryl Gross, née Ivory

(1926-) Br. stage, film actress
Jane **Baxter**: Feodora Forde (1909-)
Br. stage, film actress
Keith **Baxter**: Keith Baxter-Wright
(1933-) Welsh stage actor
Nora **Bayes**: Dora Goldberg (1880-1928) U.S. vaudeville, musical comedy actress
William **Baylebridge**: Charles William Blocksidge (1883-1942) Australian poet, short story writer
Hervé **Bazin**: Jean-Pierre Hervé-Bazin (1911-) Fr. poet, novelist, short story writer
°**B.B.**: [1] °Lewis Carroll. [2] Denys James Watkins-Pitchford (1905-) Eng. writer of books about the countryside
Beachcomber: [1] Dominic Bevan Wyndham Lewis (1894-1969) Br. humorous columnist. [2] John Cameron Andrieu Bingham Michael Morton (1893-1979) Br. humorous columnist [44]
John **Beal**: Alexander Bliedung (1909-) U.S. stage, film actor
°Orson **Bean**: Dallas Frederick Burroughs (1928-) U.S. stage actor, comedian
Beatrice: Anne Manning (1807-1879) Eng. novelist, miscellaneous writer
°**Warren Beatty**: Warren Beaty (1937-) U.S. film actor
Philip **Beauchamp**: George Grote (1794-1871) Eng. historian
Balthasar de **Beaujoyeux**: Baldassare di Belgiojoso (-1587) It. violinist, composer
Pierre-Augustin Caron de **Beaumarchais**: Pierre-Augustin Caron (1732-1799) Fr. dramatist
Beauménard: Rose-Perrine le Roy de la Corbinaye (-) Fr. actress, wife of °Bellecour
André **Beaumont**: Jean Conneau (1880-1937) Fr. aviator
Charles **Beaumont**: Charles Nutt (1929-1967) U.S. SF writer
Susan **Beaumont**: Susan Black (1936-) Br. film actress
Roger de **Beauvoir**: Edouard Roger de Bully (1809-1866) Fr. novelist
Allen **Beck**: Hugh Barnett Cave (1910-) Eng.-born U.S. horror fiction writer

Christopher **Beck**: Thomas Charles Budges (1868-1944) Eng. writer of stories for boys
Lily Adams **Beck**: Eliza Louisa Moresby Beck (-1931) Eng. author
°Cuthbert **Bede**: [Rev.] Edward Bradley (1827-1889) Br. humorist
Donald **Bedford**: Henry James O'Brien Bedford-Jones (1887-1949) Can.-born U.S. writer of historical adventures
°Demyan **Bedny**: Yefim Alekseyevich Pridvorov (1883-1945) Russ. Socialist, poet
Widow **Bedott**: Frances Miriam Whitcher (1814-1852) U.S. humorous writer
Jon (or George) **Bee**: John Badcock (?-?1830) Br. sporting writer
Janet **Beecher**: Janet Beecher Meysenburg (1884-1955) U.S. film actress
°Francis **Beeding**: John Leslie Palmer (1885-1944) Br. thriller writer. + Hilary Aidan St. George Saunders (1898-1951) Br. thriller writer
Mrs. **Beeton**: Isabella Mary Beeton, née Mayson (1836-1865) Eng. housewifery expert, cook [29]
Beggerstaff Brothers: [Sir] William Newzam Prior Nicholson (1872-1949) Eng. poster artist. + James Pryde (1866-1941) Eng. poster artist
Maurice **Béjart**: Maurice-Jean de Berger (1928-) Fr. ballet dancer, opera director
Barbara **Bel Geddes**: Barbara Geddes Lewis (1922-) U.S. stage, film actress
Belita: Gladys Jepson-Turner (1924-) Br. ice-skater, dancer, film actress
Ivan Petrovich **Belkin**: Aleksandr Sergeyevich Pushkin (1799-1837) Russ. poet, dramatist
Acton **Bell**: Ann Brontë (1820-1849) Eng. novelist, poet [23]
°Currer **Bell**: Charlotte Brontë (1816-1855) Eng. novelist [23]
Ellis **Bell**: Emily Brontë (1818-1848) Eng. novelist, sister of Anne and Charlotte [23]
Josephine **Bell**: Doris Bell Ball, née Collier (1897-) Eng. detective novelist, doctor
Marie **Bell**: Marie-Jeanne Bellon-

Downey (1900-) Fr. stage, film actress

°Neil **Bell**: Stephen H. Critten (1887-1964) Eng. novelist, short story writer

Paul **Bell**: Henry Fothergill Chorley (1808-1872) Eng. journalist, novelist, music critic

Rex **Bell**: George F. Beldam (1905-1962) U.S. film actor

George **Bellairs**: Harold Blundell (1902-) Eng. mystery novelist

Madge **Bellamy**: Margaret Philpott (1903-) U.S. film actress

°**Bellecour**: Jean-Claude-Gilles Colson (1725-1778) Fr. playwright, comic actor

Bellerose: Pierre Le Messier (c.1592-1670) Fr. actor

°**Belleville**: Henri Legrand (?-1637) Fr. actor

Bessie **Bellwood**: Elizabeth Ann Katherine Mahony (1847-1896) Ir. music hall artiste

°N. **Beltov**: Georgy Valentinovich Plekhanov (1857-1918) Russ. Socialist

Andrey **Bely**: Boris Nikolayevich Bugayev (1880-1934) Russ. symbolist poet, writer, literary critic

Benauly: Benjamin Vaughan Abbott (1830-1890) U.S. author. + Austin Abbott (1831-1896) U.S. author, his brother. + [Rev.] Lyman Abbott (1835-1922) U.S. author, their brother.

°**Bendigo**: William Thompson (1811-1889) Br. boxer, prizefighter

Benedict XI: Niccolò Boccasini (1240-1304) It. pope [50]

Benedict XII: Jacques Fournier (-1342) Fr. pope

Benedict XIII: Vincenzo Maria Orsini (1649-1730) It. pope

Benedict XIV: Prospero Lambertini (1675-1758) It. pope

Benedict XV: Giacomo della Chiesa (1854-1922) It. pope [50]

Richard **Benedict**: Riccardo Benedetto (1916-) U.S. film actor

David **Ben-Gurion**: David Gruen (1886-1973) Pol.-born Israeli prime minister

Bruce **Bennett**: Herman Brix (1909-) U.S. film actor

Lennie **Bennett**: Michael Berry (1939-) Eng. stage, TV entertainer

Tony **Bennett**: Anthony Dominick Benedetto (1926-) U.S. popular singer

°**Jack Benny**: Benjamin Kubelsky (1894-1974) U.S. stage, radio, TV comedian

Carl **Benson**: Charles Astor Bristed (1820-1874) U.S. author

Brook **Benton**: Benjamin Franklin Peay (1931-) U.S. black rock singer

Gertrude **Berg**: Gertrude Edelstein (1899-1966) U.S. TV, radio, film actress

Teresa **Berganza**: Teresa Vargas (1935-) Sp. opera singer

Polly **Bergen**: Neillie Burgini (1929-) U.S. stage, radio, TV singer, film actress

E. **Berger**: Elizabeth Sara Sheppard (1830-1862) U.S. novelist

Ludwig **Berger**: Ludwig Bamberger (1892-1969) Ger. film director

Elisabeth **Bergner**: Elisabeth Ettel (1898-) Austr. stage, film actress

Anthony **Berkeley**: Anthony Berkeley Cox (1893-1971) Eng. detective novelist

Busby **Berkeley**: William Berkeley Enos (1895-1976) U.S. director of film musicals [28, 36]

Milton **Berle**: Mendel Berlinger (1908-) U.S. TV, stage, film comedian [27]

°Irving **Berlin**: Israel Baline (1888-) Russ.-born U.S. composer, writer of popular songs

Paul **Bern**: Paul Levy (1889-1932) U.S. film director

[Saint] **Bernadette**: Marie-Bernarde Soubirous (1844-1879) Fr. peasant girl, visionary [37]

Carl **Bernhard**: Andreas Nicolai de Saint-Aubin (1798-1865) Dan. novelist, chronicler

Sarah **Bernhardt**: Rosine Bernard (1844-1923) Fr. tragic actress

L'Abbé **Bernier**: Paul Thiry [baron] d'Holbach (1723-1789) Fr. materialist, atheist philosopher

Claude **Berri**: Claude Langmann (1934-) Fr. film director

Judith M. **Berrisford**: Mary Lewis

(1921-) Eng. writer of books on animals for children. +Clifford Lewis (1912-) Eng. writer of books on animals for children, her husband [56]

Chuck **Berry**: Charles Edward Anderson Berry (1926-) U.S. blues songwriter, singer

Dave **Berry**: David Grundy (1941-) Eng. pop singer

Jules **Berry**: Jules Paufichet (1883-1951) Fr. film actor

Vic **Berton**: Vic Cohen (1896-1953) Fr. film actor

Charles **Bertram**: James Bassett (1853-1907) Eng. magician

°Mary **Berwick**: Adelaide Anne Proctor (1825-1864) Eng. poet

Don **Betteridge**: Bernard Newman (1897-1968) Br. novelist, author of travel books

Billy **Bevan**: William Bevan Harris (1887-1957) Eng.-born U.S. film actor

Isla **Bevan**: Isla Buckley (1910-) Br. film actress

Bhaskar: Bhaskar Roy Chowdhury (1930-) Indian ballet dancer, teacher, working in U.S.

Ernesto **Bianco**: Oscar Ernesto Pelicori (1923-1977) Argentinian stage actor

Jacob **Bibliophile**: Paul Lacroix (1806-1884) Fr. historical write

John **Bickerdyke**: Charles Henry Cook (1858-1933) Eng. sporting writer, novelist

Richard **Bickers**: Richard Leslie Townshend Bickers (1917-) Eng. writer of war stories

°Isaac **Bickerstaff**: [1] Jonathan Swift (1667-1745) Ir.-born Br. satirist, cleric. [2] [Sir] Richard Steele (1672-1729) Ir. essayist, dramatist. [3] Benjamin West (1730-1813) U.S. mathematician.

Big **Bopper**: J P Richardson (1932-1959) U.S. rock songwriter

Big **Daddy**: Shirley Crabtree (1935-) Eng. heavyweight wrestler

Hosea **Biglow**: James Russell Lowell (1819-1891) U.S. humorist, satirist, poet

Big **Maybelle**: Mabel Smith (1926-1972) U.S. blues singer

Bilitis: Pierre Louÿs (1870-1925) Belg.-born Fr. novelist [21]

Vladimir Naumovich **Bill-Belotserkovsky**: Vladimir Naumovich Belotserkovsky (1884-1970) Russ. dramatist

Josh **Billings**: Henry Wheeler Shaw (1818-1885) U.S. humorist [57]

Billy the Kid: William H. Bonney (1859-1881) U.S. desperado

°**Bim**: Ivan Semyonovich Radunsky (1872-1955) Russ. clown, teaming with Bom (*q.v.*)

Satané **Binet**: Francisque Sarcey (1828-1899) Fr. dramatic critic, novelist

W. **Bird**: Jack Butler Yeats (1871-1957) Ir. painter, cartoonist

Tata **Birell**: Natalie Bierle (1908-1959) Pol.-Austr. film actress, working in U.S.

George A. **Birmingham**: [Rev.] James Owen Hannay (1865-1950) Ir.-born Br. author of light novels

Joey **Bishop**: Joseph Abraham Gottlieb (1918-) U.S. TV, film comedian

George **Bizet**: George T Bisset Smith (-) Br. writer of Scottish lawbooks

Brynjolf **Bjarme**: Henrik Ibsen (1828-1906) Norw. poet, dramatist

Dinna **Bjorn**: Dinna Bjorn Larsen (1947-) Dan. ballet dancer

Cilla **Black**: Priscilla Maria Veronica White (1943-) Eng. popular singer, film, TV actress [42]

Ivory **Black**: Thomas Allibone Janvier (1849-1913) U.S. novelist

Karen **Black**: Karen Ziegeler (1943-) U.S. film actress

Lionel **Black**: Dudley Barker (1910-) Eng. novelist, nonfiction writer

Harry **Blackstone**: Henri Bouton (1885-1965) U.S. magician

Scrapper **Blackwell**: Frankie Black (c.1900-) U.S. black jazz guitarist

Vivian **Blaine**: Vivienne Stapleton (1921-) U.S. stage, film actress, singer

Betsy **Blair**: Elizabeth Boger (1923-) U.S. film actress

David **Blair**: David Butterfield (1932-1976) Eng. ballet dancer

Janet **Blair**: Martha Lafferty (1921-) U.S. film actress

Joyce **Blair**: Joyce Sheridan Taylor,

née Ogus (1932-) Eng. stage actress
Lionel **Blair**: Lionel Ogus (1913-) Eng. stage actor, dancer, choreographer
Anne **Blaisdell**: Elizabeth Linington (1921-) U.S. writer of history, mystery novels
Amanda **Blake**: Beverly Louise Neill (1929-) U.S. stage, film actress
°Nicholas **Blake**: Cecil Day-Lewis (1904-1972) Ir.-born Br. poet
Robert **Blake**: Michael Gubitosi (1934-) U.S. film actor
Neltje **Blanchan**: Neltje Doubleday, née de Graff (1865-1918) U.S. author of books on nature subjects
Alexander **Bland**: Nigel Gosling (1909-) Eng. ballet critic. + Maude Gosling, née Lloyd (1908-) S.A.-born Eng. ballerina, ballet critic, his wife.
°Fabian **Bland**: Hubert Bland (1856-1914) Br. author. + Edith Nesbit (1858-1924) Br. author, his wife.
Sally **Blane**: Elizabeth Jung (1910-) U.S. film actress
Docteur **Blasius**: Paschal Grousset (1845-1909) Fr. journalist
Charles Stuart **Blayds**: Charles Stuart Calverley (1831-1884) Br. poet, parodist
Christopher **Blayre**: Edward Heron-Allen (1861-1943) Eng. writer of fantasy fiction
Henri **Blaze**: Ange Henri Blaze de Bury (1813-1888) Fr. author
Émile **Blémont**: Léon-Émile Petitdidier (1839-1927) Fr. critic, dramatic author, poet
Belinda **Blinders**: Desmond F T Coke (1879-1931) Br. novelist
Helena **Bliss**: Helena Louise Lipp (1917-) U.S. stage actress, singer
Reginald **Bliss**: Herbert George Wells (1866-1946) Eng. novelist, sociological writer, historian
Levi **Blodgett**: Theodore Parker (1810-1860) U.S. religious writer
Blondin: Jean-François Gravelet (1824-1897) Fr. tight-rope walker
Claire **Bloom**: Claire Blume (1931-) Eng. stage, film actress
Ben **Blue**: Benjamin Bernstein (1900-1975) U.S. film comedian
David **Blue**: David Cohen (1941-)
U.S. pop songwriter
°Nelly **Bly**: Elizabeth Cochrane Seaman (1867-1922) U.S. journalist
Larry **Blyden**: Ivan Lawrence Blieden (1925-) U.S. stage actor, director
Betty **Blythe**: Elizabeth Blythe Slaughter (1893-1972) U.S. film actress
Jimmy **Blythe**: Sammy Price (1908-) U.S. black jazz pianist
Tim **Bobbin**: John Collier (1708-1786) Eng. author, painter
Willie **Bobo**: William Correa (1934-) U.S. jazz musician
Bocage: Pierre-Martinien Tousez (1797-1863) Fr. actor
Dirk **Bogarde**: Derek Gentron Gaspart Ulric van den Bogaerde (1920-) Br. stage, film actor
Boisgilbert: Ignatius Donnelly (1831-1901) U.S. author, politician
°Marc **Bolan**: Marc Feld (1947-1977) Br. pop musician
Rolf **Boldrewood**: Thomas Alexander Browne (1826-1915) Eng.-born Australian author of popular novels
Richard **Boleslawski**: Boleslaw Ryszart Srzednicki (1889-1937) Pol. stage director
William **Bolitho**: William Bolitho Ryall (1831-1930) S.A.-born Br. journalist, author [28]
°Isabel **Bolton**: Mary Britton Miller (1883-) U.S. poet, novelist
Bom: [1] F Cortesi (?-1897) It.-born Russ. clown, teaming with °Bim. [2] Mechislav Antonovich Stanevsky (1879-1927) Russ. clown, of Pol. parentage, teaming with °Bim. [3] Nikolay Iosifovich Viltzak (1880-1960) Russ. clown, of Czech parentage, teaming with °Bim. [4] N A Kamsky (1894-1966) Russ. clown, teaming with °Bim
Bombardinio: William Maginn (1793-1842) Ir. author
Father **Bonaventura**: Charles Edward Stuart (1720-1788) Sc. prince ("The Young Pretender")
Beulah **Bondi**: Beulah Bondy (1888-1981) U.S. film actress
Gary U.S. **Bonds**: Gary Anderson (1939-) U.S. rock composer
Captain Ralph **Bonehill**: Edward

Stratemeyer (1863-1930) U.S. writer of fiction for boys

John and Emery **Bonett**: John Hubert Arthur Coulson (1906-) Eng. mystery writer. + Felicity Winifred Carter (1906-) Eng. mystery writer, his wife

°**Bon Gaultier**: William Edmondstone Aytoun (1813-1865) Sc. poet. + [Sir] Theodore Martin (1814-1909) Sc. poet

Ali **Bongo**: William Wallace (-) Eng. magician

Jacques **Bonhomme**: Guillaume Cale (or Caillet) (?-1358) Fr. peasant leader

°**Boniface**: Wynfrith (Winfrid?) (?680-755) Eng. missionary, martyr [52]

Boniface VIII: Benedetto Caetani (?1235-1303) It. pope

Boniface IX: Pietro Tomacelli (?1355-1404) It. pope

Issy **Bonn**: Benjamin Levin (1903-1977) Eng. comedian, singer

Richard **Bonnelli**: Richard Bunn (-) U.S. opera singer

Sherwood **Bonner**: Katherine Sherwood Bonner Macdowell (1849-1883) U.S. short story writer [28]

Roger **Bontemps**: Roger de Collerye (?1470-1540) Fr. poet

°William **Boot**: °Tom Stoppard (*q.v.*)

Edwina **Booth**: Josephine Constance Woodruff (1909-) U.S. film actress

James **Booth**: James Geeves-Booth (1933-) Eng. stage actor

Shirley **Booth**: Thelma Booth Ford (1907-) U.S. stage actress

Cornell **Borchers**: Cornelia Bruch (1925-) Ger. film actress

Petrus **Borel**: Joseph-Pierre Borel (or Borel d'Hauterive) (1809-1859) Fr. poet, novelist, critic

°Ludwig **Börne**: Löb Baruch (1786-1837) Ger. political writer, satirist

Francesco **Borromini**: Francesco Castelli (1599-1667) It. architect

°**Bos**: Thomas Peckett Prest (-) Eng. author of stories for boys

Hieronymus **Bosch**: Jerom van Aeken (?1450-?1516) Du. painter

Abbé **Bossut**: [Sir] Richard Phillips (1767-1840) Eng. writer

Boston Bard: Robert S. Coffin (1797-1827) U.S. poet

A **Bostonian**: Edgar Allan Poe (1809-1849) U.S. poet, short story writer

Sandro **Botticelli**: Alessandro di Mariano dei Filipepi (1445-1510) It. painter [33]

Anthony **Boucher**: William Anthony Parker White (1911-1968) U.S. editor, SF, detective story writer

Dion **Boucicault**: Dionysius Lardner Boursiquot (?1820-1890) Ir.-born U.S. actor, playwright

Nicholas **Boulanger**: Paul Thiry [Baron d'Holbach] (1723-1789) Fr. materialist, atheist philosopher

Houari **Boumédienne**: Mohammed Ben Brahim Boukharrouba (1927-1978) Algerian head of state

Benjamin **Bounce**: Henry Carey (?-1743) Eng. poet, composer

George **Bourne**: George Sturt (1863-1927) Eng. author of books on rural themes

Bourvil: Andre Raimbourg (1917-1970) Fr. film comedian

B. **Bouverie**: William Ewart Gladstone (1809-1898) Br. prime minister

Marjorie **Bowen**: Gabrielle Margaret Vere Long, née Campbell (1886-1952) Eng. novelist, biographer

°David **Bowie**: David Hayward-Jones (1947-) Eng. rock musician

Edgar **Box**: Gore Vidal (1925-) U.S. novelist

Boy: Tadeusz Zeleński (1874-1941) Pol. writer

John **Boyd**: Boyd Bradfield Upchurch (1919-) U.S. SF writer

Nancy **Boyd**: Edna St. Vincent Millay (1892-1950) U.S. poet

Neil **Boyd**: Peter De Rosa (-) Br. writer of books on life of Rom. Cath. priest

Stephen **Boyd**: William Millar (1928-) Ir. film actor

Katie **Boyle**: Caterina Irene Helen Imperiali di Francavilla (1929-) It.-born Eng. TV panelist, writer

Kay **Boyle**: [Baroness] Joseph von Franckenstein (1903-) U.S. novelist, short story writer

René **Boylesve**: René-Marie-Auguste Tardiveau (1867-1926) Fr. novelist

°**Boz**: Charles Dickens (1812-1870) Eng. novelist

Edward P. **Bradbury**: Michael Moorcock (1939-) Eng. SF writer

Scott **Brady**: Gerald Tierney (1924-) U.S. film actor

June **Brae**: June Bear (1917-) Eng. ballet dancer

John **Braham**: John Abraham (?1774-1856) Eng. opera singer

Ernest **Bramah**: Ernest Bramah Smith (1868-1942) Br. author

Donato **Bramante**: Pascuccio d'Antonio (1444-1514) It. architect, painter

Christianna **Brand**: Mary Christianna Milne Lewis (1907-) Eng. detective writer

Max **Brand**: Frederick Schiller Faust (1892-1944) U.S. novelist

Henry **Brandon**: Henry Kleinbach (1910-) U.S. film actor

°Willy **Brandt**: Herbert Ernst Karl Frahm (1913-) West Ger. politician

°**Brassaï**: Gyula Halész (1899-) Hung.-born Fr. photographer

Pierre **Brasseur**: Albert Espinasse (1905-1972) Fr. stage, film actor, playwright

Wellman **Braud**: Wellman Breaux (1891-1966) U.S. black jazz bassist

Hans **Breitmann**: Charles Godfrey Leland (1824-1903) U.S. humorous writer, editor

Marie **Brema**: Minny Fehrmann (1856-1925) Eng. opera singer

Edith **Brendall**: Eddy Charly Bertin (1944-) Ger.-born Belg. writer of horror stories

Evelyn **Brent**: Mary Elizabeth Riggs (1899-1975) U.S. film actress

George **Brent**: George Brent Nolan (1904-1979) Ir.-born U.S. film actor

Romney **Brent**: Romulo Larralde (1902-1976) Mexican-born U.S. stage, film actor, dramatist

Edward **Breon**: Edmund MacLaverty (1882-1951) Ir. stage, film actor, working in U.S. and U.K.

Ford **Brereton**: Samuel Rutherford Crockett (1860-1914) Sc. novelist, journalist

Jeremy **Brett**: Peter Jeremy William Huggins (1935-) Eng. stage, film actor

James **Brian**: Arthur George Street (1892-1966) Eng. author of books on country life

Mary **Brian**: Louise Dantzler (1908-) U.S. film actress [27]

°Fanny **Brice**: Fannie Borach (1891-1951) U.S. singer, comedienne

Ann **Bridge**: [Lady] Mary Dalling O'Malley, née Sanders (1891-1974) Eng. novelist

Bonar **Bridge**: [Rev.] W W Tulloch (1846-1920) Sc. biographer, editor

James **Bridie**: Osborne Henry Mavor (1888-1951) Sc. playwright [15]

Bright Eyes: Susette La Flesche (1854-1903) U.S.-Indian writer, lecturer

Carl **Brisson**: Carl Pedersen (1895-1958) Dan. film actor, working in U.K.

Elton **Britt**: James Britt Baker (1917-1972) U.S. country singer

May **Britt**: Maybritt Wilkens (1933-) Swe. film actress [29]

Colonel **Britton**: Douglas E Ritchie (1905-) Br. radio news director

Barbara **Britton**: Barbara Brantingham Czukor (1920-) U.S. film actress

Geffery **Broadbottom**: Philip Dormer Stanhope [Earl of Chesterfield] (1694-1773) Eng. statesman

Lynn **Brock**: Alister McAllister (1877-1943) Ir. author

Lea **Brodie**: Lea Dregham (1951-) Eng. TV actress

Steve **Brodie**: John Stevens (1919-) U.S. film actor

James **Brolin**: James Bruderlin (1940-) U.S. film, TV actor

John **Bromfield**: Farron Bromfield (1922-) U.S. film actor

°Charles **Bronson**: Charles Buchinski (1922-) U.S. film actor

Hillary **Brooke**: Beatrice Peterson (1916-) U.S. film actress

Elkie **Brooks**: Elaine Bookbinder (1945-) Eng. pop singer

Geraldine **Brooks**: Geraldine Stroock (1925-1977) U.S. film actress [27]

Leslie **Brooks**: Lesli Gettman (1922-) U.S. film actress

°Mel **Brooks**: Melvin Kaminsky (1927-) U.S. film comedy writer, producer

Phyllis **Brooks**: Phyllis Weiler (1914-) U.S. film actress

Mr. **Brown**: William Makepeace Thackeray (1811-1863) Eng. novelist

Mrs. **Brown**: George Rose (1817-1882) Eng. humorous writer, entertainer

Arthur **Brown**: Arthur Wilton (1944-) Eng. rock musician, comedian

Georgia **Brown**: Lillian Klot (1933-) Eng. stage, film, TV actress

Teddy **Brown**: Abraham Himmebrand (1900-1946) U.S. music hall instrumentalist

Vanessa **Brown**: Smylla Brind (1928-) U.S. film actress

Coral **Browne**: Coral Brown (1913-) Australian stage actress

Henriette **Browne**: Sophie de Saux, née de Boutellier (1829-1901) Fr. painter, etcher

Matthew **Browne**: William Brightly Rands (1823-1882) Br. writer of poems, fairy tales for children

H. **Brownrigg**: Douglas William Jarrold (1803-1857) Eng. author, playwright, humorist

Thomas **Brown** the Younger: Thomas Moore (1779-1852) Ir. poet, satirist

Arthur Loring **Bruce**: Francis Welch Crowninshield (1872-) U.S. editor

David **Bruce**: Marden McBroom (1914-1976) U.S. film actor

°Lenny **Bruce**: Leonard Alfred Schneider (1925-1966) U.S. comedian

Virginia **Bruce**: Helen Virginia Briggs (1910-) U.S. film actress

Erik **Bruhn**: Belton Evers (1928-) Dan. ballet dancer, director

Henri **Brulard**: °Stendhal

°Dora **Bryan**: Dora May Lawton, née Broadbent (1923-) Eng. stage, film, TV comedienne

Jane **Bryan**: Jane O'Brien (1918-) U.S. film actress

Rudy **Bryans**: Bernard Godet (c.1945-) Fr. ballet dancer

James **Bryce**: Alexander Anderson (1862-1949) Sc. novelist

Bryher: Annie Winifred Ellerman (1894-) Eng. novelist

°Yul **Brynner**: Youl Bryner (1915-) U.S. film actor

B.T.B.: [Lord] Basil Blackwood (1870-) Br. illustrator

Bubbles: John Sublett (c.1900-) U.S. black tap-dancer

°Martin **Bucer**: Martin Kuhhorn (1491-1551) Ger. Protestant reformer [31]

°**Buffalo Bill**: William Frederick Cody (1846-1917) U.S. scout, showman

°Lawsona **Bukowski**: Ruth Davies (1965-) Eng. child TV actress, daughter of writer Beryl Bainbridge

Bunny: Carl Emil Schultze (1866-1939) U.S. cartoonist

°Ned **Buntline**: Edward Zane Carroll Judson (1823-1886) U.S. adventurer, trapper, author

Eleanor **Burford**: Eleanor Alice Burford Hibbert (1906-) Eng. novelist

David **Burg**: Alexander Dolberg (1933-) Russ.-born Eng. writer, translator from Russ.

Anthony **Burgess**: John Burgess Wilson (1917-) Eng. novelist, critic

Betty **Burke**: Charles Edward Stuart (1720-1788) Sc. prince ("The Young Pretender")

°Billie **Burke**: Mary William Ethelbert Appleton Burke (1885-1970) U.S. stage, film actress

Fielding **Burke**: Olive Dargan, née Tilford (1869-1963) U.S. poet, novelist

Jonathan **Burn**: Henry Jonas Jonathan Burn-Forti (1939-) Eng. stage, TV actor

George **Burns**: Nathan Birnbaum (1896-) U.S. stage, TV comedian

Katherine **Burns**: Katharine Hepburn (1909-) U.S. stage, film actress

Tommy **Burns**: Noah Brusso (1881-1955) Can. heavyweight boxer

Burton Junior: Charles Lamb (1775-1834) Eng. essayist, critic

°Richard **Burton**: Richard Walter Jenkins (1925-) Welsh stage, film actor

Robert **Burton**: Nathaniel Crouch (?1632-?1725) Eng. miscellaneous author

°[Sir] Alexander **Bustamente**: William Alexander Clarke (1884-1977) Jamaican prime minister

The **Busy-Body**: Benjamin Franklin (1706-1790) U.S. statesman, scientist, philosopher

Hilda **Butsova**: Hilda Boot (-1976) Eng. ballet dancer

William **Butterworth**: Henry Schroeder (1774-1853) Eng. topographer, engraver

Myra **Buttle**: Victor William Williams Saunders Purcell (1896-1965) Br. author of books on China

°Red **Buttons**: Aaron Schwatt (1918-) U.S. stage, screen, TV comedian

°Max **Bygraves**: Walter William Bygraves (1922-) Eng. comedian

Robert **Byr**: Karl Robert Emmerich von Bayer (1935-1902) Austr. novelist, writer on military subjects

James **Byrne**: Edward William Garnett (1868-1937) Br. writer, literary adviser

Edd **Byrnes**: Edward Breitenberger (1933-) U.S. juvenile TV actor

Marion **Byron**: Miriam Bilenkin (1911-) U.S. film actress

Walter **Byron**: Walter Butler (1899-) U.S. film actor

The **Bystander**: Goldwin Smith (1823-1910) Eng. historian, publicist, working in Canada

C

Roy **C.**: Roy Charles Hammond (1943-) U.S. pop singer

Fernan **Caballero**: Cecilia Böhl de Faber (1796-1877) Sp. novelist

Bruce **Cabot**: Étienne Pelissier de Pujac (1904-1972) U.S. film actor

Susan **Cabot**: Harriet Shapiro (1927-) U.S. film actress

[Sir] Stanford **Cade**: Stanford Kadinsky (1895-1973) Russ.-born Br. surgeon

°**Cadenus**: Jonathan Swift (1667-1745) Ir. satirist, cleric

George **Cadwalader**, Gent.: George Bubb Dodington [Baron Melcombe] (1691-1762) Eng. politician, pamphleteer, verse writer

Caffarelli: Gaetano Majorano (1710-1783) It. male soprano

Count Alessandro di **Cagliostro**: Giuseppe Balsamo (1743-1795) It. impostor, magician

André **Calleux**: André de Cayeux de Sénarpent (1907-) Fr. geologist

°Marti **Caine**: Lynda Denise Crapper (1945-) Eng. TV singer, entertainer

°Michael **Caine**: Maurice Joseph Micklewhite (1933-) Eng. film, TV actor

Calamity Jane: Martha Burk (or Cannary) (?1852-1903) U.S. popular heroine of the West

Calchas: James Louis Garvin (1868-1947) Eng. newspaper editor

John William **Calcraft**: John William Cole (-) Eng. writer

Taylor **Caldwell**: Janet Miriam Taylor Reback, née Caldwell (1900-) Eng.-born U.S. novelist

°Louis **Calhern**: Carl Henry Vogt (1895-1956) U.S. stage, film actor

Rory **Calhoun**: Francis Timothy Durgin (1922-) U.S. film actor

Caliban: [1] Robert Williams Buchanan (1841-1901) Eng. poet, novelist. [2] Auguste Émile Bergerat (1845-1923) Fr. poet, novelist, dramatist

Caligula: Gaius Julius Caesar (12-41 A.D.) Roman emperor [33]

Calixtus II: Guido di Borgogne (?-1124) It. pope

Calixtus III: Alfonso de Borgia (1378-1458) Sp. pope

Michael **Callan**: Martin Caliniff (1935-) U.S. dancer, film actor

Colonel Tony **Callan**: Costas Giorgiou (1955-1976) Gk. mercenary leader, exiled to Angola

°Maria **Callas**: Cecilia Sophia Anna Maria Meneghini, née Kalogeropoulos (1923-1977) U.S. opera singer, of Gk. parentage

Joseph **Calleia**: Joseph Spurin-Calleja (1897-1976) Maltese-born U.S. film actor

Callum Beg: [Captain] J G O Mack (1872-) Br. writer on military matters

Emma **Calvé**: Rosa Noémie Emma Calvet de Roquer (1858-1942) Fr. opera singer

Mary **Calvert**: Mary Danby (1941-) Eng. novelist, writer of horror stories

°Phyllis **Calvert**: Phyllis Bickle (1915-) Eng. stage, film, TV actress

Corinne **Calvet**: Corinne Dibos (1925-)

Fr. film actress

Marie **Camargo**: Marie Anne de Cupis (1710-1770) Belg. ballet dancer

Elizabeth **Cambridge**: Barbara K. Hodges, née Webber (1893-1949) Br. novelist, short story writer

John **Cameron**: Archibald Gordon Macdonell (1895-1941) Sc. author

Rod **Cameron**: Nathan Cox (1910-) Can. film actor, appearing in U.S. films

Camillus: [1] Alexander Hamilton (1757-1804) U.S. statesman, pamphleteer, author. [2] Fisher Ames (1758-1808) U.S. statesman, orator, political writer

Angus **Campbell**: Ronald Chetwynd-Hayes (1919-) Eng. writer of horror fiction

Herbert Edward **Campbell**: Herbert Edward Story (1844-1904) Br. music hall artiste

Judy **Campbell**: Judy Birkin, née Gamble (1916-) Eng. stage, screen, TV actress

Mrs. Patrick **Campbell**: Beatrice Stella Campbell, née Tanner (1865-1940) Eng. stage actress

[Sir] Henry **Campbell-Bannerman**: Henry Campbell (1836-1908) Sc.-born Br. prime minister

°**Cañadas**: Henry Higgins (1944-1978) Colombian-born Eng. bullfighter, working in Spain

Canaletto: Giovanni Antonio Canal(e) (1697-1768) It. painter [33]

Ann **Candler**: Ann More (1740-1814) Eng. poet (the "Suffolk cottager")

Denis **Cannan**: Denis Pullein-Thompson (1919-) Br. actor, playwright

Charles **Cannell**: Evelyn Charles Vivian (1882-1947) Eng. writer of adventure, detective stories

Effie **Canning**: Effie Carlton, née Crockett (1857-1940) U.S. stage actress

Dyan **Cannon**: Samile Diane Friesen (1938-) U.S. film actress

Freddie **Cannon**: Frederick Anthony Picariello (1940-) U.S. rock musician

°**Cantinflas**: Mario Moreno Reyes (1913-) Mexican clown, bullfighter, stage and film comedian

Eddie **Cantor**: Edward Israel Iskowitz (1892-1964) U.S. singer, entertainer, film actor

°Robert **Capa**: Andrei Friedmann (1913-1954) Hung.-born U.S. photojournalist

Truman **Capote**: Truman Persons (1924-) U.S. writer [34]

Al **Capp**: Alfred Gerald Caplin (1909-1979) U.S. cartoonist, originator of "Li'l Abner" strip

Capucine: Germaine Lefebvre (1933-) Fr. stage, film actress

°**Caran d'Ache**: Emmanuel Poiré (1858-1909) Fr. caricaturist

Caravaggio: Michelangelo Merisi (da Caravaggio) (1573-1610) It. painter [41]

Francis **Carco**: François Marie Alexandre Carcopino-Tussoli (1886-1958) Fr. poet, writer

Cardini: Richard Valentine Pitchford (1895-1973) Welsh magician

Carette: Julien Carette (1897-1966) Fr. film actor

°Joyce **Carey**: Joyce Lawrence (1898-) Br. stage, film actress

Madame **Cariba**: Kate Williams (1921-) Eng. clairvoyant

Richard **Carle**: Charles Carleton (1871-1941) U.S. film actor

Kitty **Carlisle**: Catherine Holzman (1915-) U.S. opera singer, film actress [27]

Carlo-Rim: Jean-Marius Richard (1905-) Fr. film writer, director

Carlos: Illich Ramirez Sánchez (1946-) Venezuelan terrorist, anti-Israeli killer

Carlota: Marie-Charlotte-Amélie-Augustine-Victoire-Clémentine-Léopoldine (1840-1927) Belg.-born empress of Mexico [29]

Felix **Carmen**: Frank Dempster Sherman (1860-1916) U.S. poet [45]

°**Carmen Sylva**: Elizabeth [queen of Romania] née Pauline Elisabeth Ottilie Luise [Princess of Wied] (1843-1916) Rom. verse, prose writer

Sue **Carol**: Evelyn Lederer (1907-) U.S. film actress

Martine **Carole**: Maryse Mourer (1921-1967) Fr. film actress

Augustus **Carp**: [Sir] Henry Howarth

Bashford (1880-1961) Br. novelist, physician

Catharine **Carr**: Rosalind Herschel Seymour, née Wade (1909-) Eng. novelist

Jane **Carr**: Rita Brunstrom (1909-1957) Br. film actress

Philippa **Carr**: Eleanor Alice Burford Hibbert (1906-) Eng. author of historical romances

Vikki **Carr**: Florencia Bisenta de Casillas Martinez Cardona (1938-) U.S. pop singer

Edward **Carrick**: Edward Anthony Craig (1905-) Br. art director, film actor

C.H. **Carroder**: Walter John Tripp (1874-) Br. writer, poet

Norman **Carrol**: Sydney Edward Brandon (1890-) Eng. music hall comedian

S. **Carrol**: Susanna(h) Centlivre, née Freeman (or Rawkins) (1667-1722) Eng. dramatist, actress

Andrea **Carroll**: Andrea Lee DeCapite (1946-) U.S. pop singer

Elisabeth **Carroll**: Elisabeth Pfister (1937-) U.S. ballet dancer

°Joan **Carroll**: Joan Felt (1932-) U.S. child film actress

John **Carroll**: Julian la Faye (1908-) U.S. film actor, singer

°Lewis **Carroll**: Charles Lutwidge Dodgson (1832-1898) Eng. children's writer

Madeleine **Carroll**: Marie Madeleine Bernadette O'Carroll (1906-) Br. film actress

Nancy **Carroll**: Ann La Hiff (1905-1965) U.S. film actress

Sydney W. **Carroll**: George Frederick Carl Whiteman (1877-1958) Australian-born Br. stage actor, critic, theatre manager

Arthur **Carron**: Arthur Cox (1900-1967) Eng. opera singer

°Jasper **Carrott**: Robert Davies (1942-) Eng. comedian

Anthony **Carson**: Peter Brooke (1907-) Eng.-born U.S. thriller writer

Jeannie **Carson**: Jean Shufflebottom (1928-) Br. film actress [14]

John **Carson**: John Derek Carson Parker (1927-) Br. stage, TV actor

Bruce **Carter**: Richard Alexander Hough (1922-) Eng. children's writer, publisher

Helena **Carter**: Helen Rickerts (1923-) U.S. film actress

Janis **Carter**: Janis Dremann (1921-) U.S. film actress

Mrs. Leslie **Carter**: Caroline Louise Dudley (1862-1937) U.S. stage actress

°Nick **Carter**: [1] John R. Coryell (1848-1924) U.S. popular fiction writer. [2] Thomas Chalmers Harbough (1849-1924) U.S. popular fiction writer. [3] Frederick Van Rensselaer Dey (?1861-1922) U.S. popular fiction writer

Anna **Carteret**: Anna Wilkinson (1942-) Br. stage actress

Richard Claude **Carton**: Richard Claude Critchett (1856-1928) Br. actor, dramatist

Louise **Carver**: Louise Spilger Murray (1868-1956) U.S. film actress

Lynn **Carver**: Virginia Reid Sampson (1909-1955) U.S. film actress

Ivan **Caryll**: Felix Tilken (1861-1921) Belg. operetta composer, working in U.K. and U.S.

Maria **Casares**: Maria Casares Quiroga (1922-) Fr.-Sp. film actress

°Justin **Case**: Hugh Barnett Cave (1910-) Eng.-born U.S. horror fiction writer

Bill **Casey**: William Weldon (1909-) U.S. black blues singer, guitarist

Sir Edwin **Caskoden**: Charles Major (1856-1913) U.S. novelist

°**Cassandra**: [Sir] William Neil Connor (1909-1967) Eng. columnist

Cassandre: Adolphe Jean-Marie Mouron (1901-) Russ.-born Fr. graphic artist [38]

William **Castle**: William Schloss (1914-) U.S. horror film director

°Butch **Cassidy**: Robert Le Roy Parker (1866-1909) U.S. bank robber

Billie **Cassin**: °Joan Crawford

Cassius: Michael Foot (1913-) Eng. politician

Castil-Blaze: François-Henri-Joseph Blaze (1784-1857) Fr. musician, ballet critic

Frances **Castle**: Evelyn Barbara

Leader, née Blackburn (1898-) Eng. novelist, playwright

Irene **Castle**: Irene Foote (1893-1969) U.S. cabaret dancer, teaming with Vernon Castle

Vernon Blythe **Castle**: Vernon Blythe (1885-1918) Br. cabaret dancer, aviator

Harry **Castlemon**: Charles Austin Fosdick (1842-1915) U.S. writer of adventure stories for boys

[Saint] **Catherine**: Caterina de Ricci (earlier Alessandra dei Ricci) (1522-1590) It. mystic

[Saint] **Catherine of Bologna**: Caterina de' Vigri (1413-1463) It. abbess, writer

[Saint] **Catherine of Genoa**: Caterina Fieschi Adorno (1447-1510) It. mystic

[Saint] **Catherine of Siena**: Caterina Benincasa (1347-1380) It. mystic

°**Cato**: [1] William Smith (1727-1803) Sc. educator, minister, working in U.S. [2] Michael Foote (1913-) Eng. politician. + Humphrey Frank Owen (1905-) Eng. journalist, author, broadcaster. + Peter Dunsmore Howard (1908-1965) Eng. publisher, writer

Christopher **Caudwell**: Christopher St. John Sprigg (1907-1937) Br. Marxist writer [16]

Christopher **Caustic**: Thomas Green Fessenden (1771-1837) U.S. author, inventor, lawyer, editor

C.P. **Cavafy**: Konstaninos Petrou Kavaphes (1863-1933) Gk. poet

Alberto **Cavalcanti**: Alberto de Almeida-Cavalcanti (1897-1926) Brazilian film actor

Pier Francesco **Cavalli**: Pier Francesco Calett Bruni (1602-1676) It. opera composer

Cavendish: Henry Jones (1831-1899) Br. authority on whist

Kay **Cavendish**: Kathleen Murray (-) Br. classical pianist, crooner, broadcaster

Pigistratus **Caxton**: [Lord] Edward George Earle Lytton Bulwer Lytton (1803-1873) Eng. novelist, playwright, statesman

Davenant **Cecil**: [Rev.] Derwent Coleridge (1800-1883) Eng. schoolmaster and author

Henry **Cecil**: Henry Cecil Leon (1902-1976) Br. author, playwright

Ceiriog: John Ceiriog Hughes (1832-1887) Welsh poet, folk musicologist

Celestine II: Guido di Città di Castello (?-1144) It. pope

Celestine III: Giacinto Bobo-Orsini (c.1106-1198) It. pope

Celestine IV: Goffredo Castiglioni (?-1241) It. pope

Celestine V: Pietro da Morrone (c.1209-1296) It. pope

Céline: Odette Sansom (1912-) Fr.-born Br. wartime agent

Louis-Ferdinand **Céline**: Louis Fuch Destouches (1894-1961) Fr. novelist

Cem: C E Martin (-) U.S. cartoonist

Blaise **Cendrars**: Frédéric Sauser-Hall (1887-1961) Fr. novelist, poet

Luigia **Cerale**: Luigia Cerallo (1859-1937) It. ballet dancer

C.W. **Ceram**: Kurt W Marek (1915-) Ger.-born U.S. writer, archaeologist

°**Cerberus**: [Sir] John Rupert Colville (1915-) Eng. diplomat, author

Frederick **Cerny**: Frederick Guthrie (1833-1886) Eng. physicist

Cham: [Comte] Amédée de Noé (1819-1879) Fr. caricaturist

Champfleury: Jules-François-Félix Husson (1821-1889) Fr. novelist, journalist

Gene **Chandler**: Eugene Dixon (1937-) U.S. pop singer, record producer

Jeff **Chandler**: Ira Grossel (1918-1961) U.S. stage, film actor

Fay **Chandos**: Irene Maude Swatridge, née Mossop (c.1905-?) Eng. novelist

Martin **Chapender**: H M Jones (c.1876-1905) Eng. magician

Jacques **Chardonne**: Jacques Boutelleau (1884-1968) Fr. novelist

°**Cyd Charisse**: Tula Ellice Finklea (1923-) U.S. film actress, dancer

Bobby **Charles**: Robert Charles Guidry (1938-) U.S. black rock songwriter

Pamela **Charles**: Pamela Foster (1932-) Eng. stage actress, singer

Ray **Charles**: Ray Charles Robinson (1932-) U.S. black popular singer

Charlotte-Elizabeth: Charlotte Elizabeth Tonna (1790-1846) Br. author

of religious and children's books
°John **Charlton**: Martin Charlton Woodhouse (1932-) Eng. author
Charo: Maria del Rosario Pilar Martinez Molina Baeza (1948-) Can. folk singer
R.D. **Charques**: Richard D Tcherkez (-1959) Russ.-born Br. writer of books on Russia
Leslie **Charteris**: Leslie Charles Bowyer Yin (1907-) Br.-born U.S. crime novelist
Alida **Chase**: Alida Anderson (1951-) Australian ballet dancer
Beatrice **Chase**: Olive Katharine Parr (1874-1911) Eng. novelist
Charlie **Chase**: Charles Parrott (1893-1940) U.S. film comedian
James Hadley **Chase**: René Raymond (1906-) Eng. thriller writer
Geoffrey **Chater**: Geoffrey Robinson (1921-) Eng. stage actor
Daniel **Chaucer**: °Ford Madox Ford (*q.v.*)
Mary **Chavelita**: Mary Chavelita Dunne (1860-1945) Australian novelist
°**Chubby Checker**: Ernest Evans (1941-) U.S. black pop musician
Cheiro: [Count] Louis Hamon (1866-1936) Br. writer on palmistry
Antosha **Chekhonte**: Anton Pavlovich Chekhov (1860-1904) Russ. short story writer, dramatist
Pierre **Chenal**: Pierre Cohen (1903-) Fr. film director
Cher: Cherilyn Sarkasia Lalier (1946-) U.S. pop singer, teaming with °Sonny (*q.v.*) [29]
Rose **Chéri**: Rose-Marie Cizos (1824-1861) Fr. actress
Gwen **Cherrell**: Gwen Chambers (1926-) Eng. stage actress
Weatherby **Chesney**: Charles John Cutliffe Wright Hyne (1865-1944) Eng. fiction writer
Peter **Cheyney**: Reginald Evelyn Peter Southhouse-Cheyney (1896-1951) Ir. crime novelist
°**Chiang Ch'ing**: Li Yun-ho (1913-) Chinese wife of Chairman Mao
Walter **Chiari**: Walter Annichiarico (1924-) It. film comedian

Charles B. **Childs**: C Vernon Frost (1903-) Eng. mystery short story writer
Alice **Cholmondeley**: Elizabeth (*q.v.*)
Linda **Christian**: Blanca Rosa Welter (1923-) Mexican film actress
Christian-Jaque: Christian Albert François Maudet (1904-) Fr. film writer, director
Lou **Christie**: Lugee Salo (1943-) U.S. male pop singer
John **Christopher**: Christopher Sam Youd (1922-) Eng. SF short story, novel writer
Korney Ivanovich **Chukovsky**: Nikolay Vasilyevich Korneychuk (1882-1969) Russ. critic, poet
°**Chung Ling Soo**: William Ellsworth Campbell (1861-1918) U.S. conjuror
Marcus Tullius **Cicero**: William Melmoth the Elder (1666-1743) Eng. religious writer, lawyer
The **Cid**: Rodrigo Diaz de Bivar (?1040-1099) Sp. national hero
°**Cimabue**: Bencivieni di Pepo (before 1251-1302) It. painter, mosaicist
Paul **Cinquevalli**: Paul Kestner (c.1860-1918) Pol.-born U.S. juggler
°**A Citizen of New York**: Alexander Hamilton (1737-1804) U.S. statesman. + James Madison (1751-1836) U.S. president. + John Jay (1745-1829) U.S. jurist, statesman
The **Citizen of the World**: Oliver Goldsmith (1728-1774) Eng. poet, playwright, novelist
René **Clair**: René-Lucien Chomette (1898-1981) Fr. film director
Ina **Claire**: Ina Fagan (1892-) U.S. stage, screen actress
Mlle **Clairon**: Claire-Josephe-Hippolyte Léris (1723-1803) Fr. tragic actress [29]
Ada **Clare**: Jane McElheney (1836-1874) U.S. writer of "passion" poetry and fiction
Fitzroy **Clarence**: William Makepeace Thackeray (1811-1863) Eng. novelist
Claribel: Charlotte Alington-Barnard (1830-1869) Ir. popular ballad writer
Clarín: Leopoldo Alas (1852-1901) Sp. novelist, critic

°**Clarinda**: Agnes Maclehose, née Craig (1759-1841) Sc. correspondent of Sylvander (*q.v.*)

The Rev. C.C. **Clark**: [Sir] Richard Phillips (1768-1840) Eng. writer

Dane **Clark**: Bernard Zanville (1913-) U.S. film actor

°The Rev. T. **Clark**: John Galt (1779-1839) Sc. novelist

John **Clarke**: Richard Cromwell (1626-1712) Eng. soldier, politician

Claude **Lorrain**: Claude Gellée (1600-1682) Fr. landscape painter

Mrs. Mary **Clavers**: Caroline Matilda Kirkland, née Stansbury (1801-1864) U.S. short story writer, novelist

Bertha M. **Clay**: Charlotte Monica Braeme (1836-1884) Eng. author of romantic novels

Lucie **Clayton**: Evelyn Florence Kark, née Gordine (1928-) Eng. fashion designer

Claudius **Clear**: [Sir] William Robertson Nicoll (1851-1923) Sc. writer

°**Jedediah Cleishbotham**: [Sir] Walter Scott (1771-1832) Sc. poet, novelist

Clement II: Suidger (?-1047) It. pope

Clement III: Paolo Scolari (?-1191) It. pope

Clement IV: Guy le Gros Foulques (?-1268) Fr. pope

Clement V: Bertrand de Got (c.1260-1314) Fr. pope

Clement VI: Pierre Roger (1291-1352) Fr. pope

Clement VII: Giulio de' Medici (1478-1534) It. pope

Clement VIII: Ippolito Aldobrandini (1536-1605) It. pope

Clement IX: Giulio Rospigliosi (1600-1669) It. pope

Clement X: Emilio Altieri (1590-1676) It. pope

Clement XI: Giovanni Francesco Albani (1649-1721) It. pope

Clement XII: Lorenzo Corsini (1652-1740) It. pope

Clement XIII: Carlo della Torre Rezzonico (1693-1769) It. pope

Clement XIV: Giovanni Vincenzo Antonio Ganganelli (1705-1774) It. pope **[50]**

Hal **Clement**: Harry Clement Stubbs

(1922-) U.S. SF writer

Van **Cliburn**: Harvey Lavan Cliburn, Jr. (1934-) U.S. pianist

E. **Clerihew**: Edmund Clerihew Bentley (1875-1956) Eng. writer, inventor of the *clerihew*

Jimmy **Cliff**: James Chambers (1948-) Jamaican pop singer ("reggae's first superstar")

Charles **Clifford**: William Henry Ireland (1777-1835) Eng. forger of Shakespearean manuscripts

Martin **Clifford**: Frank Richards (*q.v.*)

Patsy **Cline**: Virginia Patterson Hensley (1932-1963) U.S. country singer

Walter **Clinton**: William Henry Davenport Adams (1828-1891) Eng. writer, editor

Clio: [1] Joseph Addison (1672-1719) Eng. poet, dramatist, essayist. [2] Thomas Rickman (1761-1834) Eng. bookseller, reformer

Colin **Clive**: Clive Greig (1898-1937) Br. film actor, working in U.S.

Kitty **Clive**: Catherine Raftor (1711-1785) Eng. actress

Clodion: Claude Michel (1738-1814) Fr. sculptor

°Anacharsis **Cloots**: Jean-Baptiste du Val-de-Grâce [baron de Cloots] (1755-1794) Fr. revolutionary

°Upton **Close**: Josef Washington Hall (1894-1960) U.S. journalist, novelist

Frank **Clune**: Francis Patrick (1909-1971) Australian author

Captain Cuthbert **Clutterbuck**: [Sir] Walter Scott (1771-1832) Sc. poet, novelist

Lee J. **Cobb**: Leo Jacob (1911-1976) U.S. stage, film actor

William **Cobb**: Jules Hippolyte Lermina (1839-1915) Fr. novelist

Tom **Cobbleigh**: Walter Raymond (1852-1931) Eng. novelist

°Charles **Coburn**: Colin Whitton McCallum (1852-1945) Sc.-born Br. music hall comedian

Merlino **Coccajo**: Teofilo Folengo (1491-1544) It. poet

Pindar **Cockloft**: William Irving (1766-1821) U.S. poet

°**Coco**: Nikolai Poliakov (1900-1974) Russ.-born Eng. clown

Lew **Cody**: Louis Coté (1884-1934)

Fr.-born U.S. film actor

Captain **Coe**: Tom Cosgrove (1902-1978) Eng. sports writer, editor

Joshua **Coffin**: Henry Wadsworth Longfellow (1807-1882) U.S. poet

Émile **Cohl**: Émile Courtet (1857-1938) Fr. film cartoonist

Claudette **Colbert**: Lily Claudette Chauchoin (1905-) Fr. stage, film actress, working in U.S. [63]

Coldstreamer: Harry Jocelyn Clive Graham (1874-1936) Eng. poet, playwright, writer

Nat King **Cole**: Nathaniel Adams Coles (1919-1965) U.S. singer, jazz pianist

Bill **Coleman**: William Coleman Johnson (1904-) U.S. black jazz trumpeter

Manning **Coles**: Adelaide Frances Oke Manning (1891-1959) Eng. spy, detective novelist. + Cyril Henry Coles (1901-1965) Eng. spy, detective novelist, her husband.

°**Colette**: Sidonie-Gabrielle Claudine Colette (1873-1954) Fr. novelist

Bonar **Colleano**: Bonar Sullivan (1924-1958) U.S. film actor

Constance **Collier**: Laura Constance Hardie (1878-1955) Eng. stage, film actress

Patience **Collier**: Rene Ritcher (1910-) Eng. stage actress

Harry **Collingwood**: W J C Lancaster (1851-c.1924) Eng. writer of boys' stories

Michael **Collins**: Dennis Lynds (1924-) U.S. mystery writer, journalist

Sam **Collins**: Samuel Thomas Collins Vegg (1827-1865) Eng. music hall singer, manager

Tom **Collins**: Joseph Furphy (1843-1912) Australian novelist

°Carlo **Collodi**: Carlo Lorenzini (1826-1890) It. writer

Bud **Collyer**: Clayton Johnson Heermanse, Jr. (1908-1969) U.S. TV personality

June **Collyer**: Dorothy Heermanse (1907-1968) U.S. film actress

Colon: Joseph Dennie (1768-1812) U.S. essayist, satirist

Christopher **Columbus**: Joseph C Morris (1903-) U.S. black jazz drummer, bandleader

Silas Tomkyn **Comberback**: Samuel Taylor Coleridge (1772-1834) Eng. poet, critic

Betty **Comden**: Elizabeth Kyle, née Cohen (1918-) U.S. film, stage writer, actress

Jan Amos **Comenius**: Jan Amos Komenský (1592-1670) Czech educationist, Moravian bishop

Cuthbert **Comment**: Abraham Tucker (1705-1774) Eng. moralist

Perry **Como**: Nick Perido (1912-) It.-U.S. crooner, film actor

Fay **Compton**: Virginia Lillian Emmeline Compton (1894-1978) Br. stage actress

Frances Snow **Compton**: Henry Brooks Adams (1838-1918) U.S. historian, novelist

Joyce **Compton**: Eleanor Hunt (1907-) U.S. film actress

Comus: Robert Michael Ballantyne (1825-1894) Sc. novelist for boys

°**Confucius**: K'ung Fu-tzu (c.551-479 B.C.) Chinese philosopher

Chester **Conklin**: Jules Cowles (1888-1971) U.S. film actor

F. Norreys **Connell**: Conal Holmes O'Connell O'Riordan (1874-1948) It. playwright, novelist

John **Connell**: John Henry Robertson (1909-1965) Br. novelist, biographer

Rearden **Conner**: Patrick Reardon Connor (1907-) Ir. novelist, short story writer [30]

Sean **Connery**: Thomas Connery (1930-) Sc. film actor [14]

John Jervis **Connington**: Alfred Walter Stewart (1880-1947) Ir. writer of detective novels

°Ralph **Connor**: Charles William Gordon (1860-1937) Can. writer of religious novels

Michael **Connors**: Kreker Jay Michael Ohanian (1925-) U.S. film, TV actor, of Armenian parentage

Owen **Conquest**: Frank Richards (q.v.)

Con **Conrad**: Conrad K. Dober (1893-1938) U.S. songwriter

Joseph **Conrad**: Jozef Teodor Konrad Naleçz Korzeniowski (1857-1924) Pol.-born novelist in English [26]

Robert **Conrad**: Conrad Robert Falk (1935-) U.S. TV, film actor

Will **Conroy**: Harry Champion (1866-1942) Eng. music hall comedian

Michael **Constantine**: Constantine Joanides (1927-) Gk.-born U.S. TV, film actor

Albert **Conti**: Albert de Conti Cedassamre (1887-) Austr. film actor

Gloria **Contreras**: Carmen Gloria Contreras Roeniger (1934-) Mexican ballet dancer, teacher

Gary **Conway**: Gareth Carmody (1938-) U.S. film, TV actor

Hugh **Conway**: Frederick John Fargus (1847-1895) Eng. novelist

Tom **Conway**: Thomas Sanders (1904-1967) Eng. film actor

William Augustus **Conway**: William Augustus Rugg (1789-1828) Ir. stage actor

Coo-ee: William Sylvester Walker (1846-?) Australian novelist

Susan **Coolidge**: Sarah Chauncey Woolsey (1835-1905) U.S. writer of books for girls

°Alice **Cooper**: Vincent Furnier (1948-) U.S. pop singer

Frank **Cooper**: William Gilmore Sims (1806-1870) U.S. novelist

°Gary **Cooper**: Frank J. Cooper (1901-1961) U.S. film actor

Jefferson **Cooper**: Gardner Francis Fox (1911-) U.S. writer of historical romances

William **Cooper**: Harry Summerfield Hoff (1910-) Ir. novelist

Joan **Copeland**: Joan Maxine Miller (1922-) U.S. stage actress, singer

Jean **Coralli**: Jean Coralli Peracini (1779-1854) It. ballet dancer, working in France

Coram: Thomas Whitaker (1883-1937) Eng. ventriloquist

°Le **Corbusier**: Charles Édouard Jeanneret (1887-1965) Fr. architect, of Swiss origin

Ellen **Corby**: Ellen Hansen (1913-) U.S. film actress

Alex **Cord**: Alexander Viespi (1931-) It.-born U.S. film actor

°Mara **Corday**: Marilyn Watts (1932-) U.S. film actress

°El **Cordobés**: Manuel Benítez Pérez (c.1936-) Sp. bullfighter

Raymond **Cordy**: Raymond Cordiaux (1898-1956) Fr. film comedian

°Marie **Corelli**: Mary Mackay (1855-1924) Br. novelist

Jill **Corey**: Norma Jean Speranza (1935-) U.S. pop singer

Lewis **Corey**: Louis C. Fraina (1894-1953) U.S. Marxist critic

Don **Cornell**: Dominico Francisco Connello (1921-) U.S. popular singer

°**Corno di Bassetto**: George Bernard Shaw (1856-1950) Ir. dramatist, critic, novelist

Barry **Cornwall**: Bryan Waller Procter (1787-1874) Eng. poet, songwriter

Correggio: Antonio Allegri (da Corregio) (c.1489-1534) It. painter

°Adrienne **Corri**: Adrienne Riccoboni (1930-) Eng. film actress, of It. descent

Ricardo **Cortez**: Jake Kranz (1899-1977) U.S. film actor

Stanley **Cortez**: Stanley Kranz (1908-) U.S. cinematographer

°Baron **Corvo**: Frederick William Serafino Austin Lewis Mary Rolfe (1860-1913) Br. writer

William Johnson **Cory**: William Johnson (1823-1892) Eng. schoolmaster, poet

Michael **Costa**: Michele Andrea Agniello (1808-1884) It. opera composer of Sp. descent, working in U.K.

°Elvis **Costello**: Declan McManus (1955-) Br. rock singer

Lou **Costello**: Louis Cristillo (1906-1959) U.S. film comedian, teaming with Bud Abbott (*q.v.*)

Peter **Cotes**: Sydney Arthur Boulting (1912-) Eng. play producer, film and TV director

A.V. **Coton**: Edward Haddakin (1906-1969) Eng. ballet critic, writer

François **Coty**: Francesco Giuseppe Spotumo (1874-1934) Corsican-born Fr. perfume manufacturer

Nicole **Courcel**: Nicole Andrieux (1930-) Fr. film actress

Georges Victor Marcel **Courteline**: Georges Victor Marcel Moineaux (1858-1929) Fr. humorist, dramatist

Peregrine **Courtenay**: Winthrop Mackworth Praed (1802-1839) Eng. poet

John **Coventry**: John Williamson Palmer (1825-1906) U.S. journalist

Joe **Cowell**: Joseph Leathley Whitshed (1792-1863) Eng. stage comic

Jane **Cowl**: Grace Bailey (1883-1950) U.S. playwright, stage, film actress

Richard **Cowper**: Colin Middleton Murry (1926-) Eng. SF writer

°Charles Egbert **Craddock**: Mary Noailles Murfree (1850-1922) U.S. novelist, short story writer

A.A. **Craig**: Poul William Anderson (1926-) U.S. SF writer

°Gordon **Craig**: Henry Edward Godwin Terry (1872-1966) Br. stage actor, designer, producer

James **Craig**: James Meador (1912-) U.S. film actor

Michael **Craig**: Michael Gregson (1928-) Eng. film actor

°Lucas **Cranach** (the Elder): Lucas Müller (1472-1553) Ger. painter [41]

John **Crane**: Duncan Charles McVarish (1856-1929) Sc. author

Phyllis **Crane**: Phyllis Francis (1912-) U.S. film actress

Vincent **Crane**: Vincent Rodney Cheesman (1943-) Eng. rock musician

°Joan **Crawford**: Lucille Le Sueur (1906-1977) U.S. film actress

Kathryn **Crawford**: Kathryn Crawford Moran (1908-) U.S. film actress

Michael **Crawford**: Michael Dumble-Smith (1942-) Eng. stage, film, TV comedian

Captain **Crawley**: George Frederick Pardon (1824-1884) Eng. writer on sports, pastimes

Geoffrey **Crayon**: Washington Irving (1783-1859) U.S. humorous writer

Joseph **Crehan**: Charles Wilson (1884-1966) U.S. film actor

Crescendo: A Kalisch (1863-1933) Eng. music critic

Dormer **Creston**: Dorothy Julia Colston-Baynes (-) Br. biographer

Paul **Creston**: Joseph Guttoveggio (1906-) U.S. composer

Paul **Creyton**: John Townsend Trowbridge (1827-1916) U.S. novelist, poet, author of boys' books

Otis **Criblecolis**: °W.C. Fields [58]

Edmund **Crispin**: Robert Bruce Montgomery (1921-1978) Eng. crime, SF writer, musical composer

Linda **Cristal**: Victoria Mayo (1936-) Mexican film actress, working in U.S.

Estil **Critchie**: Arthur J Burks (1898-1974) U.S. fantasy fiction writer

Chrystal **Croftangry**: [Sir] Walter Scott (1771-1832) Sc. poet, novelist

Richmal **Crompton**: Richmal Crompton Lamburn (1890-1969) Eng. (female) author of books for boys

Richard **Cromwell**: [1] Richard Williams (-) Welsh great-grandfather of Oliver Cromwell. [2] Roy Radebaugh (1910-1960) U.S. film actor

Hume **Cronyn**: Hume Blake (1911-) Can. film actor

°Bing **Crosby**: Harry Lillis Crosby (1904-1977) U.S. crooner, film actor

Henri-Edmond **Cross**: Henri Delacroix (1856-1910) Fr. neoimpressionist painter

Christopher **Crowfield**: Harriet Elizabeth Beecher Stowe (1811-1896) U.S. novelist

Aleister **Crowley**: Edward Alexander Crowley (1875-1947) Eng. writer on the occult

Alfred **Crowquill**: Alfred Henry Forrester (1805-1872) Eng. illustrator, cartoonist. + Charles Robert Forrester (1803-1850) Eng. illustrator, cartoonist, his brother.

James **Cruze**: Jens Cruz Bosen (1884-1942) U.S. film director, of Dan. parentage

Constance **Cummings**: Constance Levy, née Halverstadt (1910-) U.S. stage, film actress [34]

Robert **Cummings**: Clarence Robert Orville Cummings (1908-) U.S. film actor

Le **Curé d'Ars**: Jean-Baptiste-Marie Vianney (1786-1859) Fr. Roman Catholic saint

Finlay **Currie**: Finlay Jefferson (1878-1968) Sc. stage, screen, TV star

Avon **Curry**: Jean Bowden (1920-) Sc. writer of romantic novels, thrillers

Alan **Curtis**: Harold Neberroth (1909-1953) U.S. film actor

Peter **Curtis**: Norah Lofts, née Robinson (1904-) Br. novelist

°Tony **Curtis**: Bernard Schwartz (1925-) U.S. film actor [14]

Michael **Curtiz**: Mihaly Kertesz (1888-1962) Hung. film actor, working in U.S.

Cynddelw: Robert Ellis (1810-1875) Welsh poet, Baptist minister

The **Czar of Muscovy**: Archibald Constable (1774-1827) Sc. publisher

D

Morton **Da Costa**: Morton Tecosky (1914-) U.S. stage musical, film director

Dagmar: Virginia Ruth Egnor (c.1930-) U.S. TV comedienne

Dagonet: George Robert Sims (1847-1922) Br. writer

Lil **Dagover**: Marta-Maria Daghofer, née Lillits (1897-1980) Ger. film actress

Julian **d'Albie**: D'Albiac Luard (1892-1978) Ir.-born Eng. stage, radio, TV actor

Margaret **Dale**: Margaret Bolan (1922-) Br. ballet dancer, choreographer, TV director

Cass **Daley**: Catherine Dailey (1915-1975) U.S. film comedienne

Dalida: Gigliotta Lolande (1933-) It. pop singer, working in France

John **Dall**: John Tenner Thompson (1918-1971) U.S. film actor

Toti **Dal Monte**: Antonietta Meneghelli (1899-) It. opera singer

Charles **Dalmorès**: Henry Alphonse Brin (1871-1939) Fr. opera singer, working in U.S.

Hamlin **Daly**: Edgar Hoffman Price (1898-) U.S. adventure fiction writer

Rann **Daly**: Edward Vance Palmer (1885-1959) Australian writer

[Father] **Damien**: Joseph Damien de Veuster (1840-1889) Belg. missionary, working in Hawaii

Lili **Damita**: Lilliane Carré (1901-) Fr. film actress

Stuart **Damon**: Stuart Michael Zonis (1937-) U.S. stage, TV actor, director

Vic **Damone**: Vito Farinola (1929-) U.S. film actor, singer

Claude **Dampier**: Claude Cowan (1885-1955) Br. stage, film comedian

°**Dana**: Rosemary Brown (1952-) Ir.-born Eng. pop singer

Viola **Dana**: Violet Flugrath (1897-) U.S. film actress

Frank **Danby**: Julia Frankau (1864-1916) Br. popular novelist

°Clemence **Dane**: Winifred Ashton (1888-1965) Eng. novelist, playwright

Hal **Dane**: Haldane M'Fall (1860-1928) Eng. soldier, author, art critic

Karl **Dane**: Karl Daen (1886-1934) Dan. film actor

John **Dangerfield**: Oswald Crawfurd (1834-1909) Eng. novelist, travel writer

Dangle: Alexander M Thompson (1861-) Eng. journalist, editor

°Bebe **Daniels**: Virginia Daniels (1901-1971) U.S. film actress

°Lisa **Daniely**: Elizabeth Bodington (1930-) Eng. film, TV actress

Gabriele **D'Annunzio**: Gabriele Rapagnetta (1863-1938) It. poet, novelist, dramatist

Dante: Harry Jansen (1882-1955) Dan.-born U.S. conjuror

Michael **Dante**: Ralph Vitti (1931-) U.S. film director

Caleb **D'Anvers**: Nicholas Amhurst (1697-1742) Eng. poet, political writer

°Lorenzo **Da Ponte**: Emmanuele Conegliano (1749-1838) It. librettist, especially of operas of Mozart

Kim **Darby**: Zerby Denby (1947-) U.S. film actress

Denise **Darcel**: Denise Billecard (1925-) Fr. film actress, working in U.S.

Alex **D'Arcy**: Alexander Sarruf (1908-) Egyptian film actor

Roy **D'Arcy**: Roy F Guisti (1894-) U.S. film actor

Phyllis **Dare**: Phyllis Dones (1890-1975) Eng. musical comedy actress

Simon **Dare**: Marjorie Huxtable (1897-) Br. author of romantic novels

Zena **Dare**: Florence Hariette Zena Dones (1887-1975) Br. film actress

Bobby **Darin**: Walden Robert Cassotto (1936-1973) U.S. pop singer, film actor [40]

Rubén **Darío**: Félix Rubén García-Sarmiento (1867-1916) Nicaraguan poet, essayist

Clark **Darlton**: Walter Ernsting (1920-) Ger. SF writer. + Karl Herbet Scheer (1928-) Ger. SF writer

Linda **Darnell**: Manetta Eloisa Darnell (1921-1965) U.S. film actress

James **Darren**: James Ercolani (1936-) U.S. film actor, pop singer

Frankie **Darro**: Frank Johnson (1917-1977) U.S. film actor

John **Darrow**: Harry Simpson (1907-) U.S. film actor

Bella **Darvi**: Bayla Wegier (1927-1971) Pol.-Fr. film actress, working in U.S.

Jane **Darwell**: Patti Woodward (1880-1967) U.S. film actress

Comtesse **Dash**: [Marquise] Gabrielle Saint-Mars (1804-1872) Fr. writer, society leader

Howard **Da Silva**: Harold Silverblatt (1909-) U.S. film actor, director [27]

Jean **Dauberval** (or d'Auberval): Jean Bercher (1742-1806) Fr. ballet dancer, choreographer

Claude **Dauphin**: Claude Franc-Nohain (1903-1978) Fr. stage, film actor

Victor **d'Auverney**: Victor-Marie Hugo (1802-1885) Fr. novelist

Lewis **Davenport**: George Ryan (1883-1916) Eng. conjuror

Jocelyn **Davey**: Chaim Raphael (1908-) Eng. crime novelist

Nuna **Davey**: Margaret Symonds (1902-1977) Eng. stage actress

°Lawrence H. **Davidson**: David Herbert Lawrence (1885-1930) Eng. novelist, short story writer

Marion **Davies**: Marion Cecilie Douras (1897-1961) U.S. film actress

Siobhan **Davies**: Sue Davies (1950-) Eng. ballet dancer, teacher, choreographer

Gordon **Daviot**: Elizabeth Mackintosh (1897-1952) Br. novelist, playwright

Bette **Davis**: Ruth Elizabeth Davis (1908-) U.S. stage, film actress

Billie **Davis**: Carol Hedges (1945-) Eng. soul singer

David **Davis**: William Eric Davis (1908-) Eng. broadcaster, children's storyteller

°Skeeter **Davis**: Mary Frances Penick (1931-) U.S. country singer

William **Davis**: Adolf Günther Kies (1933-) Ger.-born Eng. writer, editor

Bobby **Day**: Robert Byrd (1934-) U.S. pop singer

°Doris **Day**: Doris Kappelhoff (1924-) U.S. singer, film actress

Laraine **Day**: Laraine Johnson (1917-) U.S. film actress

Henri **de Alleber**: Henri di Lappomeraye (1839-1891) Fr. critic, lecturer

Eddie **Dean**: Edgar Dean Glossop (?1908-) U.S. film actor

Isabel **Dean**: Isabel Hodgkinson (1918-) Eng. stage, film actress

James **Dean**: James Byron (1931-1955) U.S. film actor

Jimmy **Dean**: Seth Ward (1928-) U.S. country singer

Charles **Deane**: Edward Saunders (1866-1910) Eng. music hall singer, songwriter

Norman **Deane**: John Creasey (1908-1973) Eng. crime novelist

[Colonel] W. **de Basil**: Vassili Grigorievitch Voskresensky (1888-1951) Russ. impresario

Yvonne **De Carlo**: Peggy Yvonne Middleton (1922-) Can. film actress [14]

Eleanora **de Cisneros**: Eleanor Broadfoot (1878-1934) U.S. opera singer

Arturo **De Cordova**: Arturo Garcia (1908-1973) Mexican film actor

°Dave **Dee**: David Harmon (1943-) Eng. pop singer, TV actor

Joey **Dee**: Joe Dinicola (1940-) U.S. rock musician

Kiki **Dee**: Pauline Matthews (1947-) Eng. pop singer

Nicholas **Dee**: Joan Aiken (1924-) Eng. thriller, children's books writer

Ruby **Dee**: Ruby Ann Wallace (1924-) U.S. black film actress

Sandra **Dee**: Alexandra Zuck (1942-) U.S. film actress

Simon **Dee**: Carl Nicholas Henty-Dodd

(1934-) Can.-born Eng. radio DJ, TV actor

°Daniel **Defoe**: Daniel Foe (?1660-1731) Eng. journalist, novelist

Richard **Dehan**: Clotilde Inez Mary Graves (1863-1932) Ir. playwright, humorous novelist

Elmyr de **Hory**: Palmer Hoffer (1906-1976) Hung. copier of master painters

Maurice **Dekobra**: Ernest Maurice Tessier (1885-1973) Fr. novelist

De **Kolta**: Joseph Buartier (1847-1903) Fr. magician, working in U.S., U.K.

E.M. **Delafield**: Edmée Elizabeth Monica Dashwood, née de la Pasture (1890-1943) Eng. novelist

°Theodore de la **Guard**: Nathaniel Ward (c.1578-1652) Eng. poet, satirist

Jeames de la **Pluche**: William Makepeace Thackeray (1811-1863) Eng. novelist

Isidore de **Lara**: Isidore Cohen (1858-1935) Eng. opera composer

Abbé de la **Tour**: Isabelle de Charrière, née Isabella van Tuyll van Servoskerken (1740-1805) Du.-born Fr. novelist

Le Vicomte Charles de **Launey**: Delphine de Girardin, née Gay (1804-1855) Fr. writer [23]

Bernard **Delfont**: Barnet Winogradsky (1909-) Russ.-born Eng. theatre, TV manager, presenter

Jean de l'**Isle**: Alphonse Daudet (1840-1897) Fr. novelist, short story writer

Belinda **Dell**: Jean Bowden (1920-) Sc. writer of romantic novels, thrillers

Claudia **Dell**: Claudia Dell Smith (1910-) U.S. film actress

Gabriel **Dell**: Gabriel del Vecchio (1930-) West Indies-born U.S. stage actor

°**Della Crusca**: Robert Merry (1755-1798) Eng. poet

Florian **Deller**: Florian Drosendorf (1729-1773) Austr. violinist, composer

Florentina del **Mar**: Carmen Conde (1907-) Sp. poet, novelist, short story writer

Danielle **Delorme**: Gabrielle Girard

(1926-) Fr. film actress

°Joseph **Delorme**: Charles-Augustin Sainte-Beuve (1804-1869) Fr. literary critic

Victoria de **Los Angeles**: Victoria Lopez Cima (1923-) Sp. opera singer

Dolores **del Rio**: Lolita Dolores Asunsolo de Martinez (1905-) Mexican film actress

Delta: [1] David Macbeth Moir (1778-1851) Sc. writer. [2] Benjamin Disraeli (1804-1881) Eng. prime minister, author

Alice **Delysia**: Alice Kolb-Bernard, née Douce (1889-) Br. stage, film actress

Katherine De **Mille**: Katherine Lester (1911-) U.S. film actress

Democritus Junior: Robert Burton (1577-1640) Eng. clergyman, author

Tirso de **Molina**: Gabriel Téllez (c.1571-1648) Sp. dramatist

Louis de **Montalte**: Blaise Pascal (1623-1662) Fr. philosopher, physicist

Peter de **Morny**: Esme Wynn-Tyson (1898-) Eng. novelist, dramatist, critic

Jack **Dempsey**: William Harrison Dempsey (1895-) U.S. heavyweight boxer

Catherine **Deneuve**: Catherine Dorléac (1943-) Fr. film actress

Richard **Denning**: Louis Albert Denninger (1916-) U.S. film actor

Reginald **Denny**: Reginald Leigh Daymore (1891-1967) Br. stage, film actor

Karl **Denver**: Angus Mackenzie (1934-) Sc. pop musician

Dan De **Quille**: William Wright (1829-1898) U.S. humorist, Far West historian

Thomas De **Quincey**: Thomas Quincey (1785-1859) Eng. essayist

Madame Marguerite de **Ponti**: Stéphane Mallarmé (1842-1898) Fr. poet

John **Derek**: Derek Harris (1926-) U.S. film actor

Tristan **Derème**: Philippe Huc (1889-1942) Fr. poet

Jean de **Reszke**: Jean Mieczislaw (1850-1925) Pol. opera singer

Father **Desiderius**: Peter Lenz (1832-1928) Ger. artist, architect

Florence **Desmond**: Florence Dawson (1905-) Eng. revue artiste, impersonator

Jerry **Desmonde**: James Robert Sadler (1908-1967) Eng. music hall comedian

Philippe Nicolas **Destouches**: Philippe Nicolas Néricault (1680-1754) Fr. playwright

André de **Toth**: Andreas Toth (1913-) Hung. film actor

Jacques **Deval**: Jacques Boularan (1890-1972) Fr. playwright, working in U.S.

[Dame] Ninette de **Valois**: Edris Connell, née Stannus (1898-) Ir.-born Br. ballet dancer, director, teacher

David **Devant**: David Wighton (1868-1941) Eng. magician

Mme de **Villedieu**: Marie Catherine H Desjardins (1631-1683) Fr. author

Justin de **Villeneuve**: Nigel Davies (1939-) Br. manager of °Twiggy

Andy **Devine**: Jeremiah Schwartz (1905-1977) U.S. film comedian

°Billy de **Wolfe**: William Andrew Jones (1907-1974) U.S. stage, film comedian, of Welsh parentage

Anthony **Dexter**: Walter Fleischmann (1919-) U.S. film actor

William **Dexter**: William T Pritchard (-) Eng. writer on magic

Robert **Dhery**: Robert Foullcy, né Héry (1921-) Fr. film comedian

°Fra **Diavolo**: Michele Pezza (1771-1806) It. brigand chief

Angie **Dickinson**: Angeline Brown (1931-) U.S. film actress

Carr **Dickson**: John Dickson Carr (1905-) U.S. detective novelist [30]

Carter **Dickson**: John Dickson Carr (1905-) U.S. detective novelist [30]

°Bo **Diddley**: Elias McDaniel (1928-) U.S. black jazz musician

Didi: Waldir Pereira (1928-) Brazilian footballer

°Marlene **Dietrich**: Marie Magdalene Dietrich von Losch (1904-) Ger.-born U.S. film actress, singer

Izak **Dinesen**: Karen Christence Blixen, née Dinesen (1885-1962) Dan.-born Eng. novelist

Ding: Jay Norwood Darling (1876-1962) U.S. cartoonist

Dion: Dion DiMucci (1939-) U.S. rock musician

Diplomat: John Franklin Carter (1897-1967) U.S. mystery novelist, biographer

Discobolus: Donald William Aldous (1914-) Eng. writer on sound recording, engineering [44]

Dick **Distich**: Alexander Pope (1688-1744) Eng. poet

Issay **Dobrowen**: Ishok Israelevich Barabeychik (1891-1953) Russ. conductor, pianist, working in Germany, Sweden

Countess Dora **D'Istria**: Helene Ginka [Princess] Kiltzof Massalsky (1828-1888) Rom. writer

°**Dito und Idem**: Elizabeth [Queen of Romania] (1843-1916) Rom. verse, prose writer. + Mite (or Marie) Kremnitz (1852-1916) Ger. writer

Dorothy **Dix**: Elizabeth Meriwether Gilmer (1861-1951) U.S. author of advice to the lovelorn

Richard **Dix**: Ernest Carlton Brimmer (1894-1949) U.S. film actor

Marmaduke **Dixey**: Geoffrey Howard (1889-) Eng. novelist, poet

Diz: Edward Jeffrey Irving Ardizzone (1900-1979) Br. cartoonist, author, illustrator

°**Don Leucadio Doblado**: °Joseph Blanco White

°**Q.K. Philander Doesticks**, P.B.: Mortimer Neal Thomson (1831-1875) U.S. humorist

Swamp **Dogg**: Jerry Williams, Jr. (1942-) U.S. rock musician

Sir Iliad **Doggrel**: [Sir] Thomas Burnet (1694-1753) Eng. writer. + George Ducket (?-1732) Eng. member of parliament

Dolbokov: Hannes Vajn Bok (1914-1964) U.S. SF writer, artist. + Boris Dolgov (-) U.S. artist

Doleman: Robert Parsons (1546-1610) Eng. Jesuit missionary, plotter

°Anton **Dolin**: Sydney Francis Patrick Chippendall Healey-Kay (1904-) Eng. ballet dancer, choreographer

Fats **Domino**: Antoine Domino (1928-) U.S. black jazz musician

Troy **Donahue**: Merle Johnson (1936-) U.S. film actor [14]

Pauline **Donalda**: Pauline Lightstone (1882-1970) Can. opera singer

Donatello: Donato di Niccolo di Betto Bardi (?1386-1466) It. sculptor

Lonnie **Donegan**: Anthony James Donegan (1931-) Eng. pop musician

Donovan: Donovan P. Leitch (1946-) Sc. rock musician

Dick **Donovan**: Joyce Emmerson Preston Muddock (1843-1934) Eng. journalist, detective fiction writer

Mr. **Dooley**: Finley Peter Dunne (1867-1936) U.S. humorist [18]

Mary **Doran**: Florence Arnot (1907-) U.S. film actress

Philip **Dorn**: Fritz van Dongen (1905-1975) Du. stage, film actor, working in U.S.

Marie **Doro**: Marie Stewart (1882-1956) U.S. film actress

°**Diana Dors**: Diana Mary Fluck (1931-) Eng. stage, film, TV actress

°**Fifi D'Orsay**: Angelina Yvonne Cecile Lussier D'Sablon (1907-) Can.-born U.S. stage, film actress

St. John **Dorset**: Hugo John Belfour (1802-1827) Eng. curate, poet

Marie **Dorval**: Marie Delaunay (1798-1849) Fr. actress

Gabrielle **Dorziat**: Gabrielle Moppert (1880-) Fr. film actress

Dosso **Dossi**: Giovanni di Lutero (?1479-1542) It. painter

Donald **Douglas**: Douglas Kinleyside (1905-1945) U.S. film actor

Felicity **Douglas**: Felicity Dowson, née Tomlin (1910-) Eng. stage, film, TV, radio author

George **Douglas**: George Douglas Brown (1869-1902) Sc. author

°**Kirk Douglas**: Issur Danielovitch Demsky (1916-) U.S. film actor, of Russ.-Jewish parentage

Melvyn **Douglas**: Melvyn Hesselberg (1901-) U.S. stage, film actor, producer, director

Olive **Douglas**: Anna Buchan (-1948) Sc. novelist

Robert **Douglas**: Robert Douglas Finlayson (1909-) Br. stage, film actor, working in U.S.

Wallace **Douglas**: Wallace Finlayson (1911-) Can. stage director

Frederick **Douglass**: Frederick Augustus Washington Dailey (?1817-1895) U.S. black lecturer, writer

°**Kent Douglass**: Robert Douglas Montgomery (1908-1966) U.S. film actor

Robert **Douglass**: Robert Douglas Montgomery (1908-1966) U.S. film actor

Stephen **Douglass**: Stephen Fitch (1921-) U.S. stage actor, singer

Billie **Dove**: Lilian Bohny (1900-) U.S. film actress

Dow Jr.: Eldred F Paige (-1859) Eng. humorist

Peggy **Dow**: Peggy Varnadow (1928-) U.S. film actress

Eddie **Dowling**: Joseph Nelson Goucher (1894-1976) U.S. stage actor, producer, playwright

Major Jack **Downing**: Seba Smith (1792-1868) U.S. humorist

Lynn **Doyle**: Leslie Alexander Montgomery (1873-1961) Ir. humorous novelist, playwright

Alfred **Drake**: Alfredo Capurro (1914-) It.-born U.S. stage singer, dancer

Charles **Drake**: Charles Ruppert (1914-) U.S. film actor

Charlie **Drake**: Charles Springall (1925-) Eng. TV, film, stage comedian

Dona **Drake**: Rita Novella (1920-) Mexican singer, dancer, film actress

Fabia **Drake**: Fabia Drake McGlinchy (1904-) Br. film actress

Tom **Drake**: Alfred Alderdice (1919-) U.S. film actor

°**M.B. Drapier**: Jonathan Swift (1667-1745) Ir. satirist, cleric

Sir Alexander **Drawcansir**: Henry Fielding (1707-1754) Eng. novelist, playwright

Alfred **Drayton**: Alfred Varick (1881-1949) Br. film actor

Carl **Dreadstone**: John Ramsey Campbell (1940-) Eng. writer of horror fiction

Sonia **Dresdel**: Lois Obee (1908-1976) Eng. stage, film actress

Louise **Dresser**: Louise Kerlin (1881-1965) U.S. film actress

Marie **Dressler**: Leila von Koerber (1869-1934) Can.-born U.S. stage, film comedienne

Ellen **Drew**: Terry Ray (1915-) U.S. film actress

Mr. and Mrs. Sidney **Drew**: Sidney White (1864-1920) U.S. stage, film actor. + Lucille McVey (1868-1925) U.S. stage, film actress

Jimmy **Driftwood**: James Morris (1917-) U.S. country singer [45]

Adam **Drinan**: Joseph Todd Gordon Macleod (1903-) Br. author, play producer

Droch: Robert Seymour Bridges (1844-1930) Eng. poet

°Joanne **Dru**: Joanne Letitia La Cock (1923-) U.S. film actress

The **Druid**: Henry Hall Dixon (1822-1870) Eng. sporting writer

Dryasdust: M.Y. Halidom (*q.v.*) [66]

The Rev. Dr. **Dryasdust**: [Sir] Walter Scott (1771-1832) Sc. poet, novelist

Leo **Dryden**: George Dryden Wheeler (1863-1939) Eng. singer of patriotic ballads in the music hall

Doggerel **Drydog**: Charles Clark (1806-1880) Br. sporting writer

Sieur **du Baudrier**: Jonathan Swift (1667-1745) Ir. satirist

Jacques **Duchesne**: Michel Jacques Saint-Denis (1897-) Fr.-born Eng. stage actor, producer

The **Duchess**: Margaret Wolfe Hungerford, née Hamilton (1855-1897) Ir. novelist

°Thomas **du Clévier**: Bonaventure Des Périers (c.1500-1543/4) Fr. story-teller, humanist writer

Pete **Duel**: Peter Deuel (1940-1971) U.S. film actor

Vernon **Duke**: Vladimir Dukelsky (1903-1969) Russ.-born U.S. popular music composer [26]

Germaine **Dulac**: Germaine Saisset-Schneider (1882-1942) Fr. film director, actress

Mlle **Dumesnil**: Marie-Françoise Marchand (1713-1803) Fr. tragic actress

Steffi **Duna**: Stephanie Berindey (1913-) Hung. dancer, film actress

Irma **Duncan**: Irma Dorette Henrietta Ehrich Grimme (1897-) Ger.-U.S. ballet dancer, teacher

"Professor" **Duncan**: John Patterson (1856-1936) Sc. music hall animal trainer

Michael **Dunn**: Gary Neil Miller (1934-1973) U.S. dwarf film actor

Augustus **Dun-shunner**: [Professor] William Edmonstone Aytoun (1813-1865) Sc. poet [16]

Amy **Dunsmuir**: Margaret Oliphant Oliphant, née Wilson (1828-1897) Sc. novelist, historical writer

T.E. **Dunville**: T.E. Wallen (c.1870-1924) Eng. eccentric music hall comedian

E.A. **Dupont**: Ewald André (1891-1956) Ger. film director

Carolus **Duran**: Charles-Auguste-Émile Durand (1837-1917) Fr. genre, portrait painter

Henry Fowle **Durant**: Henry Welles Smith (1822-1881) U.S. lawyer, lay preacher

Deanna **Durbin**: Edna Mae Durbin (1921-) Can. film actress, singer

Frank **Duveneck**: Frank Decker (1848-1919) U.S. painter, sculptor, etcher

Henri **Duvernois**: Henri Schwabacher (1875-1937) Fr. novelist, playwright

Ann **Dvorak**: Ann McKim (1912-1979) U.S. film actress [34]

°Bob **Dylan**: Robert Alan Zimmerman (1941-) U.S. rock musician, poet, composer

E

Solomon **Eagle**: [Sir] John Collings Squire (1884-1958) Br. poet, essayist, short story writer

Edward **Eastaway**: Philip Edward Thomas (1878-1917) Br. essayist, poet, of Welsh parentage

Barbara **Eden**: Barbara Huffman (1934-) U.S. film actress

Sir John **Edgar**: [Sir] Richard Steele (1672-1729) Eng. essayist, dramatist

Jack **Edge**: Jack Haylon (1891-) Eng. music hall comedian

Charles **Edmonds**: Charles Edmund Carrington (1897-) Eng. writer, lecturer

Paul **Edmonds**: Henry Kittner (1915-1958) U.S. fantasy fiction writer

G.C. **Edmondson**: José Mario Garry Ordonez Edmonson y Cotton (1922-)

Guatemalan-born U.S. SF writer

George Alden **Edson**: Paul Ernst (1900-) U.S. writer of horror stories

Albert **Edwards**: Arthur Bullard (1879-1929) U.S. journalist, writer

Blake **Edwards**: William Blake McEdwards (1922-) U.S. film producer, director

Gus **Edwards**: Gustave Edward Simon (1881-1945) U.S. songwriter

Vince **Edwards**: Vincent Edward Zorrio (1928-) U.S. film actor

Edwin: Thomas Vaughan (-) Eng. poet of Dellacruscan school

°Jean **Effel**: François Lejeune (1918-) Fr. cartoonist [30]

°Philippe **Égalité**: Louis Philippe Joseph [duc d'Orléans] (1747-1793) Fr. statesman

H.M. **Egbert**: Victor Rousseau Emanuel (1879-1960) Eng.-born U.S. pulp magazine writer

°George **Egerton**: Mary Chavelita Dunne (1860-1945) Australian novelist

Georg **Egestorff**: [Baron] Georg von Ompteda (1863-1931) Ger. writer, translator

John **Eglinton**: William Kirkpatrick Magee (1868-1962) Ir. essayist, poet, biographical writer

Eha: Edward Hamilton Aitken (1851-) Eng. writer on India, natural history

Marc **Elder**: Marcel Tendron (1884-) Fr. novelist

Florence **Eldridge**: Florence McKechnie (1901-) U.S. stage actress

Gus **Elen**: Ernest Augustus (1862-1940) Eng. music hall artiste, singer of Cockney ditties

Avril **Elgar**: Arril Williams (1932-) Eng. stage actress

El **Hakim**: Barry Walls (1937-) Eng. circus fakir

°**Elia**: Charles Lamb (1775-1834) Eng. writer, poet

°George **Eliot**: Mary Ann (later Marian) Evans (1819-1880) Eng. novelist

Elizabeth: Mary Annette [Countess] von Arnim (later Russell), née Beauchamp (1866-1941) Australian author [25, 35]

Duke **Ellington**: Edward Kennedy Ellington (1899-1974) U.S. black jazz musician

Cass **Elliott**: Ellen Naomi Cohen (1942-1974) U.S. pop singer

Maxine **Elliott**: Jessie Dermot (1868-1940) U.S. stage actress

Mary **Ellis**: Mary Elsas (1900-) U.S. film actress, singer

Patricia **Ellis**: Patricia Gene O'Brien (1916-1970) U.S. film actress

James **Ellison**: James Ellison Smith (1910-) U.S. film actor

Ziggy **Elman**: Harry Finkelman (1914-1968) U.S. jazz trumpeter

Isobel **Elsom**: Isobel Reed (1893-) Br. stage, film actress, working in U.S.

Julian **Eltinge**: William Julian Dalton (1882-1941) U.S. female impersonator

Geoffrey Rudolph **Elton**: Geoffrey Rudolph Ehrenberg (1921-) Ger.-born Eng. historian

Paul **Éluard**: Eugène Grindel (1895-1952) Fr. poet

Maurice **Elvey**: William Folkard (1887-1967) Br. film director

Violetta **Elvin**: Violetta Prokhorova (1925-) Russ. ballet dancer

Gilbert **Emery**: Gilbert Emery Bensley Pottle (1875-1945) Eng.-born U.S. film actor, playwright

Mehmet **Emin Pasha**: Eduard Schnitzler (1840-1892) Ger. traveller, explorer in Africa

Emmwood: John Musgrove-Wood (1915-) Eng. cartoonist

Frederick **Engelheart**: Lafayette Ronald Hubbard (1911-) U.S. fantasy fiction writer

S. **England**: Richard Porson (1759-1808) Eng. classical scholar

An **English Opium-Eater**: Thomas De Quincey (*q.v.*)

Ephemera: Edward Fitzgibbon (1803-1857) Eng. journalist, author of books on angling

Ephesian: Carl Eric Bechhofer Roberts (1894-1949) Br. biographer, novelist, playwright

Epsilon: James Baldwin Brown (1785-1843) Eng. barrister, miscellaneous writer

Desiderius **Erasmus**: Gerhard Gerharhards (or Geert Geerts) (?1466-1536) Du. humanist, theologian

Thomas **Erastus**: Thomas Lieber (or Liebler) (1524-1583) Ger.-Swiss theologian, physician, philosopher

S.W. **Erdnase**: Milton Andrews (or E.S. Andrews) (-) Eng. writer on card-gambling

Leif **Erickson**: William Anderson (1911-) U.S. film actor

John **Ericson**: Joseph Meibes (1927-) Ger.-born U.S. film actor

Erratic Enrique: Henry Clay Lukens (1838-?1900) U.S. humorous writer, poet, journalist

°**Erté**: Romain de Tirtoff (1892-) Russ.-born Fr. costume designer, illustrator

Patrick **Ervin**: Robert E Howard (1906-1936) U.S. SF writer

Uncle **Esek**: Henry Wheeler Shaw (1818-1885) U.S. humorist

Carl **Esmond**: Willy Eichberger (1905-) Austr. film actor, working in U.K., U.S.

°Dr. **Esperanto**: [Dr.] Lazar Ludwik Zamenhof (1859-1917) Pol. physician, inventor of Esperanto

[Don] Miguel Alvarez **Espriella**: Robert Southey (1774-1843) Eng. poet, prose writer

David **Essex**: David Albert Cook (1947-) Eng. pop singer

Martin **Esslin**: Martin Julius Pereszlenyi (1918-) Eng. radio producer, drama critic, of Austr.-Hung. parentage

Robert **Estienne**: Robert le Bonnières (1850-1895) Fr. writer

Étienne: Lev Yefimovich Manevich (1898-1945) Russ. spy

°Partenio **Etiro**: Pietro Aretino (q.v.) [66, 67]

Robert **Eton**: Laurence Walker Meynell (1899-) Eng. author

Eugène: Hugo Arnot (1749-1786) Fr. historical writer

Eugenius III: Bernardo Paganelli (or Pignatelli) (?-1153) It. pope

Eugenius IV: Gabriele Condolmieri (c.1383-1447) It. pope

°**Eusébio**: Eusébio Ferreira da Silva (1942-) Mozambiquan-born Port. footballer (the "Black Panther")

Eusebius: Edmund Ruck (?1735-1787) Eng. writer on religion, agriculture

Eutrapel: Noël du Fail (1520-1591) Fr. writer

Dale **Evans**: Frances Octavia Smith (1912-) U.S. film actress

Jessie **Evans**: Jessie Thomas (1918-) Welsh stage actress

Joan **Evans**: Joan Eunson (1934-) U.S. film actress

Judith **Evelyn**: Judith Evelyn Allen (1913-1967) U.S. stage, film actress

Chad **Everett**: Raymon Lee Cramton (1939-) U.S. TV, film actor

Kenny **Everett**: Maurice James Cole (1944-) Eng. radio, TV DJ, entertainer, presenter

°**Evoe**: Edmund George Valpy Knox (1881-1971) Eng. essayist, humorist

Tom **Ewell**: S. Yewell Tompkins (1909-) U.S. film comedian, stage actor

Ex-Private X: Alfred McLelland Burrage (1889-1956) Eng. novelist, fantasy story writer

Clive **Exton**: Clive Brooks (1930-) Eng. playwright

An **Eye-Witness**: Charles Lamb (1775-1834) Eng. essayist, critic

F

Fabian: Fabiano Forte Bonaparte (1943-) U.S. pop singer, film actor [29]

Nanette **Fabray**: Nanette Fabares (1920-) U.S. film comedienne, singer

°Philippe **Fabre d'Églantine**: Philippe François Nazaire Fabre (1750-1794) Fr. playwright, revolutionary pol.

Georg **Fabricius**: Georg Goldschmied (1516-1571) Ger. scholar [31]

Barent **Fabritius**: Barent Pieterz (1624-1673) Du. painter

Carel **Fabritius**: Carel Pieterz (1622-1654) Du. painter

°**Fabulous Moolah**: Lillian Ellison (c.1930-) U.S. woman wrestler

Frederick **Fag**: [Dr.] James Johnson (1777-1845) Eng. writer

A.A. **Fair**: Erle Stanley Gardner (1889-1970) U.S. crime novelist

°Douglas **Fairbanks**: Douglas Elton Thomson Ullman (1883-1939) U.S. film actor

Douglas **Fairbanks, Jr.**: Douglas Elton Thomas Ullman, Jr. (1909-) U.S. film actor

Sydney **Fairbrother**: Sydney Tapping (1873-1941) Eng. film actress

Frank **Fairleigh**: Francis Edward Smedley (1818-1864) Eng. novelist

Michael **Fairless**: Margaret Fairless Barber (1869-1901) Eng. writer, essayist

°Adam **Faith**: Terence Nelhams (1940-) Eng. pop singer

Johan Petter **Falkberget**: John Petter Lillebakken (1879-1967) Norw. novelist

Hans **Fallada**: Friedrich Rudolf Ditzen (1893-1947) Ger. novelist

°Georgie **Fame**: Clive Powell (1943-) Eng. pop musician

Violet **Fane**: Baroness Mary Montgomerie Currie, née Lamb (1843-1905) Eng. novel, verse writer

Eben **Fardd**: Ebenezer Thomas (1802-1863) Welsh poet, bard

Carlo **Farinelli**: Carlo Broschi (1705-1782) It. castrato singer

Ralph Milne **Farley**: Roger Sherman Hoar (1887-1963) U.S. SF writer

Chris **Farlowe**: John Deighton (1940-) Eng. pop singer

Marianne **Farningham**: Marianne Hearn (1834-1909) Eng. religious writer, hymnwriter

Martha **Farquharson**: Martha Farquharson Finley (1828-1909) U.S. children's writer

°Walli **Farrad**: Wallace D Fard (c.1877-?1934) U.S. Black Muslim leader

M.J. **Farrell**: Mary Nesta Keane, née Skrine (1905-) Ir. author

Suzanne **Farrell**: Roberta Sue Ficker (1945-) U.S. ballet dancer

Julia **Farron**: Julia Farron-Smith (1929-) Br. ballet dancer

Helen **Faucit**: Helena Saville (1817-1898) Br. stage actress

William **Faulkner**: William Harrison Falkner (1897-1962) U.S. novelist, short story writer

Catherine **Fawcett**: Catherine Ann Cookson, née McMullan (1906-) Eng. novelist

Alice **Faye**: Alice Leppert (1912-) U.S. film actress

Joey **Faye**: Joseph Anthony Palladino (1910-) U.S. stage comedian

°Irving **Fazola**: Irving Henry Prestopnik (1912-1949) U.S. jazz clarinettist

Justinus **Febronius**: Johann Nikolaus von Hontheim (1701-1790) Ger. Roman Catholic prelate

Charles K. **Feldman**: Charles Gould (1904-1968) U.S. film producer

Felix: Felix Fernandez García (c.1896-1941) Sp. ballet dancer

°N. **Felix**: Nicholas Wanostrocht (1804-1876) Eng. schoolmaster, writer on cricket

Freddy **Fender**: Baldemar Huerta (1936-) U.S. rock singer

Lavinia **Fenton**: Lavinia Beswick (1708-1760) Eng. opera singer

Shane **Fenton**: °Alvin Stardust

Fanny **Fern**: Sara Payson Parton, née Willis (1811-1872) U.S. children's author

°**Fernandel**: Fernand-Joseph-Desiré Constandin (1903-1971) Fr. film comedian

Elizabeth X. **Ferrars**: Morna Doris Brown, née MacTaggart (1907-) Eng. novelist, mystery writer

José **Ferrer**: José Vincente Ferrer Otero y Cintrón (1912-) U.S. stage, film actor

Ernest **Fest**: Eduard Heinrich Mayer (1821-1907) Ger. poet

°Stepin **Fetchit**: Lincoln Theodore Perry (1898-) U.S. black film actor

Edwige **Feuillère**: Edwige Cunati (1907-) Fr. stage, film actress

Jacques **Feyder**: Jacques Frédérix (1887-1948) Belg.-born Fr. film director

°Michael **ffolkes**: Brian Davis (1925-) Eng. cartoonist

John **Field**: John Greenfield (1921-) Eng. ballet dancer, director

Martyn **Field**: Frederick William Horner (1854-) Eng. politician, administrator, author

Michael **Field**: Katharine Harris Bradley (1848-1914) Eng. poet. + Edith Emma Cooper (1862-1913) Eng. poet

Virginia **Field**: Margaret Cynthia Field (1917-) Eng. film actress

Fieldfare: [Sir] Alexander Balmain Bruce Valentine (1899-) Sc. transport executive, writer

Gabriel **Fielding**: Alan Gabriel Barnsley (1916-) Br. novelist

°Gracie **Fields**: Grace Stansfield (1898-1979) Eng. singer, comedienne

Lew **Fields**: Lewis Maurice Shanfields (1867-1941) U.S. stage comedian

Stanley **Fields**: Walter L. Agnew (1884-1941) U.S. film actor

Tommy **Fields**: Thomas Stansfield (1908-) Eng. music hall comedian

Totie **Fields**: Sophie Feldman (?1930-1978) U.S. nightclub, TV comedienne

°**W.C. Fields**: William Claude Dukinfield (1879-1946) U.S. film comedian

Figaro: Henry Clapp (1814-1875) U.S. journalist, editor

Filaret: Vasily Mikhaylovich Drozdov (1782-1867) Russ. Orthodox churchman, archbishop of Moscow

Filarete: Antonio di Pietro Averlino (or Averalino) (c.1400-1469) It. architect, sculptor

Filinto Elisio: Francisio Manuel do Nascimento (1734-1819) Port. poet, working in France

Fin-Bec: William Blanchard Jerrold (1826-1884) Eng. playwright, novelist

Peter **Finch**: William Mitchell (1916-1977) Eng. stage, film actor

Richard **Findlater**: Kenneth Bruce Findlater Bain (1921-) Eng. editor, writer

Fiore della Neve: Martinus Gesinus Lambert van Loghem (1849-1934) Du. poet, fiction writer

John **Fiske**: Edmund Fisk Green (1842-1901) U.S. philosopher, historian

Minnie Maddern **Fiske**: Marie Augusta Fiske, née Davey (1865-1932) U.S. stage actress

Tarleton **Fiske**: Robert Bloch (1917-) U.S. writer of horror, fantasy fiction

Mary **Fitt**: Kathleen Freeman (1897-1959) Br. writer of books on Greek subjects, detective novelist

George Savage **Fitz-Boodle**: William

Makepeace Thackeray (1811-1863) Eng. novelist

°Barry **Fitzgerald**: William Shields (1888-1961) Ir. film actor

Walter **Fitzgerald**: Walter Fitzgerald Bond (1896-1977) Eng. stage, film actor

Sir Thomas **Fitzosborne**: William Melmoth (1710-1799) Eng. writer

John **Fitzvictor**: Percy Bysshe Shelley (1792-1822) Eng. poet

Francis **Flagg**: Henry George Weiss (1898-1946) U.S. SF writer

°Bud **Flanagan**: Chaim Reuben Weintrop (1896-1968) Eng. stage, film comedian, of Pol.-Jewish parentage

°**Fléchelles**: Hugues Guéru (-1633) Fr. actor

George **Fleming**: Constance Fletcher (1858-1938) U.S. novelist, playwright

Oliver **Fleming**: Philip MacDonald (?1890-) Eng. writer of detective novels

Rhonda **Fleming**: Marilyn Louis (1923-) U.S. film actress

Herbert **Flemming**: Arif Nicolaiih El-Michelle (1905-) Tunisian jazz trombonist

George U. **Fletcher**: Fletcher Pratt (1897-1956) U.S. naval, American historian, fantasy writer

Robert **Fletcher**: Robert Fletcher Wyckoff (1923-) U.S. theatre designer

Fleury: Abraham-Joseph Benard (1750-1822) Fr. comic actor

William Jermyn **Florence**: Bernard Conlin (1831-1891) U.S. comedian

°**Floridor**: Josias de Soulas [Sieur de Prinefosse] (?1608-1671/2) Fr. actor

°**Florizel**: George IV (1762-1830) king of Great Britain

Flotsam: Bentley Collingwood Hilliam (1890-1968) Eng. composer, pianist, entertainer, teaming with Jetsam (*q.v.*)

Barbara **Flynn**: Barbara McMurray (1948-) Eng. stage, TV actress

Josiah **Flynt**: Josiah Flint Willard (1869-1907) U.S. writer on experiences as a tramp

Nina **Foch**: Nina Fock (1924-) Du. stage actress, working in U.S.

Jonathan Lituleson **Fogarty**: James T Farrell (1904-) U.S. novelist, critic

°Joan **Fontaine**: Joan de Beauvoir de Havilland (1917-) Eng.-born U.S. stage, film actress

Roy **Fontaine**: Archibald Thomson Hall (1925-) Sc. butler, murderer

Wayne **Fontana**: Glyn Ellis (1947-) Eng. rock musician

°[Dame] Margot **Fonteyn**: Margot Fonteyn de Arias, née Margaret Hookham (1919-) Eng. ballet dancer

Athel **Forbes**: [Rev.] Forbes Phillips (1866-) Eng. novelist, dramatist

Brenda **Forbes**: Brenda Taylor (1909-) Eng. stage actress

Bryan **Forbes**: Brian Clarke (1926-) Eng. film actor, screenwriter

Meriel **Forbes**: Meriel Forbes-Robertson (1913-) Eng. stage, film actress

Stanton **Forbes**: Deloris Stanton Forbes (1923-) U.S. mystery writer

Elbur **Ford**: Eleanor Hibbert (1906-) Eng. novelist

°**Ford** Madox **Ford**: Ford Hermann Hueffer (1873-1939) Br. novelist, editor

Francis **Ford**: Francis Feeney (1883-1953) U.S. film actor

°Gerald Randolph **Ford, Jr.**: Leslie Lynch King, Jr. (1913-) U.S. president

Glenn **Ford**: Gwyllyn Ford (1916-) Can. film actor, working in U.S.

John **Ford**: Sean O'Feeny (1895-1973) Ir.-born U.S. film director

Leslie **Ford**: Zenith Brown, née Jones (1898-) U.S. detective novelist

Paul **Ford**: Paul Ford Weaver (1901-1976) U.S. stage actor

Wallace **Ford**: Samuel Jones Grundy (1897-1966) Eng.-born U.S. film actor

Florrie **Forde**: Florence Flanagan (1876-1940) Australian-born Eng. music hall singer

Walter **Forde**: Thomas Seymour (1896-) Br. film director

Keith **Fordyce**: Keith Marriot (1928-) Eng. radio, TV interviewer, compère, DJ

Mark **Forest**: Lou Degni (1933-) U.S. film actor

Forester: Thomas Paine (1737-1809) Eng. political writer, working in U.S.

Fanny **Forester**: Emily Chubbuck Judson (1817-1854) U.S. novelist

Frank **Forester**: Henry William Herbert (1807-1858) Eng. author, editor, working in U.S.

°**Forez**: François Mauriac (1885-1970) Fr. novelist, poet, playwright

°George **Formby**: George Hoy Booth (1904-1961) Eng. comedian, singer, ukelele player

Sally **Forrest**: Katharine Scully Feeney (1928-) U.S. film actress

Steve **Forrest**: William Forrest Andrews (1924-) U.S. film actor

John **Forsell**: Carl Johan Jacob (1868-1941) Swe. opera singer

Bruce **Forsyth**: Bruce Joseph Forsyth Johnson (1928-) Eng. stage, TV actor, compère

Jean **Forsyth**: Jean Newton McIlwraith (1871-1938) Can. short story, magazine article writer

John **Forsythe**: John Lincoln Freund (1918-) U.S. stage, film actor

George **Forth**: Harold Frederic (1856-1898) U.S. novelist

Fortis: Leslie Forse (1907-1978) Eng. journalist, editor

Dion **Fortune**: Violet Mary Firth (1890-1946) U.S. writer of occult novels [45]

Lukas **Foss**: Lukas Fuchs (1922-) Ger. born U.S. composer, conductor

Dianne **Foster**: Dianne Laruska (1928-) Can. film actress

Norman **Foster**: Norman Hoeffer (1900-1976) U.S. film actor

Richard **Foster**: Kendall Foster Crossen (1910-) U.S. author, journalist

°Susanna **Foster**: Susan DeLis Flanders Larson (1924-) U.S. film actress

°**Fougasse**: Cyril Kenneth Bird (1887-1965) Eng. artist, cartoonist, editor

Adam **Fouleweather**: Thomas Nash (1567-1601) Eng. satirical pamphleteer, dramatist [59, 60]

Hugh **Foulis**: David Storrar Meldrum (1865-) Br. novelist, journalist

Oliver **Foulis**: David Lloyd (1635-1692) Eng. miscellaneous writer

Sydney **Fowler**: Sydney Fowler Wright (1874-) Eng. poet, novelist, biographer, anthropologist

G.L. **Fox**: George Washington Lafayette (1825-1877) U.S. stage actor, pantomimist

William **Fox**: William Friedman (1879-1952) Hung.-born U.S. film executive

°Redd **Foxx**: John Elroy Sanford (1922-) U.S. film, TV comedian

Eddie **Foy**, Jr.: Edwin Fitzgerald (1905-) U.S. stage actor, dancer, son of Eddie Foy, Sr. (*q.v.*)

Eddie **Foy**, Sr.: Edwin Fitzgerald (1856-1928) U.S. stage actor, vaudeville player

F.P.A.: Franklin Pierce Adams (1881-) U.S. journalist, humorist

Harry **Fragson**: Leon Vince Philip Pott (1869-1913) Eng.-Fr. music hall comedian, singer

Celia **Franca**: Celia Franks (1921-) Eng. ballet dancer, director, choreographer

°Anatole **France**: Jacques Anatole François Thibault (1844-1924) Fr. novelist, poet, playwright

[Mother] **Frances** Mary Theresa: Frances Ball (1794-1861) Eng. religious, founder of Loretto Nuns, Ireland

Anthony **Franciosa**: Anthony Papaleo (1928-) It.-born U.S. film actor

Arthur **Francis**: Ira Gershwin (1896-) U.S. songwriter

Connie **Francis**: Constance Franconero (1938-) U.S. pop singer, film actress

Kaye **Francis**: Katherine Gibbs (1905-1968) U.S. stage, film actress

M.E. **Francis**: Mary Francis Blundell, née Sweetman (c.1855-1930) Ir. novelist

°[Saint] **Francis of Assisi**: Giovanni di Pietro di Bernardone (1182-1226) It. monk, preacher

Harry **Franco**: Charles Frederick Briggs (1804-1877) U.S. journalist, author

Jacob **Frank**: Jacob Leibowicz (1726-1791) Pol. founder ("false messiah") of Zoharist sect

Pat **Frank**: Harry Hart (1907-) U.S. SF writer

Jane **Frazee**: Mary Jane Frahse (1918-) U.S. singer, film actress

Frédérick: Antoine-Louis-Prosper Lemaître (1800-1876) Fr. actor

Pauline **Frederick**: Pauline Libby (1885-1938) U.S. stage, film actress

Arthur **Freed**: Arthur Grossman (1894-1973) U.S. film producer

Mrs. **Freeman**: Sarah Churchill, Duchess of Marlborough (1660-1744) Eng. aristocrat [25]

Paul **French**: Isaac Asimov (1920-) Russ.-born U.S. SF writer

Peter **French**: John Nicholas ffrench (1935-) Welsh stage, TV actor

Pierre **Fresnay**: Pierre-Jules-Louis Laudenbach (1897-1975) Fr. stage, film actor

Ruby **Freugon**: Rubie Constance Ashby (1899-) Eng. writer of mystery novels

Trixie **Friganza**: Delia O'Callahan (1870-1955) U.S. actress, singer

Freddie **Frinton**: Frederick Hargate (1911-1968) Eng. comedian

Joachim **Frizius**: Fobert Flud (1574-1637) Eng. physician, Rosicrucian

David **Frome**: Zenith Brown, née Jones (1898-) U.S. novelist

Christopher **Fry**: Christopher Harris (1907-) Eng. playwright

Elmer **Fudpucker**: Hollis Champion (1935-) Can. country & western singer, comedian

Fu **Manchu**: David Bamberg (1904-1974) U.S. magician, son of Okito (*q.v.*)

Joseph **Fume**: William Andrew Chatto (1799-1864) Eng. miscellaneous writer

Billy **Fury**: Ronald Wycherly (1941-) Eng. pop singer

G

Franceska **Gaal**: Fanny Zilveritch (1909-) Hung. film actress

Jean **Gabin**: Jean Alexis Moncorgé (1904-1976) Fr. film actor

Naum **Gabo**: Naum Neemia Pevsner (1890-1977) Russ. constructivist sculptor, working abroad

Zsa Zsa **Gabor**: Sari Gabor (1919-) Hung. film actress

Major **Goliah Gahagan**: William Makepeace Thackeray (1811-1863) Eng. novelist

Galen: Vasily Konstantinovich Blücher (1889-1938) Russ. general

Vincenzo **Galeotti**: Vincenzo Tomazelli (1733-1816) It. ballet dancer, teacher

Anna **Galina**: Evelyne Cournand (1936-) U.S. ballet dancer

Geoffrey **Gambado**: Henry William Bembury (1750-1811) Eng. artist, society caricaturist

Ganconagh: William Butler Yeats (1865-1939) Ir. poet, dramatist

Sir Gregory **Gander**: George Ellis (1753-1815) Eng. author

Joe **Gans**: Joseph Gaines (1874-1910) U.S. lightweight boxer

°**Greta Garbo**: Greta Lovisa Gustafsson (1905-) Swe.-born U.S. film actress

Ava **Gardner**: Lucy Johnson (1922-) U.S. film actress

John **Garfield**: Julius Garfinkle (1913-1952) U.S. film actor

Beverly **Garland**: Beverly Fessenden (1926-) U.S. film, TV actress

°**Judy Garland**: Frances Ethel Gumm (1922-1969) U.S. film actress

Robert **Garloch**: Robert Sutherland (1909-) Br. poet

James **Garner**: James Baumgartner (1928-) U.S. film actor

Edward **Garrett**: Isabella Fyvie Mayo (1843-1914) Br. novelist, journalist

John **Garrick**: Reginald Doudy (1902-) Br. stage, film actor

Garrincha: Manoel Francisco dos Santos (1933-) Chilean footballer

Andrew **Garve**: Paul Winterton (1908-) Eng. journalist, mystery writer

Romain **Gary**: Romain Kacewgary (or Kassevgari) (1914-1980) Russ.-born (Georgian) Fr. author

Gaston-Marie: Alphonse Daudet (1840-1897) Fr. novelist

°**Pearly Gates**: Viola Billups (1946-) U.S. black popular singer

Gath: George Alfred Townsend (1841-1914) U.S. journalist, war correspondent, fiction writer

°**Paul Gavarni**: Sulpice Guillaume Chevalier (1804-1866) Fr. illustrator, caricaturist

John **Gawsworth**: Terence Ian Fytton Armstrong (1912-1970) Eng. poet, critic, editor, horror story writer

Joseph **Gay**: John Durant Breval (?1680-1738) Eng. miscellaneous writer

Maisie **Gay**: Maisie Munro-Noble (1883-) Eng. film actress

°**Noel Gay**: Reginald Armitage (1898-1954) Eng. popular songwriter, music publisher

Crystal **Gayle**: Brenda Gayle Webb (1951-) U.S. pop singer

Janet **Gaynor**: Laura Gainor (1906-) U.S. film actress

Mitzi **Gaynor**: Francesca Mitzi Marlene deChamey von Gerber (1930-) U.S. film actress

Clara **Gazul**: Prosper Mérimée (1803-1870) Fr. novelist, historian [21]

George **Ge**: George Grönfeldt (1893-1962) Finn. ballet dancer, choreographer

Nicolai **Gedda**: Nicolai Ustinov (1925-) Swe. opera singer, of Russ. origin

Will **Geer**: William Ghere (1902-1978) U.S. stage actor

[Dame] Adeline **Genée**: Anina Jensen (1878-1970) Dan.-born Br. ballet dancer

Genêt: Janet Flanner (1892-) U.S. foreign correspondent, novelist, art critic

°**Genghis Khan**: Temujin (or Temuchin) (1662-1227) Mongol conqueror

A **Gentleman** of the University of Oxford: Percy Bysshe Shelley (1792-1822) Eng. poet

A **Gentleman** who has left his Lodgings [Lord] John Russell (1792-1878) Eng. statesman

A **Gentleman** with a Duster: Harold Begbie (1871-1929) Eng. novelist, biographer, popular religious writer

Mlle **George**: Marguerite-Joséphine Weymer (1787-1867) Fr. actress

Daniel **George**: Daniel George Bunting (1890-1967) Br. essayist, critic, anthologist

Gladys **George**: Gladys Clare (1900-1954) U.S. film actress

Jim **Gerald**: Jacques Guenod (1889-1958) Fr. stage, film actor

°**Geraldo**: Gerald Bright (1904-1974) Br. dance-band leader

Morice **Gerard**: [Rev.] J Jessop Teague (1856-) Eng. novelist, reviewer

Steve **Geray**: Stefan Gyergyay (1904-1976) Hung. film actor, working in U.K, U.S.

°William **Gerhardie**: William Alexander Gerhardi (1895-1977) Russ.-born Eng. writer

Karl **Germain**: Charles Mattmueller (1878-1959) U.S. magician, of Ger. parentage

[Sir] Edward **German**: Edward German Jones (1862-1936) Br. light opera composer

Gene **Gerrard**: Eugene Maurice O'Sullivan (1892-1971) Br. music hall comedian, film actor

George **Gershwin**: Jacob Gershvin (1898-1937) U.S. composer, of Russ.-Jewish parentage

John **Gerstad**: John Gjerstad (1924-) U.S. stage actor, producer, director, playwright

Gertrude: Jame Cross Simpson (1811-1886) Eng. writer of hymns, stories, poems

Tamara **Geva**: Tamara Gevergeyeva (1908-) Russ. ballet dancer, working in U.S.

G.G.: H G Harper (1851-) Eng. sporting journalist

Lorenzo **Ghiberti**: Lorenzo di Cione di Ser Buonaccorso (1378-1455) It. goldsmith, painter, sculptor

°Domenico **Ghirlandaio**: Domenico di Tommaso Bigordi (1449-1494) It. painter

Lewis Grassic **Gibbon**: James Leslie Mitchell (1901-1935) Sc. novelist, short story writer

Chloë **Gibson**: Chloë Cawdle (1899-) Eng. stage director

J. **Gifford**: John Richard Green (1837-1883) Eng. historian

John **Gifford**: Edward Foss (1787-1870) Eng. biographer

Theo **Gift**: Theodora Boulger, née Havers (1847-1923) Eng. writer of children's stories, fantasy fiction

Anthony **Gilbert**: Lucy Beatrice Balleson (1899-1973) Eng. writer of detective novels, short stories

Jean **Gilbert**: Max Winterfield (1879-1942) Ger. operetta composer

°John **Gilbert**: John Pringle (1897-1936) U.S. film actor

Lou **Gilbert**: Lou Gitlitz (1909-) U.S. stage actor

Paul **Gilbert**: Paul MacMahon (1924-) U.S. film comedian, dancer

Gilderoy: Patrick Macgregor (-1638) Sc. robber, cattlestealer

Giles: Carl Ronald Giles (1916-) Br. cartoonist [29]

André **Gill**: Louis-André Gosset (1840-1885) Fr. caricaturist

Geneviève **Gilles**: Geneviève Gillaizeau (1946-) Fr. film actress

Ann **Gillis**: Alma O'Connor (1927-) U.S. film actress

Virgina **Gilmore**: Sherman Poole (1919-) U.S. film actress

Barbara **Gilson**: Charles Gibson (1878-1943) Eng. soldier, writer of children's stories

Giorgione: Giorgio Barbarelli (da Castelfranco) (1477-1510) It. painter

Zinaida **Gippius**: Zinaida Nikolayevna Merezhkovskaya (1869-1945) Russ. writer, working in France

Albert **Giraud**: Marie Émile Albert Kayenbergh (1860-1929) Belg. poet

Dorothy **Gish**: Dorothy de Guiche (1898-1968) U.S. film actress

Lillian **Gish**: Lillian de Guiche (1896-) U.S. film actress

°Gertie **Gitana**: Gertrude Mary Astbury (1889-1957) Br. music hall singer

Jac **Glan-y-Dors**: John Jones (1766-1821) Welsh satirical poet, social reformer

°Gary **Glitter**: Paul Gadd (1944-) Eng. pop singer

Gluck: Gluckstein (1895-1978) U.S.-born Eng. artist

Alma **Gluck**: Reba Fiersohn (1884-1938) U.S. opera singer, of Rom. parentage

Tito **Gobbi**: Tito Weiss (1915-) It. opera singer

Paulette **Goddard**: Marion Levy (1911-) U.S. film actress

Rumer **Godden**: Margaret Rumer Haynes Dixon, née Godden (1907-) Eng. novelist

John **Godey**: Morton Freedgood

(1912-) U.S. writer of mystery short stories

Charles **Godfrey**: Paul Lacey (1851-1900) Eng. music hall artiste

Michael **Gold**: Irwin Granich (1893-1967) U.S. Communist writer, critic

Horace **Goldwin**: Hyman Goldstein (1873-1939) Pol.-born U.S. illusionist

Peter **Goldsmith**: John Boynton Priestley (1894-) Eng. novelist, essayist, dramatist. + George Billam (-) Eng. writer

°Samuel **Goldwyn**: Samuel Goldfish (1882-1974) U.S. film producer, of Pol.-Jewish parentage

Lemmie B. **Good**: Limmie Snell (c.1945-) U.S. pop singer [45]

Will B. **Good**: Rosco ("Fatty") Arbuckle (1887-1933) U.S. comic film actor, comedy director [45]

Goodliffe: C Goodliffe Neale (-) Eng. magician, writer, publisher of books on magic

Myles na **Gopaleen**: Brian O'Nolan (1912-1966) Ir. novelist

Gale **Gordon**: Gaylord Aldrich (1906-) U.S. TV actress

Janet **Gordon**: Cecil Blanche Woodham-Smith, née Fitzgerald (1896-) Welsh novelist [16]

Neil **Gordon**: Archibald Gordon Macdonell (1895-1941) Sc. writer

Richard **Gordon**: Gordon Ostlere (1921-) Br. novelist [16]

Ruth **Gordon**: Ruth Gordon Jones (1896-) U.S. stage, film actress, screenwriter

Gorgeous George: George Raymond Wagner (1915-1963) U.S. wrestler

°Maxim **Gorky**: Aleksei Maksimovich Peshkov (1868-1936) Russ. writer

Tobio **Gorria**: Arrigo Boito (1842-1918) It. composer, librettist

Sirak **Goryan**: William Saroyan (1908-) U.S. novelist, short story writer, of Armenian parentage

°Jeremias **Gotthelf**: Albert Bitzius (1797-1854) Swiss novelist, short story writer

Bernard **Gould**: [Sir] Bernard Partridge (1861-1945) Br. actor, cartoonist

Elliott **Gould**: Elliot Goldstein (1938-) U.S. stage, film actor

Caius **Gracchus**: François-Émile (or Noël) Babeuf (1760-1797) Fr. revolutionary politician

[Baron] Lew **Grade**: Louis Winogradsky (1906-) Br. TV executive, brother of Bernard Delfont (q.v.)

A **Graduate of Oxford**: John Ruskin (1819-1900) Eng. writer, art critic

Bruce **Graeme**: Graham Montague Jeffries (1900-) Eng. novelist

Rodney **Graeme**: Roderic Graeme Jeffries (1926-) Eng. mystery writer

Bill **Graham**: Wolfgang Grajonca (1931-) Ger.-born U.S. rock promoter

Ennis **Graham**: Mary Louisa Molesworth (Mrs. Molesworth), née Stewart (1839-1921) Sc. novelist

°Sheilah **Graham**: Lily Sheil (?1910-) Eng. writer, biographer

Gloria **Grahame**: Gloria Grahame Hallward (1925-) U.S. stage, film, TV actress

Sarah **Grand**: Frances Elizabeth McFall, née Clarke (1862-1943) Ir. novelist

Grandville: Jean Ignace Isidore Gérard (1803-1847) Fr. illustrator, caricaturist

°Stewart **Granger**: James Lablache Stewart (1913-) Eng. film actor

°Cary **Grant**: Alexander Archibald Leach (1904-) Eng. film actor, working in U.S.

Joan **Grant**: Joan Kelsey, née Marshall (1907-) Eng. novelist

Kathryn **Grant**: Katherine Grandstaff (1933-) U.S. film actress

Kirby **Grant**: Kirby Grant Horn (1914-) U.S. film actor

Lee **Grant**: Lyova Rosenthal (1929-) U.S. stage, film actress

Mary **Grant**: Angela Willans (-) Eng. agony columnist

°Ingahild **Grathmer**: Margrethe II (1940-) Queen of Denmark

Peter **Graves**: Peter Aurness (1925-) U.S. film actor, brother of James Arness (q.v.)

Fernand **Gravet**: Fernand Martens (1904-1970) Fr. film actor

Barry **Gray**: Robert Barry Coffin (1797-1857) U.S. author

Colleen **Gray**: Doris Jensen (1922-)

U.S. film actress

Donald **Gray**: Eldred Tidbury (1914-) Eng. film, TV actor

Dulcie **Gray**: Dulcie Winifred Catherine Denison, née Bailey (1920-) Eng. stage, film actress, thriller writer [34]

E. Conder **Gray**: Alexander Hay Japp (1837-1905) Sc. author, publisher

Ellington **Gray**: Naomi Ellington Jacob (1889-) Eng. novelist

Gilda **Gray**: Marianna Michalska (1901-1959) Pol. dancer, film actress, working in U.S.

Linda **Gray**: Linda Baxter (1910-) Eng. stage actress, singer

Michael **Gray**: Michael Grealis (1947-) Eng. TV reporter

Nadia **Gray**: Nadia Kujnir-Herescu (1923-) Russ.-Rom. film actress

Sally **Gray**: Constance Stevens (1916-) Br. film actress

Simon **Gray**: [Sir] Alexander Boswell (1775-1822) Eng. antiquary, poet

David **Grayson**: Ray Stannard Baker (1870-1946) U.S. essayist

Diane **Grayson**: Diane Guinibert (1948-) Flemish-born Eng. stage, film, TV dancer, actress

Kathryn **Grayson**: Zelma Hedrick (1922-) U.S. film actress, singer

°Larry **Grayson**: William White (1923-) Eng. TV entertainer, compère

The **Great Carmo**: Harry Cameron (1881-1944) Australian-born Eng. magician

The **Great Lafayette**: Sigmund Neuberger (1872-1911) Ger. magician

The **Great Nicola**: William Mozart Nicol (1880-1946) U.S. illusionist

El **Greco**: Domenikos Theotokopoulos (?1548-?1614) Gk.-born Sp. painter

Henry **Green**: Henry Vincent Yorke (1905-1973) Br. novelist

Martyn **Green**: William Martyn-Green (1899-) Eng. stage actor, singer

Mitzi **Green**: Elizabeth Keno (1920-1969) U.S. film actress

Max **Greene**: Mutz Greenbaum (1896-1968) Ger. cinematographer, working in U.K.

Grace **Greenwood**: Sara Jane (Clarke)

Lippincott (1823-1904) U.S. poet, newspaper writer, essayist

[Sir] Ben **Greet**: Philip Barling (1857-1936) Br. stage actor, manager

Gregory V: Brunone di Carinzia (972-999) Ger. pope [10]

Gregory VI: Giovanni Graziano (972-1048) It. pope

[Saint] **Gregory VII**: Hildebrand (c.1020-1085) It. pope

Gregory VIII: Alberto de Morra (?1142-1187) It. pope

Gregory IX: Ugo (or Ugolino) di Segni (?-1241) It. pope

Gregory X: Teobaldo Visconti (1210-1276) It. pope

Gregory XI: Pierre-Roger de Beaufort (1331-1378) Fr. pope

Gregory XII: Angelo Corrario (?1327-1417) It. pope

Gregory XIII: Ugo Buoncompagni (1502-1585) It. pope

Gregory XIV: Niccolò Sfondrato (1535-1591) It. pope

Gregory XV: Alessandro Ludovisi (1554-1623) It. pope

Gregory XVI: Bartolommeo Alberto Cappellarri (1765-1846) It. pope

Gregory XVII: Clement Dominguez (-) Sp. schismatic "pope" (elected 1978)

Paul **Gregory**: Jason Lenhart (?1905-) U.S. impresario, film producer

Maysie **Greig**: Maysie Sopoushek, née Greig-Smith (1901-) Australian novelist

Stephen **Grendon**: August William Derleth (1909-1971) U.S. writer of horror fiction

Henry **Gréville**: Alice Durand, née Fleury (1842-1902) Fr. novelist

Greville Minor: John Alfred Spender (1862-1942) Eng. journalist, editor

Leo **Grex**: Leonard Reginald Gribble (1908-) Eng. detective fiction writer

Anne **Grey**: Aileen Ewing (1907-) Br. film actress

°Beryl **Grey**: Beryl Svenson, née Groom (1927-) Br. ballet dancer, artistic director

°Joel **Grey**: Noel Katz (1932-) U.S. stage actor

Mary **Grey**: Ada Bevan ap Rees Bryant (1878-1974) Welsh stage actress

Nan **Grey**: Eschal Miller (1918-) U.S. film actress

°**Grey Owl**: Archibald Stansfield Belaney (1888-1938) Eng. author of books on the Canadian Indians

R.E.H. **Greyson**: Henry Rogers (1806-1877) Eng. reviewer, Christian apologist

Gabbler **Gridiron**: Joseph Haselwood (1793-1833) Eng. antiquary

Francis **Grierson**: Benjamin Henry Jesse Francis Shepard (1848-1927) Eng.-born U.S. writer, singer, pianist

Alan **Griff**: Donald Suddaby (1901-1964) Br. author of SF for boys

Ethel **Griffies**: Ethel Woods (1878-1975) Eng. stage, film actress, working in U.S.

Arthur **Griffinhoofe**: George Colman [the younger] (1762-1836) Eng. dramatist

Fred **Griffiths**: Frederick George Delaney (1856-1940) Eng. music hall artiste

Romayne **Grigorova**: Romayne Austin (1926-) Eng. dancer, teacher [32]

Dod **Grile**: Ambrose Gwinett Bierce (1842-1914) U.S. short story writer

Carleton **Grindle**: Gerald W Page (1939-) U.S. SF, horror fiction writer, editor

Harry **Gringo**: Henry Augustus Wise (1819-1869) U.S. author of melodramatic novels

David **Grinnell**: Donald A Wollheim (1914-) U.S. SF, fantasy writer, publisher

Juan **Gris**: José Victoriano González (1887-1927) Sp.-born Fr. artist

°**Grock**: Adrien Wettach (1880-1959) Swiss clown

Anton **Grot**: Antocz Franziszek Groszewski (1884-) Pol. film art director, working in U.S.

Anastasius **Grün**: Anton Alexander von Auersperg (1806-1876) Austr. poet, statesman

Matthias **Grünewald**: Matthias Nithardt (Nithart) [or Neithardt (Neithart)] (?1470/5-1528) Ger. painter

Nathaniel **Gubbins**: Edward Spencer Mott (1844-1910) Eng. sporting writer

°**Guercino**: Giovanni Francesco Barbieri (1591-1666) It. painter, illustrator

Jules **Guesde**: Mathieu Basile (1845-1922) Fr. Marxist author, orator

George **Guess**: Sequoyah (?1770-1843) U.S.-Indian language teacher, writer

Georges **Guétary**: Lambros Worloou (1915-) Gk.-Egyptian singer, working mainly in France

°**Che Guevara**: Ernesto Guevara de la Serna (1928-1967) Argentine socialist revolutionary

Guitar Slim: Eddie Jones (1926-1959) U.S. blues singer

Sigrid **Gurie**: Sigrid Gurie Haukelid (1911-1969) Norw.-born U.S. film actress

Angelina **Gushington**: Charles Wallwyn Radcliffe-Cooke (1841-1911) Br. writer

Impulsia **Gushington**: Helena Selina Sheridan [Lady Dufferin] (1806-1867) Eng. song, ballad writer

°**Johannes Gutenberg**: Johann Gensfleisch (c.1398-1468) Ger. printing inventor

Anne **Gwynne**: Marguerite Gwynne Trice (1918-) U.S. film actress

Greta **Gynt**: Greta Woxholt (1916-) Norw.-born Eng. film actress

°**Gyp**: Sibylle Gabrielle Marie Antoinette, née de Riquetti de Mirabeau [Comtesse de Martel de Janville] (1850-1932) Fr. novelist

H

Buddy **Hackett**: Leonard Hucker (1924-) U.S. film comedian

Albert **Haddock**: Alan Patrick Herbert (1890-1971) Eng. journalist, writer

Christopher **Haddon**: John Leslie Palmer (1885-1944) Eng. novelist, theatre critic

Peter **Haddon**: Peter Tildsley (1898-1962) Br. film actor

John **Hadham**: [Rev.] James William Parker (1896-) Eng. writer on Jewish affairs

Reed **Hadley**: Reed Herring (1911-1974) U.S. film actor

Jean **Hagen**: Jean Verhagen (1924-) U.S. film actress

William **Haggard**: Richard Henry Michael Clayton (1907-) Eng. author of spy, mystery novels

Fenil **Haig**: °Ford Madox Ford

°**Haile Selassie**: Ras Tafari Makonnen (1891-1975) Ethiopian emperor

Alan **Hale**: Rufus Alan McKahan (1892-1950) U.S. film actor

Binnie **Hale**: Bernice Hale Monro (1899-) Eng. stage comedienne, sister of Sonnie Hale (*q.v.*)

Creighton **Hale**: Patrick Fitzgerald (1882-1965) U.S. film actor

Jonathan **Hale**: Jonathan Hatley (189-1966) U.S. film actor

Sonnie **Hale**: John Robert Hale Monro (1902-1959) Eng. stage, film comedian

Fromental **Halévy**: Jacques Fromental Élie Lévy (1799-1862) Fr. musical composer

Hugh **Haliburton**: James Logie Robertson (1846-1922) Sc. poet, prose writer

M.Y. **Halidom**: ? (-) Br. (?) horror story writer(s) (*v.* Dryasdust) [66]

Adam **Hall**: Elleston Trevor (1920-) Eng. spy thriller writer

Holworthy **Hall**: Harold Everett Porter (1887-1936) U.S. novelist, short story writer

Huntz **Hall**: Henry Hall (1920-) U.S. film actor

James **Hall**: James Brown (1900-1940) U.S. film actor

Jon **Hall**: Charles Locher (1913-1979) U.S. film actor

Ruth **Hall**: Ruth Hale Ibanez (1912-) U.S. film actress

[Sir] Charles **Hallé**: Karl Halle (1819-1895) Ger.-born Eng. pianist, orchestra conductor

Joseph **Haller**: Henry Nelson Coleridge (1798-1843) Eng. lawyer, writer

Hugh **Halliburton**: James Logie Robertson (1846-1922) Sc. poetry, prose writer

°**Brett Halliday**: Davis Dresser (1904-) U.S. author of "private eye" stories

James **Halliday**: David Symington (1904-) Eng. writer on India, Africa

Johnny **Halliday**: Jean-Philippe Smet (1943-) Fr. pop singer

Michael **Halliday**: John Creasey (1908-1973) Eng. crime novelist

Friedrich **Halm**: [Baron] Eligius F J von Münch-Bellinghausen (1806-1871) Ger. dramatist

Clive **Hamilton**: Clive Staples Lewis (1898-1963) Br. writer on literary, religious subjects, novelist

Cosmo **Hamilton**: Cosmo Gibbs (1879-1942) Eng. playwright, novelist

David **Hamilton**: David Pilditch (1939-) Eng. radio, TV announcer, compère

°[Lady] Emma **Hamilton**: Amy Lyon (1765-1815) Eng. society leader, mistress of Nelson

°**Gail Hamilton**: Mary Abigail Dodge (1833-1896) U.S. popular writer, essayist

Paul **Hamlyn**: Paul Bertrand Hamburger (1926-) Br. publisher [35]

Hans **Hammergafferstein**: Henry Wadsworth Longfellow (1807-1882) U.S. poet

Alexander **Hammid**: Alexander Hackenschmied (?1910-) Ger. maker of film documentaries, working in U.S.

Kay **Hammond**: Dorothy Katherine Clements, née Standing (1909-1980) Eng. stage, film actress [35]

Pierre **Hamp**: Henri Louis Bourillon (1876-1962) Fr. novelist

Walter **Hampden**: Walter Hampden Dougherty (1879-1955) U.S. stage, film actor

Olphar **Hamst**: Ralph Thomas (-) Br. bibliophile, pseudonymist [24, 30, 44, 47, 60]

Knut **Hamsun**: Knut Petersen (1859-1952) Norw. novelist

Justin **Hannaford**: Shafto Justin Adair Fitzgerald (1859-) Eng. novelist, dramatist

John **Hanson**: John Watts (1922-) Can.-born Eng. stage singer, actor

Han **Suyin**: Elizabeth Comber, née Chow (1917-) Br. novelist

Robert **Harbin**: Ned Williams (1910-1978) S.A.-born Eng. conjuror

Ephraim **Hardcastle**: William Henry Pyne (1769-1843) Eng. painter, author

Theo **Hardeen**: Theodore Weiss (1876-1944) U.S. illusionist, brother of °Houdini

Ty **Hardin**: Orton Hungerford (1930-) U.S. TV, film actor

Wes **Hardin**: Clay Allison (1914-) Eng. writer of westerns

Ann **Harding**: Dorothy Gatley (1902-) U.S. stage, film actress

°Cyril **Hare**: Alfred Alexander Gordon Clark (1900-1958) Eng. crime novelist

[Sir] John **Hare**: John Fairs (1844-1921) Br. stage actor, manager

Martin **Hare**: Zoë Zajdler, née Girling (c.1907-) Ir. writer

Marion **Harland**: Mary Virginia Terhune, née Hawes (1830-1922) U.S. popular writer

Steve **Harley**: Steven Nice (1951-) Eng. pop musician

Jean **Harlow**: Harlean Carpentier (1911-1937) U.S. film actress

Rolf **Harolde**: Rolf Harolde Wigger (1899-1974) U.S. film actor

Slim **Harpo**: James Moore (1924-1970) U.S. popular harmonica player, singer

James **Harpole**: James Johnston Abraham (1876-) Ir. author

George F. **Harrington**: William Mumford Baker (1825-1883) U.S. clergyman, novelist

Mr. and Mrs. **Harris**: Peregrine Francis Adelbert Cust [Lord Brownlow] (1899-1978) Eng. politician + Wallis Simpson, née Warfield [Duchess of Windsor] (1896-) Eng. noblewoman

Rex **Harrison**: Reginald Carey Harrison (1908-) Eng. stage, film actor

Uncle **Harry**: John Habberton (1842-1921) U.S. journalist, writer

Dolores **Hart**: Dolores Hicks (1939-) U.S. film actress

°Laurence **Harvey**: Larushka Mischa Skikne (1928-1973) Lithuanian-born U.S. film director

Signe **Hasso**: Signe Larsson (1915-) Swe. film actress

Hugh **Hastings**: Hugh Williamson (1917-) Australian stage actor, dramatist

Minnie **Hauk**: Mignon Hauck (1851-1929) U.S. opera singer

June **Haver**: June McMurray, née Stovenour (1926-) U.S. film actress

June **Havoc**: June Hovick (1916-) U.S. stage, film actress, director

Jeremy **Hawk**: Jeremy Lange (1918-) S.A.-born Eng. stage actor

Dale **Hawkins**: Delmar Allen (1938-) U.S. rock musician

Allan **Hawkwood**: Henry James O'Brien Bedford-Jones (1887-1949) Can.-born U.S. historical fiction, fantasy writer

Alice **Hawthorne**: Septimus Winner (1827-1902) U.S. popular songwriter

Rainey **Hawthorne**: Charlotte Eliza Lawson Riddell, née Cowan (1832-1906) Ir.-born Eng. writer

Charles **Hawtrey**: Charles Hartree (1914-) Br. film comedian

Ian **Hay**: John Hay Beith (1876-1952) Sc. novelist

Melissa **Hayden**: Mildred Herman (1923-) U.S. ballet dancer

Russell **Hayden**: Pate Lucid (1912-) U.S. film actor, TV producer

Sterling **Hayden**: John Hamilton (1917-) U.S. film actor

Helen **Haye**: Helen Hay (1874-1957) Br. stage, film actress

Helen **Hayes**: Helen MacArthur, née Brown (1900-) U.S. stage, film actress [34]

Henry **Hayes**: Ellen Warner Kirk, née Olney (1842-1928) U.S. popular fiction writer

Giant **Haystacks**: Luke McMasters (1947-) Br. wrestler, actor [44, 56]

Joan **Haythorne**: Joan Haythornthwaite (1915-) Eng. stage, film actress

Louis **Hayward**: Seafield Grant (1909-) S.A. film actor, working in U.S.

Susan **Hayward**: Edythe Marriner (1918-1975) U.S. film actor

Richard **Haywarde**: Frederick Swartwout Cozzens (1818-1869) U.S. humorous writer

Haywire Mac: Harry Kirby McClintock (1882-1957) U.S. country singer [46]

Rita **Hayworth**: Marguerita Carmen Cansino (1918-) U.S. stage, film actress [42]

Désiré **Hazard**: Octave Feuillet (1821-1890) Fr. novelist, dramatist

Hy **Hazell**: Hyacinth Hazel O'Higgins (1920-1970) Br. revue, musical comedy artiste

H.B.: [1] John Doyle (1797-1868) Ir.-born Eng. caricaturist. [2] Hilaire Belloc (1870-1953) Eng. author

H.D.: Hilda Doolittle (1886-1961) U.S. poet, novelist

Matthew **Head**: John Canaday (1907-) U.S. art critic, mystery novel writer

David **Hedison**: Ara Heditsian (1928-) U.S. film, TV actor

Van **Heflin**: Emmett Evan Heflin, Jr. (1910-1971) U.S. stage, film actor

Gerard **Heinz**: Gerard Hinze (1904-) Ger. stage actor, working in U.K.

Amalie **Heiter**: Amalie Marie Friedrike Auguste (1794-1870) Ger. dramatist, composer

Heldau: [Colonel] J C L Subanski (-1907) Eng. writer of military romances

Ernest **Helfenstein**: Elizabeth Oakes Smith (1806-1893) U.S. popular novelist, magazine writer

Heliogabalus (or Elagabalus): Varius Avitus Bassianus (204-222) Roman emperor

Robert **Heller**: William Henry Palmer (c.1830-1878) Eng. magician, working in U.S.

Brigitte **Helm**: Gisele Eve Schiltenhelm (1907-) Ger. film actress

Mary **Henderson**: James Bridie (q.v.)

Paul **Henderson**: Ruth France (1913-1968) N.Z. novelist, poet [16]

Jimi **Hendrix**: James Marshall Hendrix (1942-1970) U.S. rock musician

Paul **Henreid**: Paul Julius von Hernreid (1908-) Austr. film actor, working in U.S.

°O. **Henry**: William Sydney Porter (1862-1910) U.S. short story writer

Gladys **Henson**: Gladys Gunn (1897-) Ir. stage, film actress

°Audrey **Hepburn**: Edda Hepburn van Heemstra (1929-) Belg.-born U.S. film actress

Francis **Herbert**: William Cullen Bryant (1794-1878) U.S. writer. + Galian Crommelia Verplanck (1786-1870) U.S. writer. + Robert

Charles **Sands** (1799-1832) U.S. writer

Homes **Herbert**: Edward Sanger (1882-1956) Br. stage, film actor, working in U.S.

Herblock: Herbert Lawrence Block (1909-) U.S. cartoonist

Hergé: Georges Rémi (-) Belg. cartoonist, originator of boy detective "Tintin"

Eileen **Herlie**: Eileen Herlihy (1919-) Sc. stage, screen actress

Herman: Peter Blair Denis Bernard Noone (1947-) Eng. pop singer

The **Hermit of Marlow**: Percy Bysshe Shelley (1792-1822) Eng. poet

James A. **Heron**: James Ahern (1839-1901) U.S. stage actor, playwright

Robert **Heron**: John Pinkerton (1758-1826) Sc. writer

James **Herriot**: James Alfred Wight (1916-) Eng. veterinary novelist

A **Hertfordshire Incumbent**: [Rev.] Joseph Williams Blakesley (1808-1885) Eng. writer of letters to *The Times*

Carl **Hertz**: Leib (or Louis) Morganstern (1859-1924) U.S. illusionist, working in U.K.

Hervé: Florimond Rongé (1825-1892) Fr. composer, organist, orchestra leader

°Aleksandr Ivanovich **Herzen** (or Gertsen): Aleksandr Ivanovich Yakovlev (1812-1870) Russ. revolutionary writer

Charlton **Heston**: Charlton Carter (1922-) U.S. stage, film actor

Martin **Hewitt**: Arthur Merrison (1863-1945) Eng. novelist, journalist

Harrington **Hext**: Eden Phillpotts (1862-1960) Eng. novelist, poet, essayist, playwright

Anne **Heywood**: Violet Pretty (1931-) Eng. film actress

H.H.: Helen Maria Hunt Jackson, née Fiske (1830-1885) U.S. poet, novelist, children's writer

Ruth **Hiatt**: Ruth Redfern (1908-) U.S. U.S. film actress

William **Hickey**: Thomas James Leasor (1923-) Eng. author

Harry **Hieover**: Charles Bindley (1795-1859) Eng. sporting writer

Nehemiah **Higginbottom**: Samuel Taylor Coleridge (1772-1834) Eng. poet, critic

Jack **Higgins**: Henry Patterson (1929-) Eng. fiction writer

Patricia **Highsmith**: Patricia Plangman (1921-) U.S. novelist

Headon **Hill**: Francis Edward Grainger (1857-1924) Eng. romantic novelist, detective fiction writer

Joe **Hill**: Joel Emanuel Hagglund (1879-1915) Swe.-born U.S. political poet, composer

Robin **Hill**: Robert Young (1811-1908) Eng. poet

Wendy **Hiller**: Wendy Gow, née Watkin (1912-) Eng. stage, film actress

Harriet **Hilliard**: Peggy Lou Snyder (1914-) U.S. film, TV actress

Thomas **Hinde**: [Sir] Thomas Willes Chitty (1926-) Br. novelist

Jerome **Hines**: Jerome Heinz (1921-) U.S. opera singer

Hi-Regan: [Captain] John Joseph Dunne (1837-1910) Eng. traveler, sports writer

His **Nibs**: Philip Poole (1909-) Eng. pen shop owner

Historicus: [1] George Grote (1794-1871) Eng. historian. [2] [Sir] William George Granville Venables Vernon Harcourt (1827-1904) Eng. statesman

°**H.L.L.**: Jane Laurie Borthwick (1813-1897) Sc. hymnwriter

Rose **Hobart**: Rose Keefer (1906-) U.S. film actress

°John Oliver **Hobbes**: Pearl Mary Teresa Craigie, née Richards (1867-1906) U.S.-born Eng. novelist

°**Ho Chi Minh**: Nguyen That Thanh (1890-1969) North Vietnamese president

Stephen **Hockaby**: Gladys Maude Winifred Mitchell (1901-) Br. crime novelist

John **Hodgkinson**: John Meadowcraft (1767-1805) Br. actor, working in U.S.

Dennis **Hoey**: Samuel David Hyams (1893-1960) Eng. film actor, working mainly in U.S.

Monckton **Hoffe**: Reaney Monckton Hoffe-Miles (1881-1951) Ir. playwright

Professor Louis **Hoffmann**: Angelo J Lewis (1839-1919) Eng. journalist, writer on conjuring

Fay **Holden**: Fay Hammerton (1894-1973) Br. stage, film actress, working in U.S.

Jan **Holden**: Jan Wilkinson (1931-) Eng. stage actress

Stanley **Holden**: Stanley Waller (1928-) Br. ballet dancer

°William **Holden**: William Franklin Beedle, Jr. (1918-) U.S. film actor

Ephraim **Holding**: George Mogridge (1787-1854) Eng. miscel. writer

Judy **Holliday**: Judith Tuvim (1923-1965) U.S. stage, film actress [32]

Earl **Holliman**: Anthony Numenka (1928-) U.S. film actor

Buddy **Holly**: Charles Hardin Holly (1936-1959) U.S. rock musician

Hanya **Holm**: Johanna Kuntze, née Eckert (c.1900-) Ger. stage choreographer, director of musicals

Ian **Holm**: Ian Holm Cuthbert (1931-) Eng. stage actor

Saxe **Holm**: Helen Maria Hunt Jackson (1830-1885) U.S. poet, novelist, children's writer

K.E. **Holme**: John Edward Christopher Hill (1912-) Eng. historian, writer

Gordon **Holmes**: Louis Tracy (1863-1928) Eng. journalist, fiction writer

H.H. **Holmes**: William Anthony Parker White (1911-1968) U.S. thriller writer

Victoria **Holt**: Eleanor Alice Burford Hibbert (1906-) Eng. novelist

Leonard **Holton**: Leonard Patrick O'Connor Wibberley (1915-) Ir. mystery writer

Cecil **Home**: Julia Augusta Webster, née Davies (1837-1894) Br. poet, dramatist

°Evelyn **Home**: Peggy Makins, née Carn (1916-) Br. advice columnist

Homer: Henry D Haynes (1918-) U.S. country singer

Geoffrey **Homes**: Daniel Mainwaring (1901-) U.S. mystery novelist, screenwriter

Homo Novus: William John Courthope (1842-1917) Eng. critic, literary historian [44]

Henry **Honeycomb**: James Henry Leigh Hunt (1784-1859) Eng. essayist, poet

Honoria: Marguerite A Power (?1815-1867) Br. author, poet

Honorius II: Lamberto Scannabecchi (?-1130) It. pope

Honorius III: Cencio Savelli (?-1227) It. pope

Honorius IV: Giacomo (or Jacobus) Savelli (?1210-1287) It. pope

Perci **Honri**: Percy Henry Thompson (1874-1953) Eng. music hall artiste

Anthony **Hope**: [Sir] Anthony Hope Hawkins (1863-1933) Eng. historical novelist, playwright

Ascott R. **Hope**: Robert Hope Moncrieff (1846-) Eng. editor, novelist, schoolbook writer

°Bob **Hope**: Leslie Townes Hope (1904-) Eng.-born U.S. film comedian

Mark **Hope**: Eustace Clare Grenville Murray (1824-1881) Eng. journalist, author

Laurence **Hope**: Adela Florence Nicolson, née Cory (1865-1904) Br. writer of "oriental" lyrics

Antony **Hopkins**: Antony Reynolds (1921-) Eng. composer, conductor, broadcaster about music

°Hedda **Hopper**: Elda Furry (1890-1966) U.S. film actress, gossip columnist

Otto **Horn**: Adolf Baüerle (1786-1859) Austr. dramatist, novelist

Adam **Hornbrook**: Thomas Cooper (1805-1892) Eng. politician, author

Horace **Hornem**: George Gordon Byron (1788-1824) Eng. poet

Isaac **Hortibonus**: Isaac Casaubon (1559-1614) Swiss theologian, classical scholar

Robert **Houdin**: Jean Eugène Robert (1805-1871) Fr. conjuror

°Harry **Houdini**: Erik Weisz (1874-1926) Hung.-born U.S. escapologist

Claude **Houghton**: Claude Houghton Oldfield (1889-1961) Br. novelist

John **Houseman**: Jacques Haussman (1902-) Rom. stage, film director, working in U.S.

Renée **Houston**: Katherina Houston Gribbin (1902-1980) Sc. vaudeville artiste, film actress

The **Howadji**: George William Curtis (1824-1892) U.S. travel-writer, newspaper correspondent

Elizabeth Jane **Howard**: Elizabeth Jane Liddon (1923-) Eng. writer, editor, reviewer

H.L. **Howard**: Charles Jeremiah Wells (?1799-1879) Eng. poet

John **Howard**: John Cox (1913-) U.S. film actor

Keble **Howard**: John Keble Bell (1875-1928) Eng. playwright, journalist

Leslie **Howard**: Leslie Stainer (1893-1943) Eng. stage, film actor

Thomas **Howard**: Jesse Woodson James (1847-1882) U.S. desperado

James Wong **Howe**: Wong Tung Jim (1899-1976) Chinese cinematographer, working in U.S.

°Frankie **Howerd**: Francis Alick Howard (1922-) Eng. stage, film, TV comedian

Howlin' Wolf: Chester Arthur Burnett (1910-1976) U.S. black blues singer, songwriter

Margaret **Howth**: Rebecca Blaine Harding Davis (1831-1910) U.S. novelist

John **Hoyt**: John Hoysradt (1905-) U.S. film actor

°Rock **Hudson**: Roy Harold Fitzgerald (1925-) U.S. film actor

Stephen **Hudson**: Sydney Schiff (?1869-1944) Eng. novelist, translator

Jean **Hugard**: John G Boyce (1872-1959) Australian magician, working in U.S.

Hazel **Hughes**: Hazel Hepenstall (1913-1974) S.A. stage actress

Kathleen **Hughes**: Betty von Gerlean (1929-) U.S. film actress

Josephine **Hull**: Josephine Sherwood (1884-1957) U.S. stage, film actress

Richard **Hull**: Richard Henry Sampson (1896-1973) Eng. detective novelist

°Engelbert **Humperdinck**: Arnold George Dorsey (1936-) Eng. pop singer

Kyle **Hunt**: John Creasey (1908-1973) Eng. crime novelist

Jeffrey **Hunter**: Henry Hunter McKinnies (1927-1969) U.S. film actor

°Kim **Hunter**: Janet Cole (1922-) U.S.

stage, film actress

Ross **Hunter**: Martin Fuss (1921-) U.S. film producer, actor

Tab **Hunter**: Arthur Andrew Gelien (1931-) U.S. film actor [63]

Frances E. **Huntly**: Ethel Colburn Mayne (-1941) Ir. biographer, writer of literary studies

Ruth **Hussey**: Ruth Carol O'Rourke (1914-) U.S. film actress

Walter **Huston**: Walter Houghston (1884-1950) Can.-born U.S. stage, film actor

°Betty **Hutton**: Elizabeth Jane Thornburg (1921-) U.S. film actress

Marion **Hutton**: Marion Thornburg (1920-) U.S. singer, film actress, sister of °Betty Hutton

Robert **Hutton**: Robert Bruce Winne (1920-) U.S. film actor

Joris Karl **Huysmans**: Charles-Marie-Georges Huysmans (1848-1907) Fr. novelist

Père **Hyacinthe**: Charles-Jean-Marie Loyson (1827-1912) Fr. priest, writer

Robin **Hyde**: Iris Guiver Wilkinson (1906-1939) S.A. novelist, poet, working in New Zealand

Wilfred **Hyde-White**: Wilfred White (1903-) Eng. stage, film actor

Ronald **Hyde**: Ronald Hens (1931-) Eng. ballet dancer, choreographer, director

I

Ianthe: Emma Catherine Embury (1806-1863) U.S. novelist [39]

Ibrahim ibn Abd Allah: Johann Ludwig Burckhardt (1784-1817) Swiss-born Eng. explorer, traveler, writer

Iconoclast: [1] Mary Agnes Hamilton, née Adamson (1884-1966) Br. novelist, biographer. [2] Charles Bradlaugh (1833-1891) Eng. secularist, social, political reformer

Idris: Arthur Henry Mee (1875-1943) Eng. journalist, editor, writer

Father **Ignatius**: Joseph Leycester Lyne (1837-1908) Br. Benedictine monk

Ignotus: James Franklin Fuller (1835-)

Eng. architect, writer

Francis **Iles**: Anthony Berkeley Cox (1893-1971) Br. writer of detective stories

M. **Ilyin**: Ilya Yakovlevich Marshak (1896-1953) Russ. author, children's writer

Immerito: Edmund Spenser (?1552-1599) Eng. poet

The **Impenitent**: Henry Dawson Lowry (1869-1906) Eng. author

Fay **Inchfawn**: Elizabeth Rebecca Ward (1881-) Br. popular writer

Colonel Frederic **Ingham**: Edward Everett Hale (1822-1909) U.S. author, editor, Unitarian clergyman

Mona **Inglesby**: Mona Kimberley (1918-) Br. ballet dancer

Ingoldsby: [Rev.] James Hildyard (1809-1897) Eng. classical scholar

Thomas **Ingoldsby**: [Rev.] Richard Harris Barham (1788-1845) Br. writer, antiquary

Rex **Ingram**: Reginald Hitchcock (1893-1950) Ir. film director

°Michael **Innes**: John Innes Mackintosh Stewart (1906-) Sc. writer of detective novels

Innocent II: Gregorio Papareschi dei Guidoni (?-1143) It. pope

Innocent III: Giovanni Lotario de' Conti (1161-1216) It. pope

Innocent IV: Sinibaldo (de') Fieschi (?-1254) It. pope

Innocent V: Pierre de Tarenlaise (c.1224-1276) Fr. pope

Innocent VI: Étienne Aubert (?-1362) Fr. pope

Innocent VII: Cosimo Gentile de' Migliorati (?1336-1406) It. pope

Innocent VIII: Giovanni Battista Cibo (1432-1492) It. pope

Innocent IX: Giovanni Antonio Facchinetti (1519-1591) It. pope

Innocent X: Giovanni Battista Pamfili (1574-1655) It. pope

Innocent XI: Benedetto Odescalchi (1611-1689) It. pope

Innocent XII: Antonio Pignatelli (1615-1700) It. pope

Innocent XIII: Michelangiolo Conti (1655-1724) It. pope [50]

Ionicus: J C Armitage (-) Eng. cartoonist

Iota: Kathleen Mannington Caffyn (-1926) Eng. author

Michael Ireland: Darrell Figgis (1882-1925) Ir. poet, writer

Irenaeus: Samuel Irenaeus Prime (1812-1885) U.S. clergyman, author

Ralph Iron: Olive Emilie Albertina Schreiner (1885-1920) Br. novelist [23]

Ironquill: Eugene Fitch Ware (1841-1911) U.S. lawyer, poet

Nestor Ironside: [1] [Rev.] Samuel Croxall (?-1752) Eng. literary scholar. [2] [Sir] Richard Steele (1672-1729) Ir. essayist, dramatist

George Irving: George Irving Sheasky (1922-) U.S. stage actor, singer

°[Sir] Henry Irving: John Henry Brodribb (1838-1905) Br. stage actor, manager

Jules Irving: Jules Israel (1925-) U.S. stage director

May Irwin: Ada Campbell (1862-1938) Can. stage actress, music hall artiste

Isa: Isa Craig Knox (1831-1903) Sc. writer

°Iskander: °Aleksandr Ivanovich Herzen

Burl Ives: Burl Icle Ivanhoe (1909-) U.S. stage, film actor, folk singer

J

Kareem Abdul Jabbar: Lew Alcindor (1947-) U.S. basketball player

Wanda Jackson: Wanda Goodman (1937-) U.S. pop singer

Cousin Jacques: Louis Abel Beffroy de Reigny (1757-1811) Fr. writer

Frank Jacson: Ramón Mercader (1914-1978) Sp. assassinator of °Leon Trotsky

Dean Jagger: Dean Jeffries (1903-) U.S. film actor

Jak: Raymond Jackson (1927-) Eng. cartoonist [30]

James James: Arthur Henry Adams (1872-1936) N.Z. novelist, poet, playwright

°Jimmy James: James Casey (1892-1965) Eng. music hall comedian

Polly James: Pauline Devaney (1941-) Eng. stage, TV actress

Sonny James: James Loden (1929-) U.S. country singer

Elsie Janis: Elsie Bierbower (1889-1956) U.S. stage actress

Emil Jannings: Theodor Friedrich Emil Janenz (1884-1950) Swiss film actor

David Janssen: David Meyer (1930-1980) U.S. film, TV actor

Janus: [1] Johann Joseph Ignaz von Döllinger (1799-1890) Ger. theologian. [2] Robert le Bonnières (1850-1895) Fr. journalist, novelist. [3] [Dr.] Johannes Friedrich (1836-1917) Ger. theologian, historian [38]

Emile Jaques-Dalcroze: Jakob Dalkes (1865-1950) Swiss music teacher

Jacques Jasmin: Jacques Boé (1798-1864) Fr. poet, "troubadour"

W.M.L. Jay: Julia Louisa Matilda Woodruff, née Curtiss (1833-1909) Eng. author

Michael Jayston: Michael James (1936-) Eng. stage actor

Gloria Jean: Gloria Jean Schoonover (1928-) U.S. film actress

Ursula Jeans: Ursula Livesey, née McMinn (1906-1973) Eng. stage actress

Mahatma Cane Jeeves: °W.C. Fields [58]

Anne Jeffreys: Anne Carmichael (1923-) U.S. stage actress, singer

Allen Jenkins: Alfred McGonegal (1900-1974) U.S. film actor

Caryl Jenner: Pamela Penelope Ripman (1917-) Eng. stage director, theatre manager

Jenneval: Hippolyte Louis Alexandre Dechet (1801-1830) Fr. comedian, poet

°Kid Jensen: David Allen Jensen (1950-) Can.-born Eng. radio, TV DJ, MC

Mary Jerrold: Mary Allen (1877-1955) Br. film actress

Jethro: Kenneth C. Burns (1923-) U.S. country singer

Jetsam: Malcolm McEachern (1884-1945) Australian singer, stage, radio entertainer, teaming with Flotsam (q.v.)

Jillana: Jillana Zimmerman (1936-) U.S. ballet dancer

Robert **Jeffrey**: Abdullah Jaffa Anver Bey Khan) (1930-) U.S. ballet dancer, choreographer

John II: Mercurius (?-535) It. pope [10]

John III: Catelinus (?-574) It. pope

John XII: Octavian (?937-964) It. pope [10]

John XIV: Pietro Canepanora (?-984) It. pope

John XVII: Giovanni Siccone (?-1003) It. pope

John XVIII: Giovanni Fasano (?-1009) It. pope

John XXI: Peter Juliani (c.1210 or 1220-1277) Sp. pope

John XXII: Jacques d'Euse (1249-1334) Fr. pope

John XXIII: Angelo Giuseppe Roncalli (1881-1963) It. pope [49]

°**Elton (Hercules) John**: Reginald Kenneth Dwight (1947-) Eng. pop musician

Evan **John**: Evan John Simpson (1901-) Br. playwright, novelist

Jasper **John**: Rosalie Muspratt Jones (1913-) Br. film, stage actress

[Brother] **John Charles**: [Rt. Rev.] John Charles Vocklet (1924-) Australian Anglican friar, writer

John of Kronshtadt: Ioann Sergiev (1821-1908) Russ. priest, alleged miracle-worker

[Saint] **John of the Cross**: Juan de Yepis y Álvarez (1542-1591) Sp. mystic, poet [37]

John Paul I: Albino Luiciani (1913-1978) It. pope [49, 51, 52]

John Paul II: Karol Wojtyla (1920-) Pol. pope [10, 49, 51, 52]

Foster **Johns**: Gilbert Vivian Seldes (1893-1970) U.S. journalist, drama critic, writer

John **Johnson**: Guy Fawkes (1570-1606) Eng. conspirator

Benjamin F. **Johnson of Boone**: James Whitcomb Riley (1854-1916) U.S. poet, journalist

°**Al Jolson**: Asa Yoelson (1886-1950) U.S. singer, stage, film actor

°**Jennifer Jones**: Phyllis Selznick, née Isley (1919-) U.S. film actress

John Paul **Jones**: John Paul (1747-1792) Sc.-born U.S. naval hero

Paul **Jones**: Paul Pond (1942-) Eng. stage actor, pop musician

Richard **Jones**: Theodore Edward Hook (1788-1841) Eng. humorist, novelist

Sheridan **Jones**: Ada Elizabeth Chesterton, née Jones (1870-1962) Br. journalist, writer

T. Percy **Jones**: William Edmonstoune Aytoun (1813-1865) Sc. humorous writer

Tom **Jones**: Thomas Jones Woodward (1940-) Welsh pop singer

Mrs. Dorothea **Jordan**: Dorothea Bland (1762-1816) Ir. comedy actress

Ivar **Jorgensen**: Paul W Fairman (1916-) U.S. writer of SF

°[Père] **Joseph**: François Leclerc du Tremblay (1577-1638) Fr. friar, diplomat

Josiah Allen's Wife: Marietta Holley (1836-1926) U.S. popular humorist

Louis **Jourdain**: Louis Gendre (1919-) Fr. film actor

Leatrice **Joy**: Leatrice Joy Zeidler (1899-) U.S. film actress

Brenda **Joyce**: Betty Leabo (1918-) U.S. film actress

Thomas **Joyce**: Arthur Joyce Lunel Carey (1888-1957) Ir. novelist

J.S. of Dale: Frederic Jesup Stimson (1855-1943) U.S. author, lawyer

Aunt **Judy**: Margaret Scott Gatty (1809-1873) Eng. children's writer

Julius II: Giuliano della Rovere (1443-1513) It. pope

Julius III: Giammaria Ciocchi del Monte (1487-1555) It. pope

Jennie **June**: Jane Croly, née Cunningham (1829-1901) Eng.-born U.S. writer

Junius Americanus: Arthur Lee (1740-1792) U.S. diplomat

E. **Junius**: Adrien Emmanuel Rouquette (1813-1887) U.S. poet, novelist

Katy **Jurado**: María Jurado García (1927-) Mexican film actress, working in U.S.

K

Vasily Ivanovich **Kachalov**: Vasily

Ivanovich Shverubovich (1875-1948) Russ. stage actor

Kalanag: Helmut Schreiber (1893-1963) Ger. illusionist

Lev Borisovich Kamenev: Lev Borisovich Rozenfeld (1883-1936) Russ. revolutionary

°Eden Kane: Richard Sarstedt (1942-) Eng. pop singer

°Karandash: Mikhail Nikolayevich Rumyantsev (1901-) Russ. clown, circus artiste

Anna Karina: Hanne Karin Beyer (1940-) Dan. film actress, appearing in Fr., U.S. films

Miriam Karlin: Miriam Samuels (1925-) Br. film revue comedienne

°Boris Karloff: William Henry Pratt (1887-1969) Eng. film actor, working mainly in U.S.

Phil Karlson: Philip N. Karlstein (1908-) U.S. film director

Maria Karnilova: Maria Dovgolenko (1920-?) U.S. ballet dancer, of Russ. parentage [35]

°Fred Karno: Frederick John Westcott (1866-1941) Eng. music hall comedian

Kurt S. Kasznar: Kurt Serwischer (1913-) Austr. stage actor

Isser Katch: Isser Kać (1896-1958) Pol. film actor, working in U.S.

Charles Kay: Charles Piff (1930-) Eng. stage actor

Danny Kaye: David Daniel Kaminsky (1913-) U.S. stage, film, TV actor [14, 31]

Nora Kaye: Nora Koreff (1920-) U.S. ballet dancer

°Elia Kazan: Elia Kazanjoglou (1909-) Turk.-born U.S. film director

Mathilda Kchessinkska: [Princess] Krassinska-Romanovska (1872-1971) Russ. ballet dancer, teacher

°Buster Keaton: Joseph Francis Keaton (1895-1966) U.S. film comedian

Diane Keaton: Diane Hall (1946-) U.S. stage, film actress

Viola Keats: Viola Smart (1911-) Sc. stage actress

Howard Keel: Harold Keel (1919-) U.S. stage, film actor, singer

Malcolm Keen: Malcolm Knee (1887-) Br. film, stage, theatre manager

Carolyn Keene: Edward L Stratemeyer (1862-1930) U.S. children's writer

Laura Keene: Mary Moss (or Foss) (c.1830-1873) U.S. actress, theatre manager

Tom Keene: George Duryea (1896-1963) U.S. film actor

David Keith: Francis Steegmuller (1906-) U.S. novelist, literary critic

Ian Keith: Keith Ross (1899-1960) U.S. film actor

Penelope Keith: Penelope Timson, née Hatfield (1940-) Eng. TV actress

Harry Kellar: Harry Keller (1849-1922) U.S. magician

°Pamela Kellino: Pamela Ostrer 1916-) Br. film actress, columnist, TV personality

Will P. Kellino: William P. Gislingham (1873-1958) Br. circus clown, acrobat, film actor, director

Kathleen Kellow: Eleanor Hibbert (1906-) Eng. novelist

Kem: Kimon Evan Marengo (1906-) Egyptian-born Br. political cartoonist, journalist

Jeremy Kemp: Edmund Walker (1934-) Eng. film, TV actor [34]

Kempferhausen: Robert Pearse Gillies (1788-1858) Eng. littérateur, autobiographer

Joan Kemp-Welch: Joan Green (1906-) Eng. stage actress, director

William Hunter Kendal: William Hunter Grimston (1843-1917) Br. stage actor, manager

Kay Kendall: Justine McCarthy (1927-1959) Eng. film actress

Suzy Kendall: Frieda Harrison (?1943-) Eng. film actress

Merna Kennedy: Merna Kahler (1908-1944) U.S. film actress

Milward Kennedy: Milward Rodon X Burge (1894-1968) Eng. journalist, mystery writer

Charles J. Kenny: Erle Stanley Gardner (1889-1970) U.S. crime novelist

Barry Kent: Barry Sautereau (1932-) Eng. stage actor

Jean Kent: Joan Summerfield (1921-) Eng. film actress

Richard Kent: Frank Owen (1893-1968) Eng. writer of "oriental" mystery fiction

°Jomo **Kenyatta**: Kamau (?1894-1978) African statesman, nationalist leader

Deborah **Kerr**: Deborah Jane Viertel, née Kerr-Trimmer (1921-) Sc. film actress [14]

Frederick **Kerr**: Frederick Grinham Keen (1858-1933) Br. stage, film actor

°**Orpheus** C. **Kerr**: Robert Henry Newell (1836-1901) U.S. humorous journalist

Norman **Kerry**: Arnold Kaiser (1889-1956) U.S. film actor

Irvin **Kershner**: Irvin Kerschner (1923-) U.S. film actor

Stanley **Ketchel**: Stanislaus Kiecal (1886-1910) U.S. middleweight boxer

The **Khalifa**: Abdullah et Taaisha (?1846-1899) Arab dervish leader in Sudan

Johnny **Kidd**: Frederick Heath (1939-1966) Eng. rock singer

Michael **Kidd**: Milton Greenwald (1919-) U.S. dancer, choreographer, theatre director

Bobbie **Kimber**: Robert Kimberley (1918-) Eng. ventriloquist, female impersonator

Andrea **King**: Georgetta Barry (1915-) Fr. U.S. film actress

°**B.B. King**: Riley B. King (1925-) U.S. black blues guitarist

Ben E. **King**: Benjamin Earl Nelson (1938-) U.S. pop singer

Carole **King**: Carole Klein (1942-) U.S. pop singer

Dennis **King**: Dennis Pratt (1897-1972) Eng. opera singer, film actor

Edith **King**: Edith Keck (1896-) U.S. stage actress

Freddie **King**: Billy Myles (1934-) U.S. black rock musician

Kennedy **King**: George Douglas Brown (1869-1902) Sc. novelist

°Nosmo **King**: Vernon Watson (?1887-1949) Eng. stage comedian

W. Scott **King**: [Rev.] William Kingscote Greenland (1868-) Eng. Wesleyan minister, writer

King Curtis: Curtis Ousley (1934-1971) U.S. jazz saxophonist

Sidney **Kingsley**: Sidney Kieschner (1906-) U.S. stage, film actor, playwright

Hugh **Kingsmill**: Hugh Kingsmill Lunn (1889-1949) Br. novelist, short story writer, biographer

Julian **Kingstead**: Francis James de Mallet Cunynghame (1884-) Br. novelist, magazine writer

Gertrude **Kingston**: Gertrude Silver, née Konstam (1866-1937) Eng. stage actress, theatre manager [26]

Mme **Kinkel**: Elizabeth Sara Sheppard (1830-1862) U.S. novelist

W. **Kinsayder**: John Marston (?1575-1634) Eng. dramatist, poet

Phyllis **Kirk**: Phyllis Kirkegaard (1926-) U.S. film actress

Edmund **Kirke**: James Roberts Gilmore (1822-1903) U.S. businessman, author

°Sergey Mironovich **Kirov**: Sergey Mironovich Kostrikov (1886-1934) Russ. statesman, Communist leader

Louise **Kirtland**: Louise Jelly (1905-) U.S. stage actress

°**Klabund**: Alfred Henschke (1890-1928) Ger. Expressionist poet, playwright, novelist

°**Klaxon**: [Commander] John Graham Bower (1886-) Eng. writer of adventure stories

Paul **Klenovsky**: [Sir] Henry Joseph Wood (1869-1944) Eng. orchestra conductor, musical arranger

Tristan **Klingsor**: Léon Leclère (1875-?) Fr. poet, art critic

°Diedrich **Knickerbocker**: Washington Irving (1783-1859) U.S. humorist [20]

David **Knight**: David Mintz (1927-) U.S. film, stage actor

Edward **Knoblock**: Edward Knoblauch (1874-1945) U.S. dramatist, working in U.K.

Edward **Knott**: Matthias Wilson (1580-1656) Eng. Jesuit writer

Teddy **Knox**: Albert Edward Cromwell-Knox (1896-1974) Eng. stage comedian, teaming with °Jimmy Nervo

Ruth **Kobart**: Ruth Maxine Kohn (1924-) U.S. stage actress, singer

John **Kobbler**: John Kelso Hunter (1802-1873) Sc. artist, author, cobbler

N. **Kokhanovskaya**: Nadezhda Stepanovna Sokhanskaya (1825-1884) Russ. writer

Al **Koran**: Edward Doe (1916-1972) Br. conjuror

Janusz **Korczak**: Genrik Goldszmidt (1878-1942) Pol. writer, educationalist, doctor

°[Sir] Alexander **Korda**: Sandro Kellner (1893-1956) Hung.-born Br. film producer

Mikhail Petrovich **Korinfsky**: Mikhail Petrovich Varentsov (1788-1851) Russ. architect

Bogomir Bogomirovich **Korsov**: Gottfried Gëring (1845-1920) Russ. opera singer

Fritz **Kortner**: Fritz Nathan Kohn (1892-1970) Austr. film actor

Sonia **Korty**: Sophia Ippar (1892-1955) Russ. ballet dancer, choreographer, teacher

Charles **Korvin**: Geza Kaiser (1907-) Czech-born U.S. film actor

Martin **Kosleck**: Nicolai Yoshkin (1907-) Russ. film actor, working in U.S.

Henry **Koster**: Hermann Kosterlitz (1905-) Ger. film director, working in U.S.

Billy J. **Kramer**: William Ashton (1943-) Eng. pop singer

Nathalie **Krassovska**: Natasha Leslie (1918-) Russ.-U.S. ballet dancer

Kreskin: George Kresge (-) Eng. conjuror

Kristine: Christine Hodgson (1950-) Eng. pop singer

°**Kukryniksy**: Mikhail Vasilyevich Kupriyanov (1903-) Russ. artist, satirical cartoonist. + Porfiry Nikitich Krylov (1902-) Russ. artist, satirical cartoonist. + Nikolai Aleksandrovich Sokolov (1903-) Russ. artist, satirical cartoonist

Hermann **Kunst**: Walter Chalmers Smith (1824-1908) Sc. poet

Thomas **Kyd**: Alfred Bennett Harbage (1901-) U.S. educator, Shakespeare scholar, detective story writer

Elisabeth **Kyle**: Agnes Mary Robertson Dunlop (-) Sc. author of children's books

L

Barbara **Laage**: Claire Colombat (1925-) Fr. film actress

Rudolph von **Laban**: Rudolf Laban de Varaljas (1879-1958) Hung. ballet dancer, choreographer

°Louise **Labé**: Louise Charly (?1524-1566) Fr. poet

Patti **Labelle**: Patricia Holt (1944-) U.S. black rock singer

Jack **La Bolina**: Augustus Victor Vecchi (1843-) It. naval writer

Simon **Lack**: Simon Macalpine (1917-1980) Sc. stage actor

François **La Colère**: Louis Aragon (1897-) Fr. poet

Ed **Lacy**: Len Zinberg (1911-1968) U.S. writer of mystery short stories

John **Lacy**: George Darley (1795-1846) Ir. poet, novelist, critic [16]

Leon **Ladulfi**: Noël du Fail (1520-1591) Fr. writer

A **Lady**: [1] Anne Finch [Countess of Winchelsea] (1661-1720) Eng. poet. [2] Sarah Fielding (1710-1768) Eng. writer. [3] Anna Brownell Jameson, née Murphy (1794-1860) Ir. writer. [4] Elizabeth Missing Sewell (1815-1906) Eng. writer [5] Susan Fenimore Cooper (1813-1894) U.S. writer [24]

Lady of Quality: Enid Bagnold (1889-) Eng. writer

Philip **Lafargue**: [Dr.] Joshua Henry Philpot (1850-) Br. editor, novelist

Lafayette: Sigmund Neuberger (1872-1911) Ger.-born U.S. illusionist

La Fleur: Robert Guérin (?-1634) Fr. actor

La Grange: Charles Varlet (1639-1692) Fr. actor

Jean **Lahor**: Henri Cazalis (1840-1909) Fr. poet

Bert **Lahr**: Irving Lahrheim (1895-1967) U.S. stage, film comedian

Cleo **Laine**: Clementine Dinah Dankworth, née Campbell (1927-) Eng. jazz singer, actress

Denny **Laine**: Brian Arthur Haynes (1944-) Eng. pop musician

°Frankie **Laine**: Frank Paul Lo Vecchio (1913-) U.S. pop singer, actor

Arthur **Lake**: Arthur Silverlake (1905-) U.S. film actor

°Veronica **Lake**: Constance Ockleman (1919-1973) U.S. film actress

Barbara **La Marr**: Reatha Watson (1896-1926) U.S. film actress

°Hedy **Lamarr**: Hedwig Kiesler (1914-) Austr. film actress, working in U.S.

Louis **Lambert**: Patrick Sarsfield Gilmore (1829-1892) Ir.-born U.S. bandmaster

La Meri: Russell Meriwether Hughes (1898-) U.S. ballet dancer, ethnologist, writer

La Messine: Juliette Adam, née Lamber (1836-1936) Fr. novelist, editor

Lamia: Alfred Austin (1835-1913) Eng. poet [39]

Miss **Lamont**: Eleanor Jourdain (-1924) Eng. author (jointly with Miss Morison—q.v.)

Dorothy **Lamour**: Dorothy Kaumeyer (1914-) U.S. film actress

Lana: Alan Kemp (1938-) Eng. female impersonator

A **Lancashire** Incumbent: [Rev.] Abraham Hume (1814-1884) Eng. antiquarian, writer of letters to *Times*

G.B. **Lancaster**: Edith Joan Balfour Lyttleton (?1865-1948) N.Z. writer

Elsa **Lanchester**: Elizabeth Sullivan (1902-) Br. stage, film actress, working in U.S. [34]

Harald **Lander**: Alfred Bernhardt Stevnsborg (1905-1971) Dan.-Fr. ballet dancer, teacher

Lew **Landers**: Lewis Friedlander (1901-1962) U.S. film director

Elissa **Landi**: Elizabeth Zanardi-Landi (1904-1948) Austr.-It. film actress

Carole **Landis**: Frances Ridste (1919-1948) U.S. film actress

Jessie Royce **Landis**: Jessie Royse Medbury (1904-1972) U.S. stage, film actress

Avice **Landon**: Avice Spitta (1910-) Eng. stage actress

Jane **Landon**: Frances Jane Leach (1947-) Australian ballet dancer

Michael **Landon**: Eugene Maurice Orowitz (1937-) U.S. film, TV actor

Allan "Rocky" **Lane**: Harry Albershart (1901-1973) U.S. film actor

Burton **Lane**: Burton Levy (1912-) Br. composer of musicals

Jane **Lane**: Elaine Dakers, née Kidner (?-1978) Eng. writer of historical novels, children's books, biographies

Lola **Lane**: Dorothy Milligan (1909-) U.S. film actress

Lupino **Lane**: Henry George Lupino (1892-1959) Br. stage, film comedian

Eddie **Lang**: Salvatore Massaroa (1903-1933) U.S. jazz guitarist

June **Lang**: June Vlasek (1915-) U.S. film actress

Launcelot **Langstaff**: Washington Irving (1783-1859) U.S. story writer, essayist, historian. + William Irving (1766-1821) U.S. politician, satirist, his brother. + James Kirke Paulding (1778-1860) U.S. writer

Lillie **Langtry**: Emilie Charlotte Langtry, née Le Breton (1853-1929) Br. stage actress

E.B. **Lanin**: Dr. Emile Joseph Dillon (1854-1933) Ir.-born Br. newspaper correspondent

Jörg **Lanner**: Jörg Langenstrass (1939-) Ger. ballet dancer

Katti **Lanner**: Katharina Lanner (1829-1908) Austr. ballet dancer, choreographer, teacher

°Mario **Lanza**: Alfredo Arnold Cocozza (1921-1959) It.-born U.S. opera singer

Eddie **Large**: Edward Hugh McGinnis (1942-) Sc.-born Br. TV comedian, teaming with Syd Little (q.v.)

Rod **La Rocque**: Roderick la Rocque de la Rour (1896-1971) U.S. film actor

Rita **La Roy**: Ina Stuart (1907-) Fr. film actress

°**Larry**: Terence Parkes (1927-) Eng. cartoonist

°Danny **La Rue**: Daniel Patrick Carroll (1928-) Ir.-born Br. revue artiste female impersonator

Jack **La Rue**: Gaspare Biondolillo (1903-) U.S. film actor

Denise **Lasalle**: Denise Craig (c.1947-) U.S. pop singer, songwriter

Lady Carolina **Lascelles**: Mary Elizabeth Maxwell, née Braddon (1837-

1915) Eng. novelist

Orlandi di **Lasso**: (or Orlandus Lassus): Roland Delattre (?1532-1594) Belg. musical composer

Frank **Latimore**: Frank Kline (1925-) U.S. film actor

Tomline **Latour**: [Sir] William Schwenk Gilbert (1836-1911) Eng. playwright, librettist

[Sir] Harry **Lauder**: Hugh MacLennan (1870-1950) Sc. music hall singer

Laura: Mary Robinson, née Darby (1758-1810) Eng. actress, novelist, poet

Stan **Laurel**: Arthur Stanley Jefferson (1890-1965) Eng. film comedian, working in U.S.

Paula **Laurence**: Paula de Lugo (1916-) U.S. stage actress

Piper **Laurie**: Rosetta Jacobs (1932-) U.S. film actress

Comte de **Lautréamont**: Isidore-Lucien Ducasse (1846-1870) Fr. poet

Anthony **Lawless**: Philip MacDonald (c.1890-?) Br. writer of detective novels

Gertrude **Lawrence**: Gertrud Alexandra Dagmar Lawrence Klasen (1898-1952) Eng. stage actress

Lars **Lawrence**: Philip Stevenson (1896-1965) U.S. author

°Slingsby **Lawrence**: George Henry Lewes (1817-1878) U.S. philosopher, literary critic

Steve **Lawrence**: Sidney Leibowitz (1935-) U.S. pop singer

Henry Hertzberg **Lawson**: Henry Hertzberg Larsen (1867-1922) Australian poet, short story writer

W.B. **Lawson**: George Charles Jenks (1850-1929) Br. printer, journalist, fiction writer, working in U.S.

Wilfred **Lawson**: Wilfred Worsnop (1900-1966) Br. stage, film actor

Halldór Kiljan **Laxness**: Halldór Kiljan Gudjonsson (1902-) Icelandic novelist

Dilys **Lay**: Dilys Laye (1934-) Eng. stage actress

A **Layman**: [1] [Dr.] William Falconer (1744-1824) Eng. miscellaneous writer. [2] [Sir] Walter Scott (1771-1832) Sc. poet, novelist, historian, biographer. [3] Richard

Monckton Milnes [Baron Houghton] (1809-1885) Eng. poet

Joe **Layton**: Joseph Lichtman (1931-) U.S. choreographer, stage director

Leadbelly: Huddie Ledbetter (1888-1949) U.S. folk singer

Evelyn **Lear**: Evelyn Schulman (1928-) U.S. opera singer

[Major] **Le Caron**: Thomas Miller Beach (1841-1894) Br. secret agent, working in U.S.

°John **Le Carré**: David John Moore Cornwell (1931-) Eng. writer of spy stories

Jean-Paul **Le Chanois**: Jean-Paul Dreyfus (1909-) Fr. film director

Andrew **Lee**: Louis (Stanton) Auchinloss (1917-) U.S. novelist

Anna **Lee**: Joanna Winnifrith (1914-) Br. film actress, working in U.S.

Brenda **Lee**: Brenda Mae Tarpley (1944-) U.S. country singer

Bruce **Lee**: Lee Yen Kam (1941-1973) U.S. film actor, of Chin. parentage

°Canada **Lee**: Leonard Lionel Cornelius Canegata (1907-1952) U.S. black stage, film actor

Dickey **Lee**: Dickey Lipscomb (1943-) U.S. pop singer

Dixie **Lee**: Wilma Wyatt (1911-1952) U.S. film actress

Dorothy **Lee**: Marjorie Millsop (1911-) U.S. film actress

°Gypsy Rose **Lee**: Rose Louise Hovick (1914-1970) U.S. stage, film actress

Holm(e) **Lee**: Harriet Parr (1828-1900) Eng. novelist [45]

Lila **Lee**: Augusta Apple (1902-1973) U.S. film actress

Michele **Lee**: Michele Dusiak (1942-) U.S. film actress, singer

Patty **Lee**: Alice Cary (1820-1871) U.S. poet, novelist

°Peggy **Lee**: Norma Dolores Egstrom (1920-) U.S. night-club singer, film actress

Steve **Lee**: Michel Patrick Parry (1947-) Eng. writer, anthologist

Vanessa **Lee**: Winifred Ruby Moule (1920-) Eng. stage actress, singer

Vernon **Lee**: Violet Paget (1856-1935) Fr.-born Eng. essayist, art critic, novelist

William **Lee**: William S. Burroughs

(1914-) U.S. novelist

Richard **Leech**: Richard Leeper Mc-Clelland (1922-) Ir. stage, film, TV actor

Andrea **Leeds**: Antoinette Lees (1914-) U.S. film actress

Herbert I. **Leeds**: Herbert I Levy (?1900-1954) U.S. film director

Ethel **Leginska**: Ethel Liggins (1890-) Eng. pianist, conductor, comp. [32]

Janet **Leigh**: Jeanette Helen Morrison (1927-) U.S. film actress

°Vivien **Leigh**: Vivian Mary Hartley (1913-1967) Eng. stage, film actress

Eino **Leino**: Armas Eino Leopold Lönnbohm (1878-1926) Finn. poet

Erich **Leinsdorf**: Erich Landauer (1912-) U.S. conductor, of Austr. parentage

Lekain: Henri-Louis Cain (1729-1778) Fr. actor

L.E.L.: Letitia Elizabeth Landon (1802-1838) Eng. poet, novelist

Sara **Leland**: Sally Harrington (1941-) U.S. ballet dancer

°[Sir] Peter **Lely**: Pieter van der Faes (1618-1680) Du. portrait painter, working in England

°**Lenare**: Leonard Green (1883-) Eng. society photographer

Nikolaus **Lenau**: Franz Niembsch Edler von Strehlenau (1802-1850) Austr. poet [27]

°**Leonid Lench**: Leonid Sergeyevich Popov (1905-) Russ. writer, dramatist

°**Lenin**: Vladimir Ilyich Ulyanov (1870-1924) Russ. Communist party founder, head of state

Dan **Leno**: George Wild Galvin (1860-1904) Eng. music hall artiste

Rula **Lenska**: [Countess] Roza-Maria Lubienska (1947-) Pol.-born Eng. TV actress

Lotte **Lenya**: Karoline Blamauer (1900-) Austr. stage actress, opera singer

[Saint] **Leo IX**: Bruno of Egisheim (1002-1054) Alsatian pope [50]

Leo X: Giovanni de' Medici (1475-1521) It. pope

Leo XI: Alessandro Ottaviano de' Medici (1535-1605) It. pope

Leo XII: Annibale Sermattei della Genga (1760-1829) It. pope

Leo XIII: Vincenzo Gioacchino Pecci (1810-1903) It. pope [50, 51]

André **Léo**: Léonie Champseix (-) Fr. writer [35]

Benny **Leonard**: Benjamin Leiner (1896-1947) U.S. lightweight boxer

Hugh **Leonard**: John Keyes Byrne (1926-) Ir. dramatist

Sheldon **Leonard**: Sheldon Bershad (1907-) U.S. film actor, TV producer

Baby **Le Roy**: Le Roy Overacker (1931-) U.S. film actor

Carole **Lesley**: Maureen Rippingale (1935-1974) Br. film actress

Frank **Leslie**: Henry Carter (1821-1821-1880) Eng. engraver, publisher, working in U.S.

°Joan **Leslie**: Joan Agnes Theresa Sadie Brodel (1925-) U.S. film actress

Natasha **Leslie**: Nathalie Krassovska (1919-) Russ. ballet dancer

Bruce **Lester**: Bruce Lister (1912-) S.A. film actor, working in U.S., U.K.

Daniel **Lesueur**: Jeanne Lapauze, née Loiseau (1860-1921) Fr. writer

Letine: George Gorin (1853-1889) Eng. acrobatic cyclist in the music hall

Daniel **Levans**: Daniel Levins (1944-) U.S. ballet dancer

Les **Levante**: Leslie George Cole (1892-1978) Australian illusionist ("The Great Levante")

Samuel **Levene**: Samuel Levine (1905-) U.S. stage actor

°Caroline **Lewis**: Harold Begbie (1871-1929) Eng. author. + M H Temple (-) Eng. author. + Stafford Ransome (-) Eng. illustrator

°Jerry **Lewis**: Joseph Levitch (1926-) U.S. film comedian, teaming with °Dean Martin

Smiley **Lewis**: Overton Amos Lemons (1920-1966) U.S. pop musician

Ted **Lewis**: Theodore Friedman (1889-1971) U.S. bandleader, entertainer, film actor

Val **Lewton**: Vladimir Ivan Leventon (1904-1951) Russ.-born U.S. horror movie director

Edward **Lexy**: Edward Gerald Little

(1897-) Br. film actor

George **Leybourne**: Joe Saunders (1842-1884) Eng. music hall artiste ("Champagne Charlie")

Liberace: Wladziu Valentino Liberace (1919-) U.S. popular pianist, film actor, entertainer

David **Lichine**: David Liechtenstein (1910-1972) Russ.-U.S. ballet dancer, choreographer

Serge **Lido**: Serge Lidoff (1906-) Russ.-Fr. ballet photographer

Lien Chi Altangi: Oliver Goldsmith (?1730-1774) Ir.-born Eng. writer

Winnie **Lightner**: Winifred Hanson (1901-1971) U.S. film comedienne

Beatrice **Lillie**: [Lady] Constance Sylvia Peel, née Munston (1898-) Can.-born Eng. stage actress

Frank **Lin**: Gertrude Franklin Atherton, née Horn (1857-1948) U.S. novelist

Abbey **Lincoln**: Anna Marie Woolridge (1930-) U.S. black film actress

Elmo **Lincoln**: Otto Elmo helter (1889-1952) U.S. film actor

Anya **Linden**: Anya Sainsbury, née Eltenton (1933-) Eng. ballet dancer

Hal **Linden**: Harold Lipshitz (1931-) U.S. stage actor, singer

Max **Linder**: Gabriel Leuvielle (1883-1925) Br. film comedian

Viveca **Lindfors**: Elsa Viveca Torstensdotter (1920-) Swe. film actress

Harry **Lindsay**: Lindsay Hudson (1858-) Br. journalist, novelist

Margaret **Lindsay**: Margaret Kies (1910-) U.S. film actress

Linesman: [Captain] Maurice Grant (1872-) Br. soldier, magazine contributor

Bambi **Linn**: Bambi Linnemeier (1926- (1926-) U.S. stage actress, dancer

Carolus **Linnaeus**: Carl von Linné (1707-1778) Swe. botanist

Virna **Lisi**: Virna Pieralisi (1937-) It. film actress

Emanuel **List**: Emanuel Fleissig (1890-1967) Austr.-born U.S. opera singer

Frances **Little**: Fannie Macaulay, née Caldwell (1863-1941) U.S. novelist

Syd **Little**: Cyril John Mead (1942-) Eng. TV comedian, teaming with Eddie Large (*q.v.*)

°Thomas **Little**: Thomas Moore (1779-1852) Ir. poet, satirist

Little Eva: Eva Narcissus Boyd (1945-) U.S. pop singer [46]

Little Milton: Milton James Campbell (1934-) U.S. blues musician [46]

Little Richard: Richard Penniman (1935-) U.S. black rock musician [46]

°**Little Tich**: Harry Ralph (1868-1928) Br. music hall comedian, of dwarfish stature

Little Walter: Marion Walter Jacobs (1930-1968) U.S. harmonica blues player

Cornelius **Littlepage**: James Fenimore Cooper (1789-1851) U.S. novelist

Mark **Littleton**: John Pendleton Kennedy (1795-1870) U.S. politician, educationalist, author

Maksim Maksimovich **Litvinov**: Maksim Maksimovich Wallach (1876-1951) Russ. revolutionary, diplomat

Emma **Livry**: Emma-Marie Emarot (1842-1863) Fr. ballet dancer

Richard **Llewellyn**: Richard Dafydd Vivian Llewellyn Lloyd (1907-) Welsh novelist

Charles **Lloyd**: Sir Charles Lloyd Birkin (1907-) Eng. horror story writer

°Lucy Vaughan **Lloyd**: John Keats (1795-1821) Eng. poet

Marie **Lloyd**: Matilda Alice Victoria Wood (1870-1922) Eng. music hall artiste

Lobo: Kent Lavoie (1943-) U.S. pop guitar player, singer

Gary **Lockwood**: John Gary Yusolfsky (1937-) U.S. film, TV actor

Margaret **Lockwood**: Margaret Mary Day (1916-) Eng. film, TV actress

John **Loder**: John Lowe (1898-) Br. film actor

Cecilia (or Cissie) **Loftus**: Marie Cecilia M'Carthy (1876-1943) Sc. stage, film actress, working in U.S.

Jimmy **Logan**: James Short (1922-) Sc. stage, TV actor, comedian

Log-roller: Richard Le Gallienne (1866-1947) Eng. poet, essayist

Herbert **Lom**: Herbert Charles Angelo Kuchacevich ze Schluderpacheru (1917-) Czech-born Br. film actor

Carole **Lombard**: Jane Alice Peters

(1908-1942) U.S. film comedian

George **London**: George Burnstein (1920-) Can. opera singer, producer

°Jack **London**: John Griffith London (1876-1916) U.S. author

Julie **London**: Julie Peck (1926-) U.S. film actress, singer

London Antiquary: Frederick William Fairholt (1814-1866) Eng. engraver, antiquarian writer

The **Londoner**: Oswald Barron (1868-1939) Br. contributor of feature articles to London *Evening News*

Professor **Longhair**: Henry Roeland Byrd (1918-) U.S. pop pianist

Pietro **Longhi**: Pietro Falca (1702-1785) It. painter

Frederick **Lonsdale**: Lionel Frederick Leonard (1881-1954) Eng. dramatist

Gordon Arnold **Lonsdale**: Konon Trofimovich Molody (1924-) Russ. spy, working in U.K. **[12]**

Looker-On: David Storrar Meldrum (1865-) Br. novelist, journalist

E.C.R. **Lorac**: Edith Caroline Rivett (1894-1958) Eng. author of detective novels **[30]**

Jack **Lord**: John Joseph Ryan (1922-) U.S. film, TV actor

Jeremy **Lord**: Ben Ray Redman (1896-) U.S. journalist, writer

°Sophia **Loren**: Sofia Scicolone (1934-) It. film actress, working in U.S.

Constance **Lorne**: Constance Mac-Laurin (1914-) Sc. stage actress

Marion **Lorne**: Marion Lorne Mac-Dougal (1886-1968) U.S. stage, film comedienne

Tommy **Lorne**: Hugh Gallagher Corcoran (1890-1935) Sc. music hall comedian

Peter **Lorre**: László Löwenstein (1904-1964) Hung. film actor, working in U.S.

Joan **Lorring**: Magdalen Ellis (1926-) Eng.-Russ. film actress, working in U.S.

Parson **Lot**: Charles Kingsley (1819-1875) Eng. clergyman, novelist

Amy **Lothrop**: Anna Bartlett Warner (1827-1915) U.S. novelist

°Pierre **Loti**: Louis-Marie-Julien Viaud (1850-1923) Fr. naval officer, traveler, novelist

Joe **Louis**: Joseph Louis Barrow (1914-1981) U.S. black heavyweight boxer

Morris **Louis**: Morris Bernstein (1912-1962) U.S. Abstract Expressionist painter

Anita **Louise**: Anita Louise Fremault (1917-1970) U.S. stage, film actress

Pierre **Louÿs**: Pierre Louis (1870-1925) Belg.-born Fr. novelist, poet **[21]**

°Bessie **Love**: Juanita Horton (1898-) U.S. film actress, working in U.K.

Darlene **Love**: Darlene Wright (1930-) U.S. pop singer

Low: [Sir] David Alexander Cecil Low (1891-1963) N.Z.-born Eng. cartoonist, caricaturist **[29]**

Robert **Lowery**: Robert Lowery Hanks (1916-1971) U.S. film actor

Woytec **Lowski**: Woiciech Wiesidlowski (1939-) Pol. ballet dancer

°Myrna **Loy**: Myrna Williams (1902-) U.S. film actress

Ignatius **Loyola**: Iñigo de Oñez y Loyola (1491-1556) Sp. soldier, churchman

°Arthur **Lucan**: Arthur Towle (1887-1954) Eng. music hall, film comedian

°Victoria **Lucas**: Sylvia Plath (1932-1963) U.S. poet

Lucas van Leyden: Lucas Hugensz (or Lucas Jacobsz) (1494-1533) Du. painter, engraver

Lasse **Lucidor**: Lars Johansson (1638-1674) Swe. poet

Lucius II: Gherardo Caccianemici (?-1145) It. pope

Lucius III: Ubaldo Allucingoli (?1097-1185) It. pope

Aunt **Lucy**: Lucy Bather (1836-1864) Eng. children's author **[46]**

Johnny **Ludlow**: Ellen Wood, née Price (1814-1887) Eng. novelist

Kazak **Lugansky**: Vladimir Ivanovich Dal' (1801-1872) Russ. novelist, philologist

Bela **Lugosi**: Bela Lugosi Blasko (1882-1956) Hung.-born U.S. film actor

Luigi: Eugene Louis Facciuto (1925-) U.S. ballet dancer, teacher

Marcel **Luipart**: Marcel Fenchel (1912-) Ger.-Austr. ballet dancer, choreographer, teacher

Luisillo: Luis Perez Davila (1928-) Mexican ballet dancer, choreographer

Paul Lukas: Paul Lugacs (1895-1971) Hung.-born U.S. film actor

Jean-Baptiste Lully: Giovanni Battista Lulli (1632-1687) It.-born Fr. composer [32]

°Lulu: Marie McDonald McLaughlin Lawrie (1948-) Sc. popular singer, stage, TV actress

Lulubelle: Myrtle Eleanor Cooper (1913-) U.S. country singer, teaming with Scotty (q.v.)

Benjamin Lumley: Benjamin Levy (1811-1875) Eng. opera manager

Sidney Luska: Henry Harland (1861-1905) U.S. novelist

David Lyall: [1] Annie Shepherd Swan (1860-1943) Sc. novelist. [2] Helen Buckingham Reeves, née Mathers (1853-1920) Eng. novelist

Edna Lyall: Ada Ellen Bayly (1857-1903) Eng. writer of popular novels

°Le Lycanthrope: Petrus Borel (1809-1859) Fr. poet, novelist

Lyddal: David Garrick (1717-1779) Eng. actor

Viola Lyel: Violet Watson (1900-1972) Eng. stage, film actress

°Moura Lympany: Mary Defries, née Johnstone (1916-) Eng. concert pianist

Barre Lyndon: Alfred Edgar (1896-1972) Eng. playwright, film scriptwriter, working in U.S.

Barbara Lynn: Barbara Lynn Ozen (1942-) U.S. blues singer

Diana Lynn: Dolores Loehr (1926-1971) U.S. film, stage, TV comedienne

Ethel Lynn: Ethelinda Beers, née Eliot (1827-1879) U.S. poet

Dr. H.S. Lynn: Hugh Simmons (1836-1899) Eng. conjuror

Jeffrey Lynn: Rognar Lind (1909-) U.S. film actor

°Vera Lynn: Vera Margaret Welch (1917-) Eng. popular singer

Gillian Lynne: Gillian Back, née Pyrke (1926-) Eng. ballet dancer, director, choreographer

Lynx: °Rebecca West

Leonard Lyons: Leonard Sucher (1906-1976) U.S. columnist

Christian Lys: Percy J Brebner (1864-) Br. novelist

M

Maarten Maartens: Jozua Marius Willem Van Der Poorten-Schwartz (1858-1915) Du.-born Eng. novelist

Uncle Mac: Derek McCulloch (1897-1967) Eng. children's author, broadcaster [46]

McArone: George Arnold (1834-1865) U.S. poet, humorist

Seosamh MacCathmhaoil: Joseph Campbell (1881-) Ir. poet

Greg McClure: Dale Easton (1918-) U.S. film actor

F.J. McCormick: Peter Judge (1891-1947) Ir. stage, film actor

Kid McCoy: Norman Selby (1873-1940) U.S. boxer (possibly the original "real McCoy")

°Hugh MacDiarmid: Christopher Murray Grieve (1892-1978) Sc. poet, critic, translator

John Ross Macdonald: Kenneth Millar (1915-) U.S. novelist, mystery writer

Marie McDonald: Marie Frye (1923-1965) U.S. film actress ("The Body")

Murray Macdonald: Walter MacDonald Honeyman (1899-) Sc. stage director, manager

Geraldine McEwan: Geraldine Crutwell, née McKeown (1932-) Eng. stage, TV actress

Stephen Macfarlane: John Keir Cross (1911-1967) Sc. fantasy fiction, children's writer

Mike McGear: Michael McCartney (1944-) Eng. pop musician

Fibber McGee: James Jordan (1897-) U.S. radio comedian, film actor

Molly McGee: Marion Jordan (1898-1961) U.S. radio comedienne, film actress, teaming with her husband Fibber McGee (q.v.)

Malcolm Macgregor: William Mason (1724-1797) Eng. poet

Sandy MacGregor: John White (1893-) Sc. music hall singer

Richard McGrory: Keith Joseph May

(1952-) U.S. accomplice of Joy(ce) McKinney (Darleen O'Connor — q.v.)

Arthur **Machen**: Arthur Llewellyn Jones (1863-1947) Welsh horror fiction, ghost story writer

Connie **Mack**: Cornelius Alexander McGillicuddy (1862-1956) U.S. baseball manager

Siobhan **McKenna**: Siobhan Giollamhuire nic Cionnaith (1923-) Ir. stage, film actress

Charles **Macklin**: Charles M'Laughlin (?1690-1797) Ir. actor, playwright

Bridget **Maclagen**: Mary Borden (1886-1968) U.S.-born Eng. novelist

Shirley **Maclaine**: Shirley Maclean Beaty (1934-) U.S. film actress, sister of °Warren Beatty

Ian **Maclaren**: John Watson (1850-1907) Sc. short story writer, essayist

°Fiona **Macleod**: William Sharp (1855-1905) Sc. author

Frank **McLowery**: Clay Allison (1914-) Eng. writer of westerns

Brinsley **Macnamara**: John Weldon (1891-1963) Ir. stage actor, dramatist

Gus **McNaughton**: Augustus Howard (1884-1969) Br. film actor

Pierre **Mac Orlan**: Pierre Dumarchey (1882-1970) Fr. novelist

°Butterfly **McQueen**: Thelma McQueen (1911-) U.S. black stage actress

Mark **Macrabin**: Allan Cunningham (1784-1842) Sc. poet, writer

Sean **MacStiofain**: John Edward Drayton Stephenson (1928-) Br.-born leading IRA member

Minnie **Maddern**: Marie Augusta Fiske, née Davey (1865-1932) U.S. stage actress, director

Rose **Maddox**: Roseea Arbana Brogdon (1926-) U.S. country singer

Jean **Madeira**: Jean Browning (1918-1972) U.S. opera singer

Madeleine: Noor Imayat Khan (1914-1944) Br. agent, working in France

Guy **Madison**: Robert Moseley (1922-) U.S. film actor

Noel **Madison**: Mathaniel Moscovitch (1898-1975) U.S. film actor

Magic Sam: Sam Marghett (1937-1969) U.S. black musician

Hyacinthe **Maglanowich**: Prosper Mérimée (1803-1870) Fr. novelist, historian

Philip **Magnus**: [Sir] Philip Magnus-Allcroft (1906-) Eng. biographer

°**Maharaj Ji**: Pratap Singh Rawat (1957-) Indian guru

Jock **Mahoney**: Jacques O'Mahoney (1919-) U.S. film actor

°**Marjorie Main**: Mary Tomlinson Krebs (1890-1975) U.S. film actress

John Wilson **Maitland**: [Sir] William Watson (1858-1935) Eng. poet

Thomas **Maitland**: Robert Williams Buchanan (1841-1901) Eng. poet, novelist

Maître Adam: Adam Billaut (1602-1662) Fr. carpenter, poet

Earl **Majors**: Alan Garreth (1953-1978) Eng. motor-cycle stunt rider

°[Archbishop] **Makarios III**: Mikhail Khristodolou Mouskos (1913-1977) Cypriot head of state

Malachi **Malagrowther**: [Sir] Walter Scott (1771-1832) Sc. poet, novelist [38]

Curzio **Malaparte**: Kurt Erich Suckert (1898-1957) It. writer, journalist

Karl **Malden**: Mladen Sekulovich (1914-) U.S. film, TV actor

Lucas **Malet**: Mary St. Leger Harrison, née Kingsley (1852-1931) Eng. novelist

Peter **Malin**: Rearden Conner (q.v.)

Max **Malini**: Max K Breit (1873-1963) Pol.-born U.S. magician

Gina **Malo**: Janet Flynn (1909-1963) Ir.-Ger.-U.S. film actress, working in U.K.

Dorothy **Malone**: Dorothy Maloney (1925-) U.S. film, TV actress

°Louis **Malone**: Louis MacNeice (1907-1963) Ir. poet

Manchecourt: Henri Léon Émile Lavedan (1859-1940) Fr. playwright, novelist

Georges **Mandel**: Jeroboam Rothschild (1885-1943) Fr. politician

Miles **Mander**: Lionel Mander (1888-1946) Eng. stage, film actor

Frederick **Manfred**: Feike Feikema (1912-) U.S. novelist

Anthony **Mann**: Emil Bundsmann

(1906-1967) U.S. film director
Hank **Mann**: David Liebermann (1887-1971) U.S. film actor
Manfred **Mann**: Mike Lubowitz (1940-) S.A.-born Eng. pop musician
Theodore **Mann**: Theodore Goldman (1924-) U.S. stage producer, director
Mary **Mannering**: Florence Friend (1876-1953) Eng. stage actress, working in U.S.
Charles **Manners**: Southcote Mansergh (1857-1935) Ir. opera singer, working in U.K.
David **Manners**: Rauff de Ryther Duan Acklom (1901-) Can. stage, film actor, novelist
Mrs. Horace **Manners**: Algernon Charles Swinburne (1837-1909) Eng. poet
Irene **Manning**: Inez Harvuot (1917-) U.S. film actress
Manolete: Manuel Laureano Rodríguez Sánchez (1917-1947) Sp. bullfighter
°Jayne **Mansfield**: Vera Jayne Palmer (1932-1967) U.S. film actress
Katherine **Mansfield**: Kathleen Mansfield Murry, née Beauchamp (1888-1923) N.Z.-born Br. novelist, short story writer
Peter **Manton**: John Creasey (1908-1973) Eng. crime novelist
E. **Manuel**: Ernest L'Épine (1826-1893) Fr. writer
Maori: James Inglis (1845-1908) N.Z. author, journalist, politician
°Le **Mapah**: Ganneau (1805-1851) Fr. sculptor, religious leader
Adele **Mara**: Adelaida Delgado (1923- Sp.-U.S. dancer, film actress
Jean **Marais**: Jean Villain-Marais (1913-) Fr. film actor
Marcel **Marceau**: Marcel Mangel (1923-) Fr. mime artist
Elspeth **March**: Elspeth MacKenzie (-) Eng. stage actress
°Fredric **March**: Frederick McIntyre Bickel (1897-1975) U.S. stage, film actor
William **March**: William Edward March Campbell (1893-1954) U.S. novelist
Catherine **Marchant**: Catherine Ann

Cookson, née McMullen (1906-) Eng. novelist
Rocky **Marciano**: Rocco Francis Marchegiano (1923-1969) U.S. heavyweight boxer
Marco II: Harold Henry Sebag-Montefiore (1924-) Eng. barrister, writer on Marco Polo
Margo: María Marguerita Guadelupe Boldao y Castilla (1918-) Mexican-born stage, film actress, dancer, working in U.S.
Marie-Jeanne: Marie-Jeanne Pelus (1920-) U.S. ballet dancer
Mariemma: Emma Martinez (1920-) Sp. ballet dancer
J.-J. **Marine**: René Oppitz (1904-1976) Belg. poet, critic, detective story writer
Mona **Maris**: Maria Capdevielle (1903-) Fr.-Argentinian film actress, working in U.S.
Sari **Maritza**: Sari Deterling-Nathan (1911-) Chinese film actress
J. **Marjoram**: Ralph Hale Mottram (1883-1971) Eng. novelist, poet
Mrs. **Markham**: Elizabeth Penrose, née Cartwright (1780-1837) Eng. novelist, children's writer
David **Markham**: Peter Basil Harrison (1913-) Eng. stage actor
°Joseph Arthur **Markham**: John Thomson Stonehouse (1925-) Eng. politician
Robert **Markham**: Kingsley Amis (1922-) Eng. novelist
[Dame] Alicia **Markova**: Lilian Alice Marks (1910-) Br. ballet dancer [32]
E. **Marlitt**: Eugenie John (1825-1887) Ger. novelist
Louis **Marlow**: Louis Umfreville Wilkinson (1881-1966) Br. novelist, biographer
Anthony **Marlowe**: Anthony Perredita (1913-) Eng. stage actor
Hugh **Marlowe**: Hugh Hipple (1914-) U.S. film actor
Julia **Marlowe**: Sarah Frances Frost (1866-1950) Eng.-born U.S. stage actress
Florence **Marly**: Hana Smekalova (1918-1978) Fr.-Czech film actress
Martin **Marprelate**: John Penry (1559-1593) Welsh Puritan writer. + John

Udall (?1560-1592) Eng. Puritan preacher. + Henry Barrow (?-1593) Eng. church reformer. + Job Throckmorton (1545-1601) Eng. Puritan

J.J. **Marric**: John Creasey (1908-1973) Eng. crime novelist

Moore **Marriott**: George Thomas Moore-Marriott (1885-1949) Br. film comedian

Mlle **Mars**: Anne-Françoise-Hippolyte Boutet (1779-1847) Fr. actress

Carol **Marsh**: Norma Simpson (1926-) Br. film actress

Garry **Marsh**: Leslie Marsh Geraghty (1902-1981) Eng. stage, film actor [34]

Joan **Marsh**: Nancy Ann Rosher (1914-) U.S. film actress

Marian **Marsh**: Violet Krauth (1913-) U.S. film actress

James **Marshal**: Sydney James Bounds (1920-) Eng. SF writer

Brenda **Marshall**: Ardis Anderson (1915-) U.S. film actress

Tully **Marshall**: Tully Marshall Phillips (1864-1943) U.S. film actor

°William **Marshall**, Gent.: Horace Walpole (1717-1797) Eng. writer

Paul **Martens**: Stephen H. Critten (1887-1964) Eng. novelist, short story writer

Fred **Marteny**: Feodor Neumann (1931-) Czech-Austr. ballet dancer, choreographer

Martin IV: Simon de Brie (?1210-1285) Fr. pope

Martin V: Oddone Colonna (1368-1431) It. pope [52]

Alan Langdon **Martin**: Jane Cowl (q.v.) + Jane Murfin (-) Eng. playwright

°Dean **Martin**: Dino Crocetti (1917-) U.S. film actor, singer, teaming with °Jerry Lewis

Ernest H. **Martin**: Ernest H Markowitz (1919-) U.S. stage mgr., producer

Richard **Martin**: John Creasey (1908-1973) Eng. crime novelist

Ross **Martin**: Martin Rosenblatt (1920-) Pol.-U.S. film actor

Stella **Martin**: Georgette Heyer (1902-1974) Br. author of historical romances, detective novels [63]

Tony **Martin**: Alvin Morris (1913-) U.S. cabaret singer, film actor

Jean Paul Égide **Martini**: Johann Paul Ägidius Schwarzendorf (1741-1816) Ger.-born Fr. composer

Al **Martino**: Alfred Cini (1927-) U.S. pop singer

L. **Martov**: Yuly Osipovich Tsederbaum (1873-1923) Russ. Menshevik leader

°Ik **Marvel**: Donald Grant Mitchell (1822-1908) U.S. essayist

°Chico **Marx**: Leonard Marx (1891-1961) U.S. film comedian

°Groucho **Marx**: Julius Henry Marx (1895-1977) U.S. film comedian

°Gummo **Marx**: Milton Marx (1893-1977) U.S. film comedian

°Harpo **Marx**: Adolph Arthur Marx (1893-1964) U.S. film comedian

°Zeppo **Marx**: Herbert Marx (1901-1979) U.S. film comedian

Mary of Arnhem: Helen Sensburg (-) Ger. Nazi propagandist, broadcasting to Br. troops

[Sister] **Mary Regis**: [Dame] Mary Maud Morant (1901-) Br. headmistress, working in Rhodesia, South Africa

Masaccio: Tommaso di Giovanni di Simone Guidi (1401-1428) It. painter [33, 34]

Masolino: Tommaso di Cristofero Fini (1383-1440 or 47) It. painter, pupil of Masaccio (q.v.) [34]

Edith **Mason**: Edith Barnes (1898-1973) U.S. opera singer

Shirley **Mason**: Leona Flugrath (1900-) U.S. film actress

Stuart **Mason**: Christopher Sclater Millard (1872-1927) Br. biographer of Oscar Wilde

°**Massachusettensis**: Daniel Leonard (1740-1829) U.S. Loyalist writer

Ilona **Massey**: Ilona Hajmassy (1912-1974) Hung.-born U.S. film actress

°Léonide **Massine**: Leonid Fedorovich Miassin (1896-1979) Russ. ballet dancer, choreographer

Lorca **Massine**: Leonide Massine (1944-) U.S. ballet dancer, choreographer, son of °Léonide Massine (q.v.)

The **Master**: John Corlett (1841-) Br.

sporting editor, newspaper proprietor

°**Mata Hari**: Gertrud Margarete Macleod, née Zelle (1876-1917) Du.-born Fr. dancer, spy

Rudolph **Mate**: Rudolf Matheh (1898-1964) Pol. film actor

Carmen **Mathé**: Margaretha Matheson (1938-) Sc. ballet dancer

Helen **Mathers**: Helen Buckingham Reeves, née Matthews (1853-1920) Eng. novelist

Mathetes: John Jones (?1821-1878) Welsh Baptist biblical writer

°**Anna Matilda**: [1] Hannay Cowley (1743-1809) Eng. dramatist, poet. [2] Hester Lynch Piozzi, née Salusbury (1741-1821) Eng. writer

Julia **Matilda**: Julia Clara Byrne, née Busk (1819-1894) Eng. author

Matteo: Matteo Marcellus Vittucci (1919-) U.S. ballet dancer, choreographer, director

°**Walter Matthau**: Walter Matuschanskayasky (1920-) U.S. stage, film actor

Thomas **Matthew**: John Rogers (1505-1555) Eng. Protestant divine, martyr, author of Matthew's Bible

Robin **Maugham**: Robert Cecil Maugham [Viscount Maugham] (1916-1981) Eng. novelist

Furnley **Maurice**: Frank Wilmost (1881-1942) Australian poet

Walter **Maurice**: [Sir] Walter Besant (1836-1901) Eng. novelist

°André **Maurois**: Émile Salomon Wilhelm Herzog (1885-1967) Fr. writer

Maxim the Greek: Mikhail Trivolis (c.1475-1556) Gk. churchman, translator

Lois **Maxwell**: Lois Hooker (1927-) Can. film actress, working in U.S., U.K.

Robert **Maxwell**: Ian Robert Hoch (1923-) Ger.-born Eng. publisher, politician, writer

Roger **Maxwell**: Roger D Latham (1900-) Eng. stage, film, TV actor

Joe **May**: Joseph Mandel (1880-1954) Austr. director of film adventure serials

Sophie **May**: Rebecca Sophia Clarke (1833-1906) U.S. children's writer

Ferdy **Mayne**: Ferdinand Mayer-Boerckel (1920-) Ger.-born Eng. stage actor

Rutherford **Mayne**: Samuel J. Waddell (1879-1967) Ir. playwright

°**Virginia Mayo**: Virginia May Jones (1922-) U.S. film actress

Joseph **Mazilier**: Giulio Mazarini (1801-1868) Fr. ballet dancer, choreographer, balletmaster

Mike **Mazurki**: Mikhail Mazurwski (1909-) U.S. film actor

Lillie Thomas (or L.T. **Meade**: Elizabeth Thomasina Meade Smith (1854-1941) Eng. writer of books for girls, mystery, detective fiction author

Kay **Medford**: Kay Regan (1920-) U.S. stage actress

Medium Tem Plum: Mostyn T Piggot (-) Eng. writer [46]

Ralph **Meeker**: Ralph Rathgeber (1920-) U.S. stage, film actor

Mehboob: Ramjankhan Mehboobkhan (1907-) Indian film director

°**Golda Meir**: Goldie Myerson, née Mabovitch (1898-1978) Russ.-born Israeli prime minister

°**Melanchthon**: Philip Schwarzerd (1497-1560) Ger. humorist, theologian [31]

Melanie: Melanie Safka (1947-) U.S. pop singer, songwriter

°[Dame] Nellie **Melba**: Helen Porter Armstrong, née Mitchell (1861-1931) Australian opera singer

Lauritz **Melchior**: Lebrecht Himml (1890-1973) U.S. opera singer, of Dan. parentage

Jill **Melford**: Jill Melford-Melford (1934-) U.S. stage actress

Courtney **Melmoth**: Samuel Jackson Pratt (1749-1814) Br. poet, prose writer

°Sebastian **Melmoth**: Oscar Wilde (1854-1900) Ir. playwright, author, poet

Alan **Melville**: Alan Caverhill (1910-) Eng. lyric writer, dramatist

Jean-Pierre **Melville**: Jean-Pierre Grumbach (1917-1973) Fr. film director

Lewis **Melville**: Lewis Samuel Benjamin (1874-1932) Br. author

Memphis Slim: Peter Chatman (1915-)

U.S. black blues singer, musician

Menander: Charles Langbridge Morgan (1894-1958) Br. novelist, essayist

°Adah Isaacs **Menken**: Dolores Adios Fuertes (?1835-1868) U.S. actress, poet

Mercator: [Dr.] James Anderson (1739-1808) Sc. economist, writer on agriculture

Gerhardus **Mercator**: Gerhard Kremer (1512-1594) Flemish map-maker [31, 32]

T. **Merchant**: Thomas John Dibdin (1771-1841) Eng. playwright, operatic composer, songwriter

Vivien **Merchant**: Ada Thomson (1929-) Eng. stage actress

Freddie **Mercury**: Frederick Bulsara (1946-) Eng. rock singer

Anne **Meredith**: Lucy Beatrice Malleson (1899-1973) Eng. crime novelist, short story writer

Burgess **Meredith**: George Burgess (1908-) U.S. film actor

Owen **Meredith**: Edward Robert Bulwer Lytton (1831-1891) Br. statesman, poet [35]

Merlin: [1] Alfred [Lord] Tennyson (1809-1892) Eng. poet. [2] David Christie Murray (1847-1907) Eng. novelist, journalist

Merlinus Anglicus: William Lilly (1602-1681) Eng. astrologer

Ethel **Merman**: Ethel Zimmerman (1908-) U.S. stage, film actress

°Mary **Merrall**: Mary Lloyd (1890-) Eng. stage, film actress

Leonard **Merrick**: Leonard Miller (1864-1939) Eng. novelist

Dina **Merrill**: Nedinia Hutton Rumbough (1925-) U.S. film, TV actress

Henry Seton **Merriman**: Hugh Stowell Scott (1862-1903) Eng. writer of historical fiction

Felix **Merry**: Evert Augustus Duychinck (1816-1878) U.S. editor

Billy **Merson**: William Henry Thompson (1881-1947) Eng. music hall artiste

Ambrose **Merton**: William John Thoms (1803-1885) Eng. antiquary, founder of *Notes and Queries*

Tristram **Merton**: Thomas Babington Macaulay (1800-1859) Eng. writer

and statesman

William **Mervyn**: William Mervyn Pickwoad (1912-1976) Eng. stage, film, TV actor

°Pietro **Metastasio**: Pietro Antonio Domenico Bonaventura Trapassi (1698-1782) It. dramatist, librettist

[Sir] Algernon Methuen Marshall **Methuen**: Algernon Methuen Marshall Stedman (1856-1924) Eng. publisher

Giacomo **Meyerbeer**: Jakob Liebmann Meyer Beer (1791-1864) Ger. opera composer, working in Italy and France

Kathleen **Michael**: Kathleen Smith (1917-) Eng. stage actress

Ralph **Michael**: Ralph Champion Shotter (1907-) Eng. film actor

Karin **Michaëlis**: Katarina Bek (1872-1950) Dan. novelist

Michelangelo: Michelagniolo di Lodovico Buonarroti Simoni (1475-1564) It. sculptor, painter, artpoet

Robert **Middleton**: Samuel G. Messer (1911-) U.S. film actor

Hans **Mikkelsen**: Ludvig von Holberg (1684-1754) Norw.-born Dan. dramatist ("Father of Danish Drama")

Miles: Stephen H. Critten (1887-1964) Eng. novelist, short story writer

Peter **Miles**: Gerald Perreau (1938-) U.S. film actor

Vera **Miles**: Vera Ralston (1930-) U.S. film actress

°Raymond Alton **Milland**: Reginald Truscott-Jones (1905-) Welsh-born Br. film actor, working in U.S.

Mary **Millar**: Mary Wetton (1936-) Eng. stage actress, singer

Ann **Miller**: Lucy Ann Collier (1919-) U.S. dancer, film actress

°Joaquin **Miller**: Cincinnatus Hiner Miller (1841-1913) U.S. poet

Marilyn **Miller**: Marilyn Reynolds (1898-1936) U.S. film actress

Martin **Miller**: Rudolph Muller (1899-1969) Czech film actor, in U.K.

Marvin **Miller**: Marvin Mueller (1913-) U.S. film actor

°Max **Miller**: Harold Sargent (1895-

1963) Eng. music hall comedian (The "Cheeky Chappie")

Wade **Miller**: Robert Wade (1920-) U.S. mystery writer. + Bill Miller (1920-1961) U.S. mystery writer

Carl **Milles**: Wilhelm Carl Emil Andersson (1875-1955) Swe. sculptor

Millie: Millicent Small (1947-) Jamaican pop singer

Alan **Mills**: Albert Miller (1914-1977) Can. folk singer

Martin **Mills**: Martin à Beckett Boyd (1893-) Eng.-Australian novelist

George **Milner**: George Edward Charles Hardinge [Baron Hardinge of Penhurst] (1921-) Eng. crime novelist

°[Cardinal] Jozsef **Mindszenty**: Jozsef Pehm (1892-1975) Hung. church dignitary

A Ministering Friend: °Daniel Defoe

Mary Miles **Minter**: Juliet Reilly (1902-) U.S. film actress

A Minute Philosopher: Charles Kingsley (1819-1875) Eng. clergyman, novelist

Jean **Mirabeau**: Paul Thiry [Baron d'Holbach] (1723-1789) Fr. materialist, atheist philosopher

°Carmen **Miranda**: María de Carmo Mirando de Cunha (1915-1955) U.S. popular singer, film actress

Isa **Miranda**: Ines Isabella Sampietro (1909-) It. stage, film actress

Miroslava: Miroslava Stern (1926-1955) Czech film actress, working in Mexico

°**Mistinguett**: Jeanne-Marie Bourgeois (1875-1956) Fr. music hall artiste

°Gabriela **Mistral**: Lucila Godoy de Alcayaga (1889-1957) Chilean poet

°Guy **Mitchell**: Al Cernick (1927-) U.S. pop singer, film actor

Joni **Mitchell**: Roberta Joan Anderson (1943-) Can. pop musician

Yvonne **Mitchell**: Yvonne Joseph (1925-1979) Eng. stage, film actress, writer [34]

Mit (or Mot) Yenda: Timothy (or Thomas) Adney (-) Eng. poet of the Dellacruscan school

°**M.le ch.X.o.a.s.s.d.s.M.S.**: Xavier de Maistre (1763-1852) Fr. novelist

°[President] **Mobutu**: Joseph-Désiré

Mobutu (1930-) African statesman, president of Zaïre

Jean-Pierre **Mocky**: Jean Mokiejeswki (1929-) Fr. film director

Helena **Modjeska**: Helena Modrzejewska, née Opid (1840-1909) Pol.-U.S. stage actress

A. **Modus**: Jonathan Swift (1667-1745) Eng. satirist

Leonide **Moguy**: Leonid Moguilevsky (1899-1976) Russ. newsreel producer, film director, working in France, U.S.

°**Molière**: Jean-Baptiste Poquelin (1622-1673) Fr. comic dramatist

Ferenc **Molnar**: Ferenc Neumann (1878-1952) Hung. dramatist, working in U.S.

°**Molotov**: Vyacheslav Mikhailovich Skryabin (1890-) Russ. diplomat

Pierre **Mondy**: Pierre Cuq (1925-) Fr. film actor

Lireve **Monett**: Everil Worrell (1893-1969) U.S. (female) writer of horror stories

Monitor: Arthur Lee (1740-1792) U.S. diplomatist

°**Marilyn Monroe**: Norma Jean Baker (or Mortenson) (1926-1962) U.S. film actress

°Nicholas **Monsarrat**: Nicholas John Turney Montserrat (1910-1979) Eng. novelist

Bull **Montana**: Luigi Montagna (1887-1950) It.-U.S. film actor

Patsy **Montana**: Rubye Blevins (1914-) U.S. country singer

°Yves **Montand**: Ivo Levi (1921-) It.-born Fr. film actor, singer

Mlle **Montansier**: Marguerite Brunet (1730-1820) Fr. actress, theatre manager

Georges **Montbard**: Charles Auguste Loyes (1841-) Fr. artist, journalist, author in English

Montdory: Guillaume des Gilberts (1594-1651) Fr. actor

Lola **Montez**: Maria Dolores Eliza Rosanna Gilbert (1818-1861) Ir. actress, working in Europe, U.S.

Maria **Montez**: María de Santo Silas (1918-1951) U.S. film actress

George **Montgomery**: George Montgomery Letz (1916-) U.S. film actor

Robert **Montgomery**: Henry Montgomery (1904-) U.S. film actor, politician

Ron **Moody**: Ronald Moodnick (1924-) Eng. stage, TV comedian

°**Moondog**: Louis Thomas Hardin (1916-) U.S. blind "popular-classical" composer

Harry **Mooney**: Harry Goodchild (1889-1972) Eng. music hall comedian

Archie **Moore**: Archibald Lee Wright (1913-) U.S. light heavyweight boxer, film actor

Colleen **Moore**: Kathleen Morrison (1900-) U.S. film actress

°**Garry Moore**: Thomas Morfit (1915-) U.S. TV comedian

Kieron **Moore**: Kieron O'Hanrahan (1925-) Ir. film actor

Terry **Moore**: Helen Koford (1929-) U.S. film actress

Wentworth **Moore**: William Hurrell Mallock (1849-1923) Eng. author, poet

Lois **Moran**: Lois Darlington Dowling (1909-) U.S. film actress

Alberto **Moravia**: Alberto Pincherle (1907-) It. novelist, short story writer

Jean **Moréas**: Ioannes Papadiamantópoulos (1856-1910) Gk.-born Fr. poet

°**Eric Morecambe**: Eric Bartholomew (1926-) Eng. TV comedian, teaming with Ernie Wise (q.v.)

André **Morell**: André Mesritz (1909-1978) Eng. stage, film actor

Sir Charles **Morell**: [Rev.] James Ridley (1736-1765) Eng. writer

Rita **Moreno**: Rosita Dolores Alverio (1931-) Puerto-Rican stage, film actress, dancer

Louis **Moresby**: Eliza Louisa Moresby Beck (-1931) Eng. novelist

Andrew **Moreton**: °Daniel Defoe

Dennis **Morgan**: Stanley Morner (1910-) U.S. film actor

Frank **Morgan**: Francis Phillip Wuppermann (1890-1949) U.S. film actor

Harry **Morgan**: Harry Bratsburg (1915-) U.S. film actor

Michèle **Morgan**: Simone Roussel (1920-) Fr. film actress

Ralph **Morgan**: Ralph Wuppermann (1882-1956) U.S. film actor, brother of Frank Morgan (q.v.)

Iolo **Morganwg**: Edward Williams (1746-1826) Welsh poet, antiquary

Miss **Morison**: Anne Moberley (-1937) Eng. author (jointly with Miss Lamont—q.v.)

Patricia **Morison**: Eileen Morrison (1915-) U.S. film actress

Gaby **Morlay**: Blanche Fumoleau (1897-1964) Fr. film actress

Karen **Morley**: Mildred Linton (1905-) U.S. film actress

Mrs. **Morley**: Anne (1665-1714) queen of England [25]

Clara **Morris**: Clara Morrison (1846-1925) U.S. stage actress

Jan **Morris**: James Morris (?1927-) Eng. author [9]

Peter **Morris**: John Gibson Lockhart (1794-1854) Sc. author

Boris **Morros**: Boris Mikhailovitch (1891-1963) Russ.-born U.S. film producer

Anthony **Morton**: John Creasey (1908-1973) Eng. crime novelist

°**Jelly Roll Morton**: Ferdinand Joseph La Menthe Morton (1885-1941) U.S. jazz composer, pianist

°**Mickie Most**: Michael Hayes (1938-) Eng. record company director, promoter

Zero **Mostel**: Samuel Joel Mostel (1915-1977) U.S. stage, film actor [33]

Mary **Motley**: [Comtesse] Guy de Renéville, née Sheridan (-1976) Eng. writer

°[Lord] Louis **Mountbatten of Burma**: [Prince] Louis Francis Albert Victor Nicholas of Battenberg (1900-1979) Eng. soldier, statesman [8]

Louis Alexander **Mountbatten** [Marquess of Milford Haven]: [Prince] Louis Alexander of Battenberg (1854-1921) Ger.-born Eng. admiral [8]

George **Mozart**: David Gillings (1864-1947) Eng. music hall comedian, musician

Leonard **Mudie**: Leonard Mudie Cheetham (1884-1965) Br. film actor, working in U.S.

°Elijah **Muhammad**: Elijah (or Robert) Poole (1897-1975) U.S. Black Muslim leader

Jean **Muir**: Jean Muir Fullerton (1911-) U.S. film actress

Maria **Muldaur**: Maria Grazia Rosa Domenica d'Amato (1943-) U.S. pop singer

°**Multatuli**: Eduard Douwes Dekker (1820-1887) Du. novelist

Claude **Muncaster**: Grahame Hall (1903-) Eng. landscape, marine painter

Talbot **Mundy**: William Lancaster Gribbon (1879-1940) Eng.-born U.S. writer of adventure novels, historical fantasies

Paul **Muni**: Meshulom Meyer Weisenfreund (1895-1967) Pol.-born U.S. stage, film actor

°Baron **Münchhausen**: Rudolfe Erich Raspe (1737-1794) Ger. scientist, anantiquarian, writer

C.K. **Munro**: Charles Walden Kirkpatrick MacMullan (1889-) Ir. playwright

Ona **Munson**: Ona Wolcott (1906-1955) U.S. film actress

Murad Effendi: Franz von Werner (1836-1881) Ger. poet

Friedrich Wilhelm (or F.W.) **Murnau**: Friedrich Wilhelm Plumpe (1889-1931) Ger. film director, working in U.S.

Dennis Jasper **Murphy**: [Rev.] Charles Robert Maturin (1782-1824) Ir. playwright, novelist

Murray: Leo Murray Carrington-Walters (-) Australian magician, escapologist

Braham **Murray**: Braham Goldstein (1943-) Eng. stage director

Brian **Murray**: Brian Bell (1937-) S.A. stage actor, working in U.K.

Hon. Mrs. **Murray**: Sarah Aust (1741-1811) Eng. topographical writer

Ken **Murray**: Don Court (1903-) U.S. film comedian, radio, TV entertainer

Mae **Murray**: Marie Adrienne Koenig (1885-1965) U.S. film actress

Sinclair **Murray**: Edward Alan Sullivan (1868-) Can. novelist

°Eadweard **Muybridge**: Edward

James Muggeridge (1830-1904) Eng.-born U.S. photographer

Le **Myosotis**: Hégésippe Moreau (1810-1838) Fr. poet

Harriet **Myrtle**: Lydia Falconer Miller, née Fraser (1811-1876) Sc. children's writer

Marmaduke **Myrtle**: [Sir] Richard Steele (1672-1729) Br. essayist, dramatist

Minnie **Myrtle**: Anna Cummings Johnson (1818-1892) U.S. writer

N

°**Nadar**: Félix Tournachon (1820-1910) Fr. photographer, illustrator, writer

A.A. **Nadir**: Achmed Abdullah (*q.v.*)

Laurence **Naismith**: Lawrence Johnson (1908-) Eng. stage, film actor

Nita **Naldi**: Anita Donna Dorley (1899-1961) It.-U.S. film actress

Lewis Bernstein **Namier**: Lewis Bernstein Namerovsky (1888-1960) Eng. historian

Alan **Napier**: Alan Napier-Clavering (1903-) Br. film actor, working in U.S.

Diana **Napier**: Molly Ellis (1908-) Br. film actress

Mark **Napier**: John Laffin (1922-) Australian novelist, journalist

Owen **Nares**: Owen Nares Ramsay (1888-1943) Br. film actor

Petroleum Vesuvius **Nasby**: David Ross Locke (1833-1888) U.S. humorous journalist [20, 21]

Daniel **Nash**: William Reginald Loader (1916-) Br. novelist

N. Richard **Nash**: Nathaniel Richard Nusbaum (1913-) U.S. dramatist

Simon **Nash**: Raymond Chapman (1924-) Welsh writer on education, theology, crime novelist

Alcofribas **Nasier**: François Rabelais (1495-1553) Fr. satirist

Nathalie **Nattier**: Nathalie Belaieff (-) Fr. film actress [27]

John-Antoine **Nau**: Antoine Torquet (1860-1918) Fr. poet, novelist

Nauticus: [1] [Sir] William Laird Clowes (1856-1905) Eng. naval writer, historian. [2] [Sir] Owen Seaman (1861-1936) Eng. editor, humorist

Andre **Navarre**: Alexander Wright (-1940) Australian music hall impressionist

Eliot **Naylor**: Pamela Frankau (1908-1967) Br. novelist, short story writer

[Dame] Anna **Neagle**: [Dame] Marjorie Wilcox, née Robertson (1904-) Eng. stage, film actress [34]

Hilary **Neal**: Olive Marion Norton (1913-) Br. children's novelist

Neera: Anna Radius Zaccari (1846-1918) It. novelist

Hildegarde **Neff**: Hildegarde Knef (1925-) Ger. film actress

Pola **Negri**: Barbara Appolonia Chalupek (1897-) Pol.-born U.S. film actress

Roy William **Neill**: Roland de Gastrio (1890-1946) Ir.-born U.S. film director

Thomas **Neill**: Thomas Neill Cream (1850-1892) Sc. physician, murderer

°Donald **Neilson**: Donald Nappey (1936-) Eng. murderer

Lilian Adelaide **Neilson**: Elizabeth Ann Brown (1848-1880) Br. actress

Perlita **Neilson**: Margaret Sowden (1933-) Eng. stage actress

Barry **Nelson**: Robert Nielson (1920-) U.S. stage, film actor

Gene **Nelson**: Gene Berg (1920-) U.S. stage, film actor, dancer

Nemo: °Phiz

°Nadia **Nerina**: Nadine Judd (1927-) S.A. ballet dancer

°**Nero**: Lucius Domitius Ahenobarbus (37-68) Roman emperor

°Pablo **Neruda**: Neftalí Ricardo Reyes (1904-1973) Chilean poet

Gérard de **Nerval**: Gérard Labrunie (1808-1855) Fr. romantic poet

°Jimmy **Nervo**: James Henry Holloway (1897-1975) Eng. stage comedian, teaming with Teddy Knox (*q.v.*)

Francis **Nesbitt**: Francis Nesbitt McCron (1809-1853) Br. actor, working in Australia

Adolf **Neuwert**: Adolf Nowaczyński (1876-1944) Pol. dramatist

Emma **Nevada**: Emma Wixom (1859-1940) U.S. opera singer

Alexander Sergeyevich **Neverov**: Alexander Sergeyevich Skobelev (1886-1923) Russ. author

Aristarchus **Newlight**: Richard Whately (1786-1863) Eng. logician, theologian

Ernest **Newman**: William Roberts (1868-1959) Eng. music critic, authority on Wagner

Margaret **Newman**: Margaret Potter (1926-) Br. crime novelist

Julie **Newmar**: Julia Newmeyer (1930-) Swe. film actress, working in U.S.

F. **Newton**: [Prof.] Eric John Ernest Hobsbawm (1917-) Eng. economist, social historian

R. **Newton**: °Sylvanus Urban

A **New Writer**: [Sir] Lewis Morris (1833-1907) Welsh lawyer, writer of verse in English

Fred **Niblo**: Federico Nobile (1874-1948) U.S. film director

Nicholas II: Gerard (?-1061) Fr. pope

Nicholas III: Giovanni Gaetano Orsini (c.1225-1280) It. pope

Nicholas IV: Girolamo Masci (1227-1292) It. pope

Nicholas V: Tommaso Parentucelli (1397-1455) It. pope

Horatio **Nicholls**: Lawrence Wright (1888-) Eng. musical composer, publisher, arranger

Barbara **Nichols**: Barbara Nicekrauer (1932-) Jamaican-born U.S. film actress

Mike **Nichols**: Michael Igor Peschkowsky (1931-) Ger.-born U.S. cabaret entertainer, film director

Nicolino: Nicolò Grimaldi (1673-1732) It. male contralto

Flora **Nielsen**: Sybil Crawley (1900-1976) Can. opera singer, singing teacher

Édouard de **Nieuport**: Édouard de Niéport (1875-1911) Fr. pilot, aircraft designer

Shmuel **Niger**: Shmuel Charmi (1884-) Russ.-born Yiddish literary critic, essayist, working in U.S.

Nikodim: Boris Georgiyevich Rotov (1929-1978) Russ. Orthodox churchman, metropolitan of Leningrad

Nikon: Nikita Minov (1605-1681) Russ.

Orthodox churchman, patriarch of Moscow and All Russia

Bee **Nilson**: Amabel Rhoda Nilson (1908-) N.Z. writer on cookery, dieting

Nilsson: Hary Edward Nelson III (1941-) U.S. pop musician

°**Nimrod**: Charles James Apperley (1777-1843) Eng. sporting writer

Nina: Ethel Florence Nelson (1923-) Can. travel writer

Sir Nicholas **Nipclose**, Bart.: David Garrick (1717-1779) Eng. actor

°**Red Nirt**: Tommy Trinder (1909-) Eng. stage comedian [30]

Greta **Nissen**: Greta Rutz-Nissen (1906-) Norw. film actress, working in U.S.

Kwame **Nkrumah**: Francis Nwia Kofi (1909-1972) Ghanaian political leader

°**Nobody**: William Stevens (1732-1807) Eng. biographer

John **Noel**: Dennis Leslie Bird (1930-) Br. writer on skating

Noël-Noël: Lucien Noël (1897-) Fr. film comedian

Victor **Noir**: Yvan Salmon (1848-1870) Fr. journalist

Mary **Nolan**: Mary Imogen Robertson (1905-) U.S. film actress

Emil **Nolde**: Emil Hansen (1867-1956) Ger. Expressionist painter

Nomad: Norman Ellison (1893-1976) Eng. naturalist, writer, broadcaster

Ed **Noon**: Michael Angelo Avallone, Jr. (1924-) U.S. thriller, horror story writer

°**Jeremiah Noon**: John Calvin (1829-1871) Br. boxer

T.R. **Noon**: Olive Marion Norton (1913-) Br. children's novelist

Tommy **Noonan**: Thomas Patrick (1922-1968) U.S. film comedian, writer

°**Noor al-Hussein**: Elizabeth Halaby (1951-) U.S. businesswoman, married King Hussein of Jordan

°**Max Simon Nordau**: Max Simon Südfeld (1849-1923) Hung.-Ger. physician, author

°**Charles Norden**: Lawrence George Durrell (1912-) Br. novelist, poet

Christine **Norden**: Mary Lydia Thorn-

ton (1924-) Br. film actress

Lillian **Nordica**: Lillian Norton (1859-1914) U.S. opera singer [33]

Norman **Norell**: Norman Levinson (1900-1972) U.S. fashion designer

Eidé **Norena**: Kaja Hansen (1884-1968) Norw. opera singer

Mabel **Normand**: Mabel Fortescue (1894-1930) U.S. film comedienne

Normy: George Norman Douglas (1868-1952) Sc. novelist

Nedra **Norris**: Nedra Gullette (1914-) U.S. film actress

°**Captain George North**: Robert Louis Balfour Stevenson (1850-1894) Sc. essayist, novelist, poet

Christopher **North**: John Wilson (1785-1854) Sc. literary critic

Gil **North**: Geoffrey Horne (1916-) Br. detective novelist

Mark **North**: Wright W. Miller (1903-1974) Br. writer on Russia

Sheree **North**: Dawn Bethel (1933-) U.S. film actress

Northerner: William Jesse Hughes (1912-) Br. writer on engineering models

Bess **Norton**: Olive Marian Norton (1913-) Br. children's author

Fleming **Norton**: Frederic Mills (1836-1895) Br. actor, entertainer

Red **Norvo**: Kenneth Norville (1908-) U.S. jazz musician

Kate **Norway**: Olive Marion Norton (1913-) Br. children's author

Max **Nosseck**: Alexander Norris (1902-1972) Pol. film director, actor, working in U.S.

Nostalgia: James William Benedict Bentley (1914-) Br. novelist

Nostradamus: Michel de Nostre-Dame (1503-1566) Fr. astrologer, doctor

Barry **Nott**: Bernard John Hurren (1907-) Br. author on aviation

°**Kim Novak**: Marily Novak (1933-) U.S. film actress

°**Novalis**: Friedrich Leopold von Hardenberg (1772-1801) Ger. romantic poet, novelist

Novanglus: John Adams (1735-1828) U.S. statesman, second president of U.S.

Ramon **Novarro**: José Ramón Gil Samaniegos (1899-1968) Mexican film actor, working in U.S.

Alec Nove: [Prof.] Alexander Novakovsky (1915-) Russ.-born Eng. economist, specialist on Soviet affairs

°Ivor Novello: David Ivor Davies (1893-1951) Welsh stage actor-manager, dramatist, composer

Aleksey Silych Novikov-Priboy: Aleksei Silych Novikov (1877-1944) Russ. author of novels of sea life

Karel Nový: Karel Novák (1890-) Czech children's writer

Zygmunt Nowakowski: Zygmunt Tempa (1891-) Pol. novelist

Owen Nox: Charles Barney Cory (1857-1921) U.S. ornithologist

Nuitter: Charles-Louis-Étienne Truinet (1828-1899) Fr. playwright, librettist

Gary Numan: Gary Webb (1957-) Eng. pop singer

Nunquam: Robert Blatchford (1851-1943) Eng. journalist, editor

Bill Nye: Edgar Wilson Nye (1850-1896) U.S. humorist, editor

O

°Jack Oakie: Lewis Delaney Offield (1903-1978) U.S. film comedian [33]

Vivian Oakland: Vivian Anderson (1895-1958) U.S. film actress

°Annie Oakley: Phoebe Anne Oakley Moses (1860-1926) U.S. sharp-shooter

Quentin Oates: ? (-) Br.(?) literary critic [66]

°Merle Oberon: Estelle Merle O'Brien Thompson (1911-1979) Eng. film actress

Hugh O'Brian: Hugh Krampke (1925-) U.S. film, TV actor

Dave O'Brien: David Barclay (1912-1969) U.S. film actor

David O'Brien: David Herd (1930-) Eng. stage actor

Flann O'Brien: Brian O'Nolan (1912-1966) Ir. novelist

Dermot O'Byrne: [Sir] Arnold Edward Trevor Bax (1883-1953) Br. composer, writer

°Sean O'Casey: John Casey (1880-1964) Ir. dramatist

°Jehu O'Cataract: John Neal (1793-1876) U.S. romantic novelist, poet

°Maria del Occidente: Maria Gowen Brooks (c.1794-1845) U.S. poet

Darleen O'Connor: Joy(ce) McKinney (1949-) U.S. model [11]

Frank O'Connor: Michael O'Donovan (1903-1966) Ir. short story writer

An Octogenarian: James Roche (1770-1853) Eng. magazine contributor

°Dawn O'Day: Dawn Paris (1918-) U.S. film actress

Odetta: Odetta Felious (1930-) U.S. folk singer

Odette: Odette Brailly (1912-) Fr. spy

Mary Odette: Odette Goimbault (1901-) Fr.-born Eng. film actress

Sir Morgan Osoherty: [Dr.] William Maginn (1793-1842) Sc. magazine-contributor

Cathy O'Donnell: Ann Steely (1923-1970) U.S. film actress

Cornelius O'Dowd: Charles James Lever (1806-1872) Eng.-born Ir. novelist

Odysseus: [Sir] Charles Norton Edgcumbe Eliot (1862-1931) Br. diplomat, scholar

Séan O'Faioláin: John Phelan (1900-) Ir. novelist, biographer

Talbot O'Farrell: William Parrot (1878-1952) Eng. music hall comedian

°Jacques Offenbach: Jakob Eberst (1819-1880) Ger.-born Fr. composer

Ogdones: [Seigneur de] Guillaume du Bellay Langey (1491-1553) Fr. general, diplomat

Le Prieur Ogier: Jean Louis Guez de Balzac (1594-1655) Fr. prose writer

Gavin Ogilvy: [Sir] James Matthew Barrie (1860-1937) Sc. novelist, dramatist

George O'Hanlan: George Rice (1917-) U.S. film comedian

Maureen O'Hara: Maureen Fitzsimmons (1920-) Ir. film actress, working in U.S.

°[Don] Ambrosio O'Higgins: Ambrose Higgins (?1720-1801) Ir. soldier, administrator, working in Chile

O.K.: Olga Alekseyevna Novikova, née Kireyeva (1840-1925) Russ. journalist, working in England [29, 30]

Dennis **O'Keefe**: Edward Vanes Flanagan (1908-1968) U.S. film, TV actor

Okito: Theodore Bamberg (1875-1963) U.S. magician, of Du. extraction

Pierre **Olaf**: Pierre-Olaf Trivier (1928-) Fr. stage actor

Sidney **Olcott**: John Sidney Alcott (1873-1949) Ir.-Can. film director, working in U.S.

°**Old Block**: Alonzo Delano (?1802-1874) U.S. playwright, humorist

An **Old Boy**: Thomas Hughes (1822-1896) Eng. author

Old Humphrey: George Mogridge (1787-1854) Eng. author of religious books, essays for children

Old Sailor: Matthew Henry Barker (1790-1846) Eng. writer of sea stories, editor

Cedric **Oldacre of Saxe Normanby**: [Rev.] John Wood Warter (1806-1878) Eng. antiquary, author

Humphrey **Oldcastle**: [1] Henry St. John (1672-1751) Eng. magazine contributor. [2] Nicholas Amhurst (1697-1742) Eng. poet, politician

John **Oldcastle**: Wilfrid Meynell (1852-1948) Br. writer, poet **[63]**

Jonathan **Oldstyle**: Washington Irving (1783-1859) U.S. essayist, short story writer, historian **[20]**

°**Oliver Oldstyle**: James Kirke Paulding (1778-1860) U.S. novelist, satirist, poet

°**Patrick Albert O'Leary**: [Dr.] Albert Marie Edmond Guérisse (1911-) Belg. army officer, serving with British Navy

°**Ole Luk-Oie**: [Sir] Ernest Dunlop Swinton (1868-1951) Br. soldier, writer

Oliver: William Oliver Swofford (1945-) U.S. pop musician

Edith **Oliver**: Edith Goldsmith (1913-) U.S. dramatic critic

Edna May **Oliver**: Edna May Cox-Oliver (1883-1942) U.S. film actress

George **Oliver**: Oliver Onions (1873-1961) Eng. novelist

Jane **Oliver**: Helen Rees (1903-1970) Sc. novelist

Vic **Oliver**: Viktor Oliver von Samek (1898-1964) Austr.-born Br. comedian, pianist, violinist, conductor

John **O'London**: Wilfred Whitten (?-1942) Br. editor, author, founder of *John O'London's Weekly*

°**Omar Khayyam**: Gheyas od-Din Abu Ol-Fath Umar ebn Ebrahim ol-Khayyami (?1048-1122) Persian poet, astronomer

Jacob **Omnium**: Matthew James Higgins (1810-1868) Eng. journalist, writer of letters to *The Times*

Philothée **O'Neddy**: Théophile Dondey (1811-1875) Fr. poet, short story writer, dramatic critic **[30]**

Sally **O'Neil**: Virginia Louise Noonan (1913-1968) U.S. film actress

Maire **O'Neill**: Maire Allgood (1885-1952) Ir. film actress

One of the **Boys**: Percy Hetherington Fitzgerald (1834-1925) Ir. sculptor, writer

Colette **O'Niel**: [Lady] Constance Annesley (1886-1975) Ir. stage actress, writer

Onlooker: George William Erskine Russell (1853-1919) Eng. writer

Max **Ophüls**: Max Oppenheimer (1902-1957) Ger.-born Fr. film director

Oliver **Optic**: William Taylor Adams (1822-1897) U.S. novelist, children's writer

Katherine **O'Regan**: Kathleen Melville (1904-) Ir. film actress

Miles **O'Reilly**: Charles Graham Halpine (1829-1868) Ir. humorist, soldier, working in U.S.

Navan **O'Reilly**: Tom Franks (1869-) Ir. ventriloquist

Max **O'Rell**: Léon Paul Blouet (1848-1903) Fr.-born Eng. humorous writer

Orinda: Katherine Philips, née Fowler (1631-1664) Eng. poet, letter-writer ("The Matchless Orinda")

Eugene **Ormandy**: Eugene Blau (1899-) Hung.-born U.S. conductor

Orwell: Walter Chalmers Smith (1824-1908) Sc. poet

°**George Orwell**: Eric Arthur Blair (1903-1950) Eng. novelist, satirist

Henry **Oscar**: Henry Wale (1891-1970) Br. stage actor, director **[63]**

Irene **Osgood**: Irene Harvey (1875-) Br. author

Osman **Pasha**: Jan Willem [Duke] of Ripperda (1680-1737) Du. adventurer, working in Spain

°Gilbert **O'Sullivan**: Raymond O'Sullivan (1946-) Ir. pop musician

Seumas **O'Sullivan**: James Sullivan Starkey (1879-1958) Ir. poet, founder of the *Dublin Magazine*

Richard **Oswald**: Richard Ornstein (1880-1963) Ger. film director

James **Otis**: James Otis Kaler (1848-1912) U.S. writer of stories for boys

Johnny **Otis**: Johnny Veliotes (1921-) U.S. rhythm & blues musician, of Gk. parentage

Rudolf **Otreb**: Robert Fludd (1574-1634) Eng. Rosicrucian, philosopher, physician

°**Ouida**: Marie Louise de la Ramée (1839-1908) Eng. novelist

Gérard **Oury**: Max-Gérard Tannenbaum (1919-) Fr. film actor

Bill **Owen**: Bill Rowbotham (1916-) Eng. stage, film comedian

John Pickard **Owen**: Samuel Butler (1835-1902) Br. satirist

Seena **Owen**: Signe Auen (1894-1966) U.S. film actress

Jesse **Owens**: John Cleveland Owens (1913-1980) U.S. black athlete

Rochelle **Owens**: Rochelle Bass (1936-) U.S. dramatist

John **Oxenham**: William Arthur Dunkerley (1852-1941) Eng. poet, novelist

Oxoniensis: [Rev.] Francis Trench (1805-1886) Eng. churchman, author

P

Pacificus: Alexander Hamilton (1757-1804) U.S. statesman

°**Philo Pacificus**: Noah Worcester (1758-1837) U.S. clergyman, editor, pacifist

Anita **Page**: Anita Pomares (1910-) U.S. film actress

Annette **Page**: Annette Hynd, née Lees (1932-) Eng. ballet dancer

Gale **Page**: Sally Rutter (1913-) U.S. film actress

H.A. **Page**: Alexander Hay Japp (1837-1905) Sc. author, publisher

Marco **Page**: Harry Kurnitz (1909-1968) U.S. playwright, novelist, filmwriter

°Patti **Page**: Clara Ann Fowler (1927-) U.S. pop singer

Stanton **Page**: Henry Blake Fuller (1857-1929) U.S. novelist

Debra **Paget**: Debralee Griffin (1933-) U.S. film actress

°Janis **Paige**: Donna Mae Jaden (1923-(1923-) U.S. film actress, singer

Robert **Paige**: John Arthur Page (1910-) U.S. film actor

Jack **Palance**: Walter Palanchik (1920-) U.S. film actor, of Russ. parentage

°**Palinurus**: Cyril Vernon Connolly (1903-1974) Br. literary critic, novelist

Andrea **Palladio**: Andrea di Pietro Monaro (1508-1580) It. architect

Jackie **Pallo**: John Gutteridge (-) Eng. wrestler, TV entertainer

Betsy **Palmer**: Patricia Brumek (1929-) U.S. film actress, TV panellist

Gregg **Palmer**: Palmer Lee (1927-) U.S. film actor

Lilli **Palmer**: Lilli Marie Peiser (1914-) Ger. film actress

Pansy: Isabella Macdonald Alden (1841-1930) U.S. children's magazine editor

Joseph **Papp**: Joseph Papirofsky (1921-) U.S. stage producer, director

°**Paracelsus**: Philippus Aureolus Theophrastus Bombast von Hohenheim (1493-1541) Swiss-Ger. physician, alchemist

Harry **Parke**: °Parkyarkarkus

Cecil **Parker**: Cecil Schwabe (1897-1971) Br. film actor **[27]**

Dorothy **Parker**: Dorothy Rothschild (1893-1967) U.S. novelist, poet

Eric **Parker**: Frederick Moore Searle (1870-1955) Eng. writer on field sports, cricket, gardening

Jean **Parker**: Mae Green (1915-) U.S. film actress

Lew **Parker**: Austin Lewis Jacobs (1906-) U.S. stage actor

Willard **Parker**: Worster van Eps (1912-) U.S. film actor

Larry **Parks**: Samuel Klausman Parks (1914-1975) U.S. film actor

°**Parkyakarkus**: Harry Einstein (1904-1958) U.S. radio comedian

°Peter **Parley**: [1] Samuel Griswold Goodrich (1793-1860) U.S. bookseller, author of children's moral tales. [2] George Mogridge (Old Humphrey) Eng. children's writer. [3] John Bennett (1865-1956) U.S. writer of boys' books. [4] William Martin (1801-1867) Eng. children's writer. [5] William Tegg (1816-1895) Eng. children's writer.

Dita **Parlo**: Gerthe Kornstadt (1906-1972) Ger. film actress [45]

Martine **Parmain**: Martine Hemmerdinger (1942-) Fr. ballet dancer

Louella **Parsons**: Louella Oettinger (1880-1972) U.S. film columnist, actress

°Mrs. **Partington**: Benjamin Penhallow Shillaber (1814-1890) U.S. humorist

Paschal II: Ranierus (?-1118) It. pope

Jules **Pascin**: Julius Pinkas (1885-1930) Fr. painter

Pasionaria: Dolores Ibárruri (1895-) Sp. Communist leader

Pasquil: [1] Thomas Nash (1567-1601) Eng. satirical pamphleteer, dramatist. [2] Nicholas Breton (?1545-?1626) Eng. poet

°Anthony **Pasquin**: John Williams (1761-1818) Eng. critic, satirist, working in U.S.

George **Paston**: Emily Morse Symonds (c.1870-1936) Br. author of "feminist" novels

Wally **Patch**: Walter Vinnicombe (1888-1971) Eng. stage, film comedian

Philip Roger **Pater**: [Dom] Gilbert Roger Hudlestone (1874-1936) Eng. Benedictine monk, ghost-story writer

Gail **Patrick**: Margaret Fitzpatrick (1911-1980) U.S. film actress, TV producer

John **Patrick**: John Patrick Goggan (1905-) U.S. playwright

Nigel **Patrick**: Nigel Wemyss (1913-) Eng. stage actor, director

Peter **Pattieson**: [Sir] Walter Scott (1771-1832) Sc. poet, novelist

°Ted **Pauker**: George Robert Acworth Conquest (1917-) Eng. poet, editor, writer on Russia

°[Saint] **Paul**: Saul (?-c.65) Christian theologian, missionary

Paul II: Pietro Barbo (1417-1471) It. pope

Paul III: Alessandro Farnese (1468-1549) It. pope

Paul IV: Gian Pietro Carafa (1476-1559) It. pope

Paul V: Camillo Borghese (1552-1621) It. pope

Paul VI: Giovanni Battista Montini (1897-1978) It. pope

Jean **Paul**: Jean Paul Friedrich Richter (1763-1825) Ger. humorist, prose writer

John **Paul**: Charles Henry Webb (1834-1905) U.S. journalist, editor

Les **Paul**: Lester Polfus (1923-) U.S. rock musician

Marisa **Pavan**: Marisa Pierangeli (1932-) It. film actress, working in U.S., sister of Pier Angeli (*q.v.*)

Pax: Mary Cholmondeley (1859-1925) Br. novelist

Philip **Paxton**: Samuel Adams Hammet (1816-1865) U.S. humorist, writer of adventure stories

Johnny **Paycheck**: Donald Lytle (1941-) U.S. country singer

Robert **Paye**: Marjorie Bowen (*q.v.*)

Drew **Pearson**: Andrew Russell (1897-1969) U.S. political columnist [63]

John **Peel**: John Robert Parker Ravenscroft (1939-) Eng. radio DJ

Jan **Peerce**: Jacob Pincus Perlemuth (1904-) U.S. opera singer

°**Pelé**: Edson Arantes do Nascimento (1940-) Brazilian footballer

M. **Pelham**: [Sir] Richard Phillips (1768-1840) Eng. journalist

Pellerin: [Baron de] Friedrich Heinrich Karl de la Motte-Fouqué (1777-1843) Ger. writer

A. **Pen, Esq.**: John Leech (1817-1864) Eng. caricaturist

Pendragon: Henry Sampson (1841-1891) Eng. sporting journalist

Joe **Penner**: Joe Pinter (1904-1941) Hung.-U.S. radio comedian, film actor

Pennsylvania Farmer: John Dickinson (1732-1800) U.S. political writer

K.N. Pepper: James M Morris (-) U.S. humorist

Pip Pepperpod: Charles Warren Stoddard (1843-1909) U.S. traveler, author

Philemon Perch: Richard Malcolm Johnson (1822-1898) U.S. humorous writer, educator

Percival: Julian Ralph (1853-1903) U.S. journalist

Edward Percy: Edward Percy Smith (1891-1968) Br. playwright, novelist

Florence Percy: Elisabeth Allen, née Chase (1832-1911) U.S. poet, literary editor

Reuben Percy: Thomas Byerley (-1826) Eng. journalist

Sholto Percy: Joseph Clinton Robertson (1788-1852) Eng. journalist, writing jointly with Reuben Percy (q.v.)

Giovanni Battista Pergolesi: Giovanni Battista Draghi (1710-1736) It. composer

François Perier: François Gabriel Pilu (1919-) Fr. stage, film actor

Paul Periwinkle: Percy Bolingbroke St. John (1821-1889) Eng. journalist, newspaper editor

Eli Perkins: Melville de Lancey Landon (1839-1910) U.S. journalist, humorous lecturer

Perley: Benjamin Perley Poore (1820-1897) U.S. journalist, author, biographer

Barry Perowne: Philip Atkey (1908-) Eng. crime, adventure, mystery short story writer

Gigi Perreau: Ghislaine Elizabeth Marie Therese Perreau-Saussine (1941-) U.S. film actress, of Fr. parentage

Edgar A. Perry: Edgar Allan Poe (1809-1849) U.S. poet, storywriter

St. John Perse: Marie-René-Auguste-Alexis Léger Saint-Leger (1887-1975) Fr. poet, working for a while in U.S.

Peregrine Persic: James Justinian Morier (?1780-1849) Br. diplomat, novelist

Pertinax: [1] Charles Gerault (1878-)

Fr. journalist. [2] Charles Joseph André Geraud (1882-1974) Fr. journalist, his successor on Écho de Paris

Pietro Perugino: Pietro di Cristoforo Vanucci (1446-1524) It. painter [41]

Pesellino: Francesco di Stefano (1422-1457) It. painter

°[Saint] Peter: Simon (or Simeon) (?-c.65) Christian leader, pope

Bernadette Peters: Bernadette Lazzara (1948-) U.S. stage actress, singer

Susan Peters: Suzanne Carnahan (1921-1952) U.S. film actress

Le Petit Homme Rouge: Ernest Alfred Vizetelly (1853-1922) Eng. newspaper correspondent, novelist

Vladimir Mikhaylovich Petrov: Afanasy Mikhaylovich Shorokhov (1907-) Russ. security chief, embassy officer in Australia

Olga Petrova: Muriel Harding (1886-) Eng. film actress, working in U.S.

Phaedrus: Polibius (c.15BC-c.AD50) Roman fabulist

Phantasus: Joseph Maximilian [Duke of Bavaria] (1808-1888) Ger. writer of novels, dramas

Alazonomastix Philalethes: [Dr.] Henry More (1614-1687) Eng. philosopher

Eugenius Philalethes: Thomas Vaughan (1622-1666) Eng. alchemist

Phil Anglus: William Penn (1776-1845) Eng. Quaker, American colonist

Phileleutharus Norfolciensis: [Dr.] Samuel Parr (1747-1825) Eng. pedagogue, Latin scholar

Philenia: Sarah Wentworth Morton, née Apthorp (1759-1846) U.S. novelist, poet

°François-André Philidor: François-André Danican (1727-1795) Fr. musical composer, chessplayer

Gérard Philipe: Gérard Philip (1922-1959) Fr. stage, film actor

Conrad Philips: Conrad Philip Havord (1930-) Eng. film, TV actor

The Philistine: John Alfred Spender (1862-1942) Eng. editor, writer

°Esther Phillips: Esther May Jones (1935-) U.S. pop singer

Philo-Criticus: Francis Hare (1671-

-1740) Eng. church polemicist

Philomela: Elizabeth Rowe (1674-1737) Eng. writer, poet

°**Phiz**: Hablot Knight Browne (1815-1882) Eng. illustrator of works by Dickens, Surtees

John **Phoenix**: George Horatio Derby (1823-1861) U.S. humorous writer, satirist

Duncan **Phyfe**: Duncan Fife (1768-1854) Sc. furniture designer, working in U.S.

°Edith **Piaf**: Edith Giovanna Gassion (1915-1963) Fr. singer, entertainer

Slim **Pickens**: Louis Bert Lindley (1919-) U.S. film actor

Jack **Pickford**: Jack Smith (1896-1933) Can. film actor, brother of Mary Pickford (*q.v.*)

Mary **Pickford**: Gladys Mary Smith (1893-1979) Can.-born U.S. film actress

Pickle: Alastair Ruadh Macdonnell (?1725-1761) Sc. Jacobite, spy

Peregrine **Pickle**: George Putnam Upton (1834-1919) U.S. journalist, music critic

Pictor Ignotus: William Blake (1757-1827) Eng. artist, poet, mystic [44]

Piero di Cosimo: Piero di Lorenzo (1462-1521) It. painter

[Abbé] **Pierre**: Henri Antoine Groués (1912-) Fr. priest, Resistance fighter

Pigpen: Ronald McKernan (1946-1973) U.S. rock musician

Martin **Pike**: David Herbert Parry (1868-1950) Eng. writer of boys' stories, military articles

°Nova **Pilbeam**: Margery Pilbeam (1919-) Br. film actress

David **Pilgrim**: John Leslie Palmer (1895-1944) Br. thriller writer. + Hilary Aidan St. George Saunders (1895-1951) Br. thriller writer

Boris **Pilnyak**: Boris Andreyevich Vogau (1894-c.1937) Russ. novelist

Pimen: Sergei Mikhailovich Izvekov (1910-) Russ. churchman, patriarch of Moscow, All Russia

Paul **Pindar**: John Yonge Akerman (1806-1873) Eng. antiquary

°Peter **Pindar**: [1] John Wolcot (1738-1819) Eng. satirical verse writer. [2] C F Lawler (1738-1819) Eng. writer

Theodore **Pine**: Emil Pataja (1915-) U.S. SF, fantasy writer

[Sir] Arthur **Pinero**: Arthur Wing Pinheiro (1855-1934) Br. dramatist, stage actor

Harold **Pinter**: Harold da Pinta (1930-) Br. dramatist, stage actor

°**Pintoricchio**: Bernardino di Betti (1454-1513) It. painter

Lazarus **Piot**: Anthony Munday (1553-1633) Eng. poet, playwright

Jeems **Pipes of Pipesville**: Stephen G Massett (1820-1898) U.S. author

Pitcher: Arthur M Binstead (1861-1914) Eng. sporting writer

Augustus Henry **Pitt-Rivers**: Augustus Henry Lane Fox (1827-1900) Eng. soldier, archaeologist

Pius II: Enea Silvio de Piccolomini (or Aeneas Silvius) (1405-1464) It. pope, scholar [51]

Pius III: Francesco Todeschini Piccolomini (1439-1503) It. pope

Pius IV: Giovanni Angelo de'Medici (1499-1565) It. pope

[Saint] **Pius V**: Michele Ghislieri (1504-1572) It. pope

Pius VI: Giovanni Angelo Braschi (1717-1799) It. pope

Pius VII: Gregorio Luigi Barnabo Chiarmonti (1742-1823) It. pope [51]

Pius VIII: Francesco Saverio Castiglioni (1761-1830) It. pope

Pius IX: Giovanni Maria Mastai-Ferretti (1792-1878) It. pope [51]

Pius X: Giuseppe Melchiorre Sarto (1835-1914) It. pope

Pius XI: Achille Ambrogio Damiano Ratti (1857-1939) It. pope

Pius XII: Eugenio Pacelli (1876-1958) It. pope [51]

Benjamin **Place**: [Rev.] Edward Thring (1821-1887) Eng. schoolmaster, educationalist

Jean **Plaidy**: Eleanor Alice Burford Hibbert (1906-) Eng. historical novelist

John **Ploughman**: [Rev.] Charles Haddon Spurgeon (1834-1892) Eng. Baptist preacher, writer

Jacques **Plowert**: Paul Adam (1862-1920) Fr. novelist

Patrick **Plum**: Michael Anthony

McConville (1925-) Eng. magazine contributor

Peter **Plymley**: Sydney Smith (1771-1845) Eng. clergyman, essayist, wit

°**Pocahontas**: Matoaka (?1595-1617) American-Indian wife of Eng. colonizer John Rolfe

William **Poel**: William Pole (1852-1934) Br. stage actor, producer

Nikolai Fyodorovich **Pogodin**: Nikolai Fyodorovich Stukalov (1900-1962) Russ. dramatist

Lou **Polan**: Lou Polansky (1904-) U.S. stage director

°**Boris Polevoy**: Boris Nikolayevich Kampov (1908-) Russ. novelist, journalist

Poliarchus: [Sir] Charles Cotterell (1615-?1687) Eng. politician, courtier, correspondent of Orinda (*q.v.*)

Polidor: Ferdinando Guillaume (1887-1977) Fr. film comedian, stage clown

Angelo **Poliziano**: Angelo Ambrogini (1454-1494) It. poet, philologist

Antonio **Pollaiuolo**: Antonio Benci (1433-1498) It. painter, sculptor, engraver

Michael J. **Pollard**: Michael J Pollack (1939-) U.S. film actor

Snub **Pollard**: Harold Fraser (1886-1962) Australian film comedian, working in U.S.

°**Pont**: Graham Laidler (1908-1940) Br. cartoonist

Pontormo: Jacopo Carrucci (1494-1557) It. painter

Poor Richard: Benjamin Franklin (1709-1790) U.S. statesman, philosopher, writer

Poor Robin: Robert Herrick (1591-1674) Eng. poet

Popski: Vladimir Peniakoff (1897-1951) Belg. military commander, of Russ. parentage

Peter **Porcupine**: William Cobbett (1763-1835) Eng. journalist, politician [**45, 60**]

Martin **Porlock**: Philip MacDonald (1890-) Br. writer of detective novels

Porphyry: Malchas (233-c.304) Gk. scholar

Porte-Crayon: David Hunter Strother (1816-1888) U.S. artist, illustrator

Sandy **Posey**: Martha Sharp (1945-) U.S. pop singer, songwriter

Adrienne **Posta**: Adrienne Poster (1948-) Eng. film actress

Gillie **Potter**: Hugh William Peel (1888-1975) Br. humorist

Jane **Powell**: Suzanne Burce (1929-) U.S. film actress, singer, dancer

Mala **Powers**: Mary Ellen Powers (1931-) U.S. film actress

Stefanie **Powers**: Stefania Zofia Federkiewicz (1942-) U.S. film, TV actress

Stephen **Powys**: Virginia Bolton, née de Lanty (1907-) U.S. playwright, short story writer

Poy: Percy Hutton Fearon (-) Br. cartoonist [**46**]

Michael **Praetorius**: Michael Schultheiss (or Schulz) (1571-1621) Ger. composer, writer on music [**31**]

George R. **Preedy**: Marjorie Bowen (*q.v.*)

Paul **Prendergast**: Douglas William Jerrold (1803-1857) Eng. novelist, dramatist, humorist

Paula **Prentiss**: Paula Ragusa (1939-) U.S. film actress

John **Presland**: Gladys Williams Bendit, née Presland (1885-) Australian-born Eng. author, poet

Micheline **Presle**: Micheline Chassagne (1927-) Fr. film actress

George F. **Preston**: [Baron] John Byrne Leicester Warren (1835-1895) Eng. poet

Robert **Preston**: Robert Preston Meservey (1918-) U.S. stage, film actor

Préville: Pierre-Louis Dubus (1721-1799) Fr. comic actor

Marie **Prévost**: Marie Bickford Dunn (1898-1937) Can.-born U.S. film actress

Dennis **Price**: Dennistoun Franklyn John Rose-Price (1915-1973) Eng. stage, film actor

Maire **Price**: Maire Nic Shiubhlaigh, née Marie Walker (-1958) Ir. stage actress

The **Prig**: Thomas Longueville (1844-1922) Br. author

Dorothy **Primrose**: Dorothy Buckley

(1916-) Sc. stage actress

Aileen **Pringle**: Aileen Bisbee (1895-) U.S. film actress

Yvonne **Printemps**: Yvonne Wigniolle (1894-1977) Fr. singer, film, stage comedienne

James **Prior**: James Prior Kirk (1851-1922) Eng. novelist

Private 19022: Frederic Manning (1887-1935) Australian-born Eng. writer

P.J. (Jim) **Proby**: James Marcus Smith (1938-) U.S. rock singer

Lozania **Prole**: Ursula Bloom (-) Eng. novelist

°**Father Prout**: Francis Sylvester Mahoney (1804-1866) Ir. humorist

Marcel **Provence**: Marcel Jouhandeau (1888-) Fr. novelist, short story writer, essayist, dramatist

Joseph **Prunier**: Guy de Maupassant (1850-1893) Fr. short story writer

°**Kozma Prutkov**: Alexei Konstantinovich Tolstoy (1817-1875) Russ. poet. +Alexei Mikhailovich Zhemchuzhnikov (1821-1908) Russ. poet. +Vladimir Mikhailovich Zhemchuzhnikov (1830-1884) Russ. poet, their cousin

Anthony **Pride**: Agnes Russell Weekes (1880-) Br. novelist

Maureen **Pryor**: Maureen Pook (1924-1977) Ir. stage, film, TV actress

George **Psalmanazar**: ? (c.1679-1763) Fr. (or Swiss) literary impostor, working in England **[64, 65]**

Pseudoplutarch: John Milton (1608-1674) Eng. poet

Publius: Alexander Hamilton (1757-1804) U.S. statesman. +James Madison (1751-1804) U.S. man, 4th president. +John Jay (1745-1829) U.S. lawyer, statesman, jurist

William Owen **Pughe**: William Owen (1759-1835) Welsh antiquarian, lexicographer

Punjabee: William Delafield Arnold (1828-1859) Eng. novelist

Reginald **Purdell**: Reginald Grasdorf (1896-1953) Br. stage, music hall, film actor

Bobby **Purify**: Robert Lee Dickey (1939-) U.S. black pop singer, team-ing with his cousin, James Purify

Eleanor **Putnam**: Harriet L. Bates, née Vose (1856-1886) U.S. writer

Isra **Putnam**: Greye La Spina, née Fanny Greye Bragg (1880-1969) U.S. horror story writer

Hanna **Puttick**: Astrid Proll (1947-) Ger. terrorist, working in U.K.

Q

Q: [1] [Sir] Arthur Thomas Quiller-Couch (1863-1944) Br. novelist, short story writer. [2] Douglas William Jerrold (1803-1857) Eng. playwright, humorist **[30]**

Q.Q.: Jane Taylor (1783-1824) Eng. writer

°**M. Quad**: Charles Bertrand Lewis (1842-1924) U.S. printer, journalist, humorist

John **Quaten**: John Oleson (1899-) Norw. film actor, working in U.S.

°**Ellery Queen**: Frederic Dannay (1905-) U.S. crime novelist. +Manfred Bennington Lee (1905-1971) U.S. crime novelist

°**Patrick Quentin**: Richard Wilson Webb (-); +Hugh Callingham Wheeler (1913-); +Martha Mott Kelly (-); +Mary Louise Aswell (-); all U.S. writers of detective fiction **[57]**

Peter **Query**, Esq.: Martin Farquhar Tupper (1810-1889) Eng. versifier

Quevedo Redivivus: George Gordon Byron (1788-1824) Eng. poet

Dan **Quin**: Alfred Henry Lewis (c.1858-1914) U.S. journalist, novelist

Peter **Quince**: [1] Isaac Story (1774-1803) U.S. satirist, poet. [2] John William McWean Thompson (1920-) Eng. editor

Quirinus: [Dr.] Johann Joseph Ignaz von Döllinger (1799-1890) Ger. theologian

Quiz: [1] [Sir] Max Beerbohm (1872-1956) Br. essayist, caricaturist. [2] Charles Dickens (1812-1870) Eng. novelist, short story writer

John **Quod**: John Treat Irving (1812-1906) U.S. writer on frontier life

Richard **Quongti**: Thomas Babington

Macaulay (1800-1859) Eng. writer, statesman

R

William **Rabbit**: Katay Don Sasorith (1904-1959) Laotian nationalist, writer of resistance pamphlets [32]

Isaac **Rabbotenus**: Philipp van Marnix Sainte Aldegonde (1538-1598) Du. statesman

István **Rabovsky**: István Rab (1930-) Hung.-U.S. ballet dancer, teacher

Mlle **Rachel**: Élisabeth Rachel Félix (1820-1858) Fr. tragedienne

Rachilde: Marguerite Vallette, née Eymery (1860-1953) Fr. literary critic, author

Charlotte **Radd**: Charlotte Lubotsky (1926-) U.S. stage actress, singer

Chips **Rafferty**: John William Goffage (1909-1971) Australian film actor

George **Raft**: George Ranft (1895-1980) U.S. film actor

C.E. **Raimond**: Elizabeth Robins (1865-1952) U.S. stage actress, novelist

Raimu: Jules-Auguste-César Muraire (1883-1946) Fr. stage, film actor

Ferdinand **Raimund**: Jakob Raimann (1790-1836) Austr. playwright, actor

Allen **Raine**: Anne Adalisa Puddicombe (1836-1908) Welsh novelist

Ella **Raines**: Ella Rauber (1921-) U.S. film actress

W.B. **Rainey**: Wyatt Rainey Blassingame (1909-) U.S. writer of children's books, reference works

Jan **Rainis**: Jan Plieksans (1865-1929) Latvian playwright, translator

Rosa **Raisa**: Rose Burchstein (1893-1963) Pol. opera singer, working in Italy, U.S.

Jesse **Ralph**: Jessie Ralph Chambers (1864-1944) U.S. film actress

Walter **Ramal**: Walter de la Mare (1873-1956) Eng. poet, anthologist, short story writer

°Marie **Rambert**: Myriam Ramberg (1888-) Eng. ballet teacher, producer, director

"Ram" **Ramirez**: Roeger Ameres (c.1915-) West Indian jazz pianist

Sally **Rand**: Helen Gould Beck (1904-1979) U.S. vaudeville dancer

James **Randi**: James Randall Zwinge (-) Can. escapologist ("The Amazing Randi")

Frank **Randle**: Arthur McEvoy (1901-1957) Eng. music hall, film comedian

Raoul: Hugh Duff McLauchlan (1920-) Sc. music hall dancer, teaming with Babette (*q.v.*) [33]

Raphael: Raffaello Santi (1483-1520) It. painter

°**Rasputin**: Grigoriy Yefimovich Novykh (1864 or 1865-1916) Russ. monk, court favorite, religious fanatic

Alexis **Rassine**: Alexis Rays (1919-) Lithuanian-Br. ballet dancer

Morgan **Rattler**: P W Banks (1806-1850) Eng. writer

Mike **Raven**: Churton Fairman (1924-) Eng. radio DJ

Aldo **Ray**: Aldo Da Re (1926-) U.S. film actor

Cyril **Ray**: Cyril Rotenberg (1908-) Eng. writer on wine

Jean **Ray**: Jean-Raymond De Kremer (1887-1964) Belg. novelist, short story writer [16]

°**Man Ray**: Emmanuel Rudnitsky (1890-1976) U.S. surrealistic painter, photographer

Nicholas **Ray**: Raymond Nicholas Kienzle (1911-1979) U.S. film director

René **Ray**: Irene Creese (1912-) Eng. stage, film actress

°**Ted Ray**: Charles Olden (c.1909-1977) Eng. comedian, violinist

Carol **Raye**: Kathleen Corkrey (1923-) Br. film actress

Martha **Raye**: Margaret Theresa Yvonne Reed (1916-) U.S. radio, TV comedienne, singer [40]

Raymond: Raymondo Pietro Carlo Bessone (1911-) Eng. hair stylist, of It. parentage ("Mr. Teasy-Weasy")

Gene **Raymond**: Raymond Guion (1908-) U.S. film, TV actor

John T. **Raymond**: John O'Brien (1836-1887) U.S. comedian

Paula **Raymond**: Paula Ramona Wright (1923-) U.S. film actress

Miss **Read**: Dora Jessie Saint, née Shafe (1913-) Eng. author

°Ronald **Reagan** [pron. "Rayg'n"]: Ronald Reagan [pron. "Reeg'n"] (1911-) 40th U.S. Pres., former film actor

The **Redeemed Captive**: John Williams (1644-1729) U.S. clergyman, Indian prisoner

Martin **Redfield**: Alice Brown (1857-1948) U.S. novelist

Ralph **Redway**: Frank Richards (*q.v.*)

Donna **Reed**: Donna Mullenger (1921-) U.S. film, TV actress

Della **Reese**: Dellareese Taliaferro, née Early (1932-) U.S. black pop singer

Ada **Reeve**: Adelaide Mary Isaacs (1874-1966) Eng. music hall comedienne

George **Reeves**: George Besselo (1914-1959) U.S. film actor

Seeley **Regester**: Metta Victoria Fuller Victor (1831-1886) U.S. writer of romantic, humorous novels

Regiomontanus: Johann Müller (1436-1476) Ger. astronomer, mathematician

Ada **Rehan**: Ada Crehan (1860-1916) U.S. stage actress

Philip **Reid**: Richard Reid Ingrams (1937-) Eng. satirical magazine editor. + Andrew Osmond (-) Eng. satirical writer

Max **Reinhardt**: Max Goldmann (1873-1943) Austr. stage actor, manager, director, working in U.S.

Hans **Reinmar**: Hans Wochinz (1895-1961) Austr. opera singer, working in Germany

Réjane: Gabrielle-Charlotte Réju (1857-1920) Fr. stage actress, theatre manager

Uncle **Remus**: Joel Chandler Harris (1848-1908) U.S. writer

Duncan **Renaldo**: Renault Renaldo Duncan (1904-) U.S. film actor, painter

°Mary **Renault**: Mary Challans (1905-) Br. novelist

Liz **Renay**: Pearl Elizabeth Dobbins (1934-) U.S. film actress

Ludwig **Renn**: Arnold Friedrich Vieth von Golssenau (1889-) East German novelist, children's writer

Emma **Renzi**: Emmarentia Scheepers (-) S.A. opera singer

Elisabeth **Rethberg**: Elisabeth Sättler (1894-1976) Ger. opera singer, working in U.S.

[Baron von] Paul Julius **Reuter**: Israel Beer Josaphat (1816-1899) Ger. founder of Reuters news agency

Reginald **Reverie**: Grenville Mellen (1799-1841) U.S. author, poet

Dorothy **Revier**: Dorothy Velegra (1904-) U.S. film actress

Fernando **Rey**: Fernando Arambillet (1915-) Sp. film actor

Monte **Rey**: James Montgomery Fyfe (1900-) Sc. radio singer

Judith **Reyn**: Judith Fisher (1944-) Rhodesian-born Eng. ballet dancer

°Debbie **Reynolds**: Mary Frances Reynolds (1932-) U.S. film actress

Marjorie **Reynolds**: Marjorie Goodspeed (1921-) U.S. film actress

Peter **Reynolds**: Peter Horrocks (1926-1975) Br. film actor

Rhäticus: Georg Joachim von Lauchen (1514-1576) Ger. astronomer, mathematician

John **Rhode**: °Honoré de Balzac

Jean **Rhys**: Jean Hamer, née Rees Williams (1894-1979) Eng. writer

°Ruggiero **Ricci**: Woodrow Wilson (later Roger) Rich (1918-) U.S. concert violinist

°Craig **Rice**: Georgiana Ann Randolph (1908-1957) U.S. mystery novelist, film scriptwriter

Dan **Rice**: Daniel McLaren (1823-1900) U.S. circus clown

°Elmer **Rice**: Elmer Lion Reizenstein (1892-1967) U.S. playwright, novelist

Irene **Rich**: Irene Luther (1891-) U.S. film actress

°Cliff **Richard**: Harold Roger Webb (1940-) Eng. pop musician, film actor

Francis **Richard**: Frank R. Stockton (1834-1902) U.S. novelist, short story writer

Frank **Richards**: Charles Harold St. John Hamilton (1875-1961) Eng. author of school stories

Hilda **Richards**: Frank Richards (*q.v.*)

Henry Handel **Richardson**: Ethel Florence Lindesay Richardson (1870-1946) Austr. novelist, working in Germany, U.K.

Richelieu: William Erigena Robinson (1814-1892) U.S. journalist, politician

Fiona **Richmond**: Julia Harrison (1947-) Eng. stage, film actress

Kane **Richmond**: Frederick W Bowditch (1906-1973) U.S. film actor

John **Ridgeley**: John Huntingdon Rea (1909-1968) U.S. film actor

Laura **Riding**: Laura Jackson, née Reichenthal (1901-) U.S. writer, poet

Robert **Rietty**: Robert Rietti (1923-) Eng. stage actor, playwright, director

°John **Ringling**: John Rüngeling (1866-1936) U.S. circus impresario

Johnny **Ringo**: Clay Allison (1914-) Eng. writer of westerns

Ringuet: Philippe Panneton (1895-1960) Fr.-Can. novelist

A. **Riposte**: Elinor Mordaunt, née Evelyn May Clowes (1877-1942) Br. novelist, travel writer

Elizabeth **Risdon**: Elizabeth Evans (1887-1958) Br. stage, film actress

Jack **Riskit**: John Evans (1879-?) Eng. gymnast, wire walker

Rita: Eliza Margaret Humphreys, née Gollan (-1938) Sc. romantic novelist

Chita **Rivera**: Concita del Rivera (1933-) U.S. stage actress, singer

Johnny **Rivers**: John Ramistella (1942-) U.S. pop musician, record company executive

Larry **Rivers**: Yitzroch Loiza Grossberg (1923-) U.S. painter

Jerome **Robbins**: Jerome Rabinowitz (1918-) U.S. stage director, choreographer

Ben **Roberts**: Benjamin Eisenberg (1916-) U.S. screenwriter

Ewan **Roberts**: Ewan Hutchison (1914-) Sc. stage actor

Lionel **Roberts**: Robert Lionel Fanthorpe (1935-) Eng. SF writer

Lynn **Roberts**: Mary Hart (1922-) U.S. film actress

E. Arnot **Robertson**: Eileen Arbuthnot Turner, née Robertson (1903-) Eng. novelist

Gilles **Roberval**: Gilles Personne (1602-1675) Fr. mathematician

[Sir] George **Robey**: George Edward Wade (1869-1954) Eng. stage, film comedian (the "Prime Minister of Mirth")

Henri **Robin**: Henri-Jospeh Dunkell (c.1805-1875) Du.-born Fr. conjuror ("The French Wizard")

Mr. and Master **Robinson**: Henry Hawley Crippen (1868-1910) Eng. murderer. + Ethel Le Neve (1893-1967) his mistress

°Edward G. **Robinson**: Emmanuel Goldenberg (1893-1973) U.S. film actor

Madeleine **Robinson**: Madeleine Svoboda (1916-) Fr. stage, film actress

Ralph **Robinson**: George III (1738-1820) king of England

°Sugar Ray **Robinson**: Walker Smith (1920-) U.S. black world champion boxer

°**Rob Roy**: [1] Robert Macgregor (1671-1734) Sc. Highlands outlaw. [2] John Macgregor (1825-1892) Eng. traveler, writer, canoe designer

Frederick **Robson**: Thomas Robson Brownhill (1821-1864) Eng. music hall actor

May **Robson**: Mary Robinson (1865-1942) Australian-born U.S. stage, film actress

Stuart **Robson**: Henry Robson Stuart (1836-1903) U.S. stage comedian

Patricia **Roc**: Felicia Riese (1918-) Br. film actress

Mark **Rochester**: William Charles Mark Kent (1823-1902) Eng. poet, miscellaneous writer

Jimmy **Rodgers**: James Snow (1933-) U.S. folk singer

William **Roerick**: William Roehrich (1912-) U.S. playwright, stage actor

°Ginger **Rogers**: Virginia Katharine McMath (1911-) U.S. stage, film actress, dancer [33]

°Roy **Rogers**: Leonard Slye (1912-) U.S. film actor

Will **Rogers**: William Penn Adair

Rogers (1879-1935) U.S. stage, film comedian

Eric **Rohmer**: Jean Maurice Scherer (1920-) Fr. film director

°**Sax Rohmer**: Arthur Sarsfield Ward (1886-1959) Eng. writer of "oriental" mystery stories

Gilbert **Roland**: Luis Antonio Dumaso de Alonso (1905-) Mexican-born U.S. film, TV actor

C.H. **Rolph**: Cecil Rolph Hewitt (1901-) Eng. writer, editor

Jules **Romains**: Louis-Henri-Jean Farigoule (1885-1972) Fr. playwright, novelist, poet

°**Michael (or Mike) Romanoff**: Harry Gerguson (1892-1971) Lithuanian-born U.S. restaurateur, film actor

Romany: George Bramwell Evans (1884-1943) Eng. writer, broadcaster on the countryside

Romark: Ronald Markham (1927-) Eng. TV hypnotist

Stewart **Rome**: Septimus William Ryott (1887-1965) Br. film actor

Edana **Romney**: Edana Rubenstein (1919-) S.A. film actress

[Sir] Landon **Ronald**: Landon Russell (1873-1938) Eng. conductor, composer

Edward **Ronns**: Edward Sidney Aarons (1916-1975) U.S. writer of detective fiction

°**Mickey Rooney**: Joe Yule, Jr. (1922-) U.S. film actor

Carl **Rosa**: Karl Rose (1842-1889) Ger. conductor, impresario, founder of Carl Rosa Opera Company

Rosario: Florencia Pérez Podilla (1918-) Sp. ballet dancer, teaming with Antonio (q.v.)

Françoise **Rosay**: Françoise Bandy de Nalèche (1891-1974) Fr. stage, film actress

Billy **Rose**: William Samuel Rosenberg (1899-1966) U.S. theatre manager, composer

Philip **Rose**: Philip Rosenberg (1921-) U.S. stage producer

[Saint] **Rose of Lima**: Isabel de Flores y del Oliva (1586-1617) Peruvian recluse, of Sp. parentage

Carl **Rosini**: John Rosen (1882-) Pol.-born magician, working in U.S.

Emperor **Rosko**: Michael Pasternak (1942-) Eng. radio DJ

Natalia **Roslavleva**: Natalia Rene (1906-1977) Russ.-born Eng. writer on ballet

°**Milton Rosmer**: Arthur Milton Lunt (1881-1971) Br. stage, film actor, director

J.H. **Rosny**: Joseph Henri Boex (1856-1940) Fr. novelist. + Seraphin Justin François Boex (1859-1948) Fr. novelist, his brother

Adrian **Ross**: Arthur Reed Ropes (1859-1933) Eng. writer of lyrics, librettos for musicals

°**Barnaby Ross**: °Ellery Queen

Leonard Q. **Ross**: Leo Calvin Rosten (1908-) Pol.-born U.S. humorous writer

°**Martin Ross**: Violet Florence Martin (1865-1915) Ir. author

Shirley **Ross**: Bernice Gaunt (1909-1975) U.S. pianist, singer, film actress

Sutherland **Ross**: Thomas Henry Callard (1912-) Eng. writer, schoolmaster

°**T.E. Ross**: Thomas Edward Lawrence (1888-1935) Eng. soldier, archaeologist, writer ("Lawrence of Arabia")

Eleanora **Rossi-Drago**: Palmina Omiccioli (1925-) It. film actress

Lillian **Roth**: Lillian Rutstein (1910-1980) U.S. film actress

Mark **Rothko**: Marcus Rothkovich (1903-1970) Russ.-born U.S. painter

Johnny **Rotten**: John Joseph Lydon (1956-) Eng. punk rock musician

The **Roving Englishman**: Eustace Clare Grenville Murray (1824-1881) Eng. traveler, writer

Effie Adelaide **Rowlands**: Effie Marie Albanesi, née Henderson (1859-1936) Br. author of romantic novels ("Madame Albanesi")

°**Samuel Roxy**: Samuel L. Rothafel (-) U.S. film distributor

Gabrielle **Roy**: Marcel Carbotte (1909-) Fr.-Can. novelist

Marie **Roze**: Hippolyte Ponsin (1846-1926) Fr. opera singer

Alma **Rubens**: Alma Smith (1897-1931) U.S. film actress

Harry **Ruby**: Harry Rubenstein (1895-1974) U.S. songwriter

Steele **Ruby**: Arthur Hoey Davis (1868-1935) Australian novelist, playwright, short story writer

°Titta **Ruffo**: Ruffo Titta (1878-1953) It. baritone opera singer

Runnymede: Benjamin Disraeli (1804-1881) Eng. prime minister, author

Anna **Russell**: Anna Claudia Russell-Brown (1911-) Br. stage entertainer

Billy **Russell**: Adam George Brown (1893-1971) Eng. music hall comedian

°Fred **Russell**: Thomas Frederick Parnell (1862-1957) Eng. ventriloquist, variety artiste

Lillian **Russell**: Helen Louise Leonard (1861-1922) U.S. stage actress, singer

Sarah **Russell**: Marghanita Laski (1915-) Br. novelist

Mark **Rutherford**: William Hale White (1831-1913) Eng. novelist

Irene **Ryan**: Irene Riordan (1903-1973) U.S. film comedienne

Bobby **Rydell**: Robert Ridarelli (1942-) U.S. pop musician

Alfred **Ryder**: Alfred Jacob Corn (1919-) U.S. stage actor, director

Poul **Rytter**: Parmo Carl Ploug (1813-1894) Dan. poet, journalist

S

Umberto **Saba**: Umberto Poli (1883-1957) It. poet

Sabrina: Norma Sykes (1928-) Eng. film, TV actress

Sabu: Sabu Dastagis (1924-1963) Indian film actor, working in U.K., U.S. [29]

Michael **Sadleir**: Michael Thomas Harvey Sadler (1888-1957) Br. novelist, biographer

°Françoise **Sagan**: Françoise Quoirez (1935-) Fr. novelist

Sagittarius: [1] Olga Miller, née Katzin (1896-) Br. author, satirical verse writer. [2] Heinrich Schütz (1585-1672) Ger. church music composer [31]

A. **Sailor**: William Falconer (1732-1769) Eng. poet

Horace de **Sainte-Aubin**: °Honoré de Balzac

Alan **St. Aubyn**: Frances Marshall, née Bridges (-) Eng. novelist

St. **Barbe**: Douglas Brooke Wheelton Sladen (1856-1947) Eng. author, critic

Michael **St. Clair**: Michael Sinclair MacAuslan Shea (1938-) Sc. writer, royal press secretary

Michel **Sainte-Denis**: Jacques Duchesne (1897-1971) Fr. theatre director, playwright, actor

Ruth **St. Denis**: Ruth Dennis (?1878-1968) U.S. dancer, teacher of dancing

Marco de **St. Hilaire**: Emile Marc Hilaire (1798-1887) Fr. writer

Xavier **Saintine**: Joseph Xavier Boniface (1798-1865) Fr. writer

Raymond **St. Jacques**: James Johnson (1930-) U.S. black film actor

Susan **Saint James**: Susan Miller (1946-) U.S. film, TV actress

Betta **St. John**: Betty Streidler (1930-) U.S. film actress

Christopher Marie **St. John**: Christabel Marshall (-1960) Br. novelist, playwright, biographer

Hector **St. John**: Michel-Guillaume Jean de Crèvecoeur (1735-1813) Fr. traveler, writer

Jill **St. John**: Jill Oppenheim (1940-) U.S. film actress

Alfred **St. Laurence**: Alfred Laurence Felkin (1856-) Eng. writer, working in U.S.

Comte de **St. Lue**: Louis Bonaparte (1778-1846) Fr. nobleman

S.Z. **Sakall**: Eugene Gero Szakall (1884-1955) Hung. film actor, working in U.S. ("Cuddles")

Alexander **Sakharoff**: Alexander Zuckermann (1886-1963) Russ. ballet dancer, teacher

°**Saki**: Hector Hugh Munro (1870-1916) Eng. short story writer

Saladin: William Stewart Ross (1844-1906) Eng. author of poems, works on agnosticism

°Soupy **Sales**: Milton Hines (1926-) U.S. TV entertainer, film actor

Felix **Salten**: Felix Salzmann (1869-1945) Hung. novelist, journalist, critic, working in Switzerland

Gregor **Samarow**: J F M O Meding (1829-) Ger. statesman, historical novelist

Galina **Samtsova**: Galina Ursulyak (1937-) Russ. ballet dancer, working in Canada

°George **Sand**: Amandine Lucile Aurore Dudevant (1804-1876) Fr. novelist

Jules **Sand**: Leonard Sylvain Jules Sandeau (1811-1883) Fr. writer

Maurice **Sand**: Maurice Dudevant (1823-1889) Fr. painter, writer, son of °George Sand

Dominique **Sanda**: Dominique Varaigne (1948-) U.S. film actress

Cora **Sandel**: Sara Fabricius (1880-1974) Norw. novelist, short story writer

Oliver **Sandys**: Marguerite Florence Hélène Evans, née Jervist (1894-) Br. writer

Sangiro: Andries Albertus Pienaar (1894-) S.A. writer in Afrikaans

George **Santayana**: Jorge Ruiz de Santayana y Borrais (1863-1952) Sp.-born U.S. writer, philosopher

Jacopo **Sansovino**: Jacopo Tatti (1486-1570) It. sculptor, architect

°**Sapper**: Herman Cyril McNeile (1888-1937) Eng. novelist

Gene **Sarazen**: Eugene Saraceni (1902-) U.S. golfer, of It. parentage

Leslie **Sarony**: Leslie Sarony-Frye (1897-) Eng. music hall singer

Andrea del **Sarto**: Andrea Domenico d'Agnolo di Francesco (1486-1531) It. painter

Lu **Säuberlich**: Liselotte Säuberlich-Lauke (1911-1976) Ger. stage, film actress

Richard **Saunders**: Benjamin Franklin (1706-1790) U.S. statesman, scientist, philosopher

George **Sava**: George Alexis Milkomanovich Milkomane (1903-) Russ.-born Br. author

Laura **Savage**: Frederic George Stephens (1828-1907) Eng. art critic

Signora Fernando **Savarese**: Violetta Elvin, née Prokhorova (1925-) Russ.-born Br. ballet dancer

Lee **Savold**: Lee Hulver (?1914-1972)

U.S. heavyweight boxer

Joseph **Sawyer**: Joseph Sauer (1901-) U.S. film comedian

John **Saxon**: Carmen Orrico (1935-) U.S. film actor

Peter **Saxon**: Wilfred McNeilly (1921-) Sc. detective, occult fiction writer

°Leo **Sayer**: Gerard Hughes Sayer (1948-) Eng. rock singer

S.B.: Herbert George Wells (1866-1946) Eng. novelist, short story writer

°**Scaeva**: John Stubbes (1541-1600) Eng. puritan zealot

Gia **Scala**: Giovanna Scoglio (1934-1972) Eng. film actress, of Ir.-It. parentage

Prunella **Scales**: Prunella West, née Illingworth (1932-) Eng. stage actress

John **Scarne**: Orlando Scarnecchia (-) U.S. conjuror, card magician

Emanuel **Schikaneder**: Johann Josef Schickeneder (1751-1812) Austr. dramatist, actor, theatre director

°Dr. **Schmidt**: Johann Christoph Friedrich von Schiller (1759-1805) Ger. poet, playwright

Romy **Schneider**: Rosemarie Albach-Retty (1938-) Austr. film actress [34]

A. **Scholar**: Samuel Wesley (1662-1735) Eng. clergyman

Lotte **Schöne**: Charlotte Bodenstein (1891-1977) Austr.-born Fr. opera singer

Gordon **Scott**: Gordon M Werschkul (1927-) U.S. film actor

Jack **Scott**: Jack Scafone (1938-) Can. rock singer

Lizabeth **Scott**: Emma Matzo (1922-) U.S. film actress

Randolph **Scott**: Randolph Crane (1903-) U.S. film actor

Raymond **Scott**: Harry Warnow (1910-) U.S. popular music composer, arranger

Sheila **Scott**: Sheila Christine Hopkins (1927-) Eng. aviator, lecturer, actress, writer

°Sir Walter **Scott**: James Kirke Paulding (1779-1860) U.S. author

W. **Scott-King**: [Rev.] William Kingscote Greenland (1868-) Eng. Wesleyan minister, journalist, novelist

Scotty: Scott Wiseman (1909-1981) U.S. country singer, teaming with Lulubelle (*q.v.*)

The Scout: Clive Graham (1913-1974) Eng. racing correspondent

Simon Scribe: Adam Black (1784-1874) Sc. publisher

H. Secundus Scriblerus: Henry Fielding (1707-1754) Eng. novelist, playwright

°Martinus Scriblerus: [1] Alexander Pope (1688-1744) Eng. poet. [2] George Crabbe (1754-1832) Eng. poet

George Julius Poulett Scrope: George Julius Poulett Thomson (1797-1876) Eng. geologist, politician [34, 35]

Scrutator: [Sir] Robert Charles Kirkwood Ensor (1877-1950) Br. historian, poet

Barbara Seagull: Barbara Hertzstein (1948-) U.S. film, TV actress

Sealion: Geoffrey Martin Bennett (1909-) Eng. novelist, naval writer

Charles Sealsfield: Karl Postl (1793-1864) Swiss monk, author, in U.S.

Edward Search: Abraham Tucker (1705-1774) Br. philosopher

January Searle: George Searle Phillips (1815-1889) Br. popular writer

Anna Seghers: Netty Radványi, née Reiling (1900-) Ger. novelist, in U.S.

Steve Sekely: Istvan Szekely (1899-) Hung. film director, working in U.S.

Elisa Selbig: Frau von Ahleberg (1781-1849) Ger. novelist

P.T. Selbit: Percy Tibbles (1879-1938) Eng. magician

Selmar: [Baron] Karl Gustav von Brinckman (1764-1847) Swe. diplomat, poet

George Selmark: Leslie Seldon Truss (1892-) Eng. thriller writer [16]

Morton Selten: Morton Richard Stubbs (1860-1940) Eng. stage, film actor

Tonio Selwart: Tonio Selmair (1896-) Ger. stage actor

Senior: [Rev.] John Penrose (1778-1859) Eng. theological writer

Mack Sennett: Michael Sinnott (1880-1960) U.S. producer of comic films (the "King of Comedy")

Sergius: Ivan Nikolayevich Stragorodsky (1867-1944) Russ. churchman, patriarch of Moscow, All Russia

Sergius IV: Peter Buccaporci (?-1012) It. pope

[Saint] Sergius of Radonezh: Bartholomew Kirillovich (1314-1392) Russ. monk, spiritual leader

Andrew Seth: Andrew Seth Pringle-Pattison (1856-1931) Sc. philosopher

Ernest Evan Thompson Seton: Ernest Evan Seton Thompson (1860-1946) Eng. author, artist, naturalist, working in Canada

Gabriel Setoun: Thomas Nicoll Hepburn (1861-1930) Sc. novelist

Dr. Seuss: Theodor Seuss Geisel (1904-) U.S. writer, illustrator of children's books

David Severn: David Storr Unwin (1918-) Eng. novelist, children's writer

°David Seville: Ross Bagdassarian (1919-1972) U.S. music, record company executive

Gordon Seymour: [Sir] Charles Waldstein (later Walston) (1856-1927) U.S.-born Br. archaeologist

Jane Seymour: Joyce Penelope Wilhelmina Frankenberg (1951-) Eng. film actress, working in U.S.

°Lynn Seymour: Lynn Berta Springbett (1939-) Can. ballet dancer

William Seymour: William Gorman Cunningham (1855-1933) U.S. stage actor

John Shadow: John Byrom (1692-1763) Eng. poet

Del Shannon: Charles Westover (1939-) U.S. pop singer

°Omar Sharif: Michel Shalhoub (1932-) Egyptian film actor

°Jack Sharkey: Joseph Paul Zukauskas (1902-) U.S. heavyweight boxer

Dee Dee Sharp: Diana LaRue (1945-) U.S. pop singer

°Luke Sharp: Robert Barr (1850-1912) Sc. novelist, working in Canada, U.K. [45]

Artie Shaw: Arthur Arshawsky (c.1904-) U.S. jazz musician, clarinettist, bandleader

Brian Shaw: Brian Earnshaw (1928-) Eng. ballet dancer

Roger Shaw: Roger Ollerearnshaw (1931-) Eng. TV announcer [14]

Sandie Shaw: Sandra Goodrich

(1948-) Eng. pop singer

Susan **Shaw**: Patsy Sloots (1929-) Eng. film actress **[57]**

T.E. **Shaw**: Thomas Edward Lawrence (1888-1935) Eng. soldier, archaeologist, writer ("Lawrence of Arabia")

Victoria **Shaw**: Jeanette Elphick (1935-) Australian film actress, working in U.S.

Dick **Shawn**: Richard Schulefand (?1929-) U.S. film comedian

Robert **Shayne**: Robert Shaen Dawe (?1910-) U.S. film actor

°N. **Shchedrin**: Mikhail Yevgrafovich Saltykov(-Shchedrin) (1826-1889) Russ. author

Al **Shean**: Alfred Schoenberg (1868-1949) Ger.-born U.S. stage, film comedian

Moira **Shearer**: Moira Shearer King (1926-) Sc. ballet dancer, stage, film actress

Joseph **Shearing**: Marjorie Bowen (*q.v.*)

Martin **Sheen**: Ramon Estevez (1940-) U.S. stage actor

Paul **Shelley**: Paul Matthews (1942-) Eng. stage, TV actor

Michael **Shepley**: Michael Shepley-Smith (1907-1961) Br. stage, film actor

Ann **Sheridan**: Clara Lou Sheridan (1915-1967) U.S. film actress (the "Oomph Girl")

Mark **Sheridan**: Fred Shaw (1867-1918) Eng. music hall singer

Paul **Sheriff**: Paul Schouvalov (or Schouvaloff) (1903-1962) Russ.-born film art director, working in U.K.

George **Shiels**: George Morshiel (1886-1949) Ir. playwright

Shirley: [Sir] John Skelton (1831-1897) Sc. lawyer, author

Anne **Shirley**: Dawn Paris (1918-) U.S. film actress

Troy **Shondell**: Gary Shelton (1940-) U.S. pop singer, producer

°Dinah **Shore**: Frances Rose Shore (1917-) U.S. singer, radio, TV actress

Bob **Short**: [1] Augustus Baldwin Longstreet (1790-1870) U.S. lawyer, educationalist, author. [2] Alexander Pope (1688-1744) Eng. poet

Abel **Shufflebottom**: Robert Southey (1774-1843) Eng. poet

Nevil **Shute**: Nevil Shute Norway (1899-1960) Br. novelist

Ethel **Shutta**: Ethel Schutte (1896-) U.S. stage actress, singer

Timothy **Shy**: Dominic Bevan Wyndham Lewis (1894-1969) Br. journalist, novelist, biographer

Edward William **Sidney**: Nathaniel Beverley Tucker (1784-1851) U.S. novelist

George **Sidney**: Sammy Greenfield (1878-1945) U.S. film comedian

Margaret **Sidney**: Harriet Mulford Lothrop, née Stone (1844-1924) U.S. children's writer

Sylvia **Sidney**: Sophia Kosow (1910-) U.S. stage, film actress

Siful **Sifadda**: Henrik Arnold T Wergeland (1808-1845) Norw. poet, satirist

Sigma: [Sir] Douglas Straight (1844-1914) Eng. author

Simone **Signoret**: Simone Henriette Charlotte Kaminker (1921-) Fr. film actress **[34, 63]**

°The **Silent Traveller**: Chiang Yee (1903-) Chinese-born Eng. writer of popular travel books

Angelus **Silesius**: Johann Scheffler (1624-1677) Pol. monk, poet

Beverly **Sills**: Belle Greenough, née Silverman (1929-) U.S. opera singer

Ignazio **Silone**: Secondo Tranquilli (1900-1978) It. anti-fascist writer, novelist

James **Silvain**: James Sullivan (-1856) Eng. ballet dancer

Silver Pen: Eliza Meteyard (1816-1879) Eng. novelist, author

°Georges **Sim**: Georges-Joseph-Christian Simeon (1903-) Belg. writer of detective fiction

John **Simm**: John Simmon (1920-) U.S. theatre critic

Ginny **Simms**: Virginia Sims (1916-) U.S. popular singer, film actress

Hilda **Simms**: Hilda Moses (1920-) U.S. stage actress

°Nina **Simone**: Eunice Wayman (1933-) U.S. black jazz musician

Konstantin **Simonov**: Kirill Mikhailovich Simonov̆ (1915-) Russ. poet, dramatist, novelist

°**Simplicissimus**: Georgy Valentinovich Plekhanov (1857-1918) Russ. socialist

Anne **Singleton**: Ruth Benedict, née Fulton (1887-1948) U.S. anthropologist, poet

Penny **Singleton**: Dorothy McNulty (1908-) U.S. film actress [63]

John **Sinjohn**: John Galsworthy (1867-1933) Eng. novelist, playwright

°**Sirin**: Vladimir Vladimirovich Nabokov (1899-1977) Russ. novelist, working in U.S.

Douglas **Sirk**: Hans Detlef Sierck (1900-) Ger. film director, of Dan. parentage, working in U.S.

Sixtus IV: Francesco della Rovere (1414-1484) It. pope [51]

Sixtus V: Felice Peretti (1521-1590) It. pope

°**Skanderbeg**: George Kastrioti (1405-1468) Albanian national hero

Arthur **Sketchley**: George Rose (1817-1882) Eng. humorous writer, entertainer

Joseph **Skillett**: [Lord] John Russell (1792-1878) Eng. statesman

Alison **Skipworth**: Alison Groom (1875-1952) Br. film actress, working in U.S.

Skitt: Harden E. Taliaferro (1818-1875) U.S. editor, sketch writer

Mia **Slavenska**: Mia Corak (1916-) Yugoslav-U.S. ballet dancer, choreographer, teacher

Jonathan **Slick**: Ann Sophia Stephens (1813-1886) U.S. historical novelist

Sam **Slock**: Thomas Chandler Haliburton (1796-1865) Can. jurist, humorist

Bumble Bee **Slim**: Amos Easton (c.1908-) U.S. black blues singer

Lightnin' **Slim**: Otis Hicks (1915-1974) U.S. blues singer

Jonathan Freke **Slingsby**: John Francis Waller (1810-1894) Ir. journalist, poet

Philip **Slingsby**: Nathaniel Parker Willis (1806-1867) U.S. journalist, poet

Ally **Sloper**: Charles H Ross (?1842-1897) Eng. humorous writer

Tony **Slydini**: Quintino Marucci (-) It.-born U.S. magician

°**Smectymnuus**: Stephen Marshall (?1594-1655) Eng. Presbyterian preacher, leader. + Edmund Calamy (1600-1666) Eng. Puritan clergyman. + Thomas Young (1587-1655) Sc. clergyman. + Matthew Newcomen (?1610-1669) Eng. clergyman. + William Spurstowe (?1605-1666) Eng. clergyman

Wentworth **Smee**: George Brown Burgin (1856-1944) Eng. novelist, journalist, critic

Sam **Smiff**: Tristram Coutts (-) Eng. author

Smilby: Francis Smith (1927-) Eng. cartoonist

Betty **Smith**: Elizabeth Keogh (1896-1972) U.S. novelist

Gamaliel **Smith**: Jeremy Bentham (1748-1832) Eng. jurist, philosopher

John **Smith**: Robert Van Order (1931-) U.S. film, TV actor

Johnston **Smith**: Stephen Crane (1871-1900) U.S. fiction writer

S.S. **Smith**: Thames Ross Williamson (1894-) U.S. fiction writer

Stevie **Smith**: Florence Margaret Smith (1902-1971) Eng. poet

°**Smokey Joe**: Joseph Sewell (1938-) Eng. "gunslinger"

Harry **Smolka**: Harry Peter Smollet (1912-) Austr.-born Eng. author, journalist

The **Snark**: Starr Wood (1870-) Eng. artist, caricaturist

Hans **Snoek**: Johanna Snoek (1906-) Du. ballet dancer, choreographer, director

°[Sir] Henry F.R. **Soame**: [Sir] Henry Edward Bunbury (1778-1860) Eng. historical writer

°**Sodoma**: Giovanni Antonio Bazzi (1477-1549) It. painter

°Lydia **Sokolova**: Hilda Munnings (1896-1974) Eng. ballet dancer

Fyodor **Sologub**: Fyodor Kuzmich Teternikov (1863-1927) Russ. writer

Solomon: Solomon Cuttner (1902-) Br. concert pianist [29]

Ikey **Solomons**: William Makepeace Thackeray (1811-1863) Eng. novelist

Somerville and Ross: Edith Anna Oenone Somerville (1858-1949) Ir. author + Violet Florence Martin (1862-1915) Ir. author, her cousin

Franca Somigli: Marin Bruce Clark (1901-1974) U.S.-It. opera singer

Elke Sommer: Elke Schletz (1940-) Ger. film actress

Somnambulus: [Sir] Walter Scott (1771-1832) Sc. poet, novelist

°Sonny: Salvatore Bono (1935-) U.S. pop singer, teaming with Cher (q.v.)

A Son of the Soil: Joseph Smith Fletcher (1863-1935) Eng. journalist, novelist, poet

Kaikhosru Shapurji Sorabji: Leon Dudley Sorabji (c.1892-) Eng. musical composer

°Jean Sorel: Jeande Rochbrune (1934-) Fr. film actor

Agnes Sorma: Martha Karoline Zaremba (1865-1927) Ger. stage actress

Ann Sothern: Harriet Lake (1909-) U.S. film, TV actress

Edward Askew Sothern: Douglas Stewart (1826-1881) Br. actor

David Soul: David Solberg (1943-) U.S. pop singer

Jimmy Soul: James McCleese (1942-) U.S. pop singer

°Suzi Soul: Suzi Quatro (1950-) U.S. pop singer

Theophilus South: Edward Chitty (1804-1863) Eng. legal reporter

Stephen Southwold: Stephen H. Critten (1887-1964) Eng. novelist, short story writer

E. Souza: Evelyn Scott (1893-) U.S. novelist, poet, short story writer

Gérard Souzay: Gérard Marcel Tisserand (1921-) Fr. opera singer

Mark Spade: Nigel Marlin Balchin (1908-1970) Br. novelist

Georg Spalatin: Georg Burkhardt (1484-1545) Ger. humanist

Tony Spargo: Anthony Sbarbaro (1897-1969) U.S. jazz musician

Godfrey Sparks: Charles Dickens (1812-1870) Eng. novelist

Ned Sparks: Edward Sparkman (1883-1957) Can. film comedian, working in U.S.

Spartakus: Karl Liebknecht (1871-1919) Ger. lawyer, Communist leader

Speckled Red: Rufus Perryman (1892-) U.S. black jazz pianist

Spectator: Arthur Bingham Walkley (1855-1926) Eng. dramatic critic, author

Speranza: [Lady] Jane Francisca Speranza Wilde, née Elgee (1826-1896) Ir. poet, mother of Oscar Wilde

Spondee: Royall Tyler (1757-1826) U.S. playwright, essayist, satirist

°Dusty Springfield: Mary O'Brien (1939-) Eng. pop singer, musician

Mercurius Spur: Cuthbert Shaw (1739-1771) Eng. poet

°Spy: [Sir] Leslie Ward (1851-1922) Eng. illustrator, caricaturist

Squibob: George Horatio Derby (1823-1861) U.S. humorous writer, satirist [46]

Ronald Squire: Ronald Squirl (1886-1958) Eng. stage, film actor

Staccato: A Kalisch (1863-1933) Br. journalist, music critic

Robert Stack: Robert Modini (1919-) U.S. film, TV actor

Hanely Stafford: Alfred John Austin (1899-1968) U.S. radio actor

P.J. Stahl: Pierre Jules Hetzel (1814-1886) Fr. publisher, author

°Stainless Stephen: Arthur Clifford Baynes (1892-1971) Eng. music hall comedian

°Joseph Stalin: Iosif Vissarionovich Dzhugashvili (1879-1953) Russ. Communist leader

John Standing: [Sir] John Ronald Leon (1934-) Eng. stage, film actor

Burt L. Standish: William Gilbert Patten (1866-1945) U.S. author of "dime novels," stories

Konstantin Stanislavsky: Konstantin Sergeevich Alekseyev (1865-1938) Russ. stage actor, producer, teacher

°[Sir] Henry Morton Stanley: John Rowlands (1841-1904) Welsh-born Br. explorer of Africa

Kim Stanley: Patricia Reid (1921-) U.S. stage, film actress

Barbara Stanwyck: Ruby Stevens (1907-) U.S. film actress

°Alvin Stardust: Bernard William Jewry (1942-) Eng. pop singer

Edwin **Starr**: Charles Hatcher (1942-) U.S. pop singer

Kay **Starr**: Catherine Starks (1923-) U.S. popular radio singer

°**Ringo Starr**: Richard Starkey (1940-) Eng. pop singer

Vargo **Statten**: John Russell Fearn (1908-1960) Eng. SF writer

Si **Stebbins**: Will H Coffrin (-) U.S. card magician

Byron **Steel**: Francis Steegmuller (1906-) U.S. novelist, literary critic

Bob **Steele**: Robert Bradbury (1907-1966) U.S. film actor

Tommy **Steele**: Thomas Hicks (1936-) Eng. pop singer, stage, film actor

Saul **Steinberg**: Saul Jacobson (1914-) Rom. cartoonist, illustrator, working in U.S.

Henry Engelhard **Steinway**: Heinrich Engelhardt Steinweg (1797-1871) Ger. piano manufacturer, working in U.S.

Stella: [1] Esther Johnson (1681-1728) Eng. letter writer, correspondent of Jonathan Swift. [2] Estella Anna Lewes (1824-1880) U.S. author

Anna **Sten**: Anjuschka Stenski Sujakevitch (1908-) Russ.-born U.S. film actress

°**Stendhal**: Marie-Henri Beyle (1783-1842) Fr. novelist

Stephen IX: Frederick of Lorraine (c.1000-1058) Fr. pope [52]

Henry **Stephenson**: Henry Stephenson Garroway (1871-1956) Br. stage, screen actor, working in U.S.

Sergei Mikhailovich **Stepnyak**: Sergei Mikhailovich Kravchinsky (1852-1895) Russ. writer, working in U.K.

Ford **Sterling**: George Ford Stitch (1883-1939) U.S. film comedian

Jan **Sterling**: Jane Sterling Adriance (1923-) U.S. film actress

Robert **Sterling**: William Sterling Hart (1917-) U.S. film actor

°Daniel **Stern**: Marie Catherine Sophie de Flavigny [Comtesse d'Agoult] (1805-1876) Fr. writer [23]

Paul Frederick **Stern**: Paul Frederick Ernst (1902-) U.S. SF writer

Stet: Thomas Earle Welby (1881-1933) Br. journalist, essayist, literary critic

Cat **Stevens**: Steven Giorgiou (1948-) Eng. pop musician, of Gk.-Swe. parentage

Connie **Stevens**: Concetta Ann Ingolia (1938-) U.S. film actress

Craig **Stevens**: Gail Shekles (1918-) U.S. film actor

Inger **Stevens**: Inger Stensland (1935-1970) Swe.-born U.S. film, TV actress

K.T. **Stevens**: Gloria Wood (1919-) U.S. film actress

Onslow **Stevens**: Onslow Ford Stevenson (1902-1977) U.S. stage, film actor

Ed **Stewart**: Edward Stewart Mainwaring (1941-) Eng. radio DJ, compère, TV actor ("Stewpot")

Elaine **Stewart**: Elsy Steinberg (1929-) U.S. film actress [27]

Karl **Stille**: Hermann Christoph Gottfried Demme (1760-1822) Ger. poet, novelist

Sting: Gordon Sumner (1950-) Eng. rock singer

Arthur **Stirling**: Upton Beall Sinclair (1878-1968) U.S. novelist

Max **Stirner**: Johann Kaspar Schmidt (1806-1856) Ger. philosopher

Wilhelmina **Stitch**: Ruth Collie (1889-1936) Br. author of popular sentimental verse

Betty **Stockfeld**: Betty Stockfield (1905-1966) Austr. film actress, working in U.K.

°Leopold **Stokes**: Leopold Antoni Stanislaw Boleslawowicz Stokowski (1882-1977) Br. orchestra conductor, working in U.S.

[Sir] Oswald **Stoll**: Oswald Gray (1866-1942) Eng. theatre manager

George E. **Stone**: George Stein (1903-1967) Pol. film actor, working in U.S.

Jesse **Stone**: Charles Calhoun (-) U.S. pop music arranger

Sly **Stone**: Sylvester Stewart (1944-) U.S. black rock musician

Stonehenge: John Henry Walsh (1810-1888) Eng. sporting writer, editor

The **Stonemason of Cromarty**: Hugh Miller (1802-1856) Sc. author, geologist

°Tom **Stoppard**: Tom Straussler (1937-) Czech-born Br. dramatist, theatre critic

Gale **Storm**: Josephine Cottle (1922-) U.S. film, TV actress

Lesley **Storm**: Margaret Clark, née Cowie (1904-1975) Sc. playwright

°Rory **Storm**: Alan Caldwell (1941-) Br. pop singer

Herbert **Strang**: George Herbert Ely (1866-1958) Eng. children's writer. + Charles James L'Estrange (-1947) Eng. children's writer

Eugene **Stratton**: Eugene Augustus Ruhlmann (1861-1918) U.S. black impersonator

Gene **Stratton-Porter**: Geneva Grace Porter, née Stratton (1863-1924) U.S. writer of books for girls

Paul Patrick **Streeten**: Paul Patrick Hornig (1917-) Austr.-born Br. economist

Hesba **Stretton**: Sarah Smith (1832-1911) Br. short story writer, novelist

Stringbean: David Akeman (1915-1973) U.S. country singer

Patience **Strong**: Winifred May (1905-) Eng. "inspirational" poet

Sheppard **Strudwick**: John Shepperd (1907-) U.S. film actor

Jan **Struther**: Joyce Maxtone Graham, née Anstruther (1901-1953) Eng. poet, short story writer, novelist

Ian **Stuart**: Alistair Maclean (1922-) Sc. novelist

John **Stuart**: John Croall (1898-1979) Sc. film, stage actor

Leslie **Stuart**: Thomas Barrett (c.1860-1928) Eng. popular songwriter

Theodore **Sturgeon**: Edward Hamilton Waldo (1918-) U.S. SF writer

Preston **Sturges**: Edmund Preston Biden (1898-1959) U.S. film writer, director

Jule **Styne**: Jule Stein (1905-) Eng. stage producer, composer of musicals

°Poly **Styrene**: Marion Elliott (1956-) Eng. punk rock singer

°Eugène **Sue**: Marie-Joseph Sue (1804-1857) Fr. novelist

Barry **Sullivan**: Patrick Barry (1912-) U.S. film actor

Charles **Summerfield**: Alfred W. Arrington (1810-1867) U.S. lawyer, writer

Prudence **Summerhayes**: Violet Prudence Alan Turner (1906-) Eng. author

°Felix **Summerly**: [Sir] Henry Cole (1808-1882) Eng. art patron, educator

Franz von **Suppé**: Francesco Esechiele Ermenegildo Suppé Demelli (1819-1895) It. operetta composer

°**Surfaceman**: Alexander Anderson (1845-1909) Sc. poet

Colonel **Surry**: John Esten Cooke (1830-1886) U.S. novelist, essayist

Comte de **Survilliers**: Joseph Bonaparte (1768-1844) Fr. nobleman

Suzy: Aileen Mehle (1952-) U.S. a "queen of aristocratic tittle-tattle"

°Italo **Svevo**: Ettore Schmitz (1861-1928) It. novelist, short story writer

°Gloria **Swanson**: Josephine Swenson (1897-) U.S. film actress

Emanuel **Swedenborg**: Emanuel Svedberg (1688-1772) Swe. scientist, philosopher, religious writer

Blanche **Sweet**: Daphne Wayne (1895-) U.S. film actress

Benjamin **Swift**: William Romaine Paterson (1871-) Eng. novelist

Nora **Swinburne**: Nora Johnson (1902-) Eng. stage actress

Urbanus **Sylvan**: Henry Charles Beeching (1859-1919) Eng. poet, essay writer

Sylvander: Robert Burns (1756-1796) Sc. poet

Sylvia: Sylvia Vanderpool (1936-) U.S. pop singer

T

T: Joseph Peter Thorp (1873-1962) Br. writer, biographer

Tad: Thomas Aloysius Dorgan (1877-1929) U.S. cartoonist, sports commentator

°**Taffrail**: [Captain] Henry Taprell Dorling (1883-1968) Br. naval correspondent, broadcaster, writer on naval affairs

°**Taffy**: Nadezhda Aleksandrovna Buchinskaya, née Likhvitskaya (1872-1952) Russ. short story writer, poet, working in France

Messrs. **Tag, Rag and Bobtail**: Isaac

Disraeli (1766-1848) Eng. writer
Aleksandr Yakovlevich **Tairov**: Aleksandr Kornblit (1885-1950) Russ. theatre producer, director
Howard **Talbot**: Richard Munkittrick (1865-1928) U.S. composer of musicals, working in U.K.
Lyle **Talbot**: Lisle Henderson (1904-) U.S. film actor
Talis Qualis: Carl Vilhelm August Strandberg (1818-1877) Swe. poet, journalist [45]
Richard **Talmadge**: Ricardo Metzetti (1896-) U.S. film actor, stunt man
°**Talvj**: Therese Albertine Louise Robinson, née von Jakob (1797-1870) Ger. author, writing in English
Helen **Tamiris**: Helen Becker (1905-1966) U.S. ballet dancer, choreographer, director
Tampa Red: Hudson Whittaker (c.1900-) U.S. black blues singer
°**Tania**: [1] Haydee Tamara Bunke (1937-1967) Russ. agent, of Ger. parentage, working in South America with °Che Guevara. [2] Patricia Campbell Hearst (1954-) U.S. liberationist
Tanya: Zoya Anatolyevna Kosmodemyanskaya (1923-1941) Russ. partisan
[Princess] Elizaveta **Tarakanova**: ? (c.1745-1775) Russ. royal pretender [65, 66]
Tasma: Jessie Couvreur, née Huybers (1860-) Australian novelist
Ellalice **Tate**: Eleanor Hibbert (1906-) Eng. novelist
Harry **Tate**: Ronald Macdonald Hutchinson (1873-1940) Eng. music hall comedian
°**Jacques Tati**: Jacques Tatischeff (1908-) Fr. comic film actor
Leo **Taxil**: Gabriel Antoine Jogand Pages (1854-1907) Fr. anticlerical, antireligious writer
Estelle **Taylor**: Estelle Boylan (1899-1958) U.S. stage, film actress
Kent **Taylor**: Louis Weiss (1907-) U.S. film actor
°**Laurette Taylor**: Laurette Cooney (1884-1946) U.S. stage, film actress
Little Johnny **Taylor**: Johnny Young (1940-) U.S. soul, blues singer

°**Robert Taylor**: Spangler Arlington Brough (1911-1969) U.S. film actor
Theodore **Taylor**: John Camden Hotten (1832-1873) Eng. author, publisher
T.B.: Arthur Christopher Benson (1862-1925) Eng. writer
Ludmila **Tcherina**: Monique Tchemerzina (1924-) Fr. ballet dancer
Conway **Tearle**: Frederick Levy (1878-1938) U.S. film actor
J. **Telio**: Charles Joilet (1832-) Fr. novelist, writer
Paul **Tell-truth**: George Saville Carey (1743-1807) Eng. humorous poet, vocalist, mimic
Anne **Telscombe**: Marie Dobbs, née Catton (-) Australian writer
[Dame] Marie **Tempest**: Mary Susan Tempest, née Etherington (1864-1942) Br. stage, film actress
Launcelot **Temple**: John Armstrong (1709-1779) Eng. poet
°**Paul Temple**: Francis Durbirdge (1912-) Eng. thriller writer. +James Douglas Rutherford McConnell (1915-) Eng. thriller writer
Laurence **Templeton**: [Sir] Walter Scott (1771-1832) Sc. poet, novelist
Kylie **Tennant**: Kylie Tennant Rodd (1912-) Australian novelist, playwright
Madison **Tensas, M.D.**: [Dr.] Henry Clay Lewis (1825-1850) U.S. humorist
Teresa: Teresa Viera-Romero (1929-) U.S.-Sp. ballet dancer
[Mother] **Teresa** (of Calcutta): Agnes Gonxha Bojaxhiu (1910-) Yugoslav-born missionary, of Albanian parentage, working in India [37]
Max **Terpis**: Max Pfister (1889-1958) Swiss ballet dancer, choreographer, teacher
°**Tammi Terrell**: Tammy Montgomery (1946-1970) U.S. pop singer
William **Terriss**: William Charles James Lewin (1847-1897) Eng. actor
C.V. **Terry**: Frank Gill Slaughter (1908-) U.S. novelist
Alice **Terry**: Alice Taafe (1899-) U.S. film actress
Don **Terry**: Donald Locher (1902-) U.S. film actor
Sonny **Terry**: Saunders Teddell (1911-)

U.S. black jazz harmonica player, blues singer

°**Terry-Thomas**: Thomas Terry Hoar-Stevens (1911-) Eng. comic stage, film actor

Phillida **Terson**: Phyllis Neilson-Terry (1892-1977) Eng. stage actress

Abram **Tertz**: Andrey Donatovich Sinyavsky (1925-) Russ. dissident writer [16]

Josephine **Tey**: Elizabeth Mackintosh (1897-1952) Sc. playwright, novelist, short story writer [35]

°[Dame] Maggie **Teyte**: [Dame] Margaret Cottingham, née Tate (1888-1976) Eng. singer

Zaré **Thalberg**: Ethel Western (1858-1915) Eng. opera singer, stage actress

°Octave **Thanet**: Alice French (1850-1934) U.S. novelist

Mlle **Théodore**: Marie-Madeleine Crépé (1760-1796) Fr. ballet dancer

°**Theodosia**: Anne Steel (1716-1778) Eng. writer of religious verse, hymns

Sylvanus **Theophrastus**: John Thelwall (1764-1834) Eng. reformer, politician, lecturer on elocution [38, 39]

[Saint] **Thérèse de Lisieux**: Marie-Françoise-Thérèse Martin (1873-1897) Fr. Carmelite nun

Denis **Thevenin**: Georges Duhamel (1884-1966) Fr. poet, playwright (the "Little Flower of Jesus")

Danny **Thomas**: Amos Jacobs (1914-) U.S. night club comedian, TV actor

Carlos **Thompson**: Juan Carlos Mundanschaffter (1916-) Argentinian stage, film actor

Sue **Thompson**: Eva Sue McKee (1926-) U.S. pop singer

°James **Thomson, B.V.**: James Thomson (1834-1882) Sc. poet

Guy **Thorne**: Cyril A E Ranger-Gill (1876-) Eng. novelist, reviewer

Frank **Thornton**: Francis Bull (1921-) Eng. stage, TV actor

Linda **Thorson**: Linda Robinson (1947-) Can. stage, TV actress

°General Tom **Thumb**: Charles Sherwood Stratton (1838-1883) U.S. midget

Chief **Thundercloud**: Victor Daniels (1900-1955) Amer.-Indian film star

°Henry T. **Thurston**: Francis Turner Palgrave (1824-1897) Eng. poet, critic

Dick **Tiger**: Dick Itehu (1929-1971) Nigerian boxer

Tikhon: Vasily Ivanovich Belyavin (?1865-1925) Russ. churchman, patriarch of Moscow, All Russia

°Vesta **Tilley**: Matilda Alice Powles (or Bowles) (1864-1952) Br. music hall, pantomime artiste, male impersonator

Alice **Tilton**: Phoebe Atwood Taylor (1909-) U.S. detective story writer

Dick **Tinto**: Frank Booth Goodrich (1826-1894) U.S. writer, son of °Peter Parley [1]

°**Tintoretto**: Jacopo Robusti (1518-1594) It. painter

Tiny Tim: Herbert Khaury (1922-) U.S. popular singer, musician

Timothy **Titcomb**: Josiah Gilbert Holland (1819-1881) U.S. novelist, poet, editor

Titian: Tiziano Vecellio (1477-1576) It. painter

°Michael Angelo **Titmarsh**: William Makepeace Thackeray (1811-1863) Eng. novelist

°**Tito**: Josip Broz (1892-1980) Yugoslav soldier, statesman

Tivoli: Horace W Bleackley (1868-) Eng. author

Harriet **Toby**: Harriet Katzman (1929-1952) U.S. ballet dancer

°**Toby, M.P.**: [Sir] Henry William Lucy (1845-1924) Eng. journalist, humorist, satirist

°Ann **Todd**: Ann Todd Mayfield (1932-) U.S. film actress

°Michael **Todd**: Avrom Hirsch Goldbogen (1907-1958) U.S. film producer

°**Tom and Jerry**: Art Garfunkel (1937-) U.S. pop singer. + Paul Simon (1940-) U.S. pop singer

Isaac **Tomkins**: Henry Peter Brougham [Baron Brougham and Vaux] (1778-1868) Sc. jurist, political leader

Jacob **Tonson**: Enoch Arnold Bennett (1867-1931) Br. novelist

Horne **Tooke**: John Horne (1736-1812) Eng. politician, philologist

Topol: Chaim Topol (1935-) Israeli

film actor [29]

Miguel **Torga**: Adolfo Correia da Rocha (1907-) Port. poet

Peter **Tork**: Peter Torkelson (1942-) U.S. pop musician [27]

Rip **Torn**: Elmore Rual Torn (1931-) U.S. stage actor, director

Torquemada: Edward Powys Mathers (1892-1939) Br. crossword compiler [36, 53]

Raquel **Torres**: Paula Marie Osterman (1908-) U.S. film actress

Malcolm **Torrie**: Gladys Maude Winifred Mitchell (1901-) Eng. writer of detective novels, children's books

Toto: [1] Antonio de Curtis-Gagliardi (1897-1967) It. stage, film comedian, circus clown. [2] Armando Novello (?-1938) Swiss circus clown

Jennie **Tourel**: Jennie Davidson (1900-1973) Fr.-Can. opera singer, of Russ. parentage

°Maurice **Tourneur**: Maurice Thomas (1876-1961) Fr. film director

Martello **Tower**: [Commander] Francis Martin Norman (1833-c.1918) Eng. author of naval books

Charles **Townshend**: Charlotte Brontë (1816-1855) Eng. novelist

Peter **Towry**: David Towry Piper (1918-) Eng. writer on art, novelist

Arthur **Tracy**: Harry Rosenberg (1903-) U.S. singer, film actor

F.G. **Trafford**: Charlotte Eliza Lawson Riddell, née Cowan (1832-1906) Ir. novelist

Peter **Traill**: Guy Mainwaring Morton (1896-1968) Eng. novelist,. playwright

B. **Traven**: Berick Traven Torsvan (?1890-1969) U.S. novelist of Swe. or Ger. parentage

Graham **Travers**: Margaret Todd (1859-1918) Sc. novelist

Henry **Travers**: Travers Heagerty (1874-1965) Br. stage, film actor, working in U.S.

Linden **Travers**: Florence Lindon-Travers (1913-) Br. stage, film actress

Richard **Travis**: William Justice (1913-) U.S. film actor

Arthur **Treacher**: Arthur Treacher Veary (1894-1975) Br. film actor, working in U.S.

Zélia **Trebelli**: Gloria Caroline Gillebert (or Le Bert) (1834-1892) Fr. opera singer

Pirmin **Trecu**: Pirnon Aldabaldetrecu (1930-) Sp. ballet dancer, teacher

°[Sir] Herbert Beerbohm **Tree**: Herbert Beerbohm (1953-1917) Eng. theatre actor, manager

Robert **Tressell**: Robert Noonan (1868-1911) Br. author

Hilda **Trevelyan**: Hilda Tucker (1880-1957) Br. stage actress

John **Trevena**: Ernest George Henham (1870-1946) Eng. poet, novelist, working in Canada

Austin **Trevor**: Austin Schilsky (1897-1978) Ir.-born Br. film, stage, radio star

Claire **Trevor**: Claire Wemlinger (1909-) U.S. film actress

Glen **Trevor**: James Hilton (1900-1954) Br. novelist

William **Trevor**: William Trevor Cox (1928-) Ir. novelist, short story writer

Trim: Louis Fortune Gustave Ratisbonne (1827-1900) Fr. writer, librarian

A. Stephen **Tring**: Laurence Walker Meynell (1899-) Eng. author

°**Trog**: Wally Fawkes (1925-) Can. cartoonist, working in U.K.

Frances **Trollope**: Paul Feval (1817-1887) Fr. writer of sentimental novels

Sven **Trost**: [Count] Carl Johan Gustav Snoilsky (1841-1903) Swe. lyric poet

°Leon **Trotsky**: Lev Davidovich Bronstein (1879-1940) Russ. revolutionary leader

Kilgore **Trout**: Philip José Farmer (1918-) U.S. SF writer

Ben **Trovato**: Samuel Lover (1797-1868) Ir. songwriter, novelist, printer

Doris **Troy**: Doris Payne (1937-) U.S. pop singer, songwriter

Henri **Troyat**: Lev Tarasov (1911-) Russ.-born Fr. novelist

°H. **Trusta**: Elizabeth Stuart Phelps (1815-1852) U.S. novelist

°Sojourner **Truth**: Isabella Van Wagener (c.1797-1883) U.S. black

evangelist, reformer
Richard **Tucker**: Reuben Ticker (1913-1975) U.S. opera singer
Sophie **Tucker**: Sophia Abuza (1884-1966) U.S. vaudeville, film actress
Tommy **Tucker**: Robert Higgenbotham (1939-) U.S. pop pianist
Antony **Tudor**: William Cook (1908-) Eng. ballet dancer, choreographer, teacher
Sonny **Tufts**: Bowen Charleston Tufts (1911-1970) U.S. film actor
Boris **Tumarin**: Boris Tumarinson (1910-) Latvian stage actor, director, teacher, working in U.S.
°Yevgeniya **Tur** (or Eugénie Tour): Yelizaveta Vasilyevna Salias-de-Turnemir (1815-1892) Russ. writer
Lana **Turner**: Julia Turner (1920-) U.S. film actress **[63]**
Sammy **Turner**: Samuel Black (1932-) U.S. pop singer
Tina **Turner**: Annie Mae Bullock (1938-) U.S. black rock singer
°Mark **Twain**: Samuel Langhorne Clemens (1835-1910) U.S. novelist, short story writer
°Helen **Twelvetrees**: Helen Jurgens (1908-1958) U.S. film actress
°**Twiggy**: Lesley Hornby (1950-) Eng. fashion model, film actress, singer
°Conway **Twitty**: Harold Jenkins (1933-) U.S. folk singer
Bonnie **Tyler**: Gaynor Sullivan (1951-) Welsh pop singer
Tom **Tyler**: Vincent Markowsky (1903-1954) U.S. film actor
T. Texas **Tyler**: David Luke Myrick (1916-1971) U.S. country singer
Sarah **Tytler**: Henrietta Keddie (1827-1914) Sc. novelist

U

°Paolo **Uccello**: Paolo di Dono (1397-1475) It. painter
Lenore **Ulric**: Lenore Ulrich (1892-1970) U.S. stage, film actress
Michael **Underwood**: John Michael Evelyn (1916-) Eng. crime novelist
Urban II: Odo of Lagery (c.1035-1099) Fr. pope
Urban III: Uberto Crivelli (-1187) It.

pope
Urban IV: Jacques Pantaléon (c.1200-1264) Fr. pope
Urban V: Guillaume de Grimoard (c.1310-1370) Fr. pope
Urban VI: Bartolomeo Prignani (c.1318-1389) It. pope
Urban VII: Giambattista Castagna (1521-1590) It. pope
Urban VIII: Maffeo Barberini (1568-1644) It. pope
°Sylvanus **Urban**: Edward Cave (1691-1754) Eng. printer, founder of *The Gentleman's Magazine*
Peter **Ustinov**: Peter Alexander von Ustinov (1921-) Br. stage, film actor, director, playwright
°Maurice **Utrillo**: Maurice Valadon (1883-1955) Fr. painter

V

"**V**": Caroline Clive, née Meysey-Wigley (1801-1873) Eng. writer of verses, novels
Roger **Vadim**: Roger Vadim Plemiannikow (1928-) Fr. film writer, director
Vagrant: Rudolph Chambers Lehmann (1856-1926) Br. journalist, Liberal politician
Vera **Vague**: Barbara Jo Allen (?1904-1974) U.S. film, radio comic **[45]**
G. **Valbert**: Charles Victor Cherbuliez (1829-1899) Swiss-born Fr. novelist, critic
Ritchie **Valens**: Richard Valenzuela (1941-1959) U.S. pop guitarist
°Rudolph **Valentino**: Rodolpho Alfonzo Raffaelo Pierre Filibert Guglielmi di Valentina d'Antonguolla (1895-1926) It.-born U.S. film actor, romantic hero
Simone **Valère**: Simone Gondoff (1923-) Fr. film actress
Alwina **Valleria**: Alwina Schoening (1848-1925) U.S. opera singer
Alida **Valli**: Alida Maria Altenburger (1921-) It. film actress
Frankie **Valli**: Frank Castelluccio (1937-) U.S. rock musician
Virginia **Valli**: Virginia McSweeney (1898-1968) U.S. film actress

Guy de **Valmont**: Guy de Maupassant (1850-1893) Fr. short story writer

Bobby **Van**: Robert King (1932-) U.S. dancer, singer, stage actor

Jan **Van Avond**: Francis Carey Salter (1876-1958) S.A. poet, novelist

[Dame] Irene **Vanbrugh**: Irene Barnes (1872-1949) Br. stage actress

Violet **Vanbrugh**: Violet Augusta Mary Barnes (1867-1942) Br. stage actress, sister of Irene Vanbrugh (*q.v.*)

Alfred Glenville **Vance**: Alfred Peck Stevens (1839-1888) Eng. music hall entertainer

Charles **Vance**: Charles Goldblatt (1929-) West Indian stage actor, director, producing manager

Ethel **Vance**: Grace Stone, née Zaring (1896-) U.S. novelist

Vivian **Vance**: Vivian Jones (1913-1979) U.S. TV actress

Margaret **Vandegrift**: Margaret Thomson Janvier (1844-1913) U.S. children's writer, sister of Ivory Black (*q.v.*)

Van Beyssel: K Josephus Albertus Alberdingk Thijm (1820-1889) Du. author, art critic

°**S.S. Van Dine**: Willard Huntington Wright (1888-1939) U.S. literary critic, detective story writer

Mamie **Van Doren**: Joan Lucille Olander (1933-) U.S. film actress

James **Van Heusen**: Edward Chester Babcock (1913-) U.S. composer of musicals, film music

Erik **Van Lhin**: Lester del Rey (or Ramón Álvarez del Rey) (1915-) U.S. SF writer

Victor **Varconi**: Mihaly Varkonyi (1896-1976) Hung. film actor, working in U.S.

John Philip **Varley**: Langdon Elwyn Mitchell (1862-1935) U.S. playwright

°**Comte Paul Vasili**: Juliette Adam, née Lamber (1836-1936) Fr. novelist, editor, founder of *La Nouvelle Revue*

Frankie **Vaughan**: Frank Abelsohn (1928-) Eng. popular singer, dancer, film actor

Kate **Vaughan**: Catherine Candelin (c.1852-1903) Br. stage actress

Peter **Vaughan**: Peter Ohm (1923-) Eng. film, TV actor

Bobby **Vee**: Robert Thomas Velline (1943-) U.S. pop singer

Conrad **Veidt**: Conrad Weidt (1893-1943) Ger. film actor

Lupe **Velez**: Guadeloupe Velez de Villalobos (1908-1944) Mexican film actress

Benay **Venuta**: Venuta Rore Crooke (1911-) U.S. stage actress, singer

°**Vera**: [1] [Lady] Gertrude Elizabeth Campbell, née Blood (-1911) Br. art critic, author. [2] Charlotte Louisa Hawkins Dempster (1835-1913) Br. author

Vera-Ellen: Vera-Ellen Westmeyr Rohe (1926-) U.S. popular singer, dancer, film actress

Verax: Henry Dunckley (1823-1896) Eng. journalist

°**Vercors**: Jean Bruller (1902-) Fr. writer, illustrator

Violette **Verdy**: Nelly Nuillerm (1933-) Fr.-born U.S. ballet dancer

V. **Veresaeff**: Vikenty Vikentievich Smidovich (1867-1945) Russ. author

Karen **Verne**: Ingabor Katrine Klinckerfuss (1915-1967) Ger. film actress, working in U.S.

Anne **Vernon**: Edith Vignaud (1925-) Fr. film actress, working in U.K., U.S.

Dai **Vernon**: David Werner (-) Can.-born magician of Ir. descent, working in U.S.

Konstanze **Vernon**: Konstanze Herzfeld (1939-) Ger. ballet dancer

Paolo **Veronese**: Paolo Cogliari (or Caliari) (1528-1588) It. painter [41]

Andrea del **Verrocchio**: Andrea di Michele Cioni (1435-1488) It. sculptor, painter, goldsmith

Odile **Versois**: Militza de Poliakoff-Baidarov (1930-1980) Fr. film actress, of Russ. origin, sister of Marina Vlady (*q.v.*)

Dziga **Vertov**: Denis Arkadyevich Kaufman (1896-1954) Russ. director of film documentaries

Stanley **Vestal**: Walter Stanley Campbell (1887-1957) U.S. author, educator

°**Madame Vestris**: Lucia Elisabetta

Vestris, née Bartolozzi (1787-1856) Eng. actress, stage singer

Victoria **Vetri**: Angela Dorian (1944-) Australian film actress

°**Vetus**: Edward Sterling (1773-1847) Eng. writer of letters to *The Times* ("The Thunderer")

Count Palmiro **Vicarion**: Christopher Logue (1926-) Eng. poet, writer

°Sid **Vicious**: John Simon Ritchie (later Beverley) (1957-1979) Eng. punk rock musician

Martha **Vickers**: Martha MacVicar (1925-1971) U.S. film actress

Vicky: Victor Weisz (1913-1966) Ger.-born Br. political cartoonist [29]

Victor II: Gebhard of Dollnstein-Hirschberg (c.1018-1057) Ger. pope

Victor III: Dauferi (1027-1087) It. pope

Victor and Cazire: Percy Bysshe Shelley (1792-1822) Eng. poet. + Elisabeth Shelley (-) Eng. poet, his sister

Florence **Vidor**: Florence Arto (1895-1977) U.S. film actress

Vigilans sed Æquus: William Thomas Arnold (1852-1904) Eng. political writer

Hugues **Vignix**: Henri François Joseph de Régnier (1864-1936) Fr. poet, novelist

Jean **Vigo**: Jean Almereyda (1905-1934) Fr. film director

Pancho **Villa**: Doroteo Arango (1878-1923) Mexican revolutionary, guerrilla leader

Frank **Villard**: François Drouineau (1917-) Fr. film actor

Henry **Villard**: Ferdinand Heinrich Gustav Hilgard (1835-1900) Ger.-born U.S. journalist

Caroline **Villiers**: Carol Friday (1949-) Eng. stage, TV actress

°François **Villon**: François de Montcorbier (1431-?) Fr. poet

Jacques **Villon**: Gaston Duchamp (1875-1963) Fr. artist

Gene **Vincent**: Eugene Vincent Craddock (1935-1971) U.S. rock musician

William **Vincent**: Thomas Holcroft (1745-1809) Eng. dramatist, miscellaneous writer

Vinkbooms: Thomas Griffiths

Wainwright (1794-1852) Eng. art critic, writer, forger

Helen **Vinson**: Helen Rulfs (1907-) U.S. film actress

Luchino **Visconti**: Luchino Visconti di Modrone (1906-1976) It. film writer, director

°**Vitalis**: Erik Sjöberg (1794-1825) Swe. poet

Monica **Vitti**: Maria Luisa Ceciarelli (1933-) It. film actress

Renée **Vivien**: Pauline Tarn (1877-1909) Fr. poet

Vivienne: Florence Entwistle (1887-) Br. portrait photographer

Marina **Vlady**: Marina de Poliakoff-Baidarov (1938-) Fr. film actress

°**Voltaire**: François Marie Arouet (1694-1778) Fr. philosopher, poet, dramatist, author

Gerhard **von Amyator**: Dagobert van Gerhardt (1831-) Ger. soldier, novelist

°Samuel Greifensohn **von Hirschfeld**: Hans Jakob Christoffel von Grimmelshausen (?1620-1676) Ger. writer

W.O. **von Horn**: Philip Friedrich Wilhelm Örtel (1798-1867) Ger. writer of popular stories

Baron **von Schlicht**: [Count] Wolf Heinrich von Bandissin (1789-1878) Ger. literary critic, translator

Sasha **von Scherler**: Alexandra-Xenia Elizabeth Anne Marie Fiesola von Schoeler (1939-) U.S. stage actress

Philander **von Siettewald**: Johann Michael Moscherosch (1601-1669) Ger. Lutheran satirist

Joseph **von Sternberg**: Josef Stern (1894-1969) Austr. film director, working in U.S.

Erich **von Stroheim**: Hans Erich Maria Stroheim von Nordenwall (1885-1957) Austr. film actor, director, working in U.S.

Baron Arminius **von Thunder-Ten-Tronckh**: Matthew Arnold (1822-1888) Eng. poet, critic

Harry **von Tilzer**: Harry Gumm (1872-1946) U.S. composer of popular songs

Curt **von Veltheim**: Ludwig Kurtze (1857-1930) Ger. adventurer

W

Henry **Wade**: [Major Sir] Henry Lancelot Aubrey-Fletcher (1887-1969) Eng. detective fiction writer

Michael **Wager**: Emanuel Weisgal (1925-) U.S. stage actor, director

Simon **Wagstaff, Esq.**: Jonathan Swift (1667-1745) Eng. satirist

Anton **Walbrook**: Adolf Wohlbrück (1900-1968) Austr. film actor, working in U.K.

Jersey Joe **Walcott**: Arnold Raymond Cream (?1914-) U.S. heavyweight boxer

Hubert **Wales**: William Pigott (1870-1943) Br. novelist, writer on psychical research

Arthur David **Waley**: Arthur David Schloss (1889-1966) Eng. museum curator, translator

John **Walker**: John Joseph Mans (1943-) U.S. pop singer

Nancy **Walker**: Anna Myrtle Swoyer (1922-) U.S. stage actress, singer

Syd **Walker**: Sidney Kirman (1887-1945) Eng. radio comedian

A **Walking** Gentleman: Thomas Colley Grattan (1792-1864) Ir. traveler, writer

°Max **Wall**: Maxwell George Lorimer (1908-) Sc.-born Br. stage, TV actor, comedian, dancer

°Edgar **Wallace**: Richard Edgar (1875-1932) Eng. novelist

Jean **Wallace**: Jean Wallasek (1923-) U.S. film actress

Nellie **Wallace**: Eleanor Jane Liddy (1870-1948) Br. music hall artiste

Lester **Wallack**: John Johnstone Wallack (1820-1888) U.S. actor, playwright, theatre manager

Fats **Waller**: Thomas Waller (1904-1943) U.S. jazz pianist, composer

Lewis **Waller**: William Waller Lewis (1860-1915) Br. theatre actor, manager

Max **Waller**: Maurice Warlomont (1866-1895) Belg. lyric poet

Stella **Walsh**: Stanislava Walasiewicz (1911-1980) Pol.-born U.S. athlete

Bruno **Walter**: Bruno Walter Schlesinger (1876-1962) Ger. opera, symphony conductor, working in U.S.

Joseph **Walton**: Joseph Losey (1909-) U.S. film director, working in U.K.

Walter **Wanger**: Walter Feuchtwanger (1894-1968) U.S. film producer

°Artemus **Ward**: Charles Farrar Browne (1834-1867) U.S. humorous writer [21]

Polly **Ward**: Byno Poluski (1908-) Br. film actress

Florence **Warden**: Florence James, née Price (1857-) Eng. novelist

Andy **Warhol**: Andrew Warhola (?1930-) U.S. artist

Derek **Waring**: Derek Barton-Chapple (-) Eng. stage actor

Richard **Waring**: Richard Stephens (1912-) Eng. stage actor

°Peter **Warlock**: [1] Philip Arnold Heseltine (1894-1930) Eng. composer, writer. [2] Alec Bell (-) Eng. magician, writer on magic

Charles **Warner**: Charles Lickfold (1846-1909) Br. stage actor

Harry Morris **Warner**: Harry Morris Eichelbaum (1881-1958) U.S. film exhibitor, producer, of Russ. parentage

°Jack **Warner**: Jack Waters (1894-) Eng. stage, film, TV actor

Jack L. **Warner**: Jack L. Eichelbaum (1892-) U.S. film producer, bother of Harry Morris Warner (*q.v.*)

Jeff **Warren**: Jeff Jones (1921-) U.S. stage director, singer

Leonard **Warren**: Leonard Warenoff (1911-1960) U.S. opera singer

Lavinia **Warren**: Mercy Lavinia Warren Bumpus (1841-1919) U.S. dwarf, married °General Tom Thumb

John **Warwick**: John McIntosh Beattie (1905-1972) Australian film actor, working in U.K.

Robert **Warwick**: Robert Taylor Bien (1878-1965) U.S. film actor

Dionne **Warwicke**: Marie Dionne Warrick (1941-) U.S. pop singer

Washboard Sam: Robert Brown (1910-) U.S. black washboard player, blues singer

Dinah **Washington**: Ruth Jones (1924-1963) U.S. black blues singer

Donna Day **Washington**: Donna Day Washington-Smith (1942-) Can.

ballet dancer

Hugo **Wast**: Gustavo Martínez Zuviría (1883-1962) Argentinian novelist, short story writer

William **Wastle**: John Gibson Lockhart (1794-1854) Br. magazine contributor, biographer

Onoto **Watanna**: Winnifred Babcock, née Eaton (1879-) U.S. novelist

Muddy **Waters**: McKinley Morganfield (1915-) U.S. blues singer, musician [45]

Dilys **Watling**: Dilys Rhys-Jones (1946-) Eng. stage actress

Claire **Watson**: Claire McLamore (1927-) U.S. opera singer

Wylie **Watson**: John Wylie Robertson (1889-1966) Br. film actor

Jonathan **Watts**: John B Leech (1933-) U.S. ballet dancer, teacher

Edward Bradwardine **Waverley**: John Wilson Croker (1780-1857) Ir.-born Br. politician, essayist [38]

Franz **Waxman**: Franz Wachsmann (1906-1967) Ger. composer of film music, working in U.S.

Wayfarer: James Bell Salmond (1891-1958) Sc. editor, poet

David **Wayne**: Wayne James McMeekan (1914-) U.S. stage, film actor

Dennis **Wayne**: Dennis Wayne Wendelken (1945-) U.S. ballet dancer

°John **Wayne**: Marion Michael Morrison (1907-1979) U.S. film actor ("Duke")

Naunton **Wayne**: Naunton Davies (1901-1970) Welsh stage, film, TV, radio actor, entertainer

Putnam **Weale**: Bertram Lenox Simpson (1877-1930) Eng. publicist

Charley **Weaver**: Clifford Arquette (1905-1974) U.S. entertainer

Clifton **Webb**: Webb Parmelee Hollenbeck (1893-1966) U.S. film actor

Vert **Weber**: Georg P L L Wachter (1762-1837) Ger. author

Frank **Wedekind**: Benjamin Franklin Wedekind (1864-1918) Ger. dramatist, stage actor

°Arthur **Weegee**: Arthur H Fellig (1899-1968) Pol.-born U.S. photographer

Frederico **Wegener**: Eduard Roschmann (1908-1977) Ger. Nazi war criminal (the "Butcher of Riga")

Barbara **Weisberger**: Barbara Linshen (c.1926-) U.S. ballet dancer, teacher, director

Horace **Welby**: John Timbs (1801-1875) Eng. author, editor

Raquel **Welch**: Raquel Tejada (1940-) U.S. film actress

Tuesday **Weld**: Susan Ker Weld (1943-) U.S. film actress

Colin **Welland**: Colin Williams (1934-) Eng. actor, playwright

Samuel **Weller**: Thomas Onwhyn (?-1886) Eng. humorous draughtsman, engraver

°Kitty **Wells**: Muriel Deason (1919-) U.S. country singer

Senor **Wences**: Wenceslas Moreno (1899-) Sp. ventriloquist, working in U.K.

John **Wengraf**: Johann Wenngraft (1901-) Austr. film actor, working in U.S.

Henry **Wenman**: Henry Newman (1875-) Br. film actor

Bessie **Wentworth**: Elizabeth Andrews (1874-1901) Eng. music hall singer

Patricia **Wentworth**: Dora Amy Elles (1878-1961) Eng. crime novelist

E. **Werner**: Elisabeth Bürstenbinder (1838-1918) Ger. novelist

Oskar **Werner**: Josef Bschliessmayer (1922-) Austr. stage, film actor

Adam **West**: William Anderson (1929-) U.S. film actor

Nathaniel **West**: Nathan Wallenstein Weinstein (1903-1940) U.S. novelist, screenwriter [27]

°[Dame] Rebecca **West**: Cicily Isabel Andrews, née Fairchild (1892-) Ir.-born Eng. novelist, critic

A **Westchester** Farmer: Samuel Seabury (1729-1796) U.S. Anglican minister, loyalist campaigner

Helen **Westcott**: Myrthas Helen Hickman (1929-) U.S. film actress

Helen **Westley**: Henrietta Remsen Meserole Manny (1879-1942) U.S. stage, film actress

Mary **Westmacott**: [Dame] Agatha Christie (1891-1976) Br. detective novelist

Elizabeth **Wetherall**: Susan Bogert Warner (1819-1885) U.S. sentimental novelist for children

Joan **Wetmore**: Joan Dixon, née Deery (1911-) Australian stage actress

Michael **Whalen**: Joseph Kenneth Shovlin (1899-1974) U.S. film actor

Anthony **Wharton**: Alister McAllister (1877-1943) Ir. author

Grace **Wharton**: Katharine Thomson, née Byerley (1797-1862) Br. author

Philip **Wharton**: John Cockburn Thomson (1834-1860) Br. author, son of Grace Wharton (*q.v.*)

°Mr. **Whatsisname**: Francis Reynolds (1934-) Ir.-born Br. law lecturer

Peetie **Wheatstraw**: William Bunch (1894-1941) U.S. black blues singer, pianist, guitarist

Jimmy **Wheeler**: Ernest Remnant (1910-1973) Eng. music hall comedian

Albert **Whelan**: Albert Waxman (1875-1962) Australian music hall entertainer

William and Robert **Whistlecraft**: John Hookham Frere (1769-1846) Eng. diplomat, author [57]

Antonia **White**: Antonia Botting (1899-1980) Eng. author, translator (mainly of books by °Colette)

Babington **White**: Mary Elizabeth Maxwell, née Braddon (1837-1915) Eng. novelist

°Chris **White**: Chris Costner Sizemore (1927-) U.S. "split personality"

Jesse **White**: Jesse Wiedenfeld (1918-) U.S. film comedian

°Joseph Blanco **White**: José María Blanco y Crespo (1775-1841) Sp.-born Eng. poet, journalist, churchman

Matthew **White**: William Prynne (1600-1669) Eng. Puritan pamphleteer

Roma **White**: Blanche Oram (1866-) Eng. novelist, journalist

°Slim **Whitman**: Otis Dewey (1924-) U.S. country singer, yodeller

Harry **Whitney**: Patrick Kennedy (1801-1873) Ir. writer, bookseller

Peter **Whitney**: Peter King Eagle (1916-1972) U.S. film actor

Violet **Whyte**: Henrietta Eliza

Vaughan Stannard, née Palmer (1856-1911) Eng. novelist

Mary **Wickes**: Mary Wickenhauser (1916-) U.S. film comedienne

Mary **Wigman**: Marie Wiegmann (1886-1973) Ger. ballet dancer, choreographer, teacher

Helene **Wildbrunn**: Helene Wehrenpfennig (1882-1972) Austr. opera singer

Marty **Wilde**: Reginald Smith (1939-) Eng. pop singer

Patricia **Wilde**: Patricia White (1930-) Can.-born U.S. ballet dancer

David **William**: David Williams (1926-) Eng. stage actor, director

Warren **William**: Warren Krech (1895-1948) U.S. film actor

Barney **Williams**: Bernard O'Flaherty (1824-1876) U.S. actor, of Ir. parentage

Bert **Williams**: Egbert Austin (c.1876-1922) U.S. black stage comedian

Bill **Williams**: William Katt (1916-) U.S. film actor

Bransby **Williams**: Bransby William Pharez (1870-1961) Br. music hall actor, literary impersonator

Cara **Williams**: Bernice Kamiat (1925-) U.S. TV, radio, film comedienne

Daniel **Williams**: Daniel Grossman (1942-) U.S. ballet dancer, teacher

F. Harold **Williams**: [Rev.] F W Orde Ward (1843-) Eng. author

Guy **Williams**: Guy Catalano (1924-) U.S. film, TV actor

Joe **Williams**: Joseph Goreed (1918-) U.S. black blues singer

°Tennessee **Williams**: Thomas Lanier Williams (1914-) U.S. dramatist

°Sonny Boy **Williamson**: Rice Miller (1897-1965) U.S. blues harmonica player, singer

James **Willington**: Oliver Goldsmith (?1730-1774) Ir.-born Eng. writer

Alfred **Willmore**: Micheál Macliammóir (1899-1978) Ir. stage actor

Willy: [1] Henri Gauthier-Villars (1859-1931) Fr. novelist, music critic, husband (1893-1906) of °Colette. [2] Emmett Kelly (-) U.S. circus clown

Charles **Wilson**: John Oldmixon (1673-

1742) Eng. Whig historian, pamphleteer

David **Wilson**: David Wilson MacArthur (1903-) Br. writer

Henry **Wilson**: Jeremiah Jones Culbath (1812-1875) U.S. statesman

J. Arbuthnot **Wilson**: Grant Allen (1848-1899) Can.-born Eng. author

Marie **Wilson**: Katherine Elizabeth White (1916-1972) U.S. film actress

Romer **Wilson**: Florence Roma Muir O'Brien, née Wilson (1891-1930) Br. novelist

Robb **Wilton**: Robert Wilton Smith (1881-1957) Eng. music hall comedian

John **Winch**: Marjorie Bowen (*q.v.*)

°Barbara **Windsor**: Barbara Anne Deeks (1937-) Eng. film, TV actress, singer

Claire **Windsor**: Olga Viola Cronk (1902-1972) U.S. film actress

Marie **Windsor**: Emily Marie Bertelson (1923-) U.S. film actress

Arthur M. **Winfield**: Edward Stratemeyer (1863-1930) U.S. author of stories for boys

George **Winslow**: George Wenzlaff (1946-) U.S. film actor **[26]**

John Strange **Winter**: Henrietta Eliza Vaughan Stannard, née Palmer (1856-1911) Eng. novelist

Shelley **Winters**: Shirley Schrift (1922-) U.S. stage, film actress

Frances **Winwar**: Francesa Vinciguerra Grebanier (1900-) Sicilian-born U.S. novelist

Estelle **Winwood**: Estelle Goodwin (1883-) Eng. stage, film actress

Norman **Wisdom**: Norman Wisden (1920-) Eng. stage, film, radio comedian

Ernie **Wise**: Ernest Wiseman (1925-) Eng. TV comedian, teaming with °Eric Morecambe

Herbert **Wise**: Herbert Weisz (1924-) Austr. stage actor, working in U.K.

Vic **Wise**: Donald Victor Bloom (1900-) Eng. music hall comedian

°Googie **Withers**: Georgina Withers (1917-) Eng. stage, film, TV actress

George **Woden**: George Wilson Slaney (1884-) Eng. novelist **[41]**

Reginald **Wolfe**: Thomas Frognall Dibdin (1776-1847) Eng. bibliographer

[Sir] Donald **Wolfit**: Donald Woolfitt (1902-1968) Br. stage, film actor, theatre manager

°Stevie **Wonder**: Stephen Judkins (or Steveland Morris Hardaway) (1950-) U.S. black blind "Motown" pop singer

A **Wonderful** Quiz: James Russell Lowell (1819-1891) U.S. author

Anna May **Wong**: Wong Liu-Tsong (1902-1960) U.S. film actress, of Chinese parentage

Brenton **Wood**: Alfred Jesse Smith (1941-) U.S. pop singer

Judith **Wood**: Helen Johnson (-) U.S. film actress

°Natalie **Wood**: Natasha Gurdin (1938-) U.S. film actress, of Russ. parentage

Wee Georgie **Wood**: George Bramlett (1895-1979) Eng. music hall comedian

°Henry **Woodhouse**: Mario Terenzio Enrico Casalegno (1884-) It.-born U.S. authority on aeronautics

Philip **Woodruff**: Philip Mason (1906-) Eng. writer

Monty **Woolley**: Edgar Montillion Woolley (1888-1963) U.S. film comedian

Woon: Ralph Wotherspoon (1897-) Eng. writer, journalist **[46]**

Christina **World**: Ina Skriver (-) Dan.-born Eng. film, TV actress

Nicholas **Worth**: Walter Hines Page (1855-1918) U.S. journalist, diplomat

John **Wray**: John Malloy (1890-1940) U.S. film actor

Reginald **Wray**: W B Home-Gall (1861-) Eng. author

Belinda **Wright**: Brenda Wright (1927-) Eng. ballet dancer

John **Wyckham**: John Suckling (1926-) Eng. theatre consultant, lighting designer

Julian **Wylie**: Julian Samuelson (1878-1934) Br. theatre manager

Bill **Wyman**: William Perks (1936-) Eng. pop musician

Jane **Wyman**: Sarah Jane Fulks (1914-) U.S. film actress

Patrick **Wymark**: Patrick Cheeseman (1926-1970) Eng. TV, film actor
[Sir] Charles **Wyndham**: Charles Culverwell (1837-1919) Eng. stage actor, theatre manager
Esther **Wyndham**: Mary Links, née Lutyens (1908-) Eng. writer
John **Wyndham**: John Benyon Harris (1903-1969) Eng. SF, short story writer
Tammy **Wynette**: Wynette Pugh (1942-) U.S. country singer
Ed **Wynn**: Isaiah Edwin Leopold (1886-1966) U.S. stage, film, radio, TV comedian **[29]**
Charles Whitworth **Wynne**: Charles William Cayzer (1869-) Eng. poet
May **Wynne**: Donna Lee Hickey (1931-) U.S. film actress
Diana **Wynyard**: Dorothy Isobel Cox (1906-1964) Br. stage actress
John **Wyse**: John Wise (1904-) Eng. stage actor

X

X: Eustace Budgell (1686-1737) Br. essayist
°**Flying Officer X**: Herbert Ernest Bates (1905-1974) Eng. novelist
°**Malcolm X**: Malcolm Little (1925-1965) U.S. black politician, campaigner for Negro rights
°**Michael X**: Michael Abdul Malik (1933-1975) Br. black power leader
Xanrof: Léon Fourneau (-) Fr. composer, songwriter **[32]**
Xavier: Joseph Xavier Boniface Saintine (1798-1865) Fr. novelist, poet, dramatist
°**Ximenes**: Derrick Somerset Macnutt (1902-1971) Eng. crossword compiler
X.L.: Julian Field (1849-1925) Br. novelist, writer

Y

A **Yankee**: Richard Grant White (1822-1885) U.S. essayist, Shakespearean critic
Yas Yas Girl: Merline Johnson (c.1915-) U.S. black blues singer
Dornford **Yates**: [Major] Cecil William Mercer (1885-1960) Eng. novelist
Yellow Bird: John Rollin Ridge (1827-1867) U.S. writer
Charles James **Yellowplush**: William Makepeace Thackeray (1811-1863) Eng. novelist
Sydney **Yendys**: Sydney Thompson Dobell (1824-1874) Br. poet, critic
Mr. **Yorick**: Laurence Sterne (1713-(1768) Ir. writer
Jeremy **York**: John Creasey (1908-1973) Eng. crime novelist
Susannah **York**: Susannah Fletcher (1941-) Eng. film actress, writer
Stephen **Yorke**: Mary Linskill (1840-1891) Eng. novelist
°**Gig Young**: Byron Ellsworth Barr (1917-1978) U.S. film, stage, TV actor
Loretta **Young**: Gretchen Young (1913-) U.S. film actress
Ysgafell: Jane Williams (1806-1885) Welsh historian, miscellaneous writer
Yuriko: Yuriko Kikuchi (1920-) U.S. ballet dancer, teacher, choreographer
Blanche **Yurka**: Blanche Jurka (1887-1974) U.S. stage, film actress
Colette **Yves**: Antoinette Huzard, née de Bergevin (1874-) Fr. novelist
Y.Y.: Robert Lynd (1879-1949) Ir. essayist

Z

Zadkiel: Richard James Morrison (1795-1874) Eng. naval officer, astrologer
Zander: Alexander Robins (1917-) Eng. crossword compiler **[55]**
Zélide: Isabelle de Charrière, née Isabella van Tuyll van Serooskerken (1740-1805) Du.-born Fr. novelist, autobiographer
Samuel **Zemurray**: Samuel Zmuri (1877-1961) Russ.-born U.S. president, financial director of United Fruit Company
Zeta: James Anthony Froude (1818-1894) Eng. historian, writer

Zico: Artur Antunes Coimbra (1954-)
Brazilian footballer

Anne **Ziegler**: Irene Eastwood (1910-)
Eng. romantic singer, teaming with
Webster Booth

Grigory Yevseyevich **Zinoviev**:
Grigory Yevseyevich Radomyslsky
(1883-1936) Russ. Bolshevik leader

Miro **Zolan**: Miroslav Zlochovsky
(1926-) Czech-Br. ballet dancer,
choreographer

Vera **Zorina**: Eva Brigitta Hartwig
(1917-) Ger. ballet dancer, stage,
film actress

°**Zouzou**: Danielle Ciarlet (1944-) Fr.
film actress

Z.Z.: Louis Zangwill (1869-) Eng.
novelist

Bright with names that men remember,
loud with names that men forget
(Algernon Charles Swinburne, "Eton: An Ode")

Appendices

The five Appendices given here are something of a curiosity. They are designed not so much for reference, although they may well fulfill this function, as for casual perusal or even entertainment. They are not random, however, and do relate specifically to the general subject of the book.

Appendix I is a complete list of the 173 pseudonyms used by °Voltaire (although not including Voltaire itself). They come from the *Bibliothèque Nationale: Catalogue Général*, ccxiv (1978), i. 162-166 (*Pseudonymes de Voltaire, noms sous lesquels il a écrit, formules ou qualifications sous lesquelles il s'est déguisé* [Pseudonyms of Voltaire, names under which he wrote, phrases and designations under which he disguised himself]). Many were for satirical writings, hence the predominance of religious and professional names and titles for this most outspoken critic of his age. English translations of some of the more obscure (and translatable) French names and titles are given.

Appendix II is a similar list of what is doubtless not all but at any rate the majority of pseudonyms used by °Daniel Defoe — 198 of them (thus overvaulting Voltaire), including Daniel Defoe itself. Many of the names were used for Defoe's pamphlets and reflect both the passion and prolificity of his political writings, as well as his fine imagination and attention to detail. In many ways the names can be directly compared to those of Voltaire: both Defoe and his French fellow writer were industrious and outspoken thinkers and polemicists, although at different levels, active in the first half of the 18th century.

Appendix III lists names that are as private as those of Voltaire and Defoe are public. They are a selection of names of sweethearts in St. Valentine's Day Messages published in *The Times* (February 14, 1978). The true identities of lover and beloved are of course unknown, but the "pet" names assumed are genuine pseudonyms, even if expressly devised for the occasion of the message. Most such messages seem to be from the man to the woman, although there is no guarantee, since there is absolutely no way of telling, that one or two *billets doux* here are not from the gal to the guy, rather than the other way round. Not surprisingly, many names are in the form of diminutives and more than a few are affectionately anthropomorphic and based on names of animals. (Bears, which are huggable, and hedgehogs, which are round and sleepy and cuddly under their prickles, are popular.)

Appendix IV gives a selection of ring names used by wrestlers. They are quoted from Jares (pp. 211-214) and are an extension to the consideration of wrestlers' names given in Chapter 6. In their own way, they are just as enjoyable as the lovers' names in Appendix III. (And are not both kinds used for an important match?)

Appendix V is somewhat different in character from the others, so has its own preamble.

I. Pseudonyms Used by °Voltaire
*(with translations where appropriate)**

Firmin Abauzit
Abbé ***
Abbé B **
Académicien B.
Un Académicien de Berlin (An Academician from Berlin)
Un Académicien de Londres, de Boulogne, de Pétersbourg, de Berlin, etc. (An Academician from London, Boulogne, Petersburg, Berlin, etc.)
Un Académicien de Lyon (An Academicien from Lyons)
Jacques Aimon
Le Docteur Akakia, médecin du pape (Doctor Akakia, physician to the Pope)
Le Rabbin Akib (Rabbi Akib)
Irénée Aléthès, professor du droit dans le canton suisse d'Uri (Irénée Aléthès, professor of law in the Swiss canton of Uri)
Ivan Aléthof, secrétaire de l'Ambassade russe (Ivan Aléthof, secretary at the Russian embassy)
Alexis, archevêque de Novogorod (Alexis, archbishop of Novogorod)
Amabed

Un Amateur de belles-lettres (A Lover of the Humanities)
Archevêque de Cantorbéry (Archbishop of Canterbury)
Abbé d'Arty
Un Auteur célèbre qui s'est retiré de France (A Famous Author Who Has Left France)
L'Auteur de "L'Homme aux quarante écus" (The Author of "The Man with Forty Crowns")
L'Auteur de la tragédie de "Sémiramis" (The Author of the tragedy "Semiramis")
L'Auteur de la tragédie des "Guèbres" (The Author of the tragedy "The Gabars")
L'Auteur du "Compère Mathieu" (The Author of "Comrade Mathieu")
Le Sieur Aveline
George Avenger
Un Avocat de Besançon (An Advocate from Besançon)
Un Avocat de province (A Provincial Advocate)
Un Bachelier ubiquiste (A Ubiquitous Graduate)
Feu l'abbé Bazin (The Late Father

*Where pseudonyms resemble first-plus-last-name or contain a surname, they are entered alphabetically under that last name; otherwise arrangement is alphabetical by first main word.

Bazin)
Beaudinet, citoyen de Neufchâtel (Beaudinet, citizen of Neufchâtel)
Une Belle Dame (A Beautiful Lady)
Ancien Avocat Belleguier (Former Advocate Belleguier)
Un Bénédictin (A Benedictine)
Un Bénédictin de Franche-Comté (A Benedictine from Franche-Comte)
Abbé Bigex
Abbé Bigore
Lord Bolingbroke
Joseph Bourdillon, professor en droit public (Joseph Bourdillon, professor of civil law)
Un Bourgeois de Genève (A Township of Geneva)
Le Pasteur Bourn
Abbé Caille
Caius Memmius Gemellus
Dom Calmet
Jérôme Carré
Cass ***, avocat au Conseil du Roi (Cass ***, advocate to the King's Council)
Cassen, avocat au Conseil du Roi (Cassen, advocate to the King's Council)
M. de Chambon
Chapelain du Cte de Chesterfield (Chaplain to the Count of Chesterfield)
Le Papa Nicolas Charisteski
Un Chrétien... (A Christian...)
Le Chrétien errant (The erring Christian)
Les Cinquante (The Fifty)
Un Citoyen de Genève (A Citizen of Geneva)
M. Clair
Clocpitre
Cte de Corbera
Lord Cornsbury
Le Corps des Pasteurs du Gévaudan (The Pastors of Gevaudan)
Robert Covelle
Cubstorf, pasteur de Helmstad (Cubstorf, pastor of Helmstad)
Le Curé de Frêne (The Vicar of Frêne)
D., chapelain de S.E. Mgr le Cte de K... (D., chaplain to His Eminence Monseigneur the Count of K...)
D*** M***

Cte Da...
Damilaville
George Aronger Dardelle
M. de la Caille
De La Lindelle
M. de La Visclède
M. de L'Écluse
Chev^r de M...re
Chev^r de Molmire
Chev^r de Morton
M. de Morza
Démad
Feu M. de Saint-Didier (The Late M. de Saint-Didier)
Chev^r de Saint-Gile
Abbé de Saint-Pierre
Des Amateurs (Some Devotees)
Desjardins
Desmahis
Gaillard d'Étallonde de Morival
Abbé de Tilladet
Cte de Tournay
Mis de Villette (Marquis de Villette)
Mis de Ximénez (Marquis de Ximenez)
John Dreamer
Anne Dubourg
Dumarsais [Du Marsay], philosophe
Dumoulin
M. le Chev^r Durand (Knight Durand)
Un Ecclésiastique (An Ecclesiastic)
R.P. Élie, carme chaussé (The Reverend Father Elias, calced Carmelite)
Ératou
Évhémère
Fatema
Formey
Le P. Fouquet (Father Fouquet)
Un Frère de la Doctrine chrétienne (A Brother of the Christian Doctrine)
Le Gardien des Capucins de Raguse (Guardian of the Capuchins of Ragusa)
Un Gentilhomme (A Gentleman)
Gérofle
Dr Good Natur'd Wellwisher
Dr Goodheart
Charles Gouju
Gabriel Grasset et associés
Un Homme de lettres (A Man of Letters)
Hude, échevin d'Amsterdam (Hude, deputy mayor of Amsterdam)
M. Huet (Hut)

L'Humble Evêque d'Alétopolis (The Humble Bishop of Alétopolis)

Hume, prêtre écossais (Hume, a Scottish priest)

L'Ignorant (The Ignorant One)

Imhof

Le Jésuite des anguilles (The Jesuit of the eels)

Un Jeune Abbé (A Young Priest)

Major Kaiserling

M. L***

Joseph Laffichard

Lantin, neveu de M. Lantin et de feu l'abbé Bazin (Lantin, nephew of M. Lantin and of the Late Father Bazin)

Le Neveu de l'abbé Bazin (The Nephew of Father Bazin)

R.P. L'Escarbotier

Mairet

M. Mamaki

Abbé Mauduit

M. de Mauléon

Maxime de Madaure

Un Membre du Conseil de Zurich (A Member of the Zurich Council)

Un Membre des nouveaux conseils (A Member of the New Council)

Un Membre d'un corps (A Member of the Body)

Le Curé Meslier

Prêtre Montmolin

Le Muphti

Naigeon

Needham

Docteur Obern

Cte Physicien de Saint-Flour

Plusieurs Aumôniers (Several Chaplains)

Jean Plokof

R.P. Polycarpe, prieur des Bernardins de (The Reverend Father Polycarp, prior of the Bernardines of Chésery)

Un Professeur de droit public (A Professor of Civil Law)

Un Proposant (A Divinity Student)

Un Quaker (A Quaker)

Le P. Quesnel

Le Dr Ralph

Genest Ramponeau

Rapterre

Don Apuleius Risorius

Josias Rossette

La Roupilière

Sadi

Saint-Hiacinte

Scarmentado

Le Secrétaire de M. de Voltaire (The Secretary to M. de Voltaire)

Le Secrétaire du Prince Dolgorouki (The Secretary to Prince Dolgorouki)

Mr Sherloc

Une Société de bacheliers en théologie (A Group of Theology Graduates)

Soranus, médecin de Trajan (Soranus, physician to Trajan)

Abbé Tamponet

Sieur Tamponet, docteur en Sorbonne (Mr. Tamponet, doctor at the Sorbonne)

Théro

Thomson

Tompson (Thomson)

Trois Avocats d'un Parlement (Three advocates from one Parliament)

Un Turc (A Turk)

Antoine Vadé

Catherine Vadé

Guillaume Vadé

Verzenot

Le Vieillard du Mont-Caucase (The Old Man of Mount Caucasus)

Un Vieux Capitaine de cavalerie (An Old Cavalry Captain)

Dr Good Natur'd Wellwisher

Youssouf

Dominico Zapata

II. Pseudonyms Used by Daniel Foe, Better Known as °Daniel Defoe

A.A.A.
A.B.
A Citizen Who Lives the Whole Time
    in London
A.G.
A.M.G.
A.Z.
Abed
Abigail
All-Hide
Aminadab
Ancient
Andronicus
Anglipolski of Lithuania
Anne
Antiaethiops
Anti-Bubble
Anti-Bubbler
Anticationist
Hen. Antifogger, Jr.
Anti-Italik
Anti-Jobber
Anti-King-Killer
Anti-Pope
Antiplot
Anthony Antiplot
Antisycoph
The Author of the
    "Trueborn Englishman"
Bankrupt
Tom Bankrupt
Barinda
Tom Beadle
Tom A. Bedlam
Obadiah Blue Hat
Betty Blueskin
Nicholas Boggle
William Bond
Anthony Broadheart
Bubble
C.M.
Callipedia
Christopher Carefull
Cataline
Caution
Henry Caution, Jr.
Sir Timothy Caution
Celibacy

Sir Malcontent Chagrin
Chesapeake
Combustion
Conscientia
A Converted Thief
The Corporal
Coventry
Credulous
D--
D.D.F.
D.F., Gent.
Daniel De Foe
Daniel Defoe
Democritus
Diogenes
Jeremiah Dry-Boots
E.S.
Eleanor
Elevator
Mr. Eminent
An English Gentleman
An Englishman at the Court of
    Hanover
Enigma
The Enquirer
Epidemicus
T. Experience
Eye Witness
Dan D. F-e
Count Kidney Face
Frank Faithfull
A Familiar Spirit
Henry Fancy, Jr.
The Farmer
The Father of Modern Prose Fiction
Penelope Firebrand
Florentina
A Freeholder
Harry Freeman
Furioso
Furious
G.
G.B.
G.M.
G.T.
G.Y.
A Gentleman
Grateful

Gunpowder
Gyaris
H.
H.R.
Thomas Horncastle
Autho' Hubble Bubble
Hubble-Bubble
Humanity
Hushai
Anthony Impartiality
Jack Indifferent
The Inoculator
Insolvent
P. Ivy
John-John
Journal
L.L.L.
A Layman
Leicestershire
Libertas
Liberty
Leonard Love-Wit
Theophilus Lovewit
Lionel Lye-Alone
Livery Man
M.G.
Tom Manywife
Lady Marjory
Miranda Meanwell
Meeting House
A Member
A Member of the Honourable
    House of Commons
Meteor
A Ministering Friend of the People
    Called Quakers
Miser
Misericordia
Modern
Moll
Andrew Moreton, Merchant
Myra
N.B.
N-- Upon Trent
Nelly
The New Convert
New Whig
Andrew Newport
Nicety
Oliver Oldway
One, Two, Three, Four
Orthodox

Patience
Abel Peaceable
Phil-Arguros
Mrs. Philo-Britannia
Philo-Royalist
Philygeia
Jonathan Problematick
Protestant Neutrality
Prudential
Quarantine
Anthony Quiet
Quietness
Quinquampoix
Arine Donna Quixota
R.R.
R.S.
Rebel
L.M. Regibus
Anthony Tom Richard
S.
S.B.
T. Sadler
Same Friend Who Wrote to Thomas
    Bradbury, etc.
Fello De Se
Sempronicus
Sincerity
Jeffrey Sing-Song
Spanish
A Sufferer
The Sunny Gentleman
T.B.
T.E.
T.L.
Talionis
T. Taylor
Tea-Table
Termagant
Theo-Philo
Thunder-Bolt
Sir Fopling Tittle-Tattle
Tranquillity
Timothy Trifle
Boatswain Trinkolo
True Love
The Trustee
Tom Turbulent
Urgentissimus
Vale
W.L.
Wallnutshire
Solomon Waryman

Weeping Winifred	Woman Witch'd
White Witch	A Young Cornish Gentleman

III. Lovers' Private Pseudonyms

From...	*To...*
The Putney Spaniard	Miss World
Baby Bear	Horrid Hedgepig
J.D.B.	J.F.
Mr. Aitch	Froggy
Champ	Fafa
Chunkle	Stravvy Baby
Ram	Ewe
Bee	Woudgie
Jon-Jon	She-She
Babes	Sexy
Pong	Ping
Gonco	Columbia Mia
Looce	Smooth
Monsieur Rochas	Princess
Egor	Dotty Bucket
R.X.	Pudding
4675	7634
Hersh	Choochy Face
Abu Ben McBurke	Wuzzie
Blue Eyes	Petalhead
Gnome	Hedgie
Incy Wincy Spider	Teapot
Elf	Snugglebunny
Shoesies	Baby Two Shoes
Major Malfunction	Captain Snortwright
Lumpy	Peter Pooh
Chublet	Booger-Face
Poodle	Biscuit
Simonpoos	Sallypot
Ptah	Nudd
Your Bird	My Little Box
Piglet	Pooh
The Boy Who Laughs	The Girl Who Sings in Squash Courts
The Man Who Does It	The Girl Who Supervises the Washing-Up
Sir Frog-Toad More	Miss Piggy
J.F.R.W.	Nancy Thunderthighs
Phoopie	Whoosie
Ploot	Cabbage
A Movie Producer	His Principal Lady

IV. Pseudonyms (Ring Names) Used by Wrestlers

Ring name	*Real name*
Abdullah the Butcher	Larry Shreeve
The Beast	Yvan Cormier
Bobby Becker	John Emerling
Sir Clement Beresford	Steven Beresford
Black Venus	Waver Pearl Bryant
Joe Bommerito	Giuseppe Mazza
Ivan Bulba	Johnny Shaw
Mildred Burke	Mildred Bliss
Man Mountain Dean	Frank Leavitt
Dick the Bruiser	Richard Afflis
Don Eagle	Carl Donald Bell
Elmer the Great	George Wagner
Heather Feather	Peggy Jones
The French Angel	Maurice Tillet
Buddy Fuller	Lester Welch
Golden Superman	Walter Podolak
Hillbilly Spunky	Frank Robinson
Happy Humphrey	William J. Cobb
Tito Infanti	Danny Frian
Paul Jones	Andy Lutse
King Curtis	Curtis Iaukea
George Koverly	Gojko Kovacovich
Dave Levin	George Wenzel
Bill Lewis	Bill Whitfield
Luther Lindsey	Luther Jacob Goodal
Little Louie	Louis Waterhouse
Johnny Long	Billy Strong
Tiger Joe Marsh	Joe Marusich
Terry McGinnis	Max Martin
Gorilla Monsoon	Gino Morella
Blackjack Mulligan	Bob Widham
Barbara Nichols	Joyce Fowler Becker
Pat O'Shocker	William Hayes Shaw
Humid Kala Pasha	Joe Rickard
The Polish Angel	Wladislaw Talun
Ivan Rasputin	Hyman Fishman
Dusty Rhodes	Virgil Reynolds
Nature Boy Buddy Rogers	Herman Rhode
Ad Santel	Adolph Ernst
Whiskers Savage	Eddie Civil
Hans Schmidt	Guy Larose
Hans Schnabel	Jake Moehler
Smasher Sloane	Donald Whittler
Ricki Starr	Rick Herman
Ray Steele	Pete Sauer
Chief Jay Strongbow	Joe Scarpa
Chief Sunni War Cloud	Sonny Chorre

The Thing	Frank Jares
Chief Thunderbird	Baptiste Paull
Sweet Daddy Watts	J.T. Holloway
Tim Woods	George Woodin
Yukon Eric	Eric Holmbeck
Stanislaus Zbysko	Stanislaus Cyganiewicz
Doc Zoko	Pedro Godoy

He telleth the number of the stars;
he calleth them all by their names (Psalm 147:4)

V. Real Names

When Sydne Rome, the American film actress, once asked at an airport if she could stop off in Nice, the clerk, after asking her name, looked at her carefully, and said, "Madam, I think you would do better to transfer to Qantas." Yet this really was her name!

This final Appendix contains a selection of 250 names that many people might suppose to be pseudonyms, since they so often resemble them. In fact they are all real names (allowing for the modification of some forenames to a pet form or even their replacement by a nickname). They are given here since, after all, there could be no pseudonyms or name changes without an original name to start with.

These names, however, were not changed — their bearers stuck by them. Indeed, in some cases their owners were quite determined *not* to change them. Of his name, the American film actor Bradford Dillman said, "Bradford Dillman sounded like a distinguished, phoney, theatrical name so I kept it."

Of a Hollywood executive who wanted to change his name to "Lennon," the American film comedian Jack Lemmon said, "I told him it had taken me most of my life to get used to the traumatic effects of being called Jack U. Lemmon, and that I was used to it now and I wasn't going to change it."

Of Rita Gam, the American stage and screen actress, Louella Parsons said, "I *do* wish she would change her name." But she didn't.

Nor did Janet Suzman, the English actress, in spite of a request when she first began on the stage to change her surname because it sounded "foreign." Instead she sent a telegram to the theatre director saying, "Imperative remain Suzman."*

---

*Quotes concerning these five persons were obtained from Telegraph Sunday Magazine, *June 3, 1979 (Sydne Rome);* Clarke, *pp. 249, 250 (Bradford Dillman, Jack Lemmon, Rita Gam);* TV Times, *April 9, 1976 (Janet Suzman).*

Even Barbra Streisand made only the smallest concession. When pressed to change *her* foreign-sounding name she simply dropped the middle vowel of her first name, Barbara.

The heavy preponderance of movie stars in the list is both accidental and intentional. It is accidental, since many actors and actresses have real names that do in fact resemble an assumed stage or screen name. One might cite such names here as Marlon Brando, Clint Eastwood, Errol Flynn, or Cesar Romero.

It is intentional to illustrate the noteworthy fact that a number of surnames listed here are also well known as assumed names of film actors. Katherine Hepburn, for example, really is a Hepburn, but °Audrey Hepburn began life as Edda Hepburn van Heemstra; Gloria Holden is indeed a true Holden, but Fay Holden was formerly Fay Hammerton and William Holden was William Beedle; Mary Martin and Millicent Martin are genuine Martins, but °Dean Martin was Dino Crocetti, Ross Martin was Martin Rosenblatt, and Tony Martin was Alvin Morris.

Other names listed may seem unlikely to be real names, yet Pearl Buck, Neil Diamond, Nelson Eddy, Bobbie Gentry, Suzi Quatro and King Vidor are here because these *are* their real names.

Apart from this, the Appendix has a further aim, which is to lay one or two popular myths to rest.

Adolf Hitler, for example, was not originally Adolf Schicklgruber (sometimes misspelled Schickelgruber) as many people suppose — or would wish to suppose. Adolf's father Alois had been of illegitimate birth, and for a time had borne his mother's name Schicklgruber. By 1876, however, 13 years before Adolf was born, Alois had established his claim to the name Hitler. True, some of Adolf's political opponents dubbed him "Herr Schicklgruber" in derision in the 1940s, but the Nazi Führer himself never used any name other than Hitler.

Again, it is often said of the English entertainer and panelist Joyce Grenfell that she was "really" Joyce Phipps, as if "Joyce Grenfell" were her adopted stage name. She was indeed born Joyce Irene Phipps, but her "stage" name is her perfectly legal married name — that of her husband Reginald Grenfell whom she married in 1929. Unusual it may be for a stage performer to prefer her married name as her professional name, but this was what Joyce Grenfell did, and as such her name is her true one and no pseudonym — at any rate according to the definition of the term made earlier in this book (see page 5).

It may seem difficult to credit that Tyrone Power used his real name, so like a typical stage name is it. Yet it has a most reputable pedigree. The star inherited his name from his father, the actor Tyrone Edmund Power (1869-1931), who in turn acquired his name from his own father, the Irish actor Tyrone Power (1795-1841).

That Berta Ruck, the novelist, married Oliver Onions, the novelist, is also somewhat hard to swallow. But it is so, and these are their real names — although Oliver Onions began life as George Oliver Onions and was known privately as George Oliver.

So all credit to Ursula Andress, Judy Dench, Gayle Hunnicutt et al. who in spite of the possible undesirable or even unfortunate connotations of their names decided, quite rightly, to keep them.

The information given for each name is the same as in the Who's Who.

Lola Albright (1925-) U.S. film actress

Bibi Andersson (1935-) Swe. film actress

Ursula Andress (1936-) Swiss-born film actress, working in U.S.

Paul Anka (1941-) U.S. pop singer

Gene Autry (1907-) U.S. film actor

Nigel Balchin (1908-1970) Eng. author

"Long" John Baldry (1941-) Eng. blues singer

Tallulah Bankhead (1902-1968) U.S. stage, film actress

Patrick Barr (1908-) Br. stage, film, TV actor

Shirley Bassey (1937-) Br.-born cabaret singer

Harry Belafonte (1927-) U.S. black popular singer, film actor

Saul Bellow (1915-) Can.-born U.S. writer

Jean-Paul Belmondo (1933-) Fr. film actor

Candice Bergen (1946-) U.S. film actress, of Swe.-U.S. parentage

Ingrid Bergman (1915-) Swe. film actress, working in U.S.

Theodore Bikel (1924-) Austr. film actor, guitarist, singer

Joan Blondell (1909-1979) U.S. film comedian

Humphrey Bogart (1899-1957) U.S. film actor

Ward Bond (1903-1960) U.S. film, TV actor

Timothy Bottoms (1949-) U.S. film actor

Clara Bow (1905-1965) U.S. film actress (the "It" girl)

Marlon Brando (1924-) U.S. film actor

Eleanor Bron (1934-) Br. TV revue actress

Pearl Buck (1892-1973) U.S. novelist,

Sid Caesar (1922-) U.S. film, TV comedian

James Cagney (1899-) U.S. film actor

Hoagy Carmichael (1899-) U.S. songwriter, lyricist

Primo Carnera (1906-1967) It. heavyweight boxer, wrestler

Leslie Caron (1931-) Fr. film actress

Enrico Caruso (1873-1921) It. opera singer

Johnny Cash (1932-) U.S. folk singer

David Cassidy (1950-) U.S. pop singer

Harry Champion (1866-1942) Eng. music hall comedian

Raymond Chandler (1888-1959) U.S. crime novelist

Lon Chaney, Sr. (1883-1930) U.S. film actor

Carol Channing (1921-) U.S. cabaret comedienne

Charlie Chaplin (1889-1972) Eng. film comedian

Maurice Chevalier (1888-1972) Fr. popular singer, film actor

Petula Clark (1932-) Eng. film actress, popular singer

Rosemary Clooney (1928-) U.S. cabaret singer

Joan Collins (1933-) Eng. film actress

Alex Comfort (1920-) Br. novelist, short story writer, writer on social problems

Ray Conniff (1916-) U.S. popular singer

Billy Connolly (1942-) Sc. comedian (the "Big Yin")

Kenneth Connor (1918-) Br. film, radio, TV comedian

Gladys Cooper (1888-1971) Br. stage, film actress, working in U.S.

Jackie Cooper (1921-) U.S. film actor

Noël Coward (1899-1973) Eng. stage, film actor, writer, composer, director

Wally Cox (1924-1976) U.S. comic film actor

Wendy Craig (1934-) Eng. stage, TV actress

Robert Cummings (1908-) U.S. film actor

Sinead Cusack (1949-) Ir. film actress

Peter Cushing (1913-) U.S. stage, film, TV actor

Dan Dailey (1914-1978) U.S. film actor, dancer

Danielle Darrieux (1917-) Fr. film actress

Olivia de Havilland (1916-) Eng.-born U.S. film actress, sister of °Joan Fontaine

Judy Dench (1934-) Eng. stage, film actress

Neil Diamond (1945-) U.S. pop singer

Bradford Dillman (1930-) U.S. film actor

Ken Dodd (1927-) Eng. vaudeville, TV comedian

Val Doonican (1927-) Ir. popular singer

Faye Dunaway (1941-) U.S. film actress

Jimmy Durante (1893-1980) U.S. film comedian

Clint Eastwood (1930-) U.S. film actor

Nelson Eddy (1901-1967) U.S. film actor, romantic singer

Noel Edmonds (1948-) Eng. disc jockey

Samantha Eggar (1939-) Eng. film actress

Anita Ekberg (1931-) Swe. film actress

Britt Ekland (1942-) Swe. film actress

Dick Emery (1918-) Eng. TV comedian

Max Factor (1876-1937) Pol. cosmetician, working in U.S.

Marianne Faithfull (1947-) Eng. film actress, singer

Lynn Farleigh (1942-) Eng. film, TV actress

Mia Farrow (1945-) U.S. film actress

Marty Feldman (1933-) Eng. TV comedian

Mel Ferrer (1917-) U.S. film actor

Roberta Flack (1937-) U.S. pop singer

Errol Flynn (1909-1959) Tasmanian film actor

Jane Fonda (1937-) U.S. film actress

Lynn Fontanne (1887-) Eng. stage actress, working in U.S.

Allen Funt (1914-) U.S. TV actor

Will Fyffe (1884-1947) Sc. film comedian, music hall singer

Clark Gable (1901-1960) U.S. film actor

Rita Gam (1928-) U.S. stage, film actress

Art Garfunkel (1937-) U.S. pop singer, once teamed with Paul Simon

Greer Garson (1908-) Eng.-Ir. film actress, working in U.S.

Leo Genn (1905-) Eng. film actor

Bobbie Gentry (1945-) U.S. (female) pop singer

Dizzy Gillespie (1917-) U.S. jazz trumpeter, composer

Hermione Gingold (1897-) Eng. revue, film comedienne

Betty Grable (1916-1973) U.S. film actress

Hughie Green (1920-) Can.-born Br. TV quizmaster, talent scout

Joyce Grenfell (1910-1979) Eng. film comedienne, solo revue performer

Zane Grey (1875-1939) U.S. author of westerns

Alec Guinness (1914-) Eng. stage, film actor

Edmund Gwenn (1875-1959) Eng. film actor

Rider Haggard (1856-1925) Eng. writer of romantic adventure stories

Susan Hampshire (1938-) Eng. film actress

Russell Harty (1934-) Eng. radio talk show host

Jack Hawkins (1910-1973) Eng. film actor

Goldie Hawn (1945-) U.S. film actress

Will Hay (1888-1949) Eng. film comedian

Sessue Hayakawa (1889-1973) Japanese film actor, working in U.S.

Gabby Hayes (1885-1969) U.S. comic film actor

Katharine Hepburn (1907-) U.S. film actress

Benny Hill (1925-) Eng. vaudeville, TV comedian

Thora Hird (1914-) Eng. film comedienne

Alfred Hitchcock (1899-1980) Eng. film director

Adolf Hitler (1889-1945) Ger. Nazi dictator

Dustin Hoffman (1937-) U.S. film actor

Gloria Holden (1908-) Eng. film actress, working in U.S.

Celeste Holm (1919-) U.S. stage, film actress

Trevor Howard (1916-) Eng. film actor

Roy Hudd (1936-) Eng. TV comedian

Rod Hull (1935-) Eng. TV comedian

Gayle Hunnicutt (1942-) U.S. film actress

John Hurt (1940-) Eng. film, TV actor

Olivia Hussey (1951-) Argentine-born Br. film actress

Hammond Innes (1913-) Eng. writer of adventure, mystery stories

Mick Jagger (1939-) Eng. pop musician

David Jason (1940-) Eng. TV comedian

Jimmy Jewell (1912-) Eng. radio, TV comedian

Glynis Johns (1923-) Eng. film actress

Ben Johnson (1919-) U.S. film actress

Janis Joplin (1943-1970) U.S. blues singer

Yootha Joyce (1927-1980) Eng. TV comedienne

Rosco Karns (1893-1970) U.S. film actor

Gene Kelly (1912-) U.S. film actor, dancer

Grace Kelly (1928-) U.S. film actress, subsequently Princess Grace of Monaco

Felicity Kendal (1947-) Eng. TV actress

Eartha Kitt (1928-) U.S. Creole cabaret singer

Kris Kristofferson (1936-) U.S. folk musician, film actor

Alan Ladd (1913-1964) U.S. film actor

Dinsdale Landen (1932-) Eng. TV actor

Ring Lardner (1885-1933) U.S. short story writer, journalist

Jack Lemmon (1925-) U.S. comic film actor

Jennie Linden (1939-) Eng. film actress

Gene Lockhart (1891-1957) Can. film actor, writer

Gina Lollobrigida (1927-) It. film actress

Anita Loos (1893-) U.S. humorist

Joanna Lumley (1946-) Eng. TV actress

Ida Lupino (1914-) Eng. film actress, daughter of Stanley Lupino

Stanley Lupino (1893-1942) Eng. stage, film comedian

Carol Lynley (1942-) U.S. film actress

Ben Lyon (1901-1979) U.S. film actor, married to °Bebe Daniels, with whom teamed

Mercedes McCambridge (1918-) U.S. film actress

Patrick Macnee (1922-) Eng. TV actor

Steve McQueen (1930-1980) U.S. film actor

Lee Majors (c.1940-) U.S. film actor

Barry Manilow (1946-) U.S. pop singer

Mary Martin (1923-) U.S. musical comedienne

Millicent Martin (1934-) Eng. stage, TV singer

Lee Marvin (1924-) U.S. film actor

James Mason (1909-) Eng. film actor

Raymond Massey (1896-) Can. stage, film actor, working in U.K.

Mireille Mathieu (1946-) Fr. film actress

Melina Mercouri (1923-) Gk. film actress

Bette Midler (1945-) U.S. rock singer

Spike Milligan (1918-) Ir. stage, radio, TV comedian

Robert Mitchum (1917-) U.S. film actor

Tom Mix (1880-1940) U.S. film actor

Roger Moore (1928-) Eng. TV actor

Patrick Mower (1940-) Eng. TV actor

Carry Nation (1846-1911) U.S. temperance reformer

Paul Newman (1925-) U.S. film actor

Robert Newton (1905-1956) Eng. film actor

Anthony Nicholls (1902-1977) Eng. stage, film actor

Derek Nimmo (1931-) Eng. film, TV comic actor

Anaïs Nin (1903-1977) U.S. novelist

Des O'Connor (1932-) Eng. popular singer

Jimmy O'Dea (1899-1965) Ir. film comedian

Oliver Onions (1872-1961) Eng. novelist, married Berta Ruck [see below]

Peter O'Toole (1932-) Eng. film actor

Dolly Parton (1946-) U.S. country singer

Gregory Peck (1916-) U.S. film actor

Sam Peckinpah (1926-) U.S. film actor

Susan Penhaligon (1950-) Eng. TV actress

Pat Phoenix (1925-) Eng. TV actress

Walter Pidgeon (1897-) Can. film actor, working in U.S.

Lili Pons (1904-1976) Fr. opera singer

Oleg Popov (1930-) Russ. clown

Cole Porter (1893-1964) U.S. songwriter, composer

Tyrone Power (1913-1958) U.S. film actor

Tom Powers (1890-1955) U.S. film actor

Elvis Presley (1935-1978) U.S. pop singer

Suzi Quatro (1950-) U.S. pop musician

Anthony Quayle (1913-) Eng. stage, film actor, director

Anthony Quinn (1915-) Mexican-born U.S. film actor

Gregory Ratoff (1897-1960) Russ.-born film actor, working in U.S., U.K.

Lee Remick (1935-) U.S. film actress

Burt Reynolds (1936-) U.S. film actor

Diana Rigg (1938-) Eng. film, TV actress

Sydne Rome (1946-) U.S. film actress

Cesar Romero (1907-) U.S. film actor

Leonard Rossiter (1927-) Eng. comic film actor

Berta Ruck (1878-1978) Eng. novelist married Oliver Onions [see above]

Charles Ruggles (1886-1970) U.S. film comedian

Damon Runyon (1884-1946) U.S. short story writer, journalist

Gail Russell (1924-1961) U.S. film actress

Robert Ryan (1909-1973) U.S. film actor

Telly Savalas (1924-) Gk.-U.S. film, TV actor

Jimmy Savile (1926-) Eng. TV host

Jean Seberg (1938-1979) U.S. film actress

Neil Sedaka (1939-) U.S. popular songwriter, performer

Pete Seeger (1919-) U.S. popular musician ("the Johnny Appleseed of folk song")

Blossom Seeley (1892-1974) U.S. nightclub entertainer

William Shatner (1931-) Can. film, TV actor

Victor Silvester (1901-1978) Eng. dance band leader

Alastair Sim (1900-1976) Sc. film actor

Jean Simmons (1929-) Eng. film actress, working in U.S.

Simone Simon (1910-) Fr. film actress

Frank Sinatra (1915-) U.S. film actor, singer

Donald Sinden (1923-) Eng. film actor

Valerie Singleton (1937-) Eng. TV host, interviewer

Cornelia Otis Skinner (1901-1979) U.S. stage, film actress

Freddie Starr (1944-) Eng. TV comedian

Rod Steiger (1925-) U.S. film actor

Rod Stewart (1945-) Eng. pop singer

Janet Street-Porter (1947-) Eng. TV host

Barbra Streisand (1942-) U.S. popular singer, entertainer, film actress

Elaine Stritch (1922-) U.S. stage, film comedienne

Booth Tarkington (1869-1946) U.S. novelist

John Thaw (1942-) Eng. TV actor

Gene Tierney (1920-) U.S. film actress

Richard Todd (1919-) Eng. film actor

Franchot Tone (1905-1968) U.S. stage, film actor

Mel Torme (1923-) U.S. ballad singer

Spencer Tracy (1900-1967) U.S. film actor

Forrest Tucker (1919-) U.S. film actor

Ben Turpin (1874-1940) U.S. film comedian

Rita Tushingham (1940-) Eng. film actress

Mary Ure (1933-1975) Eng. stage, film actress

Rudy Vallee (1901-) U.S. film comedian, crooner

Robert Vaughn (1932-) U.S. film actor

Gore Vidal (1925-) U.S. writer

King Vidor (1894-) U.S. film director

Booker T. Washington (1856-1915)

U.S. black educator, reformer
Ethel Waters (1900-1977) U.S. black
  film actress, singer
Orson Welles (1915-) U.S. film actor,
  producer, director, writer
Mae West (1892-1980) U.S. film ac-
  tress
Timothy West (1934-) Eng. film, TV
  actor
Cornel Wilde (1915-) U.S. film actor
Michael Wilding (1912-) Eng. film
  actor
Esther Williams (1923-) U.S. film ac-
  tress
Frank Windsor (1926-) Eng. TV actor
Terry Wogan (1938-) Ir. radio disk
  jockey, host
Fay Wray (1907-) U.S. film actress
Tessa Wyatt (1948-) Eng. TV actress
Frank Zappa (1940-) U.S. rock musi-
  cian

Bibliography

Agee, Patrick. *Where Are They Now?* London: Everest Books, 1977.

Ash, Brian. *Who's Who in Science Fiction*. London: Elm Tree Books, 1976.

Ashley, Leonard R.N. "Flicks, Flacks, and Flux: Tides of Taste in the Onomasticon of the Moving Picture Industry," *Names: Journal of the American Name Society* 23:4 (December 1975).

Ashley, Mike. *Who's Who in Horror and Fantasy Fiction*. London: Elm Tree Books, 1977.

Atkinson, Frank. *Dictionary of Pseudonyms and Pen-Names*. London: Clive Bingley, 1975.

————. *Dictionary of Literary Pseudonyms*. London: Clive Bingley, 1977.

Attwater, Donald. *The Penguin Dictionary of Saints*. Harmondsworth: Penguin Books, 1965.

The Author's and Writer's Who's Who. London: Burke's Peerage, 5th ed. 1963, 6th ed. 1971.

Bateman, Michael. *Funny Way to Earn a Living: A Book of Cartoons and Cartoonists*. London: Leslie Frewin, 1966.

Benét, William Rose. *The Reader's Encyclopaedia*. London: A & C Black, 1973.

Browning, D.C., comp. *Everyman's Dictionary of Literary Biography, English and American*. London: Dent, 1969.

Busby, Roy. *The British Music Hall: An Illustrated Who's Who from 1850 to the Present Day*. London: Paul Elek, 1976.

Case, Brian, and Stan Britt. *The Illustrated Encyclopedia of Jazz*. London: Salamander Books, 1978.

Chaneles, S., and A. Wolsky. *The Movie Makers*. London: Octopus Books, 1974.

Clarke, J.F. *Pseudonyms*. London: Elm Tree Books, 1977.

Coston, Henry. *Dictionnaires des Pseudonymes*. Paris: Lectures Françaises, 1965 (vol. I), 1969 (vol. II).

Crosland, Margaret. *Ballet Carnival: A Companion to Ballet*. London: Arco Publications, 1957.

Crowther, Jonathan, ed. *The AZED Book of Crosswords*. London: Pan Books, 1977.

Cummings, William H. *Biographical Dictionary of Musicians*. London: Novello, Ewer & Co., 1892.

Curthoys, Alan, and John Doyle, eds. *Who's Who on Television*. London: Independent Television Books, 1980.

Dauzat, Albert. *Dictionnaire Étymologique des Noms et Prénoms de France*. Paris: Larousse, 1976.

Dawson, Lawrence H. *Nicknames and Pseudonyms: Including Sobriquets of Persons in History, Literature, and the Arts Generally, Titles Given to Monarchs, and the Nicknames of the British Regiments and the States of North America*. London: Routledge, 1908.

346

Dearling, Robert, and Celia Dearling, with Brian Rust. *The Guinness Book of Music Facts and Feats.* Enfield, England: Guinness Superlatives, 1976.
Dmitriev, V.G. *Skryvshie Svoyo Imya (iz Istorii Anonimov i Psevdonimov)* ["Those Who Hid Their Names (from the History of Anonyms and Pseudonyms)"], 2d enl. ed. Moscow: Nauka, 1977.
Dunkling, Leslie Alan. *First Names First.* London: Dent, 1977.
Dunkling, Leslie. *The Guinness Book of Names.* Enfield, England: Guinness Superlatives, 1974.
Encyclopaedia Britannica, 5th ed. 1976.
Farmer, David Hugh. *The Oxford Dictionary of Saints.* Oxford: Clarendon Press, 1978.
Fisher, John. *Funny Way to Be a Hero.* St. Albans: Paladin, 1976.
Gammond, Peter and Peter Clayton. *A Guide to Popular Music.* London: Phoenix House, 1960.
Gaye, Freda. *Who's Who in the Theatre.* London: Pitman, 14th ed. 1967.
Geipel, John. *The Cartoon: A Short History of Graphic Comedy and Satire.* Newton Abbot, England: David & Charles, 1972.
Halliwell, Leslie. *The Filmgoer's Companion.* St. Albans, England: Paladin, 4th ed. 1972, 5th ed. 1974, 6th ed. 1977.
Hamst, Olphar. *Handbook of Fictitious Names (Being a Guide to Authors, Chiefly in the Lighter Literature of the XIXth Century, Who Have Written under Assumed Names; And to Literary Forgers, Impostors, Plagiarists, and Imitators).* London: John Russell Smith, 1868.
Hardy, Phil, and Dave Laing, eds. *Encyclopedia of Rock: 1955-75.* London: Aquarius Books, 1977.
Hart, James D. *The Oxford Companion to American Literature,* 4th ed. New York: Oxford University Press, 1965.
Hartnoll, Phyllis. *Concise Oxford Companion to the Theatre.* Oxford: Oxford University Press, 1972.
Harvey, Sir Paul, ed. *The Oxford Companion to English Literature,* rev. by Dorothy Eagle, 4th ed. Oxford University Press, 1967. Reprinted with corrections 1973.
_____, and J.E. Heseltine, comps. and ed. *The Oxford Companion to French Literature.* Oxford: Oxford University Press, 1961.
Hildreth, Peter. *Name Dropper.* London: McWhirter, 1970.
Hughes, James Pennethorne. *How You Got Your Name: The Origin and Meaning of Surnames.* London: Phoenix House, 1959.
_____. *Is Thy Name Wart? The Origins of Some Curious and Other Surnames.* London: Phoenix House, 1959.
Illustrated Encyclopaedia of World Theatre. London: Thames & Hudson, 1977.
Jares, Joe. *Whatever Happened to Gorgeous George?* New York: Grosset & Dunlap, 1974.
Jasper, Tony. *The 70's: A Book of Records.* London: Macdonald Futura, 1980.
Johnson, Charles, and Linwood Sleigh. *The Harrap Book of Boys' and Girls' Names.* London: George Harrap, 1973.
Jones, Maldwyn A. *Destination America.* London: Book Club Associates, 1976.
Josling, J.F. *Change of Name,* 11th ed. London: Oyez Publishing, 1978. (Oyez Practice Notes No. 1).
Kaganoff, Benzion C. *A Dictionary of Jewish Names and Their History.* London: Routledge & Kegan Paul, 1978.
Kálmán, Béla. *The World of Names: A Study in Hungarian Onomatology.* Budapest: Akadémiai Kiadó, 1978.
Klymasz, R.B. *A Classified Dictionary of Slavic Surname Changes in Canada.* Winnipeg: Ukrainian Free Academy of Sciences, 1961. (Onomastica No. 22.).

Koegler, Horst. *The Concise Oxford Dictionary of Ballet*. Oxford: Oxford University Press, 1977.

Lamb, Geoffrey. *Magic Illustrated Dictionary*. London: Kaye & Ward, 1979.

McCormick, Donald. *Who's Who in Spy Fiction*. London: Elm Tree Books, 1977.

Murray, Peter, and Linda Murray. *A Dictionary of Art and Artists*. Harmondsworth: Penguin Books, 1969.

Masanov, I.F. *Slovar Psevdonimov Russkikh Pisateley, Uchyonykh i Obshchestvennykh Deyateley* ["Dictionary of Pseudonyms of Russian Writers, Scholars and Public Figures"]. Moscow: Izdatelstvo Vsesoyuznoy Knizhnoy Palaty, 1956. 4 vols.

Meades, Jonathan. *This Is Your Life: An Insight into the Unseen Lives of Your Favourite T.V. Personalities*. London: Salamander Books, 1979.

Mencken, H.L. *The American Language*. London: Routledge & Kegan Paul, 1963.

Miller, Casey, and Kate Swift. *Words and Women: New Language in New Times*. Harmondsworth, England: Penguin Books, 1979.

Miller, Maud M., ed. *Winchester's Screen Encyclopedia*. London, 1948.

Morgan, Jane; Christopher O'Neill, and Rom Harré. *Nicknames: Their Origins and Social Consequences*. London: Routledge & Kegan Paul, 1979.

National Union Catalog: Pre-1956 Imprints. London: Mansell Publishing, 1979.

New Catholic Encyclopaedia. New York: McGraw-Hill, 1967.

Noble, Peter, ed. *1979-80 Screen International Film and TV Year Book*. London: Screen International, 1979.

Panassié, Hugues, and Madeleine Gautier. *Dictionary of Jazz*. London: Cassell, 1956.

Parker, John, orig. comp. *Who's Who in the Theatre*, 15th ed. London: Pitman, 1972.

Parish, James Robert. *Great Child Stars*. New York: Ace Books, 1976.

Pascall, Jeremy, and Rob Burt. *The Stars and Superstars of Black Music*. London: Phoebus, 1977.

Petit Larousse Illustré. Paris: Librairie Larousse, 1978.

Phoebus Publishing Co., comps. *The Story of Pop*. London: Octopus Books, 1974.

Pine, L.G. *The Story of Surnames*. Newton Abbot, England: David & Charles, 1969.

Podolskaya, N.V. *Slovar Russkoy Onomasticheskoy Terminologii* ["Dictionary of Russian Onomastic Terminology"]. Moscow: Nauka, 1978.

Reaney, P.H. *A Dictionary of British Surnames*, 2d ed. with corrections and additions by R.M. Wilson. London: Routledge & Kegan Paul, 1976.

Reyna, Ferdina. *Concise Encyclopedia of Ballet*. London: Collins, 1974.

Roberts, Frank C., comp. *Obituaries from The Times 1961-1970*. Reading, England: Newspaper Archive Developments, 1975; *...1971-75*, 1978; *...1951-1960*, 1979.

Robinson, Kenneth, ed. *Twentieth Century Writing: A Reader's Guide to Contemporary Literature*. London: Newnes Books, 1969.

Rosenthal, Harold, and John Warrack. *The Concise Oxford Dictionary of Opera*, 2d ed. Oxford: Oxford University Press, 1979.

Roxon, Lillian. *Rock Encyclopedia*. New York: Grosset & Dunlap, 1971.

Seth, Ronald. *Encyclopedia of Espionage*. London: Book Club Associates, 1974.

Sharp, Harold S., comp. *Handbook of Pseudonyms and Personal Nicknames*. Metuchen, N.J.: Scarecrow Press, 1972. *First Supplement*, 1975.

Shestack, Melvin. *The Country Music Encyclopaedia*. London: Omnibus Press, 1977.

Shneyer, A.Ya, and R.Ye. Slavsky. *Tsirk: Malenkaya Entsiklopediya* ["The Circus: A Little Encyclopedia"]. Moscow: Sovetskaya Entsiklopediya, 1979.

Stambler, Irwin. *Encyclopaedia of Pop, Rock and Soul.* London: St. James Press, 1974.

Stevens, Andy. *World of Stars: Your 200 Favourite Personalities.* London: Fontana, 1980.

Thomson, David. *A Biographical Dictionary of the Cinema.* London: Secker & Warburg, 1975.

Thomson, Ronald W. *Who's Who of Hymn Writers.* London: Epworth Press, 1967.

Thorne, J.O., ed. *Chambers's Biographical Dictionary.* Edinburgh: Chambers, 1968.

Train, John, comp. *Remarkable Names of Real People or How to Name Your Baby.* Hassocks, England: Harvester Press, 1978.

The TV Times Guide to Movies on Television. London: Independent Television Publications, 1979.

TV Times Staff, comps. *Who's Who on Television.* London: Independent Television Publications, 1970.

Unbegaun, B.O. *Russian Surnames.* Oxford: Oxford University Press, 1972.

Verstappen, Peter. *The Book of Surnames.* London: Pelham, 1980.

Wagner, Leopold. *Names and Their Meanings.* London: T. Fisher Unwin, 1892.

Wallechinsky, David, Irving Wallace and Amy Wallace. *The Book of Lists.* London: Cassell, 1977.

Ward, A.C. *Longman Companion to Twentieth Century Literature.* London: Longman, 1st ed. 1970, 2d ed. 1975.

Webster's Biographical Dictionary. Springfield, Mass.: Merriam, 1st ed. 1943, 21st ed. 1974.

Weekley, Ernest. *Jack and Jill: A Study in Our Christian Names.* London: John Murray, 1939.

Wheeler, William A. *A Dictionary of the Noted Names of Fiction (Including Also Familiar Pseudonyms, Surnames Bestowed on Eminent Men, and Analogous Popular Appellations Often Referred to in Literature and Conversation).* London: George Bell & Son, 1892.

Who's Who. London: A & C Black, 1971, 1978.

Williams, Sir Edgar, ed. *Dictionary of National Biography.* Oxford: Oxford University Press, 1975.

Winchester, Clarence, ed. *The World Film Encyclopedia.* London: Amalgamated Press, 1933.

Withycombe, E.G. *The Oxford Dictionary of English Christian Names,* 3d ed. Oxford: Clarendon Press, 1977.

The World Almanac & Book of Facts. New York: Newspaper Enterprise Association, 1980.

Zec, Donald. *Some Enchanted Egos.* London: Allison & Busby, 1972.